Praise for the First Edition

The definitive guide to Hibernate and to object/relational mapping in enterprise computing.
—From the Foreword by Linda DeMichiel
Sun Microsystems

This book is the ultimate solution. If you are going to use Hibernate in your application, you have no other choice; go rush to the store and get this book.
—Meera Subbarao
JavaLobby

Java Persistence with Hibernate *is the most comprehensive, authoritative, and definitive guide, tutorial, and reference to OR-mapped Java persistence.*
—Will Wagers
C#online.net

A definitive source on Hibernate. Great for any developer.
—Patrick Peak, CTO
BrowserMedia, Author of *Hibernate Quickly*

I wholeheartedly recommend this book!
—Stuart Caborn
ThoughtWorks

Great topic, great content—and there is a great need for this book!
—Ryan Daigle, RTP Region
ALTERthought

This is the most complete book on Hibernate on the market. It covers everything, and I mean everything. From mapping to annotations to whatever … it's in here.
—Liz Hills
Amazon reviewer

Java Persistence with Hibernate

SECOND EDITION

CHRISTIAN BAUER
GAVIN KING
GARY GREGORY

MANNING
SHELTER ISLAND

For online information and ordering of this and other Manning books, please visit
www.manning.com. The publisher offers discounts on this book when ordered in quantity.
For more information, please contact

    Special Sales Department
    Manning Publications Co.
    20 Baldwin Road
    PO Box 761
    Shelter Island, NY 11964
    Email: orders@manning.com

Manning Publications Co.
20 Baldwin Road
PO Box 761
Shelter Island, NY 11964

Development editor:	Christina Taylor
Technical development editor:	Palak Mathur
Copyeditor:	Tiffany Taylor
Proofreaders:	Katie Tennant, Barbara Mirecki
Technical proofreader:	Christian Alfano
Typesetter:	Dottie Marsico
Cover designer:	Marija Tudor

ISBN 9781617290459
Printed in the United States of America
1 2 3 4 5 6 7 8 9 10 – EBM – 20 19 18 17 16 15

To Alexander, for teaching me how to teach him
　　　　　　　　　　　　　　　　　　　　　　—GG

brief contents

    14 ■ Creating and executing queries   345
    15 ■ The query languages   369
    16 ■ Advanced query options   408
    17 ■ Customizing SQL   426

PART 5   BUILDING APPLICATIONS 469

    18 ■ Designing client/server applications   471
    19 ■ Building web applications   498
    20 ■ Scaling Hibernate   532

contents

foreword to the first edition

Relational databases are indisputably at the core of the modern enterprise. While modern programming languages, including Java, provide an intuitive, object-oriented view of application-level business entities, the enterprise data underlying these entities is heavily relational in nature. Further, the main strength of the relational model—over earlier navigational models as well as over later OODB models—is that by design it is intrinsically agnostic to the programmatic manipulation and application-level view of the data that it serves up. Many attempts have been made to bridge relational and object-oriented technologies, or to replace one with the other, but the gap between the two is one of the hard facts of enterprise computing today. It is this challenge—to provide a bridge between relational data and Java objects—that Hibernate takes on through its object/relational mapping (ORM) approach. Hibernate meets this challenge in a very pragmatic, direct, and realistic way.

As Christian Bauer and Gavin King demonstrate in this book, the effective use of ORM technology in all but the simplest of enterprise environments requires understanding and configuring how the mediation between relational data and objects is performed. This demands that the developer be aware and knowledgeable both of the application and its data requirements, and of the SQL query language, relational storage structures, and the potential for optimization that relational technology offers. Not only does Hibernate provide a full-function solution that meets these requirements head-on, it is also a flexible and configurable architecture. Hibernate's developers designed it with modularity, pluggability, extensibility, and user customization in mind. As a result, in the few years since its initial release, Hibernate has rapidly become one of the leading ORM technologies for enterprise developers—and deservedly so.

This book provides a comprehensive overview of Hibernate. It covers how to use its type-mapping capabilities and facilities for modeling associations and inheritance; how to retrieve objects efficiently using the Hibernate query language; how to configure Hibernate for use in both managed and unmanaged environments; and how to use its tools. In addition, throughout the book the authors provide insight into the underlying issues of ORM and into the design choices behind Hibernate. These insights give the reader a deep understanding of the effective use of ORM as an enterprise technology. *Hibernate in Action* is the definitive guide to using Hibernate and to object/relational mapping in enterprise computing today.

LINDA DEMICHIEL
LEAD ARCHITECT, ENTERPRISE JAVABEANS
SUN MICROSYSTEMS
NOVEMBER 2012

preface

This is our third book about Hibernate, an open source project that is almost 15 years old. In a recent poll, Hibernate was among the top five tools used by many Java developers every day. This shows that SQL databases are still the preferred technology for reliable data storage and management, especially in the Java enterprise software development space. It's also a testament to the quality of specifications and tools available, which today make it easy to start a project and to estimate and reduce risk when building large, complex applications.

The fifth major Hibernate release is now available, as well as the second major version of the Java Persistence API specification (JPA) implemented by Hibernate. The core of Hibernate, or what is now called object/relational mapping (ORM), has been mature for a long time, and many small improvements have been made over the years. Other related projects such as Hibernate Search, Hibernate Bean Validation, and more recently Hibernate object/grid mapping (OGM) are delivering new and innovative solutions that make Hibernate a complete tool kit for a diverse range of data-management tasks.

When we wrote the previous edition of this book, Hibernate was undergoing some significant changes: grown organically and driven by an open source community and the daily requirements of Java developers, Hibernate had to become more formal and implement the first version of the JPA specification. The last edition was therefore a large book, because many examples had to be shown in the old form and the new, standardized form.

Today this gap has almost completely disappeared, and we can now first and foremost rely on the standardized API and architecture of Java Persistence. There are of course also many excellent Hibernate features, which we discuss in this edition. Although the number of pages has been reduced compared with the previous edition, we used this space for numerous new examples. We also cover how JPA fits into the larger picture of Java EE, and how your application architecture can integrate Bean Validation, EJB, CDI, and JSF.

Let this new edition be a guide through your first Hibernate project. We hope it will replace the last edition as the Hibernate reference documentation you keep on your desk.

acknowledgments

We couldn't have created this book without the help of many people. Palak Mathur and Christian Alfano did an excellent job as the technical reviewers of our book; thank you for the many hours you spent editing our broken code examples.

We'd also like to thank our peer reviewers for taking the time and providing invaluable feedback during the development phase: Chris Bakar, Gaurav Bhardwaj, Jacob Bosma, José Diaz, Marco Gambini, Sergio Fernandez Gonzalez, Jerry Goodnough, John Griffin, Stephan Heffner, Chad Johnston, Christophe Martini, Robby O'Connor, Anthony Patricio, and Denis Wang.

Manning's publisher Marjan Bace again assembled a great production team at Manning: Christina Taylor edited our crude manuscript and turned it into a real book. Tiffany Taylor found all our typos and made the book readable. Dottie Marsico was responsible for typesetting and gave the book its great look. Mary Piergies coordinated and organized the production process. We'd like to thank you all for working with us.

Finally, special thanks to Linda DeMichiel for writing the foreword to the first edition.

GARY GREGORY

I'd like to thank my parents for getting me started on my journey, providing me with the opportunity for a great education, and giving me the freedom to choose my path. I'm eternally grateful to my wife Lori and my son Alexander for giving me the time to pursue yet another project like this one, my third book.

Along the way, I've studied and worked with truly exceptional individuals like George Bosworth, Lee Breisacher, Christoper Hansen, Deborah Lewis, and many others. My father-in-law, Buddy Martin, deserves a special mention for providing wisdom and insights through great conversations and storytelling born of decades spent writing about sports (go Gators!). I always find inspiration in music, especially that of Wilco (*Impossible Germany*), Tom Waits (*Blue Valentine*), Donald Fagen (*The Nightfly, A just machine to make big decisions/Programmed by fellows with compassion and vision*), David Lindley, and Bach. Finally, I thank my coauthor Christian Bauer for sharing his knowledge, and all of the people at Manning for their support, professionalism, and great feedback.

A special "thank you" goes out to Tiffany Taylor at Manning for a giving the book a great polish. Don Wanner, thank you, period.

about this book

This book is both a tutorial and a reference for Hibernate and Java Persistence. If you're new to Hibernate, we suggest that you start reading the book with chapter 1 and begin coding with the "Hello World" tutorial in chapter 2. If you've used an older version of Hibernate, you should read the first two chapters quickly to get an overview and then jump into the middle with chapter 3. We will, whenever appropriate, tell you if a particular section or subject is optional or reference material that you can safely skip during your first read.

Roadmap

This book is divided into five major parts.

In part 1, "Getting started with ORM," we discuss the fundamentals behind object/relational mapping. We walk through a hands-on tutorial to get you started with your first Hibernate project. We look at Java application design for domain models and at the options for creating object/relational mapping metadata.

Part 2, "Mapping strategies," focuses on Java classes and their properties, and how they map to SQL tables and columns. We explore all basic and advanced mapping options in Hibernate and Java Persistence. We show you how to deal with inheritance, collections, and complex class associations. Finally, we discuss integration with legacy database schemas and some mapping strategies that are especially tricky.

Part 3, "Transactional data processing," is all about loading and storing data with Hibernate and Java Persistence. We introduce the programming interfaces, how to write transactional applications, and how Hibernate can load data from the database most efficiently.

With part 4, "Writing queries," we introduce the data query features and cover query languages and APIs in detail. Not all chapters in this part are written in a tutorial style; we expect you'll browse this part of the book frequently when building an application and looking up a solution for a particular query problem.

In part 5, "Building applications," we discuss the design and implementation of layered and conversation-aware Java database applications. We discuss the most common design patterns that are used with Hibernate, such as the Data Access Object (DAO). You see how you can test your Hibernate application easily and learn what other best practices are relevant if you work with an object/relational mapping software in web and client/server applications in general.

Who should read this book?

Readers of this book should have basic knowledge of object-oriented software development and should have used this knowledge in practice. To understand the application examples, you should be familiar with the Java programming language and the Unified Modeling Language.

Our primary target audience consists of Java developers who work with SQL-based database systems. We'll show you how to substantially increase your productivity by using ORM. If you're a database developer, the book can be part of your introduction to object-oriented software development.

If you're a database administrator, you'll be interested in how ORM affects performance and how you can tune the performance of the SQL database-management system and persistence layer to achieve performance targets. Because data access is the bottleneck in most Java applications, this book pays close attention to performance issues. Many DBAs are understandably nervous about entrusting performance to tool-generated SQL code; we seek to allay those fears and also to highlight cases where applications shouldn't use tool-managed data access. You may be relieved to discover that we don't claim that ORM is the best solution to every problem.

Code conventions

This book provides copious examples, which include all the Hibernate application artifacts: Java code, Hibernate configuration files, and XML mapping metadata files. Source code in listings or in text is in a fixed-width font like this to separate it from ordinary text. Additionally, Java method names, component parameters, object properties, and XML elements and attributes in text are also presented using fixed-width font.

Java, HTML, and XML can all be verbose. In many cases, the original source code (available online) has been reformatted; we've added line breaks and reworked indentation to accommodate the available page space in the book. In rare cases, even this was not enough, and listings include line-continuation markers (➥). Additionally, comments in the source code have often been removed from the listings when the code is described in the text. Code annotations accompany some of the source code listings, highlighting important concepts. In some cases, numbered bullets link to explanations that follow the listing.

Source code downloads

Hibernate is an open source project released under the Lesser GNU Public License. Directions for downloading Hibernate packages, in source or binary form, are available from the Hibernate website: www.hibernate.org. The source code for all examples in this book is available from http://jpwh.org/. You can also download the code for the examples in this book from the publisher's website at www.manning.com/books/java-persistence-with-hibernate-second-edition.

Author Online

The purchase of *Java Persistence with Hibernate, Second Edition* includes free access to a private web forum run by Manning Publications, where you can make comments about the book, ask technical questions, and receive help from the authors and from other users. To access the forum and subscribe to it, point your web browser to www.manning.com/books/java-persistence-with-hibernate-second-edition. This page provides information on how to get on the forum once you are registered, what kind of help is available, and the rules of conduct on the forum.

Manning's commitment to our readers is to provide a venue where a meaningful dialogue between individual readers and between readers and the authors can take place. It is not a commitment to any specific amount of participation on the part of the authors, whose contribution to the forum remains voluntary (and unpaid). We suggest you try asking the authors some challenging questions lest their interest stray!

The Author Online forum and the archives of previous discussions will be accessible from the publisher's website as long as the book is in print.

About the authors

CHRISTIAN BAUER is a member of the Hibernate developer team; he works as a trainer and consultant.

GAVIN KING is the founder of the Hibernate project and a member of the original Java Persistence expert group (JSR 220). He also led the standardization effort of CDI (JSR 299). Gavin is currently creating a new programming language called Ceylon.

GARY GREGORY is a principal software engineer at Rocket Software working on application servers and legacy integration. He is the coauthor of Manning's *JUnit in Action* and *Spring Batch in Action* and a member of the Project Management Committees for the Apache Software Foundation projects: Commons, HttpComponents, Logging Services, and Xalan.

about the cover illustration

The illustration on the cover of *Java Persistence with Hibernate, Second Edition* is taken from a collection of costumes of the Ottoman Empire published on January 1, 1802, by William Miller of Old Bond Street, London. The title page is missing from the collection and we have been unable to track it down to date. The book's table of contents identifies the figures in both English and French, and each illustration bears the names of two artists who worked on it, both of whom would no doubt be surprised to find their art gracing the front cover of a computer programming book ... 200 years later.

The pictures from the Ottoman collection, like the other illustrations that appear on our covers, bring to life the richness and variety of dress customs of two centuries ago. They recall the sense of isolation and distance of that period—and of every other historic period except our own hyperkinetic present. Dress codes have changed since then, and the diversity by region, so rich at the time, has faded away. It is now often hard to tell the inhabitants of one continent from another. Perhaps, trying to view it optimistically, we have traded a cultural and visual diversity for a more varied personal life—or a more varied and interesting intellectual and technical life.

We at Manning celebrate the inventiveness, the initiative, and, yes, the fun of the computer business with book covers based on the rich diversity of regional life of two centuries ago, brought back to life by the pictures from this collection.

Part 1

Getting started with ORM

In part 1, we'll show you why object persistence is such a complex topic and what solutions you can apply in practice. Chapter 1 introduces the object/relational paradigm mismatch and several strategies to deal with it, foremost object/relational mapping (ORM). In chapter 2, we'll guide you step by step through a tutorial with Hibernate and Java Persistence—you'll implement and test a "Hello World" example. Thus prepared, in chapter 3 you'll be ready to learn how to design and implement complex business domain models in Java, and which mapping metadata options you have available.

After reading this part of the book, you'll understand why you need ORM and how Hibernate and Java Persistence work in practice. You'll have written your first small project, and you'll be ready to take on more complex problems. You'll also understand how real-world business entities can be implemented as a Java domain model and in what format you prefer to work with ORM metadata.

Understanding object/relational persistence 1

This book is about Hibernate; our focus is on using Hibernate as a provider of the Java Persistence API. We cover basic and advanced features and describe some ways to develop new applications using Java Persistence. Often, these recommendations aren't specific to Hibernate. Sometimes they're our own ideas about the *best* ways to do things when working with persistent data, explained in the context of Hibernate.

The approach to managing persistent data has been a key design decision in every software project we've worked on. Given that persistent data isn't a new or unusual requirement for Java applications, you'd expect to be able to make a simple choice among similar, well-established persistence solutions. Think of web application frameworks (JavaServer Faces versus Struts versus GWT), GUI component frameworks (Swing versus SWT), or template engines (JSP versus Thymeleaf). Each of the competing solutions has various advantages and disadvantages, but they all share the same scope and overall approach. Unfortunately, this isn't yet the case with persistence technologies, where we see some wildly differing solutions to the same problem.

Persistence has always been a hot topic of debate in the Java community. Is persistence a problem that is already solved by SQL and extensions such as stored procedures, or is it a more pervasive problem that must be addressed by special Java component models, such as EJBs? Should we hand-code even the most primitive CRUD (create, read, update, delete) operations in SQL and JDBC, or should this work be automated? How do we achieve portability if every database management system has its own SQL dialect? Should we abandon SQL completely and adopt a different database technology, such as object database systems or NoSQL systems? The debate may never end, but a solution called *object/relational mapping* (ORM) now has wide acceptance, thanks in large part to the innovations of Hibernate, an open source ORM service implementation.

Before we can get started with Hibernate, you need to understand the core problems of object persistence and ORM. This chapter explains why you need tools like Hibernate and specifications such as the *Java Persistence API* (JPA).

First we define persistent data management in the context of object-oriented applications and discuss the relationship of SQL, JDBC, and Java, the underlying technologies and standards that Hibernate builds on. We then discuss the so-called *object/relational paradigm mismatch* and the generic problems we encounter in object-oriented software development with SQL databases. These problems make it clear that we need tools and patterns to minimize the time we have to spend on the persistence-related code in our applications.

The best way to learn Hibernate isn't necessarily linear. We understand that you may want to try Hibernate right away. If this is how you'd like to proceed, skip to the next chapter and set up a project with the "Hello World" example. We recommend that you return here at some point as you go through this book; that way, you'll be prepared and have all the background concepts you need for the rest of the material.

1.1 *What is persistence?*

Almost all applications require persistent data. Persistence is one of the fundamental concepts in application development. If an information system didn't preserve data when it was powered off, the system would be of little practical use. *Object persistence* means individual objects can outlive the application process; they can be saved to a data store and be re-created at a later point in time. When we talk about persistence in Java, we're normally talking about mapping and storing object instances in a database using SQL. We start by taking a brief look at the technology and how it's used in Java. Armed with this information, we then continue our discussion of persistence and how it's implemented in object-oriented applications.

1.1.1 *Relational databases*

You, like most other software engineers, have probably worked with SQL and relational databases; many of us handle such systems every day. Relational database management systems have SQL-based application programming interfaces; hence, we call today's relational database products SQL *database management systems* (DBMS) or, when we're talking about particular systems, SQL *databases*.

Relational technology is a known quantity, and this alone is sufficient reason for many organizations to choose it. But to say only this is to pay less respect than is due. Relational databases are entrenched because they're an incredibly flexible and robust approach to data management. Due to the well-researched theoretical foundation of the relational data model, relational databases can guarantee and protect the integrity of the stored data, among other desirable characteristics. You may be familiar with E.F. Codd's four-decades-old introduction of the relational model, *A Relational Model of Data for Large Shared Data Banks* (Codd, 1970). A more recent compendium worth reading, with a focus on SQL, is C. J. Date's *SQL and Relational Theory* (Date, 2009).

Relational DBMSs aren't specific to Java, nor is an SQL database specific to a particular application. This important principle is known as *data independence*. In other words, and we can't stress this important fact enough, *data lives longer than any application does*. Relational technology provides a way of sharing data among different applications, or among different parts of the same overall system (the data entry application and the reporting application, for example). Relational technology is a common denominator of many disparate systems and technology platforms. Hence, the relational data model is often the foundation for the common enterprise-wide representation of business entities.

Before we go into more detail about the practical aspects of SQL databases, we have to mention an important issue: although marketed as relational, a database system providing only an SQL data language interface isn't really relational and in many ways isn't even close to the original concept. Naturally, this has led to confusion. SQL practitioners blame the relational data model for shortcomings in the SQL language, and relational data management experts blame the SQL standard for being a weak implementation of the relational model and ideals. Application engineers are stuck somewhere in the middle, with the burden of delivering something that works. We highlight some important and significant aspects of this issue throughout this book, but generally we focus on the practical aspects. If you're interested in more background material, we highly recommend *Practical Issues in Database Management: A Reference for the Thinking Practitioner* by Fabian Pascal (Pascal, 2000) and *An Introduction to Database Systems* by Chris Date (Date, 2003) for the theory, concepts, and ideals of (relational) database systems. The latter book is an excellent reference (it's big) for all questions you may possibly have about databases and data management.

1.1.2   Understanding SQL

To use Hibernate effectively, you must start with a solid understanding of the relational model and SQL. You need to understand the relational model and topics such as normalization to guarantee the integrity of your data, and you'll need to use your knowledge of SQL to tune the performance of your Hibernate application. Hibernate automates many repetitive coding tasks, but your knowledge of persistence technology must extend beyond Hibernate itself if you want to take advantage of the full power of modern SQL databases. To dig deeper, consult the bibliography at the end of this book.

You've probably used SQL for many years and are familiar with the basic operations and statements written in this language. Still, we know from our own experience that SQL is sometimes hard to remember, and some terms vary in usage.

Let's review some of the SQL terms used in this book. You use SQL as a *data definition language* (DDL) when *creating*, *altering*, and *dropping* artifacts such as tables and constraints in the catalog of the DBMS. When this *schema* is ready, you use SQL as a *data manipulation language* (DML) to perform operations on data, including *insertions*, *updates*, and *deletions*. You retrieve data by executing queries with *restrictions, projections*, and *Cartesian products*. For efficient reporting, you use SQL to *join, aggregate*, and *group* data as necessary. You can even nest SQL statements inside each other—a technique that uses *subselects*. When your business requirements change, you'll have to modify the database schema again with DDL statements after data has been stored; this is known as *schema evolution*.

If you're an SQL veteran and you want to know more about optimization and how SQL is executed, get a copy of the excellent book *SQL Tuning*, by Dan Tow (Tow, 2003). For a look at the practical side of SQL through the lens of how not to use SQL, *SQL Antipatterns: Avoiding the Pitfalls of Database Programming* (Karwin, 2010) is a good resource.

Although the SQL database is one part of ORM, the other part, of course, consists of the data in your Java application that needs to be persisted to and loaded from the database.

1.1.3   Using SQL in Java

When you work with an SQL database in a Java application, you issue SQL statements to the database via the Java Database Connectivity (JDBC) API. Whether the SQL was written by hand and embedded in the Java code or generated on the fly by Java code, you use the JDBC API to bind arguments when preparing query parameters, executing the query, scrolling through the query result, retrieving values from the result set, and so on. These are low-level data access tasks; as application engineers, we're more interested in the business problem that requires this data access. What we'd really like to write is code that saves and retrieves instances of our classes, relieving us of this low-level drudgery.

Because these data access tasks are often so tedious, we have to ask, are the relational data model and (especially) SQL the right choices for persistence in object-oriented applications? We answer this question unequivocally: yes! There are many reasons why SQL databases dominate the computing industry—relational database management systems are the only proven generic data management technology, and they're almost always a *requirement* in Java projects.

Note that we aren't claiming that relational technology is *always* the best solution. There are many data management requirements that warrant a completely different approach. For example, internet-scale distributed systems (web search engines, content distribution networks, peer-to-peer sharing, instant messaging) have to deal with exceptional transaction volumes. Many of these systems don't require that after a data update completes, all processes see the same updated data (strong transactional consistency). Users might be happy with weak consistency; after an update, there might be a window of inconsistency before all processes see the updated data. Some scientific applications work with enormous but very specialized datasets. Such systems and their unique challenges typically require equally unique and often custom-made persistence solutions. Generic data management tools such as ACID-compliant transactional SQL databases, JDBC, and Hibernate would play only a minor role.

Relational systems at internet scale

To understand why relational systems, and the data-integrity guarantees associated with them, are difficult to scale, we recommend that you first familiarize yourself with the *CAP theorem*. According to this rule, a distributed system can't be *consistent*, *available*, and *tolerant against partition failures* all at the same time.

A system may guarantee that all nodes will see the same data at the same time and that data read and write requests are always answered. But when a part of the system fails due to a host, network, or data center problem, you must either give up strong consistency (linearizability) or 100% availability. In practice, this means you need a strategy that detects partition failures and restores either consistency or availability to a certain degree (for example, by making some part of the system temporarily unavailable for data synchronization to occur in the background). Often it depends on the data, the user, or the operation whether strong consistency is necessary.

For relational DBMSs designed to scale easily, have a look at VoltDB (www.voltdb.com) and NuoDB (www.nuodb.com). Another interesting read is how Google scales its most important database, for the advertising business, and why it's relational/SQL, in "F1 - The Fault-Tolerant Distributed RDBMS Supporting Google's Ad Business" (Shute, 2012).

In this book, we'll think of the problems of data storage and sharing in the context of an object-oriented application that uses a *domain model*. Instead of directly working with the rows and columns of a `java.sql.ResultSet`, the business logic of an application interacts with the application-specific object-oriented domain model. If the SQL database schema of an online auction system has ITEM and BID tables, for example, the Java application defines Item and Bid classes. Instead of reading and writing the value of a particular row and column with the ResultSet API, the application loads and stores instances of Item and Bid classes.

At runtime, the application therefore operates with instances of these classes. Each instance of a Bid has a reference to an auction Item, and each Item may have a collection of references to Bid instances. The business logic isn't executed in the database (as an SQL stored procedure); it's implemented in Java and executed in the application tier. This allows business logic to use sophisticated object-oriented concepts such as inheritance and polymorphism. For example, we could use well-known design patterns such as *Strategy, Mediator,* and *Composite* (see *Design Patterns: Elements of Reusable Object-Oriented Software* [Gamma, 1995]), all of which depend on polymorphic method calls.

Now a caveat: not all Java applications are designed this way, nor should they be. Simple applications may be much better off without a domain model. Use the JDBC ResultSet if that's all you need. Call existing stored procedures, and read their SQL result sets, too. Many applications need to execute procedures that modify large sets of data, close to the data. You might implement some reporting functionality with plain SQL queries and render the result directly onscreen. SQL and the JDBC API are perfectly serviceable for dealing with tabular data representations, and the JDBC RowSet makes CRUD operations even easier. Working with such a representation of persistent data is straightforward and well understood.

But in the case of applications with nontrivial business logic, the domain model approach helps to improve code reuse and maintainability significantly. In practice, *both* strategies are common and needed.

For several decades, developers have spoken of a *paradigm mismatch.* This mismatch explains why every enterprise project expends so much effort on persistence-related concerns. The *paradigms* referred to are object modeling and relational modeling, or, more practically, object-oriented programming and SQL.

With this realization, you can begin to see the problems—some well understood and some less well understood—that an application that combines both data representations must solve: an object-oriented domain model and a persistent relational model. Let's take a closer look at this so-called paradigm mismatch.

1.2 *The paradigm mismatch*

The object/relational paradigm mismatch can be broken into several parts, which we examine one at a time. Let's start our exploration with a simple example that is problem free. As we build on it, you'll see the mismatch begin to appear.

Suppose you have to design and implement an online e-commerce application. In this application, you need a class to represent information about a user of the system, and you need another class to represent information about the user's billing details, as shown in figure 1.1.

Figure 1.1 A simple UML diagram of the User and BillingDetails entities

In this diagram, you can see that a User has many BillingDetails. You can navigate the relationship between the classes in both directions; this means you can iterate through collections or call methods to get to the "other" side of the relationship. The classes representing these entities may be extremely simple:

```java
public class User {

    String username;
    String address;
    Set billingDetails;

    // Accessor methods (getter/setter), business methods, etc.
}

public class BillingDetails {

    String account;
    String bankname;
    User user;

    // Accessor  methods (getter/setter), business methods, etc.
}
```

Note that you're only interested in the state of the entities with regard to persistence, so we've omitted the implementation of property accessors and business methods, such as getUsername() or billAuction().

It's easy to come up with an SQL schema design for this case:

```sql
create table USERS (
    USERNAME varchar(15) not null primary key,
    ADDRESS varchar(255) not null
);

create table BILLINGDETAILS (
    ACCOUNT varchar(15) not null primary key,
    BANKNAME varchar(255) not null,
    USERNAME varchar(15) not null,
    foreign key (USERNAME) references USERS
);
```

The foreign key–constrained column USERNAME in BILLINGDETAILS represents the relationship between the two entities. For this simple domain model, the object/relational mismatch is barely in evidence; it's straightforward to write JDBC code to insert, update, and delete information about users and billing details.

Now let's see what happens when you consider something a little more realistic. The paradigm mismatch will be visible when you add more entities and entity relationships to your application.

1.2.1 *The problem of granularity*

The most glaringly obvious problem with the current implementation is that you've designed an address as a simple `String` value. In most systems, it's necessary to store street, city, state, country, and ZIP code information separately. Of course, you could add these properties directly to the `User` class, but because it's highly likely that other classes in the system will also carry address information, it makes more sense to create an `Address` class. Figure 1.2 shows the updated model.

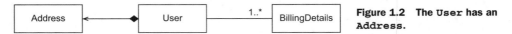

Figure 1.2 **The `User` has an `Address`.**

Should you also add an `ADDRESS` table? Not necessarily; it's common to keep address information in the `USERS` table, in individual columns. This design is likely to perform better, because a table join isn't needed if you want to retrieve the user and address in a single query. The nicest solution may be to create a new SQL data type to represent addresses, and to add a single column of that new type in the `USERS` table instead of several new columns.

You have the choice of adding either several columns or a single column (of a new SQL data type). This is clearly a problem of *granularity*. Broadly speaking, granularity refers to the relative size of the types you're working with.

Let's return to the example. Adding a new data type to the database catalog, to store `Address` Java instances in a single column, sounds like the best approach:

```
create table USERS (
    USERNAME varchar(15) not null primary key,
    ADDRESS address not null
);
```

A new `Address` type (class) in Java and a new `ADDRESS` SQL data type should guarantee interoperability. But you'll find various problems if you check the support for user-defined data types (UDTs) in today's SQL database management systems.

UDT support is one of a number of so-called *object-relational extensions* to traditional SQL. This term alone is confusing, because it means the database management system has (or is supposed to support) a sophisticated data type system—something you take for granted if somebody sells you a system that can handle data in a relational fashion. Unfortunately, UDT support is a somewhat obscure feature of most SQL DBMSs and certainly isn't portable between different products. Furthermore, the SQL standard supports user-defined data types, but poorly.

This limitation isn't the fault of the relational data model. You can consider the failure to standardize such an important piece of functionality as fallout from the object-relational database wars between vendors in the mid-1990s. Today, most engineers accept that SQL products have limited type systems—no questions asked. Even with a sophisticated UDT system in your SQL DBMS, you would still likely duplicate the type declarations, writing the new type in Java and again in SQL. Attempts to find a better solution for the Java space, such as SQLJ, unfortunately, have not had much success. DBMS products rarely support deploying and executing Java classes directly on the database, and if support is available, it's typically limited to very basic functionality and complex in everyday usage.

For these and whatever other reasons, use of UDTs or Java types in an SQL database isn't common practice in the industry at this time, and it's unlikely that you'll encounter a legacy schema that makes extensive use of UDTs. You therefore can't and won't store instances of your new Address class in a single new column that has the same data type as the Java layer.

The pragmatic solution for this problem has several columns of built-in vendor-defined SQL types (such as Boolean, numeric, and string data types). You usually define the USERS table as follows:

```
create table USERS (
    USERNAME varchar(15) not null primary key,
    ADDRESS_STREET varchar(255) not null,
    ADDRESS_ZIPCODE varchar(5) not null,
    ADDRESS_CITY varchar(255) not null
);
```

Classes in the Java domain model come in a range of different levels of granularity: from coarse-grained entity classes like User, to finer-grained classes like Address, down to simple SwissZipCode extending AbstractNumericZipCode (or whatever your desired level of abstraction is). In contrast, just two levels of type granularity are visible in the SQL database: relation types created by you, like USERS and BILLINGDETAILS, and built-in data types such as VARCHAR, BIGINT, or TIMESTAMP.

Many simple persistence mechanisms fail to recognize this mismatch and so end up forcing the less flexible representation of SQL products on the object-oriented model, effectively flattening it.

It turns out that the granularity problem isn't especially difficult to solve. We probably wouldn't even discuss it, were it not for the fact that it's visible in so many existing systems. We describe the solution to this problem in section 4.1.

A much more difficult and interesting problem arises when we consider domain models that rely on *inheritance*, a feature of object-oriented design you may use to bill the users of your e-commerce application in new and interesting ways.

1.2.2 *The problem of subtypes*

In Java, you implement type inheritance using superclasses and subclasses. To illustrate why this can present a mismatch problem, let's add to your e-commerce application so that you now can accept not only bank account billing, but also credit and debit cards. The most natural way to reflect this change in the model is to use inheritance for the BillingDetails superclass, along with several concrete subclasses: CreditCard, BankAccount, and so on. Each of these subclasses defines slightly different data (and completely different functionality that acts on that data). The UML class diagram in figure 1.3 illustrates this model.

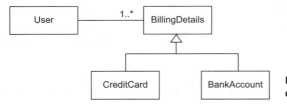

Figure 1.3   Using inheritance for different billing strategies

What changes must you make to support this updated Java class structure? Can you create a table CREDITCARD that *extends* BILLINGDETAILS? SQL database products don't generally implement table inheritance (or even data type inheritance), and if they do implement it, they don't follow a standard syntax and might expose us to data integrity problems (limited integrity rules for updatable views).

We aren't finished with inheritance. As soon as we introduce inheritance into the model, we have the possibility of *polymorphism*.

The User class has an association to the BillingDetails superclass. This is a *polymorphic association*. At runtime, a User instance may reference an instance of any of the subclasses of BillingDetails. Similarly, you want to be able to write *polymorphic queries* that refer to the BillingDetails class, and have the query return instances of its subclasses.

SQL databases also lack an obvious way (or at least a standardized way) to represent a polymorphic association. A foreign key constraint refers to exactly one target table; it isn't straightforward to define a foreign key that refers to multiple tables. You'd have to write a procedural constraint to enforce this kind of integrity rule.

The result of this mismatch of subtypes is that the inheritance structure in a model must be persisted in an SQL database that doesn't offer an inheritance mechanism. In chapter 6, we discuss how ORM solutions such as Hibernate solve the problem of persisting a class hierarchy to an SQL database table or tables, and how polymorphic behavior can be implemented. Fortunately, this problem is now well understood in the community, and most solutions support approximately the same functionality.

The next aspect of the object/relational mismatch problem is the issue of *object identity*. You probably noticed that the example defined USERNAME as the primary key of the USERS table. Was that a good choice? How do you handle identical objects in Java?

1.2.3   *The problem of identity*

Although the problem of identity may not be obvious at first, you'll encounter it often in your growing and expanding e-commerce system, such as when you need to check whether two instances are identical. There are three ways to tackle this problem: two in the Java world and one in your SQL database. As expected, they work together only with some help.

Java defines two different notions of *sameness*:

- Instance identity (roughly equivalent to memory location, checked with a == b)
- Instance equality, as determined by the implementation of the equals() method (also called *equality by value*)

On the other hand, the identity of a database row is expressed as a comparison of primary key values. As you'll see in section 10.1.2, neither equals() nor == is always equivalent to a comparison of primary key values. It's common for several non-identical instances in Java to simultaneously represent the same row of the database—for example, in concurrently running application threads. Furthermore, some subtle difficulties are involved in implementing equals() correctly for a persistent class and understanding when this might be necessary.

Let's use an example to discuss another problem related to database identity. In the table definition for USERS, USERNAME is the primary key. Unfortunately, this decision makes it difficult to change a user's name; you need to update not only the row in USERS, but also the foreign key values in (many) rows of BILLINGDETAILS. To solve this problem, later in this book we recommend that you use *surrogate keys* whenever you can't find a good natural key. We also discuss what makes a good primary key. A surrogate key column is a primary key column with no meaning to the application user—in other words, a key that isn't presented to the application user. Its only purpose is identifying data inside the application.

For example, you may change your table definitions to look like this:

```
create table USERS (
    ID bigint not null primary key,
    USERNAME varchar(15) not null unique,
    ...
);

create table BILLINGDETAILS (
    ID bigint not null primary key,
    ACCOUNT varchar(15) not null,
    BANKNAME varchar(255) not null,
    USER_ID bigint not null,
    foreign key (USER_ID) references USERS
);
```

The ID columns contain system-generated values. These columns were introduced purely for the benefit of the data model, so how (if at all) should they be represented in the Java domain model? We discuss this question in section 4.2, and we find a solution with ORM.

In the context of persistence, identity is closely related to how the system handles caching and transactions. Different persistence solutions have chosen different strategies, and this has been an area of confusion. We cover all these interesting topics—and show how they're related—in section 10.1.

So far, the skeleton e-commerce application you've designed has exposed the paradigm mismatch problems with mapping granularity, subtypes, and identity. You're almost ready to move on to other parts of the application, but first we need to discuss the important concept of *associations*: how the relationships between entities are mapped and handled. Is the foreign key constraint in the database all you need?

1.2.4 *Problems relating to associations*

In your domain model, associations represent the relationships between entities. The User, Address, and BillingDetails classes are all associated; but unlike Address, BillingDetails stands on its own. BillingDetails instances are stored in their own table. Association mapping and the management of entity associations are central concepts in any object persistence solution.

Object-oriented languages represent associations using *object references*; but in the relational world, a *foreign key–constrained column* represents an association, with copies of key values. The constraint is a rule that guarantees integrity of the association. There are substantial differences between the two mechanisms.

Object references are inherently directional; the association is from one instance to the other. They're pointers. If an association between instances should be navigable in both directions, you must define the association *twice*, once in each of the associated classes. You've already seen this in the domain model classes:

```
public class User {
    Set billingDetails;
}

public class BillingDetails {
    User user;
}
```

Navigation in a particular direction has no meaning for a relational data model because you can create arbitrary data associations with *join* and *projection* operators. The challenge is to map a completely open data model, which is independent of the application that works with the data, to an application-dependent navigational model—a constrained view of the associations needed by this particular application.

Java associations can have *many-to-many* multiplicity. For example, the classes could look like this:

```
public class User {
    Set billingDetails;
}

public class BillingDetails {
    Set users;
}
```

But the foreign key declaration on the BILLINGDETAILS table is a *many-to-one* association: each bank account is linked to a particular user. Each user may have multiple linked bank accounts.

If you wish to represent a *many-to-many* association in an SQL database, you must introduce a new table, usually called a *link table*. In most cases, this table doesn't appear anywhere in the domain model. For this example, if you consider the relationship between the user and the billing information to be *many-to-many*, you define the link table as follows:

```
create table USER_BILLINGDETAILS (
    USER_ID bigint,
    BILLINGDETAILS_ID bigint,
    primary key (USER_ID, BILLINGDETAILS_ID),
    foreign key (USER_ID) references USERS,
    foreign key (BILLINGDETAILS_ID) references BILLINGDETAILS
);
```

You no longer need the `USER_ID` foreign key column and constraint on the `BILLING-DETAILS` table; this additional table now manages the links between the two entities. We discuss association and collection mappings in detail in chapter 7.

So far, the issues we've considered are mainly *structural*: you can see them by considering a purely static view of the system. Perhaps the most difficult problem in object persistence is a *dynamic* problem: how data is accessed at runtime.

1.2.5 *The problem of data navigation*

There is a fundamental difference in how you access data in Java and in a relational database. In Java, when you access a user's billing information, you call `someUser.getBillingDetails().iterator().next()` or something similar. This is the most natural way to access object-oriented data, and it's often described as *walking the object network*. You navigate from one instance to another, even iterating collections, following prepared pointers between classes. Unfortunately, this isn't an efficient way to retrieve data from an SQL database.

The single most important thing you can do to improve the performance of data access code is to *minimize the number of requests to the database*. The most obvious way to do this is to minimize the number of SQL queries. (Of course, other, more sophisticated, ways—such as extensive caching—follow as a second step.)

Therefore, efficient access to relational data with SQL usually requires joins between the tables of interest. The number of tables included in the join when retrieving data determines the depth of the object network you can navigate in memory. For example, if you need to retrieve a `User` and aren't interested in the user's billing information, you can write this simple query:

```
select * from USERS u where u.ID = 123
```

On the other hand, if you need to retrieve a `User` and then subsequently visit each of the associated `BillingDetails` instances (let's say, to list all the user's bank accounts), you write a different query:

```
select * from USERS u
    left outer join BILLINGDETAILS bd
        on bd.USER_ID = u.ID
where u.ID = 123
```

As you can see, to use joins efficiently you need to know what portion of the object network you plan to access when you retrieve the initial instance *before* you start navigating the object network! Careful, though: if you retrieve too much data (probably more than you might need), you're wasting memory in the application tier. You may also overwhelm the SQL database with huge *Cartesian product* result sets. Imagine retrieving not only users and bank accounts in one query, but also all orders paid from each bank account, the products in each order, and so on.

Any object persistence solution worth its salt provides functionality for fetching the data of associated instances only when the association is first accessed in Java code. This is known as *lazy loading*: retrieving data on demand only. This piecemeal style of data access is fundamentally inefficient in the context of an SQL database, because it requires executing one statement for each node or collection of the object network that is accessed. This is the dreaded *n+1 selects* problem.

This mismatch in the way you access data in Java and in a relational database is perhaps the single most common source of performance problems in Java information systems. Yet although we've been blessed with innumerable books and articles advising us to use `StringBuffer` for string concatenation, avoiding the *Cartesian product* and *n+1 selects* problems is still a mystery for many Java programmers. (Admit it: you just thought `StringBuilder` would be much better than `StringBuffer`.)

Hibernate provides sophisticated features for efficiently and transparently fetching networks of objects from the database to the application accessing them. We discuss these features in chapter 12.

We now have quite a list of object/relational mismatch problems, and it can be costly (in time and effort) to find solutions, as you may know from experience. It will take us most of this book to provide a complete answer to these questions and to demonstrate ORM as a viable solution. Let's get started with an overview of ORM, the Java Persistence standard, and the Hibernate project.

1.3   *ORM and JPA*

In a nutshell, object/relational mapping is the automated (and transparent) persistence of objects in a Java application to the tables in an SQL database, using metadata that describes the mapping between the classes of the application and the schema of the SQL database. In essence, ORM works by transforming (reversibly) data from one representation to another. Before we move on, you need to understand what Hibernate *can't* do for you.

A supposed advantage of ORM is that it shields developers from messy SQL. This view holds that object-oriented developers can't be expected to understand SQL or relational databases well and that they find SQL somehow offensive. On the contrary, we believe that Java developers must have a sufficient level of familiarity with—and appreciation of—relational modeling and SQL in order to work with Hibernate. ORM is an advanced technique used by developers who have already done it the hard way. To use Hibernate effectively, you must be able to view and interpret the SQL statements it issues and understand their performance implications.

Let's look at some of the benefits of Hibernate:

- *Productivity*—Hibernate eliminates much of the grunt work (more than you'd expect) and lets you concentrate on the business problem. No matter which application-development strategy you prefer—top-down, starting with a domain model, or bottom-up, starting with an existing database schema—Hibernate, used together with the appropriate tools, will significantly *reduce development time.*
- *Maintainability*—Automated ORM with Hibernate reduces lines of code (LOC), making the system *more understandable* and *easier to refactor.* Hibernate provides a buffer between the domain model and the SQL schema, insulating each model from minor changes to the other.
- *Performance*—Although hand-coded persistence might be faster in the same sense that assembly code can be faster than Java code, automated solutions like Hibernate allow the use of many optimizations *at all times.* One example of this is efficient and easily tunable caching in the application tier. This means developers can spend more energy hand-optimizing the few remaining real bottlenecks instead of prematurely optimizing everything.
- *Vendor independence*—Hibernate can help mitigate some of the risks associated with vendor lock-in. Even if you plan never to change your DBMS product, ORM tools that support a number of different DBMSs enable *a certain level of portability.* In addition, DBMS independence helps in development scenarios where *engineers use a lightweight local database* but deploy for testing and production on a different system.

The Hibernate approach to persistence was well received by Java developers, and the standard Java Persistence API was designed along similar lines.

JPA became a key part of the simplifications introduced in recent EJB and Java EE specifications. We should be clear up front that neither Java Persistence nor Hibernate are limited to the Java EE environment; they're general-purpose solutions to the persistence problem that any type of Java (or Groovy, or Scala) application can use.

The JPA specification defines the following:

- A facility for specifying mapping metadata—how persistent classes and their properties relate to the database schema. JPA relies heavily on Java annotations in domain model classes, but you can also write mappings in XML files.
- APIs for performing basic CRUD operations on instances of persistent classes, most prominently `javax.persistence.EntityManager` to store and load data.
- A language and APIs for specifying queries that refer to classes and properties of classes. This language is the Java Persistence Query Language (JPQL) and looks similar to SQL. The standardized API allows for programmatic creation of *criteria queries* without string manipulation.
- How the persistence engine interacts with transactional instances to perform dirty checking, association fetching, and other optimization functions. The latest JPA specification covers some basic caching strategies.

Hibernate implements JPA and supports all the standardized mappings, queries, and programming interfaces.

1.4 Summary

- With *object persistence*, individual objects can outlive their application process, be saved to a data store, and be re-created later. The object/relational mismatch comes into play when the data store is an SQL-based relational database management system. For instance, a network of objects can't be saved to a database table; it must be disassembled and persisted to columns of portable SQL data types. A good solution for this problem is object/relational mapping (ORM).

- ORM isn't a silver bullet for all persistence tasks; its job is to relieve the developer of 95% of object persistence work, such as writing complex SQL statements with many table joins and copying values from JDBC result sets to objects or graphs of objects.

- A full-featured ORM middleware solution may provide database portability, certain optimization techniques like caching, and other viable functions that aren't easy to hand-code in a limited time with SQL and JDBC.

- Better solutions than ORM might exist someday. We (and many others) may have to rethink everything we know about data management systems and their languages, persistence API standards, and application integration. But the evolution of today's systems into true relational database systems with seamless object-oriented integration remains pure speculation. We can't wait, and there is no sign that any of these issues will improve soon (a multibillion-dollar industry isn't very agile). ORM is the best solution currently available, and it's a time-saver for developers facing the object/relational mismatch every day.

Starting a project 2

In this chapter

- Overview of Hibernate projects
- "Hello World" with Hibernate and Java Persistence
- Configuration and integration options

In this chapter, you'll start with Hibernate and Java Persistence using a step-by-step example. You'll see both persistence APIs and how to benefit from using either native Hibernate or standardized JPA. We first offer you a tour through Hibernate with a straightforward "Hello World" application. Before you start coding, you must decide which Hibernate modules to use in your project.

2.1 Introducing Hibernate

Hibernate is an ambitious project that aims to provide a complete solution to the problem of managing persistent data in Java. Today, Hibernate is not only an ORM service, but also a collection of data management tools extending well beyond ORM.

The Hibernate project suite includes the following:

- *Hibernate ORM*—Hibernate ORM consists of a core, a base service for persistence with SQL databases, and a native proprietary API. Hibernate ORM is the foundation for several of the other projects and is the oldest Hibernate

19

project. You can use Hibernate ORM on its own, independent of any framework or any particular runtime environment with all JDKs. It works in every Java EE/J2EE application server, in Swing applications, in a simple servlet container, and so on. As long as you can configure a data source for Hibernate, it works.

- *Hibernate EntityManager*—This is Hibernate's implementation of the standard Java Persistence APIs, an optional module you can stack on top of Hibernate ORM. You can fall back to Hibernate when a plain Hibernate interface or even a JDBC Connection is needed. Hibernate's native features are a superset of the JPA persistence features in every respect.

- *Hibernate Validator*—Hibernate provides the reference implementation of the Bean Validation (JSR 303) specification. Independent of other Hibernate projects, it provides declarative validation for your domain model (or any other) classes.

- *Hibernate Envers*—Envers is dedicated to audit logging and keeping multiple versions of data in your SQL database. This helps you add data history and audit trails to your application, similar to version control systems you might already be familiar with such as Subversion and Git.

- *Hibernate Search*—Hibernate Search keeps an index of your domain model data up to date in an Apache Lucene database. It lets you query this database with a powerful and naturally integrated API. Many projects use Hibernate Search in addition to Hibernate ORM, adding full-text search capabilities. If you have a free text search form in your application's user interface, and you want happy users, work with Hibernate Search. Hibernate Search isn't covered in this book; you can find more information in *Hibernate Search in Action* by Emmanuel Bernard (Bernard, 2008).

- *Hibernate OGM*—The most recent Hibernate project is the object/grid mapper. It provides JPA support for NoSQL solutions, reusing the Hibernate core engine but persisting mapped entities into a key/value-, document-, or graph-oriented data store. Hibernate OGM isn't covered in this book.

Let's get started with your first Hibernate and JPA project.

2.2   *"Hello World" with JPA*

In this section, you'll write your first Hibernate application, which stores a "Hello World" message in the database and then retrieves it. Let's start by installing and configuring Hibernate.

We use Apache Maven as the project build tool, as we do for all the examples in this book. Declare the dependency on Hibernate:

```
<dependency>
    <groupId>org.hibernate</groupId>
    <artifactId>hibernate-entitymanager</artifactId>
    <version>5.0.0.Final</version>
</dependency>
```

The `hibernate-entitymanager` module includes transitive dependencies on other modules you'll need, such as `hibernate-core` and the Java Persistence interface stubs.

Your starting point in JPA is the *persistence unit*. A persistence unit is a pairing of your domain model class mappings with a database connection, plus some other configuration settings. Every application has at least one persistence unit; some applications have several if they're talking to several (logical or physical) databases. Hence, your first step is setting up a persistence unit in your application's configuration.

2.2.1 Configuring a persistence unit

The standard configuration file for persistence units is located on the classpath in META-INF/persistence.xml. Create the following configuration file for the "Hello World" application:

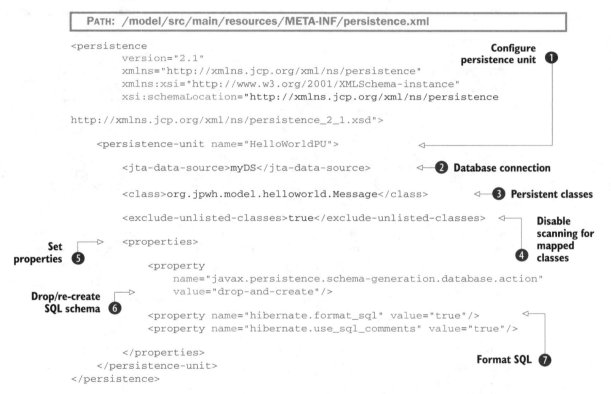

PATH: /model/src/main/resources/META-INF/persistence.xml

```
<persistence
        version="2.1"                                                        Configure
        xmlns="http://xmlns.jcp.org/xml/ns/persistence"              persistence unit ❶
        xmlns:xsi="http://www.w3.org/2001/XMLSchema-instance"
        xsi:schemaLocation="http://xmlns.jcp.org/xml/ns/persistence

http://xmlns.jcp.org/xml/ns/persistence_2_1.xsd">

    <persistence-unit name="HelloWorldPU">

        <jta-data-source>myDS</jta-data-source>              ❷ Database connection

        <class>org.jpwh.model.helloworld.Message</class>          ❸ Persistent classes

        <exclude-unlisted-classes>true</exclude-unlisted-classes>       Disable
                                                                        scanning for
        Set                                                             mapped
    properties ❺  <properties>                                    ❹  classes

            <property
                name="javax.persistence.schema-generation.database.action"
    Drop/re-create        value="drop-and-create"/>
    SQL schema ❻
            <property name="hibernate.format_sql" value="true"/>
            <property name="hibernate.use_sql_comments" value="true"/>

        </properties>
    </persistence-unit>                                          Format SQL ❼
</persistence>
```

❶ The persistence.xml file configures at least one persistence unit; each unit must have a unique name.

❷ Each persistence unit must have a database connection. Here you delegate to an existing `java.sql.DataSource`. Hibernate will find the data source by name with a JNDI lookup on startup.

❸ A persistent unit has persistent (mapped) classes. You list them here.

4 Hibernate can scan your classpath for mapped classes and add them automatically to your persistence unit. This setting disables that feature.

5 Standard or vendor-specific options can be set as properties on a persistence unit. Any standard properties have the `javax.persistence` name prefix; Hibernate's settings use `hibernate`.

6 The JPA engine should drop and re-create the SQL schema in the database automatically when it boots. This is ideal for automated testing, when you want to work with a clean database for every test run.

H When printing SQL in logs, let Hibernate format the SQL nicely and generate comments into the SQL string so you know why Hibernate executed the SQL statement. Most applications need a pool of database connections, with a certain size and optimized thresholds for the environment. You also want to provide the DBMS host and credentials for your database connections.

> **Logging SQL**
>
> All SQL statements executed by Hibernate can be logged—an invaluable tool during optimization. To log SQL, in persistence.xml, set the properties `hibernate.format_sql` and `hibernate.use_sql_comments` to `true`. This will cause Hibernate to format SQL statements with causation comments. Then, in your logging configuration (which depends on your chosen logging implementation), set the categories `org.hibernate.SQL` and `org.hibernate.type.descriptor.sql.BasicBinder` to the finest debug level. You'll then see all SQL statements executed by Hibernate in your log output, including the bound parameter values of prepared statements.

For the "Hello World" application, you delegate database connection handling to a Java Transaction API (JTA) provider, the open source *Bitronix* project. Bitronix offers connection pooling with a managed `java.sql.DataSource` and the standard `javax.transaction.UserTransaction` API in any Java SE environment. Bitronix binds these objects into JNDI, and Hibernate interfaces automatically with Bitronix through JNDI lookups. Setting up Bitronix in detail is outside of the scope of this book; you can find the configuration for our examples in `org.jpwh.env.TransactionManagerSetup`.

In the "Hello World" application, you want to store messages in the database and load them from the database. Hibernate applications define persistent classes that are mapped to database tables. You define these classes based on your analysis of the business domain; hence, they're a model of the domain. This example consists of one class and its mapping.

Let's see what a simple persistent class looks like, how the mapping is created, and some of the things you can do with instances of the persistent class in Hibernate.

2.2.2 *Writing a persistent class*

The objective of this example is to store messages in a database and retrieve them for display. The application has a simple persistent class, `Message`:

> PATH: /model/src/main/java/org/jpwh/model/helloworld/Message.java

```java
package org.jpwh.model.helloworld;

import javax.persistence.Entity;
import javax.persistence.GeneratedValue;
import javax.persistence.Id;

@Entity                                        ①  @Entity required
public class Message {

    @Id                                        ②  @Id required
    @GeneratedValue
    private Long id;                           ③  Enables auto ID generation

    private String text;                       ④  Maps attribute

    public String getText() {
        return text;
    }

    public void setText(String text) {
        this.text = text;
    }
}
```

① Every persistent entity class must have at least the `@Entity` annotation. Hibernate maps this class to a table called MESSAGE.

② Every persistent entity class must have an identifier attribute annotated with `@Id`. Hibernate maps this attribute to a column named ID.

③ Someone must generate identifier values; this annotation enables automatic generation of IDs.

④ You usually implement regular attributes of a persistent class with private or protected fields and public getter/setter method pairs. Hibernate maps this attribute to a column called TEXT.

The identifier attribute of a persistent class allows the application to access the database identity—the primary key value—of a persistent instance. If two instances of `Message` have the same identifier value, they represent the same row in the database.

This example uses `Long` for the type of the identifier attribute, but this isn't a requirement. Hibernate allows virtually anything for the identifier type, as you'll see later.

You may have noticed that the `text` attribute of the `Message` class has JavaBeans-style property accessor methods. The class also has a (default) constructor with no parameters. The persistent classes we show in the examples will usually look something like this. Note that you don't need to implement any particular interface or extend any special superclass.

Instances of the Message class can be managed (made persistent) by Hibernate, but they don't have to be. Because the Message object doesn't implement any persistence-specific classes or interfaces, you can use it just like any other Java class:

```
Message msg = new Message();
msg.setText("Hello!");
System.out.println(msg.getText());
```

It may look like we're trying to be cute here; in fact, we're demonstrating an important feature that distinguishes Hibernate from some other persistence solutions. You can use the persistent class in any execution context—no special container is needed.

You don't have to use annotations to map a persistent class. Later we'll show you other mapping options, such as the JPA orm.xml mapping file, and native hbm.xml mapping files, and when they're a better solution than source annotations.

The Message class is now ready. You can store instances in your database and write queries to load them again into application memory.

2.2.3 *Storing and loading messages*

What you really came here to see is Hibernate, so let's save a new Message to the database. First you need an EntityManagerFactory to talk to your database. This API represents your persistence unit; most applications have one EntityManagerFactory for one configured persistence unit:

> **PATH:** /examples/src/est/java/org/jpwh/helloworld/HelloWorldJPA.java

```
EntityManagerFactory emf =
    Persistence.createEntityManagerFactory("HelloWorldPU");
```

Once it starts, your application should create the EntityManagerFactory; the factory is thread-safe, and all code in your application that accesses the database should share it.

You can now work with the database in a demarcated unit—a transaction—and store a Message:

> **PATH:** /examples/src/test/java/org/jpwh/helloworld/HelloWorldJPA.java

```
UserTransaction tx = TM.getUserTransaction();      ①  Accesses UserTransaction
tx.begin();

EntityManager em = emf.createEntityManager();      ②  Creates EntityManager

Message message = new Message();                   ③  Creates Message
message.setText("Hello World!");

em.persist(message);                        ④  Makes instance persistent

tx.commit();                                                          ⑤  Commits
// INSERT into MESSAGE (ID, TEXT) values (1, 'Hello World!')             transaction

em.close();                          ⑥  Closes EntityManager
```

❶ Get access to the standard transaction API `UserTransaction`, and begin a transaction on this thread of execution.

❷ Begin a new session with the database by creating an `EntityManager`. This is your context for all persistence operations.

❸ Create a new instance of the mapped domain model class `Message`, and set its `text` property.

❹ Enlist the transient instance with your persistence context; you make it persistent. Hibernate now knows that you wish to store that data, but it doesn't necessarily call the database immediately.

❺ Commit the transaction. Hibernate automatically checks the persistence context and executes the necessary SQL `INSERT` statement.

❻ If you create an `EntityManager`, you must close it.

To help you understand how Hibernate works, we show the automatically generated and executed SQL statements in source code comments when they occur. Hibernate inserts a row in the `MESSAGE` table, with an automatically generated value for the `ID` primary key column, and the `TEXT` value.

You can later load this data with a database query:

PATH: /examples/src/test/java/org/jpwh/helloworld/HelloWorldJPA.java

```java
UserTransaction tx = TM.getUserTransaction();    // ❶ Transaction boundary
tx.begin();

EntityManager em = emf.createEntityManager();
                                                 // ❷ Executes query
List<Message> messages =
    em.createQuery("select m from Message m").getResultList();
// SELECT * from MESSAGE

assertEquals(messages.size(), 1);
assertEquals(messages.get(0).getText(), "Hello World!");    // ❸ Changes property value

messages.get(0).setText("Take me to your leader!");

tx.commit();
// UPDATE MESSAGE set TEXT = 'Take me to your leader!' where ID = 1

em.close();                                      // Executes UPDATE ❹
```

❶ Every interaction with your database should occur within explicit transaction boundaries, even if you're only reading data.

❷ Execute a query to retrieve all instances of `Message` from the database.

❸ You can change the value of a property. Hibernate detects this automatically because the loaded `Message` is still attached to the persistence context it was loaded in.

❹ On commit, Hibernate checks the persistence context for dirty state and executes the SQL `UPDATE` automatically to synchronize in-memory with the database state.

The query language you've seen in this example isn't SQL, it's the Java Persistence Query Language (JPQL). Although there is syntactically no difference in this trivial example, the Message in the query string doesn't refer to the database table name, but to the persistent class name. If you map the class to a different table, the query will still work.

Also, notice how Hibernate detects the modification to the text property of the message and automatically updates the database. This is the automatic dirty-checking feature of JPA in action. It saves you the effort of explicitly asking your persistence manager to update the database when you modify the state of an instance inside a transaction.

You've now completed your first Hibernate and JPA application. Maybe you've already noticed that we prefer to write examples as executable tests, with assertions that verify the correct outcome of each operation. We've taken all the examples in this book from test code, so you (and we) can be sure they work properly. Unfortunately, this also means you need more than one line of code to create the EntityManager-Factory when starting the test environment. We've tried to keep the setup of the tests as simple as possible. You can find the code in org.jpwh.env.JPASetup and org.jpwh.env.JPATest; use it as a starting point for writing your own test harness.

Before we work on more-realistic application examples, let's have a quick look at the native Hibernate bootstrap and configuration API.

2.3   *Native Hibernate configuration*

Although basic (and extensive) configuration is standardized in JPA, you can't access all the configuration features of Hibernate with properties in persistence.xml. Note that most applications, even quite sophisticated ones, don't need such special configuration options and hence don't have to access the bootstrap API we show in this section. If you aren't sure, you can skip this section and come back to it later, when you need to extend Hibernate type adapters, add custom SQL functions, and so on.

The native equivalent of the standard JPA EntityManagerFactory is the org.hibernate.SessionFactory. You have usually one per application, and it's the same pairing of class mappings with database connection configuration.

Hibernate's native bootstrap API is split into several stages, each giving you access to certain configuration aspects. In its most compact form, building a Session-Factory looks like this:

> PATH: /examples/src/test/java/org/jpwh/helloworld/HelloWorldHibernate.java

```
SessionFactory sessionFactory = new MetadataSources(
    new StandardServiceRegistryBuilder()
        .configure("hibernate.cfg.xml").build()
).buildMetadata().buildSessionFactory();
```

This loads all settings from a Hibernate configuration file. If you have an existing Hibernate project, you most likely have this file on your classpath. Similar to persistence.xml, this configuration file contains database connection details, as well as a list of persistent classes and other configuration properties.

Let's deconstruct this bootstrap snippet and look at the API in more detail. First, create a `ServiceRegistry`:

PATH: /examples/src/test/java/org/jpwh/helloworld/HelloWorldHibernate.java

```
StandardServiceRegistryBuilder serviceRegistryBuilder =        ◁────❶ Builder
    new StandardServiceRegistryBuilder();

serviceRegistryBuilder                                          ◁
    .applySetting("hibernate.connection.datasource", "myDS")           Configures
    .applySetting("hibernate.format_sql", "true")                      services
    .applySetting("hibernate.use_sql_comments", "true")           ❷    registry
    .applySetting("hibernate.hbm2ddl.auto", "create-drop");

ServiceRegistry serviceRegistry = serviceRegistryBuilder.build();
```

❶ This builder helps you create the immutable service registry with chained method calls.
❷ Configure the services registry by applying settings.

If you want to externalize your service registry configuration, you can load settings from a properties file on the classpath with `StandardServiceRegistryBuilder#load-Properties(file)`.

With the `ServiceRegistry` built and immutable, you can move on to the next stage: telling Hibernate which persistent classes are part of your mapping metadata. Configure the metadata sources as follows:

PATH: /examples/src/test/java/org/jpwh/helloworld/HelloWorldHibernate.java

```
MetadataSources metadataSources = new MetadataSources(serviceRegistry); ◁─┐

metadataSources.addAnnotatedClass(                             ◁
    org.jpwh.model.helloworld.Message.class                        Requires service registry ❶
);

// Add hbm.xml mapping files                                       Adds persistent classes
// metadataSources.addFile(...);                              ❷    to metadata sources

// Read all hbm.xml mapping files from a JAR
// metadataSources.addJar(...)

MetadataBuilder metadataBuilder = metadataSources.getMetadataBuilder();
```

❶ This builder helps you create the immutable service registry with chained method calls.
❷ Configure the services registry by applying settings.

The `MetadataSources` API has many methods for adding mapping sources; check the Javadoc for more information. The next stage of the boot procedure is building all the metadata needed by Hibernate, with the `MetadataBuilder` you obtained from the metadata sources.

You can then query the metadata to interact with Hibernate's completed configuration programmatically, or continue and build the final `SessionFactory`:

> **PATH:** /examples/src/test/java/org/jpwh/helloworld/HelloWorldHibernate.java

```
Metadata metadata = metadataBuilder.build();

assertEquals(metadata.getEntityBindings().size(), 1);

SessionFactory sessionFactory = metadata.buildSessionFactory();
```

> **Creating an EntityManagerFactory from a SessionFactory**
>
> At the time of writing, Hibernate has no convenient API to build an `EntityManager-Factory` programmatically. You can use an internal API for this purpose: the `org.hibernate.jpa.internal.EntityManagerFactoryImpl` has a constructor that accepts a `SessionFactory`.

Let's see if this configuration works by storing and loading a message with Hibernate's native equivalent of `EntityManager`, `org.hibernate.Session`. You can create a `Session` with the `SessionFactory`, and you must close it just as you have to close your own `EntityManager`.

Or, using another Hibernate feature, you can let Hibernate take care of creating and closing the `Session` with `SessionFactory#getCurrentSession()`:

> **PATH:** /examples/src/ test/java/org/jpwh/helloworld/HelloWorldHibernate.java

```
UserTransaction tx = TM.getUserTransaction();        ◁——❶ Accesses UserTransaction
tx.begin();

Session session =
    sessionFactory.getCurrentSession();              ◁——❷ Gets org.hibernate.Session

Message message = new Message();
message.setText("Hello World!");

session.persist(message);                            ◁——❸ Hibernate API and JPA are similar.

tx.commit();                                         ◁—┐
// INSERT into MESSAGE (ID, TEXT) values (1, 'Hello World!')
                                                        │
                                     Commits transaction ❹
```

❶ Get access to the standard transaction API `UserTransaction`, and begin a transaction on this thread of execution.

❷ Whenever you call `getCurrentSession()` in the same thread, you get the same `org.hibernate.Session`. It's bound automatically to the ongoing transaction and is closed for you automatically when that transaction commits or rolls back.

❸ The native Hibernate API is very similar to the standard Java Persistence API, and most methods have the same names.

❹ Hibernate synchronizes the session with the database and automatically closes the "current" session on commit of the bound transaction.

Accessing the current `Session` results in compact code:

> PATH: /examples/src/test/java/org/jpwh/helloworld/HelloWorldHibernate.java

```java
UserTransaction tx = TM.getUserTransaction();
tx.begin();

List<Message> messages =                              ⟵──❶ Criteria query
    sessionFactory.getCurrentSession().createCriteria(
        Message.class
    ).list();
// SELECT * from MESSAGE

assertEquals(messages.size(), 1);
assertEquals(messages.get(0).getText(), "Hello World!");

tx.commit();
```

❶ A Hibernate criteria query is a type-safe programmatic way to express queries, automatically translated into SQL.

Most of the examples in this book don't use the `SessionFactory` or `Session` API. From time to time, when a particular feature is only available in Hibernate, we show you how to `unwrap()` the native interface given a standard API.

2.4 Summary

- You've completed your first JPA project.
- You wrote a persistent class and its mapping with annotations.
- You've seen how to configure and bootstrap a persistence unit, and how to create the `EntityManagerFactory` entry point. Then you called the `Entity-Manager` to interact with the database, storing and loading instances of your persistent domain model class.
- We discussed some of the more advanced native Hibernate bootstrap and configuration options, as well as the equivalent basic Hibernate APIs, `Session-Factory` and `Session`.

Domain models
and metadata

The "Hello World" example in the previous chapter introduced you to Hibernate; certainly, it isn't useful for understanding the requirements of real-world applications with complex data models. For the rest of the book, we use a much more sophisticated example application—CaveatEmptor, an online auction system—to demonstrate Hibernate and Java Persistence. (*Caveat emptor* means "Let the buyer beware".)

> **Major new features in JPA 2**
> - A JPA persistence provider now integrates automatically with a Bean Validation provider. When data is stored, the provider automatically validates constraints on persistent classes.
> - The `Metamodel` API has been added. You can obtain (unfortunately not change) the names, properties, and mapping metadata of the classes in a persistence unit.

We'll start our discussion of the application by introducing a layered application architecture. Then, you'll learn how to identify the business entities of a problem domain. You'll create a conceptual model of these entities and their attributes, called a *domain model*, and you'll implement it in Java by creating persistent classes. We'll spend some time exploring exactly what these Java classes should look like and where they fit within a typical layered application architecture. We'll also look at the persistence capabilities of the classes and how this aspect influences the design and implementation. We'll add *Bean Validation*, which helps to automatically verify the integrity of the domain model data not only for persistent information but all business logic.

We'll then explore mapping metadata options—the ways you tell Hibernate how your persistent classes and their properties relate to database tables and columns. This can be as simple as adding annotations directly in the Java source code of the classes or writing XML documents that you eventually deploy along with the compiled Java classes that Hibernate accesses at runtime. After reading this chapter, you'll know how to design the persistent parts of your domain model in complex real-world projects, and what mapping metadata option you'll primarily prefer and use. Let's start with the example application.

3.1 The example CaveatEmptor application

The CaveatEmptor example is an online auction application that demonstrates ORM techniques and Hibernate functionality. You can download the source code for the application from www.jpwh.org. We won't pay much attention to the user interface in this book (it could be web based or a rich client); we'll concentrate instead on the data access code. When a design decision about data access code that has consequences for the user interface has to be made, we'll naturally consider both.

In order to understand the design issues involved in ORM, let's pretend the CaveatEmptor application doesn't yet exist and that you're building it from scratch. Let's start by looking at the architecture.

3.1.1 A layered architecture

With any nontrivial application, it usually makes sense to organize classes by concern. Persistence is one concern; others include presentation, workflow, and business logic. A typical object-oriented architecture includes layers of code that represent the concerns.

Cross-cutting concerns

There are also so-called *cross-cutting* concerns, which may be implemented generically—by framework code, for example. Typical cross-cutting concerns include logging, authorization, and transaction demarcation.

A layered architecture defines interfaces between code that implements the various concerns, allowing changes to be made to the way one concern is implemented without significant disruption to code in the other layers. Layering determines the kinds of inter-layer dependencies that occur. The rules are as follows:

- Layers communicate from top to bottom. A layer is dependent only on the interface of the layer directly below it.
- Each layer is unaware of any other layers except for the layer just below it.

Different systems group concerns differently, so they define different layers. The typical, proven, high-level application architecture uses three layers: one each for presentation, business logic, and persistence, as shown in figure 3.1.

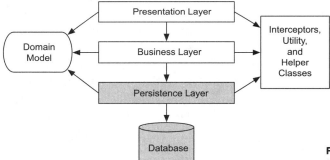

Figure 3.1   A persistence layer is the basis in a layered architecture.

- *Presentation layer*—The user interface logic is topmost. Code responsible for the presentation and control of page and screen navigation is in the presentation layer. The user interface code may directly access business entities of the shared *domain model* and render them on the screen, along with controls to execute actions. In some architectures, business entity instances might not be directly accessible by user interface code: for example, if the presentation layer isn't running on the same machine as the rest of the system. In such cases, the presentation layer may require its own special data-transfer model, representing only a transmittable subset of the domain model.
- *Business layer*—The exact form of the next layer varies widely between applications. It's generally agreed that the business layer is responsible for implementing any business rules or system requirements that would be understood by users as part of the problem domain. This layer usually includes some kind of

controlling component—code that knows when to invoke which business rule. In some systems, this layer has its own internal representation of the business domain entities. Alternatively, it relies on a domain model implementation, shared with the other layers of the application.

- *Persistence layer*—The persistence layer is a group of classes and components responsible for storing data to, and retrieving it from, one or more data stores. This layer needs a model of the business domain entities for which you'd like to keep persistent state. The persistence layer is where the bulk of JPA and Hibernate use takes place.
- *Database*—The database is usually external, shared by many applications. It's the actual, persistent representation of the system state. If an SQL database is used, the database includes a schema and possibly stored procedures for execution of business logic close to the data.
- *Helper and utility classes*—Every application has a set of infrastructural helper or utility classes that are used in every layer of the application (such as `Exception` classes for error handling). These shared infrastructural elements don't form a layer because they don't obey the rules for inter-layer dependency in a layered architecture.

Now that you have a high-level architecture, you can focus on the business problem.

3.1.2 *Analyzing the business domain*

At this stage, you, with the help of domain experts, analyze the business problems your software system needs to solve, identifying the relevant main entities and their interactions. The motivating goal behind the analysis and design of a domain model is to capture the essence of the business information for the application's purpose.

Entities are usually notions understood by users of the system: payment, customer, order, item, bid, and so forth. Some entities may be abstractions of less concrete things the user thinks about, such as a pricing algorithm, but even these are usually understandable to the user. You can find all these entities in the conceptual view of the business, sometimes called a *business model.*

From this business model, engineers and architects of object-oriented software create an object-oriented model, still at the conceptual level (no Java code). This model may be as simple as a mental image existing only in the mind of the developer, or it may be as elaborate as a UML class diagram. Figure 3.2 shows a simple model expressed in UML.

This model contains entities that you're bound to find in any typical e-commerce system: category, item, and user. This model of the problem domain represents all the entities and their relationships (and perhaps their attributes). We call this kind of object-oriented model of entities from the problem domain, encompassing only

Figure 3.2   A class diagram of a typical online auction model

those entities that are of interest to the user, a *domain model*. It's an abstract view of the real world.

Instead of an object-oriented model, engineers and architects may start the application design with a data model (possibly expressed with an entity-relationship diagram). We usually say that, with regard to persistence, there is little difference between the two; they're merely different starting points. In the end, what modeling language you use is secondary; we're most interested in the structure and relationships of the business entities. We care about the rules that have to be applied to guarantee the integrity of data (for example, the multiplicity of relationships) and the code procedures used to manipulate the data.

In the next section, we complete our analysis of the CaveatEmptor problem domain. The resulting domain model will be the central theme of this book.

3.1.3   *The CaveatEmptor domain model*

The CaveatEmptor site auctions many different kinds of items, from electronic equipment to airline tickets. Auctions proceed according to the English auction strategy: users continue to place bids on an item until the bid period for that item expires, and the highest bidder wins.

In any store, goods are categorized by type and grouped with similar goods into sections and onto shelves. The auction catalog requires some kind of hierarchy of item categories so that a buyer can browse these categories or arbitrarily search by category and item attributes. Lists of items appear in the category browser and search result screens. Selecting an item from a list takes the buyer to an item-detail view where an item may have images attached to it.

An auction consists of a sequence of bids, and one is the winning bid. User details include name, address, and billing information.

The result of this analysis, the high-level overview of the domain model, is shown in figure 3.3. Let's briefly discuss some interesting features of this model.

Each item can be auctioned only once, so you don't need to make Item distinct from any auction entities. Instead, you have a single auction item entity named Item. Thus, Bid is associated directly with Item. You model the Address information of a User as a separate class, a User may have three addresses, for home, billing, and shipping. You do allow the user to have many BillingDetails. Subclasses of an abstract class represent the various billing strategies (allowing future extension).

The application may nest a Category inside another Category, and so on. A recursive association, from the Category entity to itself, expresses this relationship. Note that a single Category may have multiple child categories but at most one parent. Each Item belongs to at least one Category.

This representation isn't the *complete* domain model but only classes for which you need persistence capabilities. You'd like to store and load instances of Category, Item, User, and so on. We have simplified this high-level overview a little; we may introduce additional classes later or make minor modifications to them when needed for more complex examples.

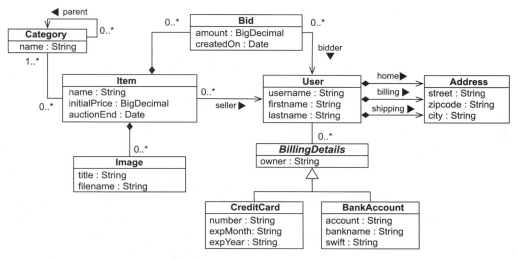

Figure 3.3   **Persistent classes of the CaveatEmptor domain model and their relationships**

Certainly, the entities in a domain model should encapsulate state and behavior. For example, the `User` entity should define the name and address of a customer *and* the logic required to calculate the shipping costs for items (to this particular customer).

There might be other classes in the domain model that have only transient runtime instances. Consider a `WinningBidStrategy` class encapsulating the fact that the highest bidder wins an auction. This might be called by the business layer (controller) code when checking the state of an auction. At some point, you might have to figure out how tax for sold items is calculated or how the system may approve a new user account. We don't consider such business rules or domain model behavior to be unimportant; rather, this concern is mostly orthogonal to the problem of persistence.

Now that you have a (rudimentary) application design with a domain model, the next step is to implement it in Java.

ORM without a domain model

Object persistence with full ORM is most suitable for applications based on a rich domain model. If your application doesn't implement complex business rules or complex interactions between entities (or if you have few entities), you may not need a domain model. Many simple and some not-so-simple problems are perfectly suited to table-oriented solutions, where the application is designed around the database data model instead of around an object-oriented domain model, often with logic executed in the database (stored procedures). Another aspect to consider is the learning curve: once you're proficient with Hibernate, you'll use it for all applications, even as a simple SQL query generator and result mapper. If you're just learning ORM, a trivial use case may not justify your invested time and overhead.

3.2   *Implementing the domain model*

You'll start with an issue that any implementation must deal with: the separation of concerns. The domain model implementation is usually a central, organizing component; it's reused heavily whenever you implement new application functionality. For this reason, you should be prepared to go to some lengths to ensure that concerns other than business aspects don't leak into the domain model implementation.

3.2.1   *Addressing leakage of concerns*

When concerns such as persistence, transaction management, or authorization start to appear in the domain model classes, this is an example of leakage of concerns. The domain model implementation is such an important piece of code that it shouldn't depend on orthogonal Java APIs. For example, code in the domain model shouldn't perform JNDI lookups or call the database via the JDBC API, not directly and not through an intermediate abstraction. This allows you to reuse the domain model classes virtually anywhere:

- The presentation layer can access instances and attributes of domain model entities when rendering views.
- The controller components in the business layer can also access the state of domain model entities and call methods of the entities to execute business logic.
- The persistence layer can load and store instances of domain model entities from and to the database, preserving their state.

Most important, preventing leakage of concerns makes it easy to unit-test the domain model without the need for a particular runtime environment or container, or the need for mocking any service dependencies. You can write unit tests that verify the correct behavior of your domain model classes without any special test harness. (We aren't talking about testing "load from the database" and "store in the database" aspects, but "calculate the shipping cost and tax" behavior.)

The Java EE standard solves the problem of leaky concerns with metadata, as annotations within your code or externalized as XML descriptors. This approach allows the runtime container to implement some predefined cross-cutting concerns—security, concurrency, persistence, transactions, and remoteness—in a generic way, by intercepting calls to application components.

Hibernate isn't a Java EE runtime environment, and it's not an application server. It's an implementation of just one specification under the Java EE umbrella—JPA— and a solution for just one of these concerns: persistence.

JPA defines the *entity class* as the primary programming artifact. This programming model enables transparent persistence, and a JPA provider such as Hibernate also offers automated persistence.

3.2.2 *Transparent and automated persistence*

We use *transparent* to mean a complete separation of concerns between the persistent classes of the domain model and the persistence layer. The persistent classes are unaware of—and have no dependency on—the persistence mechanism. We use *automatic* to refer to a persistence solution (your annotated domain, the layer, and mechanism) that relieves you of handling low-level mechanical details, such as writing most SQL statements and working with the JDBC API.

The `Item` class of the CaveatEmptor domain model, for example, shouldn't have any runtime dependency on any Java Persistence or Hibernate API. Furthermore:

- JPA doesn't require that any special superclasses or interfaces be inherited or implemented by persistent classes. Nor are any special classes used to implement attributes and associations. (Of course, the option to use both techniques is always there.)

- You can reuse persistent classes outside the context of persistence, in unit tests or in the presentation layer, for example. You can create instances in any runtime environment with the regular Java `new` operator, preserving testability and reusability.

- In a system with transparent persistence, instances of entities aren't aware of the underlying data store; they need not even be aware that they're being persisted or retrieved. JPA externalizes persistence concerns to a generic persistence manager API.

- Hence, most of your code, and certainly your complex business logic, doesn't have to concern itself with the current state of a domain model entity instance in a single thread of execution.

We regard transparency as a requirement because it makes an application easier to build and maintain. Transparent persistence should be one of the primary goals of any ORM solution. Clearly, no automated persistence solution is completely transparent: Every automated persistence layer, including JPA and Hibernate, imposes some requirements on the persistent classes. For example, JPA requires that collection-valued attributes be typed to an interface such as `java.util.Set` or `java.util.List` and not to an actual implementation such as `java.util.HashSet` (this is a good practice anyway). Or, a JPA entity class has to have a special attribute, called the *database identifier* (which is also less of a restriction but usually convenient).

You now know why the persistence mechanism should have minimal impact on how you implement a domain model, and that transparent and automated persistence are required. Our preferred programming model to archive this is POJO.

Around 10 years ago, many developers started talking about POJO, a back-to-basics approach that essentially revives JavaBeans, a component model for UI development, and reapplies it to the other layers of a system. Several revisions of the EJB and JPA specifications brought us new lightweight entities, and it would be appropriate to call

POJO

POJO is the acronym for Plain Old Java Objects. Martin Fowler, Rebecca Parsons, and Josh Mackenzie coined this term in 2000.

them *persistence-capable JavaBeans*. Java engineers often use all these terms as synonyms for the same basic design approach.

You shouldn't be too concerned about what terms we use in this book; the ultimate goal is to apply the persistence aspect as transparently as possible to Java classes. Almost any Java class can be persistence-capable if you follow some simple practices. Let's see how this looks in code.

3.2.3   *Writing persistence-capable classes*

Working with fine-grained and rich domain models is a major Hibernate objective. This is a reason we work with POJOs. In general, using fine-grained objects means more classes than tables.

A persistence-capable plain-old Java class declares attributes, which represent state, and business methods, which define behavior. Some attributes represent associations to other persistence-capable classes.

A POJO implementation of the User entity of the domain model is shown in the following listing. Let's walk through the code.

Listing 3.1   POJO implementation of the User class

PATH: /model/src/main/java/org/jpwh/model/simple/User.java

```java
public class User implements Serializable {

    protected String username;

    public User() {
    }

    public String getUsername() {
        return username;
    }

    public void setUsername(String username) {
        this.username = username;
    }

    public BigDecimal calcShippingCosts(Address fromLocation) {
        // Empty implementation of business method
        return null;
    }

    // ...
}
```

JPA doesn't require that persistent classes implement `java.io.Serializable`. But when instances are stored in an `HttpSession` or passed by value using RMI, serialization is necessary. Although this might not occur in your application, the class will be serializable without any additional work, and there are no downsides to declaring that. (We aren't going to declare it on every example, assuming that you know when it will be necessary.)

The class can be abstract and, if needed, extend a non-persistent class or implement an interface. It must be a top-level class, not nested within another class. The persistence-capable class and any of its methods *can't* be final (a requirement of the JPA specification).

Unlike the JavaBeans specification, which requires no specific constructor, Hibernate (and JPA) require a constructor with no arguments for every persistent class. Alternatively, you might not write a constructor at all; Hibernate will then use the Java default constructor. Hibernate calls classes using the Java reflection API on such a no-argument constructor to create instances. The constructor may not be public, but it has to be at least package-visible if Hibernate will use runtime-generated proxies for performance optimization. Also, consider the requirements of other specifications: the EJB standard requires public visibility on session bean constructors, just like the JavaServer Faces (JSF) specification requires for its managed beans. There are other situations when you'd want a public constructor to create an "empty" state: for example, query-by-example building.

The properties of the POJO implement the attributes of the business entities—for example, the `username` of `User`. You usually implement properties as private or protected member fields, together with public or protected property accessor methods: for each field a method for retrieving its value and a method for setting the value. These methods are known as the *getter* and *setter*, respectively. The example POJO in listing 3.1 declares getter and setter methods for the `username` property.

The JavaBean specification defines the guidelines for naming accessor methods; this allows generic tools like Hibernate to easily discover and manipulate property values. A getter method name begins with `get`, followed by the name of the property (the first letter in uppercase); a setter method name begins with `set` and similarly is followed by the name of the property. You may begin getter methods for Boolean properties with `is` instead of `get`.

Hibernate doesn't require accessor methods. You can choose how the state of an instance of your persistent classes should be persisted. Hibernate will either directly access fields or call accessor methods. Your class design isn't disturbed much by these considerations. You can make some accessor methods non-public or completely remove them—then configure Hibernate to rely on field access for these properties.

Should property fields and accessor methods be private, protected, or package visible?

Typically, you want to discourage direct access to the internal state of your class, so you don't make attribute fields public. If you make fields or methods private, you're effectively declaring that nobody should ever access them; only you're allowed to do that (or a service like Hibernate). This is a definitive statement. There are often good reasons for someone to access your "private" internals—usually to fix one of your bugs—and you only make people angry if they have to fall back to reflection access in an emergency. Instead, you might assume or know that the engineer who comes after you has access to your code and knows what they're doing.

The protected visibility then is a more reasonable default. You're forbidding direct public access, indicating that this particular member detail is internal, but allowing access by subclasses if need be. You trust the engineer who creates the subclass. Package visibility is rude: you're forcing someone to create code in the same package to access member fields and methods; this is extra work for no good reason. Most important, these recommendations for visibility are relevant for environments without security policies and a runtime SecurityManager. If you have to keep your internal code private, make it private.

Although trivial accessor methods are common, one of the reasons we like to use Java-Beans-style accessor methods is that they provide encapsulation: you can change the hidden internal implementation of an attribute without any changes to the public interface. If you configure Hibernate to access attributes through methods, you abstract the internal data structure of the class—the instance variables—from the design of the database.

For example, if your database stores the name of a user as a single NAME column, but your User class has firstname and lastname fields, you can add the following persistent name property to the class.

Listing 3.2   POJO implementation of the User class with logic in accessor methods

```
public class User {

    protected String firstname;
    protected String lastname;

    public String getName() {
        return firstname + ' ' + lastname;
    }

    public void setName(String name) {
        StringTokenizer t = new StringTokenizer(name);
        firstname = t.nextToken();
        lastname = t.nextToken();
    }
}
```

Later, you'll see that a custom type converter in the persistence service is a better way to handle many of these kinds of situations. It helps to have several options.

Another issue to consider is *dirty checking*. Hibernate automatically detects state changes in order to synchronize the updated state with the database. It's usually safe to return a different instance from the getter method than the instance passed by Hibernate to the setter. Hibernate compares them by value—not by object identity—to determine whether the attribute's persistent state needs to be updated. For example, the following getter method doesn't result in unnecessary SQL UPDATEs:

```
public String getFirstname() {                    ◁——— This is OK.
    return new String(firstname);
}
```

There is one important exception to this: collections are compared by identity! For a property mapped as a persistent collection, you should return exactly the same collection instance from the getter method that Hibernate passed to the setter method. If you don't, Hibernate will update the database, even if no update is necessary, every time the state held in memory is synchronized with the database. You should usually avoid this kind of code in accessor methods:

```
protected String[] names = new String[0];

public void setNames(List<String> names) {
    this.names = names.toArray(new String[names.size()]);
}

public List<String> getNames() {                    Don't do this if Hibernate
    return Arrays.asList(names);                ◁——┘ accesses the methods!
}
```

Of course, this won't be a problem if Hibernate is accessing the names field directly, ignoring your getter and setter methods.

How does Hibernate handle exceptions when your accessor methods throw them? If Hibernate uses accessor methods when loading and storing instances and a RuntimeException (unchecked) is thrown, the current transaction is rolled back, and the exception is yours to handle in the code that called the Java Persistence (or Hibernate native) API. If you throw a checked application exception, Hibernate wraps the exception into a RuntimeException.

The example in listing 3.2 also defines a business method that calculates the cost of shipping an item to a particular user (we left out the implementation of this method).

Next, we'll focus on the relationships between entities and associations between persistent classes.

3.2.4 *Implementing POJO associations*

You'll now see how to associate and create different kinds of relationships between objects: one-to-many, many-to-one, and bidirectional relationships. We'll look at the scaffolding code needed to create these associations, how to simplify relationship management, and how to enforce the integrity of these relationships.

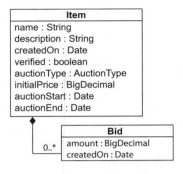

You create properties to express associations between classes, and you (typically) call accessor methods to navigate from instance to instance at runtime. Let's consider the associations defined by the Item and Bid persistent classes, as shown in figure 3.4.

As with all of our UML class diagrams, we left out the association-related attributes, Item#bids and Bid#item. These properties and the methods that manipulate their values are called *scaffolding code*. This is what the scaffolding code for the Bid class looks like:

Figure 3.4 Associations between the Item and Bid classes

PATH: /model/src/main/java/org/jpwh/model/simple/Bid.java

```java
public class Bid {

    protected Item item;

    public Item getItem() {
        return item;
    }

    public void setItem(Item item) {
        this.item = item;
    }
}
```

The item property allows navigation from a Bid to the related Item. This is an association with *many-to-one* multiplicity; users can make many bids for each item. Here is the Item class's scaffolding code:

PATH: /model/src/main/java/org/jpwh/model/simple/Item.java

```java
public class Item {

    protected Set<Bid> bids = new HashSet<Bid>();

    public Set<Bid> getBids() {
        return bids;
    }

    public void setBids(Set<Bid> bids) {
        this.bids = bids;
    }
}
```

This association between the two classes allows *bidirectional* navigation: the *many-to-one* is from this perspective a *one-to-many* multiplicity (again, one item can have many bids). The scaffolding code for the bids property uses a collection interface type, `java.util.Set`. JPA requires interfaces for collection-typed properties, where you must use `java.util.Set`, `java.util.List`, or `java.util.Collection` rather than `HashSet`, for example. It's good practice to program to collection interfaces anyway, rather than concrete implementations, so this restriction shouldn't bother you.

You choose a `Set` and initialize the field to a new `HashSet` because the application disallows duplicate bids. This is good practice because you avoid any `NullPointer-Exceptions` when someone is accessing the property of a new `Item` without any bids. The JPA provider is also required to set a non-empty value on any mapped collection-valued property: for example, when an `Item` without bids is loaded from the database. (It doesn't have to use a `HashSet`; the implementation is up to the provider. Hibernate has its own collection implementations with additional capabilities—for example, dirty checking.)

Shouldn't bids on an item be stored in a list?

The first reaction is often to preserve the order of elements as they're entered by users, because this may also be the order in which you will show them later. Certainly, in an auction application there has to be some defined order in which the user sees bids for an item—for example, highest bid first or newest bid last. You might even work with a `java.util.List` in your user interface code to sort and display bids of an item. That doesn't mean this display order should be durable; data integrity isn't affected by the order in which bids are displayed. You need to store the amount of each bid, so you can find the highest bid, and you need to store a timestamp for each bid when it's created, so you can find the newest bid. When in doubt, keep your system flexible and sort the data when it's retrieved from the datastore (in a query) and/or shown to the user (in Java code), not when it's stored.

Just like for basic properties, accessor methods for associations need to be declared `public` only if they're part of the external interface of the persistent class used by the application logic to create a link between two instances. We'll now focus on this issue, because managing the link between an `Item` and a `Bid` is much more complicated in Java code than it is in an SQL database, with declarative foreign key constraints. In our experience, engineers are often unaware of this complication arising from a network object model with bidirectional references (pointers). Let's walk through the issue step by step.

The basic procedure for linking a `Bid` with an `Item` looks like this:

```
anItem.getBids().add(aBid);
aBid.setItem(anItem);
```

Whenever you create this bidirectional link, two actions are required:

- You must add the `Bid` to the `bids` collection of the `Item`.
- The `item` property of the `Bid` must be set.

JPA doesn't manage persistent associations. If you want to manipulate an association, you must write exactly the same code you would write without Hibernate. If an association is bidirectional, you must consider both sides of the relationship. If you ever have problems understanding the behavior of associations in JPA, just ask yourself, "What would I do without Hibernate?" Hibernate doesn't change the regular Java semantics.

We recommend that you add convenience methods that group these operations, allowing reuse and helping ensure correctness, and in the end guaranteeing data integrity (a `Bid` *is required* to have a reference to an `Item`). The next listing shows such a convenience method in the `Item` class.

> **Listing 3.3   A convenience method simplifies relationship management**
>
> PATH: /model/src/main/java/org/jpwh/model/simple/Item.java

```
public void addBid(Bid bid) {
    if (bid == null)                                              ◁——— Be defensive
        throw new NullPointerException("Can't add null Bid");
    if (bid.getItem() != null)
        throw new IllegalStateException("Bid is already assigned to an
    ➥ Item");

    getBids().add(bid);
    bid.setItem(this);
}
```

The `addBid()` method not only reduces the lines of code when dealing with `Item` and `Bid` instances, but also enforces the cardinality of the association. You avoid errors that arise from leaving out one of the two required actions. You should always provide this kind of grouping of operations for associations, if possible. If you compare this with the relational model of foreign keys in an SQL database, you can easily see how a network and pointer model complicates a simple operation: instead of a declarative constraint, you need procedural code to guarantee data integrity.

Because you want `addBid()` to be the only externally visible mutator method for the bids of an item (possibly in addition to a `removeBid()` method), you can make the `Item#setBids()` method private or drop it and configure Hibernate to directly access fields for persistence. Consider making the `Bid#setItem()` method package-visible, for the same reason.

The `Item#getBids()` getter method still returns a modifiable collection, so clients can use it to make changes that aren't reflected on the inverse side. Bids added directly to the collection wouldn't have a reference to an item—an inconsistent state, according to your database constraints. To prevent this, you can wrap the internal collection before returning it from the getter method, with `Collections.unmodifiable-Collection(c)` and `Collections.unmodifiableSet(s)`. The client then gets an exception if it tries to modify the collection; you therefore force every modification to go through the relationship management method that guarantees integrity. Note that in this case you'll have to configure Hibernate for field access, because the collection returned by the getter method is then not the same as the one given to the setter method.

An alternative strategy is immutable instances. For example, you could enforce integrity by requiring an `Item` argument in the constructor of `Bid`, as shown in the following listing.

> **Listing 3.4 Enforcing integrity of relationships with a constructor**
>
> PATH: /model/src/main/java/org/jpwh/model/simple/Bid.java

```
public class Bid {

    protected Item item;

    public Bid(Item item) {
        this.item = item;
        item.getBids().add(this);          ←—— Bidirectional
    }

    public Item getItem() {
        return item;
    }
}
```

In this constructor, the `item` field is set; no further modification of the field value should occur. The collection on the "other" side is also updated for a bidirectional relationship. There is no `Bid#setItem()` method, and you probably shouldn't expose a public `Item#setBids()` method.

There are several problems with this approach. First, Hibernate can't call this constructor. You need to add a no-argument constructor for Hibernate, and it needs to be at least package-visible. Furthermore, because there is no `setItem()` method, Hibernate would have to be configured to access the `item` field directly. This means the field can't be `final`, so the class isn't guaranteed to be immutable.

In the examples in this book, we'll sometimes write scaffolding methods such as the `Item#addBid()` shown earlier, or we may have additional constructors for required values. It's up to you how many convenience methods and layers you want to wrap around the persistent association properties and/or fields, but we recommend being consistent and applying the same strategy to all your domain model classes. For the sake of readability, we won't always show convenience methods, special constructors, and other such scaffolding in future code samples and assume you'll add them according to your own taste and requirements.

You now have seen domain model classes, how to represent their attributes, and the relationships between them. Next, we'll increase the level of abstraction, adding metadata to the domain model implementation and declaring aspects such as validation and persistence rules.

3.3   *Domain model metadata*

Metadata is data about data, so domain model metadata is information about your domain model. For example, when you use the Java reflection API to discover the names of classes of your domain model or the names of their attributes, you're accessing domain model metadata.

ORM tools also require metadata, to specify the mapping between classes and tables, properties and columns, associations and foreign keys, Java types and SQL types, and so on. This object/relational mapping metadata governs the transformation between the different type systems and relationship representations in object-oriented and SQL systems. JPA has a metadata API, which you can call to obtain details about the persistence aspects of your domain model, such as the names of persistent entities and attributes. First, it's your job as an engineer to create and maintain this information.

JPA standardizes two metadata options: annotations in Java code and externalized XML descriptor files. Hibernate has some extensions for native functionality, also available as annotations and/or XML descriptors. Usually we prefer either annotations or XML files as the primary source of mapping metadata. After reading this section, you'll have the background information to make an educated decision for your own project.

We'll also discuss *Bean Validation* (JSR 303) and how it provides declarative validation for your domain model (or any other) classes. The reference implementation of this specification is the *Hibernate Validator* project. Most engineers today prefer Java annotations as the primary mechanism for declaring metadata.

3.3.1   *Annotation-based metadata*

The big advantage of annotations is to put metadata next to the information it describes, instead of separating it physically into a different file. Here's an example:

PATH: /model/src/main/java/org/jpwh/model/simple/Item.java

```
import javax.persistence.Entity;

@Entity
public class Item {

}
```

You can find the standard JPA mapping annotations in the javax.persistence package. This example declares the Item class as a persistent entity using the @javax .persistence.Entity annotation. All of its attributes are now automatically persistent with a default strategy. That means you can load and store instances of Item, and all properties of the class are part of the managed state.

(If you followed the previous chapter, you probably notice the missing required @Id annotation and identifier property. If you want to try the Item example, you'll have to add an identifier property. We'll discuss identifier properties again in the next chapter, in section 4.2.)

Annotations are type-safe, and the JPA metadata is included in the compiled class files. Hibernate then reads the classes and metadata with Java reflection when the application starts. The IDE can also easily validate and highlight annotations—they're regular Java types, after all. If you refactor your code, you rename, delete, or move classes and properties all the time. Most development tools and editors can't refactor XML element and attribute values, but annotations are part of the Java language and are included in all refactoring operations.

Is my class now dependent on JPA?

Yes, but it's a compile-time only dependency. You need JPA libraries on your classpath when compiling the source of your domain model class. The Java Persistence API isn't required on the classpath when you create an instance of the class: for example, in a desktop client application that doesn't execute any JPA code. Only when you access the annotations through reflection at runtime (as Hibernate does internally when it reads your metadata) will you need the packages on the classpath.

When the standardized Java Persistence annotations are insufficient, a JPA provider may offer additional annotations.

USING VENDOR EXTENSIONS

Even if you map most of your application's model with JPA-compatible annotations from the `javax.persistence` package, you'll have to use vendor extensions at some point. For example, some performance-tuning options you'd expect to be available in high-quality persistence software are only available as Hibernate-specific annotations. This is how JPA providers compete, so you can't avoid annotations from other packages—there's a reason why you picked Hibernate.

This is the `Item` entity source code again with a Hibernate-only mapping option:

```
import javax.persistence.Entity;

@Entity
@org.hibernate.annotations.Cache(
    usage = org.hibernate.annotations.CacheConcurrencyStrategy.READ_WRITE
)
public class Item {

}
```

We prefer to prefix Hibernate annotations with the full `org.hibernate.annotations` package name. Consider this good practice, because you can easily see what metadata for this class is from the JPA specification and which is vendor-specific. You can also easily search your source code for "org.hibernate.annotations" and get a complete overview of all nonstandard annotations in your application in a single search result.

If you switch your Java Persistence provider, you only have to replace the vendor-specific extensions where you can expect a similar feature set to be available with most mature JPA implementations. Of course, we hope you'll never have to do this, and it doesn't happen often in practice—just be prepared.

Annotations on classes only cover metadata that is applicable to that particular class. You often need metadata at a higher level, for an entire package or even the whole application.

GLOBAL ANNOTATION METADATA

The `@Entity` annotation maps a particular class. JPA and Hibernate also have annotations for global metadata. For example, a `@NamedQuery` has global scope; you don't apply it to a particular class. Where should you place this annotation?

Although it's possible to place such global annotations in the source file of a class (any class, really, at the top), we'd rather keep global metadata in a separate file. Package-level annotations are a good choice; they're in a file called package-info.java in a particular package directory. You can see an example of global named query declarations in the following listing.

> **Listing 3.5   Global metadata in a package-info.java file**
>
> PATH: /model/src/main/java/org/jpwh/model/querying/package-info.java

```
@org.hibernate.annotations.NamedQueries({
    @org.hibernate.annotations.NamedQuery(
        name = "findItemsOrderByName",
        query = "select i from Item i order by i.name asc"
    )
    ,
    @org.hibernate.annotations.NamedQuery(
        name = "findItemBuyNowPriceGreaterThan",
        query = "select i from Item i where i.buyNowPrice > :price",
        timeout = 60,                                              ◁─────┐
        comment = "Custom SQL comment"                                   │  Seconds!
    )
})

package org.jpwh.model.querying;
```

Unless you've used package-level annotations before, the syntax of this file with the package and import declarations at the bottom is probably new to you.

There is a reason the previous code example only includes annotations from the Hibernate package and no Java Persistence annotations. We ignored the standardized JPA `@org.javax.persistence.NamedQuery` annotation and used the Hibernate alternative. The JPA annotations don't have package applicability—we don't know why. In fact, JPA doesn't allow annotations in a package-info.java file. The native Hibernate annotations offer the same, and sometimes even more, functionality, so this shouldn't be too much of a problem. If you don't want to use the Hibernate annotations, you'll have to either put the JPA annotations at the top of any class (you could have an otherwise empty `MyNamedQueries` class as part of your domain model) or use an XML file, as you'll see later in this section.

Annotations will be our primary tool throughout this book for ORM metadata, and there is much to learn about this subject. Before we look at some alternative mapping styles with XML files, let's use some simple annotations to improve the domain model classes with validation rules.

3.3.2   *Applying Bean Validation rules*

Most applications contain a multitude of data-integrity checks. You've seen what happens when you violate one of the simplest data-integrity constraints: you get a `Null-PointerException` when you expect a value to be available. Other examples are a string-valued property that shouldn't be empty (remember, an empty string isn't `null`), a string that has to match a particular regular expression pattern, and a number or date value that must be within a certain range.

These business rules affect every layer of an application: The user interface code has to display detailed and localized error messages. The business and persistence layers must check input values received from the client before passing them to the datastore. The SQL database has to be the final validator, ultimately guaranteeing the integrity of durable data.

The idea behind Bean Validation is that declaring rules such as "This property can't be null" or "This number has to be in the given range" is much easier and less error-prone than writing if-then-else procedures repeatedly. Furthermore, declaring these rules on the central component of your application, the domain model implementation, enables integrity checks in every layer of the system. The rules are then available to the presentation and persistence layers. And if you consider how data-integrity constraints affect not only your Java application code but also your SQL database schema—which is a collection of integrity rules—you might think of Bean Validation constraints as additional ORM metadata.

Look at the following extended `Item` domain model class.

Listing 3.6   Applying validation constraints on `Item` entity fields

PATH: /model/src/main/java/org/jpwh/model/simple/Item.java

```
import javax.validation.constraints.Future;
import javax.validation.constraints.NotNull;
import javax.validation.constraints.Size;

@Entity
public class Item {

    @NotNull
    @Size(
        min = 2,
        max = 255,
        message = "Name is required, maximum 255 characters."
    )
    protected String name;
```

```
@Future
protected Date auctionEnd;
}
```

You add two more attributes—the name of an item and the auctionEnd date—when an auction concludes. Both are typical candidates for additional constraints: you want to guarantee that the name is always present and human readable (one-character item names don't make much sense), but it shouldn't be too long—your SQL database will be most efficient with variable-length strings up to 255 characters, and your user interface also has some constraints on visible label space. The ending time of an auction obviously should be in the future. If you don't provide an error message, a default message will be used. Messages can be keys to external properties files, for internationalization.

The validation engine will access the fields directly if you annotate the fields. If you prefer calls through accessor methods, annotate the getter method with validation constraints, not the setter. Then constraints are part of the class's API and included in its Javadoc, making the domain model implementation easier to understand. Note that this is independent from access by the JPA provider; that is, Hibernate Validator may call accessor methods, whereas Hibernate ORM may call fields directly.

Bean Validation isn't limited to the built-in annotations; you can create your own constraints and annotations. With a custom constraint, you can even use class-level annotations and validate several attribute values at the same time on an instance of the class. The following test code shows how you can manually check the integrity of an Item instance.

> **Listing 3.7   Testing an Item instance for constraint violations**
>
> PATH: /examples/src/test/java/org/jpwh/test/simple/ModelOperations.java

```
ValidatorFactory factory = Validation.buildDefaultValidatorFactory();
Validator validator = factory.getValidator();

Item item = new Item();                                    One validation error:
item.setName("Some Item");                                 auction end date not
item.setAuctionEnd(new Date());                                   in the future!

Set<ConstraintViolation<Item>> violations = validator.validate(item);

assertEquals(1, violations.size());

ConstraintViolation<Item> violation = violations.iterator().next();
String failedPropertyName =
        violation.getPropertyPath().iterator().next().getName();

assertEquals(failedPropertyName, "auctionEnd");

if (Locale.getDefault().getLanguage().equals("en"))
    assertEquals(violation.getMessage(), "must be in the future");
```

We're not going to explain this code in detail but offer it for you to explore. You'll rarely write this kind of validation code; most of the time, this aspect is automatically handled by your user interface and persistence framework. It's therefore important to look for Bean Validation integration when selecting a UI framework. JSF version 2 and newer automatically integrates with Bean Validation, for example.

Hibernate, as required from any JPA provider, also automatically integrates with Hibernate Validator if the libraries are available on the classpath and offers the following features:

- You don't have to manually validate instances before passing them to Hibernate for storage.
- Hibernate recognizes constraints on persistent domain model classes and triggers validation before database insert or update operations. When validation fails, Hibernate throws a `ConstraintViolationException`, containing the failure details, to the code calling persistence-management operations.
- The Hibernate toolset for automatic SQL schema generation understands many constraints and generates SQL DDL-equivalent constraints for you. For example, an `@NotNull` annotation translates into an SQL `NOT NULL` constraint, and an `@Size(n)` rule defines the number of characters in a `VARCHAR(n)`-typed column.

You can control this behavior of Hibernate with the `<validation-mode>` element in your persistence.xml configuration file. The default mode is `AUTO`, so Hibernate will only validate if it finds a Bean Validation provider (such as Hibernate Validator) on the classpath of the running application. With mode `CALLBACK`, validation will always occur, and you'll get a deployment error if you forget to bundle a Bean Validation provider. The `NONE` mode disables automatic validation by the JPA provider.

You'll see Bean Validation annotations again later in this book; you'll also find them in the example code bundles. At this point we could write much more about Hibernate Validator, but we'd only repeat what is already available in the project's excellent reference guide. Have a look, and find out more about features such as validation groups and the metadata API for discovery of constraints.

The Java Persistence and Bean Validation standards embrace annotations aggressively. The expert groups have been aware of the advantages of XML deployment descriptors in certain situations, especially for configuration metadata that changes with each deployment.

3.3.3 *Externalizing metadata with XML files*

You can replace or override every annotation in JPA with an XML descriptor element. In other words, you don't have to use annotations if you don't want to, or if keeping mapping metadata separate from source code is for whatever reason advantageous to your system design.

XML METADATA WITH JPA

The following listing shows a JPA XML descriptor for a particular persistence unit.

Listing 3.8   JPA XML descriptor containing the mapping metadata of a persistence unit

```
<entity-mappings
        version="2.1"
        xmlns="http://xmlns.jcp.org/xml/ns/persistence/orm"
        xmlns:xsi="http://www.w3.org/2001/XMLSchema-instance"
        xsi:schemaLocation="http://xmlns.jcp.org/xml/ns/persistence/orm
            http://xmlns.jcp.org/xml/ns/persistence/orm_2_1.xsd">

    <persistence-unit-metadata>

        <xml-mapping-metadata-complete/>

        <persistence-unit-defaults>
            <delimited-identifiers/>
        </persistence-unit-defaults>

    </persistence-unit-metadata>

    <entity class="org.jpwh.model.simple.Item" access="FIELD">
        <attributes>
            <id name="id">
                <generated-value strategy="AUTO"/>
            </id>
            <basic name="name"/>
            <basic name="auctionEnd">
                <temporal>TIMESTAMP</temporal>
            </basic>
        </attributes>
    </entity>

</entity-mappings>
```

Annotations: **First, global metadata** → `<persistence-unit-metadata>`. **Ignore all annotations and all mapping metadata in XML files.** → `<xml-mapping-metadata-complete/>`. **Some default settings** → `<persistence-unit-defaults>`. **Escape all SQL column, table, and other names: for example, if your SQL names are keywords (such as a "USER").**

The JPA provider automatically picks up this descriptor if you place it in a META-INF/orm.xml file on the classpath of the persistence unit. If you prefer to use a different name or several files, you'll have to change the configuration of the persistence unit in your META-INF/persistence.xml file:

PATH: /model/src/main/resources/META-INF/persistence.xml

```
<persistence-unit name="SimpleXMLCompletePU">
    ...

    <mapping-file>simple/Mappings.xml</mapping-file>
    <mapping-file>simple/Queries.xml</mapping-file>
    ...
</persistence-unit>
```

If you include the `<xml-mapping-metadata-complete>` element, the JPA provider ignores all annotations on your domain model classes in this persistence unit and relies only on the mappings as defined in the XML descriptor(s). You can (redundantly in this case) enable this on an entity level, with `<metadata-complete="true"/>`. If enabled, the JPA provider assumes that you mapped all attributes of the entity in XML and that it should ignore all annotations for this particular entity.

Instead, if you don't want to ignore but override the annotation metadata, don't mark the XML descriptors as "complete", and name the class and property to override:

```
<entity class="org.jpwh.model.simple.Item">
    <attributes>
        <basic name="name">                          ◁─┐  Override SQL
            <column name="ITEM_NAME"/>                  │  column name
        </basic>
    </attributes>
</entity>
```

Here you map the name property to the ITEM_NAME column; by default, the property would map to the NAME column. Hibernate will now ignore any existing annotations from the javax.persistence.annotation and org.hibernate.annotations packages on the name property of the Item class. But Hibernate doesn't ignore Bean Validation annotations and still applies them for automatic validation and schema generation! All other annotations on the Item class are also recognized. Note that you don't specify an access strategy in this mapping, so field access or accessor methods are used, depending on the position of the @Id annotation in Item. (We'll get back to this detail in the next chapter.)

We won't talk much about JPA XML descriptors in this book. The syntax of these documents is a 1:1 mirror of the JPA annotation syntax, so you shouldn't have any problems writing them. We'll focus on the important aspect: the mapping strategies. The syntax used to write down metadata is secondary.

Unfortunately, like many other schemas in the Java EE world, the JPA orm_2_0.xsd doesn't allow vendor extensions. You can't have elements and attributes from another namespace in the JPA XML mapping documents. Consequently, using vendor extensions and Hibernate native features requires falling back to a different XML syntax.

HIBERNATE XML MAPPING FILES

The native Hibernate XML mapping file format was the original metadata option before JDK 5 introduced annotations. By convention, you name these files with the suffix .hbm.xml. The following listing shows a basic Hibernate XML mapping document.

Listing 3.9 Metadata document in Hibernate's native XML syntax

PATH: /model/src/main/resources/simple/Native.hbm.xml

```
<?xml version="1.0"?>
<hibernate-mapping
        xmlns="http://www.hibernate.org/xsd/orm/hbm"
        package="org.jpwh.model.simple"
        default-access="field">                        ◁──❶ Declare metadata
    <class name="Item">
        <id name="id">
            <generator class="native"/>
        </id>
        <property name="name"/>
        <property name="auctionEnd" type="timestamp"/>
```

Entity class mapping ├─▷

```
    </class>                                                        Externalized
                                                                    queries
    <query name="findItemsHibernate">select i from Item i</query>

    <database-object>
        <create>create index ITEM_NAME_IDX on ITEM(NAME)</create>
        <drop>drop index if exists
    ITEM_NAME_IDX</drop>                                            Auxiliary
    </database-object>                                              schema
                                                                    DDL
</hibernate-mapping>
```

1 Metadata is declared ion a <hibernate-mapping> root element. Attributes such as package name and default-access apply to all mappings in this file. You may include as many entity class mappings as you like.

Note that this XML file declares a default XML namespace for all elements; this is a new option in Hibernate 5. If you have existing mapping files for Hibernate 4 or older with XML document type declarations, you can continue using them.

Although it's possible to declare mappings for multiple classes in one mapping file by using multiple <class> elements, many older Hibernate projects are organized with one mapping file per persistent class. The convention is to give the file the same name and package as the mapped class: for example, my/model/Item.hbm.xml for the my.model.Item class.

A class mapping in a Hibernate XML document is a "complete" mapping; that is, any other mapping metadata for that class, whether in annotations or JPA XML files, will trigger a "duplicate mapping" error on startup. If you map a class in a Hibernate XML file, this declaration has to include all mapping details. You can't override individual properties or extend an existing mapping. In addition, you have to list and map all persistent properties of an entity class in a Hibernate XML file. If you don't map a property, Hibernate considers it transient state. Compare this with JPA mappings, where the @Entity annotation alone will make all properties of a class persistent.

Hibernate native XML files are no longer the primary choice for declaring the bulk of a project's ORM metadata. Most engineers now prefer annotations. Native XML metadata files are mostly used to gain access to special Hibernate features that aren't available as annotations or are easier to maintain in XML files (for example, because it's deployment-dependent configuration metadata). You aren't required to have *any* <class> elements in a Hibernate XML mapping file. Thus, all metadata in these files can be global to the persistence unit, such as externalized (even native SQL) query strings, custom type definitions, auxiliary SQL DDL for particular DBMS products, dynamic persistence context filters, and so on.

When we later discuss such advanced and native Hibernate features, we'll show you how to declare them in Hibernate XML files. As already mentioned, your focus should be on understanding the essence of a mapping strategy, and most of our examples will use JPA and Hibernate annotations to express these strategies.

The approaches we've described so far assume that all ORM metadata is known at development (or deployment) time. Suppose that some information isn't known before the application starts. Can you programmatically manipulate the mapping metadata at runtime? We've also mentioned the JPA metadata API for access to persistence unit details. How does that work, and when is it useful?

3.3.4 Accessing metadata at runtime

The JPA specification provides programming interfaces for accessing the metamodel of persistent classes. There are two flavors of the API. One is more dynamic in nature and similar to basic Java reflection. The second option is a static metamodel, typically produced by a Java 6 annotation processor. For both options, access is read-only; you can't modify the metadata at runtime.

Hibernate also offers a native metamodel API that supports read and write access and much more detail about the ORM. We don't cover this native API (found in `org.hibernate.cfg.Configuration`) in the book because it was already deprecated, and a replacement API wasn't available at the time of writing. Please refer to the Hibernate documentation for the latest updates on this feature.

THE DYNAMIC METAMODEL API IN JAVA PERSISTENCE

Sometimes—for example, when you want to write some custom validation or generic UI code—you'd like to get programmatic access to the persistent attributes of an entity. You'd like to know what persistent classes and attributes your domain model has dynamically. The code in the next listing shows how to read metadata with Java Persistence interfaces.

> **Listing 3.10 Obtaining entity type information with the `Metamodel` API**
>
> PATH: /examples/src/test/java/org/jpwh/test/simple/AccessJPAMetamodel.java

```
Metamodel mm = entityManagerFactory.getMetamodel();

Set<ManagedType<?>> managedTypes = mm.getManagedTypes();
assertEquals(managedTypes.size(), 1);

ManagedType itemType = managedTypes.iterator().next();
assertEquals(
    itemType.getPersistenceType(),
    Type.PersistenceType.ENTITY
);
```

You can get the `Metamodel` from either the `EntityManagerFactory`, of which you typically have only one instance in an application per data source, or, if it's more convenient, from calling `EntityManager#getMetamodel()`. The set of managed types contains information about all persistent entities and embedded classes (which we'll discuss in the next chapter). In this example, there's only one: the `Item` entity. This is how you can dig deeper and find out more about each attribute.

Listing 3.11   Obtaining entity attribute information with the `Metamodel` API

PATH: **/examples/src/test/java/org/jpwh/test/simple/AccessJPAMetamodel.java**

```
SingularAttribute nameAttribute =
    itemType.getSingularAttribute("name");            ◁——— ❶ Entity attribute
assertEquals(
    nameAttribute.getJavaType(),
    String.class
);
assertEquals(
    nameAttribute.getPersistentAttributeType(),
    Attribute.PersistentAttributeType.BASIC
);
assertFalse(
    nameAttribute.isOptional()
);

SingularAttribute auctionEndAttribute =
    itemType.getSingularAttribute("auctionEnd");      ◁——— ❷ Entity attribute
assertEquals(
    auctionEndAttribute.getJavaType(),
    Date.class
);
assertFalse(
    auctionEndAttribute.isCollection()
);
assertFalse(
    auctionEndAttribute.isAssociation()
);
```

NOT NULL ⟶ (points to `nameAttribute.isOptional()`)

The attributes of the entity are accessed with a string: `name` ❶ and `auctionEnd` ❷. This obviously isn't type-safe, and if you change the names of the attributes, this code becomes broken and obsolete. The strings aren't automatically included in the refactoring operations of your IDE.

JPA also offers a static type-safe metamodel.

USING A STATIC METAMODEL

Java (at least up to version 8) has no first-class support for properties. You can't access the fields or accessor methods of a bean in a type-safe fashion—only by their names, using strings. This is particularly inconvenient with JPA criteria querying, a type-safe alternative to string-based query languages. Here's an example:

```
CriteriaBuilder cb = entityManager.getCriteriaBuilder();

CriteriaQuery<Item> query =
    cb.createQuery(Item.class);                       ◁———  This query is
Root<Item> fromItem = query.from(Item.class);              the equivalent
query.select(fromItem);                                    of "select i
                                                           from Item i."
List<Item> items =
    entityManager.createQuery(query)
        .getResultList();

assertEquals(items.size(), 2);
```

This query returns all items in the database; here there are two. If you now want to restrict this result and only return items with a particular name, you have to use a `like` expression, comparing the `name` attribute of each item with the pattern set in a parameter:

```
Path<String> namePath = fromItem.get("name");            ◄─┐ "where i.name
query.where(                                                │  like :pattern"
    cb.like(
        namePath,                                        ◄─┐ Has to be a Path<String>
        cb.parameter(String.class, "pattern")            │  for like() operator!
    )
);

items =
    entityManager.createQuery(query)
        .setParameter("pattern", "%some item%")          ◄─── Wildcards!
        .getResultList();

assertEquals(items.size(), 1);
assertEquals(items.iterator().next().getName(), "This is some item");
```

Notice how the `namePath` lookup requires the `name` string. This is where the type-safety of the criteria query breaks down. You can rename the `Item` entity class with your IDE's refactoring tools, and the query will still work. But as soon as you touch the `Item#name` property, manual adjustments are necessary. Luckily, you'll catch this when the test fails.

A much better approach, safe for refactoring and detecting mismatches at compile-time and not runtime, is the type-safe static metamodel:

```
query.where(
    cb.like(
        fromItem.get(Item_.name),                        ◄─── Static Item_ metamodel!
        cb.parameter(String.class, "pattern")
    )
);
```

The special class here is `Item_`; note the underscore. This class is a metadata class and lists all the attributes of the `Item` entity class:

```
@javax.persistence.metamodel.StaticMetamodel(Item.class)
public abstract class Item_ {

    public static volatile SingularAttribute<Item, Long> id;
    public static volatile SingularAttribute<Item, String> name;
    public static volatile SingularAttribute<Item, Date> auctionEnd;

}
```

You can write this class by hand or, as intended by the designers of this API, have it automatically generated by the *annotation processing tool (apt)* of the Java compiler. The *Hibernate JPA2 Metamodel Generator* (a distinct subproject of the Hibernate suite) uses this extension point. Its only purpose is to generate static metamodel classes from your managed persistent classes. You can download its JAR file and integrate it with your IDE (or your Maven build, as in the example code for this book). It will run automatically whenever you compile (or modify, depending on the IDE) the Item entity class and generate the appropriate Item_ metadata class.

What is the annotation processing tool (apt)?

Java includes the command-line utility apt, or annotation processing tool, which finds and executes annotation processors based on annotations in source code. An annotation processor uses reflection APIs to process program annotations (JSR 175). The apt APIs provide a build-time, source file, and read-only view of programs to model the Java type system. Annotation processors may first produce new source code and files, which apt can then compile along with the original source.

Although you've seen some mapping constructs in the previous sections, we haven't introduced more sophisticated class and property mappings so far. You should now decide which mapping metadata strategy you'd like to use in your project—we recommend annotations, and XML only when necessary—and then read more about class and property mappings in the next chapter.

3.4   *Summary*

- You've implemented persistent classes free of any crosscutting concerns like logging, authorization, and transaction demarcation; your persistent classes only depend on JPA at compile time. Even persistence-related concerns should not leak into the domain model implementation.
- Transparent persistence is important if you want to execute and test your business objects independently and easily.
- You've learned the best practices and requirements for the POJO and JPA entity programming model, and what concepts they have in common with the old JavaBean specification.
- You're ready to write more complex mappings, possibly with a combination of JDK annotations or JPA/Hibernate XML mapping files.

Part 2

Mapping strategies

This part is all about actual ORM, from classes and properties to tables and columns. Chapter 4 starts with regular class and property mappings and explains how you can map fine-grained Java domain models. Next, in chapter 5, you'll see how to map basic properties and embeddable components, and how to control mapping between Java and SQL types. In chapter 6, you'll map inheritance hierarchies of entities to the database using four basic inheritance-mapping strategies; you'll also map polymorphic associations. Chapter 7 is all about mapping collections and entity associations: you map persistent collections, collections of basic and embeddable types, and simple many-to-one and one-to-many entity associations. Chapter 8 dives deeper with advanced entity association mappings like mapping one-to-one entity associations, one-to-many mapping options, and many-to-many and ternary entity relationships. Finally, you'll find chapter 9 most interesting if you need to introduce Hibernate in an existing application, or if you have to work with legacy database schemas and handwritten SQL. We'll also talk about customized SQL DDL for schema generation in this chapter.

After reading this part of the book, you'll be ready to create even the most complex mappings quickly and with the right strategy. You'll understand how the problem of inheritance mapping can be solved and how to map collections and associations. You'll also be able to tune and customize Hibernate for integration with any existing database schema or application.

Mapping persistent classes

This chapter presents some fundamental mapping options and explains how to map entity classes to SQL tables. We show and discuss how you can handle database identity and primary keys, and how you can use various other metadata settings to customize how Hibernate loads and stores instances of your domain model classes. All mapping examples use JPA annotations. First, though, we define the essential distinction between entities and value types, and explain how you should approach the object/relational mapping of your domain model.

Major new feature in JPA 2

You can globally enable escaping of all names in generated SQL statements with the `<delimited-identifiers>` element in the persistence.xml configuration file.

61

4.1   *Understanding entities and value types*

When you look at your domain model, you'll notice a difference between classes: some of the types seem more important, representing first-class business objects (the term *object* is used here in its natural sense). Examples are the Item, Category, and User classes: these are entities in the real world you're trying to represent (refer back to figure 3.3 for a view of the example domain model). Other types present in your domain model, such as Address, String, and Integer, seem less important. In this section, we look at what it means to use fine-grained domain models and making the distinction between entity and value types.

4.1.1   *Fine-grained domain models*

A major objective of Hibernate is support for fine-grained and rich domain models. It's one reason we work with POJOs. In crude terms, *fine-grained* means more classes than tables.

For example, a user may have a home address in your domain model. In the database, you may have a single USERS table with the columns HOME_STREET, HOME_CITY, and HOME_ZIPCODE. (Remember the problem of SQL types we discussed in section 1.2.1?)

In the domain model, you could use the same approach, representing the address as three string-valued properties of the User class. But it's much better to model this using an Address class, where User has a homeAddress property. This domain model achieves improved cohesion and greater code reuse, and it's more understandable than SQL with inflexible type systems.

JPA emphasizes the usefulness of fine-grained classes for implementing type safety and behavior. For example, many people model an email address as a string-valued property of User. A more sophisticated approach is to define an EmailAddress class, which adds higher-level semantics and behavior—it may provide a prepareMail() method (it shouldn't have a sendMail() method, because you don't want your domain model classes to depend on the mail subsystem).

This granularity problem leads us to a distinction of central importance in ORM. In Java, all classes are of equal standing—all instances have their own identity and life cycle. When you introduce persistence, some instances may not have their own identity and life cycle but depend on others. Let's walk through an example.

4.1.2   *Defining application concepts*

Two people live in the same house, and they both register user accounts in Caveat-Emptor. Let's call them John and Jane.

An instance of User represents each account. Because you want to load, save, and delete these User instances independently, User is an entity class and not a value type. Finding entity classes is easy.

The User class has a homeAddress property; it's an association with the Address class. Do both User instances have a runtime reference to the same Address instance,

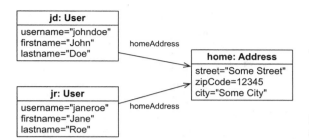

Figure 4.1 Two `User` instances have a reference to a single `Address`.

or does each `User` instance have a reference to its own `Address`? Does it matter that John and Jane live in the same house?

In figure 4.1, you can see how two `User` instances share a single `Address` instance (this is a UML object diagram, not a class diagram). If `Address` is supposed to support shared runtime references, it's an entity type. The `Address` instance has its own life, you can't delete it when John removes his `User` account—Jane might still have a reference to the `Address`.

Now let's look at the alternative model where each `User` has a reference to its own `homeAddress` instance, as shown in figure 4.2. In this case, you can make an instance of `Address` dependent on an instance of `User`: you make it a value type. When John removes his `User` account, you can safely delete his `Address` instance. Nobody else will hold a reference.

Hence, we make the following essential distinction:

- You can retrieve an instance of *entity type* using its persistent identity: for example, a `User`, `Item`, or `Category` instance. A reference to an entity instance (a pointer in the JVM) is persisted as a reference in the database (a foreign key–constrained value). An entity instance has its own life cycle; it may exist independently of any other entity. You map selected classes of your domain model as entity types.

- An instance of *value type* has no persistent identifier property; it belongs to an entity instance. Its lifespan is bound to the owning entity instance. A value type instance doesn't support shared references. The most obvious value types are all JDK-defined classes such as `String`, `Integer`, and even primitives. You can also map your own domain model classes as value types: for example, `Address` and `MonetaryAmount`.

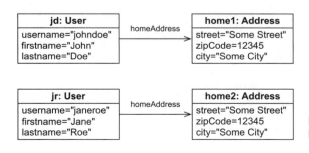

Figure 4.2 Two `User` instances each have their own dependent `Address`.

If you read the JPA specification, you'll find the same concept. But value types in JPA are called *basic property types* or *embeddable classes*. We come back to this in the next chapter; first our focus is on entities.

Identifying entities and value types in your domain model isn't an ad hoc task but follows a certain procedure.

4.1.3 *Distinguishing entities and value types*

You may find it helpful to add stereotype (a UML extensibility mechanism) information to your UML class diagrams so you can immediately recognize entities and value types. This practice also forces you to think about this distinction for all your classes, which is a first step to an optimal mapping and well-performing persistence layer. Figure 4.3 shows an example.

The Item and User classes are obvious entities. They each have their own identity, their instances have references from many other instances (shared references), and they have independent lifespans.

Marking the Address as a value type is also easy: a single User instance references a particular Address instance. You know this because the association has been created as a composition, where the User instance has been made fully responsible for the life cycle of the referenced Address instance. Therefore, Address instances can't be referenced by anyone else and don't need their own identity.

The Bid class could be a problem. In object-oriented modeling, this is marked as a composition (the association between Item and Bid with the diamond). Thus, an Item is the owner of its Bid instances and holds a collection of references. At first, this seems reasonable, because bids in an auction system are useless when the item they were made for is gone.

But what if a future extension of the domain model requires a User#bids collection, containing all bids made by a particular User? Right now, the association between Bid and User is unidirectional; a Bid has a bidder reference. What if this was bidirectional?

In that case, you have to deal with possible shared references to Bid instances, so the Bid class needs to be an entity. It has a dependent life cycle, but it must have its own identity to support (future) shared references.

You'll often find this kind of mixed behavior; but your first reaction should be to make everything a value typed class and promote it to an entity only when absolutely necessary. Try to simplify your associations: persistent collections, for example, frequently add complexity without offering any advantages. Instead of mapping

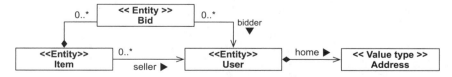

Figure 4.3   Diagramming stereotypes for entities and value types

`Item#bids` and `User#bids` collections, you can write queries to obtain all the bids for an `Item` and those made by a particular `User`. The associations in the UML diagram would point from the `Bid` *to* the `Item` and `User`, unidirectionally, and not the other way. The stereotype on the `Bid` class would then be `<<Value type>>`. We come back to this point again in chapter 7.

Next, take your domain model diagram and implement POJOs for all entities and value types. You'll have to take care of three things:

- *Shared references*—Avoid shared references to value type instances when you write your POJO classes. For example, make sure only one `User` can reference an `Address`. You can make `Address` immutable with no public `setUser()` method and enforce the relationship with a public constructor that has a `User` argument. Of course, you still need a no-argument, probably protected constructor, as we discussed in the previous chapter, so Hibernate can also create an instance.
- *Life cycle dependencies*—If a `User` is deleted, its `Address` dependency has to be deleted as well. Persistence metadata will include the cascading rules for all such dependencies, so Hibernate (or the database) can take care of removing the obsolete `Address`. You must design your application procedures and user interface to respect and expect such dependencies—write your domain model POJOs accordingly.
- *Identity*—Entity classes need an identifier property in almost all cases. Value type classes (and of course JDK classes such as `String` and `Integer`) don't have an identifier property, because instances are identified through the owning entity.

We come back to references, associations, and life cycle rules when we discuss more-advanced mappings throughout later chapters in this book. Object identity and identifier properties are our next topic.

4.2 Mapping entities with identity

Mapping entities with identity requires you to understand Java identity and equality before we can walk through an entity class example and its mapping. After that, we'll be able to dig in deeper and select a primary key, configure key generators, and finally go through identifier generator strategies. First, it's vital to understand the difference between Java object identity and object equality before we discuss terms like *database identity* and the way JPA manages identity.

4.2.1 Understanding Java identity and equality

Java developers understand the difference between Java object identity and equality. Object identity (`==`) is a notion defined by the Java virtual machine. Two references are identical if they point to the same memory location.

On the other hand, object equality is a notion defined by a class's `equals()` method, sometimes also referred to as *equivalence*. Equivalence means two different (non-identical) instances have the same value—the same state. Two different instances of String are equal if they represent the same sequence of characters, even though each has its own location in the memory space of the virtual machine. (If you're a Java guru, we acknowledge that String is a special case. Assume we used a different class to make the same point.)

Persistence complicates this picture. With object/relational persistence, a persistent instance is an in-memory representation of a particular row (or rows) of a database table (or tables). Along with Java identity and equality, we define database identity. You now have three methods for distinguishing references:

- Objects are identical if they occupy the same memory location in the JVM. This can be checked with the a == b operator. This concept is known as *object identity*.
- Objects are equal if they have the same state, as defined by the a.equals(Object b) method. Classes that don't explicitly override this method inherit the implementation defined by java.lang.Object, which compares object identity with ==. This concept is known as *object equality*.
- Objects stored in a relational database are identical if they share the same table and primary key value. This concept, mapped into the Java space, is known as *database identity*.

We now need to look at how database identity relates to object identity and how to express database identity in the mapping metadata. As an example, you'll map an entity of a domain model.

4.2.2 *A first entity class and mapping*

We weren't completely honest in the previous chapter: the @Entity annotation isn't enough to map a persistent class. You also need an @Id annotation, as shown in the following listing.

> **Listing 4.1 Mapped Item entity class with an identifier property**
>
> PATH: /model/src/main/java/org/jpwh/model/simple/Item.java

```
@Entity
public class Item {

    @Id
    @GeneratedValue(generator = "ID_GENERATOR")
    protected Long id;

    public Long getId() {              ◁──── Optional but useful
        return id;
    }
}
```

This is the most basic entity class, marked as "persistence capable" with the @Entity annotation, and with an @Id mapping for the database identifier property. The class maps by default to a table named ITEM in the database schema.

Every entity class has to have an @Id property; it's how JPA exposes database identity to the application. We don't show the identifier property in our diagrams; we assume that each entity class has one. In our examples, we always name the identifier property id. This is a good practice for your own project; use the same identifier property name for all your domain model entity classes. If you specify nothing else, this property maps to a primary key column named ID of the ITEM table in your database schema.

Hibernate will use the field to access the identifier property value when loading and storing items, not getter or setter methods. Because @Id is on a field, Hibernate will now enable every field of the class as a persistent property by default. The rule in JPA is this: if @Id is on a field, the JPA provider will access fields of the class directly and consider all fields part of the persistent state by default. You'll see how to override this later in this chapter—in our experience, field access is often the best choice, because it gives you more freedom for accessor method design.

Should you have a (public) getter method for the identifier property? Well, the application often uses database identifiers as a convenient handle to a particular instance, even outside the persistence layer. For example, it's common for web applications to display the results of a search screen to the user as a list of summaries. When the user selects a particular element, the application may need to retrieve the selected item, and it's common to use a lookup by identifier for this purpose—you've probably already used identifiers this way, even in applications that rely on JDBC.

Should you have a setter method? Primary key values never change, so you shouldn't allow modification of the identifier property value. Hibernate won't update a primary key column, and you shouldn't expose a public identifier setter method on an entity.

The Java type of the identifier property, java.lang.Long in the previous example, depends on the primary key column type of the ITEM table and how key values are produced. This brings us to the @GeneratedValue annotation and primary keys in general.

4.2.3 Selecting a primary key

The database identifier of an entity is mapped to some table primary key, so let's first get some background on primary keys without worrying about mappings. Take a step back and think about how you identify entities.

A *candidate key* is a column or set of columns that you could use to identify a particular row in a table. To become the primary key, a candidate key must satisfy the following requirements:

- The value of any candidate key column is never null. You can't identify something with data that is unknown, and there are no nulls in the relational model. Some SQL products allow defining (composite) primary keys with nullable columns, so you must be careful.
- The value of the candidate key column(s) is a unique value for any row.
- The value of the candidate key column(s) never changes; it's immutable.

Must primary keys be immutable?

The relational model defines that a candidate key must be unique and irreducible (no subset of the key attributes has the uniqueness property). Beyond that, picking a candidate key as *the* primary key is a matter of taste. But Hibernate expects a candidate key to be immutable when used as the primary key. Hibernate doesn't support updating primary key values with an API; if you try to work around this requirement, you'll run into problems with Hibernate's caching and dirty-checking engine. If your database schema relies on updatable primary keys (and maybe uses ON UPDATE CASCADE foreign key constraints), you must change the schema before it will work with Hibernate.

If a table has only one identifying attribute, it becomes, by definition, the primary key. But several columns or combinations of columns may satisfy these properties for a particular table; you choose between candidate keys to decide the best primary key for the table. You should declare candidate keys not chosen as the primary key as unique keys in the database if their value is indeed unique (but maybe not immutable).

Many legacy SQL data models use natural primary keys. A *natural key* is a key with business meaning: an attribute or combination of attributes that is unique by virtue of its business semantics. Examples of natural keys are the US Social Security Number and Australian Tax File Number. Distinguishing natural keys is simple: if a candidate key attribute has meaning outside the database context, it's a natural key, regardless of whether it's automatically generated. Think about the application users: if they refer to a key attribute when talking about and working with the application, it's a natural key: "Can you send me the pictures of item #123-abc?"

Experience has shown that natural primary keys usually cause problems in the end. A good primary key must be unique, immutable, and never null. Few entity attributes satisfy these requirements, and some that do can't be efficiently indexed by SQL databases (although this is an implementation detail and shouldn't be the deciding factor for or against a particular key). In addition, you should make certain that a candidate key definition never changes throughout the lifetime of the database. Changing the value (or even definition) of a primary key, and all foreign keys that refer to it, is a frustrating task. Expect your database schema to survive decades, even if your application won't.

Furthermore, you can often only find natural candidate keys by combining several columns in a *composite* natural key. These composite keys, although certainly appropriate for some schema artifacts (like a link table in a many-to-many relationship), potentially make maintenance, ad hoc queries, and schema evolution much more difficult. We talk about composite keys later in the book, in section 9.2.1.

For these reasons, we strongly recommend that you add synthetic identifiers, also called *surrogate keys*. Surrogate keys have no business meaning—they have unique values generated by the database or application. Application users ideally don't see or refer to these key values; they're part of the system internals. Introducing a surrogate key column is also appropriate in the common situation when there are no candidate keys. In other words, (almost) every table in your schema should have a dedicated surrogate primary key column with only this purpose.

There are a number of well-known approaches to generating surrogate key values. The aforementioned `@GeneratedValue` annotation is how you configure this.

4.2.4 Configuring key generators

The `@Id` annotation is required to mark the identifier property of an entity class. Without the `@GeneratedValue` next to it, the JPA provider assumes that you'll take care of creating and assigning an identifier value before you save an instance. We call this an *application-assigned* identifier. Assigning an entity identifier manually is necessary when you're dealing with a legacy database and/or natural primary keys. We have more to say about this kind of mapping in a dedicated section, 9.2.1.

Usually you want the system to generate a primary key value when you save an entity instance, so you write the `@GeneratedValue` annotation next to `@Id`. JPA standardizes several value-generation strategies with the `javax.persistence.GenerationType` enum, which you select with `@GeneratedValue(strategy = ...)`:

- `GenerationType.AUTO`—Hibernate picks an appropriate strategy, asking the SQL dialect of your configured database what is best. This is equivalent to `@GeneratedValue()` without any settings.

- `GenerationType.SEQUENCE`—Hibernate expects (and creates, if you use the tools) a sequence named `HIBERNATE_SEQUENCE` in your database. The sequence will be called separately before every `INSERT`, producing sequential numeric values.

- `GenerationType.IDENTITY`—Hibernate expects (and creates in table DDL) a special auto-incremented primary key column that automatically generates a numeric value on `INSERT`, in the database.

- `GenerationType.TABLE`—Hibernate will use an extra table in your database schema that holds the next numeric primary key value, one row for each entity class. This table will be read and updated accordingly, before `INSERT`s. The default table name is `HIBERNATE_SEQUENCES` with columns `SEQUENCE_NAME` and `SEQUENCE_NEXT_HI_VALUE`. (The internal implementation uses a more complex but efficient hi/lo generation algorithm; more on this later.)

Although `AUTO` seems convenient, you need more control, so you usually shouldn't rely on it and explicitly configure a primary key generation strategy. In addition, most applications work with database sequences, but you may want to customize the name and other settings of the database sequence. Therefore, instead of picking one of the JPA strategies, we recommend a mapping of the identifier with `@Generated-Value(generator = "ID_GENERATOR")`, as shown in the previous example.

This is a *named* identifier generator; you are now free to set up the `ID_GENERATOR` configuration independently from your entity classes.

JPA has two built-in annotations you can use to configure named generators: `@javax`
`.persistence.SequenceGenerator` and `@javax.persistence.TableGenerator`. With
these annotations, you can create a named generator with your own sequence and
table names. As usual with JPA annotations, you can unfortunately only use them at the
top of a (maybe otherwise empty) class, and not in a package-info.java file.

For this reason, and because the JPA annotations don't give us access to the full Hibernate feature set, we prefer an alternative: the native `@org.hibernate.annotations`
`.GenericGenerator` annotation. It supports all Hibernate identifier generator strategies and their configuration details. Unlike the rather limited JPA annotations, you can
use the Hibernate annotation in a package-info.java file, typically in the same package
as your domain model classes. The next listing shows a recommended configuration.

> **Listing 4.2   Hibernate identifier generator configured as package-level metadata**
>
> PATH: **/model/src/main/java/org/jpwh/model/package-info.java**

```
@org.hibernate.annotations.GenericGenerator(
  name = "ID_GENERATOR",
  strategy = "enhanced-sequence",                    ①  enhanced-sequence strategy
  parameters = {
     @org.hibernate.annotations.Parameter(
        name = "sequence_name",                       ②  sequence_name
        value = "JPWH_SEQUENCE"
     ),
     @org.hibernate.annotations.Parameter(
        name = "initial_value",                       ③  initial_value
        value = "1000"
     )
})
```

This Hibernate-specific generator configuration has the following advantages:

- The `enhanced-sequence` ① strategy produces sequential numeric values. If
  your SQL dialect supports sequences, Hibernate will use an actual database
  sequence. If your DBMS doesn't support native sequences, Hibernate will manage and use an extra "sequence table," simulating the behavior of a sequence.
  This gives you real portability: the generator can always be called before performing an SQL INSERT, unlike, for example, auto-increment identity columns,
  which produce a value on INSERT that has to be returned to the application
  afterward.
- You can configure the `sequence_name` ②. Hibernate will either use an existing
  sequence or create it when you generate the SQL schema automatically. If your
  DBMS doesn't support sequences, this will be the special "sequence table"
  name.

- You can start with an `initial_value` ❸ that gives you room for test data. For example, when your integration test runs, Hibernate will make any new data insertions from test code with identifier values greater than 1000. Any test data you want to import before the test can use numbers 1 to 999, and you can refer to the stable identifier values in your tests: "Load item with id 123 and run some tests on it." This is applied when Hibernate generates the SQL schema and sequence; it's a DDL option.

You can share the same database sequence among all your domain model classes. There is no harm in specifying `@GeneratedValue(generator = "ID_GENERATOR")` in all your entity classes. It doesn't matter if primary key values aren't contiguous for a particular entity, as long as they're unique within one table. If you're worried about contention, because the sequence has to be called prior to every `INSERT`, we discuss a variation of this generator configuration later, in section 20.1.

Finally, you use `java.lang.Long` as the type of the identifier property in the entity class, which maps perfectly to a numeric database sequence generator. You could also use a `long` primitive. The main difference is what `someItem.getId()` returns on a new item that hasn't been stored in the database: either `null` or `0`. If you want to test whether an item is new, a `null` check is probably easier to understand for someone else reading your code. You shouldn't use another integral type such as `int` or `short` for identifiers. Although they will work for a while (perhaps even years), as your database size grows, you may be limited by their range. An `Integer` would work for almost two months if you generated a new identifier each millisecond with no gaps, and a `Long` would last for about 300 million years.

Although recommended for most applications, the `enhanced-sequence` strategy as shown in listing 4.2 is just one of the strategies built into Hibernate.

Hibernate Feature

4.2.5 *Identifier generator strategies*

Following is a list of all available Hibernate identifier generator strategies, their options, and our usage recommendations. If you don't want to read the whole list now, enable `GenerationType.AUTO` and check what Hibernate defaults to for your database dialect. It's most likely `sequence` or `identity`—a good but maybe not the most efficient or portable choice. If you require consistent portable behavior, and identifier values to be available before `INSERT`s, use `enhanced-sequence`, as shown in the previous section. This is a portable, flexible, and modern strategy, also offering various optimizers for large datasets.

We also show the relationship between each standard JPA strategy and its native Hibernate equivalent. Hibernate has been growing organically, so there are now two sets of mappings between standard and native strategies; we call them *Old* and *New* in the list. You can switch this mapping with the `hibernate.id.new_generator_mappings`

Generating identifiers before or after INSERT: what's the difference?

An ORM service tries to optimize SQL INSERTs: for example, by batching several at the JDBC level. Hence, SQL execution occurs as late as possible during a unit of work, not when you call entityManager.persist(someItem). This merely queues the insertion for later execution and, if possible, assigns the identifier value. But if you now call someItem.getId(), you might get null back if the engine wasn't able to generate an identifier before the INSERT. In general, we prefer *pre-insert* generation strategies that produce identifier values independently, before INSERT. A common choice is a shared and concurrently accessible database sequence. Auto-incremented columns, column default values, or trigger-generated keys are only available after the INSERT.

setting in your persistence.xml file. The default is true; hence the New mapping. Software doesn't age quite as well as wine:

- native—Automatically selects other strategies, such as sequence or identity, depending on the configured SQL dialect. You have to look at the Javadoc (or even the source) of the SQL dialect you configured in persistence.xml. Equivalent to JPA GenerationType.AUTO with the Old mapping.

- sequence—Uses a native database sequence named HIBERNATE_SEQUENCE. The sequence is called before each INSERT of a new row. You can customize the sequence name and provide additional DDL settings; see the Javadoc for the class org.hibernate.id.SequenceGenerator.

- sequence-identity—Generates key values by calling a database sequence on insertion: for example, insert into ITEM(ID) values (HIBERNATE_SEQUENCE .nextval). The key value is retrieved after INSERT, the same behavior as the identity strategy. Supports the same parameters and property types as the sequence strategy; see the Javadoc for the class org.hibernate.id.Sequence-IdentityGenerator and its parent.

- enhanced-sequence—Uses a native database sequence when supported; otherwise falls back to an extra database table with a single column and row, emulating a sequence. Defaults to name HIBERNATE_SEQUENCE. Always calls the database "sequence" before an INSERT, providing the same behavior independently of whether the DBMS supports real sequences. Supports an org.hibernate .id.enhanced.Optimizer to avoid hitting the database before each INSERT; defaults to no optimization and fetching a new value for each INSERT. You can find more examples in chapter 20. For all parameters, see the Javadoc for the class org.hibernate.id.enhanced.SequenceStyleGenerator. Equivalent to JPA GenerationType.SEQUENCE and GenerationType.AUTO with the New mapping enabled, most likely your best option of the built-in strategies.

- seqhilo—Uses a native database sequence named HIBERNATE_SEQUENCE, optimizing calls before INSERT by combining hi/lo values. If the hi value retrieved from the sequence is 1, the next 9 insertions will be made with key values 11, 12, 13, ..., 19. Then the sequence is called again to obtain the next hi value (2 or higher), and the procedure repeats with 21, 22, 23, and so on. You can configure the maximum lo value (9 is the default) with the `max_lo` parameter. Unfortunately, due to a quirk in Hibernate's code, you can *not* configure this strategy in `@GenericGenerator`. The only way to use it is with JPA `Generation-Type.SEQUENCE` and the Old mapping. You can configure it with the standard JPA `@SequenceGenerator` annotation on a (maybe otherwise empty) class. See the Javadoc for the class `org.hibernate.id.SequenceHiLoGenerator` and its parent for more information. Consider using `enhanced-sequence` instead, with an optimizer.

- `hilo`—Uses an extra table named `HIBERNATE_UNIQUE_KEY` with the same algorithm as the `seqhilo` strategy. The table has a single column and row, holding the next value of the sequence. The default maximum lo value is 32767, so you most likely want to configure it with the `max_lo` parameter. See the Javadoc for the class `org.hibernate.id.TableHiLoGenerator` for more information. We don't recommend this legacy strategy; use `enhanced-sequence` instead with an optimizer.

- `enhanced-table`—Uses an extra table named `HIBERNATE_SEQUENCES`, with one row by default representing the sequence, storing the next value. This value is selected and updated when an identifier value has to be generated. You can configure this generator to use multiple rows instead: one for each generator; see the Javadoc for `org.hibernate.id.enhanced.TableGenerator`. Equivalent to JPA `GenerationType.TABLE` with the New mapping enabled. Replaces the outdated but similar `org.hibernate.id.MultipleHiLoPerTableGenerator`, which is the Old mapping for JPA `GenerationType.TABLE`.

- `identity`—Supports `IDENTITY` and auto-increment columns in DB2, MySQL, MS SQL Server, and Sybase. The identifier value for the primary key column will be generated on `INSERT` of a row. Has no options. Unfortunately, due to a quirk in Hibernate's code, you can *not* configure this strategy in `@GenericGenerator`. The only way to use it is with JPA `GenerationType.IDENTITY` and the Old or New mapping, making it the default for `GenerationType.IDENTITY`.

- `increment`—At Hibernate startup, reads the maximum (numeric) primary key column value of each entity's table and increments the value by one each time a new row is inserted. Especially efficient if a non-clustered Hibernate application has exclusive access to the database; but don't use it in any other scenario.

- `select`—Hibernate won't generate a key value or include the primary key column in an `INSERT` statement. Hibernate expects the DBMS to assign a (default in schema or by trigger) value to the column on insertion. Hibernate then retrieves the primary key column with a `SELECT` query after insertion. Required parameter is `key`, naming the database identifier property (such as `id`) for the

SELECT. This strategy isn't very efficient and should only be used with old JDBC drivers that can't return generated keys directly.

- uuid2—Produces a unique 128-bit UUID in the application layer. Useful when you need globally unique identifiers across databases (say, you merge data from several distinct production databases in batch runs every night into an archive). The UUID can be encoded either as a java.lang.String, a byte[16], or a java.util.UUID property in your entity class. Replaces the legacy uuid and uuid.hex strategies. You configure it with an org.hibernate.id.UUIDGeneration-Strategy; see the Javadoc for the class org.hibernate.id.UUIDGenerator for more details.

- guid—Uses a globally unique identifier produced by the database, with an SQL function available on Oracle, Ingres, MS SQL Server, and MySQL. Hibernate calls the database function before an INSERT. Maps to a java.lang.String identifier property. If you need full control over identifier generation, configure the strategy of @GenericGenerator with the fully qualified name of a class that implements the org.hibernate.id.IdentityGenerator interface.

To summarize, our recommendations on identifier generator strategies are as follows:

- In general, we prefer pre-insert generation strategies that produce identifier values independently before INSERT.

- Use enhanced-sequence, which uses a native database sequence when supported and otherwise falls back to an extra database table with a single column and row, emulating a sequence.

We assume from now on that you've added identifier properties to the entity classes of your domain model and that after you complete the basic mapping of each entity and its identifier property, you continue to map the value-typed properties of the entities. We talk about value-type mappings in the next chapter. Read on for some special options that can simplify and enhance your class mappings.

4.3   *Entity-mapping options*

You've now mapped a persistent class with @Entity, using defaults for all other settings, such as the mapped SQL table name. The following section explores some class-level options and how you control them:

- Naming defaults and strategies
- Dynamic SQL generation
- Entity mutability

These are options; you can skip this section and come back later when you have to deal with a specific problem.

4.3.1   *Controlling names*

Let's first talk about the naming of entity classes and tables. If you only specify @Entity on the persistence-capable class, the default mapped table name is the same as the class name. Note that we write SQL artifact names in UPPERCASE to make them easier to distinguish—SQL is actually case insensitive. So the Java entity class `Item` maps to the `ITEM` table. You can override the table name with the JPA `@Table` annotation, as shown next.

Listing 4.3   @Table annotation overrides the mapped table name

PATH: /model/src/main/java/org/jpwh/model/simple/User.java

```
@Entity
@Table(name = "USERS")
public class User implements Serializable {

    // ...
}
```

The `User` entity would map to the `USER` table; this is a reserved keyword in most SQL DBMSs. You can't have a table with that name, so you instead map it to `USERS`. The `@javax.persistence.Table` annotation also has `catalog` and `schema` options, if your database layout requires these as naming prefixes.

If you really have to, quoting allows you to use reserved SQL names and even work with case-sensitive names.

QUOTING SQL IDENTIFIERS

From time to time, especially in legacy databases, you'll encounter identifiers with strange characters or whitespace, or wish to force case sensitivity. Or, as in the previous example, the automatic mapping of a class or property would require a table or column name that is a reserved keyword.

Hibernate 5 knows the reserved keywords of your DBMS through the configured database dialect. Hibernate 5 can automatically put quotes around such strings when generating SQL. You can enable this automatic quoting with `hibernate.auto_quote _keyword=true` in your persistence unit configuration. If you're using an older version of Hibernate, or you find that the dialect's information is incomplete, you must still apply quotes on names manually in your mappings if there is a conflict with a keyword.

If you quote a table or column name in your mapping with backticks, Hibernate always quotes this identifier in the generated SQL. This still works in latest versions of Hibernate, but JPA 2.0 standardized this functionality as *delimited identifiers* with double quotes.

This is the Hibernate-only quoting with backticks, modifying the previous example:

```
@Table(name = "`USER`")
```

To be JPA-compliant, you also have to escape the quotes in the string:

```
@Table(name = "\"USER\"")
```

Either way works fine with Hibernate. It knows the native quote character of your dialect and now generates SQL accordingly: [USER] for MS SQL Server, 'USER' for MySQL, "USER" for H2, and so on.

If you have to quote *all* SQL identifiers, create an orm.xml file and add the setting <delimited-identifiers/> to its <persistence-unit-defaults> section, as shown in listing 3.8. Hibernate then enforces quoted identifiers everywhere.

You should consider renaming tables or columns with reserved keyword names whenever possible. Ad hoc SQL queries are difficult to write in an SQL console if you have to quote and escape everything properly by hand.

Next, you'll see how Hibernate can help when you encounter organizations with strict conventions for database table and column names.

Hibernate Feature

IMPLEMENTING NAMING CONVENTIONS

Hibernate provides a feature that allows you to enforce naming standards automatically. Suppose that all table names in CaveatEmptor should follow the pattern CE_<table name>. One solution is to manually specify an @Table annotation on all entity classes. This approach is time-consuming and easily forgotten. Instead, you can implement Hibernate's PhysicalNamingStrategy interface or override an existing implementation, as in the following listing.

> **Listing 4.4 PhysicalNamingStrategy, overriding default naming conventions**
>
> PATH: /shared/src/main/java/org/jpwh/shared/CENamingStrategy.java

```java
public class CENamingStrategy extends
    org.hibernate.boot.model.naming.PhysicalNamingStrategyStandardImpl {

    @Override
    public Identifier toPhysicalTableName(Identifier name,
                                    JdbcEnvironment context) {
        return new Identifier("CE_" + name.getText(), name.isQuoted());
    }

}
```

The overridden method toPhysicalTableName() prepends CE_ to all generated table names in your schema. Look at the Javadoc of the PhysicalNamingStrategy interface; it offers methods for custom naming of columns, sequences, and other artifacts.

You have to enable the naming-strategy implementation in persistence.xml:

```xml
<persistence-unit>name="CaveatEmptorPU">
    ...
    <properties>
        <property name="hibernate.physical_naming_strategy"
                value="org.jpwh.shared.CENamingStrategy"/>
    </properties>
</persistence-unit>
```

A second option for naming customization is `ImplicitNamingStrategy`. Whereas the physical naming strategy acts at the lowest level, when schema artifact names are ultimately produced, the implicit-naming strategy is called before. If you map an entity class and don't have an `@Table` annotation with an explicit name, the implicit-naming strategy implementation is asked what the table name should be. This is based on factors such as the entity name and class name. Hibernate ships with several strategies to implement legacy- or JPA-compliant default names. The default strategy is `Implicit-NamingStrategyJpaCompliantImpl`.

Let's have a quick look at another related issue, the naming of entities for queries.

NAMING ENTITIES FOR QUERYING

By default, all entity names are automatically imported into the namespace of the query engine. In other words, you can use short class names without a package prefix in JPA query strings, which is convenient:

```
List result = em.createQuery("select i from Item i")
                .getResultList();
```

This only works when you have one `Item` class in your persistence unit. If you add another `Item` class in a different package, you should rename one of them for JPA if you want to continue using the short form in queries:

```
package my.other.model;

@javax.persistence.Entity(name = "AuctionItem")
public class Item {
    // ...
}
```

The short query form is now `select i from AuctionItem i` for the `Item` class in the `my.other.model` package. Thus you resolve the naming conflict with another `Item` class in another package. Of course, you can always use fully qualified long names with the package prefix.

This completes our tour of the naming options in Hibernate. Next, we discuss how Hibernate generates the SQL that contains these names.

Hibernate Feature

4.3.2 *Dynamic SQL generation*

By default, Hibernate creates SQL statements for each persistent class when the persistence unit is created, on startup. These statements are simple create, read, update, and delete (CRUD) operations for reading a single row, deleting a row, and so on. It's cheaper to store these in memory up front, instead of generating SQL strings every time such a simple query has to be executed at runtime. In addition, prepared statement caching at the JDBC level is much more efficient if there are fewer statements.

How can Hibernate create an UPDATE statement on startup? After all, the columns to be updated aren't known at this time. The answer is that the generated SQL statement updates all columns, and if the value of a particular column isn't modified, the statement sets it to its old value.

In some situations, such as a legacy table with hundreds of columns where the SQL statements will be large for even the simplest operations (say, only one column needs updating), you should disable this startup SQL generation and switch to dynamic statements generated at runtime. An extremely large number of entities can also impact startup time, because Hibernate has to generate all SQL statements for CRUD up front. Memory consumption for this query statement cache will also be high if a dozen statements must be cached for thousands of entities. This can be an issue in virtual environments with memory limitations, or on low-power devices.

To disable generation of INSERT and UPDATE SQL statements on startup, you need native Hibernate annotations:

```
@Entity
@org.hibernate.annotations.DynamicInsert
@org.hibernate.annotations.DynamicUpdate
public class Item {
    // ...
}
```

By enabling dynamic insertion and updates, you tell Hibernate to produce the SQL strings when needed, not up front. The UPDATE will only contain columns with updated values, and the INSERT will only contain non-nullable columns.

We talk again about SQL generation and customizing SQL in chapter 17. Sometimes you can avoid generating an UPDATE statement altogether, if your entity is immutable.

Hibernate Feature

4.3.3   *Making an entity immutable*

Instances of a particular class may be immutable. For example, in CaveatEmptor, a Bid made for an item is immutable. Hence, Hibernate never needs to execute UPDATE statements on the BID table. Hibernate can also make a few other optimizations, such as avoiding dirty checking, if you map an immutable class as shown in the next example. Here, the Bid class is immutable and instances are never modified:

```
@Entity
@org.hibernate.annotations.Immutable
public class Bid {
    // ...
}
```

A POJO is immutable if no public setter methods for any properties of the class are exposed—all values are set in the constructor. Hibernate should access the fields directly when loading and storing instances. We talked about this earlier in this chapter: if the @Id annotation is on a field, Hibernate will access the fields directly, and you are free to design your getter and setter methods as you see fit. Also, remember that not all frameworks work with POJOs without setter methods; JSF, for example, doesn't access fields directly to populate an instance.

When you can't create a view in your database schema, you can map an immutable entity class to an SQL SELECT query.

Hibernate Feature

4.3.4 *Mapping an entity to a subselect*

Sometimes your DBA won't allow you to change the database schema; even adding a new view might not be possible. Let's say you want to create a view that contains the identifier of an auction Item and the number of bids made for that item.

Using a Hibernate annotation, you can create an application-level view, a read-only entity class mapped to an SQL SELECT:

> PATH: /model/src/main/java/org/jpwh/model/advanced/ItemBidSummary.java

```
@Entity
@org.hibernate.annotations.Immutable
@org.hibernate.annotations.Subselect(
    value = "select i.ID as ITEMID, i.ITEM_NAME as NAME, " +
            "count(b.ID) as NUMBEROFBIDS " +
            "from ITEM i left outer join BID b on i.ID = b.ITEM_ID " +
            "group by i.ID, i.ITEM_NAME"
)

@org.hibernate.annotations.Synchronize({"Item", "Bid"})       ⊲──┐ TODO: table names
public class ItemBidSummary {                                       are case sensitive
                                                                   (Hibernate bug
    @Id                                                            HHH-8430)
    protected Long itemId;

    protected String name;

    protected long numberOfBids;

    public ItemBidSummary() {
    }

    // Getter methods...

    // ...
}
```

When an instance of ItemBidSummary is loaded, Hibernate executes your custom SQL SELECT as a subselect:

> PATH: /examples/src/test/java/org/jpwh/test/advanced/MappedSubselect.java

```
ItemBidSummary itemBidSummary = em.find(ItemBidSummary.class, ITEM_ID);
// select * from (
```

```
//      select i.ID as ITEMID, i.ITEM_NAME as NAME, ...
// ) where ITEMID = ?
```

You should list all table names referenced in your SELECT in the @org.hibernate .annotations.Synchronize annotation. (At the time of writing, Hibernate has a bug tracked under issue HHH-8430[1] that makes the synchronized table names case sensitive.) Hibernate will then know it has to flush modifications of Item and Bid instances before it executes a query against ItemBidSummary:

PATH: **/examples/src/test/java/org/jpwh/test/advanced/MappedSubselect.java**

```
Item item = em.find(Item.class, ITEM_ID);                              No flush before retrieval
item.setName("New name");                                                  by the identifier

// ItemBidSummary itemBidSummary = em.find(ItemBidSummary.class, ITEM_ID); <──

Query query = em.createQuery(                                          <────
    "select ibs from ItemBidSummary ibs where ibs.itemId = :id"
);
ItemBidSummary itemBidSummary =
    (ItemBidSummary)query.setParameter("id", ITEM_ID).getSingleResult();

                                                        Automatic flush before queries if
                                                        synchronized tables are affected
```

Note that Hibernate doesn't flush automatically before a find() operation—only before a Query is executed, if necessary. Hibernate detects that the modified Item will affect the result of the query, because the ITEM table is synchronized with ItemBid-Summary. Hence, a flush and the UPDATE of the ITEM row are necessary to avoid the query returning stale data.

4.4   Summary

- Entities are the coarser-grained classes of your system. Their instances have an independent life cycle and their own identity, and many other instances can reference them.
- Value types, on the other hand, are dependent on a particular entity class. A value type instance is bound to its owning entity instance, and only one entity instance can reference it—it has no individual identity.
- We looked at Java identity, object equality, and database identity, and at what makes good primary keys. You learned which generators for primary key values Hibernate provides out of the box, and how to use and extend this identifier system.
- We discussed some useful class mapping options, such as naming strategies and dynamic SQL generation.

---

[1]   See https://hibernate.atlassian.net/browse/HHH-8430.

Mapping value types

In this chapter

- Mapping basic properties
- Mapping embeddable components
- Controlling mapping between Java and SQL types

After spending the previous chapter almost exclusively on entities and the respective class- and identity-mapping options, we now focus on value types in their various forms. We split value types into two categories: basic value-typed classes that come with the JDK, such as String, Date, primitives, and their wrappers; and developer-defined value-typed classes, such as Address and MonetaryAmount in CaveatEmptor.

In this chapter, we first map persistent properties with JDK types and learn the basic mapping annotations. You see how to work with various aspects of properties: overriding defaults, customizing access, and generated values. You also see how SQL is used with derived properties and transformed column values. We wrap up basic properties with temporal properties and mapping enumerations. We then discuss custom value-typed classes and map them as embeddable components. You learn how classes relate to the database schema and make your classes embeddable, while allowing for overriding embedded attributes. We complete embeddable components by mapping nested components. Finally, we discuss how to customize loading and storing of property values at a lower level with flexible JPA converters, a standardized extension point of every JPA provider.

81

Major new features in JPA 2

- Switchable access through either field or property getter/setter methods for an entity hierarchy, or individual properties, with the `@Access` annotation
- Nesting multiple levels of embeddable component classes, and the ability to apply `@AttributeOverride` to nested embedded properties with dot notation
- Addition of `Converter` API for basic-typed attributes, so you can control how values are loaded and stored and transform them if necessary

5.1   *Mapping basic properties*

When you map a persistent class, whether it's an entity or an embeddable type (more about these later, in section 5.2), all of its properties are considered persistent by default. The default JPA rules for properties of persistent classes are these:

- If the property is a primitive or a primitive wrapper, or of type `String`, `BigInteger`, `BigDecimal`, `java.util.Date`, `java.util.Calendar`, `java.sql.Date`, `java.sql .Time`, `java.sql.Timestamp`, `byte[]`, `Byte[]`, `char[]`, or `Character[]`, it's automatically persistent. Hibernate loads and stores the value of the property in a column with an appropriate SQL type and the same name as the property.
- Otherwise, if you annotate the class of the property as `@Embeddable`, or you map the property itself as `@Embedded`, Hibernate maps the property as an embedded component of the owning class. We discuss embedding of components later in this chapter, with the `Address` and `MonetaryAmount` embeddable classes of CaveatEmptor.
- Otherwise, if the type of the property is `java.io.Serializable`, its value is stored in its serialized form. This typically isn't what you want, and you should always map Java classes instead of storing a heap of bytes in the database. Imagine maintaining a database with this binary information when the application is gone in a few years.
- Otherwise, Hibernate will throw an exception on startup, complaining that it doesn't understand the type of the property.

This *configuration by exception* approach means you don't have to annotate a property to make it persistent; you only have to configure the mapping in an exceptional case. Several annotations are available in JPA to customize and control basic property mappings.

5.1.1   *Overriding basic property defaults*

You might not want all properties of an entity class to be persistent. For example, although it makes sense to have a persistent `Item#initialPrice` property, an `Item#totalPriceIncludingTax` property shouldn't be persistent if you only compute and use its value at runtime, and hence shouldn't be stored in the database. To

exclude a property, mark the field or the getter method of the property with the
@javax.persistence.Transient annotation or use the Java transient keyword. The
transient keyword usually only excludes fields for Java serialization, but it's also recognized by JPA providers.

We'll come back to the placement of the annotation on fields or getter methods in
a moment. Let's assume as we have before that Hibernate will access fields directly
because @Id has been placed on a field. Therefore, all other JPA and Hibernate mapping annotations are also on fields.

If you don't want to rely on property mapping defaults, apply the @Basic annotation to a particular property—for example, the initialPrice of an Item:

```
@Basic(optional = false)
BigDecimal initialPrice;
```

We have to admit that this annotation isn't very useful. It only has two parameters: the
one shown here, optional, marks the property as not optional at the Java object level.
By default, all persistent properties are nullable and optional; an Item may have an
unknown initialPrice. Mapping the initialPrice property as non-optional makes
sense if you have a NOT NULL constraint on the INITIALPRICE column in your SQL
schema. If Hibernate is generating the SQL schema, it will include a NOT NULL constraint automatically for non-optional properties.

Now, when you store an Item and forget to set a value on the initialPrice field,
Hibernate will complain with an exception before hitting the database with an SQL
statement. Hibernate knows that a value is required to perform an INSERT or UPDATE.
If you don't mark the property as optional and try to save a NULL, the database will
reject the SQL statement, and Hibernate will throw a constraint-violation exception.
There isn't much difference in the end result, but it's cleaner to avoid hitting the database with a statement that fails. We'll talk about the other parameter of @Basic, the
fetch option, when we explore optimization strategies later, in section 12.1.

Instead of @Basic, most engineers use the more versatile @Column annotation to
declare nullability:

```
@Column(nullable = false)
BigDecimal initialPrice;
```

We've now shown you three ways to declare whether a property value is required: with
the @Basic annotation, the @Column annotation, and earlier with the Bean Validation
@NotNull annotation in section 3.3.2. All have the same effect on the JPA provider:
Hibernate does a null check when saving and generates a NOT NULL constraint in the
database schema. We recommend the Bean Validation @NotNull annotation so you
can manually validate an Item instance and/or have your user interface code in the
presentation layer execute validation checks automatically.

The @Column annotation can also override the mapping of the property name to
the database column:

```
@Column(name = "START_PRICE", nullable = false)
BigDecimal initialPrice;
```

The @Column annotation has a few other parameters, most of which control SQL-level details such as catalog and schema names. They're rarely needed, and we only show them throughout this book when necessary.

Property annotations aren't always on fields, and you may not want Hibernate to access fields directly.

5.1.2   *Customizing property access*

The persistence engine accesses the properties of a class either directly through fields or indirectly through getter and setter methods. An annotated entity inherits the default from the position of the mandatory @Id annotation. For example, if you've declared @Id on a field, not a getter method, all other mapping annotations for that entity are expected on fields. Annotations are never on the setter methods.

The default access strategy isn't only applicable to a single entity class. Any @Embedded class inherits the default or explicitly declared access strategy of its owning root entity class. We cover embedded components later in this chapter. Furthermore, Hibernate accesses any @MappedSuperclass properties with the default or explicitly declared access strategy of the mapped entity class. Inheritance is the topic of chapter 6.

The JPA specification offers the @Access annotation for overriding the default behavior, with the parameters AccessType.FIELD and AccessType.PROPERTY. If you set @Access on the class/entity level, Hibernate accesses all properties of the class according to the selected strategy. You then set any other mapping annotations, including the @Id, on either fields or getter methods, respectively.

You can also use the @Access annotation to override the access strategy of individual properties. Let's explore this with an example.

> **Listing 5.1   Overriding access strategy for the name property**
>
> PATH: /model/src/main/java/org/jpwh/model/advanced/Item.java

```
@Entity
public class Item {

    @Id                                                        ❶ @Id is on a field.
    @GeneratedValue(generator = Constants.ID_GENERATOR)
    protected Long id;
                                                               ❷ Switches property
    @Access(AccessType.PROPERTY)                                 to runtime access
    @Column(name = "ITEM_NAME")
    protected String name;
                                                               ❸ Called when
    public String getName() {                                    loading/storing
        return name;
    }
```

Mappings are still expected here!

```
public void setName(String name) {
    this.name =
        !name.startsWith("AUCTION: ") ? "AUCTION: " + name : name;
}
}
```

❶ The Item entity defaults to field access. The @Id is on a field. (You also move the brittle ID_GENERATOR string into a constant.)

❷ The @Access(AccessType.PROPERTY) setting on the name field switches this particular property to runtime access through getter/setter methods by the JPA provider.

❸ Hibernate calls getName() and setName() when loading and storing items.

Note that the position of other mapping annotations like @Column doesn't change—only how instances are accessed at runtime.

Now turn it around: if the default (or explicit) access type of the entity would be through property getter and setter methods, @Access(AccessType.FIELD) on a getter method would tell Hibernate to access the field directly. All other mapping information would still have to be on the getter method, not the field.

Hibernate Feature

Hibernate has a rarely needed extension: the noop property accessor. This sounds strange, but it lets you refer to a virtual property in queries. This is useful if you have a database column you'd like to use only in JPA queries. For example, let's say the ITEM database table has a VALIDATED column and your Hibernate application won't access this column through the domain model. It might be a legacy column or a column maintained by another application or database trigger. All you want is to refer to this column in a JPA query such as select i from Item i where i.validated = true or select i.id, i.validated from Item i. The Java Item class in your domain model doesn't have this property; hence there is no place to put annotations. The only way to map such a virtual property is with an hbm.xml native metadata file:

```
<hibernate-mapping>
    <class name="Item">
        <id name="id">
            ...
        </id>
        <property name="validated"
                  column="VALIDATED"
                  access="noop"/>
    </class>
</hibernate-mapping>
```

This mapping tells Hibernate that you'd like to access the virtual Item#validated property, mapped to the VALIDATED column, in queries; but for value read/writes at runtime, you want "no operation" on an instance of Item. The class doesn't have that attribute. Remember that such a native mapping file has to be complete: any annotations on the Item class are now ignored!

If none of the built-in access strategies are appropriate, you can define your own customized property-access strategy by implementing the interface `org.hibernate.property.PropertyAccessor`. You enable a custom accessor by setting its fully qualified name in a Hibernate extension annotation: `@org.hibernate.annotations.AttributeAccessor("my.custom.Accessor")`. Note that `AttributeAccessor` is new in Hibernate 4.3 and replaces the deprecated `org.hibernate.annotations.AccessType`, which was easily confused with the JPA enum `javax.persistence.AccessType`.

Some properties don't map to a column. In particular, a derived property takes its value from an SQL expression.

5.1.3 Using derived properties

The value of a derived property is calculated at runtime by evaluating an SQL expression declared with the `@org.hibernate.annotations.Formula` annotation; see the next listing.

> **Listing 5.2 Two read-only derived properties**

```
@org.hibernate.annotations.Formula(
    "substr(DESCRIPTION, 1, 12) || '...'"
)
protected String shortDescription;

@org.hibernate.annotations.Formula(
    "(select avg(b.AMOUNT) from BID b where b.ITEM_ID = ID)"
)
protected BigDecimal averageBidAmount;
```

The given SQL formulas are evaluated every time the `Item` entity is retrieved from the database and not at any other time, so the result may be outdated if other properties are modified. The properties never appear in an SQL `INSERT` or `UPDATE`, only in `SELECT`s. Evaluation occurs in the database; Hibernate embeds the SQL formula in the `SELECT` clause when loading the instance.

Formulas may refer to columns of the database table, they can call SQL functions, and they may even include SQL subselects. In the previous example, the `SUBSTR()` function is called, as well as the `||` concat operator. The SQL expression is passed to the underlying database as is; if you aren't careful, you may rely on vendor-specific operators or keywords and bind your mapping metadata to a particular database product. Notice that unqualified column names refer to columns of the table of the class to which the derived property belongs.

The database evaluates SQL expressions in formulas only when Hibernate retrieves an entity instance from the database. Hibernate also supports a variation of formulas called *column transformers*, allowing you to write a custom SQL expression for reading *and* writing a property value.

5.1.4 *Transforming column values*

Let's say you have a database column called IMPERIALWEIGHT, storing the weight of an Item in pounds. The application, however, has the property Item#metricWeight in kilograms, so you have to convert the value of the database column when reading *and* writing a row from and to the ITEM table. You can implement this with a Hibernate extension: the @org.hibernate.annotations.ColumnTransformer annotation.

Listing 5.3   Transforming column values with SQL expressions

```
@Column(name = "IMPERIALWEIGHT")
@org.hibernate.annotations.ColumnTransformer(
    read = "IMPERIALWEIGHT / 2.20462",
    write = "? * 2.20462"
)
protected double metricWeight;
```

When reading a row from the ITEM table, Hibernate embeds the expression IMPERIALWEIGHT / 2.20462, so the calculation occurs in the database and Hibernate returns the metric value in the result to the application layer. For writing to the column, Hibernate sets the metric value on the mandatory, single placeholder (the question mark), and your SQL expression calculates the actual value to be inserted or updated.

Hibernate also applies column converters in query restrictions. For example, the following query retrieves all items with a weight of two kilograms:

```
List<Item> result =
    em.createQuery("select i from Item i where i.metricWeight = :w")
        .setParameter("w", 2.0)
        .getResultList();
```

The actual SQL executed by Hibernate for this query contains the following restriction in the WHERE clause:

```
// ...
where
    i.IMPERIALWEIGHT / 2.20462=?
```

Note that your database probably won't be able to rely on an index for this restriction; you'll see a full table scan, because the weight for *all* ITEM rows has to be calculated to evaluate the restriction.

Another special kind of property relies on database-generated values.

5.1.5   *Generated and default property values*

The database sometimes generates a property value, usually when you insert a row for the first time. Examples of database-generated values are a creation timestamp, a default price for an item, and a trigger that runs for every modification.

Typically, Hibernate applications need to refresh instances that contain any properties for which the database generates values, after saving. This means you would have to make another round trip to the database to read the value after inserting or updating a row. Marking properties as generated, however, lets the application delegate this responsibility to Hibernate. Essentially, whenever Hibernate issues an SQL INSERT or UPDATE for an entity that has declared generated properties, it does a SELECT immediately afterward to retrieve the generated values.

You mark generated properties with the @org.hibernate.annotations.Generated annotation.

Listing 5.4   Database-generated property values

```
@Temporal(TemporalType.TIMESTAMP)
@Column(insertable = false, updatable = false)
@org.hibernate.annotations.Generated(
    org.hibernate.annotations.GenerationTime.ALWAYS
)
protected Date lastModified;

@Column(insertable = false)
@org.hibernate.annotations.ColumnDefault("1.00")
@org.hibernate.annotations.Generated(
    org.hibernate.annotations.GenerationTime.INSERT
)
protected BigDecimal initialPrice;
```

Available settings for GenerationTime are ALWAYS and INSERT.

With ALWAYS, Hibernate refreshes the entity instance after every SQL UPDATE or INSERT. The example assumes that a database trigger will keep the lastModified property current. The property should also be marked read-only, with the updatable and insertable parameters of @Column. If both are set to false, the property's column(s) never appear in the INSERT or UPDATE statements, and you let the database generate the value.

With GenerationTime.INSERT, refreshing only occurs after an SQL INSERT, to retrieve the default value provided by the database. Hibernate also maps the property as not insertable. The @ColumnDefault Hibernate annotation sets the default value of the column when Hibernate exports and generates the SQL schema DDL.

Timestamps are frequently automatically generated values, either by the database, as in the previous example, or by the application. Let's have a closer look at the @Temporal annotation you saw in listing 5.4.

5.1.6 Temporal properties

The `lastModified` property of the last example was of type `java.util.Date`, and a database trigger on SQL `INSERT` generated its value. The JPA specification requires that you annotate temporal properties with `@Temporal` to declare the accuracy of the SQL data type of the mapped column. The Java temporal types are `java.util.Date`, `java.util.Calendar`, `java.sql.Date`, `java.sql.Time`, and `java.sql.Timestamp`. Hibernate also supports the classes of the `java.time` package available in JDK 8. (Actually, the annotation isn't required if a *converter* is applied or applicable for the property. You'll see converters again later in this chapter.)

The next listing shows a JPA-compliant example: a typical "this item was created on" timestamp property that is saved once but never updated.

Listing 5.5   Property of a temporal type that must be annotated with `@Temporal`

```
@Temporal(TemporalType.TIMESTAMP)
@Column(updatable = false)
@org.hibernate.annotations.CreationTimestamp
protected Date createdOn;

// Java 8 API
// protected Instant reviewedOn;
```

JPA says @Temporal is required, but Hibernate defaults to TIMESTAMP without it.

Available `TemporalType` options are `DATE`, `TIME`, and `TIMESTAMP`, establishing what part of the temporal value should be stored in the database.

Hibernate Feature

Hibernate defaults to `TemporalType.TIMESTAMP` when no `@Temporal` annotation is present. Furthermore, you've used the `@CreationTimestamp` Hibernate annotation to mark the property. This is a sibling of the `@Generated` annotation from the previous section: it tells Hibernate to generate the property value automatically. In this case, Hibernate sets the value to the current time before it inserts the entity instance into the database. A similar built-in annotation is `@UpdateTimestamp`. You can also write and configure custom value generators, running in the application or database. Have a look at `org.hibernate.annotations.GeneratorType` and `ValueGenerationType`.

Another special property type is enumerations.

5.1.7 Mapping enumerations

An *enumeration type* is a common Java idiom where a class has a constant (small) number of immutable instances. In CaveatEmptor, for example, you can apply this to auctions:

```
public enum AuctionType {
    HIGHEST_BID,
    LOWEST_BID,
    FIXED_PRICE
}
```

You can now set the appropriate `auctionType` on each `Item`:

```
@NotNull
@Enumerated(EnumType.STRING)
protected AuctionType auctionType = AuctionType.HIGHEST_BID;
```

**Defaults to
ORDINAL**

Without the `@Enumerated` annotation, Hibernate would store the `ORDINAL` position of the value. That is, it would store 1 for `HIGHEST_BID`, 2 for `LOWEST_BID`, and 3 for `FIXED_PRICE`. This is a brittle default; if you make changes to the `AuctionType` enum, existing values may no longer map to the same position. The `EnumType.STRING` option is therefore a better choice; Hibernate stores the label of the enum value as is.

This completes our tour of basic properties and their mapping options. So far, we have been showing properties of JDK-supplied types such as `String`, `Date`, and `Big-Decimal`. Your domain model also has custom value-typed classes, those with a composition association in the UML diagram.

5.2   *Mapping embeddable components*

So far, the classes of the domain model you've mapped have all been entity classes, each with its own life cycle and identity. The `User` class, however, has a special kind of association with the `Address` class, as shown in figure 5.1.

Figure 5.1   Composition of `User` and `Address`

In object-modeling terms, this association is a kind of *aggregation*—a *part-of* relationship. Aggregation is a strong form of association; it has some additional semantics with regard to the life cycle of objects. In this case, you have an even stronger form, *composition*, where the life cycle of the part is fully dependent on the life cycle of the whole. A composed class in UML such as `Address` is often a candidate value type for your object/relational mapping.

5.2.1   *The database schema*

Let's map such a composition relationship with `Address` as a value type, with the same semantics as `String` or `BigDecimal`, and `User` as an entity. First, have a look at the SQL schema you're targeting, in figure 5.2.

There is only one mapped table, `USERS`, for the `User` entity. This table embeds all details of the components, where a single row holds a particular `User` and their `homeAddress` and `billingAddress`. If another entity has a reference to an `Address`—for

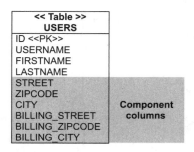

Figure 5.2   The columns of the components are embedded in the entity table.

example, `Shipment#deliveryAddress`—then the `SHIPMENT` table will also have all columns needed to store an `Address`.

This schema reflects value type semantics: a particular `Address` can't be shared; it doesn't have its own identity. Its primary key is the mapped database identifier of the owning entity. An embedded component has a dependent life cycle: when the owning entity instance is saved, the component instance is saved. When the owning entity instance is deleted, the component instance is deleted. Hibernate doesn't even have to execute any special SQL for this; all the data is in a single row.

Having "more classes than tables" is how Hibernate supports fine-grained domain models. Let's write the classes and mapping for this structure.

5.2.2 *Making classes embeddable*

Java has no concept of composition—a class or property can't be marked as a component or composition life cycle. The only difference from an entity is the database identifier: a component class has no individual identity; hence, the component class requires no identifier property or identifier mapping. It's a simple POJO, as you can see in the following listing.

Listing 5.6   Address class: an embeddable component

PATH: /model/src/main/java/org/jpwh/model/simple/Address.java

---

```java
@Embeddable
public class Address {

    @NotNull
    @Column(nullable = false)
    protected String street;

    @NotNull
    @Column(nullable = false, length = 5)
    protected String zipcode;

    @NotNull
    @Column(nullable = false)
    protected String city;

    protected Address() {
    }

    public Address(String street, String zipcode, String city) {
        this.street = street;
        this.zipcode = zipcode;
        this.city = city;
    }

    public String getStreet() {
        return street;
    }

    public void setStreet(String street) {
        this.street = street;
    }
```

@Embeddable instead of @Entity ❶

Ignored for DDL generation ▷ (street)

Used for DDL generation

Overrides VARCHAR(255) ▷ (zipcode)

No-args constructor ❷

Convenience constructor ❸

```
    public String getZipcode() {
        return zipcode;
    }

    public void setZipcode(String zipcode) {
        this.zipcode = zipcode;
    }

    public String getCity() {
        return city;
    }

    public void setCity(String city) {
        this.city = city;
    }
}
```

❶ Instead of @Entity, this component POJO is marked with @Embeddable. It has no identifier property.

❷ Hibernate calls this no-argument constructor to create an instance and then populates the fields directly.

❸ You can have additional (public) constructors for convenience.

The properties of the embeddable class are all by default persistent, just like the properties of a persistent entity class. You can configure the property mappings with the same annotations, such as @Column or @Basic. The properties of the Address class map to the columns STREET, ZIPCODE, and CITY and are constrained with NOT NULL.

Issue: Hibernate Validator doesn't generate NOT NULL constraints

At the time of writing, an open issue remains with Hibernate Validator: Hibernate won't map @NotNull constraints on embeddable component properties to NOT NULL constraints when generating your database schema. Hibernate will only use @NotNull on your components' properties at runtime, for Bean Validation. You have to map the property with @Column(nullable = false) to generate the constraint in the schema. The Hibernate bug database is tracking this issue as HVAL-3.

That's the entire mapping. There's nothing special about the User entity:

PATH: /model/src/main/java/org/jpwh/model/simple/User.java

```
@Entity
@Table(name = "USERS")
public class User implements Serializable {

    @Id
    @GeneratedValue(generator = Constants.ID_GENERATOR)
    protected Long id;

    public Long getId() {
        return id;
```

```
    }

    protected Address homeAddress;          The Address is @Embeddable;
                                            no annotation is needed here.
    public Address getHomeAddress() {
        return homeAddress;
    }

    public void setHomeAddress(Address homeAddress) {
        this.homeAddress = homeAddress;
    }

    // ...
}
```

Hibernate detects that the `Address` class is annotated with `@Embeddable`; the `STREET`, `ZIPCODE`, and `CITY` columns are mapped on the `USERS` table, the owning entity's table.

When we talked about property access earlier in this chapter, we mentioned that embeddable components inherit their access strategy from their owning entity. This means Hibernate will access the properties of the `Address` class with the same strategy as for `User` properties. This inheritance also affects the placement of mapping annotations in embeddable component classes. The rules are as follows:

- If the owning `@Entity` of an embedded component is mapped with field access, either implicitly with `@Id` on a field or explicitly with `@Access(AccessType.FIELD)` on the class, all mapping annotations of the embedded component class are expected on fields of the component class. Hibernate expects annotations on the fields of the `Address` class and reads/writes the fields directly at runtime. Getter and setter methods on `Address` are optional.

- If the owning `@Entity` of an embedded component is mapped with property access, either implicitly with `@Id` on a getter method or explicitly with `@Access(AccessType.PROPERTY)` on the class, all mapping annotations of the embedded component class are expected on getter methods of the component class. Hibernate then reads and writes values by calling getter and setter methods on the embeddable component class.

- If the embedded property of the owning entity class—`User#homeAddress` in the last example—is marked with `@Access(AccessType.FIELD)`, Hibernate expects annotations on the fields of the `Address` class and access fields at runtime.

- If the embedded property of the owning entity class—`User#homeAddress` in the last example—is marked with `@Access(AccessType.PROPERTY)`, Hibernate expects annotations on getter methods of the `Address` class and access getter and setter methods at runtime.

- If `@Access` annotates the embeddable class itself, Hibernate will use the selected strategy for reading mapping annotations on the embeddable class and runtime access.

There's one more caveat to remember: there's no elegant way to represent a null reference to an Address. Consider what would happen if the columns STREET, ZIPCODE, and CITY were nullable. When Hibernate loads a User without any address information, what should be returned by someUser.getHomeAddress()? Hibernate returns a null in this case. Hibernate also stores a null embedded property as NULL values in all mapped columns of the component. Consequently, if you store a User with an "empty" Address (you have an Address instance but all its properties are null), no Address instance will be returned when you load the User. This can be counterintuitive; on the other hand, you probably shouldn't have nullable columns anyway and avoid ternary logic.

You should override the equals() and hashCode() methods of Address and compare instances by value. This isn't critically important as long as you don't have to compare instances: for example, by putting them in a HashSet. We'll discuss this issue later, in the context of collections; see section 7.2.1.

In a more realistic scenario, a user would probably have separate addresses for different purposes. Figure 5.1 showed an additional composition relationship between User and Address: the billingAddress.

5.2.3   *Overriding embedded attributes*

The billingAddress is another embedded component property of the User class, so another Address has to be stored in the USERS table. This creates a mapping conflict: so far, you only have columns in the schema to store one Address in STREET, ZIPCODE, and CITY.

You need additional columns to store another Address for each USERS row. When you map the billingAddress, override the column names:

PATH: /model/src/main/java/org/jpwh/model/simple/User.java

```
@Entity
@Table(name = "USERS")
public class User implements Serializable {

    @Embedded                                    <──── Not necessary
    @AttributeOverrides({
            @AttributeOverride(name = "street",
                    column = @Column(name = "BILLING_STREET")),
            @AttributeOverride(name = "zipcode",
                    column = @Column(name = "BILLING_ZIPCODE", length = 5)),
            @AttributeOverride(name = "city",
                    column = @Column(name = "BILLING_CITY"))
    })
    protected Address billingAddress;

    public Address getBillingAddress() {
        return billingAddress;
    }
```

NULLable! ──▷ (annotation pointing at the BILLING_STREET line)

```
        public void setBillingAddress(Address billingAddress) {
            this.billingAddress = billingAddress;
        }

        // ...
    }
```

The `@Embedded` annotation actually isn't necessary. It's an alternative to `@Embeddable`: mark either the component class or the property in the owning entity class (both doesn't hurt but has no advantage). The `@Embedded` annotation is useful if you want to map a third-party component class without source and no annotations, but using the right getter/setter methods (like regular JavaBeans).

The `@AttributeOverrides` selectively overrides property mappings of the embedded class; in this example, you override all three properties and provide different column names. Now you can store two `Address` instances in the `USERS` table, each instance in a different set of columns (check the schema again in figure 5.2).

Each `@AttributeOverride` for a component property is "complete": any JPA or Hibernate annotation on the overridden property is ignored. This means the `@Column` annotations on the `Address` class are ignored—all BILLING_* columns are NULLable! (Bean Validation still recognizes the `@NotNull` annotation on the component property, though; Hibernate only overrides persistence annotations.)

You can further improve reusability of your domain model, and make it more fine-grained, by nesting embedded components.

5.2.4 *Mapping nested embedded components*

Let's consider the `Address` class and how it encapsulates address details: instead of a simple `city` string, you could move this detail into a new `City` embeddable class. Look at the changed domain model diagram in figure 5.3. The SQL schema we're targeting for the mapping still has only one `USERS` table, as shown in figure 5.4.

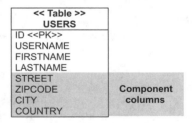

Figure 5.3 Nested composition of `Address` and `City`

Figure 5.4 Embedded columns hold `Address` and `City` details.

An embeddable class can have an embedded property. Address has a city property:

PATH: /model/src/main/java/org/jpwh/model/advanced/Address.java

```
@Embeddable
public class Address {

    @NotNull
    @Column(nullable = false)
    protected String street;

    @NotNull
    @AttributeOverrides(
        @AttributeOverride(
            name = "name",
            column = @Column(name = "CITY", nullable = false)
        )
    )
    protected City city;

    // ...
}
```

The embeddable City class has only basic properties:

PATH: /model/src/main/java/org/jpwh/model/advanced/City.java

```
@Embeddable
public class City {

    @NotNull
    @Column(nullable = false, length = 5)          ⟵——— Override VARCHAR(255).
    protected String zipcode;

    @NotNull
    @Column(nullable =  false)
    protected String name;

    @NotNull
    @Column(nullable =  false)
    protected String country;

    // ...
}
```

You could continue this kind of nesting by creating a Country class, for example. All embedded properties, no matter how deep they are in the composition, are mapped to columns of the owning entity's table—here, the USERS table.

You can declare @AttributeOverrides at any level, as you do for the name property of the City class, mapping it to the CITY column. This can be achieved with either (as shown) an @AttributeOverride in Address or an override in the root entity class, User. Nested properties can be referenced with dot notation: for example, on User#address, @AttributeOveride(name = "city.name") references the Address #City#name attribute.

We'll come back to embedded components later, in section 7.2. You can even map collections of components or have references from a component to an entity.

At the beginning of this chapter, we talked about basic properties and how Hibernate maps a JDK type such as `java.lang.String`, for example, to an appropriate SQL type. Let's find out more about this type system and how values are converted at a lower level.

5.3 Mapping Java and SQL types with converters

Until now, you've assumed that Hibernate selects the right SQL type when you map a `java.lang.String` property. Nevertheless, what is the correct mapping between the Java and SQL types, and how can you control it?

5.3.1 Built-in types

Any JPA provider has to support a minimum set of Java-to-SQL type conversions; you saw this list at the beginning of this chapter, in section 5.1. Hibernate supports all of these mappings, as well as some additional adapters that aren't standard but are useful in practice. First, the Java primitives and their SQL equivalents.

PRIMITIVE AND NUMERIC TYPES

The built-in types shown in table 5.1 map Java primitives, and their wrappers, to appropriate SQL standard types. We've also included some other numeric types.

Table 5.1 Java primitive types that map to SQL standard types

Name	Java type	ANSI SQL type
integer	int, java.lang.Integer	INTEGER
long	long, java.lang.Long	BIGINT
short	short, java.lang.Short	SMALLINT
float	float, java.lang.Float	FLOAT
double	double, java.lang.Double	DOUBLE
byte	byte, java.lang.Byte	TINYINT
boolean	boolean, java.lang.Boolean	BOOLEAN
big_decimal	java.math.BigDecimal	NUMERIC
big_integer	java.math.BigInteger	NUMERIC

The names are Hibernate-specific; you'll need them later when customizing type mappings.

You probably noticed that your DBMS product doesn't support some of the mentioned SQL types. These SQL type names are ANSI-standard type names. Most DBMS vendors ignore this part of the SQL standard, usually because their legacy type systems predate the standard. But JDBC provides a partial abstraction of vendor-specific data types, allowing Hibernate to work with ANSI-standard types when executing DML statements such as INSERT and UPDATE. For product-specific schema generation, Hibernate translates from the ANSI-standard type to an appropriate vendor-specific type using the configured SQL dialect. This means you usually don't have to worry about SQL data types if you let Hibernate create the schema for you.

If you have an existing schema and/or you need to know the native data type for your DBMS, look at the source of your configured SQL dialect. For example, the H2Dialect shipping with Hibernate contains this mapping from the ANSI NUMERIC type to the vendor-specific DECIMAL type: registerColumnType(Types.NUMERIC, "decimal($p,$s)").

The NUMERIC SQL type supports decimal precision and scale settings. The default precision and scale setting, for a BigDecimal property, for example, is NUMERIC(19, 2). To override this for schema generation, apply the @Column annotation on the property and set its precision and scale parameters.

Next are types that map to strings in the database.

CHARACTER TYPES

Table 5.2 shows types that map character and string value representations.

Table 5.2   Adapters for character and string values

Name	Java type	ANSI SQL type
string	java.lang.String	VARCHAR
character	char[], Character[], java.lang.String	CHAR
yes_no	boolean, java.lang.Boolean	CHAR(1), 'Y' or 'N'
true_false	boolean, java.lang.Boolean	CHAR(1), 'T' or 'F'
class	java.lang.Class	VARCHAR
locale	java.util.Locale	VARCHAR
timezone	java.util.TimeZone	VARCHAR
currency	java.util.Currency	VARCHAR

The Hibernate type system picks an SQL data type depending on the declared length of a string value: if your String property is annotated with @Column(length = ...) or @Length of Bean Validation, Hibernate selects the right SQL data type for the given string size. This selection also depends on the configured SQL dialect. For example, for MySQL, a length of up to 65,535 produces a regular VARCHAR(length) column when the schema is generated by Hibernate. For a length of up to 16,777,215, a MySQL-specific MEDIUMTEXT data type is produced, and even greater lengths use a LONGTEXT. The default length of Hibernate for all java.lang.String properties is 255, so without any further mapping, a String property maps to a VARCHAR(255) column. You can customize this type selection by extending the class of your SQL dialect; read the dialect documentation and source code to find out more details for your DBMS product.

A database usually enables internationalization of text with a sensible (UTF-8) default character set for your entire database, or at least whole tables. This is a DBMS-specific setting. If you need more fine-grained control and want to switch to NVARCHAR, NCHAR, or NCLOB column types, annotate your property mapping with @org.hibernate .annotations.Nationalized.

Also built in are some special converters for legacy databases or DBMSs with limited type systems, such as Oracle. The Oracle DBMS doesn't even have a truth-valued data type, the only data type required by the relational model. Many existing Oracle schemas therefore represent Boolean values with Y/N or T/F characters. Or—and this is the default in Hibernate's Oracle dialect—a column of type NUMBER(1,0) is expected and generated. Again, we refer you to the SQL dialect of your DBMS if you want to know all mappings from ANSI data type to vendor-specific type.

Next are types that map to dates and times in the database.

DATE AND TIME TYPES

Table 5.3 lists types associated with dates, times, and timestamps.

Table 5.3   Date and time types

Name	Java type	ANSI SQL type
date	java.util.Date, java.sql.Date	DATE
time	java.util.Date, java.sql.Time	TIME
timestamp	java.util.Date, java.sql.Timestamp	TIMESTAMP
calendar	java.util.Calendar	TIMESTAMP
calendar_date	java.util.Calendar	DATE
duration	java.time.Duration	BIGINT
instant	java.time.Instant	TIMESTAMP
localdatetime	java.time.LocalDateTime	TIMESTAMP
localdate	java.time.LocalDate	DATE
localtime	java.time.LocalTime	TIME
offsetdatetime	java.time.OffsetDateTime	TIMESTAMP
offsettime	java.time.OffsetTime	TIME
zoneddatetime	java.time.ZonedDateTime	TIMESTAMP

In your domain model, you may choose to represent date and time data as either java.util.Date, java.util.Calendar, or the subclasses of java.util.Date defined in the java.sql package. This is a matter of taste, and we leave the decision to you—

make sure you're consistent. You might not want to bind the domain model to types from the JDBC package.

You can also use the Java 8 API in the `java.time` package. Note that this is Hibernate-specific and not standardized in JPA 2.1.

Hibernate's behavior for `java.util.Date` properties might surprise you at first: when you store a `java.util.Date`, Hibernate won't return a `java.util.Date` after loading. It will return a `java.sql.Date`, a `java.sql.Time`, or a `java.sql.Timestamp`, depending on whether you mapped the property with `TemporalType.DATE`, `TemporalType.TIME`, or `TemporalType.TIMESTAMP`.

Hibernate has to use the JDBC subclass when loading data from the database because the database types have higher accuracy than `java.util.Date`. A `java.util.Date` has millisecond accuracy, but a `java.sql.Timestamp` includes nano-second information that may be present in the database. Hibernate won't cut off this information to fit the value into `java.util.Date`. This Hibernate behavior may lead to problems if you try to compare `java.util.Date` values with the `equals()` method; it's not symmetric with the `java.sql.Timestamp` subclass's `equals()` method.

The solution is simple, and not even specific to Hibernate: don't call `aDate.equals(bDate)`. You should always compare dates and times by comparing Unix time milliseconds (assuming you don't care about the nanoseconds): `aDate.getTime() > bDate.getTime()`, for example, is `true` if `aDate` is a later time than `bDate`. Be careful: collections such as `HashSet` call the `equals()` method as well. Don't mix `java.util.Date` and `java.sql.Date|Time|Timestamp` values in such a collection. You won't have this kind of problem with a `Calendar` property. If you store a `Calendar` value, Hibernate will always return a `Calendar` value, created with `Calendar.getInstance()` (the actual type depends on locale and time zone).

Alternatively, you can write your own *converter*, as shown later in this chapter, and transform any instance of a `java.sql` temporal type, given to you by Hibernate, into a plain `java.util.Date` instance. A custom converter is also a good starting point if, for example, a `Calendar` instance should have a non-default time zone after loading the value from the database.

Next are types that map to binary data and large values in the database.

BINARY AND LARGE VALUE TYPES

Table 5.4 lists types for handling binary data and large values. Note that only `binary` is supported as the type of an identifier property.

First, consider how Hibernate represents your potentially large value, as binary or text.

Table 5.4 Binary and large value types

Name	Java type	ANSI SQL type
binary	byte[], java.lang.Byte[]	VARBINARY
text	java.lang.String	CLOB

Table 5.4 Binary and large value types *(continued)*

Name	Java type	ANSI SQL type
clob	java.sql.Clob	CLOB
blob	java.sql.Blob	BLOB
serializable	java.io.Serializable	VARBINARY

If a property in your persistent Java class is of type byte[], Hibernate maps it to a VAR-BINARY column. The real SQL data type depends on the dialect; for example, in Post-greSQL, the data type is BYTEA, and in Oracle DBMS, it's RAW. In some dialects, the length set with @Column also has an effect on the selected native type: for example, LONG RAW for length of 2000 and greater in Oracle.

A java.lang.String property is mapped to an SQL VARCHAR column, and the same for char[] and Character[]. As we've discussed, some dialects register different native types depending on declared length.

In both cases, Hibernate initializes the property value right away, when the entity instance that holds the property variable is loaded. This is inconvenient when you have to deal with potentially large values, so you usually want to override this default mapping. The JPA specification has a convenient shortcut annotation for this purpose, @Lob:

```
@Entity
public class Item {

    @Lob
    protected byte[] image;

    @Lob
    protected String description;

    // ...
}
```

This maps the byte[] to an SQL BLOB data type and the String to a CLOB. Unfortunately, you still don't get lazy loading with this design. Hibernate would have to intercept field access and, for example, load the bytes of the image when you call someItem.getImage(). This approach requires bytecode instrumentation of your classes after compilation, for the injection of extra code. We'll discuss lazy loading through bytecode instrumentation and interception in section 12.1.3.

Alternatively, you can switch the type of property in your Java class. JDBC supports locator objects (LOBs) directly. If your Java property is java.sql.Clob or java.sql.Blob, you get lazy loading without bytecode instrumentation:

```
@Entity
public class Item {

    @Lob
    protected java.sql.Blob imageBlob;
```

```
@Lob
protected java.sql.Clob description;

// ...
}
```

What does BLOB/CLOB mean?

Jim Starkey, who came up with the idea of LOBs, says that the marketing department created the terms BLOB and CLOB and that they don't mean anything. You can interpret them any way you like. We prefer *locator objects*, as a hint that they're placeholders that help us locate and access the real thing.

These JDBC classes include behavior to load values on demand. When the owning entity instance is loaded, the property value is a placeholder, and the real value isn't immediately materialized. Once you access the property, within the same transaction, the value is materialized or even streamed directly (to the client) without consuming temporary memory:

> PATH: /examples/src/test/java/org/jpwh/test/advanced/LazyProperties.java

```
Item item = em.find(Item.class, ITEM_ID);

InputStream imageDataStream = item.getImageBlob().getBinaryStream();

ByteArrayOutputStream outStream = new ByteArrayOutputStream();
StreamUtils.copy(imageDataStream, outStream);
byte[] imageBytes = outStream.toByteArray();
```

You can stream the bytes directly ...

... or materialize them into memory.

The downside is that your domain model is then bound to JDBC; in unit tests, you can't access LOB properties without a database connection.

Hibernate Feature

To create and set a `Blob` or `Clob` value, Hibernate offers some convenience methods. This example reads `byteLength` bytes from an `InputStream` directly into the database, without consuming temporary memory:

```
Session session = em.unwrap(Session.class);
Blob blob = session.getLobHelper()
      .createBlob(imageInputStream, byteLength);

someItem.setImageBlob(blob);
em.persist(someItem);
```

Need the native Hibernate API

Need to know the number of bytes you want to read from the stream

Finally, Hibernate provides fallback serialization for any property type that is `java.io.Serializable`. This mapping converts the value of the property to a byte stream stored in a `VARBINARY` column. Serialization and deserialization occur when the owning entity instance is stored and loaded. Naturally, you should use this strategy with extreme caution, because data lives longer than applications. One day, nobody will know what those bytes in your database mean. Serialization is sometimes useful for temporary data, such as user preferences, login session data, and so on.

Hibernate will pick the right type adapter depending on the Java type of your property. If you don't like the default mapping, read on to override it.

Hibernate Feature

SELECTING A TYPE ADAPTER

You have seen many adapters and their Hibernate names in the previous sections. Use the name when you override Hibernate's default type selection, and explicitly select a particular adapter:

```
@Entity
public class Item {

    @org.hibernate.annotations.Type(type = "yes_no")
    protected boolean verified = false;
}
```

Instead of `BIT`, this `boolean` now maps to a `CHAR` column with values `Y` or `N`.

You can also override an adapter globally in the Hibernate boot configuration with a custom user type, which you'll learn how to write later in this chapter:

```
metaBuilder.applyBasicType(new MyUserType(), new String[]{"date"});
```

This setting will override the built-in `date` type adapter and delegate value conversion for `java.util.Date` properties to your custom implementation.

We consider this extensible type system one of Hibernate's core features and an important aspect that makes it so flexible. Next, we explore the type system and JPA custom converters in more detail.

5.3.2 Creating custom JPA converters

A new requirement for the online auction system is multiple currencies. Rolling out this kind of change can be complex. You have to modify the database schema, you may have to migrate existing data from the old to the new schema, and you have to update all applications that access the database. In this section, we show you how JPA converters and the extensible Hibernate type system can assist you in this process, providing an additional, flexible buffer between your application and the database.

To support multiple currencies, let's introduce a new class in the CaveatEmptor domain model: `MonetaryAmount`, shown in the following listing.

Listing 5.7   Immutable `MonetaryAmount` value-type class

PATH: **/model/src/main/java/org/jpwh/model/advanced/MonetaryAmount.java**

```
public class MonetaryAmount implements Serializable {          ◄──    ❶ Value-typed class is
    protected final BigDecimal value;                    ◄──              java.io.Serializable
    protected final Currency currency;                        ❷ No special constructor needed

    public MonetaryAmount(BigDecimal value, Currency currency) {
        this.value = value;
        this.currency = currency;
    }

    public BigDecimal getValue() {
        return value;
    }

    public Currency getCurrency() {
        return currency;
    }                                                         ❸ Implements equals()
                                                                  and hashcode()
    public boolean equals(Object o) {                    ◄──

        if (this == o) return true;
        if (!(o instanceof MonetaryAmount)) return false;

        final MonetaryAmount monetaryAmount = (MonetaryAmount) o;

        if (!value.equals(monetaryAmount.value)) return false;
        if (!currency.equals(monetaryAmount.currency)) return false;

        return true;
    }                                                    ❸ Implements equals()
                                                             and hashcode()
    public int hashCode() {                          ◄──
        int result;
        result = value.hashCode();
        result = 29 * result + currency.hashCode();
        return result;
    }                                                ❹ Creates instance from
                                                         String
    public String toString() {                   ◄──
        return getValue() + " " + getCurrency();
    }

    public static MonetaryAmount fromString(String s) {
        String[] split = s.split(" ");
        return new MonetaryAmount(
            new BigDecimal(split[0]),
            Currency.getInstance(split[1])
        );
    }
}
```

❶ This value-typed class should be `java.io.Serializable`: when Hibernate stores entity instance data in the shared second-level cache (see section 20.2), it *disassembles* the entity's state. If an entity has a `MonetaryAmount` property, the serialized representation of the property value is stored in the second-level cache region. When entity data is retrieved from the cache region, the property value is deserialized and reassembled.

2 The class doesn't need a special constructor. You can make it immutable, even with `final` fields, because your code will be the only place an instance is created.

3 You should implement the `equals()` and `hashCode()` methods and compare monetary amounts "by value."

4 You need a `String` representation of a monetary amount. Implement the `toString()` method and a static method to create an instance from a `String`.

Next, you update other parts of the auction domain model and use `MonetaryAmount` for all properties involving money, such as `Item#buyNowPrice` and `Bid#amount`.

CONVERTING BASIC PROPERTY VALUES

As is often the case, the database folks can't implement multiple currencies right away and need more time. All they can provide quickly is a column data type change, in the database schema. They suggest that you store the BUYNOWPRICE in the ITEM table in a VARCHAR column and that you append the currency code of the monetary amount to its string value. You store, for example, the value `11.23 USD` or `99 EUR`.

You have to convert an instance of `MonetaryAmount` to such a `String` representation when storing data. When loading data, you convert the `String` back into a `Monetary-Amount`.

The simplest solution is a `javax.persistence.AttributeConverter`, as shown in the next listing, a standardized extension point in JPA.

Listing 5.8   Converting between strings and `MonetaryValue`

PATH: /model/src/main/java/org/jpwh/converter/MonetaryAmountConverter.java

```java
@Converter(autoApply = true)                                        ⬅━┐ Default for
public class MonetaryAmountConverter                                    MonetaryAmount
    implements AttributeConverter<MonetaryAmount, String> {             properties

    @Override
    public String convertToDatabaseColumn(MonetaryAmount monetaryAmount) {
        return monetaryAmount.toString();
    }

    @Override
    public MonetaryAmount convertToEntityAttribute(String s) {
        return MonetaryAmount.fromString(s);
    }
}
```

A converter has to implement the `AttributeConverter` interface; the two type arguments are the type of the Java property and the type in the database schema. The Java type is `MonetaryAmount`, and the database type is `String`, which maps, as usual, to an SQL VARCHAR. You must annotate the class with `@Converter` or declare it as such in the orm.xml metadata. With `autoApply` enabled, any `MonetaryAmount` property in your domain model, be it of an entity or an embeddable class, without further mapping will now be handled by this converter automatically. (Don't be distracted by the convert-ToEntityAttribute() method of the AttributeConverter interface; it's not the best name.)

An example of such a MonetaryAmount property in the domain model is Item#buyNowPrice:

PATH: /model/src/main/java/org/jpwh/model/advanced/converter/Item.java

```
@Entity
public class Item {

    @NotNull
    @Convert(                                          Optional: autoApply
        converter = MonetaryAmountConverter.class,     is enabled.
        disableConversion = false)
    @Column(name = "PRICE", length = 63)
    protected MonetaryAmount buyNowPrice;

    // ...
}
```

The @Convert annotation is optional: apply it to override or disable a converter for a particular property. @Column renames the mapped database column PRICE; the default is BUYNOWPRICE. For automatic schema generation, define it as VARCHAR with a length of 63 characters.

Later, when your DBA upgrades the database schema and offers you separate columns for the monetary amount value and currency, you only have to change your application in a few places. Drop the MonetaryAmountConverter from your project and make MonetaryAmount an @Embeddable; it then maps automatically to two database columns. It's easy to selectively enable and disable converters, too, if some tables in the schema haven't been upgraded.

The converter you just wrote is for MonetaryAmount, a new class in the domain model. Converters aren't limited to custom classes: you can even override Hibernate's built-in type adapters. For example, you could create a custom converter for some or even all java.util.Date properties in your domain model.

You can apply converters to properties of entity classes, like Item#buyNowPrice in the last example. You can also apply them to properties of embeddable classes.

CONVERTING PROPERTIES OF COMPONENTS

We've been making the case for fine-grained domain models in this chapter. Earlier, you isolated the address information of the User and mapped the Address embeddable class. Let's continue this process and introduce inheritance, with an abstract Zipcode class as shown in figure 5.5.

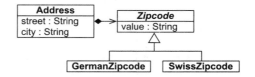

Figure 5.5   The abstract **Zipcode** class has two concrete subclasses.

The Zipcode class is trivial, but don't forget to implement equality by value:

PATH: **/model/src/main/java/org/jpwh/model/advanced/converter/Zipcode.java**

```
abstract public class Zipcode {

    protected String value;

    public Zipcode(String value) {
        this.value = value;
    }

    public String getValue() {
        return value;
    }

    @Override
    public boolean equals(Object o) {
        if (this == o) return true;
        if (o == null || getClass() != o.getClass()) return false;
        Zipcode zipcode = (Zipcode) o;
        return value.equals(zipcode.value);
    }

    @Override
    public int hashCode() {
        return value.hashCode();
    }
}
```

You can now encapsulate domain subclasses, the difference between German and Swiss postal codes, and any processing:

PATH: **/model/src/main/java/org/jpwh/model/advanced/converter/ GermanZipcode.java**

```
public class GermanZipcode extends Zipcode {

    public GermanZipcode(String value) {
        super(value);
    }
}
```

You haven't implemented any special processing in the subclass. Let's start with the most obvious difference: German zip codes are five numbers long, Swiss are four. A custom converter will take care of this:

PATH: **/model/src/main/java/org/jpwh/converter/ZipcodeConverter.java**

```
@Converter
public class ZipcodeConverter
    implements AttributeConverter<Zipcode, String> {

    @Override
    public String convertToDatabaseColumn(Zipcode attribute) {
```

```
        return attribute.getValue();
    }

    @Override
    public Zipcode convertToEntityAttribute(String s) {
        if (s.length() == 5)
            return new GermanZipcode(s);
        else if (s.length() == 4)
            return new SwissZipcode(s);

        throw new IllegalArgumentException(
            "Unsupported zipcode in database: " + s
        );
    }
}
```

If you get to this point, consider cleaning up your database ... or create an InvalidZipCode subclass and return it here.

Hibernate calls the convertToDatabaseColumn() method of this converter when storing a property value; you return a String representation. The column in the schema is VARCHAR. When loading a value, you examine its length and create either a German-Zipcode or SwissZipcode instance. This is a custom type discrimination routine; you can pick the Java type of the given value.

Now apply this converter on some Zipcode properties—for example, the embedded homeAddress of a User:

> **PATH:** /model/src/main/java/org/jpwh/model/advanced/converter/User.java

```
@Entity
@Table(name = "USERS")
public class User implements Serializable {

    @Convert(
        converter = ZipcodeConverter.class,
        attributeName = "zipcode"
    )
    protected Address homeAddress;

    // ...
}
```

Group multiple attribute conversions with @Converts

Or "city.zipcode" for nested embeddables

The attributeName declares the zipcode attribute of the embeddable Address class. This setting supports a dot syntax for the attribute path; if zipcode isn't a property of the Address class but is a property of a nested embeddable City class (as shown earlier in this chapter), reference it with city.zipcode, its nested path.

If several @Convert annotations are required on a single embedded property, to convert several attributes of the Address, for example, you can group them within an @Converts annotation. You can also apply converters to values of collections and maps, if their values and/or keys are of basic or embeddable type. For example, you can add the @Convert annotation on a persistent Set<Zipcode>. We'll show you how to map persistent collections later, with @ElementCollection, in chapter 7.

For persistent maps, the attributeName option of the @Convert annotation has some special syntax:

- On a persistent `Map<Address, String>`, you can apply a converter for the `zipcode` property of each map key with the attribute name `key.zipcode`.
- On a persistent `Map<String, Address>`, you can apply a converter for the `zipcode` property of each map value with the attribute name `value.zipcode`.
- On a persistent `Map<Zipcode, String>`, you can apply a converter for the key of each map entry with the attribute name `key`.
- On a persistent `Map<String, Zipcode>`, you can apply a converter for the value of each map entry by not setting any `attributeName`.

As before, the attribute name can be a dot-separated path if your embeddable classes are nested; you can write `key.city.zipcode` to reference the `zipcode` property of the `City` class, in a composition with the `Address` class.

Some limitations of the JPA converters are as follows:

- You can't apply them to identifier or version properties of an entity.
- You shouldn't apply a converter on a property mapped with `@Enumerated` or `@Temporal`, because these annotations already declare what kind of conversion has to occur. If you want to apply a custom converter for enums or date/time properties, don't annotate them with `@Enumerated` or `@Temporal`.
- You can apply a converter to a property mapping in an hbm.xml file, but you have to prefix the name: `type="converter:qualified.ConverterName"`.

Let's get back to multiple currency support in CaveatEmptor. The database administrators changed the schema again and asked you to update the application.

Hibernate Feature

5.3.3   *Extending Hibernate with UserTypes*

Finally, you've added new columns to the database schema to support multiple currencies. The ITEM table now has a BUYNOWPRICE_AMOUNT and a separate column for the currency of the amount, BUYNOWPRICE_CURRENCY. There are also INITIALPRICE_AMOUNT and INITIALPRICE_CURRENCY columns. You have to map these columns to the `MonetaryAmount` properties of the `Item` class, buyNowPrice and initialPrice.

Ideally, you don't want to change the domain model; the properties already use the `MonetaryAmount` class. Unfortunately, the standardized JPA converters don't support transformation of values from/to multiple columns. Another limitation of JPA converters is integration with the query engine. You can't write the following query: `select i from Item i where i.buyNowPrice.amount > 100`. Thanks to the converter from the previous section, Hibernate knows how to convert a `MonetaryAmount` to and from a string. It doesn't know that `MonetaryAmount` has an amount attribute, so it can't parse such a query.

A simple solution would be to map `MonetaryAmount` as `@Embeddable`, as discussed earlier in this chapter for the `Address` class. Each property of `MonetaryAmount`— amount and currency—maps to its respective database column.

Your database admins, however, add a twist to their requirements: because other, old applications also access the database, you have to convert each amount to a target currency before storing it in the database. For example, Item#buyNowPrice should be stored in US dollars, and Item#initialPrice should be stored in Euros. (If this example seems far-fetched, we can assure you that you'll see worse in the real world. Evolution of a shared database schema can be costly but is of course necessary because data always lives longer than applications.) Hibernate offers a native converter API: an extension point that allows much more detailed and low-level customization access.

THE EXTENSION POINTS

Hibernate's extension interfaces for its type system can found in the org.hibernate .usertype package. The following interfaces are available:

- UserType—You can transform values by interacting with the plain JDBC PreparedStatement (when storing data) and ResultSet (when loading data). By implementing this interface, you can also control how Hibernate caches and dirty-checks values. The adapter for MonetaryAmount has to implement this interface.

- CompositeUserType—This extends UserType, providing Hibernate with more details about your adapted class. You can tell Hibernate that the Monetary-Amount component has two properties: amount and currency. You can then reference these properties in queries with dot notation: for example, select avg(i.buyNowPrice.amount) from Item i.

- ParameterizedUserType—This provides settings to your adapter in mappings. You have to implement this interface for the MonetaryAmount conversion, because in some mappings you want to convert the amount to US dollars and in other mappings to Euros. You only have to write a single adapter and can customize its behavior when mapping a property.

- DynamicParameterizedType—This more powerful settings API gives you access to dynamic information in the adapter, such as the mapped column and table names. You might as well use this instead of ParameterizedUserType; there is no additional cost or complexity.

- EnhancedUserType—This is an optional interface for adapters of identifier properties and discriminators. Unlike JPA converters, a UserType in Hibernate can be an adapter for any kind of entity property. Because MonetaryAmount won't be the type of an identifier property or discriminator, you won't need it.

- UserVersionType—This is an optional interface for adapters of version properties.

- UserCollectionType—This rarely needed interface is used to implement custom collections. You have to implement it to persist a non-JDK collection and preserve additional semantics.

The custom type adapter for MonetaryAmount will implement several of these interfaces.

IMPLEMENTING THE USERTYPE

Because `MonetaryAmountUserType` is a large class, we examine it in several steps. These are the interfaces you implement:

> PATH: /model/src/main/java/org/jpwh/converter/MonetaryAmountUserType.java

```java
public class MonetaryAmountUserType
    implements CompositeUserType, DynamicParameterizedType {

    // ...
}
```

First you implement `DynamicParameterizedType`. You need to configure the target currency for the conversion by examining a mapping parameter:

> PATH: /model/src/main/java/org/jpwh/converter/MonetaryAmountUserType.java

```java
protected Currency convertTo;

public void setParameterValues(Properties parameters) {          ❶ Accesses
                                                                    dynamic
    ParameterType parameterType =                                   parameters
        (ParameterType) parameters.get(PARAMETER_TYPE);
    String[] columns = parameterType.getColumns();
    String table = parameterType.getTable();
    Annotation[] annotations = parameterType.getAnnotationsMethod();

    String convertToParameter = parameters.getProperty("convertTo");
    this.convertTo = Currency.getInstance(
        convertToParameter != null ? convertToParameter : "USD"
    );
}                                                    Determines target currency ❷
```

❶ You can access some dynamic parameters here, such as the name of the mapped columns, the mapped (entity) table, or even the annotations on the field/getter of the mapped property. You don't need them in this example, though.

❷ You only use the `convertTo` parameter to determine the target currency when saving a value into the database. If the parameter hasn't been set, default to US dollars.

Next, here's some scaffolding code that any `UserType` must implement:

> PATH: /model/src/main/java/org/jpwh/converter/MonetaryAmountUserType.java

```java
public Class returnedClass() {              ◀────── ❶ Adapts class
    return MonetaryAmount.class;
}

public boolean isMutable() {                ◀────── ❷ Enables optimizations
    return false;
}

public Object deepCopy(Object value) {      ◀────── ❸ Copies value
    return value;
}
```

4 Returns Serializable representation

```
public Serializable disassemble(Object value,
                            SessionImplementor session) {
    return value.toString();
}
```

5 Creates MonetaryAmount instance

```
public Object assemble(Serializable cached,
                    SessionImplementor session, Object owner) {
    return MonetaryAmount.fromString((String) cached);
}
```

6 Returns copy of original

```
public Object replace(Object original, Object target,
                    SessionImplementor session, Object owner) {
    return original;
}


public boolean equals(Object x, Object y) {
    return x == y || !(x == null || y == null) && x.equals(y);
}
```

Determines whether value has changed **7**

```
public int hashCode(Object x) {
    return x.hashCode();
}
```

1 The method returnedClass adapts the given class, in this case MonetaryAmount.

2 Hibernate can enable some optimizations if it knows that MonetaryAmount is immutable.

3 If Hibernate has to make a copy of the value, it calls this method. For simple immutable classes like MonetaryAmount, you can return the given instance.

4 Hibernate calls disassemble when it stores a value in the global shared second-level cache. You need to return a Serializable representation. For MonetaryAmount, a String representation is an easy solution. Or, because MonetaryAmount is Serializable, you could return it directly.

5 Hibernate calls this method when it reads the serialized representation from the global shared second-level cache. You create a MonetaryAmount instance from the String representation. Or, if you stored a serialized MonetaryAmount, you could return it directly.

6 This is called during EntityManager#merge() operations. You need to return a copy of the original. Or, if your value type is immutable, like MonetaryAmount, you can return the original.

7 Hibernate uses value equality to determine whether the value was changed and the database needs to be updated. You rely on the equality routine you already wrote on the MonetaryAmount class.

The real work of the adapter happens when values are loaded and stored, as implemented with the following methods:

PATH: /model/src/main/java/org/jpwh/converter/MonetaryAmountUserType.java

```java
public Object nullSafeGet(ResultSet resultSet,                     // ❶ Reads ResultSet
                         String[] names,
                         SessionImplementor session,
                         Object owner) throws SQLException {
    BigDecimal amount = resultSet.getBigDecimal(names[0]);
    if (resultSet.wasNull())
        return null;
    Currency currency =
        Currency.getInstance(resultSet.getString(names[1]));
    return new MonetaryAmount(amount, currency);
}

public void nullSafeSet(PreparedStatement statement,              // ❷ Stores
                        Object value,                            //   MonetaryAmount
                        int index,
                        SessionImplementor session) throws SQLException {
    if (value == null) {
        statement.setNull(
            index,
            StandardBasicTypes.BIG_DECIMAL.sqlType());
        statement.setNull(
            index + 1,
            StandardBasicTypes.CURRENCY.sqlType());        // When
    } else {                                               // saving,
        MonetaryAmount amount = (MonetaryAmount) value;    // convert
        MonetaryAmount dbAmount = convert(amount, convertTo);  // to target
        statement.setBigDecimal(index, dbAmount.getValue());   // currency
        statement.setString(index + 1, convertTo.getCurrencyCode());
    }
}

protected MonetaryAmount convert(MonetaryAmount amount,           // ❸ Converts
                                 Currency toCurrency) {          //   currency
    return new MonetaryAmount(
        amount.getValue().multiply(new BigDecimal(2)),
        toCurrency
    );
}
```

❶ This is called to read the ResultSet when a MonetaryAmount value has to be retrieved from the database. You take the amount and currency values as given in the query result and create a new instance of MonetaryAmount.

❷ This is called when a MonetaryAmount value has to be stored in the database. You convert the value to the target currency and then set the amount and currency on the provided PreparedStatement (unless MonetaryAmount was null, in which case you call setNull() to prepare the statement).

❸ Here you can implement whatever currency conversion routine you need. For the sake of the example, you double the value so you can easily test whether conversion was successful. You'll have to replace this code with a real currency converter in a real application. It's not a method of the Hibernate `UserType` API.

Finally, following are the methods required by the `CompositeUserType` interface, providing the details of the `MonetaryAmount` properties so Hibernate can integrate the class with the query engine:

PATH: /model/src/main/java/org/jpwh/converter/MonetaryAmountUserType.java

```java
public String[] getPropertyNames() {
    return new String[]{"value", "currency"};
}

public Type[] getPropertyTypes() {
    return new Type[]{
        StandardBasicTypes.BIG_DECIMAL,
        StandardBasicTypes.CURRENCY
    };
}

public Object getPropertyValue(Object component,
                               int property) {
    MonetaryAmount monetaryAmount = (MonetaryAmount) component;
    if (property == 0)
        return monetaryAmount.getValue();
    else
        return monetaryAmount.getCurrency();
}

public void setPropertyValue(Object component,
                             int property,
                             Object value) {
    throw new UnsupportedOperationException(
        "MonetaryAmount is immutable"
    );
}
```

The `MonetaryAmountUserType` is now complete, and you can already use it in mappings with its fully qualified class name in `@org.hibernate.annotations.Type`, as shown in the section "Selecting a type adapter." This annotation also supports parameters, so you can set the `convertTo` argument to the target currency.

But we recommend that you create *type definitions*, bundling your adapter with some parameters.

USING TYPE DEFINITIONS

You need an adapter that converts to US dollars and an adapter that converts to Euros. If you declare these parameters once as a *type definition*, you don't have to repeat them in property mappings. A good location for type definitions is package metadata, in a package-info.java file:

PATH: /model/src/main/java/org/jpwh/converter/package-info.java

```
@org.hibernate.annotations.TypeDefs({
    @org.hibernate.annotations.TypeDef(
        name = "monetary_amount_usd",
        typeClass = MonetaryAmountUserType.class,
        parameters = {@Parameter(name = "convertTo", value = "USD")}
    ),
    @org.hibernate.annotations.TypeDef(
        name = "monetary_amount_eur",
        typeClass = MonetaryAmountUserType.class,
        parameters = {@Parameter(name = "convertTo", value = "EUR")}
    )
})
package org.jpwh.converter;

import org.hibernate.annotations.Parameter;
```

You're now ready to use the adapters in mappings, using the names `monetary_amount_usd` and `monetary_amount_eur`.

Let's map the `buyNowPrice` and `initialPrice` of `Item`:

PATH: /model/src/main/java/org/jpwh/model/advanced/usertype/Item.java

```
@Entity
public class Item {

    @NotNull
    @org.hibernate.annotations.Type(
        type = "monetary_amount_usd"
    )
    @org.hibernate.annotations.Columns(columns = {
        @Column(name = "BUYNOWPRICE_AMOUNT"),
        @Column(name = "BUYNOWPRICE_CURRENCY", length = 3)
    })
    protected MonetaryAmount buyNowPrice;

    @NotNull
    @org.hibernate.annotations.Type(
        type = "monetary_amount_eur"
    )
    @org.hibernate.annotations.Columns(columns = {
        @Column(name = "INITIALPRICE_AMOUNT"),
        @Column(name = "INITIALPRICE_CURRENCY", length = 3)
    })
    protected MonetaryAmount initialPrice;

    // ...
}
```

If `UserType` transforms values for only a single column, you don't need an `@Column` annotation. `MonetaryAmountUserType`, however, accesses two columns, so you need to explicitly declare two columns in the property mapping. Because JPA doesn't support multiple `@Column` annotations on a single property, you have to group them with the proprietary @org.hibernate.annotations.Columns annotation. Note that order of the annotations is now important! Re-check the code for MonetaryAmountUserType; many operations rely on indexed access of arrays. The order when accessing PreparedStatement or ResultSet is the same as that of the declared columns in the mapping. Also note that the number of columns isn't relevant for your choice of UserType versus CompositeUserType—only your desire to expose value type properties for queries.

With MonetaryAmountUserType, you've extended the buffer between the Java domain model and the SQL database schema. Both representations are now more robust to changes, and you can handle even rather eccentric requirements without modifying the essence of the domain model classes.

5.4   Summary

- We discussed the mapping of basic and embedded properties of an entity class.
- You saw how to override basic mappings, how to change the name of a mapped column, and how to use derived, default, temporal, and enumeration properties.
- We covered embeddable component classes and how you can create fine-grained domain models.
- You can map the properties of several Java classes in a composition, such as Address and City, to one entity table.
- We looked at how Hibernate selects Java to SQL type converters, and what types are built into Hibernate.
- You wrote a custom type converter for the MonetaryAmount class with the standard JPA extension interfaces, and then a low-level adapter with the native Hibernate UserType API.

Mapping inheritance

We deliberately haven't talked much about inheritance mapping so far. Mapping a hierarchy of classes to tables can be a complex issue, and we present various strategies in this chapter.

A basic strategy for mapping classes to database tables might be "one table for every entity persistent class." This approach sounds simple enough and indeed works well, until we encounter inheritance.

Inheritance is such a visible structural mismatch between the object-oriented and relational worlds because object-oriented systems model both *is a* and *has a* relationships. SQL-based models provide only *has a* relationships; SQL database management systems don't support type inheritance—and even when it's available, it's usually proprietary or incomplete.

There are four different strategies for representing an inheritance hierarchy:

- Use one table per concrete class and default runtime polymorphic behavior.
- Use one table per concrete class but discard polymorphism and inheritance relationships completely from the SQL schema. Use SQL UNION queries for runtime polymorphic behavior.

117

- Use one table per class hierarchy: enable polymorphism by denormalizing the SQL schema and relying on row-based discrimination to determine super/subtypes.
- Use one table per subclass: represent *is a* (inheritance) relationships as *has a* (foreign key) relationships, and use SQL JOIN operations.

This chapter takes a top-down approach, assuming that you're starting with a domain model and trying to derive a new SQL schema. The mapping strategies described are just as relevant if you're working bottom-up, starting with existing database tables. We show some tricks along the way to help you deal with imperfect table layouts.

6.1   Table per concrete class with implicit polymorphism

Suppose we stick with the simplest approach suggested: exactly one table for each concrete class. You can map all properties of a class, including inherited properties, to columns of this table, as shown in figure 6.1.

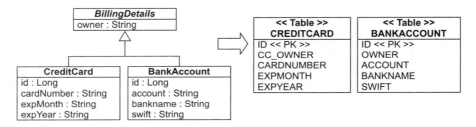

Figure 6.1   Mapping all concrete classes to an independent table

If you're relying on this implicit polymorphism, you map concrete classes with @Entity, as usual. By default, properties of the superclass are ignored and not persistent! You have to annotate the superclass with @MappedSuperclass to enable embedding of its properties in the concrete subclass tables; see the following listing.

Listing 6.1   Mapping BillingDetails (abstract superclass) with implicit polymorphism

PATH: /model/src/main/java/org/jpwh/model/inheritance/mappedsuperclass/
        BillingDetails.java

```
@MappedSuperclass
public abstract class BillingDetails {

    @NotNull
    protected String owner;

    // ...
}
```

Now map the concrete subclasses.

Listing 6.2 Mapping `CreditCard` (concrete subclass)

PATH: /model/src/main/java/org/jpwh/model/inheritance/mappedsuperclass/
      CreditCard.java

```java
@Entity
@AttributeOverride(
        name = "owner",
        column = @Column(name = "CC_OWNER", nullable = false))
public class CreditCard extends BillingDetails {

    @Id
    @GeneratedValue(generator = Constants.ID_GENERATOR)
    protected Long id;

    @NotNull
    protected String cardNumber;

    @NotNull
    protected String expMonth;

    @NotNull
    protected String expYear;

    // ...
}
```

The mapping for the `BankAccount` class looks the same, so we won't show it here.

You can override column mappings from the superclass in a subclass with the `@AttributeOverride` annotation or several with `@AttributeOverrides`. The previous example renamed the `OWNER` column to `CC_OWNER` in the `CREDITCARD` table.

You could declare the identifier property in the superclass, with a shared column name and generator strategy for all subclasses, so you wouldn't have to repeat it. We haven't done this in the examples to show you that it's optional.

The main problem with implicit inheritance mapping is that it doesn't support polymorphic associations very well. In the database, you usually represent associations as foreign key relationships. In the schema shown in figure 6.1, if the subclasses are all mapped to different tables, a polymorphic association to their superclass (abstract `BillingDetails`) can't be represented as a simple foreign key relationship. You can't have another entity mapped with a foreign key "referencing `BILLINGDETAILS`"—there is no such table. This would be problematic in the domain model, because `Billing-Details` is associated with `User`; both the `CREDITCARD` and `BANKACCOUNT` tables would need a foreign key reference to the `USERS` table. None of these issues can be easily resolved, so you should consider an alternative mapping strategy.

Polymorphic queries that return instances of all classes that match the interface of the queried class are also problematic. Hibernate must execute a query against the superclass as several SQL `SELECT`s, one for each concrete subclass. The JPA query `select bd from BillingDetails bd` requires two SQL statements:

```
select
    ID, OWNER, ACCOUNT, BANKNAME, SWIFT
from
    BANKACCOUNT
select
    ID, CC_OWNER, CARDNUMBER, EXPMONTH, EXPYEAR
from
    CREDITCARD
```

Hibernate uses a separate SQL query for each concrete subclass. On the other hand, queries against the concrete classes are trivial and perform well—Hibernate uses only one of the statements.

A further conceptual problem with this mapping strategy is that several different columns, of different tables, share exactly the same semantics. This makes schema evolution more complex. For example, renaming or changing the type of a superclass property results in changes to multiple columns in multiple tables. Many of the standard refactoring operations offered by your IDE would require manual adjustments, because the automatic procedures usually don't account for things like @Attribute- Overrides. It also makes it much more difficult to implement database integrity constraints that apply to all subclasses.

We recommend this approach (only) for the top level of your class hierarchy, where polymorphism isn't usually required, and when modification of the superclass in the future is unlikely. It isn't a good fit for the CaveatEmptor domain model, where queries and other entities refer to BillingDetails.

With the help of the SQL UNION operation, you can eliminate most of the issues with polymorphic queries and associations.

6.2 *Table per concrete class with unions*

First, let's consider a union subclass mapping with BillingDetails as an abstract class (or interface), as in the previous section. In this situation, you again have two tables and duplicate superclass columns in both: CREDITCARD and BANKACCOUNT. What's new is an inheritance strategy known as TABLE_PER_CLASS, declared on the superclass, as shown next.

Listing 6.3   Mapping BillingDetails with TABLE_PER_CLASS

PATH: /model/src/main/java/org/jpwh/model/inheritance/tableperclass/
        BillingDetails.java

```
@Entity
@Inheritance(strategy = InheritanceType.TABLE_PER_CLASS)
public abstract class BillingDetails {

    @Id
    @GeneratedValue(generator = Constants.ID_GENERATOR)
    protected Long id;

    @NotNull
```

```
    protected String owner;

    // ...
}
```

The database identifier and its mapping have to be present in the superclass, to share it in all subclasses and their tables. This is no longer optional, as it was for the previous mapping strategy. The CREDITCARD and BANKACCOUNT tables both have an ID primary key column. All concrete class mappings inherit persistent properties from the superclass (or interface). An @Entity annotation on each subclass is all that is required.

Listing 6.4 Mapping `CreditCard`

PATH: /model/src/main/java/org/jpwh/model/inheritance/tableperclass/Credit-Card.java

---

```
@Entity
public class CreditCard extends BillingDetails {

    @NotNull
    protected String cardNumber;

    @NotNull
    protected String expMonth;

    @NotNull
    protected String expYear;

    // ...
}
```

Keep in mind that the SQL schema still isn't aware of the inheritance; the tables look exactly alike, as shown in figure 6.1.

Note that the JPA standard specifies that TABLE_PER_CLASS is optional, so not all JPA implementations may support it. The implementation is also vendor dependent—in Hibernate, it's equivalent to a <union-subclass> mapping in the old native Hibernate XML metadata (don't worry about this if you've never used native Hibernate XML files).

If BillingDetails were concrete, you'd need an additional table to hold instances. We have to emphasize again that there is still no relationship between the database tables, except for the fact that they have some (many) similar columns.

The advantages of this mapping strategy are clearer if we examine polymorphic queries. For example, the query select bd from BillingDetails bd generates the following SQL statement:

```
select
    ID, OWNER, EXPMONTH, EXPYEAR, CARDNUMBER,
    ACCOUNT, BANKNAME, SWIFT, CLAZZ_
 from
    ( select
        ID, OWNER, EXPMONTH, EXPYEAR, CARDNUMBER,
        null as ACCOUNT,
        null as BANKNAME,
```

```
        null as SWIFT,
        1 as CLAZZ_
    from
        CREDITCARD
    union all
    select
        id, OWNER,
        null as EXPMONTH,
        null as EXPYEAR,
        null as CARDNUMBER,
        ACCOUNT, BANKNAME, SWIFT,
        2 as CLAZZ_
    from
        BANKACCOUNT
) as BILLINGDETAILS
```

This SELECT uses a FROM-clause subquery to retrieve all instances of BillingDetails from all concrete class tables. The tables are combined with a UNION operator, and a literal (in this case, 1 and 2) is inserted into the intermediate result; Hibernate reads this to instantiate the correct class given the data from a particular row. A union requires that the queries that are combined project over the same columns; hence, you have to pad and fill nonexistent columns with NULL. You may ask whether this query will really perform better than two separate statements. Here you can let the database optimizer find the best execution plan to combine rows from several tables, instead of merging two result sets in memory as Hibernate's polymorphic loader engine would do.

Another much more important advantage is the ability to handle polymorphic associations; for example, an association mapping from User to BillingDetails would now be possible. Hibernate can use a UNION query to simulate a single table as the target of the association mapping. We cover this topic in detail later in this chapter.

So far, the inheritance-mapping strategies we've discussed don't require extra consideration with regard to the SQL schema. This situation changes with the next strategy.

6.3   *Table per class hierarchy*

You can map an entire class hierarchy to a single table. This table includes columns for all properties of all classes in the hierarchy. The value of an extra type discriminator column or formula identifies the concrete subclass represented by a particular row. Figure 6.2 shows this approach.

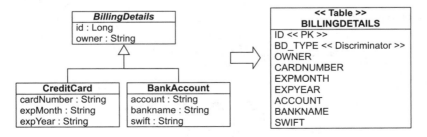

Figure 6.2   Mapping an entire class hierarchy to a single table

This mapping strategy is a winner in terms of both performance and simplicity. It's the best-performing way to represent polymorphism—both polymorphic and non-polymorphic queries perform well—and it's even easy to write queries by hand. Ad hoc reporting is possible without complex joins or unions. Schema evolution is straightforward.

There is one major problem: data integrity. You must declare columns for properties declared by subclasses to be nullable. If your subclasses each define several non-nullable properties, the loss of NOT NULL constraints may be a serious problem from the point of view of data correctness. Imagine that an expiration date for credit cards is required, but your database schema can't enforce this rule because all columns of the table can be NULL. A simple application programming error can lead to invalid data.

Another important issue is normalization. You've created functional dependencies between non-key columns, violating the third normal form. As always, denormalization for performance reasons can be misleading, because it sacrifices long-term stability, maintainability, and the integrity of data for immediate gains that may be also achieved by proper optimization of the SQL execution plans (in other words, ask your DBA).

Use the SINGLE_TABLE inheritance strategy to create a table-per-class hierarchy mapping, as shown in the following listing.

Listing 6.5 Mapping `BillingDetails` with `SINGLE_TABLE`

PATH: /model/src/main/java/org/jpwh/model/inheritance/singletable/
BillingDetails.java

```
@Entity
@Inheritance(strategy = InheritanceType.SINGLE_TABLE)
@DiscriminatorColumn(name = "BD_TYPE")
public abstract class BillingDetails {

    @Id
    @GeneratedValue(generator = Constants.ID_GENERATOR)
    protected Long id;

    @NotNull
    @Column(nullable = false)          ◁——┐ Ignored by Hibernate for
    protected String owner;                │ schema generation!

    // ...
}
```

The root class `BillingDetails` of the inheritance hierarchy is mapped to the table BILLINGDETAILS automatically. Shared properties of the superclass can be NOT NULL in the schema; every subclass instance must have a value. An implementation quirk of Hibernate requires that you declare nullability with @Column because Hibernate ignores Bean Validation's @NotNull when it generates the database schema.

You have to add a special discriminator column to distinguish what each row represents. This isn't a property of the entity; it's used internally by Hibernate. The column name is BD_TYPE, and the values are strings—in this case, "CC" or "BA". Hibernate automatically sets and retrieves the discriminator values.

If you don't specify a discriminator column in the superclass, its name defaults to DTYPE and the value are strings. All concrete classes in the inheritance hierarchy can have a discriminator value, such as CreditCard.

> **Listing 6.6   Mapping CreditCard**
>
> PATH: /model/src/main/java/org/jpwh/model/inheritance/singletable/
>   CreditCard.java

```
@Entity
@DiscriminatorValue("CC")
public class CreditCard extends BillingDetails {

    @NotNull
    protected String cardNumber;                    Ignored by Hibernate
                                                    for DDL generation!
    @NotNull
    protected String expMonth;

    @NotNull
    protected String expYear;

    // ...
}
```

Hibernate Feature

Without an explicit discriminator value, Hibernate defaults to the fully qualified class name if you use Hibernate XML files and the simple entity name if you use annotations or JPA XML files. Note that JPA doesn't specify a default for non-string discriminator types; each persistence provider can have different defaults. Therefore, you should always specify discriminator values for your concrete classes.

Annotate every subclass with @Entity, and then map properties of a subclass to columns in the BILLINGDETAILS table. Remember that NOT NULL constraints aren't allowed in the schema, because a BankAccount instance won't have an expMonth property, and the EXPMONTH column must be NULL for that row. Hibernate ignores the @NotNull for schema DDL generation, but it observes it at runtime, before inserting a row. This helps you avoid programming errors; you don't want to accidentally save credit card data without its expiration date. (Other, less well-behaved applications can of course still store incorrect data in this database.)

Hibernate generates the following SQL for select bd from BillingDetails bd:

```
select
    ID, OWNER, EXPMONTH, EXPYEAR, CARDNUMBER,
    ACCOUNT, BANKNAME, SWIFT, BD_TYPE
from
    BILLINGDETAILS
```

To query the CreditCard subclass, Hibernate adds a restriction on the discriminator column:

```
select
    ID, OWNER, EXPMONTH, EXPYEAR, CARDNUMBER
from
    BILLINGDETAILS
where
    BD_TYPE='CC'
```

Hibernate Feature

Sometimes, especially in legacy schemas, you don't have the freedom to include an extra discriminator column in your entity tables. In this case, you can apply an expression to calculate a discriminator value for each row. Formulas for discrimination aren't part of the JPA specification, but Hibernate has an extension annotation, @DiscriminatorFormula.

> **Listing 6.7 Mapping `BillingDetails` with a `@DiscriminatorFormula`**
>
> PATH: /model/src/main/java/org/jpwh/model/inheritance/singletableformula/
> BillingDetails.java

```
@Entity
@Inheritance(strategy = InheritanceType.SINGLE_TABLE)
@org.hibernate.annotations.DiscriminatorFormula(
        "case when CARDNUMBER is not null then 'CC' else 'BA' end"
)
public abstract class BillingDetails {
    // ...
}
```

There is no discriminator column in the schema, so this mapping relies on an SQL CASE/WHEN expression to determine whether a particular row represents a credit card or a bank account (many developers have never used this kind of SQL expression; check the ANSI standard if you aren't familiar with it). The result of the expression is a literal, CC or BA, which you declare on the subclass mappings.

The disadvantages of the table-per-class hierarchy strategy may be too serious for your design—considering denormalized schemas can become a major burden in the long term. Your DBA may not like it at all. The next inheritance-mapping strategy doesn't expose you to this problem.

6.4   *Table per subclass with joins*

The fourth option is to represent inheritance relationships as SQL foreign key associations. Every class/subclass that declares persistent properties—including abstract classes and even interfaces—has its own table.

Unlike the table-per-concrete-class strategy we mapped first, the table of a concrete @Entity here contains columns only for each non-inherited property, declared by the subclass itself, along with a primary key that is also a foreign key of the superclass table. This is easier than it sounds; have a look at figure 6.3.

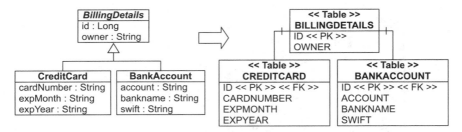

Figure 6.3   Mapping all classes of the hierarchy to their own table

If you make an instance of the `CreditCard` subclass persistent, Hibernate inserts two rows. The values of properties declared by the `BillingDetails` superclass are stored in a new row of the `BILLINGDETAILS` table. Only the values of properties declared by the subclass are stored in a new row of the `CREDITCARD` table. The primary key shared by the two rows links them together. Later, the subclass instance may be retrieved from the database by joining the subclass table with the superclass table.

The primary advantage of this strategy is that it normalizes the SQL schema. Schema evolution and integrity-constraint definition are straightforward. A foreign key referencing the table of a particular subclass may represent a polymorphic association to that particular subclass. Use the `JOINED` inheritance strategy to create a table-per-subclass hierarchy mapping.

Listing 6.8   Mapping `BillingDetails` with `JOINED`

PATH: /model/src/main/java/org/jpwh/model/inheritance/joined/BillingDetails.java

```
@Entity
@Inheritance(strategy = InheritanceType.JOINED)
public abstract class BillingDetails {

    @Id
    @GeneratedValue(generator = Constants.ID_GENERATOR)
    protected Long id;

    @NotNull
    protected String owner;

    // ...
}
```

The root class `BillingDetails` is mapped to the table `BILLINGDETAILS`. Note that no discriminator is required with this strategy.

In subclasses, you don't need to specify the join column if the primary key column of the subclass table has (or is supposed to have) the same name as the primary key column of the superclass table.

Listing 6.9   Mapping `BankAccount` (concrete class)

PATH: /model/src/main/java/org/jpwh/model/inheritance/joined/BankAccount.java

```
@Entity
public class BankAccount extends BillingDetails {

    @NotNull
    protected String account;

    @NotNull
    protected String bankname;

    @NotNull
    protected String swift;

    // ...
}
```

This entity has no identifier property; it automatically inherits the ID property and column from the superclass, and Hibernate knows how to join the tables if you want to retrieve instances of BankAccount. Of course, you can specify the column name explicitly.

Listing 6.10   Mapping `CreditCard`

PATH: /model/src/main/java/org/jpwh/model/inheritance/joined/CreditCard.java

```
@Entity
@PrimaryKeyJoinColumn(name = "CREDITCARD_ID")
public class CreditCard extends BillingDetails {

    @NotNull
    protected String cardNumber;

    @NotNull
    protected String expMonth;

    @NotNull
    protected String expYear;

    // ...
}
```

The primary key columns of the BANKACCOUNT and CREDITCARD tables each also have a foreign key constraint referencing the primary key of the BILLINGDETAILS table.

Hibernate relies on an SQL outer join for `select bd from BillingDetails bd`:

```
select
    BD.ID, BD.OWNER,
    CC.EXPMONTH, CC.EXPYEAR, CC.CARDNUMBER,
    BA.ACCOUNT, BA.BANKNAME, BA.SWIFT,
    case
        when CC.CREDITCARD_ID is not null then 1
        when BA.ID is not null then 2
```

```
        when BD.ID is not null then 0
    end
from
    BILLINGDETAILS BD
    left outer join CREDITCARD CC on BD.ID=CC.CREDITCARD_ID
    left outer join BANKACCOUNT BA on BD.ID=BA.ID
```

The SQL CASE ... WHEN clause detects the existence (or absence) of rows in the sub-class tables CREDITCARD and BANKACCOUNT, so Hibernate can determine the concrete subclass for a particular row of the BILLINGDETAILS table.

For a narrow subclass query like select cc from CreditCard cc, Hibernate uses an inner join:

```
select
    CREDITCARD_ID, OWNER, EXPMONTH, EXPYEAR, CARDNUMBER
from
    CREDITCARD
    inner join BILLINGDETAILS on CREDITCARD_ID=ID
```

As you can see, this mapping strategy is more difficult to implement by hand—even ad hoc reporting is more complex. This is an important consideration if you plan to mix Hibernate code with handwritten SQL.

Furthermore, even though this mapping strategy is deceptively simple, our experience is that performance can be unacceptable for complex class hierarchies. Queries always require a join across many tables, or many sequential reads.

Inheritance with joins and discriminator
Hibernate doesn't need a special discriminator database column to implement the InheritanceType.JOINED strategy, and the JPA specification doesn't contain any requirements either. The CASE ... WHEN clause in the SQL SELECT statement is a smart way to distinguish the entity type of each retrieved row. Some JPA examples you might find elsewhere, however, use InheritanceType.JOINED *and* an @DiscriminatorColumn mapping. Apparently some other JPA providers don't use CASE ... WHEN clauses and rely only on a discriminator value, even for the InheritanceType.JOINED strategy. Hibernate doesn't need the discriminator but uses a declared @DiscriminatorColumn, even with a JOINED mapping strategy. If you prefer to ignore the discriminator mapping with JOINED (it was ignored in older Hibernate versions), enable the configuration property hibernate.discriminator .ignore_explicit_for_joined.

Before we show you when to choose which strategy, let's consider mixing inheritance-mapping strategies in a single class hierarchy.

6.5   *Mixing inheritance strategies*

You can map an entire inheritance hierarchy with the TABLE_PER_CLASS, SINGLE_TABLE, or JOINED strategy. You can't mix them—for example, to switch from a

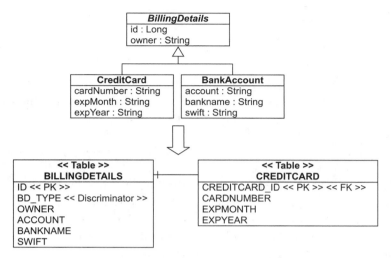

Figure 6.4 **Breaking out a subclass to its own secondary table**

table-per-class hierarchy with a discriminator to a normalized table-per-subclass strategy. Once you've made a decision for an inheritance strategy, you have to stick with it.

This isn't completely true, however. By using some tricks, you can switch the mapping strategy for a particular subclass. For example, you can map a class hierarchy to a single table, but, for a particular subclass, switch to a separate table with a foreign key–mapping strategy, just as with table-per-subclass. Look at the schema in figure 6.4.

Map the superclass `BillingDetails` with `InheritanceType.SINGLE_TABLE`, as you did before. Now map the subclass you want to break out of the single table to a secondary table.

Listing 6.11 Mapping `CreditCard`

PATH: /model/src/main/java/org/jpwh/model/inheritance/mixed/CreditCard.java

---

```
@Entity
@DiscriminatorValue("CC")
@SecondaryTable(
        name = "CREDITCARD",
        pkJoinColumns = @PrimaryKeyJoinColumn(name = "CREDITCARD_ID")
)
public class CreditCard extends BillingDetails {
```
◁── Ignored by JPA for DDL; the strategy is **SINGLE_TABLE!**

```
    @NotNull
    @Column(table = "CREDITCARD", nullable = false)
    protected String cardNumber;
```
◁── Override the primary table.

```
    @Column(table = "CREDITCARD", nullable = false)
    protected String expMonth;
```

```
@Column(table = "CREDITCARD", nullable = false)
protected String expYear;

// ...
}
```

The @SecondaryTable and @Column annotations group some properties and tell Hibernate to get them from a secondary table. You map all properties that you moved into the secondary table with the name of that secondary table. This is done with the table parameter of @Column, which we haven't shown before. This mapping has many uses, and you'll see it again later in this book. In this example, it separates the Credit-Card properties from the single table strategy into the CREDITCARD table.

The CREDITCARD_ID column of this table is at the same time the primary key, and it has a foreign key constraint referencing the ID of the single hierarchy table. If you don't specify a primary key join column for the secondary table, the name of the primary key of the single inheritance table is used—in this case, ID.

Remember that InheritanceType.SINGLE_TABLE enforces all columns of subclasses to be nullable. One of the benefits of this mapping is that you can now declare columns of the CREDITCARD table as NOT NULL, guaranteeing data integrity.

At runtime, Hibernate executes an outer join to fetch BillingDetails and all subclass instances polymorphically:

```
select
    ID, OWNER, ACCOUNT, BANKNAME, SWIFT,
    EXPMONTH, EXPYEAR, CARDNUMBER,
    BD_TYPE
from
    BILLINGDETAILS
    left outer join CREDITCARD on ID=CREDITCARD_ID
```

You can also use this trick for other subclasses in your class hierarchy. If you have an exceptionally wide class hierarchy, the outer join can become a problem. Some database systems (Oracle, for example) limit the number of tables in an outer join operation. For a wide hierarchy, you may want to switch to a different fetching strategy that executes an immediate second SQL select instead of an outer join.

Hibernate Feature

Switching the fetching strategy for this mapping isn't available in JPA or Hibernate annotations at the time of writing, so you have to map the class in a native Hibernate XML file:

PATH: /model/src/main/resources/inheritance/mixed/FetchSelect.hbm.xml

```
<subclass name="CreditCard"
        discriminator-value="CC">
    <join table="CREDITCARD" fetch="select">
        ...
    </join>
</subclass>
```

So far, we've only been talking about entity inheritance. Although the JPA specification is silent about inheritance and polymorphism of `@Embeddable` classes, Hibernate offers a mapping strategy for component types.

Hibernate Feature

6.6 *Inheritance of embeddable classes*

An embeddable class is a component of its owning entity; hence, the normal entity inheritance rules presented in this chapter don't apply. As a Hibernate extension, you can map an embeddable class that inherits some persistent properties from a superclass (or interface). Consider these two new attributes of an auction item: dimensions and weight.

An item's dimensions are its width, height, and depth, expressed in a given unit and its symbol: for example, inches (") or centimeters (cm). An item's weight also carries a unit of measurement: for example, pounds (lbs) or kilograms (kg). To capture the common attributes (name and symbol) of measurement, you define a superclass for `Dimension` and `Weight` called `Measurement`.

> **Listing 6.12   Mapping the `Measurement` abstract embeddable superclass**
>
> PATH: /model/src/main/java/org/jpwh/model/inheritance/embeddable/
>   Measurement.java

```
@MappedSuperclass
public abstract class Measurement {

    @NotNull
    protected String name;

    @NotNull
    protected String symbol;

    // ...
}
```

Use the `@MappedSuperclass` annotation on the superclass of the embeddable class you're mapping just like you would for an entity. Subclasses will inherit the properties of this class as persistent properties.

You define the `Dimensions` and `Weight` subclasses as `@Embeddable`. For `Dimensions`, override all the superclass attributes and add a column-name prefix.

> **Listing 6.13   Mapping the `Dimensions` class**
>
> PATH: /model/src/main/java/org/jpwh/model/inheritance/embeddable/
>   Dimensions.java

```
@Embeddable
@AttributeOverrides({
        @AttributeOverride(name = "name",
                column = @Column(name = "DIMENSIONS_NAME")),
```

```
        @AttributeOverride(name = "symbol",
                column = @Column(name = "DIMENSIONS_SYMBOL"))
})
public class Dimensions extends Measurement {

    @NotNull
    protected BigDecimal depth;

    @NotNull
    protected BigDecimal height;

    @NotNull
    protected BigDecimal width;

    // ...
}
```

Without this override, an `Item` embedding both `Dimension` and `Weight` would map to a table with conflicting column names. Following is the `Weight` class; its mapping also overrides the column names with a prefix (for uniformity, we avoid the conflict with the previous override).

Listing 6.14 Mapping the `Weight` class

PATH: /model/src/main/java/org/jpwh/model/inheritance/embeddable/Weight.java

```
@Embeddable
@AttributeOverrides({
        @AttributeOverride(name = "name",
                column = @Column(name = "WEIGHT_NAME")),
        @AttributeOverride(name = "symbol",
                column = @Column(name = "WEIGHT_SYMBOL"))
})
public class Weight extends Measurement {

    @NotNull
    @Column(name = "WEIGHT")
    protected BigDecimal value;

    // ...
}
```

The owning entity `Item` defines two regular persistent embedded properties.

Listing 6.15 Mapping the `Item` class

PATH: /model/src/main/java/org/jpwh/model/inheritance/embeddable/Item.java

```
@Entity
public class Item {

    protected Dimensions dimensions;

    protected Weight weight;

    // ...
}
```

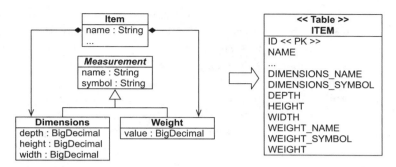

Figure 6.5   Mapping concrete embeddable classes with their inherited properties

Figure 6.5 illustrates this mapping. Alternatively, you could override the conflicting `Measurement` column names of the embedded properties in the `Item` class, as shown in section 5.2. Instead, we prefer to override them once, in the `@Embeddable` classes, so *any* consumers of these classes don't have to resolve the conflict.

A pitfall to watch out for is embedding a property of abstract superclass type (like `Measurement`) in an entity (like `Item`). This can never work; the JPA provider doesn't know how to store and load `Measurement` instances polymorphically. It doesn't have the information necessary to decide whether the values in the database are `Dimension` or `Weight` instances, because there is no discriminator. This means although you *can* have an `@Embeddable` class inherit some persistent properties from a `@MappedSuperclass`, the reference *to* an instance isn't polymorphic—it always names a concrete class.

Compare this with the alternative inheritance strategy for embeddable classes shown in the section "Converting properties of components," in chapter 5, which supported polymorphism but required some custom type-discrimination code.

Next, we give you more tips about how to choose an appropriate combination of mapping strategies for your application's class hierarchies.

6.7   *Choosing a strategy*

Picking the right inheritance-mapping strategy depends on usage of the superclasses of your entity hierarchy. You have to consider how frequently you query for instances of the superclasses and whether you have associations targeting the superclasses. Another important aspect is the attributes of super- and subtypes: whether subtypes have many additional attributes or only different behavior than their supertypes. Here are some rules of thumb:

- If you don't require polymorphic associations or queries, lean toward table-per-concrete class—in other words, if you never or rarely `select bd from Billing-Details bd` and you have no class that has an association to `BillingDetails`. An explicit `UNION`-based mapping with `InheritanceType.TABLE_PER_CLASS` should be preferred, because (optimized) polymorphic queries and associations will then be possible later.

- If you do require polymorphic associations (an association to a superclass, hence to all classes in the hierarchy with dynamic resolution of the concrete class at runtime) or queries, and subclasses declare relatively few properties (particularly if the main difference between subclasses is in their behavior), lean toward InheritanceType.SINGLE_TABLE. Your goal is to minimize the number of nullable columns and to convince yourself (and your DBA) that a denormalized schema won't create problems in the long run.

- If you do require polymorphic associations or queries, and subclasses declare many (non-optional) properties (subclasses differ mainly by the data they hold), lean toward InheritanceType.JOINED. Alternatively, depending on the width and depth of your inheritance hierarchy and the possible cost of joins versus unions, use InheritanceType.TABLE_PER_CLASS. This decision might require evaluation of SQL execution plans with real data.

By default, choose InheritanceType.SINGLE_TABLE only for simple problems. Otherwise, for complex cases, or when a data modeler insisting on the importance of NOT NULL constraints and normalization overrules you, you should consider the InheritanceType.JOINED strategy. At that point, ask yourself whether it may not be better to remodel inheritance as delegation in the class model. Complex inheritance is often best avoided for all sorts of reasons unrelated to persistence or ORM. Hibernate acts as a buffer between the domain and relational models, but that doesn't mean you can ignore persistence concerns completely when designing your classes.

When you start thinking about mixing inheritance strategies, remember that implicit polymorphism in Hibernate is smart enough to handle exotic cases. Also, consider that you can't put inheritance annotations on interfaces; this isn't standardized in JPA.

For example, consider an additional interface in the example application: ElectronicPaymentOption. This is a business interface that doesn't have a persistence aspect—except that in the application, a persistent class such as CreditCard will likely implement this interface. No matter how you map the BillingDetails hierarchy, Hibernate can answer the query select o from ElectronicPaymentOption o correctly. This even works if other classes, which aren't part of the BillingDetails hierarchy, are mapped as persistent and implement this interface. Hibernate always knows what tables to query, which instances to construct, and how to return a polymorphic result.

You can apply all mapping strategies to abstract classes. Hibernate won't try to instantiate an abstract class, even if you query or load it.

We mentioned the relationship between User and BillingDetails several times and how it influences the selection of an inheritance-mapping strategy. In the following and last section of this chapter, we explore this more advanced topic in detail: polymorphic associations. If you don't have such a relationship in your model right now, you may want to read this material later, when you encounter the issue in your application.

6.8   *Polymorphic associations*

Polymorphism is a defining feature of object-oriented languages like Java. Support for polymorphic associations and polymorphic queries is a fundamental feature of an ORM solution like Hibernate. Surprisingly, we've managed to get this far without needing to talk much about polymorphism. Refreshingly, there isn't much to say on the topic—polymorphism is so easy to use in Hibernate that we don't need to expend a lot of effort explaining it.

To provide an overview, we first consider a *many-to-one* association to a class that may have subclasses, and then a *one-to-many* relationship. For both examples, the classes of the domain model are the same; see figure 6.6.

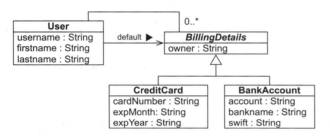

Figure 6.6   **A user has either a credit card or a bank account as the default billing details.**

6.8.1   *Polymorphic many-to-one associations*

First, consider the `defaultBilling` property of `User`. It references one particular `BillingDetails` instance, which at runtime can be any concrete instance of that class.

You map this unidirectional association to the abstract class `BillingDetails` as follows:

> PATH: /model/src/main/java/org/jpwh/model/inheritance/associations/manytoone/
> User.java

```
@Entity
@Table(name = "USERS")
public class User {

    @ManyToOne(fetch = FetchType.LAZY)
    protected BillingDetails defaultBilling;

    // ...
}
```

The USERS table now has the join/foreign key column DEFAULTBILLING_ID representing this relationship. It's a nullable column because a User might not have a default billing method assigned. Because BillingDetails is abstract, the association must refer to an instance of one of its subclasses—CreditCard or BankAccount—at runtime.

You don't have to do anything special to enable polymorphic associations in Hibernate; if the target class of an association is mapped with @Entity and @Inheritance, the association is naturally polymorphic.

The following code demonstrates the creation of an association to an instance of the `CreditCard` subclass:

> **PATH:** /examples/src/test/java/org/jpwh/test/inheritance/
> **PolymorphicManyToOne.java**

```
CreditCard cc = new CreditCard(
    "John Doe", "1234123412341234", "06", "2015"
);
User johndoe = new User("johndoe");
johndoe.setDefaultBilling(cc);

em.persist(cc);
em.persist(johndoe);
```

Now, when you navigate the association in a second unit of work, Hibernate automatically retrieves the `CreditCard` instance:

> **PATH:** /examples/src/test/java/org/jpwh/test/inheritance/
> **PolymorphicManyToOne.java**

```
User user = em.find(User.class, USER_ID);

user.getDefaultBilling().pay(123);
```
Invokes pay() method on concrete subclass of BillingDetails

There's just one thing to watch out for: because the `defaultBilling` property is mapped with `FetchType.LAZY`, Hibernate will proxy the association target. In this case, you wouldn't be able to perform a typecast to the concrete class `CreditCard` at runtime, and even the `instanceof` operator would behave strangely:

> **PATH:** /examples/src/test/java/org/jpwh/test/inheritance/
> **PolymorphicManyToOne.java**

```
User user = em.find(User.class, USER_ID);

BillingDetails bd = user.getDefaultBilling();

assertFalse(bd instanceof CreditCard);

// CreditCard creditCard = (CreditCard) bd;
```
Don't do this— ClassCastException!

The `bd` reference isn't a `CreditCard` instance in this case; it's a runtime-generated special subclass of `BillingDetails`, a Hibernate proxy. When you invoke a method on the proxy, Hibernate delegates the call to an instance of `CreditCard` that it fetches lazily. Until this initialization occurs, Hibernate doesn't know what the subtype of the given instance is—this would require a database hit, which you try to avoid with lazy loading in the first place. To perform a proxy-safe typecast, use `em.getReference()`:

```
PATH:  /examples/src/test/java/org/jpwh/test/inheritance/
       PolymorphicManyToOne.java
```

```
User user = em.find(User.class, USER_ID);

BillingDetails bd = user.getDefaultBilling();

CreditCard creditCard =
    em.getReference(CreditCard.class, bd.getId());          ◁——— No SELECT

assertTrue(bd != creditCard);                               ◁——— Careful!
```

After the `getReference()` call, `bd` and `creditCard` refer to two different proxy instances, both of which delegate to the same underlying `CreditCard` instance. The second proxy has a different interface, though, and you can call methods like `creditCard.getExpMonth()` that apply only to this interface. (Note that `bd.getId()` *will* trigger a `SELECT` if you map the `id` property with field access.)

You can avoid these issues by avoiding lazy fetching, as in the following code, using an eager fetch query:

```
PATH:  /examples/src/test/java/org/jpwh/test/inheritance/
       PolymorphicManyToOne.java
```

```
User user = (User) em.createQuery(
    "select u from User u " +
        "left join fetch u.defaultBilling " +      No proxy has been used:
        "where u.id = :id")                          BillingDetails instance
    .setParameter("id", USER_ID)                        fetched eagerly
    .getSingleResult();

CreditCard creditCard = (CreditCard) user.getDefaultBilling();   ◁——┘
```

Truly object-oriented code shouldn't use `instanceof` or numerous typecasts. If you find yourself running into problems with proxies, you should question your design, asking whether there is a more polymorphic approach. Hibernate also offers bytecode instrumentation as an alternative to lazy loading through proxies; we'll get back to fetching strategies in chapter 12.

You can handle *one-to-one* associations the same way. What about plural associations, like the collection of `billingDetails` for each `User`? Let's look at that next.

6.8.2 *Polymorphic collections*

A `User` may have references to many `BillingDetails`, not only a single default (one of the many is the default; let's ignore that for now). You can map this with a bidirectional *one-to-many* association:

PATH: /model/src/main/java/org/jpwh/model/inheritance/associations/onetomany/
       User.java

```java
@Entity
@Table(name = "USERS")
public class User {

    @OneToMany(mappedBy = "user")
    protected Set<BillingDetails> billingDetails = new HashSet<>();

    // ...
}
```

Next, here's the owning side of the relationship (declared with mappedBy in the previous mapping):

PATH: /model/src/main/java/org/jpwh/model/inheritance/associations/onetomany/
       BillingDetails.java

```java
@Entity
@Inheritance(strategy = InheritanceType.TABLE_PER_CLASS)
public abstract class BillingDetails {

    @ManyToOne(fetch = FetchType.LAZY)
    protected User user;

    // ...
}
```

So far, there is nothing special about this association mapping. The BillingDetails class hierarchy can be mapped with TABLE_PER_CLASS, SINGLE_TABLE, or a JOINED inheritance type. Hibernate is smart enough to use the right SQL queries, with either JOIN or UNION operators, when loading the collection elements.

There is one limitation, however: the BillingDetails class can't be a @Mapped-Superclass, as shown in section 6.1. It has to be mapped with @Entity and @Inheritance.

Associations with implicit polymorphism

Hibernate offers a "last resort" technique, if you really have to map an association to a class hierarchy without mapping the class hierarchy explicitly with @Inheritance. This is possible with Hibernate native XML mappings and the <any/> element. We recommend that you look this one up in the Hibernate documentation or a previous edition of this book if needed, but try to avoid it whenever possible because it results in ugly schemas.

6.9 *Summary*

- Table per concrete class with implicit polymorphism is the simplest strategy to map inheritance hierarchies of entities, but it doesn't support polymorphic associations very well. In addition, different columns from different tables share exactly the same semantics, making schema evolution more complex. We recommend this approach for the top level of your class hierarchy only, where polymorphism isn't usually required and when modification of the superclass in the future is unlikely.

- The table-per-concrete-class-with-unions strategy is optional, and JPA implementations may not support it, but it does handles polymorphic associations.

- The table-per-class-hierarchy strategy is a winner in terms of both performance and simplicity; ad hoc reporting is possible without complex joins or unions, and schema evolution is straightforward. The one major problem is data integrity, because you must declare some columns as nullable. Another issue is normalization: this strategy creates functional dependencies between non-key columns, violating the third normal form.

- The table-per-subclass-with-joins strategy's primary advantage is that it normalizes the SQL schema, making schema evolution and integrity constraint definition straightforward. The disadvantages are that it's more difficult to implement by hand, and performance can be unacceptable for complex class hierarchies.

Mapping collections and entity associations

From our experience with the Hibernate user community, the first thing many developers try to do when they begin using Hibernate is to map a *parent/children relationship*. This is usually the first time they encounter collections. It's also the first time they have to think about the differences between entities and value types, or get lost in the complexity of ORM.

Managing the associations between classes and the relationships between tables is at the heart of ORM. Most of the difficult problems involved in implementing an ORM solution relate to collections and entity association management. Feel free to come back to this chapter to grok this topic fully. We start this chapter with basic collection-mapping concepts and simple examples. After that, you'll be prepared for the first collection in an entity association—although we'll come back to more complicated entity association mappings in the next chapter. To get the full picture, we recommend you read both this chapter and the next.

> **Major new features in JPA 2**
> - Support for collections and maps of basic and embeddable types.
> - Support for persistent lists where the index of each element is stored in an additional database column.
> - One-to-many associations now have an orphan-removal option.

7.1 Sets, bags, lists, and maps of value types

Java has a rich collection API, from which you can choose the interface and implementation that best fits your domain model design. Let's walk through the most common collection mappings, repeating the same `Image` and `Item` example with minor variations. We'll start by looking at the database schema and creating and mapping a collection property in general. Then we'll proceed to how to select a specific collection interface and map various collection types: a set, identifier bag, list, map, and finally sorted and ordered collections.

7.1.1 The database schema

Let's extend CaveatEmptor and support attaching images to auction items. Ignore the Java code for now, and take a step back to consider only the database schema.

You need an `IMAGE` table in the database to hold the images, or maybe just the filenames of images. This table also has a foreign key column, say `ITEM_ID`, referencing the `ITEM` table. Look at the schema shown in figure 7.1.

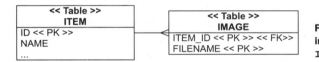

Figure 7.1 The `IMAGE` table holds image filenames, each referencing an `ITEM_ID`.

That's all there is to the schema—no collections or composition life cycle. (You could have an `ON DELETE CASCADE` option on the `ITEM_ID` foreign key column. When the application deletes an `ITEM` row, the database automatically deletes `IMAGE` rows referencing this `ITEM` in the database. Let's assume for now that this isn't the case.)

7.1.2 Creating and mapping a collection property

How would you map this `IMAGE` table with what you know so far? You'd probably map it as an `@Entity` class named `Image`. Later in this chapter, you'll map a foreign key column with an `@ManyToOne` property. You'd also need a composite primary key mapping for the entity class, as shown in section 9.2.2.

There are no mapped collections; they aren't necessary. When you need an item's images, you write and execute a query in the JPA query language: `select img from Image img where img.item = :itemParameter`. Persistent collections are *always* optional—a feature. Why would you map a collection?

The collection you could create is `Item#images`, referencing all images for a particular item. You create and map this collection property to do the following:

- Execute the SQL query `SELECT * from IMAGE where ITEM_ID = ?` automatically when you call `someItem.getImages()`. As long as your domain model instances are in a *managed* state (more later), you can read from the database on-demand while navigating the associations between your classes. You don't have to manually write and execute a query with the `EntityManager` to load data. On the other hand, the collection query when you start iterating the collection is always "all images for this item," never "only images that match criteria XYZ."

- Avoid saving each `Image` with `entityManager.persist()`. If you have a mapped collection, adding the `Image` to the collection with `someItem.getImages()`.`add()` will make it persistent automatically when the `Item` is saved. This cascading persistence is convenient because you can save instances without calling `EntityManager`.

- Have a dependent life cycle of `Images`. When you delete an `Item`, Hibernate deletes all attached `Images` with an extra SQL `DELETE`. You don't have to worry about the life cycle of images and cleaning up orphans (assuming your database foreign key constraint doesn't `ON DELETE CASCADE`). The JPA provider handles the composition life cycle.

It's important to realize that although these benefits sound great, the price you pay is additional mapping complexity. We've seen many JPA beginners struggle with collection mappings, and frequently the answer to "Why are you doing this?" has been "I thought this collection was required."

Analyzing the scenario with images for auction items, you'd benefit from a collection mapping. The images have a dependent life cycle; when you delete an item, all the attached images should be deleted. When an item is stored, all attached images should be stored. And when you display an item, you often also display all images, so `someItem.getImages()` is convenient in UI code. You don't have to call the persistence service again to get the images; they're just *there*.

Now, on to choosing the collection interface and implementation that best fits your domain model design. Let's walk through the most common collection mappings, repeating the same `Image` and `Item` example with minor variations.

7.1.3   *Selecting a collection interface*

The idiom for a collection property in the Java domain model is

```
<<Interface>> images = new <<Implementation>>();
// Getter and setter methods
// ...
```

Use an interface to declare the type of the property, not an implementation. Pick a matching implementation, and initialize the collection right away; doing so avoids uninitialized collections. We don't recommend initializing collections late, in constructors or setter methods.

Using generics, here's a typical `Set`:

```
Set<String> images = new HashSet<String>();
```

Raw collections without generics

If you don't specify the type of collection elements with generics, or the key/value types of a map, you need to tell Hibernate the type(s). For example, instead of a `Set<String>`, you map a raw `Set` with `@ElementCollection(targetClass= String.class)`. This also applies to type parameters of a `Map`. Specify the key type of a `Map` with `@MapKeyClass`. All the examples in this book use generic collections and maps, and so should you.

Out of the box, Hibernate supports the most important JDK collection interfaces and preserves the semantics of JDK collections, maps, and arrays in a persistent fashion. Each JDK interface has a matching implementation supported by Hibernate, and it's important that you use the right combination. Hibernate wraps the collection you've already initialized on declaration of the field, or sometimes replaces it, if it's not the right one. It does that to enable, among other things, lazy loading and dirty checking of collection elements.

Without extending Hibernate, you can choose from the following collections:

- A `java.util.Set` property, initialized with a `java.util.HashSet`. The order of elements isn't preserved, and duplicate elements aren't allowed. All JPA providers support this type.
- A `java.util.SortedSet` property, initialized with a `java.util.TreeSet`. This collection supports stable order of elements: sorting occurs in-memory, after Hibernate loads the data. This is a Hibernate-only extension; other JPA providers may ignore the "sorted" aspect of the set.
- A `java.util.List` property, initialized with a `java.util.ArrayList`. Hibernate preserves the position of each element with an additional index column in the database table. All JPA providers support this type.
- A `java.util.Collection` property, initialized with a `java.util.ArrayList`. This collection has *bag* semantics; duplicates are possible, but the order of elements isn't preserved. All JPA providers support this type.
- A `java.util.Map` property, initialized with a `java.util.HashMap`. The key and value pairs of a map can be preserved in the database. All JPA providers support this type.
- A `java.util.SortedMap` property, initialized with a `java.util.TreeMap`. It supports stable order of elements: sorting occurs in-memory, after Hibernate loads

the data. This is a Hibernate-only extension; other JPA providers may ignore the "sorted" aspect of the map.

- Hibernate supports persistent arrays, but JPA doesn't. They're rarely used, and we won't show them in this book: Hibernate can't wrap array properties, so many benefits of collections, such as on-demand lazy loading, won't work. Only use persistent arrays in your domain model if you're sure you won't need lazy loading. (You can load arrays on-demand, but this requires interception with bytecode enhancement, as explained in section 12.1.3.)

Hibernate Feature

If you want to map collection interfaces and implementations not directly supported by Hibernate, you need to tell Hibernate about the semantics of your custom collections. The extension point in Hibernate is the `PersistentCollection` interface in the `org.hibernate.collection.spi` package, where you usually extend one of the existing `PersistentSet`, `PersistentBag`, and `PersistentList` classes. Custom persistent collections aren't easy to write, and we don't recommend doing this if you aren't an experienced Hibernate user. You can find an example in the source code for the Hibernate test suite.

For the auction item and images example, assume that the image is stored somewhere on the file system and that you keep just the filename in the database.

Transactional file systems

If you only keep the filenames of images in your SQL database, you have to store the binary data of each picture—the files—somewhere. You could store the image data in your SQL database, in `BLOB` columns (see the section "Binary and large value types" in chapter 5). If you decide not to store the images in the database, but as regular files, you should be aware that the standard Java file system APIs, `java.io.File` and `java.nio.file.Files`, aren't transactional. File system operations aren't enlisted in a (JTA) system transaction; a transaction might successfully complete, with Hibernate writing the filename into your SQL database, but then storing or deleting the file in the file system might fail. You won't be able to roll back these operations as one atomic unit, and you won't get proper isolation of operations.

Fortunately, open source transactional file system implementations for Java are available, such as XADisk (see https://xadisk.java.net). You can easily integrate XADisk with a system transaction manager such as Bitronix, used by the examples of this book. File operations are then enlisted, committed, and rolled back together with Hibernate's SQL operations in the same `UserTransaction`.

Let's map a collection of image filenames of an `Item`.

7.1.4   *Mapping a set*

The simplest implementation is a `Set` of `String` image filenames. Add a collection property to the `Item` class, as shown in the following listing.

> **Listing 7.1   Images mapped as a simple set of strings**
> PATH: /model/src/main/java/org/jpwh/model/collections/setofstrings/Item.java

```
@Entity
public class Item {

    @ElementCollection
    @CollectionTable(                                          ← Defaults to ITEM_IMAGES
            name = "IMAGE",                          ←
            joinColumns = @JoinColumn(name = "ITEM_ID"))  ←—— Default
    @Column(name = "FILENAME")                       ←
    protected Set<String> images = new                        ← Defaults to IMAGES
            HashSet<String>();                       ←

    // ...                                              ← Initialize the field here.
}
```

The `@ElementCollection` JPA annotation is required for a collection of value-typed elements. Without the `@CollectionTable` and `@Column` annotations, Hibernate would use default schema names. Look at the schema in figure 7.2: the primary key columns are underlined.

ITEM

ID	NAME
1	Foo
2	B
3	C

IMAGE

ITEM_ID	FILENAME
1	foo.jpg
1	bar.jpg
1	baz.jpg
2	b.jpg

Figure 7.2   Table structure and example data for a set of strings

The `IMAGE` table has a composite primary key of both the `ITEM_ID` and `FILENAME` columns. That means you can't have duplicate rows: each image file can only be attached once to one item. The order of images isn't stored. This fits the domain model and `Set` collection.

It doesn't seem likely that you'd allow the user to attach the same image more than once to the same item, but let's suppose you did. What kind of mapping would be appropriate in that case?

7.1.5   *Mapping an identifier bag*

A *bag* is an unordered collection that allows duplicate elements, like the `java.util.Collection` interface. Curiously, the Java Collections framework doesn't include a bag implementation. You initialize the property with an `ArrayList`, and Hibernate ignores the index of elements when storing and loading elements.

Listing 7.2   Bag of strings, allowing duplicate elements

PATH: **/model/src/main/java/org/jpwh/model/collections/bagofstrings/Item.java**

```
@Entity
public class Item {

    @ElementCollection
    @CollectionTable(name = "IMAGE")
    @Column(name = "FILENAME")
    @org.hibernate.annotations.CollectionId(
            columns = @Column(name = "IMAGE_ID"),
            type = @org.hibernate.annotations.Type(type = "long"),
            generator = Constants.ID_GENERATOR)
    protected Collection<String> images = new ArrayList<String>();

    // ...
}
```

Surrogate primary key allows duplicates

1 Surrogate primary key column

No BagImpl in JDK

2 Hibernate-only annotation

3 Configures primary key

This looks much more complex: you can't continue with the same schema as before. The `IMAGE` collection table needs a different primary key to allow duplicate `FILENAME` values for each `ITEM_ID`. You introduce a surrogate primary key column named `IMAGE_ID` **1**, and you use a Hibernate-only annotation **2** to configure how the primary key is generated **3**. If you don't remember key generators, read section 4.2.4. The modified schema is shown in figure 7.3.

Here's an interesting question: if all you see is this schema, can you tell how the tables are mapped in Java? The `ITEM` and `IMAGE` tables look the same: each has a surrogate primary key column and some other normalized columns. Each table could be mapped with an `@Entity` class. We decided to use a JPA feature and map a collection to `IMAGE`, however, even with a composition life cycle. This is, effectively, a decision

ITEM

ID	NAME
1	Foo
2	B
3	C

IMAGE

IMAGE_ID	ITEM_ID	FILENAME
1	1	foo.jpg
2	1	bar.jpg
3	1	baz.jpg
4	1	baz.jpg
5	2	b.jpg

Figure 7.3   Surrogate primary key column for a bag of strings

that some predefined query and manipulation rules are all you need for this table, instead of the more generic @Entity mapping. When you make such a decision, be sure you know the reasons and consequences.

The next mapping technique preserves the order of images with a list.

7.1.6 *Mapping a list*

When you haven't used ORM software before, a persistent list seems to be a very powerful concept; imagine how much work storing and loading a java.util.List <String> is with plain JDBC and SQL. If you add an element to the middle of the list, depending on the list implementation, the list shifts all subsequent elements to the right or rearranges pointers. If you remove an element from the middle of the list, something else happens, and so on. If the ORM software can do all of this automatically for database records, this makes a persistent list look more appealing than it actually is.

As we noted in section 3.2.4, the first reaction is often to preserve the order of data elements as users enter them. You often have to show them later in the same order. But if another criterion can be used for sorting the data, like an entry timestamp, you should sort the data when querying and not store the display order. What if the display order changes? The order the data is displayed in is most likely not an integral part of the data, but an orthogonal concern. Think twice before you map a persistent List; Hibernate isn't as smart as you might think, as you'll see in the next example.

First, let's change the Item entity and its collection property.

Listing 7.3   Persistent list, preserving the order of elements in the database

PATH: /model/src/main/java/org/jpwh/model/collections/listofstrings/Item.java

---

```
@Entity
public class Item {

    @ElementCollection                          Enables persistent
    @CollectionTable(name = "IMAGE")            order; defaults to
    @OrderColumn                            ◁── IMAGES_ORDER
    @Column(name = "FILENAME")
    protected List<String> images = new ArrayList<String>();

    // ...
}
```

There is a new annotation in this example: @OrderColumn. This column stores an index in the persistent list, starting at zero. Note that Hibernate stores and expects the index to be contiguous in the database. If there are gaps, Hibernate will add null elements when loading and constructing the List. Look at the schema in figure 7.4.

The primary key of the IMAGE table is a composite of ITEM_ID and IMAGES_ORDER. This allows duplicate FILENAME values, which is consistent with the semantics of a List.

We said earlier that Hibernate isn't as smart as you might think. Consider modifications to the list: say the list has the three elements A, B, and C, in that order. What happens if you remove A from the list? Hibernate executes one SQL DELETE for that

ITEM	
ID	NAME
1	Foo
2	B
3	C

IMAGE		
ITEM_ID	IMAGES_ORDER	FILENAME
1	0	foo.jpg
1	1	bar.jpg
1	2	baz.jpg
1	3	baz.jpg
2	0	b1jpg
2	1	b2.jpg

Figure 7.4   The collection table preserves the position of each list element.

row. Then it executes two UPDATEs, for B and C, shifting their position to the left to close the gap in the index. For each element to the right of the deleted element, Hibernate executes an UPDATE. If you write SQL for this by hand, you can do it with one UPDATE. The same is true for insertions in the middle of the list. Hibernate shifts all existing elements to the right one by one. At least Hibernate is smart enough to execute a single DELETE when you clear() the list.

Now, suppose the images for an item have user-supplied names in addition to the filename. One way to model this in Java is with a map, using key/value pairs.

7.1.7   Mapping a map

Again, make a small change to the Java class to use a Map property.

> **Listing 7.4   Persistent map storing its key and value pairs**
>
> **PATH: /model/src/main/java/org/jpwh/model/collections/mapofstrings/Item.java**

```
@Entity
public class Item {

    @ElementCollection                                          ❶ Maps key
    @CollectionTable(name = "IMAGE")
    @MapKeyColumn(name = "FILENAME")                            ❷ Maps value
    @Column(name = "IMAGENAME")
    protected Map<String, String> images = new HashMap<String, String>();

    // ...
}
```

Each map entry is a key/value pair. Here you map the key with @MapKeyColumn to FILENAME ❶ and the value to the IMAGENAME column ❷. This means the user can only use a file once, because a Map doesn't allow duplicate keys.

As you can see from the schema in figure 7.5, the primary key of the collection table is a composite of ITEM_ID and FILENAME. The example uses a String as the key for the map; but Hibernate supports any basic type, such as BigDecimal and Integer. If the key is a Java enum, you must use @MapKeyEnumerated. With any temporal types such as java.util.Date, use @MapKeyTemporal. We discussed these options, albeit not for collections, in sections 5.1.6 and 5.1.7.

The map in the previous example was unordered. What should you do to always sort map entries by filename?

ITEM	
ID	NAME
1	Foo
2	B
3	C

IMAGE		
ITEM_ID	FILENAME	IMAGENAME
1	foo.jpg	Foo
1	bar.jpg	Bar
1	baz.jpg	Baz
2	b1.jpg	B1
2	b2.jpg	B2

Figure 7.5   Tables for a map, using strings as indexes and elements

Hibernate Feature

7.1.8   Sorted and ordered collections

In a startling abuse of the English language, the words *sorted* and *ordered* mean different things when it comes to persistent collections in Hibernate. You *sort* a collection in memory using a Java comparator. You *order* a collection when it's loaded from the database, using an SQL query with an ORDER BY clause.

Let's make the map of images a sorted map. You need to change the Java property and the mapping.

Listing 7.5   Sorting map entries in memory, using a comparator

PATH: /model/src/main/java/org/jpwh/model/collections/sortedmapofstrings/
       Item.java

```
@Entity
public class Item {

    @ElementCollection
    @CollectionTable(name = "IMAGE")
    @MapKeyColumn(name = "FILENAME")
    @Column(name = "IMAGENAME")
    @org.hibernate.annotations.SortComparator(ReverseStringComparator.class)
    protected SortedMap<String, String> images =
        new TreeMap<String, String>();

    // ...
}
```

Sorted collections are a Hibernate feature; hence the org.hibernate.annotations .SortComparator annotation with an implementation of java.util.Comparator. We won't show you this trivial class here; it sorts strings in reverse order.

The database schema doesn't change, which is also the case for all following examples. Look at the illustrations in the previous sections if you need a reminder.

You map a java.util.SortedSet as shown next.

> **Listing 7.6   Sorting set elements in memory with `String#compareTo()`**
>
> PATH: /model/src/main/java/org/jpwh/model/collections/sortedsetof-
>   strings/Item.java

```
@Entity
public class Item {

    @ElementCollection
    @CollectionTable(name = "IMAGE")
    @Column(name = "FILENAME")
    @org.hibernate.annotations.SortNatural
    protected SortedSet<String> images = new TreeSet<String>();

    // ...
}
```

Here natural sorting is used, falling back on the `String#compareTo()` method.

Unfortunately, you can't sort a bag; there is no `TreeBag`. The indexes of list elements predefine their order.

Alternatively, instead of switching to `Sorted*` interfaces, you may want to retrieve the elements of a collection in the right order from the database, and not sort in memory. Instead of a `java.util.SortedSet`, a `java.util.LinkedHashSet` is used in the following example.

> **Listing 7.7   `LinkedHashSet` offers insertion order for iteration**
>
> PATH: /model/src/main/java/org/jpwh/model/collections/setofstringsorderby/
>   Item.java

```
@Entity
public class Item {

    @ElementCollection
    @CollectionTable(name = "IMAGE")
    @Column(name = "FILENAME")
    // @javax.persistence.OrderBy                                    ⭤   Only one possible
    @org.hibernate.annotations.OrderBy(clause = "FILENAME desc")         order: "FILENAME asc"
    protected Set<String> images = new LinkedHashSet<String>();

    // ...
}
```

The `LinkedHashSet` class has a stable iteration order over its elements, and Hibernate will fill it in the right order when loading a collection. To do this, Hibernate applies an ORDER BY clause to the SQL statement that loads the collection. You must declare this SQL clause with the proprietary `@org.hibernate.annotations.OrderBy` annotation. You could even call an SQL function, like `@OrderBy("substring(FILENAME, 0, 3) desc")`, which would sort by the first three letters of the filename. Be careful to check that the DBMS supports the SQL function you're calling. Furthermore, you can use the SQL:2003 syntax ORDER BY ... NULLS FIRST|LAST, and Hibernate will automatically transform it into the dialect supported by your DBMS.

Hibernate @OrderBy vs. JPA @OrderBy

You can apply the annotation `@org.hibernate.annotations.OrderBy` to any collection; its parameter is a plain SQL fragment that Hibernate attaches to the SQL statement loading the collection. Java Persistence has a similar annotation, `@javax.persistence.OrderBy`. Its (only) parameter is not SQL but `someProperty DESC|ASC`. A `String` or `Integer` element value has no properties. Hence, when you apply JPA's `@OrderBy` annotation on a collection of basic type, as in the previous example with a `Set<String>`, the specification says, "the ordering will be by value of the basic objects." This means you can't change the order: in the previous example, the order will always be by `FILENAME asc` in the generated SQL query. We use the JPA annotation later when the element value class has persistent properties and isn't of basic/scalar type, in section 7.2.2.

The next example shows the same ordering at load time with a bag mapping.

Listing 7.8   `ArrayList` provides stable iteration order

PATH: /model/src/main/java/org/jpwh/model/collections/bagofstringsorderby/
Item.java

```java
@Entity
public class Item {

    @ElementCollection
    @CollectionTable(name = "IMAGE")
    @Column(name = "FILENAME")
    @org.hibernate.annotations.CollectionId(
            columns = @Column(name = "IMAGE_ID"),
            type = @org.hibernate.annotations.Type(type = "long"),
            generator = Constants.ID_GENERATOR)
    @org.hibernate.annotations.OrderBy(clause = "FILENAME desc")
    protected Collection<String> images = new ArrayList<String>();

    // ...
}
```

Surrogate primary key allows duplicates

Finally, you can load ordered key/value pairs with a `LinkedHashMap`.

Listing 7.9   `LinkedHashMap` keeps key/value pairs in order

PATH: /model/src/main/java/org/jpwh/model/collections/mapofstringsorderby/
Item.java

```java
@Entity
public class Item {

    @ElementCollection
    @CollectionTable(name = "IMAGE")
    @MapKeyColumn(name = "FILENAME")
    @Column(name = "IMAGENAME")
    @org.hibernate.annotations.OrderBy(clause = "FILENAME desc")
    protected Map<String, String> images = new LinkedHashMap<String, String>();

    // ...
}
```

Keep in mind that the elements of ordered collections are only in the desired order when they're loaded. As soon as you add and remove elements, the iteration order of the collections might be different than "by filename"; they behave like regular linked sets, maps, or lists.

In a real system, it's likely that you'll need to keep more than just the image name and filename. You'll probably need to create an `Image` class for this extra information. This is the perfect use case for a collection of components.

7.2 *Collections of components*

You mapped an embeddable component earlier: the `address` of a `User` in section 5.2. The current situation is different because an `Item` has many references to an `Image`, as shown in figure 7.6. The association in the UML diagram is a composition (the black diamond); hence, the referenced `Images` are bound to the life cycle of the owning `Item`.

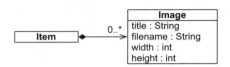

Figure 7.6   Collection of `Image` components in `Item`

The code in the next listing shows the new `Image` embeddable class, capturing all the properties of an image that interest you.

Listing 7.10   Encapsulating all properties of an image

PATH: /model/src/main/java/org/jpwh/model/collections/setofembeddables/ Image.java

---

```
@Embeddable
public class Image {

    @Column(nullable = false)
    protected String title;

    @Column(nullable = false)
    protected String filename;

    protected int width;

    protected int height;

    // ...
}
```

First, note that all properties are non-optional, NOT NULL. The size properties are non-nullable because their values are primitives. Second, you have to consider equality and how the database and Java tier compare two images.

7.2.1 *Equality of component instances*

Let's say you keep several `Image` instances in a `HashSet`. You know that sets don't allow duplicate elements. How do sets detect duplicates? The `HashSet` calls the `equals()` method on each `Image` you put in the `Set`. (It also calls the `hashCode()` method to get a hash, obviously.) How many images are in the following collection?

```
someItem.getImages().add(new Image(
        "Foo", "foo.jpg", 640, 480
));
someItem.getImages().add(new Image(
        "Bar", "bar.jpg", 800, 600
));
someItem.getImages().add(new Image(
        "Baz", "baz.jpg", 1024, 768
));
someItem.getImages().add(new Image(
        "Baz", "baz.jpg", 1024, 768
));
assertEquals(someItem.getImages().size(), 3);
```

Did you expect four images instead of three? You're right: the regular Java equality check relies on identity. The `java.lang.Object#equals()` method compares instances with a==b. Using this procedure, you'd have four instances of `Image` in the collection. Clearly, three is the "correct" answer for this use case.

For the `Image` class, you don't rely on Java identity—you override the `equals()` and `hashCode()` methods.

> **Listing 7.11 Implementing custom equality with `equals()` and `hashCode()`**
>
> PATH: /model/src/main/java/org/jpwh/model/collections/setofembeddables/
>   Image.java

```
@Embeddable
public class Image {

    @Override
    public boolean equals(Object o) {                    ①  Equality check
        if (this == o) return true;
        if (o == null || getClass() != o.getClass()) return false;

        Image other = (Image) o;

        if (!title.equals(other.title)) return false;
        if (!filename.equals(other.filename)) return false;
        if (width != other.width) return false;
        if (height != other.height) return false;

        return true;
    }

    @Override                                            ②  Must be
    public int hashCode() {                                  symmetric
        int result = title.hashCode();
        result = 31 * result + filename.hashCode();
        result = 31 * result + width;
        result = 31 * result + height;
        return result;
    }

    // ...
}
```

This custom equality check in equals() ❶ compares all values of one Image to the values of another Image. If all values are the same, then the images must be the same. The hashCode() ❷ method has to be symmetric; if two instances are equal, they must have the same hash code.

Why didn't you override equality before, when you mapped the Address of a User, in section 5.2? Well, the truth is, you probably should have done that. Our only excuse is that you won't have any problems with the regular identity equality unless you put embeddable components into a Set or use them as keys in a Map. Then you should redefine equality based on values, not identity. It's best if you override these methods on every @Embeddable class; all value types should be compared "by value."

Now consider the database primary key: Hibernate will generate a schema that includes all non-nullable columns of the IMAGE collection table in a composite primary key. The columns have to be non-nullable because you can't identify what you don't know. This reflects the equality implementation in the Java class. You'll see the schema in the next section, with more details about the primary key.

> **NOTE**   We have to mention a minor issue with Hibernate's schema generator: if you annotate an embeddable's property with @NotNull instead of @Column(nullable=false), Hibernate won't generate a NOT NULL constraint for the collection table's column. A Bean Validation check of an instance works as expected, only the database schema is missing the integrity rule. Use @Column(nullable=false) if your embeddable class is mapped in a collection, and the property should be part of the primary key.

The component class is now ready, and you can use it in collection mappings.

7.2.2 *Set of components*

You map a Set of components as shown next.

> **Listing 7.12   Set of embeddable components with an override**
>
> PATH: /model/src/main/java/org/jpwh/model/collections/setofembeddables/
>   Item.java

```
@Entity
public class Item {

    @ElementCollection                              ⬅─❶ Required
    @CollectionTable(name = "IMAGE")            ⬅──┐
    @AttributeOverride(                            └─❷ Overrides collection table name
            name = "filename",
            column = @Column(name = "FNAME", nullable = false)
    )
    protected Set<Image> images = new HashSet<Image>();

    // ...
}
```

As before, the @ElementCollection annotation ❶ is required. Hibernate automatically knows that the target of the collection is an @Embeddable type, from your declaration of a generic collection. The @CollectionTable annotation ❷ overrides the default name for the collection table, which would have been ITEM_IMAGES.

The Image mapping defines the columns of the collection table. Just as for a single embedded value, you can use @AttributeOverride to customize the mapping without modifying the target embeddable class. Look at the database schema in figure 7.7.

ITEM

ID	NAME
1	Foo
2	B
3	C

IMAGE

ITEM_ID	TITLE	FNAME	WIDTH	HEIGHT
1	Foo	foo.jpg	640	480
1	Bar	bar.jpg	800	600
1	Baz	baz.jpg	1024	768
2	B	b.jpg	640	480

Figure 7.7 Example data tables for a collection of components

You're mapping a set, so the primary key of the collection table is a composite of the foreign key column ITEM_ID and all "embedded" non-nullable columns: TITLE, FNAME, WIDTH, and HEIGHT.

The ITEM_ID value wasn't included in the overridden equals() and hashCode() methods of Image, as discussed in the previous section. Therefore, if you mix images of different items in one set, you'll run into equality problems in the Java tier. In the database table, you obviously can distinguish images of different items, because the item's identifier is included in primary key equality checks.

If you want to include the Item in the equality routine of the Image, to be symmetric with the database primary key, you need an Image#item property. This is a simple back-pointer, provided by Hibernate when Image instances are loaded:

> PATH: /model/src/main/java/org/jpwh/model/collections/setofembeddables/
>   Image.java

```
@Embeddable
public class Image {

    @org.hibernate.annotations.Parent
    protected Item item;

    // ...
}
```

You can now get the parent Item value in the equals() and hashCode() implementations and write, for example, a comparison with this.getItem().getId().equals (other.getItem().getId()). Be careful if the Item isn't persistent and has no identifier value; we'll explore this problem in more depth in section 10.3.2.

If you need load-time ordering of elements and a stable iteration order with a LinkedHashSet, use the JPA @OrderBy annotation:

PATH: /model/src/main/java/org/jpwh/model/collections/setofembeddablesor-
      derby/Item.java

```
@Entity
public class Item {

    @ElementCollection
    @CollectionTable(name = "IMAGE")
    @OrderBy("filename, width DESC")
    protected Set<Image> images = new LinkedHashSet<Image>();

    // ...
}
```

The arguments of the @OrderBy annotation are properties of the Image class, followed by either ASC for ascending or DESC for descending order. The default is
ascending, so this example sorts ascending by image filename and then descending
by the width of each image. Note that this is different from the proprietary
@org.hibernate.annotations.OrderBy annotation, which takes a plain SQL clause,
as discussed in section 7.1.8.

Declaring all properties of Image as @NotNull may not be something you want. If any
of the properties are optional, you need a different primary key for the collection table.

7.2.3 Bag of components

You used the @org.hibernate.annotations.CollectionId annotation before to add
a surrogate key column to the collection table. The collection type however, was not a
Set but a Collection, a bag. This is consistent with the udpated schema: If you have a
surrogate primary key column, duplicate "element values" are allowed. Let's walk
through this with an example.

First, the Image class may now have nullable properties:

PATH: /model/src/main/java/org/jpwh/model/collections/bagofembeddables/
      Image.java

```
@Embeddable
public class Image {

    @Column(nullable = true)          ◁─┐  Can be null if you have a
    protected String title;             │  surrogate primary key

    @Column(nullable = false)
    protected String filename;

    protected int width;

    protected int height;

    // ...
}
```

Remember to account for the optional title of the Image in your overridden
equals() and hashCode() methods, when you compare instances "by value".

Next, the mapping of the bag collection in `Item`:

> PATH: **/model/src/main/java/org/jpwh/model/collections/bagofembeddables/**
>   **Item.java**

```
@Entity
public class Item {

    @ElementCollection
    @CollectionTable(name = "IMAGE")
    @org.hibernate.annotations.CollectionId(
            columns = @Column(name = "IMAGE_ID"),
            type = @org.hibernate.annotations.Type(type = "long"),
            generator = Constants.ID_GENERATOR)
    protected Collection<Image> images = new ArrayList<Image>();

    // ...
}
```

Hibernate Feature

As before, in section 7.1.5, you declare an additional surrogate primary key column
`IMAGE_ID` with the proprietary `@org.hibernate.annotations.CollectionId` annotation. Figure 7.8 shows the database schema.

ITEM

ID	NAME
1	Foo
2	B
3	C

IMAGE

IMAGE_ID	ITEM_ID	TITLE	FILENAME	WIDTH	HEIGHT
1	1	Foo	foo.jpg	640	480
2	1		bar.jpg	800	600
3	1	Baz	baz.jpg	1024	768
4	1	Baz	baz.jpg	1024	768
5	2	B	b.jpg	640	480

Figure 7.8   Collection of components table with a surrogate primary key column

The `title` of the `Image` with identifier 2 is `null`.

Next, we look at another way to change the primary key of the collection table with a `Map`.

7.2.4   *Map of component values*

If the `Images` are stored in a `Map`, the filename can be the map key:

> Path: **/model/src/main/java/org/jpwh/model/collections/**
>   **mapofstringsembeddables/Item.java**

```
@Entity
public class Item {

    @ElementCollection
    @CollectionTable(name = "IMAGE")
```

```
@MapKeyColumn(name = "FILENAME")
protected Map<String, Image> images = new HashMap<String, Image>();

// ...                                            Optional; defaults to IMAGES_KEY
}
```

The primary key of the collection table, as shown in figure 7.9, is now the foreign key column ITEM_ID and the key column of the map, FILENAME.

ITEM

ID	NAME
1	Foo
2	B
3	C

IMAGE

ITEM_ID	FILENAME	TITLE	WIDTH	HEIGHT
1	foo.jpg	Foo	640	480
1	bar.jpg		800	600
1	baz.jpg	Baz	1024	768
2	b.jpg	B	640	480

Figure 7.9   Database tables for a map of components

The embeddable Image class maps all other columns, which may be nullable:

> PATH: /model/src/main/java/org/jpwh/model/collections/
>   mapofstringsembeddables/Image.java

```
@Embeddable
public class Image {

    @Column(nullable = true)              Can be null; not part
    protected String title;               of the primary key

    protected int width;

    protected int height;

    // ...
}
```

In the previous example, the values in the map were instances of an embeddable component class and the keys of the map a basic string. Next, you use embeddable types for both key and value.

7.2.5   *Components as map keys*

Our final example is a mapping a Map, with both keys and values of embeddable type, as you can see in figure 7.10.

Instead of a string representation, you can represent a filename with a custom type, as shown next.

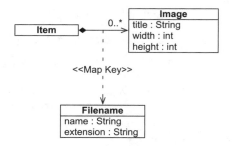

Figure 7.10   The Item has a Map keyed by Filename.

Listing 7.13   Representing a filename with a custom type

PATH: /model/src/main/java/org/jpwh/model/collections/mapofembeddables/
      Filename.java

```
@Embeddable
public class Filename {

    @Column(nullable = false)
    protected String name;                    ◁─┐  Must be NOT NULL: part
                                                 │  of the primary key
    @Column(nullable = false)                    │
    protected String extension;               ◁─┘

    @Override
    public boolean equals(Object o) {
        if (this == o) return true;
        if (o == null || getClass() != o.getClass()) return false;

        Filename filename = (Filename) o;

        if (!extension.equals(filename.extension)) return false;
        if (!name.equals(filename.name)) return false;

        return true;
    }

    @Override
    public int hashCode() {
        int result = name.hashCode();
        result = 31 * result + extension.hashCode();
        return result;
    }

    // ...
}
```

If you want to use this class for the keys of a map, the mapped database columns can't be nullable, because they're all part of a composite primary key. You also have to override the equals() and hashCode() methods, because the keys of a map are a set, and each Filename must be unique within a given key set.

You don't need any special annotations to map the collection:

PATH: /model/src/main/java/org/jpwh/model/collections/mapofembeddables/
      Item.java

```
@Entity
public class Item {

    @ElementCollection
    @CollectionTable(name = "IMAGE")
    protected Map<Filename, Image> images = new HashMap<Filename, Image>();

    // ...
}
```

ITEM			IMAGE					
ID	NAME		ITEM_ID	NAME	EXTENSION	TITLE	WIDTH	HEIGHT
1	Foo		1	foo	jpg	Foo	640	480
2	B		1	bar	jpg		800	600
3	C		1	baz	jpg	Baz	1024	768
			2	b	jpg	B	640	480

Figure 7.11   Database tables for a Map of Images keyed on Filenames

In fact, you can't apply @MapKeyColumn and @AttributeOverrides; they have no effect when the map's key is an @Embeddable class. The composite primary key of the IMAGE table includes the ITEM_ID, NAME, and EXTENSION columns, as you can see in figure 7.11.

A composite embeddable class like Image isn't limited to simple properties of basic type. You've already seen how you can nest other components, such as City in Address. You could extract and encapsulate the width and height properties of Image in a new Dimensions class.

An embeddable class can also own collections.

7.2.6   Collection in an embeddable component

Suppose that for each Address, you want to store a list of contacts. This is a simple Set<String> in the embeddable class:

```
Path: /model/src/main/java/org/jpwh/model/collections/embeddablesetofstrings/
      Address.java
```

```
@Embeddable
public class Address {

    @NotNull
    @Column(nullable = false)
    protected String street;

    @NotNull
    @Column(nullable = false, length = 5)
    protected String zipcode;

    @NotNull
    @Column(nullable = false)
    protected String city;

    @ElementCollection
    @CollectionTable(                                              Defaults to USER_CONTACTS
            name = "CONTACT",
            joinColumns = @JoinColumn(name = "USER_ID"))       Default
    @Column(name = "NAME", nullable = false)
    protected Set<String> contacts = new HashSet<String>();
    // ...
}                                                    Defaults to CONTACTS
```

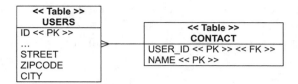

Figure 7.12 USER_ID **has a foreign key constraint referencing** USERS.

The @ElementCollection is the only required annotation; the table and column names have default values. Look at the schema in figure 7.12: the USER_ID column has a foreign key constraint referencing the owning entity's table, USERS. The primary key of the collection table is a composite of the USER_ID and NAME columns, preventing duplicate elements appropriate for a Set.

Instead of a Set, you could map a list, bag, or map of basic types. Hibernate also supports collections of embeddable types, so instead of a simple contact string, you could write an embeddable Contact class and have Address hold a collection of Contacts.

Although Hibernate gives you a lot of flexibility with component mappings and fine-grained models, be aware that code is read more often than written. Think about the next developer who has to maintain this in a few years.

Switching focus, we turn our attention to entity associations: in particular, simple *many-to-one* and *one-to-many* associations.

7.3 *Mapping entity associations*

At the beginning of this chapter, we promised to talk about parent/children relationships. So far, you've mapped an entity, Item. Let's say this is the parent. It has a collection of children: the collection of Image instances. The term *parent/child* implies some kind of life cycle dependency, so a collection of strings or embeddable components is appropriate. The children are fully dependent on the parent; they will be saved, updated, and removed always with the parent, never alone. You already mapped a parent/child relationship! The parent was an entity, and the many children were of value type.

Now you want to map a relationship of a different kind: an association between two entity classes. Their instances don't have a dependent life cycle. An instance can be saved, updated, and removed without affecting any other. Naturally, *sometimes* you have dependencies even between entity instances. You need more fine-grained control of how the relationship between two classes affects instance state, not completely dependent (embedded) types. Are we still talking about a parent/child relationship? It turns out that *parent/child* is vague, and everyone has their own definition. We'll try not to use that term from now on and will instead rely on more-precise or at least well-defined vocabulary.

The relationship we'll explore in the following sections is always the same, between the Item and Bid entity classes, as shown in figure 7.13. The association from Bid to Item is a *many-to-one*

Figure 7.13 Relationship between Item **and** Bid

association. Later you'll make this association bidirectional, so the inverse association from Item to Bid will be *one-to-many*.

The *many-to-one* association is the simplest, so we'll talk about it first. The other associations, *many-to-many* and *one-to-one*, are more complex and we'll discuss them in the next chapter.

Let's start with the *many-to-one* association.

7.3.1 *The simplest possible association*

We call the mapping of the Bid#item property a *unidirectional many-to-one association*. Before we discuss this mapping, look at the database schema in figure 7.14.

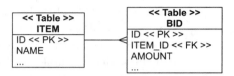

Figure 7.14   A *many-to-one* relationship in the SQL schema

Listing 7.14   Bid has a single reference to an Item

PATH: /model/src/main/java/org/jpwh/model/associations/onetomany/
        bidirectional/Bid.java

```
@Entity
public class Bid {

    @ManyToOne(fetch = FetchType.LAZY)          ⟵——— Defaults to EAGER
    @JoinColumn(name = "ITEM_ID", nullable = false)
    protected Item item;

    // ...
}
```

The @ManyToOne annotation marks a property as an entity association, and it's required. Unfortunately, its fetch parameter defaults to EAGER: this means the associated Item is loaded whenever the Bid is loaded. We usually prefer lazy loading as a default strategy, and we'll talk more about it later in section 12.1.1.

A *many-to-one* entity association maps naturally to a foreign key column: ITEM_ID in the BID table. In JPA, this is called the *join column*. You don't need anything but the @ManyToOne annotation on the property. The default name for the join column is ITEM_ID: Hibernate automatically uses a combination of the target entity name and its identifier property, separated with an underscore.

You can override the foreign key column with the @JoinColumn annotation. We used it here for a different reason: to make the foreign key column NOT NULL when Hibernate generates the SQL schema. A bid always has to have a reference to an item; it can't survive on its own. (Note that this already indicates some kind of life cycle dependency you have to keep in mind.) Alternatively, you could mark this association as non-optional with either @ManyToOne(optional = false) or, as usual, Bean Validation's @NotNull.

This was easy. It's critically important to realize that you can write a complete and complex application without using anything else.

You don't need to map the other side of this relationship; you can ignore the *one-to-many* association from `Item` to `Bid`. There is only a foreign key column in the database schema, and you've already mapped it. We are serious about this: when you see a foreign key column and two entity classes involved, you should probably map it with `@ManyToOne` and nothing else. You can now get the `Item` of each `Bid` by calling `someBid.getItem()`. The JPA provider will dereference the foreign key and load the `Item` for you; it also takes care of managing the foreign key values. How do you get all of an item's bids? Well, you write a query and execute it with `EntityManager`, in whatever query language Hibernate supports. For example, in JPQL, you'd use `select b from Bid b where b.item = :itemParameter`. One of the reasons you use a full ORM tool like Hibernate is, of course, that you don't want to write and execute that query yourself.

7.3.2　*Making it bidirectional*

At the beginning of this chapter, we had a list of reasons a mapping of the collection `Item#images` was a good idea. Let's do the same for the collection `Item#bids`. This collection would implement the *one-to-many* association between `Item` and `Bid` entity classes. If you create and map this collection property, you get the following:

- Hibernate executes the SQL query `SELECT * from BID where ITEM_ID = ?` automatically when you call `someItem.getBids()` and start iterating through the collection elements.
- You can *cascade* state changes from an `Item` to all referenced `Bids` in the collection. You can select what life cycle events should be transitive: for example, you could declare that all referenced `Bid` instances should be saved when the `Item` is saved, so you don't have to call `EntityManager#persist()` repeatedly for all bids.

Well, that isn't a very long list. The primary benefit of a *one-to-many* mapping is navigational access to data. It's one of the core promises of ORM, enabling you to access data by calling only methods of your Java domain model. The ORM engine is supposed to take care of loading the required data in a smart way while you work with a high-level interface of your own design: `someItem.getBids().iterator().next().getAmount()`, and so on.

The fact that you can optionally cascade some state changes to related instances is a nice bonus. Consider, though, that some dependencies indicate value types at the Java level, not entities. Ask yourself if any table in the schema will have a `BID_ID` foreign key column. If not, map the `Bid` class as `@Embeddable`, not `@Entity`, using the same tables as before but with a different mapping with fixed rules for transitive state changes. If any other table has a foreign key reference on any `BID` row, you need a shared `Bid` entity; it can't be mapped embedded with an `Item`.

So, should you map the `Item#bids` collection at all? You get navigational data access, but the price you pay is additional Java code and significantly more complexity. This is frequently a difficult decision. How often will you call `someItem.getBids()` in your application and then access/display *all* bids in a predefined order? If you only want to display a subset of bids, or if you need to retrieve them in a different order every time, then you need to write and execute queries manually anyway. The *one-to-many* mapping and its collection would only be maintenance baggage. In our experience, this is a frequent source of problems and bugs, especially for ORM beginners.

In CaveatEmptor's case, the answer is yes, you frequently call `someItem.getBids()` and then show a list to the user who wants to participate in an auction. Figure 7.15 shows the updated UML diagram with this bidirectional association.

The mapping of the collection and the *one-to-many* side is as follows.

Figure 7.15 Bidirectional association between `Item` and `Bid`

Listing 7.15 `Item` has a collection of `Bid` references

PATH: /model/src/main/java/org/jpwh/model/associations/onetomany/
       bidirectional/Item.java

```
@Entity
public class Item {                                    Required for
                                                       bidirectional
    @OneToMany(mappedBy = "item",                      association
                fetch = FetchType.LAZY)          <──── Default
    protected Set<Bid> bids = new HashSet<>();
    // ...
}
```

The `@OneToMany` annotation is required. In this case, you also have to set the `mappedBy` parameter. The argument is the name of the property on the "other side."

Look again at the other side: the *many-to-one* mapping in listing 7.15. The property name in the `Bid` class is `item`. The bid side is responsible for the foreign key column, `ITEM_ID`, which you mapped with `@ManyToOne`. `mappedBy` tells Hibernate to "load this collection using the foreign key column already mapped by the given property"—in this case, `Bid#item`. The `mappedBy` parameter is always required when the *one-to-many* is bidirectional, when you already mapped the foreign key column. We'll talk about that again in the next chapter.

The default for the `fetch` parameter of a collection mapping is always `Fetch-Type.LAZY`. You won't need this option in the future. It's a good default setting; the opposite would be the rarely needed `EAGER`. You don't want all the `bids` eagerly loaded every time you load an `Item`. They should be loaded when accessed, on demand.

The second reason for mapping the `Item#bids` collection is the ability to cascade state changes.

7.3.3 Cascading state

If an entity state change can be cascaded across an association to another entity, you need fewer lines of code to manage relationships. The following code creates a new `Item` and a new `Bid` and then links them:

```
Item someItem = new Item("Some Item");

Bid someBid = new Bid(new BigDecimal("123.00"), someItem);
someItem.getBids().add(someBid);                          <──── Don't forget!
```

You have to consider both sides of this relationship: the `Bid` constructor accepts an item, used to populate `Bid#item`. To maintain integrity of the instances in memory, you need to add the bid to `Item#bids`. Now the link is complete from the perspective of your Java code; all references are set. If you aren't sure why you need this code, please see section 3.2.4.

Let's save the item and its bids in the database, first without and then with transitive persistence.

ENABLING TRANSITIVE PERSISTENCE

With the current mapping of `@ManyToOne` and `@OneToMany`, you need the following code to save a new `Item` and several `Bid` instances.

> **Listing 7.16 Managing independent entity instances separately**
>
> PATH: /examples/src/test/java/org/jpwh/test/associations/
> OneToManyBidirectional.java

```java
Item someItem = new Item("Some Item");
em.persist(someItem);

Bid someBid = new Bid(new BigDecimal("123.00"), someItem);
someItem.getBids().add(someBid);                          <──── Don't forget!
em.persist(someBid);

Bid secondBid = new Bid(new BigDecimal("456.00"), someItem);
someItem.getBids().add(secondBid);
em.persist(secondBid);

tx.commit();                          <──── Dirty checking; SQL execution
```

When you create several bids, calling `persist()` on each seems redundant. New instances are transient and have to be made persistent. The relationship between `Bid` and `Item` doesn't influence their life cycle. If `Bid` were to be a value type, the state of a `Bid` would be automatically the same as the owning `Item`. In this case, however, `Bid` has its own completely independent state.

We said earlier that fine-grained control is sometimes necessary to express the dependencies between associated entity classes; this is such a case. The mechanism for this in JPA is the `cascade` option. For example, to save all bids when the item is saved, map the collection as shown next.

> **Listing 7.17 Cascading persistent state from `Item` to all `bids`**
>
> PATH: /model/src/main/java/org/jpwh/model/associations/onetomany/
> cascadepersist/Item.java

```java
@Entity
public class Item {

    @OneToMany(mappedBy = "item", cascade = CascadeType.PERSIST)
    protected Set<Bid> bids = new HashSet<>();

    // ...
}
```

Cascading options are per operation you'd like to be transitive, so you use Cascade-Type.PERSIST for the EntityManager#persist() operation. You can now simplify the code that links items and bids and then saves them.

> **Listing 7.18   All referenced bids are automatically made persistent**
>
> PATH: /examples/src/test/java/org/jpwh/test/associations/
>   OneToManyCascadePersist.java

```
Item someItem = new Item("Some Item");        ← Saves the bids automatically
em.persist(someItem);                            (later, at flush time)

Bid someBid = new Bid(new BigDecimal("123.00"), someItem);
someItem.getBids().add(someBid);

Bid secondBid = new Bid(new BigDecimal("456.00"), someItem);
someItem.getBids().add(secondBid);            ← Dirty checking;
                                                 SQL execution
tx.commit();
```

At commit time, Hibernate examines the managed/persistent Item instance and looks into the bids collection. It then calls persist() internally on each of the referenced Bid instances, saving them as well. The value stored in the column BID#ITEM_ID is taken from each Bid by inspecting the Bid#item property. The foreign key column is "mapped by" with @ManyToOne on that property.

The @ManyToOne annotation also has the cascade option. You won't use this often. For example, we can't really say "when the bid is saved, also save the item". The item has to exist beforehand; otherwise, the bid won't be valid in the database. Think about another possible @ManyToOne: the Item#seller property. The User has to exist before they can sell an Item.

Transitive persistence is a simple concept, frequently useful with @OneToMany or @ManyToMany mappings. On the other hand, you have to apply transitive deletion carefully.

CASCADING DELETION

It seems reasonable that deletion of an item implies deletion of all the bids for the item, because they're no longer relevant alone. This is what the composition (the filled-out diamond) in the UML diagram means. With the current cascading options, you have to write the following code to delete an item:

> PATH: /examples/src/test/java/org/jpwh/test/associations/
>   OneToManyCascadePersist.java

```
Item item = em.find(Item.class, ITEM_ID);

for (Bid bid : item.getBids()) {
    em.remove(bid);              ← ❶ Removes bids
}

em.remove(item);                 ← ❷ Removes owner
```

First you remove the bids ❶, and then you remove the owner: the Item ❷. The deletion order is important. If you remove the Item first, you'll get a foreign key–constraint violation, because SQL operations are queued in the order of your remove() calls. First the row(s) in the BID table have to be deleted, and then the row in the ITEM table.

JPA offers a cascading option to help with this. The persistence engine can remove an associated entity instance automatically.

Listing 7.19 Cascading removal from Item to all bids

PATH: /model/src/main/java/org/jpwh/model/associations/onetomany/
     cascaderemove/Item.java

```
@Entity
public class Item {

    @OneToMany(mappedBy = "item",
               cascade = {CascadeType.PERSIST, CascadeType.REMOVE})
    protected Set<Bid> bids = new HashSet<>();

    // ...
}
```

Just as before with PERSIST, Hibernate now cascades the remove() operation on this association. If you call EntityManager#remove() on an Item, Hibernate loads the bids collection elements and internally calls remove() on each instance:

PATH: /examples/src/test/java/org/jpwh/test/associations/
     OneToManyCascadeRemove.java

```
Item item = em.find(Item.class, ITEM_ID);          ⟵ Deletes bids one by
em.remove(item);                                        one after loading them
```

The collection must be loaded because each Bid is an independent entity instance and has to go through the regular life cycle. If there is an @PreRemove callback method present on the Bid class, Hibernate has to execute it. You'll see more on object states and callbacks in chapter 13.

This deletion process is inefficient: Hibernate must always load the collection and delete each Bid individually. A single SQL statement would have the same effect on the database: delete from BID where ITEM_ID = ?.

You know this because nobody in the database has a foreign key reference on the BID table. Hibernate doesn't know this and can't search the whole database for any row that might have a BID_ID.

If Item#bids was instead a collection of embeddable components, someItem .getBids().clear() would execute a single SQL DELETE. With a collection of value types, Hibernate assumes that nobody can possibly hold a reference to the bids, and removing only the reference from the collection makes it orphan removable data.

ENABLING ORPHAN REMOVAL

JPA offers a (questionable) flag that enables the same behavior for @OneToMany (and only @OneToMany) entity associations.

> **Listing 7.20   Enabling orphan removal on a @OneToMany collection**
>
> PATH: /model/src/main/java/org/jpwh/model/associations/onetomany/
>   orphanremoval/Item.java

```
@Entity
public class Item {

    @OneToMany(mappedBy = "item",
               cascade = CascadeType.PERSIST,       ┐ Includes
               orphanRemoval = true)              ◄─┘ CascadeType.REMOVE
    protected Set<Bid> bids = new HashSet<>();
    // ...
}
```

The orphanRemoval=true argument tells Hibernate that you want to permanently remove a Bid when it's removed from the collection. Here is an example of deleting a single Bid:

> Path: /examples/src/test/java/org/jpwh/test/associations/
>   OneToManyOrphanRemoval.java

```
Item item = em.find(Item.class, ITEM_ID);
Bid firstBid = item.getBids().iterator().next();
item.getBids().remove(firstBid);              ◄──── One bid removed
```

Hibernate monitors the collection and on transaction commit will notice that you removed an element from the collection. Hibernate now considers the Bid to be orphaned. You guarantee that nobody else had a reference to it; the only reference was the one you just removed from the collection. Hibernate automatically executes an SQL DELETE to remove the Bid instance in the database.

You still won't get the clear() one-shot DELETE as with a collection of components. Hibernate respects the regular entity-state transitions, and the bids are all loaded and removed individually.

Why is orphan removal questionable? Well, it's fine in this example case. There is so far no other table in the database with a foreign key reference on BID. There are no consequences to deleting a row from the BID table; the only in-memory references to bids are in Item#bids. As long as all of this is true, there is no problem with enabling orphan removal. It's a convenient option, for example, when your presentation layer can remove an element from a collection to delete something; you only work with domain model instances, and you don't need to call a service to perform this operation.

Consider what happens when you create a User#bids collection mapping—another @OneToMany, as shown in figure 7.16. This is a good time to test your knowledge of Hibernate: what will the tables and schema look like after this change? (Answer: The BID table has a BIDDER_ID foreign key column, referencing USERS.)

Figure 7.16 Bidirectional associations between `Item`, `Bid`, and `User`

The test shown in the following listing won't pass.

> **Listing 7.21   Hibernate doesn't clean up in-memory references after database removal**
>
> **PATH:** /examples/src/test/java/org/jpwh/test/associations/
>   OneToManyOrphanRemoval.java

```
User user = em.find(User.class, USER_ID);
assertEquals(user.getBids().size(), 2);          ◁—— User made two bids

Item item = em.find(Item.class, ITEM_ID);
Bid firstBid = item.getBids().iterator().next();
item.getBids().remove(firstBid);                 ◁—— One bid removed

// FAILURE!
// assertEquals(user.getBids().size(), 1);
assertEquals(user.getBids().size(), 2);          ◁—— Still two!
```

Hibernate thinks the removed `Bid` is orphaned and deletable; it will be deleted automatically in the database, but you still hold a reference to it in the other collection, `User#bids`. The database state is fine when this transaction commits; the deleted row of the `BID` table contained both foreign keys, `ITEM_ID` and `BIDDER_ID`. You have an inconsistency in memory, because saying, "Remove the entity instance when the reference is removed from the collection" naturally conflicts with shared references.

Instead of orphan removal, or even `CascadeType.REMOVE`, always consider a simpler mapping. Here, `Item#bids` would be fine as a collection of components, mapped with `@ElementCollection`. The `Bid` would be `@Embeddable` and have an `@ManyToOne` `bidder` property, referencing a `User`. (Embeddable components can own unidirectional associations to entities.)

This would provide the life cycle you're looking for: a full dependency on the owning entity. You have to avoid shared references; the UML diagram (figure 7.16) makes the association from `Bid` to `User` unidirectional. Drop the `User#bids` collection; you don't need this `@OneToMany`. If you need all the bids made by a user, write a query: `select b from Bid b where b.bidder = :userParameter`. (In the next chapter, you'll complete this mapping with an `@ManyToOne` in an embeddable component.)

Hibernate Feature

ENABLING **ON DELETE CASCADE** ON THE FOREIGN KEY

All the removal operations we've shown are inefficient; bids have to be loaded into memory, and many SQL `DELETE`s are necessary. SQL databases support a more efficient foreign key feature: the `ON DELETE` option. In DDL, it looks like this: `foreign key (ITEM_ID) references ITEM on delete cascade` for the `BID` table.

This option tells the database to maintain referential integrity of composites transparently for all applications accessing the database. Whenever you delete a row in the ITEM table, the database will automatically delete any row in the BID table with the same ITEM_ID key value. You only need one DELETE statement to remove all dependent data recursively, and nothing has to be loaded into application (server) memory.

You should check whether your schema already has this option enabled on foreign keys. If you want this option added to the Hibernate-generated schema, use the Hibernate @OnDelete annotation.

> **Listing 7.22 Generating foreign key ON DELETE CASCADE in the schema**
>
> PATH: /model/src/main/java/org/jpwh/model/associations/onetomany/
>   ondeletecascade/Item.java

```
                                              Hibernate quirk: schema options
                                              are usually on the mappedBy side.
@Entity
public class Item {

    @OneToMany(mappedBy = "item", cascade = CascadeType.PERSIST)
    @org.hibernate.annotations.OnDelete(                              ◁────┐
        action = org.hibernate.annotations.OnDeleteAction.CASCADE
    )
    protected Set<Bid> bids = new HashSet<>();

    // ...
}
```

One of the Hibernate quirks is visible here: the @OnDelete annotation affects only schema generation by Hibernate. Settings that affect schema generation are usually on the "other" mappedBy side, where the foreign key/join column is mapped. The @OnDelete annotation is usually next to the @ManyToOne in Bid. When the association is mapped bidirectional, however, Hibernate will only recognize it on the @OneToMany side.

Enabling foreign key cascade deletion in the database doesn't influence Hibernate's runtime behavior. You can still run into the same problem as shown in listing 7.21. Data in memory may no longer accurately reflect the state in the database. If all related rows in the BID table are automatically removed when a row in the ITEM table is deleted, your application code is responsible for cleaning up references and catching up with database state. If you aren't careful, you may even end up saving something that you or someone else previously deleted.

The Bid instances don't go through the regular life cycle, and callbacks such as @PreRemove have no effect. Additionally, Hibernate doesn't automatically clear the optional second-level global cache, which potentially contains stale data. Fundamentally, the kinds of problems you may encounter with database-level foreign key cascading are the same as when another application besides yours is accessing the same database or any other database trigger makes changes. Hibernate can be a very effective utility in such a scenario, but there are other moving parts to consider. We'll talk more about concurrency and caching later in this book.

If you work on a new schema, the easiest approach is to not enable database-level cascading and map a composition relationship in your domain model as embedded/embeddable, not as an entity association. Hibernate can then execute efficient SQL DELETE operations to remove the entire composite. We made this recommendation in the previous section: if you can avoid shared references, map the Bid as an @ElementCollection in Item, not as a standalone entity with @ManyToOne and @OneTo-Many associations. Alternatively, of course, you might not map any collections at all and use only the simplest mapping: a foreign key column with @ManyToOne, unidirectional between @Entity classes.

7.4 Summary

- Using simple collection mappings, such as a Set<String>, you worked through a rich set of interfaces and implementations.
- You know how sorted collections work as well as Hibernate's options for letting the database return the collection elements in the desired order.
- We discussed complex collections of user-defined embeddable types and sets, bags, and maps of components.
- You saw how to use components as both keys and values in maps, and a collection in an embeddable component.
- Mapping the first foreign key column to an entity many-to-one association makes it bidirectional as a one-to-many. You also learned about several cascading options.
- We covered key concepts of object/relational mapping. Once you've mapped your first @ManyToOne and maybe a simple collection of strings, the worst will be behind you.
- Be sure you try the code (and watch the SQL log)!

Advanced entity
association mappings

In this chapter
- Mapping *one-to-one* entity associations
- *One-to-many* mapping options
- *Many-to-many* and ternary entity relationships

In the previous chapter, we demonstrated a unidirectional *many-to-one* association, made it bidirectional, and finally enabled transitive state changes with cascading options. One reason we discuss more advanced entity mappings in a separate chapter is that we consider quite a few of them rare, or at least optional. It's possible to only use component mappings and *many-to-one* (occasionally *one-to-one*) entity associations. You can write a sophisticated application without ever mapping a collection! We've shown the particular benefits you gain from collection mappings in the previous chapter; the rules for when a collection mapping is appropriate also apply to all examples in this chapter. Always make sure you actually need a collection before you attempt a complex collection mapping.

Let's start with mappings that don't involve collections: *one-to-one* entity associations.

> **Major new features in JPA 2**
> - *Many-to-one* and *one-to-one* associations may now be mapped with an intermediate join/link table.
> - Embeddable component classes may have unidirectional associations to entities, even many-valued with collections.

8.1 One-to-one associations

We argued in section 5.2 that the relationships between User and Address (the user has a billingAddress, homeAddress, and shippingAddress) are best represented with an @Embeddable component mapping. This is usually the simplest way to represent *one-to-one* relationships, because the life cycle is typically dependent in such a case. It's either an aggregation or a composition in UML.

What about using a dedicated ADDRESS table and mapping both User and Address as entities? One benefit of this model is the possibility for shared references—another entity class (let's say Shipment) can also have a reference to a particular Address instance. If a User also has a reference to this instance, as their shippingAddress, the Address instance has to support shared references and needs its own identity.

In this case, User and Address classes have a true *one-to-one* association. Look at the revised class diagram in figure 8.1.

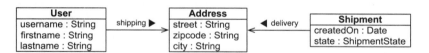

Figure 8.1 `Address` **as an entity with two associations, supporting shared references**

There are several possible mappings for *one-to-one* associations. The first strategy we consider is a shared primary key value.

8.1.1 Sharing a primary key

Rows in two tables related by a primary key association share the same primary key values. The User has the same primary key value as their (shipping-) Address. The main difficulty with this approach is ensuring that associated instances are assigned the same primary key value when the instances are saved. Before we look at this issue, let's create the basic mapping. The Address class is now a standalone entity; it's no longer a component.

Listing 8.1   Address class as a standalone entity

PATH: /model/src/main/java/org/jpwh/model/associations/onetoone/
        sharedprimarykey/Address.java

```
@Entity
public class Address {

    @Id
    @GeneratedValue(generator = Constants.ID_GENERATOR)
    protected Long id;

    @NotNull
    protected String street;

    @NotNull
    protected String zipcode;

    @NotNull
    protected String city;

    // ...
}
```

The User class is also an entity, with the shippingAddress association property.

Listing 8.2   User entity and shippingAddress association

PATH: /model/src/main/java/org/jpwh/model/associations/onetoone/
        sharedprimarykey/User.java

```
@Entity
@Table(name = "USERS")
public class User {                                    ❶ Uses application-assigned
                                                          identifier value
    @Id
    protected Long id;
                                                       ❷ Marks entity-valued property as a
                                                          one-to-one association
    @OneToOne(
        fetch = FetchType.LAZY,
Defaults    optional = false                           ❹ Required for lazy loading with proxies
to EAGER ❸ )
    @PrimaryKeyJoinColumn
    protected Address shippingAddress;
                                                       ❺ Selects shared primary
    protected User() {                                    key strategy
    }

    public User(Long id, String username) {            ❻ Identifier
        this.id = id;                                     required
        this.username = username;
    }
    // ...
}
```

For the `User`, you don't declare an identifier generator ❶. As mentioned in section 4.2.4, this is one of the rare cases when you use an *application-assigned* identifier value. You can see that the constructor design (weakly) enforces this ❻: the public API of the class requires an identifier value to create an instance.

Two new annotations are present in the example. `@OneToOne` ❷ does what you'd expect: it's required to mark an entity-valued property as a *one-to-one* association. As usual, you should prefer the lazy-loading strategy, so you override the default `Fetch-Type.EAGER` with `LAZY` ❸. The second new annotation is `@PrimaryKeyJoinColumn` ❺, selecting the shared primary key strategy you'd like to map. This is now a unidirectional shared primary key *one-to-one* association mapping, from `User` to `Address`.

The `optional=false` switch ❹ defines that a `User` must have a `shippingAddress`. The Hibernate-generated database schema reflects this with a foreign key constraint. The primary key of the `USERS` table also has a foreign key constraint referencing the primary key of the `ADDRESS` table. See the tables in figure 8.2.

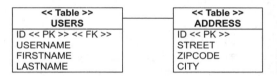

Figure 8.2   **The USERS table has a foreign key constraint on its primary key.**

The JPA specification doesn't include a standardized method to deal with the problem of shared primary key generation. This means you're responsible for setting the identifier value of a `User` instance correctly before you save it, to the identifier value of the linked `Address` instance:

> **PATH:** /examples/src/test/java/org/jpwh/test/associations/
>   OneToOneSharedPrimaryKey.java

```
Address someAddress =
    new Address("Some Street 123", "12345", "Some City");

em.persist(someAddress);                              ◁——  Generates
                                                            identifier value
User someUser =
    new User(
        someAddress.getId(),                          ◁——  Assigns the same
        "johndoe"                                           identifier value
    );

em.persist(someUser);

someUser.setShippingAddress(someAddress);             ◁——  Optional
```

After persisting the `Address`, you take its generated identifier value and set it on the `User` before saving it, too. The last line of this example is optional: your code now expects a value when calling `someUser.getShippingAddress()`, so you should set it. Hibernate won't give you an error if you forget this last step.

There are three problems with the mapping and code:

- You have to remember that the `Address` must be saved first and then get its identifier value after the call to `persist()`. This is only possible if the `Address` entity has an identifier generator that produces values on `persist()` before the `INSERT`, as we discussed in section 4.2.5. Otherwise, `someAddress.getId()` returns `null`, and you can't manually set the identifier value of the `User`.

- Lazy loading with proxies only works if the association is non-optional. This is often a surprise for developers new to JPA. The default for `@OneToOne` is `Fetch-Type.EAGER`: when Hibernate loads a `User`, it loads the `shippingAddress` right away. Conceptually, lazy loading with proxies only makes sense if Hibernate knows that there is a linked `shippingAddress`. If the property were nullable, Hibernate would have to check in the database whether the property value is `NULL`, by querying the `ADDRESS` table. If you have to check the database, you might as well load the value right away, because there would be no benefit in using a proxy.

- The *one-to-one* association is unidirectional; sometimes you need bidirectional navigation.

The first issue has no other solution, and it's one of the reasons you should always prefer identifier generators capable of producing values before any SQL `INSERT`.

An `@OneToOne(optional=true)` association doesn't support lazy loading with proxies. This is consistent with the JPA specification. `FetchType.LAZY` is a hint for the persistence provider, not a requirement. You could get lazy loading of nullable `@OneToOne` with bytecode instrumentation, as we'll show in section 12.1.3.

As for the last problem, if you make the association bidirectional, you can also use a special Hibernate-only identifier generator to help with assigning key values.

8.1.2   *The foreign primary key generator*

A bidirectional mapping always requires a `mappedBy` side. Here, pick the `User` side (this is a matter of taste and perhaps other, secondary requirements):

> PATH: /model/src/main/java/org/jpwh/model/associations/onetoone/
>   foreigngenerator/User.java

```
@Entity
@Table(name = "USERS")
public class User {

    @Id
    @GeneratedValue(generator = Constants.ID_GENERATOR)
    protected Long id;

    @OneToOne(
        mappedBy = "user",
        cascade = CascadeType.PERSIST
    )
    protected Address shippingAddress;
    // ...
}
```

Compare this with the previous mapping: you add the mappedBy option, telling Hibernate that the lower-level details are now mapped by the "property on the other side," named user. As a convenience, you enable CascadeType.PERSIST; transitive persistence will make it easier to save the instances in the right order. When you make the User persistent, Hibernate makes the shippingAddress persistent and generates the identifier for the primary key automatically.

Next, let's look at the "other side": the Address.

Listing 8.3 Address has the special foreign key generator

PATH: /model/src/main/java/org/jpwh/model/associations/onetoone/
foreigngenerator/Address.java

```java
@Entity
public class Address {

    @Id
    @GeneratedValue(generator = "addressKeyGenerator")          ❶ Defines a primary
    @org.hibernate.annotations.GenericGenerator(                   key value generator
        name = "addressKeyGenerator",
        strategy = "foreign",
        parameters =
            @org.hibernate.annotations.Parameter(
                name = "property", value = "user"
            )
    )
    protected Long id;
                                                               ❷ Creates foreign
    @OneToOne(optional = false)                                    key constraint
    @PrimaryKeyJoinColumn
    protected User user;                                        ❸ Address must have a
                                                                  reference to a User
    protected Address() {
    }

    public Address(User user) {                     Public
        this.user = user;                    constructors  ❹
    }                                        of Address
    public Address(User user, String street, String zipcode, String city) {
        this.user = user;
        this.street = street;
        this.zipcode = zipcode;
        this.city = city;
    }
    // ...
}
```

That's quite a bit of new code. Let's start with the identifier property and then the *one-to-one* association.

Hibernate Feature

The @GenericGenerator on the identifier property ❶ defines a special-purpose primary key value generator with the Hibernate-only foreign strategy. We didn't mention this generator in the overview in section 4.2.5; the shared primary key *one-to-one* association is its only use case. When you persist an instance of Address, this special generator grabs the value of the user property and takes the identifier value of the referenced entity instance, the User.

Let's continue with the @OneToOne mapping ❷. The user property is marked as a shared primary key entity association with the @PrimaryKeyJoinColumn annotation ❸. It's set to optional=false, so an Address must have a reference to a User. The public constructors of Address ❹ now require a User instance. The foreign key constraint reflecting optional=false is now on the primary key column of the ADDRESS table, as you can see in the schema in figure 8.3.

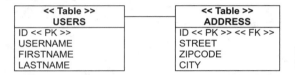

Figure 8.3   The ADDRESS table has a foreign key constraint on its primary key.

You no longer have to call someAddress.getId() or someUser.getId() in your unit of work. Storing data is simplified:

PATH: /examples/src/test/java/org/jpwh/test/associations/
       OneToOneForeignGenerator.java

```
User someUser = new User("johndoe");

Address someAddress =
    new Address(
        someUser,
        "Some Street 123", "12345", "Some City"
    );                                                    Link

someUser.setShippingAddress(someAddress);

em.persist(someUser);          ⟵————    Transitive persistence of shippingAddress
```

Don't forget that you must link both sides of a bidirectional entity association. Note that with this mapping, you won't get lazy loading of User#shippingAddress (it's optional/nullable), but you can load Address#user on demand with proxies (it's non-optional).

Shared primary key *one-to-one* associations are relatively rare. Instead, you'll often map a "to-one" association with a foreign key column and a unique constraint.

8.1.3 Using a foreign key join column

Instead of sharing a primary key, two rows can have a relationship based on a simple additional foreign key column. One table has a foreign key column that references the primary key of the associated table. (The source and target of this foreign key constraint can even be the same table: we call this a *self-referencing relationship*.)

Let's change the mapping for User#shippingAddress. Instead of the shared primary key, you now add a SHIPPINGADDRESS_ID column in the USERS table. Additionally, the column has a UNIQUE constraint, so no two users can reference the same shipping address. Look at the schema in figure 8.4.

Figure 8.4 A one-to-one join column association between the USERS and ADDRESS tables

The Address is a regular entity class, like the first one we showed in this chapter in listing 8.1. The User entity class has the shippingAddress property, implementing this unidirectional association:

> PATH: /model/src/main/java/org/jpwh/model/associations/onetoone/foreignkey/
>   User.java

```
@Entity
@Table(name = "USERS")
public class User {

    @Id
    @GeneratedValue(generator = Constants.ID_GENERATOR)
    protected Long id;

    @OneToOne(
        fetch = FetchType.LAZY,
        optional = false,              <————  NOT NULL
        cascade = CascadeType.PERSIST
    )
    @JoinColumn(unique = true)         <————  Defaults to SHIPPINGADDRESS_ID
    protected Address shippingAddress;

    // ...
}
```

You don't need any special identifier generators or primary key assignment; instead of @PrimaryKeyJoinColumn, you apply the regular @JoinColumn. If you're more familiar with SQL than JPA, it helps to think "foreign key column" every time you see @JoinColumn in a mapping.

You should enable lazy loading for this association. Unlike for shared primary keys, you don't have a problem with lazy loading here: When a row of the USERS table has been loaded, it contains the value of the SHIPPINGADDRESS_ID column. Hibernate therefore knows whether an ADDRESS row is present, and a proxy can be used to load the Address instance on demand.

In the mapping, though, you set optional=false, so the user must have a shipping address. This won't affect loading behavior but is a logical consequence of the unique=true setting on the @JoinColumn. This setting adds the unique constraint to the generated SQL schema. If the values of the SHIPPINGADDRESS_ID column must be unique for all users, only one user could possibly have "no shipping address." Hence, nullable unique columns typically aren't meaningful.

Creating, linking, and storing instances is straightforward:

> **PATH:** /examples/src/test/java/org/jpwh/test/associations/
> OneToOneForeignKey.java

```
User someUser =
    new User("johndoe");

Address someAddress =
    new Address("Some Street 123", "12345", "Some City");

someUser.setShippingAddress(someAddress);              ⟵——————  Link

em.persist(someUser);           ⟵————— Transitive persistence of shippingAddress
```

You've now completed two basic *one-to-one* association mappings: the first with a shared primary key, the second with a foreign key reference and a unique column constraint. The last option we want to discuss is a bit more exotic: mapping a *one-to-one* association with the help of an additional table.

8.1.4   *Using a join table*

You've probably noticed that nullable columns can be problematic. Sometimes a better solution for optional values is an intermediate table, which contains a row if a link is present, or doesn't if not.

Let's consider the Shipment entity in CaveatEmptor and discuss its purpose. Sellers and buyers interact in CaveatEmptor by starting and bidding on auctions. Shipping goods seems outside the scope of the application; the seller and the buyer agree on a method of shipment and payment after the auction ends. They can do this offline, outside of CaveatEmptor.

On the other hand, you could offer an escrow service in CaveatEmptor. Sellers would use this service to create a trackable shipment once the auction ends. The buyer would pay the price of the auction item to a trustee (you), and you'd inform the seller that the money was available. Once the shipment arrived and the buyer accepted it, you'd transfer the money to the seller.

If you've ever participated in an online auction of significant value, you've probably used such an escrow service. But you want more in CaveatEmptor: not only will you provide trust services for completed auctions, but you also allow users to create a trackable and trusted shipment for any deal they make outside an auction, outside CaveatEmptor.

This scenario calls for a `Shipment` entity with an optional *one-to-one* association to `Item`. Look at the class diagram for this domain model in figure 8.5.

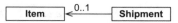

Figure 8.5   A `Shipment` has an optional link with an auction `Item`.

NOTE   We briefly considered abandoning the CaveatEmptor example for this section, because we couldn't find a natural scenario that requires optional *one-to-one* associations. If this escrow example seems contrived, consider the equivalent problem of assigning employees to workstations. This is also an optional *one-to-one* relationship.

In the database schema, you add an intermediate link table called `ITEM_SHIPMENT`. A row in this table represents a `Shipment` made in the context of an auction. Figure 8.6 shows the tables.

Figure 8.6   The intermediate table links items and shipments.

Note how the schema enforces uniqueness and the *one-to-one* relationship: the primary key of `ITEM_SHIPMENT` is the `SHIPMENT_ID` column, and the `ITEM_ID` column is unique. An item can therefore be in only one shipment. Of course, that also means a shipment can contain only one item.

You map this model with an `@OneToOne` annotation in the `Shipment` entity class:

> PATH: **/model/src/main/java/org/jpwh/model/associations/onetoone/jointable/ Shipment.java**

```
@Entity
public class Shipment {

    @OneToOne(fetch = FetchType.LAZY)
    @JoinTable(
        name = "ITEM_SHIPMENT",                          <————— Required!
        joinColumns =
            @JoinColumn(name = "SHIPMENT_ID"),           <————— Defaults to ID
        inverseJoinColumns =
            @JoinColumn(name = "ITEM_ID",                <————— Defaults to AUCTION_ID
                        nullable = false,
                        unique = true)
    )
    protected Item auction;

    public Shipment() {
    }

    public Shipment(Item auction) {
        this.auction = auction;
    }

    // ...
}
```

Lazy loading has been enabled, with a twist: when Hibernate loads a `Shipment`, it queries both the `SHIPMENT` and the `ITEM_SHIPMENT` join table. Hibernate has to know if there is a link to an `Item` present before it can use a proxy. It does that in one outer join SQL query, so you won't see any extra SQL statements. If there is a row in `ITEM_SHIPMENT`, Hibernate uses an `Item` placeholder.

The `@JoinTable` annotation is new; you always have to specify the name of the intermediate table. This mapping effectively hides the join table; there is no corresponding Java class. The annotation defines the column names of the `ITEM_SHIPMENT` table, and Hibernate generates in the schema the `UNIQUE` constraint on the `ITEM_ID` column. Hibernate also generates the appropriate foreign key constraints on the columns of the join table.

Here you store a `Shipment` without `Item`s and another linked to a single `Item`:

> **PATH:** **/examples/src/test/java/org/jpwh/test/associations/OneToOneJoinTable.java**

```
Shipment someShipment = new Shipment();
em.persist(someShipment);

Item someItem = new Item("Some Item");
em.persist(someItem);

Shipment auctionShipment = new Shipment(someItem);
em.persist(auctionShipment);
```

This completes our discussion of *one-to-one* association mappings. To summarize, use a shared primary key association if one of the two entities is always stored before the other and can act as the primary key source. Use a foreign key association in all other cases, and a hidden intermediate join table when your *one-to-one* association is optional.

We now focus on plural, or *many-valued* entity associations, beginning by exploring some advanced options for *one-to-many*.

8.2   *One-to-many associations*

A *plural entity association* is by definition a collection of entity references. You mapped one of these, a *one-to-many* association, in the previous chapter, section 7.3.2. *One-to-many* associations are the most important kind of entity association that involves a collection. We go so far as to discourage the use of more complex association styles when a simple bidirectional *many-to-one/one-to-many* will do the job.

Also, remember that you don't have to map any collection of entities if you don't want to; you can always write an explicit query instead of direct access through iteration. If you decide to map collections of entity references, you have a few options, and we discussed some more complex situations now.

8.2.1 Considering one-to-many bags

So far, you have only seen a @OneToMany on a Set, but it's possible to use a bag mapping instead for a bidirectional *one-to-many* association. Why would you do this?

Bags have the most efficient performance characteristics of all the collections you can use for a bidirectional *one-to-many* entity association. By default, collections in Hibernate are loaded when they're accessed for the first time in the application. Because a bag doesn't have to maintain the index of its elements (like a list) or check for duplicate elements (like a set), you can add new elements to the bag without triggering the loading. This is an important feature if you're going to map a possibly large collection of entity references.

On the other hand, you can't eager-fetch two collections of bag type simultaneously: for example, if bids and images of an Item were *one-to-many* bags. This is no big loss, because fetching two collections simultaneously always results in a Cartesian product; you want to avoid this kind of operation whether the collections are bags, sets, or lists. We'll come back to fetching strategies in chapter 12. In general, we'd say that a bag is the best inverse collection for a *one-to-many* association, if mapped as a @OneToMany(mappedBy = "...").

To map a bidirectional *one-to-many* association as a bag, you have to replace the type of the bids collection in the Item entity with a Collection and an ArrayList implementation. The mapping for the association between Item and Bid remains essentially unchanged:

> PATH: /model/src/main/java/org/jpwh/model/associations/oneto-
> many/bag/Item.java

```
@Entity
public class Item {

    @OneToMany(mappedBy = "item")
    public Collection<Bid> bids = new ArrayList<>();

    // ...
}
```

The Bid side with its @ManyToOne (which is the "mapped by" side), and even the tables, are the same as in section 7.3.1.

A bag also allows duplicate elements, which the set you mapped earlier didn't:

> PATH: /examples/src/test/java/org/jpwh/test/associations/OneToManyBag.java

```
Item someItem = new Item("Some Item");
em.persist(someItem);

Bid someBid = new Bid(new BigDecimal("123.00"), someItem);
someItem.getBids().add(someBid);
someItem.getBids().add(someBid);                    ⟵——————  No persistent effect!
em.persist(someBid);

assertEquals(someItem.getBids().size(), 2);
```

It turns out this isn't relevant in this case, because *duplicate* means you've added a particular reference to the same `Bid` instance several times. You wouldn't do this in your application code. Even if you add the same reference several times to this collection, though, Hibernate ignores it. The side relevant for updates of the database is the `@ManyToOne`, and the relationship is already "mapped by" that side. When you load the `Item`, the collection doesn't contain the duplicate:

PATH: /examples/src/test/java/org/jpwh/test/associations/OneToManyBag.java

```
Item item = em.find(Item.class, ITEM_ID);
assertEquals(item.getBids().size(), 1);
```

As mentioned, the advantage of bags is that the collection doesn't have to be initialized when you add a new element:

PATH: /examples/src/test/java/org/jpwh/test/associations/OneToManyBag.java

```
Item item = em.find(Item.class, ITEM_ID);

Bid bid = new Bid(new BigDecimal("456.00"), item);
item.getBids().add(bid);                       ⟵——— No SELECT!
em.persist(bid);
```

This code example triggers one SQL `SELECT` to load the `Item`. If you use `em.get-Reference()` instead of `em.find()`, Hibernate still initializes and returns an `Item` proxy with a `SELECT` as soon as you call `item.getBids()`. But as long as you don't iterate the `Collection`, no more queries are necessary, and an `INSERT` for the new `Bid` will be made without loading all the bids. If the collection is a `Set` or a `List`, Hibernate loads all the elements when you add another element.

Let's change the collection to a persistent `List`.

8.2.2 *Unidirectional and bidirectional list mappings*

If you need a real list to hold the position of the elements in a collection, you have to store that position in an additional column. For the *one-to-many* mapping, this also means you should change the `Item#bids` property to `List` and initialize the variable with an `ArrayList`:

PATH: /model/src/main/java/org/jpwh/model/associations/onetomany/
list/Item.java

```
@Entity
public class Item {

    @OneToMany
    @JoinColumn(
        name = "ITEM_ID",
        nullable = false
    )
    @OrderColumn(
```

```
        name = "BID_POSITION",              ◄─────────  Defaults to BIDS_ORDER
        nullable = false
    )
    public List<Bid> bids = new ArrayList<>();

    // ...
}
```

This is a unidirectional mapping: there is no other "mapped by" side. The Bid doesn't have a @ManyToOne property. The new annotation @OrderColumn is required for persistent list indexes, where, as usual, you should make the column NOT NULL. The database view of the BID table, with the join and order columns, is shown in figure 8.7.

BID

ID	ITEM_ID	BID_POSITION	AMOUNT
1	1	0	99.00
2	1	1	100.00
3	1	2	101.00
4	2	0	4.99

Figure 8.7   The BID table

The stored index of each collection starts at zero and is contiguous (there are no gaps). Hibernate will execute potentially many SQL statements when you add, remove, and shift elements of the List. We talked about this performance issue in section 7.1.6.

Let's make this mapping bidirectional, with a @ManyToOne property on the Bid entity:

PATH: /model/src/main/java/org/jpwh/model/associations/onetomany/list/Bid.java

```
@Entity
public class Bid {

    @ManyToOne
    @JoinColumn(
        name = "ITEM_ID",
        updatable = false, insertable = false      ◄─────────  Disable writing!
    )
    @NotNull                                        ◄─────────  For schema generation
    protected Item item;

    // ...
}
```

You probably expected different code—maybe @ManyToOne(mappedBy="bids") and no additional @JoinColumn annotation. But @ManyToOne doesn't have a mappedBy attribute: it's always the "owning" side of the relationship. You'd have to make the other side, @OneToMany, the mappedBy side. Here you run into a conceptual problem and some Hibernate quirks.

The Item#bids collection is no longer read-only, because Hibernate now has to store the index of each element. If the Bid#item side was the owner of the relationship, Hibernate would ignore the collection when storing data and not write the element indexes. You have to map the @JoinColumn twice and then disable writing on the

@ManyToOne side with `updatable=false` and `insertable=false`. Hibernate now considers the collection side when storing data, including the index of each element. The @ManyToOne is effectively read-only, as it would be if it had a `mappedBy` attribute.

> **Bidirectional list with mappedBy**
> Several existing bug reports related to this issue are open on Hibernate; a future version might allow the JPA-compliant usage of the @OneToMany(`mappedBy`) and @OrderColumn on a collection. At the time of writing, the shown mapping is the only working variation for a bidirectional *one-to-many* with a persistent `List`.

Finally, the Hibernate schema generator always relies on the @JoinColumn of the @ManyToOne side. Hence, if you want the correct schema produced, you should add the @NotNull on this side or declare @JoinColumn(`nullable=false`). The generator ignores the @OneToMany side and its join column if there is a @ManyToOne.

In a real application, you wouldn't map the association with a `List`. Preserving the order of elements in the database seems like a common use case but on second thought isn't very useful: sometimes you want to show a list with the highest or newest bid first, or only bids made by a certain user, or bids made within a certain time range. None of these operations requires a persistent list index. As mentioned in section 3.2.4, avoid storing a display order in the database; keep it flexible with queries instead of hardcoded mappings. Furthermore, maintaining the index when the application removes, adds, or shifts elements in the list can be expensive and may trigger many SQL statements. Map the foreign key join column with @ManyToOne, and drop the collection.

Next is one more scenario with a *one-to-many* relationship: an association mapped to an intermediate join table.

8.2.3 *Optional one-to-many with a join table*

A useful addition to the `Item` class is a `buyer` property. You can then call `someItem.getBuyer()` to access the `User` who made the winning bid. If made bidirectional, this association will also help to render a screen that shows all auctions a particular user has won: you call `someUser.getBoughtItems()` instead of writing a query.

From the point of view of the `User` class, the association is *one-to-many*. Figure 8.8 shows the classes and their relationship.

Why is this association different from the one between `Item` and `Bid`? The multiplicity *0..** in UML indicates that the reference is optional. This doesn't influence the Java domain model much, but it has consequences for the underlying tables. You expect a `BUYER_ID` foreign key column in the `ITEM` table. The column has to be nullable, because a user may not have bought a particular `Item` (as long as the auction is still running).

Figure 8.8   The `User`-`Item` "bought" relationship

You could accept that the foreign key column can be NULL and apply additional constraints: "Allowed to be NULL only if the auction end time hasn't been reached or if no bid has been made." We always try to avoid nullable columns in a relational database schema. Unknown information degrades the quality of the data you store. Tuples represent propositions that are true; you can't assert something you don't know. Moreover, in practice, many developers and DBAs don't create the right constraint and rely on often buggy application code to provide data integrity.

An optional entity association, be it *one-to-one* or *one-to-many*, is best represented in an SQL database with a join table. Figure 8.9 shows an example schema.

Figure 8.9 An intermediate table links users and items.

You added a join table earlier in this chapter, for a *one-to-one* association. To guarantee the multiplicity of *one-to-one*, you applied a unique constraint on a foreign key column of the join table. In the current case, you have a *one-to-many* multiplicity, so only the ITEM_ID primary key column has to be unique: only one User can buy any given Item, once. The BUYER_ID column isn't unique because a User can buy many Items.

The mapping of the User#boughtItems collection is simple:

> PATH: **/model/src/main/java/org/jpwh/model/associations/onetomany/jointable/ User.java**

```
@Entity
@Table(name = "USERS")
public class User {

    @OneToMany(mappedBy = "buyer")
    protected Set<Item> boughtItems = new HashSet<Item>();

    // ...
}
```

This is the usual read-only side of a bidirectional association, with the actual mapping to the schema on the "mapped by" side, the Item#buyer:

> PATH: **/model/src/main/java/org/jpwh/model/associations/onetomany/jointable/ Item.java**

```
@Entity
public class Item {

    @ManyToOne(fetch = FetchType.LAZY)
    @JoinTable(
        name = "ITEM_BUYER",
        joinColumns =
            @JoinColumn(name = "ITEM_ID"),          ◁————  Defaults to ID
        inverseJoinColumns =
            @JoinColumn(nullable = false)           ◁————  Defaults to BUYER_ID
```

```
    )
    protected User buyer;

    // ...
}
```

This is now a clean, optional *one-to-many/many-to-one* relationship. If an Item hasn't been bought, there is no corresponding row in the join table ITEM_BUYER. You don't have any problematic nullable columns in your schema. Still, you should write a procedural constraint and a trigger that runs on INSERT, for the ITEM_BUYER table: "Only allow insertion of a buyer if the auction end time for the given item has been reached and the user made the winning bid."

The next example is our last with *one-to-many* associations. So far, you've seen *one-to-many* associations from an entity to another entity. An embeddable component class may also have a *one-to-many* association to an entity.

8.2.4 *One-to-many association in an embeddable class*

Consider again the embeddable component mapping you've been repeating for a few chapters: the Address of a User. You now extend this example by adding a *one-to-many* association from Address to Shipment: a collection called deliveries. Figure 8.10 shows the UML class diagram for this model.

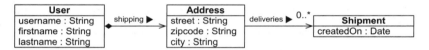

Figure 8.10   The one-to-may relationship from `Address` to `Shipment`

The Address is an @Embeddable class, not an entity. It can own a unidirectional association to an entity; here it's *one-to-many* multiplicity to Shipment. (You see an embeddable class having a *many-to-one* association with an entity in the next section.)

The Address class has a Set<Shipment> representing this association:

> PATH: /model/src/main/java/org/jpwh/model/associations/onetomany/
>   embeddable/Address.java

```
@Embeddable
public class Address {

    @NotNull
    @Column(nullable = false)
    protected String street;

    @NotNull
    @Column(nullable = false, length = 5)
    protected String zipcode;

    @NotNull
    @Column(nullable = false)
```

```
    protected String city;

    @OneToMany
    @JoinColumn(
        name = "DELIVERY_ADDRESS_USER_ID",    ⟵——— Defaults to DELIVERIES_ID
        nullable = false
    )
    protected Set<Shipment> deliveries = new HashSet<Shipment>();
    // ...
}
```

The first mapping strategy for this association is with an `@JoinColumn` named `DELIVERY_ADDRESS_USER_ID`. This foreign key-constrained column is in the `SHIPMENT` table, as you can see in figure 8.11.

Figure 8.11 A primary key in the USERS table links the USERS and SHIPMENT tables

Embeddable components don't have their own identifier, so the value in the foreign key column is the value of a `User`'s identifier, which embeds the `Address`. Here you also declare the join column `nullable = false`, so a `Shipment` must have an associated delivery address. Of course, bidirectional navigation isn't possible: the `Shipment` can't have a reference to the `Address`, because embedded components can't have shared references.

Figure 8.12 Using an intermediate table between USERS and SHIPMENT to represent an optional association

If the association is optional and you don't want a nullable column, you can map the association to an intermediate join/link table, as shown in figure 8.12. The mapping of the collection in `Address` now uses an `@JoinTable` instead of an `@JoinColumn`:

> Path: /model/src/main/java/org/jpwh/model/associations/onetomany/
>   embeddablejointable/Address.java

```
@Embeddable
public class Address {

    @NotNull
    @Column(nullable = false)
    protected String street;
```

```
@NotNull
@Column(nullable = false, length = 5)
protected String zipcode;

@NotNull
@Column(nullable = false)
protected String city;

@OneToMany
@JoinTable(
    name = "DELIVERIES",              ◁——— Defaults to USERS_SHIPMENT
    joinColumns =
    @JoinColumn(name = "USER_ID"),        ◁——— Defaults to USERS_ID
    inverseJoinColumns =
    @JoinColumn(name = "SHIPMENT_ID")   ◁——— Defaults to SHIPMENTS_ID
)
protected Set<Shipment> deliveries = new HashSet<Shipment>();
// ...
}
```

Note that if you declare neither `@JoinTable` nor `@JoinColumn`, the `@OneToMany` in an embeddable class defaults to a join table strategy.

From within the owning entity class, you can override property mappings of an embedded class with `@AttributeOverride`, as shown in section 5.2.3. If you want to override the join table or column mapping of an entity association in an embeddable class, use `@AssociationOverride` in the owning entity class instead. You can't, however, switch the mapping strategy; the mapping in the embeddable component class decides whether a join table or join column is used.

A join table mapping is of course also applicable in true *many-to-many* mappings.

8.3   *Many-to-many and ternary associations*

The association between `Category` and `Item` is a *many-to-many* association, as you can see in figure 8.13. In a real system, you may not have a *many-to-many* association. Our experience is that there is almost always other information that must be attached to each link between associated instances. Some examples are the timestamp when an `Item` was added to a `Category` and the `User` responsible for creating the link. We expand the example later in this section to cover such a case. You should start with a regular and simpler *many-to-many* association.

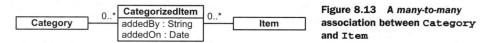

Figure 8.13   A *many-to-many* association between `Category` and `Item`

8.3.1   *Unidirectional and bidirectional many-to-many associations*

A join table in the database represents a regular *many-to-many* association, which some developers also call the *link table*, or *association table*. Figure 8.14 shows a *many-to-many* relationship with a link table.

The link table CATEGORY_ITEM has two columns, both with a foreign key constraint referencing the CATEGORY and ITEM tables, respectively. Its primary key is a composite key of both columns. You can only link a particular Category and Item once, but you can link the same item to several categories.

In JPA, you map *many-to-many* associations with @ManyToMany on a collection:

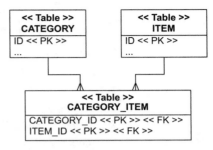

Figure 8.14 A *many-to-many* **relationship with a link table**

PATH: /model/src/main/java/org/jpwh/model/associations/manytomany/bidirectional/Category.java

```
@Entity
public class Category {

    @ManyToMany(cascade = CascadeType.PERSIST)
    @JoinTable(
        name = "CATEGORY_ITEM",
        joinColumns = @JoinColumn(name = "CATEGORY_ID"),
        inverseJoinColumns = @JoinColumn(name = "ITEM_ID")
    )
    protected Set<Item> items = new HashSet<Item>();

    // ...
}
```

As usual, you can enable CascadeType.PERSIST to make it easier to save data. When you reference a new Item from the collection, Hibernate makes it persistent. Let's make this association bidirectional (you don't have to, if you don't need it):

PATH: /model/src/main/java/org/jpwh/model/associations/manytomany/bidirectional/Item.java

```
@Entity
public class Item {

    @ManyToMany(mappedBy = "items")
    protected Set<Category> categories = new HashSet<Category>();

    // ...
}
```

As for any bidirectional mapping, one side is "mapped by" the other side. The Item#categories collection is effectively read-only; Hibernate will analyze the content of the Category#items side when storing data. Next you create two categories and two items and link them with *many-to-many* multiplicity:

PATH: /examples/src/test/java/org/jpwh/test/associations/
      ManyToManyBidirectional.java

```
Category someCategory = new Category("Some Category");
Category otherCategory = new Category("Other Category");

Item someItem = new Item("Some Item");
Item otherItem = new Item("Other Item");

someCategory.getItems().add(someItem);
someItem.getCategories().add(someCategory);

someCategory.getItems().add(otherItem);
otherItem.getCategories().add(someCategory);

otherCategory.getItems().add(someItem);
someItem.getCategories().add(otherCategory);

em.persist(someCategory);
em.persist(otherCategory);
```

Because you enabled transitive persistence, saving the categories makes the entire network of instances persistent. On the other hand, the cascading options ALL, REMOVE, and orphan deletion (see section 7.3.3) aren't meaningful for *many-to-many* associations. This is a good point to test whether you understand entities and value types. Try to come up with reasonable answers as to why these cascading types don't make sense for a *many-to-many* association.

Can you use a List instead of a Set, or even a bag? The Set matches the database schema perfectly, because there can be no duplicate links between Category and Item.

A bag implies duplicate elements, so you need a different primary key for the join table. The proprietary @CollectionId annotation of Hibernate can provide this, as shown in section 7.1.5. One of the alternative *many-to-many* strategies we discuss in a moment is a better choice if you need to support duplicate links.

You can map indexed collections such as a List with the regular @ManyToMany, but only on one side. Remember that in a bidirectional relationship one side has to be "mapped by" the other side, meaning its value is ignored when Hibernate synchronizes with the database. If both sides are lists, you can only make persistent the index of one side.

A regular @ManyToMany mapping hides the link table; there is no corresponding Java class, only some collection properties. So whenever someone says, "My link table has more columns with information about the link"—and, in our experience, someone always says this sooner rather than later—you need to map this information to a Java class.

8.3.2   *Many-to-many with an intermediate entity*

You may always represent a *many-to-many* association as two *many-to-one* associations to an intervening class. You don't hide the link table but represent it with a Java class. This model is usually more easily extensible, so we tend not to use regular *many-to-*

many associations in applications. It's a lot of work to change code later, when inevitably more columns are added to a link table; so before you map an @ManyToMany as shown in the previous section, consider the alternative shown in figure 8.15.

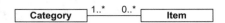

Figure 8.15 `CategorizedItem` is the link between `Category` and `Item`.

Imagine that you need to record some information each time you add an Item to a Category. The CategorizedItem captures the timestamp and user who created the link. This domain model requires additional columns on the join table, as you can see in figure 8.16.

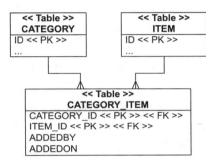

Figure 8.16 Additional columns on the join table in a *many-to-many* relationship

The new CategorizedItem entity maps to the link table, as shown next.

Listing 8.4 Mapping a *many-to-many* relationship with `CategorizedItem`

PATH: /model/src/main/java/org/jpwh/model/associations/manytomany/linkentity/
       CategorizedItem.java

```
@Entity
@Table(name = "CATEGORY_ITEM")
@org.hibernate.annotations.Immutable                    ◄──❶ Declares class immutable
public class CategorizedItem {

    @Embeddable
    public static class Id implements Serializable {     ◄──┐ Encapsulates
                                                          ❷ composite key
        @Column(name = "CATEGORY_ID")
        protected Long categoryId;

        @Column(name = "ITEM_ID")
        protected Long itemId;

        public Id() {
        }

        public Id(Long categoryId, Long itemId) {
            this.categoryId = categoryId;
            this.itemId = itemId;
        }
```

```
public boolean equals(Object o) {
    if (o != null && o instanceof Id) {
        Id that = (Id) o;
        return this.categoryId.equals(that.categoryId)
            && this.itemId.equals(that.itemId);
    }
    return false;
}

public int hashCode() {
    return categoryId.hashCode() + itemId.hashCode();
}
}
```

3 Maps identifier property and composite key columns

```
@EmbeddedId
protected Id id = new Id();
```

```
@Column(updatable = false)
@NotNull
protected String addedBy;
```

4 Maps username

```
@Column(updatable = false)
@NotNull
protected Date addedOn = new Date();
```

5 Maps timestamp

```
@ManyToOne
@JoinColumn(
    name = "CATEGORY_ID",
    insertable = false, updatable = false)
protected Category category;
```

6 Maps category

```
@ManyToOne
@JoinColumn(
    name = "ITEM_ID",
    insertable = false, updatable = false)
protected Item item;
```

7 Maps item

```
public CategorizedItem(
    String addedByUsername,
    Category category,
    Item item) {
```

8 Constructs CategorizedItem

```
    this.addedBy = addedByUsername;
    this.category = category;
    this.item = item;
```

Sets fields

```
    this.id.categoryId = category.getId();
    this.id.itemId = item.getId();
```

Sets identifier values

```
    category.getCategorizedItems().add(this);
    item.getCategorizedItems().add(this);
}

// ...
}
```

Guarantees referential integrity if made bidirectional

This is a large chunk of code with some new annotations. First, it's an immutable entity class, so you'll never update properties after creation. Hibernate can do some optimizations, such avoiding dirty checking during flushing of the persistence context, if you declare the class immutable ❶.

An entity class needs an identifier property. The primary key of the link table is the composite of CATEGORY_ID and ITEM_ID. Hence, the entity class also has a composite key, which you encapsulate in a static nested embeddable component class ❷ for convenience. You can externalize this class into its own file, of course. The new @EmbeddedId annotation ❸ maps the identifier property and its composite key columns to the entity's table.

Next are two basic properties mapping the addedBy username ❹ and the addedOn timestamp ❺ to columns of the join table. This is the "additional information about the link" that interests you.

Then two @ManyToOne properties, category ❻ and item ❼, map columns that are already mapped in the identifier. The trick here is to make them read-only, with the updatable=false, insertable=false setting. This means Hibernate writes the values of these columns by taking the identifier value of CategorizedItem. At the same time, you can read and browse the associated instances through categorizedItem.get-Item() and getCategory(), respectively. (If you map the same column twice without making one mapping read-only, Hibernate will complain on startup about a duplicate column mapping.)

You can also see that constructing a CategorizedItem ❽ involves setting the values of the identifier—the application always assigns composite key values; Hibernate doesn't generate them. Pay extra attention to the constructor and how it sets the field values and guarantees referential integrity by managing collections on both sides of the association. You map these collections next, to enable bidirectional navigation.

This is a unidirectional mapping and enough to support the *many-to-many* relationship between Category and Item. To create a link, you instantiate and persist a CategorizedItem. If you want to break a link, you remove the CategorizedItem. The constructor of CategorizedItem requires that you provide already persistent Category and Item instances.

If bidirectional navigation is required, map an @OneToMany collection in Category and/or Item:

> **PATH:** /model/src/main/java/org/jpwh/model/associations/manytomany/linkentity/
> Category.java

```
@Entity
public class Category {

    @OneToMany(mappedBy = "category")
    protected Set<CategorizedItem> categorizedItems = new HashSet<>();

    // ...
}
```

PATH: /model/src/main/java/org/jpwh/model/associations/manytomany/
       linkentity/Item.java

```
@Entity
public class Item {

    @OneToMany(mappedBy = "item")
    protected Set<CategorizedItem> categorizedItems = new HashSet<>();

    // ...
}
```

Both sides are "mapped by" the annotations in `CategorizedItem`, so Hibernate already knows what to do when you iterate through the collection returned by either `getCategorizedItems()` method.

This is how you create and store links:

PATH: /examples/src/test/java/org/jpwh/test/associations/
       ManyToManyLinkEntity.java

```
Category someCategory = new Category("Some Category");
Category otherCategory = new Category("Other Category");
em.persist(someCategory);
em.persist(otherCategory);

Item someItem = new Item("Some Item");
Item otherItem = new Item("Other Item");
em.persist(someItem);
em.persist(otherItem);

CategorizedItem linkOne = new CategorizedItem(
    "johndoe", someCategory, someItem
);

CategorizedItem linkTwo = new CategorizedItem(
    "johndoe", someCategory, otherItem
);

CategorizedItem linkThree = new CategorizedItem(
    "johndoe", otherCategory, someItem
);

em.persist(linkOne);
em.persist(linkTwo);
em.persist(linkThree);
```

The primary advantage of this strategy is the possibility for bidirectional navigation: you can get all items in a category by calling `someCategory.getCategorizedItems()` and then also navigate from the opposite direction with `someItem.getCategorized-Items()`. A disadvantage is the more complex code needed to manage the `CategorizedItem` entity instances to create and remove links, which you have to save and delete independently. You also need some infrastructure in the `CategorizedItem` class, such as the composite identifier. One small improvement would be to enable

CascadeType.PERSIST on some of the associations, reducing the number of calls to persist().

In the previous example, you stored the user who created the link between Category and Item as a simple name string. If the join table instead had a foreign key column called USER_ID, you'd have a ternary relationship. The CategorizedItem would have a @ManyToOne for Category, Item, and User.

In the following section, you see another *many-to-many* strategy. To make it a bit more interesting, we make it a ternary association.

8.3.3 *Ternary associations with components*

In the previous section, you represented a *many-to-many* relationship with an entity class mapped to the link table. A potentially simpler alternative is a mapping to an embeddable component class:

> **PATH:** /model/src/main/java/org/jpwh/model/associations/manytomany/ternary/
> CategorizedItem.java

```java
@Embeddable
public class CategorizedItem {

    @ManyToOne
    @JoinColumn(
        name = "ITEM_ID",
        nullable = false, updatable = false
    )
    protected Item item;

    @ManyToOne
    @JoinColumn(
        name = "USER_ID",
        updatable = false
    )
    @NotNull
    protected User addedBy;

    @Temporal(TemporalType.TIMESTAMP)
    @Column(updatable = false)
    @NotNull
    protected Date addedOn = new Date();

    protected CategorizedItem() {
    }

    public CategorizedItem(User addedBy,
                           Item item) {
        this.addedBy = addedBy;
        this.item = item;
    }

    // ...
}
```

Doesn't generate an SQL constraint, so not part of the primary key

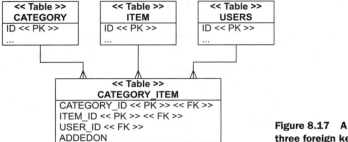

Figure 8.17   A link table with three foreign key columns

The new mappings here are @ManyToOne associations in an @Embeddable, and the additional foreign key join column USER_ID, making this a ternary relationship. Look at the database schema in figure 8.17.

The owner of the embeddable component collection is the Category entity:

> **PATH:** /model/src/main/java/org/jpwh/model/associations/manytomany/ternary/
>   Category.java

```
@Entity
public class Category {

    @ElementCollection
    @CollectionTable(
        name = "CATEGORY_ITEM",
        joinColumns = @JoinColumn(name = "CATEGORY_ID")
    )
    protected Set<CategorizedItem> categorizedItems = new HashSet<>();

    // ...
}
```

Unfortunately, this mapping isn't perfect: when you map an @ElementCollection of embeddable type, all properties of the target type that are nullable=false become part of the (composite) primary key. You want all columns in CATEGORY_ITEM to be NOT NULL. Only CATEGORY_ID and ITEM_ID columns should be part of the primary key, though. The trick is to use the Bean Validation @NotNull annotation on properties that shouldn't be part of the primary key. In that case (because it's an embeddable class), Hibernate ignores the Bean Validation annotation for primary key realization and SQL schema generation. The downside is that the generated schema won't have the appropriate NOT NULL constraints on the USER_ID and ADDEDON columns, which you should fix manually.

The advantage of this strategy is the implicit life cycle of the link components. To create an association between a Category and an Item, add a new CategorizedItem instance to the collection. To break the link, remove the element from the collection. No extra cascading settings are required, and the Java code is simplified (albeit spread over more lines):

```
PATH:  /examples/src/test/java/org/jpwh/test/associations/
       ManyToManyTernary.java
```

```java
Category someCategory = new Category("Some Category");
Category otherCategory = new Category("Other Category");
em.persist(someCategory);
em.persist(otherCategory);

Item someItem = new Item("Some Item");
Item otherItem = new Item("Other Item");
em.persist(someItem);
em.persist(otherItem);

User someUser = new User("johndoe");
em.persist(someUser);

CategorizedItem linkOne = new CategorizedItem(
    someUser, someItem
);
someCategory.getCategorizedItems().add(linkOne);

CategorizedItem linkTwo = new CategorizedItem(
    someUser, otherItem
);
someCategory.getCategorizedItems().add(linkTwo);

CategorizedItem linkThree = new CategorizedItem(
    someUser, someItem
);
otherCategory.getCategorizedItems().add(linkThree);
```

There is no way to enable bidirectional navigation: an embeddable component, such as CategorizedItem by definition, can't have shared references. You can't navigate from Item to CategorizedItem, and there is no mapping of this link in Item. Instead, you can write a query to retrieve the categories given an Item:

```
PATH:  /examples/src/test/java/org/jpwh/test/associations/
       ManyToManyTernary.java
```

```java
Item item = em.find(Item.class, ITEM_ID);

List<Category> categoriesOfItem =
    em.createQuery(
        "select c from Category c " +
            "join c.categorizedItems ci " +
            "where ci.item = :itemParameter")
    .setParameter("itemParameter", item)
    .getResultList();

assertEquals(categoriesOfItem.size(), 2);
```

You've now completed your first ternary association mapping. In the previous chapters, you saw ORM examples with maps; the keys and values of the shown maps were always of basic or embeddable type. In the following section, you see more complex key/value pair types and their mappings.

8.4   *Entity associations with Maps*

Map keys and values can be references to other entities, providing another strategy for mapping *many-to-many* and ternary relationships. First, let's assume that only the value of each map entry is a reference to another entity.

8.4.1   *One-to-many with a property key*

If the value of each map entry is a reference to another entity, you have a *one-to-many* entity relationship. The key of the map is of a basic type: for example, a `Long` value.

An example of this structure would be the `Item` entity with a map of `Bid` instances, where each map entry is a pair of `Bid` identifier and reference to a `Bid` instance. When you iterate through `someItem.getBids()`, you iterate through map entries that look like (1, <reference to `Bid` with PK 1>), (2, <reference to `Bid` with PK 2>), and so on:

> PATH: **/examples/src/test/java/org/jpwh/test/associations/MapsMapKey.java**

```
Item item = em.find(Item.class, ITEM_ID);
assertEquals(item.getBids().size(), 2);

for (Map.Entry<Long, Bid> entry : item.getBids().entrySet()) {
    assertEquals(entry.getKey(),
        entry.getValue().getId());          ⟵── Key is the identifier of each Bid
}
```

The underlying tables for this mapping are nothing special; you have an `ITEM` and a `BID` table, with an `ITEM_ID` foreign key column in the `BID` table. This is the same schema as shown in figure 7.14 for a *one-to-many/many-to-one* mapping with a regular collection instead of a `Map`. Your motivation here is a slightly different representation of the data in the application.

In the `Item` class, include a `Map` property named `bids`:

> PATH: **/model/src/main/java/org/jpwh/model/associations/maps/mapkey/**
>   **Item.java**

```
@Entity
public class Item {

    @MapKey(name = "id")
    @OneToMany(mappedBy = "item")
    protected Map<Long, Bid> bids = new HashMap<>();

    // ...
}
```

New here is the `@MapKey` annotation. It maps a property of the target entity, in this case the `Bid` entity, as the key of the map. The default if you omit the `name` attribute is the identifier property of the target entity, so the `name` option here is redundant. Because the keys of a map form a set, you should expect values to be unique for a particular map. This is the case for `Bid` primary keys but likely not for any other property of `Bid`. It's up to you to ensure that the selected property has unique values—Hibernate won't check.

The primary, and rare, use case for this mapping technique is the desire to iterate map entries with some property of the entry entity value as the entry key, maybe because it's convenient for how you'd like to render the data. A more common situation is a map in the middle of a ternary association.

8.4.2 Key/Value ternary relationship

You may be a little bored by now, but we promise this is the last time we show another way to map the association between `Category` and `Item`. Previously, in section 8.3.3, you used an embeddable `CategorizedItem` component to represent the link. Here we show a representation of the relationship with a `Map`, instead of an additional Java class. The key of each map entry is an `Item`, and the related value is the `User` who added the `Item` to the `Category`, as shown in figure 8.18.

The link/join table in the schema, as you can see in figure 8.19, has three columns: `CATEGORY_ID`, `ITEM_ID`, and `USER_ID`. The `Map` is owned by the `Category` entity:

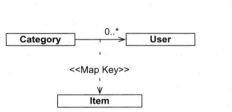

Figure 8.18 A `Map` with entity associations as key/value pairs

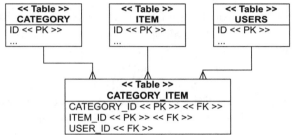

Figure 8.19 The link table represents the `Map` key/value pairs.

> PATH: /model/src/main/java/org/jpwh/model/associations/maps/ternary/
> Category.java

```
@Entity
public class Category {

    @ManyToMany(cascade = CascadeType.PERSIST)          Defaults to
    @MapKeyJoinColumn(name = "ITEM_ID")            ⟵── ITEMADDEDBY_KEY
    @JoinTable(
        name = "CATEGORY_ITEM",
        joinColumns = @JoinColumn(name = "CATEGORY_ID"),
        inverseJoinColumns = @JoinColumn(name = "USER_ID")
    )
    protected Map<Item, User> itemAddedBy = new HashMap<>();

    // ...
}
```

The @MapKeyJoinColumn is optional; Hibernate would default to the column name ITEMADDEDBY_KEY for the join/foreign key column referencing the ITEM table.

To create a link between all three entities, all instances must already be in persistent state and then put into the map:

PATH: /examples/src/test/java/org/jpwh/test/associations/MapsTernary.java

```
someCategory.getItemAddedBy().put(someItem, someUser);
someCategory.getItemAddedBy().put(otherItem, someUser);
otherCategory.getItemAddedBy().put(someItem, someUser);
```

To remove the link, remove the entry from the map. This is a convenient Java API for managing a complex relationship, hiding a database link table with three columns. But remember that in practice, link tables often grow additional columns, and changing all the Java application code later is expensive if you depend on a Map API. Earlier we had an ADDEDON column with a timestamp when the link was created, but we had to drop it for this mapping.

8.5   *Summary*

- You learned how to map complex entity associations using *one-to-one* associations, *one-to-many* associations, *many-to-many* associations, ternary associations, and entity associations with maps.
- Simplify the relationships between your classes, and you'll rarely need many of the techniques we've shown. In particular, you can often best represent *many-to-many* entity associations as two *many-to-one* associations from an intermediate entity class, or with a collection of components.
- Before you attempt a complex collection mapping, always make sure you actually need a collection. Ask yourself whether you frequently iterate through its elements.
- The Java structures shown in this chapter may make data access easier sometimes, but typically they complicate data storage, updates, and deletion.

Complex and legacy schemas

In this chapter, we focus on the most important part of your system: the database schema, where your collection of integrity rules resides—the model of the real world that you've created. If your application can auction an item only once in the real world, your database schema should guarantee that. If an auction always has a starting price, your database model should include an appropriate constraint. If data satisfies all integrity rules, the data is *consistent*, a term you'll meet again in section 11.1.

We also assume that consistent data is *correct*: everything the database states, either explicitly or implicitly, is true; everything else is false. If you want to know more about the theory behind this approach, look up the *closed-world assumption* (CWA).

Major new features in JPA 2

- Schema generation and execution of custom SQL scripts during bootstrap is now standardized and can be configured on a persistence unit.
- You can map and customize schema artifacts such as indexes and foreign key names with standard annotations.
- You can map foreign keys/*many-to-one* associations in composite primary keys with @MapsId as "derived identity."

Sometimes you can start a project top-down. There is no existing database schema and maybe not even any data—your application is completely new. Many developers like to let Hibernate automatically generate the scripts for a database schema. You'll probably also let Hibernate deploy the schema on the test database on your development machine or your continuous build systems for integration testing. Later, a DBA will take the generated scripts and write an improved and final schema for production deployment. The first part of this chapter shows you how to improve the schema from within JPA and Hibernate, to make your DBA happy.

At the other end of the spectrum are systems with existing, possibly complex schemas, with years' worth of data. Your new application is just a small gear in a big machine, and your DBA won't allow any (sometimes even non-disruptive) changes to the database. You need a flexible object/relational mapping so you don't have to twist and bend the Java classes too much when things don't fit right away. This will be the subject of the second half of this chapter, including a discussion of composite primary and foreign keys.

Let's start with a clean-room implementation and Hibernate-generated schemas.

9.1 *Improving the database schema*

Hibernate reads your Java domain model classes and mapping metadata and generates schema DDL statements. You can export them into a text file or execute them directly on your database whenever you run integration tests. Because schema languages are mostly vendor-specific, every option you put in your mapping metadata has the potential to bind the metadata to a particular database product—keep this in mind when using schema features.

Hibernate creates the basic schema for your tables and constraints automatically; it even creates sequences, depending on the identifier generator you select. But there are some schema artifacts Hibernate can't and won't create automatically. These include all kinds of highly vendor-specific performance options and any other artifacts that are relevant only for the physical storage of data (tablespaces, for example). Besides these physical concerns, your DBA will often supply custom additional schema statements to improve the generated schema. DBAs should get involved early and verify the automatically generated schema from Hibernate. Never go into production with an unchecked automatically generated schema.

If your development process allows, changes made by the DBA can flow back into your Java systems, for you to add to mapping metadata. In many projects, the mapping metadata can contain all the necessary schema changes from a DBA. Then Hibernate can generate the final production schema during the regular build by including all comments, constraints, indexes, and so on.

In the following sections, we show you how to customize the generated schema and how to add auxiliary database schema artifacts (we call them *objects* sometimes; we don't mean Java objects here). We discuss custom data types, additional integrity rules, indexes, and how you can replace some of the (sometimes ugly) auto-generated artifact names produced by Hibernate.

Exporting the schema script to a file

Hibernate bundles the class `org.hibernate.tool.hbm2ddl.SchemaExport` with a `main()` method you can run from the command line. This utility can either talk to your DBMS directly and create the schema or write a text file with the DDL script for further customization by your DBA.

First, let's look at how you can add custom SQL statements to Hibernate's automatic schema-generation process.

9.1.1 Adding auxiliary database objects

You can hook the following three types of custom SQL scripts into Hibernate's schema-generation process:

- The *create* script executes when the schema is generated. A custom create script can run before, after, or instead of Hibernate's automatically generated scripts. In other words, you can write an SQL script that runs before or after Hibernate generates tables, constraints, and so on from your mapping metadata.
- The *drop* script executes when Hibernate removes schema artifacts. Just like the create script, a drop script can run before, after, or instead of Hibernate's automatically generated statements.
- The *load* script always executes after Hibernate generates the schema, as the last step after creation. Its main purpose is importing test or master data, before your application or unit test runs. It can contain any kind of SQL statement, including DDL statements such as ALTER, if you want to further customize the schema.

This customization of the schema-generation process is actually standardized; you configure it with JPA properties in persistence.xml for a persistence unit.

Listing 9.1   Custom schema-generation properties in persistence.xml

Path: /model/src/main/resources/META-INF/persistence.xml

---

1 Switches to multiline extractor

2 Defines when scripts should be executed

```
<property name="hibernate.Ohbm2ddl.import_files_sql_extractor"
        value="org.hibernate.tool.hbm2ddl.
        ➥MultipleLinesSqlCommandExtractor"/>

<property name="javax.persistence.schema-generation.create-source"
        value="script-then-metadata"/>
<property name="javax.persistence.schema-generation.drop-source"
        value="metadata-then-script"/>

<property name="javax.persistence.schema-generation.create-script-source"
        value="complexschemas/CreateScript.sql.txt"/>

<property name="javax.persistence.schema-generation.drop-script-source"
        value="complexschemas/DropScript.sql.txt"/>

<property name="javax.persistence.sql-load-script-source"
        value="complexschemas/LoadScript.sql.txt"/>
```

3 Custom SQL script to create schema

4 Custom SQL script to drop schema

5 Load script

1 By default, Hibernate expects one SQL statement per line in scripts. This switches to the more convenient multiline extractor. SQL statements in scripts are terminated with semicolon. You can write your own `org.hibernate.tool.hbm2ddl.ImportSqlCommand-Extractor` implementation if you want to handle the SQL script in a different way.

2 This property defines when the create and drop scripts should be executed. Your custom SQL scripts will contain `CREATE DOMAIN` statements, which must be executed before the tables using these domains are created. With these settings, the schema generator runs the create script first before reading your ORM metadata (annotations, XML files) and creating the tables. The drop script executes after Hibernate drops the tables, giving you a chance to clean up anything you created. Other options are `metadata` (ignore custom script sources) and `script` (only use a custom script source; ignore ORM metadata in annotations and XML files).

3 This is the location of the custom SQL script for creation of the schema. The path is (a) the location of the script resource on the classpath; (b) the location of the script as a file:// URL; or, if neither (a) nor (b) matches, (c) the absolute or relative file path on the local file system. This example uses (a).

4 This is the custom SQL script for dropping the schema.

5 This load script runs after the tables have been created.

We've mentioned that DDL is usually highly vendor-specific. If your application has to support several database dialects, you may need several sets of create/drop/load scripts to customize the schema for each database dialect. You can solve this with several persistence unit configurations in the persistence.xml file.

Alternatively, Hibernate has its own proprietary configuration for schema customization in an hbm.xml mapping file.

Listing 9.2 Custom schema generation with a Hibernate proprietary configuration

```
<hibernate-mapping xmlns="http://www.hibernate.org/xsd/orm/hbm">

    <database-object>
        <create>
            CREATE ...
        </create>
        <drop>
            DROP ...
        </drop>
        <dialect-scope name="org.hibernate.dialect.H2Dialect"/>
        <dialect-scope name="org.hibernate.dialect.PostgreSQL82Dialect"/>
    </database-object>

</hibernate-mapping>
```

Hibernate Feature

Place your custom SQL fragments into the <create> and <drop> elements. Hibernate executes these statements *after* creating the schema for your domain model classes, which is after creating your tables and *before* dropping the automatically generated part of the schema. This behavior can't be changed, so the standard JPA schema-generation script settings offer more flexibility.

The <dialect-scope> elements restrict your SQL statements to a particular set of configured database dialects. Without any <dialect-scope> elements, the SQL statements are always applied.

Hibernate also supports a load script: if Hibernate finds a file called import.sql in the root of your classpath, it executes that file after the schema has been created. Alternatively, if you have several import files, you can name them as a comma-separated list with the hibernate.hbm2ddl.import_files property in your persistence unit configuration.

Finally, if you need more programmatic control over the generated schema, implement the org.hibernate.mapping.AuxiliaryDatabaseObject interface. Hibernate comes bundled with a convenience implementation that you can subclass and override selectively.

Listing 9.3 Controlling the generated schema programmatically

```
package org.jpwh.model.complexschemas;

import org.hibernate.dialect.Dialect;
import org.hibernate.boot.model.relational.AbstractAuxiliaryDatabaseObject;

public class CustomSchema
```

```
        extends AbstractAuxiliaryDatabaseObject {

    public CustomSchema() {
        addDialectScope("org.hibernate.dialect.Oracle9Dialect");
    }

    @Override
    public String[] sqlCreateStrings(Dialect dialect) {
        return new String[]{"[CREATE statement]"};
    }

    @Override
    public String[] sqlDropStrings(Dialect dialect) {
        return new String[]{"[DROP statement]"};
    }
}
```

You can add dialect scopes programmatically and even access some mapping information in the `sqlCreateString()` and `sqlDropString()` methods. You have to enable this custom class in an hbm.xml file:

```
<hibernate-mapping xmlns="http://www.hibernate.org/xsd/orm/hbm">

    <database-object>
        <definition class="org.jpwh.model.complexschemas.CustomSchema"/>
        <dialect-scope name="org.hibernate.dialect.H2Dialect"/>
        <dialect-scope name="org.hibernate.dialect.PostgreSQL82Dialect"/>
    </database-object>

</hibernate-mapping>
```

Additional dialect scopes are cumulative; the previous example applies to three dialects.

Let's write some custom create/drop/load scripts and implement additional schema integrity rules recommended by any good DBA. First, some background information on integrity rules and SQL constraints.

9.1.2   *SQL constraints*

Systems that ensure data integrity only in application code are prone to data corruption and often degrade the quality of the database over time. If the data store doesn't enforce rules, a trivial undetected application bug can cause unrecoverable problems such as incorrect or lost data.

In contrast to ensuring data consistency in procedural (or object-oriented) application code, database management systems allow you to implement integrity rules with declarations, as a database schema. The advantages of declarative rules are fewer possible errors in code and a chance for the DBMS to optimize data access.

In SQL databases, we identify four kinds of rules:

- *Domain constraints*—A domain is (loosely speaking, and in the database world) a data type in a database. Hence, a domain constraint defines the range of possible values a particular data type can handle. For example, an INTEGER data type is usable for integer values. A CHAR data type can hold character strings: for example, all characters defined in ASCII or some other encoding. Because we mostly use data types built-in the DBMS, we rely on the domain constraints as defined by the vendor. If supported by your SQL database, you can use the (often limited) support for custom domains to add additional constraints for particular existing data types, or create user-defined data types (UDT).

- *Column constraints*—Restricting a column to hold values of a particular domain and type creates a column constraint. For example, you declare in the schema that the EMAIL column holds values of VARCHAR type. Alternatively, you could create a new domain called EMAIL_ADDRESS with further constraints and apply it to a column instead of VARCHAR. A special column constraint in an SQL database is NOT NULL.

- *Table constraints*—An integrity rule that applies to several columns or several rows is a table constraint. A typical declarative table constraint is UNIQUE: all rows are checked for duplicate values (for example, each user must have a distinct email address). A rule affecting only a single row but multiple columns is "the auction end time has to be after the auction start time."

- *Database constraints*—If a rule applies to more than one table, it has database scope. You should already be familiar with the most common database constraint, the foreign key. This rule guarantees the integrity of references between rows, usually in separate tables, but not always (self-referencing foreign key constraints aren't uncommon). Other database constraints involving several tables aren't uncommon: for example, a bid can only be stored if the auction end time of the referenced item hasn't been reached.

Most (if not all) SQL database management systems support these kinds of constraints and the most important options of each. In addition to simple keywords such as NOT NULL and UNIQUE, you can usually also declare more complex rules with the CHECK constraint that applies an arbitrary SQL expression. Still, integrity constraints are one of the weak areas in the SQL standard, and solutions from vendors can differ significantly.

Furthermore, non-declarative and procedural constraints are possible with database triggers that intercept data-modification operations. A trigger can then implement the constraint procedure directly or call an existing stored procedure.

Integrity constraints can be checked immediately when a data-modification statement is executed, or the check can be deferred until the end of a transaction. The violation response in SQL databases is usually rejection without any possibility of customization. Foreign keys are special because you can typically decide what should happen with ON DELETE or ON UPDATE for referenced rows.

Hibernate passes on database constraint violations in error exceptions; check whether the exception in your transaction has a cause, somewhere in the exception chain, of type org.hibernate.exception.ConstraintViolationException. This exception can provide more information about the error, such as the name of the failed database constraint.

Displaying validation error messages

It sounds almost too good to be true: The database layer will throw a `Constraint-ViolationException` that includes all the details, so why not show this to the user? The user can then change the invalid value on their screen and submit the form again until the data passes validation. Unfortunately, this doesn't work, and many who have tried to implement this strategy have failed.

First, every DBMS has different error messages, and Hibernate doesn't guarantee correct parsing of the error. The details available on `ConstraintViolation-Exception` are a best guess; they're usually wrong and only good enough for developer log messages. Should SQL standardize this? Of course, but it doesn't.

Second, an application shouldn't pass invalid data to the database to see what sticks and what doesn't. The DBMS is the last line of defense, not the first validator. Use Bean Validation in the Java application tier instead, and show your users nice validation error messages in their own language.

Let's take a closer look at the implementation of integrity constraints.

ADDING DOMAIN AND COLUMN CONSTRAINTS

The SQL standard includes domains, which unfortunately are rather limited and often not supported by the DBMS. If your system supports SQL domains, you can use them to add constraints to data types.

In your custom SQL create script, define an EMAIL_ADDRESS domain based on the VARCHAR data type:

> **PATH:** **/model/src/main/resources/complexschemas/CreateScript.sql.txt**

```
create domain if not exists
  EMAIL_ADDRESS as varchar
  check (position('@', value) > 1);
```

The additional constraint is a check of the presence of an @ symbol in the string. The (relatively minor) advantage of such domains in SQL is the abstraction of common constraints into a single location. Domain constraints are always checked immediately when data is inserted and modified.

You can now use this domain in your mappings, like a built-in data type:

> **PATH:** **/model/src/main/java/org/jpwh/model/complexschemas/custom/User.java**

```
@Entity
public class User {

    @Column(                                        ⟵          Column constraint
        nullable = false,
        unique = true,                              ⟵── Table multirow constraint
        columnDefinition = "EMAIL_ADDRESS(255)"     ⟵
    )                                                          Applies domain constraint
```

```
    protected String email;

    // ...
}
```

Several constraints are present in this mapping. The NOT NULL constraint is common; you've seen it many times before. The second is a UNIQUE column constraint; users can't have duplicate email addresses. At the time of writing, there was unfortunately no way to customize the name of this single-column unique constraint in Hibernate; it will get an ugly auto-generated name in your schema. Last, the columnDefinition refers to the domain you've added with your custom create script. This definition is an SQL fragment, exported into your schema directly, so be careful with database-specific SQL.

If you don't want to create domains first, apply the CHECK keyword directly as a single-column constraint:

> **PATH: /model/src/main/java/org/jpwh/model/complexschemas/custom/User.java**

```
@Entity
public class User {

    @Column(columnDefinition =
        "varchar(15) not null unique" +
        " check (not substring(lower(USERNAME), 0, 5) = 'admin')"
    )
    protected String username;          ◄── @org.hibernate.annotations.Check
                                            currently isn't supported on
    // ...                                   properties
}
```

This constraint restricts valid username values to a maximum length of 15 characters, and the string can't begin with *admin* to avoid confusion. You can call any SQL functions supported by your DBMS; the columnDefinition is always passed through into the exported schema.

Note that you have a choice: creating and using a domain or adding a single-column constraint has the same effect. Domains are usually easier to maintain and avoid duplicating.

At the time of writing, Hibernate doesn't support its proprietary annotation @org.hibernate.annotations.Check on individual properties; you use it for table-level constraints.

Hibernate Feature

TABLE-LEVEL CONSTRAINTS

An auction can't end before it starts. So far you have no rule in your SQL schema, or even in your Java domain model, that implements this restriction. You need a single-row table constraint:

PATH: /model/src/main/java/org/jpwh/model/complexschemas/custom/Item.java

```
@Entity
@org.hibernate.annotations.Check(
    constraints = "AUCTIONSTART < AUCTIONEND"
)
public class Item {

    @NotNull
    protected Date auctionStart;

    @NotNull
    protected Date auctionEnd;

    // ...
}
```

Hibernate appends table constraints to the generated CREATE TABLE statement, which can contain arbitrary SQL expressions.

You can implement multirow table constraints with expressions that are more complex. You may need a subselect in the expression to do this, which may not be supported by your DBMS. But there are some common multirow table constraints, like UNIQUE, that you can add directly in the mappings. You've already seen the @Column(unique = true|false) option in the previous section.

If your unique constraint spans multiple columns, use the uniqueConstraints option of the @Table annotation:

PATH: /model/src/main/java/org/jpwh/model/complexschemas/custom/User.java

```
@Entity
@Table(
    name = "USERS",
    uniqueConstraints =
        @UniqueConstraint(
            name = "UNQ_USERNAME_EMAIL",
            columnNames = { "USERNAME", "EMAIL" }
        )
)
public class User {

    // ...
}
```

Now all pairs of USERNAME and EMAIL must be unique, for all rows in the USERS table. If you don't provide a name for the constraint—here, UNQ_USERNAME_EMAIL—an automatically generated and probably ugly name is used.

The last kinds of constraints we discuss are database-wide rules that span several tables.

DATABASE CONSTRAINTS

A user can only make bids until an auction ends. Your database should guarantee that invalid bids can't be stored so that whenever a row is inserted into the BID table, the

CREATEDON timestamp of the bid is checked against the auction ending time. This kind of constraint involves two tables: BID and ITEM.

You can create a rule that spans several tables with a join in a subselect in any SQL CHECK expression. Instead of referring only to the table on which the constraint is declared, you may query (usually for the existence or nonexistence of a particular piece of information) a different table. The problem is that you can't use the @org.hibernate.annotations.Check annotation on either the Bid or Item class. You don't know which table Hibernate will create first.

Therefore, put your CHECK constraint into an ALTER TABLE statement that executes after all the tables have been created. A good place is the load script, because it always executes at that time:

> **PATH: /model/src/main/resources/complexschemas/LoadScript.sql.txt**

```
alter table BID
  add constraint AUCTION_BID_TIME
  check(
    CREATEDON <= (
      select i.AUCTIONEND from ITEM i where i.ID = ITEM_ID
    )
  );
```

A row in the BID table is now valid if its CREATEDON value is less than or equal to the auction end time of the referenced ITEM row.

By far the most common rules that span several tables are referential integrity rules. They're widely known as foreign keys, which are a combination of two things: a key value copy from a related row and a constraint that guarantees that the referenced value exists. Hibernate creates foreign key constraints automatically for all foreign key columns in association mappings. If you check the schema produced by Hibernate, you'll notice that these constraints also have automatically generated database identifiers—names that aren't easy to read and that make debugging more difficult. You see this kind of statement in the generated schema:

```
alter table BID add constraint FKCFAEEDB471BF59FF
    foreign key (ITEM_ID) references ITEM
```

This statement declares the foreign key constraint for the ITEM_ID column in the BID table, referencing the primary key column of the ITEM table. You can customize the name of the constraint with the foreignKey option in an @JoinColumn mapping:

> **PATH: /model/src/main/java/org/jpwh/model/complexschemas/custom/Bid.java**

```
@Entity
public class Bid {

    @ManyToOne
    @JoinColumn(
        name = "ITEM_ID",
        nullable = false,
```

```
        foreignKey = @ForeignKey(name = "FK_ITEM_ID")
    )
    protected Item item;

    // ...
}
```

A `foreignKey` attribute is also supported in `@PrimaryKeyJoinColumn`, `@MapKeyJoin-`
`Column`, `@JoinTable`, `@CollectionTable`, and `@AssociationOverride` mappings.

The `@ForeignKey` annotation has some rarely needed options we haven't shown:

- You can write your own `foreignKeyDefinition`, an SQL fragment such as
  `FOREIGN KEY ([column]) REFERENCES [table]([column]) ON UPDATE [action]`.
  Hibernate will use this SQL fragment instead of the provider-generated fragment, it can be in the SQL dialect supported by your DBMS.

- The `ConstraintMode` setting is useful if you want to disable foreign key generation completely, with the value `NO_CONSTRAINT`. You can then write the foreign
  key constraint yourself with an `ALTER TABLE` statement, probably in a load script
  as we've shown.

Naming constraints properly is not only good practice, but also helps significantly
when you have to read exception messages.

This completes our discussion of database integrity rules. Next, we look at some
optimization you might want to include in your schema for performance reasons.

9.1.3   *Creating indexes*

Indexes are a key feature when optimizing the performance of a database application.
The query optimizer in a DBMS can use indexes to avoid excessive scans of the data
tables. Because they're relevant only in the physical implementation of a database,
indexes aren't part of the SQL standard, and the DDL and available indexing options
are product specific. You can, however, embed the most common schema artifacts for
typical indexes in mapping metadata.

Many queries in CaveatEmptor will probably involve the `username` of a `User` entity.
You can speed up these queries by creating an index for the column of this property.
Another candidate for an index is the combination of `USERNAME` and `EMAIL` columns,
which you also use frequently in queries. You can declare single or multicolumn
indexes on the entity class with the `@Table` annotation and its `indexes` attribute:

```
PATH:  /model/src/main/java/org/jpwh/model/complexschemas/custom/User.java
```

```
@Entity
@Table(
    name = "USERS",
    indexes = {
        @Index(
            name = "IDX_USERNAME",
            columnList = "USERNAME"
        ),
```

```
        @Index(
            name = "IDX_USERNAME_EMAIL",
            columnList = "USERNAME, EMAIL"
        )
    }
)
public class User {

    // ...
}
```

If you don't provide a name for the index, a generated name is used.

We don't recommend adding indexes to your schema ad hoc because it feels like an index could help with a performance problem. Get the excellent book *SQL Tuning* by Dan Tow (Tow, 2003) if you want to learn efficient database-optimization techniques and especially how indexes can get you closer to the best-performing execution plan for your queries.

Customizing the database schema is often possible only if you're working on a new system with no existing data. If you have to deal with an existing legacy schema, one of the most common issues is working with natural and composite keys.

9.2 Handling legacy keys

We mentioned in section 4.2.3 that we think natural primary keys can be a bad idea. Natural keys often make it difficult to change the data model when business requirements change. They may even, in extreme cases, impact performance. Unfortunately, many legacy schemas use (natural) composite keys heavily; and for the reason we discourage the use of composite keys, it may be difficult to change the legacy schema to use non-composite natural or surrogate keys. Therefore, JPA supports natural and composite primary and foreign keys.

9.2.1 Mapping a natural primary key

If you encounter a USERS table in a legacy schema, it's likely that USERNAME is the primary key. In this case, you have no surrogate identifier that Hibernate generates automatically. Instead, your application has to assign the identifier value when saving an instance of the User class:

> **PATH:** /examples/src/test/java/org/jpwh/test/complexschemas/
> **NaturalPrimaryKey.java**

```
User user = new User("johndoe");
em.persist(user);
```

Here the user's name is an argument of the only public constructor of the User class:

PATH: /model/src/main/java/org/jpwh/model/complexschemas/naturalprimarykey/
User.java

```
@Entity
@Table(name = "USERS")
public class User {

    @Id
    protected String username;

    protected User() {
    }

    public User(String username) {
        this.username = username;
    }

    // ...
}
```

Hibernate calls the protected no-argument constructor when it loads a `User` from the database and then assigns the `username` field value directly. When you instantiate a `User`, call the public constructor with a `username`. If you don't declare an identifier generator on the `@Id` property, Hibernate expects the application to take care of the primary key value assignment.

Composite (natural) primary keys require a bit more work.

9.2.2 *Mapping a composite primary key*

Suppose the primary key of the USERS table is a composite of the two columns USER-NAME and DEPARTMENTNR. You write a separate composite identifier class that declares just the key properties and call this class `UserId`:

PATH: /model/src/main/java/org/jpwh/model/complexschemas/compositekey/
embedded/UserId.java

```
@Embeddable                                          ①  @Embeddable, Serializable class
public class UserId implements Serializable {

    protected String username;                       ②  Automatically NOT NULL

    protected String departmentNr;

    protected UserId() {                             ③  Protected constructor
    }

    public UserId(String username, String departmentNr) {    ④  Public
        this.username = username;                                constructor
        this.departmentNr = departmentNr;
    }
                                                     ⑤  Overrides equals()
    @Override                                           and hashCode()
    public boolean equals(Object o) {
        if (this == o) return true;
```

```
        if (o == null || getClass() != o.getClass()) return false;
        UserId userId = (UserId) o;
        if (!departmentNr.equals(userId.departmentNr)) return false;
        if (!username.equals(userId.username)) return false;
        return true;
    }

    @Override
    public int hashCode() {
        int result = username.hashCode();
        result = 31 * result + departmentNr.hashCode();
        return result;
    }

    // ...
}
```

❺ Overrides equals() and hashCode()

❶ This class has to be @Embeddable and Serializable—any type used as an identifier type in JPA must be Serializable.

❷ You don't have to mark the properties of the composite key as @NotNull; their database columns are automatically NOT NULL when embedded as the primary key of an entity.

❸ The JPA specification requires a public no-argument constructor for an embeddable identifier class. Hibernate accepts protected visibility.

❹ The only public constructor should have the key values as arguments.

❺ You have to override the equals() and hashCode() methods with the same semantics the composite key has in your database. In this case, this is a straightforward comparison of the username and departmentNr values.

These are the important parts of the UserId class. You probably will also have some getter methods to access the property values.

Now map the User entity with this identifier type as an @EmbeddedId:

PATH: /model/src/main/java/org/jpwh/model/complexschemas/compositekey/
      embedded/User.java

```
@Entity
@Table(name = "USERS")
public class User {

    @EmbeddedId
    protected UserId id;                        ◁——— Optional: @AttributeOverrides

    public User(UserId id) {
        this.id = id;
    }

    // ...
}
```

Just as for regular embedded components, you can override individual attributes and their mapped columns, as you saw in section 5.2.3. Figure 9.1 shows the database schema.

Any public constructor of `User` should require an instance of `UserId`, to force you to provide a value before saving the `User` (an entity class must have another, no-argument constructor, of course):

| << Table >> |
| USERS |
| USERNAME << PK >> |
| DEPARTMENTNR << PK >> |
| ... |

Figure 9.1 The USERS table has a composite primary key.

> **PATH:** /examples/src/test/java/org/jpwh/test/complexschemas/
> CompositeKeyEmbeddedId.java

```
UserId id = new UserId("johndoe", "123");
User user = new User(id);
em.persist(user);
```

This is how you load an instance of `User`:

> **PATH:** /examples/src/test/java/org/jpwh/test/complexschemas/
> CompositeKeyEmbeddedId.java

```
UserId id = new UserId("johndoe", "123");
User user = em.find(User.class, id);
assertEquals(user.getId().getDepartmentNr(), "123");
```

Next, suppose `DEPARTMENTNR` is a foreign key referencing a `DEPARTMENT` table, and that you wish to represent this association in the Java domain model as a *many-to-one* association.

9.2.3 *Foreign keys in composite primary keys*

Look at the schema in figure 9.2.

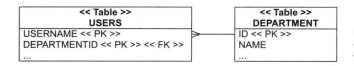

Figure 9.2 Part of the USERS composite primary key is also a foreign key.

Your first mapping option is with a dedicated annotation `@MapsId`, designed for this purpose. Start by renaming the `departmentNr` property to `departmentId` in the `UserId` embedded identifier class introduced in the previous section:

```
PATH:   /model/src/main/java/org/jpwh/model/complexschemas/compositekey/
        mapsid/UserId.java
```

```java
@Embeddable
public class UserId implements Serializable {

    protected String username;

    protected Long departmentId;

    // ...
}
```

The type of the property is now `Long`, not `String`. Next, add the `department` association with an `@ManyToOne` mapping to the `User` entity class:

```
PATH:   /model/src/main/java/org/jpwh/model/complexschemas/compositekey/
        mapsid/User.java
```

```java
@Entity
@Table(name = "USERS")
public class User {

    @EmbeddedId
    protected UserId id;

    @ManyToOne
    @MapsId("departmentId")
    protected Department department;

    public User(UserId id) {
        this.id = id;
    }

    // ...
}
```

The `@MapsId` annotation tells Hibernate to ignore the value of `UserId#departmentId` when saving an instance of `User`. Hibernate uses the identifier of the `Department` assigned to `User#department` when saving a row into the `USERS` table:

```
PATH:   /examples/src/test/java/org/jpwh/test/complexschemas/
        CompositeKeyMapsId.java
```

```java
Department department = new Department("Sales");
em.persist(department);

UserId id = new UserId("johndoe", null);          ⟵── Null?
User user = new User(id);
user.setDepartment(department);                    ⟵── Required
em.persist(user);
```

Hibernate ignores whatever value you set as the `UserId#departmentId` when saving; here it's even set to `null`. This means you always need a `Department` instance when storing a `User`. JPA calls this a derived identifier mapping.

When you load a `User`, only the identifier of a `Department` is necessary:

> **PATH: /examples/src/test/java/org/jpwh/test/complexschemas/**
> **CompositeKeyMapsId.java**

```
UserId id = new UserId("johndoe", DEPARTMENT_ID);
User user = em.find(User.class, id);
assertEquals(user.getDepartment().getName(), "Sales");
```

We don't like this mapping strategy much. This is a better variation without `@MapsId`:

> **PATH: /model/src/main/java/org/jpwh/model/complexschemas/compositekey/**
> **readonly/User.java**

```
@Entity
@Table(name = "USERS")
public class User {

    @EmbeddedId
    protected UserId id;

    @ManyToOne
    @JoinColumn(
        name = "DEPARTMENTID",              ⟵┤ Defaults to DEPARTMENT_ID
        insertable = false, updatable = false   ⟵┐
    )                                            ┤ Make it read-only
    protected Department department;

    public User(UserId id) {
        this.id = id;
    }

    // ...
}
```

With a simple `insertable=false, updatable=false`, you make the `User#department` property read-only. That means you can only query data by calling `someUser.getDepartment()`, and you have no public `setDepartment()` method. The property responsible for the database updates of the `DEPARTMENTID` column in the `USERS` table is `UserId#departmentId`.

Therefore, you now have to set the department's identifier value when saving a new `User`:

> **PATH: /examples/src/test/java/org/jpwh/test/complexschemas/**
> **CompositeKeyReadOnly.java**

```
Department department = new Department("Sales");
em.persist(department);                              ⟵── Assigns primary key value

UserId id = new UserId("johndoe", department.getId());   ⟵──  Required
```

```
User user = new User(id);
em.persist(user);

assertNull(user.getDepartment());          <──── Careful!
```

Note that `User#getDepartment()` returns `null` because you didn't set the value of this property. Hibernate only populates it when you load a `User`:

> PATH: /examples/src/test/java/org/jpwh/test/complexschemas/
> CompositeKeyReadOnly.java

```
UserId id = new UserId("johndoe", DEPARTMENT_ID);
User user = em.find(User.class, id);
assertEquals(user.getDepartment().getName(), "Sales");
```

Many developers prefer to encapsulate all these concerns in a constructor:

> PATH: /model/src/main/java/org/jpwh/model/complexschemas/compositekey/
> readonly/User.java

```java
@Entity
@Table(name = "USERS")
public class User {

    public User(String username, Department department) {
        if (department.getId() == null)
            throw new IllegalStateException(
                "Department is transient: " + department
            );
        this.id = new UserId(username, department.getId());
        this.department = department;
    }

    // ...
}
```

This defensive constructor enforces how a `User` has to be instantiated and correctly sets all identifier and property values.

If the `USERS` table has a composite primary key, a foreign key referencing the table must also be a composite key.

9.2.4 *Foreign keys to composite primary keys*

For example, the association from `Item` to `User`, the `seller`, could require a mapping of a composite foreign key. Look at the schema in figure 9.3.

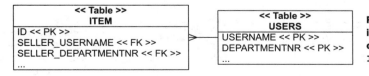

Figure 9.3 The item's seller is represented with a composite foreign key in the ITEM table.

Hibernate can hide this detail in the Java domain model. Here's the mapping of the `Item#seller` property:

> PATH: /model/src/main/java/org/jpwh/model/complexschemas/compositekey/
>   manytoone/Item.java

```
@Entity
public class Item {

    @NotNull
    @ManyToOne
    @JoinColumns({
        @JoinColumn(name = "SELLER_USERNAME",
                    referencedColumnName = "USERNAME"),
        @JoinColumn(name = "SELLER_DEPARTMENTNR",
                    referencedColumnName = "DEPARTMENTNR")
    })
    protected User seller;

    // ...
}
```

You might not have seen the `@JoinColumns` annotation before; it's a list of the composite foreign key columns underlying this association. Make sure you provide the `referencedColumnName` attribute, to link the source and target of the foreign key. Hibernate unfortunately won't complain if you forget, and you may end up with a wrong column order in the generated schema.

In legacy schemas, a foreign key sometimes doesn't reference a primary key.

9.2.5   *Foreign key referencing non-primary keys*

A foreign key constraint on the `SELLER` column in the `ITEM` table ensures that the seller of the item exists by requiring the same seller value to be present on *some* column in *some* row on *some* table. There are no other rules; the target column doesn't need a primary key constraint or even a unique constraint. The target table can be any table. The value can be a numeric identifier of the seller or a customer number string; only the type has to be the same for the foreign key reference source and target.

Of course, a foreign key constraint usually references primary key column(s). Nevertheless, legacy databases sometimes have foreign key constraints that don't follow this simple rule. Sometimes a foreign key constraint references a simple unique column—a natural non-primary key. Let's assume that in CaveatEmptor, and as shown in figure 9.4, you need to handle a legacy natural key column called `CUSTOMERNR` on the `USERS` table:

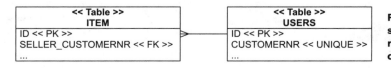

Figure 9.4 The item's seller foreign key references a non-primary column in USERS

```
PATH:  /model/src/main/java/org/jpwh/model/complexschemas/naturalforeignkey/
       User.java
```

```java
@Entity
@Table(name = "USERS")
public class User implements Serializable {

    @Id
    @GeneratedValue(generator = Constants.ID_GENERATOR)
    protected Long id;

    @NotNull
    @Column(unique = true)
    protected String customerNr;

    // ...
}
```

So far, this is nothing special; you've seen such a simple unique property mapping before. The legacy aspect is the SELLER_CUSTOMERNR column in the ITEM table, with a foreign key constraint referencing the user's CUSTOMERNR instead of the user's ID:

```
PATH:  /model/src/main/java/org/jpwh/model/complexschemas/naturalforeignkey/
       Item.java
```

```java
@Entity
public class Item {

    @NotNull
    @ManyToOne
    @JoinColumn(
        name = "SELLER_CUSTOMERNR",
        referencedColumnName = "CUSTOMERNR"
    )
    protected User seller;

    // ...
}
```

You specify the referencedColumnName attribute of @JoinColumn to declare this relationship. Hibernate now knows that the referenced target column is a natural key, and not the primary key, and manages the foreign key relationship accordingly.

If the target natural key is a composite key, use @JoinColumns instead as in the previous section. Fortunately, it's often straightforward to clean up such a schema by refactoring foreign keys to reference primary keys—if you can make changes to the database that don't disturb other applications sharing the data.

This completes our discussion of natural, composite, and foreign key–related problems you may have to deal with when you try to map a legacy schema. Let's move on to another interesting special strategy: mapping basic or embedded properties of an entity to a secondary table.

9.3   *Mapping properties to secondary tables*

We've already shown the @SecondaryTable annotation in an inheritance mapping in section 6.5. It helped to break out properties of a particular subclass into a separate table. This generic functionality has more uses—but be aware that a properly designed system should have, simplified, more classes than tables.

Suppose that in a legacy schema, you aren't keeping a user's billing address information with the other user details in the USERS main entity table, but in a separate table. Figure 9.5 shows this schema. The user's home address is stored in the columns STREET, ZIPCODE, and CITY of the USERS table. The user's billing address is stored in the BILLING_ADDRESS table, which has the primary key column USER_ID, which is also a foreign key constraint referencing the ID primary key of the USERS table.

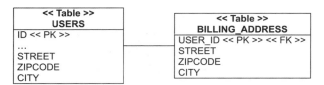

Figure 9.5   Breaking out the billing address data into a secondary table

To map this schema, declare the secondary table for the User entity and then how Hibernate should join it with @SecondaryTable:

> PATH: /model/src/main/java/org/jpwh/model/complexschemas/secondarytable/
> User.java

```
@Entity
@Table(name = "USERS")
@SecondaryTable(
    name = "BILLING_ADDRESS",
    pkJoinColumns = @PrimaryKeyJoinColumn(name = "USER_ID")
)
public class User {

    protected Address homeAddress;

    @AttributeOverrides({
        @AttributeOverride(name = "street",
            column = @Column(table = "BILLING_ADDRESS",
                             nullable = false)),
        @AttributeOverride(name = "zipcode",
            column = @Column(table = "BILLING_ADDRESS",
                             length = 5,
                             nullable = false)),
        @AttributeOverride(name = "city",
            column = @Column(table = "BILLING_ADDRESS",
                             nullable = false))
    })
    protected Address billingAddress;

    // ...
}
```

The `User` class has two properties of embedded type: `homeAddress` and `billing-Address`. The first is a regular embedded mapping, and the `Address` class is `@Embeddable`.

Just as in section 5.2.3, you can use the `@AttributeOverrides` annotation to override the mapping of embedded properties. Then, `@Column` maps the individual properties to the `BILLING_ADDRESS` table, with its `table` option. Remember that an `@AttributeOverride` replaces all mapping information for a property: any annotations on the `Address` fields are ignored if you override. Therefore, you have to specify nullability and length again in the `@Column` override.

We've shown you a secondary table mapping example with an embeddable property. Of course, you could also break out simple basic properties like the `username` string in a secondary table. Keep in mind that reading and maintaining these mappings can be a problem, though; you should only map legacy unchangeable schemas with secondary tables.

9.4 Summary

- Focus on the database schema.
- You can add additional integrity rules to a Hibernate-generated database schema. You now know how to execute custom create, drop, and load SQL scripts.
- We discussed using SQL constraints: domain, columns, table, and database constraints.
- We also covered using custom SQL data types, as well as check, unique, and foreign key constraints.
- You saw some common issues you have to resolve when dealing with legacy schemas, and specifically keys.
- You learned about several types of mapping: natural primary keys, composite primary keys, foreign keys in composite primary keys, foreign keys to composite primary keys, and foreign keys referencing non-primary keys.
- You saw how to move properties of an entity to a secondary table.

Part 3

Transactional data processing

In part 3, you'll load and store data with Hibernate and Java Persistence. You'll introduce the programming interfaces, how to write transactional applications, and how Hibernate can load data from the database most efficiently.

Starting with chapter 10, you'll learn the most important strategies for interacting with entity instances in a JPA application. You'll see the life cycle of entity instances: how they become persistent, detached, and removed. This chapter is where you'll get to know the most important interface in JPA: the EntityManager. Next, chapter 11 defines database and system transaction essentials and how to control concurrent access with Hibernate and JPA. You'll also see nontransactional data access. In chapter 12, we'll go through lazy and eager loading, fetch plans, strategies, and profiles, and wrap up with optimizing SQL execution. Finally, chapter 13 covers cascading state transitions, listening to and intercepting events, auditing and versioning with Hibernate Envers, and filtering data dynamically.

After reading this part, you'll know how to work with Hibernate and Java Persistence programming interfaces and how to load, modify, and store objects efficiently. You'll understand how transactions work and why conversational processing can open up new approaches for application design. You'll be ready to optimize any object-modification scenario and apply the best fetching and caching strategy to increase performance and scalability.

Managing data

10

You now understand how Hibernate and ORM solve the static aspects of the object/relational mismatch. With what you know so far, you can create a mapping between Java classes and an SQL schema, solving the structural mismatch problem. For a reminder of the problems you're solving, see section 1.2.

An efficient application solution requires something more: you must investigate strategies for runtime data management. These strategies are crucial to the performance and correct behavior of your applications.

In this chapter, we discuss the life cycle of entity instances—how an instance becomes persistent, and how it stops being considered persistent—and the method calls and management operations that trigger these transitions. The JPA Entity-Manager is your primary interface for accessing data.

Before we look at the API, let's start with entity instances, their life cycle, and the events that trigger a change of state. Although some of the material may be formal, a solid understanding of the persistence life cycle is essential.

> **Major new features in JPA 2**
> - You can get a vendor-specific variation of the persistence manager API with `EntityManager#unwrap()`: for example, the `org.hibernate.Session` API. Use `EntityManagerFactory#unwrap()` to obtain the `org.hibernate.SessionFactory`.
> - The new `detach()` operation provides fine-grained management of the persistence context, evicting individual entity instances.
> - From an existing `EntityManager`, you can obtain the `EntityManagerFactory` used to create the persistence context with `getEntityManagerFactory()`.
> - The new static `Persistence(Unit)Util` helper methods determine whether an entity instance (or one of its properties) was fully loaded or is an uninitialized reference (Hibernate proxy or unloaded collection wrapper.)

10.1 *The persistence life cycle*

Because JPA is a transparent persistence mechanism—classes are unaware of their own persistence capability—it's possible to write application logic that's unaware whether the data it operates on represents persistent state or temporary state that exists only in memory. The application shouldn't necessarily need to care that an instance is persistent when invoking its methods. You can, for example, invoke the `Item#calculateTotalPrice()` business method without having to consider persistence at all (for example, in a unit test).

Any application with persistent state must interact with the persistence service whenever it needs to propagate state held in memory to the database (or vice versa). In other words, you have to call the Java Persistence interfaces to store and load data.

When interacting with the persistence mechanism that way, the application must concern itself with the state and life cycle of an entity instance with respect to persistence. We refer to this as the *persistence life cycle*: the states an entity instance goes through during its life. We also use the term *unit of work*: a set of (possibly) state-changing operations considered one (usually atomic) group. Another piece of the puzzle is the *persistence context* provided by the persistence service. Think of the persistence context as a service that remembers all the modifications and state changes you made to data in a particular unit of work (this is somewhat simplified, but it's a good starting point).

We now dissect all these terms: entity states, persistence contexts, and managed scope. You're probably more accustomed to thinking about what SQL statements you have to manage to get stuff in and out of the database; but one of the key factors of your success with Java Persistence is your understanding of *state management*, so stick with us through this section.

10.1.1 *Entity instance states*

Different ORM solutions use different terminology and define different states and state transitions for the persistence life cycle. Moreover, the states used internally may be different from those exposed to the client application. JPA defines four states, hiding the complexity of Hibernate's internal implementation from the client code. Figure 10.1 shows these states and their transitions.

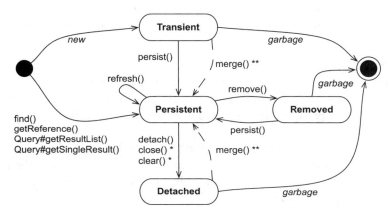

* Affects all instances in the persistence context
** Merging returns a persistent instance, original doesn't change state

Figure 10.1 Entity instance states and their transitions

The state chart also includes the method calls to the `EntityManager` (and `Query`) API that trigger transitions. We discuss this chart in this chapter; refer to it whenever you need an overview. Let's explore the states and transitions in more detail.

TRANSIENT STATE

Instances created with the `new` Java operator are *transient*, which means their state is lost and garbage-collected as soon as they're no longer referenced. For example, `new Item()` creates a transient instance of the `Item` class, just like `new Long()` and `new BigDecimal()`. Hibernate doesn't provide any rollback functionality for transient instances; if you modify the price of a transient `Item`, you can't automatically undo the change.

For an entity instance to transition from transient to persistent state, to become managed, requires either a call to the `EntityManager#persist()` method or the creation of a reference from an already-persistent instance and enabled cascading of state for that mapped association.

PERSISTENT STATE

A *persistent* entity instance has a representation in the database. It's stored in the database—or it will be stored when the unit of work completes. It's an instance with a database identity, as defined in section 4.2; its database identifier is set to the primary key value of the database representation.

The application may have created instances and then made them persistent by calling `EntityManager#persist()`. There may be instances that became persistent when the application created a reference to the object from another persistent instance that the JPA provider already manages. A persistent entity instance may be an instance retrieved from the database by execution of a query, by an identifier lookup, or by navigating the object graph starting from another persistent instance.

Persistent instances are always associated with a persistence context. You see more about this in a moment.

REMOVED STATE

You can delete a persistent entity instance from the database in several ways: For example, you can remove it with `EntityManager#remove()`. It may also become available for deletion if you remove a reference to it from a mapped collection with *orphan removal* enabled.

An entity instance is then in the *removed state:* the provider will delete it at the end of a unit of work. You should discard any references you may hold to it in the application after you finish working with it—for example, after you've rendered the removal-confirmation screen your users see.

DETACHED STATE

To understand *detached* entity instances, consider loading an instance. You call `EntityManager#find()` to retrieve an entity instance by its (known) identifier. Then you end your unit of work and close the persistence context. The application still has a *handle*—a reference to the instance you loaded. It's now in the detached state, and the data is becoming stale. You could discard the reference and let the garbage collector reclaim the memory. Or, you could continue working with the data in the detached state and later call the `merge()` method to save your modifications in a new unit of work. We'll discuss detachment and merging again later in this chapter, in a dedicated section.

You should now have a basic understanding of entity instance states and their transitions. Our next topic is the persistence context: an essential service of any Java Persistence provider.

10.1.2 *The persistence context*

In a Java Persistence application, an `EntityManager` has a persistence context. You create a persistence context when you call `EntityManagerFactory#createEntity-Manager()`. The context is closed when you call `EntityManager#close()`. In JPA terminology, this is an *application-managed* persistence context; your application defines the scope of the persistence context, demarcating the unit of work.

The persistence context monitors and manages all entities in persistent state. The persistence context is the centerpiece of much of the functionality of a JPA provider.

The persistence context allows the persistence engine to perform *automatic dirty checking*, detecting which entity instances the application modified. The provider then synchronizes with the database the state of instances monitored by a persistence context, either automatically or on demand. Typically, when a unit of work completes, the provider propagates state held in memory to the database through the execution of SQL `INSERT`, `UPDATE`, and `DELETE` statements (all part of the Data Modification Language [DML]). This *flushing* procedure may also occur at other times. For example, Hibernate may synchronize with the database before execution of a query. This ensures that queries are aware of changes made earlier during the unit of work.

The persistence context acts as a *first-level cache*; it remembers all entity instances you've handled in a particular unit of work. For example, if you ask Hibernate to load an entity instance using a primary key value (a lookup by identifier), Hibernate can first check the current unit of work in the persistence context. If Hibernate finds the entity instance in the persistence context, no database hit occurs—this is a repeatable read for an application. Consecutive `em.find(Item.class, ITEM_ID)` calls with the same persistence context will yield the same result.

This cache also affects results of arbitrary queries, executed for example with the `javax.persistence.Query` API. Hibernate reads the SQL result set of a query and transforms it into entity instances. This process first tries to resolve every entity instance in the persistence context by identifier lookup. Only if an instance with the same identifier value can't be found in the current persistence context does Hibernate read the rest of the data from the result-set row. Hibernate ignores any potentially newer data in the result set, due to read-committed transaction isolation at the database level, if the entity instance is already present in the persistence context.

The persistence context cache is always on—it can't be turned off. It ensures the following:

- The persistence layer isn't vulnerable to stack overflows in the case of circular references in an object graph.
- There can never be conflicting representations of the same database row at the end of a unit of work. The provider can safely write all changes made to an entity instance to the database.
- Likewise, changes made in a particular persistence context are always immediately visible to all other code executed inside that unit of work and its persistence context. JPA guarantees repeatable entity-instance reads.

The persistence context provides a *guaranteed scope of object identity*; in the scope of a single persistence context, only one instance represents a particular database row. Consider the comparison of references `entityA == entityB`. This is true only if both are references to the same Java instance on the heap. Now, consider the comparison `entityA.getId().equals(entityB.getId())`. This is true if both have the same database identifier value. Within one persistence context, Hibernate guarantees that both comparisons will yield the same result. This solves one of the fundamental O/R mismatch problems we introduced in section 1.2.3.

> **Would process-scoped identity be better?**
>
> For a typical web or enterprise application, persistence context-scoped identity is preferred. Process-scoped identity, where only one in-memory instance represents the row in the entire process (JVM), would offer some potential advantages in terms of cache utilization. In a pervasively multithreaded application, though, the cost of always synchronizing shared access to persistent instances in a global identity map is too high a price to pay. It's simpler and more scalable to have each thread work with a distinct copy of the data in each persistence context.

The life cycle of entity instances and the services provided by the persistence context can be difficult to understand at first. Let's look at some code examples of dirty checking, caching, and how the guaranteed identity scope works in practice. To do this, you work with the persistence manager API.

10.2 The EntityManager interface

Any transparent persistence tool includes a persistence manager API. This persistence manager usually provides services for basic CRUD (create, read, update, delete) operations, query execution, and controlling the persistence context. In Java Persistence applications, the main interface you interact with is the `EntityManager`, to create units of work.

10.2.1 The canonical unit of work

In Java SE and some EE architectures (if you only have plain servlets, for example), you get an `EntityManager` by calling `EntityManagerFactory#createEntity-Manager()`. Your application code shares the `EntityManagerFactory`, representing one persistence unit, or one logical database. Most applications have only one shared `EntityManagerFactory`.

You use the `EntityManager` for a single unit of work in a single thread, and it's inexpensive to create. The following listing shows the canonical, typical form of a unit of work.

Listing 10.1 A typical unit of work

PATH: /examples/src/test/java/org/jpwh/test/simple/SimpleTransitions.java

```
EntityManager em = null;
UserTransaction tx = TM.getUserTransaction();
try {
    tx.begin();
    em = JPA.createEntityManager();          <───────  Application-managed
```

```
    // ...

    tx.commit();                              <————  Synchronizes/flushes persistence context
} catch (Exception ex) {
    // Transaction rollback, exception handling
    // ...
} finally {
    if (em != null && em.isOpen())
        em.close();                           <————  You create it, you close it!
}
```

(The TM class is a convenience class bundled with the example code of this book. Here it simplifies the lookup of the standard UserTransaction API in JNDI. The JPA class provides convenient access to the shared EntityManagerFactory.)

Everything between tx.begin() and tx.commit() occurs in one transaction. For now, keep in mind that all database operations in transaction scope, such as the SQL statements executed by Hibernate, completely either succeed or fail. Don't worry too much about the transaction code for now; you'll read more about concurrency control in the next chapter. We'll look at the same example again with a focus on the transaction and exception-handling code. Don't write empty catch clauses in your code, though—you'll have to roll back the transaction and handle exceptions.

Creating an EntityManager starts its persistence context. Hibernate won't access the database until necessary; the EntityManager doesn't obtain a JDBC Connection from the pool until SQL statements have to be executed. You can create and close an EntityManager without hitting the database. Hibernate executes SQL statements when you look up or query data and when it flushes changes detected by the persistence context to the database. Hibernate joins the in-progress system transaction when an EntityManager is created and waits for the transaction to commit. When Hibernate is notified (by the JTA engine) of the commit, it performs dirty checking of the persistence context and synchronizes with the database. You can also force dirty checking synchronization manually by calling EntityManager#flush() at any time during a transaction.

You decide the scope of the persistence context by choosing when to close() the EntityManager. You have to close the persistence context at some point, so always place the close() call in a finally block.

How long should the persistence context be open? Let's assume for the following examples that you're writing a server, and each client request will be processed with one persistence context and system transaction in a multithreaded environment. If you're familiar with servlets, imagine the code in listing 10.1 embedded in a servlet's service() method. Within this unit of work, you access the EntityManager to load and store data.

10.2.2 *Making data persistent*

Let's create a new instance of an entity and bring it from transient into persistent state:

> PATH: /examples/src/test/java/org/jpwh/test/simple/SimpleTransitions.java

```
Item item = new Item();
item.setName("Some Item");                    ◁——————  Item#name is NOT NULL.

em.persist(item);

Long ITEM_ID = item.getId();                  ◁——————  Has been assigned
```

You can see the same unit of work and how the `Item` instances changes state in figure 10.2.

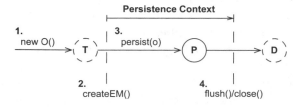

Figure 10.2 **Making an instance persistent in a unit of work**

A new transient `Item` is instantiated as usual. Of course, you may also instantiate it before creating the `EntityManager`. A call to `persist()` makes the transient instance of `Item` persistent. It's now managed by and associated with the current persistence context.

To store the `Item` instance in the database, Hibernate has to execute an SQL `INSERT` statement. When the transaction of this unit of work commits, Hibernate flushes the persistence context, and the `INSERT` occurs at that time. Hibernate may even batch the `INSERT` at the JDBC level with other statements. When you call `persist()`, only the identifier value of the `Item` is assigned. Alternatively, if your identifier generator isn't *pre-insert*, the `INSERT` statement will be executed immediately when `persist()` is called. You may want to review section 4.2.5.

Detecting entity state using the identifier

Sometimes you need to know whether an entity instance is transient, persistent, or detached. An entity instance is in persistent state if `EntityManager#contains(e)` returns `true`. It's in transient state if `PersistenceUnitUtil#getIdentifier(e)` returns `null`. It's in detached state if it's not persistent, and `Persistence-UnitUtil#getIdentifier(e)` returns the value of the entity's identifier property. You can get to the `PersistenceUnitUtil` from the `EntityManagerFactory`.

There are two issues to look out for. First, be aware that the identifier value may not be assigned and available until the persistence context is flushed. Second, Hibernate (unlike some other JPA providers) never returns `null` from `Persistence-UnitUtil#getIdentifier()` if your identifier property is a primitive (a `long` and not a `Long`).

It's better (but not required) to fully initialize the Item instance before managing it with a persistence context. The SQL INSERT statement contains the values that were held by the instance at the point when persist() was called. If you don't set the name of the Item before making it persistent, a NOT NULL constraint may be violated. You can modify the Item after calling persist(), and your changes will be propagated to the database with an additional SQL UPDATE statement.

If one of the INSERT or UPDATE statements made when flushing fails, Hibernate causes a rollback of changes made to persistent instances in this transaction at the database level. But Hibernate doesn't roll back in-memory changes to persistent instances. If you change the Item#name after persist(), a commit failure won't roll back to the old name. This is reasonable because a failure of a transaction is normally non-recoverable, and you have to discard the failed persistence context and Entity-Manager immediately. We'll discuss exception handling in the next chapter.

Next, you load and modify the stored data.

10.2.3 *Retrieving and modifying persistent data*

You can retrieve persistent instances from the database with the EntityManager. For the next example, we assume you've kept the identifier value of the Item stored in the previous section somewhere and are now looking up the same instance in a new unit of work by identifier:

> **PATH: /examples/src/test/java/org/jpwh/test/simple/SimpleTransitions.java**

```
Item item = em.find(Item.class, ITEM_ID);        Hits database if not already in
                                                  persistence context
if (item != null)
    item.setName("New Name");                     Modify
```

Figure 10.3 shows this transition graphically.

You don't need to cast the returned value of the find() operation; it's a generic method, and its return type is set as a side effect of the first parameter. The retrieved entity instance is in persistent state, and you can now modify it inside the unit of work.

If no persistent instance with the given identifier value can be found, find() returns null. The find() operation always hits the database if there was no hit for the given entity type and identifier in the persistence context cache. The entity instance is always initialized during loading. You can expect to have all of its values available later in detached state: for example, when rendering a screen after you close the persistence context. (Hibernate may not hit the database if its optional second-level cache is enabled; we'll discuss this shared cache in section 20.2.)

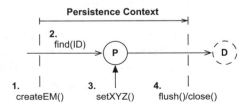

Figure 10.3 Making an instance persistent in a unit of work

You can modify the Item instance, and the persistence context will detect these changes and record them in the database automatically. When Hibernate flushes the persistence context during commit, it executes the necessary SQL DML statements to synchronize the changes with the database. Hibernate propagates state changes to the database as late as possible, toward the end of the transaction. DML statements usually create locks in the database that are held until the transaction completes, so Hibernate keeps the lock duration in the database as short as possible.

Hibernate writes the new Item#name to the database with an SQL UPDATE. By default, Hibernate includes all columns of the mapped ITEM table in the SQL UPDATE statement, updating unchanged columns to their old values. Hence, Hibernate can generate these basic SQL statements at startup, not at runtime. If you want to include only modified (or non-nullable for INSERT) columns in SQL statements, you can enable dynamic SQL generation as discussed in section 4.3.2.

Hibernate detects the changed name by comparing the Item with a snapshot copy it took before, when the Item was loaded from the database. If your Item is different from the snapshot, an UPDATE is necessary. This snapshot in the persistence context consumes memory. Dirty checking with snapshots can also be time consuming, because Hibernate has to compare all instances in the persistence context with their snapshot during flushing.

You may want to customize how Hibernate detects dirty state, using an extension point. Set the property hibernate.entity_dirtiness_strategy in your persistence.xml configuration file to a class name that implements org.hibernate.CustomEntityDirtinessStrategy. See the Javadoc of this interface for more information. org.hibernate.Interceptor is another extension point used to customize dirty checking, by implementing its findDirty() method. You can find an example interceptor in section 13.2.2.

We mentioned earlier that the persistence context enables repeatable reads of entity instances and provides an object-identity guarantee:

PATH: /examples/src/test/java/org/jpwh/test/simple/SimpleTransitions.java

```
Item itemA = em.find(Item.class, ITEM_ID);
Item itemB = em.find(Item.class, ITEM_ID);          <————    Repeatable read

assertTrue(itemA == itemB);
assertTrue(itemA.equals(itemB));
assertTrue(itemA.getId().equals(itemB.getId()));
```

The first find() operation hits the database and retrieves the Item instance with a SELECT statement. The second find() is resolved in the persistence context, and the same cached Item instance is returned.

Sometimes you need an entity instance but you don't want to hit the database.

10.2.4   *Getting a reference*

If you don't want to hit the database when loading an entity instance, because you aren't sure you need a fully initialized instance, you can tell the `EntityManager` to attempt the retrieval of a hollow placeholder—a proxy:

> **PATH: /examples/src/test/java/org/jpwh/test/simple/SimpleTransitions.java**

```
Item item = em.getReference(Item.class, ITEM_ID);            ❶ getReference()

PersistenceUnitUtil persistenceUtil =                                    Helper
    JPA.getEntityManagerFactory().getPersistenceUnitUtil();     ❷ method
assertFalse(persistenceUtil.isLoaded(item));

// assertEquals(item.getName(), "Some Item");                 ❸ Initializes proxy
// Hibernate.initialize(item);
                                                              ❹ Loads proxy data
tx.commit();
em.close();

assertEquals(item.getName(), "Some Item");                          item in
                                                              ❺ detached state
```

❶ If the persistence context already contains an `Item` with the given identifier, that `Item` instance is returned by `getReference()` without hitting the database. Furthermore, if *no* persistent instance with that identifier is currently managed, Hibernate produces a hollow placeholder: a proxy. This means `getReference()` won't access the database, and it doesn't return `null`, unlike `find()`.

❷ JPA offers `PersistenceUnitUtil` helper methods such as `isLoaded()` to detect whether you're working with an uninitialized proxy.

❸ As soon as you call any method such as `Item#getName()` on the proxy, a `SELECT` is executed to fully initialize the placeholder. The exception to this rule is a mapped database identifier getter method, such as `getId()`. A proxy may look like the real thing, but it's only a placeholder carrying the identifier value of the entity instance it represents. If the database record no longer exists when the proxy is initialized, an `EntityNotFoundException` is thrown. Note that the exception can be thrown when `Item#getName()` is called.

❹ Hibernate has a convenient static `initialize()` method that loads the proxy's data.

❺ After the persistence context is closed, `item` is in detached state. If you don't initialize the proxy while the persistence context is still open, you get a `LazyInitialization-Exception` if you access the proxy. You can't load data on demand once the persistence context is closed. The solution is simple: load the data before you close the persistence context.

We'll have much more to say about proxies, lazy loading, and on-demand fetching in chapter 12.

If you want to remove the state of an entity instance from the database, you have to make it transient.

10.2.5 *Making data transient*

To make an entity instance transient and delete its database representation, call the remove() method on the EntityManager:

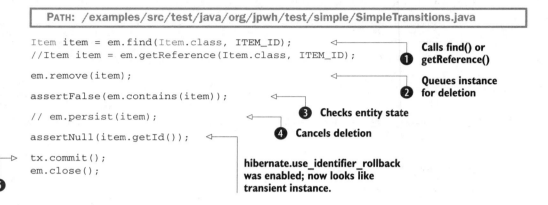

PATH: /examples/src/test/java/org/jpwh/test/simple/SimpleTransitions.java

```
Item item = em.find(Item.class, ITEM_ID);          ◁                          ❶ Calls find() or
//Item item = em.getReference(Item.class, ITEM_ID);                              getReference()

em.remove(item);                                   ◁                          ❷ Queues instance
                                                                                for deletion
assertFalse(em.contains(item));                    ◁
                                                        ❸ Checks entity state
// em.persist(item);                               ◁
                                                        ❹ Cancels deletion
assertNull(item.getId());                     ◁
                                                       hibernate.use_identifier_rollback
tx.commit();                                           was enabled; now looks like
em.close();                                            transient instance.
```

Commits transaction commits ❺

❶ If you call find(), Hibernate executes a SELECT to load the Item. If you call get-Reference(), Hibernate attempts to avoid the SELECT and returns a proxy.

❷ Calling remove() queues the entity instance for deletion when the unit of work completes; it's now in *removed* state. If remove() is called on a proxy, Hibernate executes a SELECT to load the data. An entity instance must be fully initialized during life cycle transitions. You may have life cycle callback methods or an entity listener enabled (see section 13.2), and the instance must pass through these interceptors to complete its full life cycle.

❸ An entity in removed state is no longer in persistent state. You can check this with the contains() operation.

❹ You can make the removed instance persistent again, cancelling the deletion.

❺ When the transaction commits, Hibernate synchronizes the state transitions with the database and executes the SQL DELETE. The JVM garbage collector detects that the item is no longer referenced by anyone and finally deletes the last trace of the data.

Figure 10.4 shows the same process.

By default, Hibernate won't alter the identifier value of a removed entity instance. This means the item.getId() method still returns the now outdated identifier value. Sometimes it's useful to work with the "deleted" data further: for example, you might want to save the removed Item again if your user decides to undo. As shown in the example, you can call persist() on a removed instance to cancel the deletion before the persistence context is flushed. Alternatively, if you

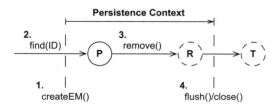

Figure 10.4 Removing an instance in a unit of work

set the property `hibernate.use_ identifier_ rollback` to `true` in persistence.xml, Hibernate will reset the identifier value after removal of an entity instance. In the previous code example, the identifier value is reset to the default value of `null` (it's a `Long`). The `Item` is now the same as in transient state, and you can save it again in a new persistence context.

Java Persistence also offers bulk operations that translate into direct SQL `DELETE` statements without life cycle interceptors in the application. We'll discuss these operations in section 20.1.

Let's say you load an entity instance from the database and work with the data. For some reason, you know that another application or maybe another thread of your application has updated the underlying row in the database. Next, we'll see how to refresh the data held in memory.

10.2.6 *Refreshing data*

The following example demonstrates refreshing a persistent entity instance:

PATH: /examples/src/test/java/org/jpwh/test/simple/SimpleTransitions.java

```
Item item = em.find(Item.class, ITEM_ID);
item.setName("Some Name");

// Someone updates this row in the database

String oldName = item.getName();
em.refresh(item);
assertNotEquals(item.getName(), oldName);
```

After you load the entity instance, you realize (how isn't important) that someone else changed the data in the database. Calling `refresh()` causes Hibernate to execute a `SELECT` to read and marshal a whole result set, overwriting changes you already made to the persistent instance in application memory. If the database row no longer exists (someone deleted it), Hibernate throws an `EntityNotFoundException` on `refresh()`.

Most applications don't have to manually refresh in-memory state; concurrent modifications are typically resolved at transaction commit time. The best use case for refreshing is with an extended persistence context, which might span several request/response cycles and/or system transactions. While you wait for user input with an open persistence context, data gets stale, and selective refreshing may be required depending on the duration of the conversation and the dialogue between the user and the system. Refreshing can be useful to undo changes made in memory during a conversation, if the user cancels the dialogue. We'll have more to say about refreshing in a conversation in section 18.3.

Another infrequently used operation is replication of an entity instance.

10.2.7 *Replicating data*

Replication is useful, for example, when you need to retrieve data from one database and store it in another. Replication takes detached instances loaded in one persistence context and makes them persistent in another persistence context. You usually open these contexts from two different `EntityManagerFactory` configurations, enabling two logical databases. You have to map the entity in both configurations.

The `replicate()` operation is only available on the Hibernate `Session` API. Here is an example that loads an `Item` instance from one database and copies it into another:

> **PATH:** /examples/src/test/java/org/jpwh/test/simple/SimpleTransitions.java

```
tx.begin();

EntityManager emA = getDatabaseA().createEntityManager();
Item item = emA.find(Item.class, ITEM_ID);

EntityManager emB = getDatabaseB().createEntityManager();
emB.unwrap(Session.class)
    .replicate(item, org.hibernate.ReplicationMode.LATEST_VERSION);

tx.commit();
emA.close();
emB.close();
```

Connections to both databases can participate in the same system transaction. `ReplicationMode` controls the details of the replication procedure:

- `IGNORE`—Ignores the instance when there is an existing database row with the same identifier in the database.
- `OVERWRITE`—Overwrites any existing database row with the same identifier in the database.
- `EXCEPTION`—Throws an exception if there is an existing database row with the same identifier in the target database.
- `LATEST_VERSION`—Overwrites the row in the database if its version is older than the version of the given entity instance, or ignores the instance otherwise. Requires enabled optimistic concurrency control with entity versioning (see section 11.2.2).

You may need replication when you reconcile data entered into different databases. An example case is a product upgrade: if the new version of your application requires a new database (schema), you may want to migrate and replicate the existing data once.

The persistence context does many things for you: automatic dirty checking, guaranteed scope of object identity, and so on. It's equally important that you know some of the details of its management, and that you sometimes influence what goes on behind the scenes.

10.2.8 *Caching in the persistence context*

The persistence context is a cache of persistent instances. Every entity instance in persistent state is associated with the persistence context.

Many Hibernate users who ignore this simple fact run into an OutOfMemoryException. This is typically the case when you load thousands of entity instances in a unit of work but never intend to modify them. Hibernate still has to create a snapshot of each instance in the persistence context cache, which can lead to memory exhaustion. (Obviously, you should execute a bulk data operation if you modify thousands of rows—we'll get back to this kind of unit of work in section 20.1.)

The persistence context cache never shrinks automatically. Keep the size of your persistence context to the necessary minimum. Often, many persistent instances in your context are there by accident—for example, because you needed only a few items but queried for many. Extremely large graphs can have a serious performance impact and require significant memory for state snapshots. Check that your queries return only data you need, and consider the following ways to control Hibernate's caching behavior.

You can call EntityManager#detach(i) to evict a persistent instance manually from the persistence context. You can call EntityManager#clear() to detach all persistent entity instances, leaving you with an empty persistence context.

The native Session API has some extra operations you might find useful. You can set the entire persistence context to read-only mode. This disables state snapshots and dirty checking, and Hibernate won't write modifications to the database:

> PATH: /examples/src/test/java/org/jpwh/test/fetching/ReadOnly.java

```
em.unwrap(Session.class).setDefaultReadOnly(true);

Item item = em.find(Item.class, ITEM_ID);
item.setName("New Name");

em.flush();        ⟵————        No UPDATE
```

You can disable dirty checking for a single entity instance:

> PATH: /examples/src/test/java/org/jpwh/test/fetching/ReadOnly.java

```
Item item = em.find(Item.class, ITEM_ID);

em.unwrap(Session.class).setReadOnly(item, true);

item.setName("New Name");

em.flush();        ⟵————        No UPDATE
```

A query with the org.hibernate.Query interface can return read-only results, which Hibernate doesn't check for modifications:

PATH: /examples/src/test/java/org/jpwh/test/fetching/ReadOnly.java

```
org.hibernate.Query query = em.unwrap(Session.class)
    .createQuery("select i from Item i");

query.setReadOnly(true).list();

List<Item> result = query.list();

for (Item item : result)
    item.setName("New Name");

em.flush();          ⟵————————  No UPDATE
```

Thanks to query hints, you can also disable dirty checking for instances obtained with the JPA standard javax.persistence.Query interface:

```
Query query = em.createQuery(queryString)
    .setHint(
        org.hibernate.annotations.QueryHints.READ_ONLY,
        true
    );
```

Be careful with read-only entity instances: you can still delete them, and modifications to collections are tricky! The Hibernate manual has a long list of special cases you need to read if you use these settings with mapped collections. You'll see more query examples in chapter 14.

So far, flushing and synchronization of the persistence context have occurred automatically, when the transaction commits. In some cases, you need more control over the synchronization process.

10.2.9 *Flushing the persistence context*

By default, Hibernate flushes the persistence context of an EntityManager and synchronizes changes with the database whenever the joined transaction is committed. All the previous code examples, except some in the last section, have used that strategy. JPA allows implementations to synchronize the persistence context at other times, if they wish.

Hibernate, as a JPA implementation, synchronizes at the following times:

- When a joined JTA system transaction is committed
- Before a query is executed—we don't mean lookup with find() but a query with javax.persistence.Query or the similar Hibernate API
- When the application calls flush() explicitly

You can control this behavior with the FlushModeType setting of an EntityManager:

> **PATH: /examples/src/test/java/org/jpwh/test/simple/SimpleTransitions.java**

```
tx.begin();
EntityManager em = JPA.createEntityManager();          ❶ Loads Item instance

Item item = em.find(Item.class, ITEM_ID);       ⤶
item.setName("New Name");                        ⤶─❷ Changes instance name

em.setFlushMode(FlushModeType.COMMIT);       ⤶      Disables flushing before queries

assertEquals(
    em.createQuery("select i.name from Item i where i.id = :id")    ⤶
        .setParameter("id", ITEM_ID).getSingleResult(),
    "Original Name"
);                                                    Gets instance name ❸

tx.commit();                        ⤶      Flush!
em.close();
```

Here, you load an Item instance ❶ and change its name ❷. Then you query the database, retrieving the item's name ❸. Usually Hibernate recognizes that data has changed in memory and synchronizes these modifications with the database before the query. This is the behavior of `FlushModeType.AUTO`, the default if you join the Entity-Manager with a transaction. With `FlushModeType.COMMIT`, you're disabling flushing before queries, so you may see different data returned by the query than what you have in memory. The synchronization then occurs only when the transaction commits.

You can at any time, while a transaction is in progress, force dirty checking and synchronization with the database by calling `EntityManager#flush()`.

This concludes our discussion of the *transient*, *persistent*, and *removed* entity states, and the basic usage of the `EntityManager` API. Mastering these state transitions and API methods is essential; every JPA application is built with these operations.

Next, we look at the *detached* entity state. We already mentioned some issues you'll see when entity instances aren't associated with a persistence context anymore, such as disabled lazy initialization. Let's explore the detached state with some examples, so you know what to expect when you work with data outside of a persistence context.

10.3 *Working with detached state*

If a reference leaves the scope of guaranteed identity, we call it a *reference* to a *detached entity instance*. When the persistence context is closed, it no longer provides an identity-mapping service. You'll run into aliasing problems when you work with detached entity instances, so make sure you understand how to handle the identity of detached instances.

10.3.1 *The identity of detached instances*

If you look up data using the same database identifier value in the same persistence context, the result is two references to the same in-memory instance on the JVM heap. Consider the two units of work shown next.

Listing 10.2   Guaranteed scope of object identity in Java Persistence

PATH: /examples/src/test/java/org/jpwh/test/simple/SimpleTransitions.java

```
tx.begin();                                    ⇐ ❶ Creates persistent context
em = JPA.createEntityManager();                ⇐ ❷ Loads entity instances

Item a = em.find(Item.class, ITEM_ID);
Item b = em.find(Item.class, ITEM_ID);              ❸ a and b have same Java identity
assertTrue(a == b);                            ⇐
assertTrue(a.equals(b));                        ⇐ ❹ a and b are equal
assertEquals(a.getId(), b.getId());             ⇐
                                                    ❺ a and b have the same
                                                       database identity
      ⇢ tx.commit();
Commits  em.close();                            ⇐
transaction ❻                                        Closes persistence
                                               ❼ context
tx.begin();
em = JPA.createEntityManager();

Item c = em.find(Item.class, ITEM_ID);              ❽ a and c aren't identical
assertTrue(a != c);                             ⇐
assertFalse(a.equals(c));                       ⇐
assertEquals(a.getId(), c.getId());             ⇐  ❾ a and c aren't equal

tx.commit();
em.close();                                        ❿ Identity test still true
```

In the first unit of work at begin() ❶, you start by creating a persistence context ❷ and loading some entity instances. Because references a and b are obtained from the same persistence context, they have the same Java identity ❸. They're equal ❹ because by default equals() relies on Java identity comparison. They obviously have the same database identity ❺. They reference the same Item instance, in persistent state, managed by the persistence context for that unit of work. The first part of this example finishes by committing the transaction ❻ and closing the persistence context ❼.

References a and b are in detached state when the first persistence context is closed. You're dealing with instances that live outside of a guaranteed scope of object identity.

You can see that a and c, loaded in a different persistence context, aren't identical ❽. The test for equality with a.equals(c) is also false ❾. A test for database identity still returns true ❿.This behavior can lead to problems if you treat entity instances as equal in detached state. For example, consider the following extension of the code, after the second unit of work has ended:

```
em.close();

Set<Item> allItems = new HashSet<>();
allItems.add(a);
allItems.add(b);
allItems.add(c);                                    That seems wrong
assertEquals(allItems.size(), 2);              ⇐    and arbitrary.
```

This example adds all three references to a Set. All are references to detached instances. Now, if you check the size of the collection—the number of elements— what result do you expect?

A Set doesn't allow duplicate elements. Duplicates are detected by the Set; whenever you add a reference, the Item#equals() method is called automatically against all other elements already in the collection. If equals() returns true for any element already in the collection, the addition doesn't occur.

By default, all Java classes inherit the equals() method of java.lang.Object. This implementation uses a double-equals (==) comparison to check whether two references refer to the same in-memory instance on the Java heap.

You may guess that the number of elements in the collection is two. After all, a and b are references to the same in-memory instance; they have been loaded in the same persistence context. You obtained reference c from another persistence context; it refers to a different instance on the heap. You have three references to two instances, but you know this only because you've seen the code that loaded the data. In a real application, you may not know that a and b are loaded in a different context than c. Furthermore, you obviously expect that the collection has exactly one element, because a, b, and c represent the same database row, the same Item.

Whenever you work with instances in detached state and you test them for equality (usually in hash-based collections), you need to supply your own implementation of the equals() *and* hashCode() *methods for your mapped entity class.* This is an important issue: if you don't work with entity instances in detached state, no action is needed, and the default equals() implementation of java.lang.Object is fine. You rely on Hibernate's guaranteed scope of object identity within a persistence context. Even if you work with detached instances: if you never check if they're equal, you never put them in a Set or use them as keys in a Map, you don't have to worry. If all you do is render a detached Item on the screen, you aren't comparing it to anything.

Many developers new to JPA think they always have to provide a custom equality routine for all entity classes, but this isn't the case. In section 18.3, we'll show you an application design with an *extended* persistence context strategy. This strategy will also extend the scope of guaranteed object identity to span an entire conversation and several system transactions. Note that you still need the discipline not to compare detached instances obtained in two conversations!

Let's assume that you want to use detached instances and that you have to test them for equality with your own method.

10.3.2 *Implementing equality methods*

You can implement equals() and hashCode() methods several ways. Keep in mind that when you override equals(), you always need to also override hashCode() so the two methods are consistent. If two instances are equal, they must have the same hash value.

A seemingly clever approach is to implement equals() to compare just the database identifier property, which is often a surrogate primary key value. Basically, if two Item instances have the same identifier returned by getId(), they must be the same. If getId() returns null, it must be a transient Item that hasn't been saved.

Unfortunately, this solution has one huge problem: identifier values aren't assigned by Hibernate until an instance becomes persistent. If a transient instance were added to a Set before being saved, then when you save it, its hash value would change while it's contained by the Set. This is contrary to the contract of java.util.Set, breaking the collection. In particular, this problem makes cascading persistent state useless for mapped associations based on sets. We strongly discourage database identifier equality.

To get to the solution that we recommend, you need to understand the notion of a *business key*. A business key is a property, or some combination of properties, that is unique for each instance with the same database identity. Essentially, it's the natural key that you would use if you weren't using a surrogate primary key instead. Unlike a natural primary key, it isn't an absolute requirement that the business key never changes—as long as it changes rarely, that's enough.

We argue that essentially every entity class should have a business key, even if it includes all properties of the class (which would be appropriate for some immutable classes). If your user is looking at a list of items on screen, how do they differentiate between items A, B, and C? The same property, or combination of properties, is your business key. The business key is what the user thinks of as uniquely identifying a particular record, whereas the surrogate key is what the application and database systems rely on. The business key property or properties are most likely constrained UNIQUE in your database schema.

Let's write custom equality methods for the User entity class; this is easier than comparing Item instances. For the User class, username is a great candidate business key. It's always required, it's unique with a database constraint, and it changes rarely, if ever.

Listing 10.3   Custom implementation of User equality

```
@Entity
@Table(name = "USERS",
       uniqueConstraints =
       @UniqueConstraint(columnNames = "USERNAME"))
public class User {

    @Override
    public boolean equals(Object other) {
        if (this == other) return true;
        if (other == null) return false;
        if (!(other instanceof User)) return false;      ◁— Use instanceof.
        User that = (User) other;
        return
      this.getUsername().equals(that.getUsername());      ◁— Use getters.
    }

    @Override
    public int hashCode() {
        return getUsername().hashCode();
    }

    // ...
}
```

You may have noticed that the `equals()` method code always accesses the properties of the "other" reference via getter methods. This is extremely important, because the reference passed as `other` may be a Hibernate proxy, not the actual instance that holds the persistent state. You can't access the `username` field of a `User` proxy directly. To initialize the proxy to get the property value, you need to access it with a getter method. This is one point where Hibernate isn't *completely* transparent, but it's good practice anyway to use getter methods instead of direct instance variable access.

Check the type of the `other` reference with `instanceof`, not by comparing the values of `getClass()`. Again, the `other` reference may be a proxy, which is a runtime-generated subclass of `User`, so `this` and `other` may not be exactly the same type but a valid super/subtype. You can find more about proxies in section 12.1.1.

You can now safely compare `User` references in persistent state:

```
tx.begin();
em = JPA.createEntityManager();

User a = em.find(User.class, USER_ID);
User b = em.find(User.class, USER_ID);
assertTrue(a == b);
assertTrue(a.equals(b));
assertEquals(a.getId(), b.getId());

tx.commit();
em.close();
```

In addition, of course, you get correct behavior if you compare references to instances in persistent and detached state:

```
tx.begin();
em = JPA.createEntityManager();

User c = em.find(User.class, USER_ID);
assertFalse(a == c);              ◁—— Still false, of course
assertTrue(a.equals(c));          ◁——————————— Now true
assertEquals(a.getId(), c.getId());

tx.commit();
em.close();

Set<User> allUsers = new HashSet();
allUsers.add(a);
allUsers.add(b);
allUsers.add(c);
assertEquals(allUsers.size(), 1);           ◁—— Correct!
```

For some other entities, the business key may be more complex, consisting of a combination of properties. Here are some hints that should help you identify a business key in your domain model classes:

- Consider what attributes users of your application will refer to when they have to identify an object (in the real world). How do users tell the difference between one element and another if they're displayed on the screen? This is probably the business key you're looking for.

- Every immutable attribute is probably a good candidate for the business key. Mutable attributes may be good candidates, too, if they're updated rarely or if you can control the case when they're updated—for example, by ensuring the instances aren't in a Set at the time.
- Every attribute that has a UNIQUE database constraint is a good candidate for the business key. Remember that the precision of the business key has to be good enough to avoid overlaps.
- Any date or time-based attribute, such as the creation timestamp of the record, is usually a good component of a business key, but the accuracy of System .currentTimeMillis() depends on the virtual machine and operating system. Our recommended safety buffer is 50 milliseconds, which may not be accurate enough if the time-based property is the single attribute of a business key.
- You can use database identifiers as part of the business key. This seems to contradict our previous statements, but we aren't talking about the database identifier value of the given entity. You may be able to use the database identifier of an associated entity instance. For example, a candidate business key for the Bid class is the identifier of the Item it matches together with the bid amount. You may even have a unique constraint that represents this composite business key in the database schema. You can use the identifier value of the associated Item because it never changes during the life cycle of a Bid—the Bid constructor can require an already-persistent Item.

If you follow our advice, you shouldn't have much difficulty finding a good business key for all your business classes. If you encounter a difficult case, try to solve it without considering Hibernate. After all, it's purely an object-oriented problem. Notice that it's almost never correct to override equals() on a subclass and include another property in the comparison. It's a little tricky to satisfy the Object identity and equality requirements that equality be both symmetric and transitive in this case; and, more important, the business key may not correspond to any well-defined candidate natural key in the database (subclass properties may be mapped to a different table). For more information on customizing equality comparisons, see *Effective Java*, 2nd edition, by Joshua Bloch (Bloch, 2008), a mandatory book for all Java programmers.

The User class is now prepared for detached state; you can safely put instances loaded in different persistence contexts into a Set. Next, we'll look at some examples that involve detached state, and you see some of the benefits of this concept.

Sometimes you might want to detach an entity instance manually from the persistence context.

10.3.3   *Detaching entity instances*

You don't have to wait for the persistence context to close. You can evict entity instances manually:

> **PATH: /examples/src/test/java/org/jpwh/test/simple/SimpleTransitions.java**

```
User user = em.find(User.class, USER_ID);

em.detach(user);

assertFalse(em.contains(user));
```

This example also demonstrates the `EntityManager#contains()` operation, which returns true if the given instance is in managed persistent state in this persistence context.

You can now work with the `user` reference in detached state. Many applications only read and render the data after the persistence context is closed.

Modifying the loaded `user` after the persistence context is closed has no effect on its persistent representation in the database. JPA allows you to merge any changes back into the database in a new persistence context, though.

10.3.4 Merging entity instances

Let's assume you've retrieved a `User` instance in a previous persistence context, and now you want to modify it and save these modifications:

> **PATH: /examples/src/test/java/org/jpwh/test/simple/SimpleTransitions.java**

```
detachedUser.setUsername("johndoe");

tx.begin();
em = JPA.createEntityManager();

User mergedUser = em.merge(detachedUser);        ⟵  Discard detachedUser
                                                     reference after merging.
mergedUser.setUsername("doejohn");                   mergedUser is in
                                                     persistent state.

tx.commit();                        ⟵── UPDATE in database
em.close();
```

Consider the graphical representation of this procedure in figure 10.5. It's not as difficult as it seems.

The goal is record the new `username` of the detached `User`. First, when you call `merge()`, Hibernate checks whether a persistent instance in the persistence context has the same database identifier as the detached instance you're merging.

In this example, the persistence context is empty; nothing has been loaded from the database. Hibernate therefore loads an instance with this identifier from the data-

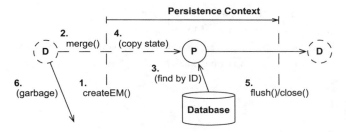

Figure 10.5 Making an instance persistent in a unit of work

base. Then, merge() copies the detached entity instance *onto* this loaded persistent instance. In other words, the new username you have set on the detached User is also set on the persistent merged User, which merge() returns to you.

Now discard the old reference to the stale and outdated detached state; the detachedUser no longer represents the current state. You can continue modifying the returned mergedUser; Hibernate will execute a single UPDATE when it flushes the persistence context during commit.

If there is no persistent instance with the same identifier in the persistence context, and a lookup by identifier in the database is negative, Hibernate instantiates a fresh User. Hibernate then copies your detached instance onto this fresh instance, which it inserts into the database when you synchronize the persistence context with the database.

If the instance you're giving to merge() is not detached but rather is transient (it doesn't have an identifier value), Hibernate instantiates a fresh User, copies the values of the transient User onto it, and then makes it persistent and returns it to you. In simpler terms, the merge() operation can handle detached *and* transient entity instances. Hibernate always returns the result to you as a persistent instance.

An application architecture based on detachment and merging may not call the persist() operation. You can merge new and detached entity instances to store data. The important difference is the returned current state and how you handle this switch of references in your application code. You have to discard the detachedUser and from now on reference the current mergedUser. Every other component in your application still holding on to detachedUser has to switch to mergedUser.

Can I reattach a detached instance?

The Hibernate Session API has a method for reattachment called saveOrUpdate(). It accepts either a transient or a detached instance and doesn't return anything. The given instance will be in persistent state after the operation, so you don't have to switch references. Hibernate will execute an INSERT if the given instance was transient or an UPDATE if it was detached. We recommend that you rely on merging instead, because it's standardized and therefore easier to integrate with other frameworks. In addition, instead of an UPDATE, merging may only trigger a SELECT if the detached data wasn't modified. If you're wondering what the saveOrUpdateCopy() method of the Session API does, it's the same as merge() on the EntityManager.

If you want to delete a detached instance, you have to merge it first. Then call remove() on the persistent instance returned by merge().

We'll look at detached state and merging again in chapter 18 and implement a more complex conversation between a user and the system using this strategy.

10.4 Summary

- We discussed the most important strategies and some optional ones for interacting with entity instances in a JPA application.
- You learned about the life cycle of entity instances and how they become persistent, detached, and removed.
- The most important interface in JPA is the EntityManager.
- In most applications, data isn't stored and loaded in isolation. Hibernate is typically integrated in a multiuser application, and the database is accessed concurrently in many threads.

Transactions and concurrency

In this chapter, we finally talk about transactions: how you create and control concurrent units of work in an application. A *unit of work* is an atomic group of operations. Transactions allow you to set unit of work boundaries and help you isolate one unit of work from another. In a multiuser application, you may also be processing these units of work concurrently.

To handle concurrency, we first focus on units of work at the lowest level: database and system transactions. You'll learn the APIs for transaction demarcation and how to define units of work in Java code. We'll talk about how to preserve isolation and control concurrent access with pessimistic and optimistic strategies.

Finally, we look at some special cases and JPA features, based on accessing the database without explicit transactions. Let's start with some background information.

> **Major new features in JPA 2**
> - There are new lock modes and exceptions for pessimistic locking.
> - You can set a lock mode, pessimistic or optimistic, on a `Query`.
> - You can set a lock mode when calling `EntityManager#find()`, `refresh()`, or `lock()`. A lock timeout hint for pessimistic lock modes is also standardized.
> - When the new `QueryTimeoutException` or `LockTimeoutException` is thrown, the transaction doesn't have to be rolled back.
> - The persistence context can now be in an *unsynchronized* mode with disabled automatic flushing. This allows you to queue modifications until you join a transaction and to decouple the `EntityManager` usage from transactions.

11.1 Transaction essentials

Application functionality requires that several things be done in one go. For example, when an auction finishes, the CaveatEmptor application must perform three different tasks:

1 Find the winning bid (highest amount) for the auction item.
2 Charge the seller of the item the cost of the auction.
3 Notify the seller and successful bidder.

What happens if you can't bill the auction costs because of a failure in the external credit-card system? The business requirements may state that either all listed actions must succeed or none must succeed. If so, you call these steps collectively a *transaction* or unit of work. If only a single step fails, the entire unit of work must fail.

11.1.1 ACID attributes

ACID stands for *atomicity, consistency, isolation, durability*. *Atomicity* is the notion that all operations in a transaction execute as an atomic unit. Furthermore, transactions allow multiple users to work concurrently with the same data without compromising the *consistency* of the data (consistent with database integrity rules). A particular transaction should not be visible to other concurrently running transactions; they should run in *isolation*. Changes made in a transaction should be *durable*, even if the system fails after the transaction has completed successfully.

In addition, you want *correctness* of a transaction. For example, the business rules dictate that the application charges the seller once, not twice. This is a reasonable assumption, but you may not be able to express it with database constraints. Hence, the correctness of a transaction is the responsibility of the application, whereas consistency is the responsibility of the database. Together, these transaction attributes define the *ACID* criteria.

11.1.2 *Database and system transactions*

We've also mentioned *system* and *database* transactions. Consider the last example again: during the unit of work ending an auction, we might mark the winning bid in a database system. Then, in the same unit of work, we talk to an external system to bill the seller's credit card. This is a transaction spanning several (sub)systems, with coordinated subordinate transactions on possibly several resources such as a database connection and an external billing processor.

Database transactions have to be short, because open transactions consume database resources and potentially prevent concurrent access due to exclusive locks on data. A single database transaction usually involves only a single batch of database operations.

To execute all of your database operations inside a system transaction, you have to set the boundaries of that unit of work. You must start the transaction and, at some point, commit the changes. If an error occurs (either while executing database operations or when committing the transaction), you have to roll back the changes to leave the data in a consistent state. This process defines a *transaction demarcation* and, depending on the technique you use, involves a certain level of manual intervention. In general, transaction boundaries that begin and end a transaction can be set either programmatically in application code or declaratively.

11.1.3 *Programmatic transactions with JTA*

In a Java SE environment, you call the JDBC API to mark transaction boundaries. You begin a transaction with setAutoCommit(false) on a JDBC Connection and end it by calling commit(). You may, at any time while the transaction is in progress, force an immediate rollback with rollback().

In an application that manipulates data in several systems, a particular unit of work involves access to more than one transactional resource. In this case, you can't achieve atomicity with JDBC alone. You need a transaction manager that can handle several resources in one system transaction. JTA standardizes system transaction management and distributed transactions so you won't have to worry much about the lower-level details. The main API in JTA is the UserTransaction interface with methods to begin() and commit() a system transaction.

> **Other transaction demarcation APIs**
>
> JTA provides a nice abstraction of the underlying resource's transaction system, with the added bonus of distributed system transactions. Many developers still believe you can only get JTA with components that run in a Java EE application server. Today, high-quality standalone JTA providers such as Bitronix (used for the example code of this book) and Atomikos are available and easy to install in any Java environment. Think of these solutions as JTA-enabled database connection pools.

You should use JTA whenever you can and avoid proprietary transaction APIs such as `org.hibernate.Transaction` or the very limited `javax.persistence` `.EntityTransaction`. These APIs were created at a time when JTA wasn't readily available outside of EJB runtime containers.

In section 10.2.1, we promised to look at transactions again with a focus on exception handling. Here is the code, this time complete with rollback and exception handling.

Listing 11.1 Typical unit of work with transaction boundaries

PATH: /examples/src/test/java/org/jpwh/test/simple/SimpleTransitions.java

```
EntityManager em = null;
UserTransaction tx = TM.getUserTransaction();
try {
    tx.begin();
    em = JPA.createEntityManager();          <───────  Application-managed

    // ...

    tx.commit();                    <───────  Synchronizes/flushes persistence context
} catch (Exception ex) {
    try {                                                    <─┐ Transaction
        if (tx.getStatus() == Status.STATUS_ACTIVE            │ rollback;
            || tx.getStatus() == Status.STATUS_MARKED_ROLLBACK) │ exception
            tx.rollback();                                     │ handling
    } catch (Exception rbEx) {
        System.err.println("Rollback of transaction failed, trace follows!");
        rbEx.printStackTrace(System.err);
    }
    throw new RuntimeException(ex);
} finally {
    if (em != null && em.isOpen())
        em.close();                <───────  You create it, you close it!
}
```

The most complicated bit of this code snippet seems to be the exception handling; we'll discuss this part in a moment. First, you have to understand how the transaction management and the `EntityManager` work together.

The `EntityManager` is lazy; we mentioned in the previous chapter that it doesn't consume any database connections until SQL statements have to be executed. The same is true for JTA: starting and committing an empty transaction is cheap when you haven't accessed any transactional resources. For example, you could execute this empty unit of work on a server, for each client request, without consuming any resources or holding any database locks.

When you create an `EntityManager`, it looks for an ongoing JTA system transaction within the current thread of execution. If the `EntityManager` finds an ongoing transaction, it *joins* the transaction by listening to transaction events. This means you should always call `UserTransaction#begin()` and `EntityManagerFactory#create-EntityManager()` on the same thread if you want them to be joined. By default, and as explained in chapter 10, Hibernate automatically flushes the persistence context when the transaction commits.

If the `EntityManager` can't find a started transaction in the same thread when it's created, it's in a special *unsynchronized* mode. In this mode, JPA won't automatically flush the persistence context. We talk more about this behavior later in this chapter; it's a convenient feature of JPA when you design more complex conversations.

FAQ: Is it faster to roll back read-only transactions?

If code in a transaction reads data but doesn't modify it, should you roll back the transaction instead of committing it? Would this be faster? Apparently, some developers found this to be faster in some special circumstances, and this belief has spread through the community. We tested this with the more popular database systems and found no difference. We also failed to discover any source of real numbers showing a performance difference. There is also no reason a database system should have a suboptimal cleanup implementation—why it shouldn't use the fastest transaction cleanup algorithm internally.

Always commit your transaction and roll back if the commit fails. Having said that, the SQL standard includes the statement SET TRANSACTION READ ONLY. We recommend that you first investigate whether your database supports this and see what the possible performance benefits are, if any.

The transaction manager will stop a transaction when it has been running for too long. Remember that you want to keep database transactions as short as possible in a busy OLTP system. The default timeout depends on the JTA provider—Bitronix, for example, defaults to 60 seconds. You can override this selectively, before you begin the transaction, with `UserTransaction#setTransactionTimeout()`.

We still need to discuss the exception handling of the previous code snippet.

11.1.4 *Handling exceptions*

If any `EntityManager` call or flushing the persistence context during a commit throws an exception, you must check the current state of the system transaction. When an exception occurs, Hibernate marks the transaction for rollback. This means the only possible outcome for this transaction is undoing all of its changes. Because you started the transaction, it's your job to check for `STATUS_MARKED_ROLLBACK`. The transaction might also still be `STATUS_ACTIVE`, if Hibernate wasn't able to mark it for rollback. In both cases, call `UserTransaction#rollback()` to abort any SQL statements that have been sent to the database within this unit of work.

All JPA operations, including flushing the persistence context, can throw a `RuntimeException`. But the methods `UserTransaction#begin()`, `commit()`, and even `rollback()` throw a checked `Exception`. The exception for rollback requires special treatment: you want to catch this exception and log it; otherwise, the original exception that led to the rollback is lost. Continue throwing the original exception after rollback. Typically, you have another layer of interceptors in your system that will finally deal with the exception, for example by rendering an error screen or contacting the operations team. An error during rollback is more difficult to handle properly; we suggest logging and escalation, because a failed rollback indicates a serious system problem.

Hibernate Feature

Hibernate throws typed exceptions, all subtypes of `RuntimeException` that help you identify errors:

- The most common, `HibernateException`, is a generic error. You have to either check the exception message or find out more about the cause by calling `get-Cause()` on the exception.
- A `JDBCException` is any exception thrown by Hibernate's internal JDBC layer. This kind of exception is always caused by a particular SQL statement, and you can get the offending statement with `getSQL()`. The internal exception thrown by the JDBC connection (the JDBC driver) is available with `getSQLException()` or `getCause()`, and the database- and vendor-specific error code is available with `getErrorCode()`.
- Hibernate includes subtypes of `JDBCException` and an internal converter that tries to translate the vendor-specific error code thrown by the database driver into something more meaningful. The built-in converter can produce `JDBC-ConnectionException`, `SQLGrammarException`, `LockAcquisitionException`, `DataException`, and `ConstraintViolationException` for the most important database dialects supported by Hibernate. You can either manipulate or enhance the dialect for your database or plug in a `SQLExceptionConverter-Factory` to customize this conversion.

Some developers get excited when they see how many fine-grained exception types Hibernate can throw. This can lead you down the wrong path. For example, you may be tempted to catch a `ConstraintViolationException` for validation purposes. If you forget to set the `Item#name` property, and its mapped column is `NOT NULL` in the database schema, Hibernate will throw this exception when you flush the persistence context. Why not catch it, display a (customized depending on the error code and text) failure message to application users, and let them correct the mistake? This strategy has two significant disadvantages.

First, throwing unchecked values against the database to see what sticks isn't the right strategy for a scalable application. You want to implement at least some data-integrity validation in the application layer. Second, exceptions are fatal for your current unit of work. But this isn't how application users will interpret a validation error: they expect to still be inside a unit of work. Coding around this mismatch is awkward and difficult. Our recommendation is that you use the fine-grained exception types to display better-looking (fatal) error messages, not for validation. For example, you could catch ConstraintViolationException separately and render a screen that says, "Application bug: someone forgot to validate data before sending it to the database. Please report it to the programmers." For other exceptions, you'd render a generic error screen.

Doing so helps you during development and also helps any customer-support engineer who has to decide quickly whether it's an application error (constraint violated, wrong SQL executed) or whether the database system is under load (locks couldn't be acquired). For validation, you have a unifying framework available with Bean Validation. From a single set of rules in annotations on entities, Hibernate can verify all domain and single-row constraints at the user interface layer and can automatically generate SQL DDL rules.

You now know what exceptions you should catch and when to expect them. One question is probably on your mind: what should you do *after* you've caught an exception and rolled back the system transaction? Exceptions thrown by Hibernate are fatal. This means you have to close the current persistence context. You aren't allowed to continue working with the EntityManager that threw an exception. Render an error screen and/or log the error, and then let the user restart the conversation with the system using a fresh transaction and persistence context.

As usual, this isn't the whole picture. Some standardized exceptions aren't fatal:

- javax.persistence.NoResultException—Thrown when a Query or Typed-Query is executed with getSingleResult() and no result was returned from the database. You can wrap the query call with exception-handling code and continue working with the persistence context. The current transaction won't be marked for rollback.

- javax.persistence.NonUniqueResultException—Thrown when a Query or TypedQuery is executed with getSingleResult() and several results were returned from the database. You can wrap the query call with exception handling code and continue working with the persistence context. Hibernate won't mark the current transaction for rollback.

- javax.persistence.QueryTimeoutException—Thrown when a Query or TypedQuery takes too long to execute. Doesn't mark the transaction for rollback. You may want to repeat the query, if appropriate.

- javax.persistence.LockTimeoutException—Thrown when a pessimistic lock couldn't be acquired. May occur during flushing or explicit locking (more on this topic later in this chapter). The transaction isn't marked for rollback, and you may want to repeat the operation. Keep in mind that endlessly hammering on a database system that is already struggling to keep up won't improve the situation.

Notably absent from this list is javax.persistence.EntityNotFoundException. It can be thrown by the EntityManager#getReference() and refresh() methods, as well as lock(), which you'll see later in this chapter. Hibernate may throw it when you try to access the reference/proxy of an entity instance and the database record is no longer available. It's a fatal exception: it marks the current transaction for rollback, and you have to close and discard the persistence context.

Programmatic transaction demarcation requires application code written against a transaction demarcation interface such as JTA's UserTransaction. Declarative transaction demarcation, on the other hand, doesn't require extra coding.

11.1.5 *Declarative transaction demarcation*

In a Java EE application, you can *declare* when you wish to work inside a transaction. It's then the responsibility of the runtime environment to handle this concern. Usually you set transaction boundaries with annotations on your managed components (EJBs, CDI beans, and so on).

You can use the older annotation @javax.ejb.TransactionAttribute to demarcate transaction boundaries declaratively on EJB components. You can find examples in section 18.2.1.

You can apply the newer and more general @javax.transaction.Transactional on any Java EE managed component. You can find an example in section 19.3.1.

All other examples in this chapter work in any Java SE environment, without a special runtime container. Hence, from now on, you'll only see programmatic transaction demarcation code until we focus on specific Java EE application examples.

Next, we focus on the most complex aspect of ACID properties: how you *isolate* concurrently running units of work from each other.

11.2 *Controlling concurrent access*

Databases (and other transactional systems) attempt to ensure transaction *isolation*, meaning that, from the point of view of each concurrent transaction, it appears that no other transactions are in progress. Traditionally, database systems have implemented isolation with locking. A transaction may place a lock on a particular item of data in the database, temporarily preventing read and/or write access to that item by other transactions. Some modern database engines implement transaction isolation with multiversion concurrency control (MVCC), which vendors generally consider more scalable. We'll discuss isolation assuming a locking model, but most of our observations are also applicable to MVCC.

How databases implement concurrency control is of the utmost importance in your Java Persistence application. Applications inherit the isolation guarantees provided by the database management system. For example, Hibernate never locks anything in memory. If you consider the many years of experience that database vendors have with implementing concurrency control, you'll see the advantage of this approach. Additionally, some features in Java Persistence, either because you explicitly use them or by design, can improve the isolation guarantee beyond what the database provides.

We discuss concurrency control in several steps. First, we explore the lowest layer: the transaction isolation guarantees provided by the database. After that, you'll see the Java Persistence features for pessimistic and optimistic concurrency control at the application level, and what other isolation guarantees Hibernate can provide.

11.2.1 *Understanding database-level concurrency*

If we're talking about isolation, you may assume that two things are either isolated or not; there is no grey area in the real world. When we talk about database transactions, complete isolation comes at a high price. You can't stop the world to access data exclusively in a multiuser OLTP system. Therefore, several isolation levels are available, which, naturally, weaken full isolation but increase performance and scalability of the system.

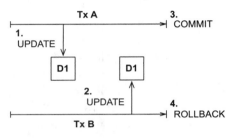

Figure 11.1 Lost update: two transactions update the same data without isolation.

TRANSACTION ISOLATION ISSUES

First, let's look at several phenomena that may occur when you weaken full transaction isolation. The ANSI SQL standard defines the standard transaction isolation levels in terms of which of these phenomena are permissible.

A *lost update* occurs if two transactions both update a data item and then the second transaction aborts, causing both changes to be lost. This occurs in systems that don't implement concurrency control, where concurrent transactions aren't isolated. This is shown in figure 11.1.

A *dirty read* occurs if a transaction reads changes made by another transaction that hasn't yet been committed. This is dangerous because the changes made by the other transaction may later be rolled back, and invalid data may be written by the first transaction; see figure 11.2.

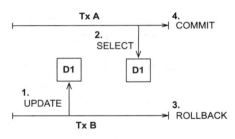

Figure 11.2 Dirty read: transaction A reads uncommitted data from transaction B.

An *unrepeatable read* occurs if a transaction reads a data item twice and reads different state each time. For example, another transaction may have written to the data item and committed between the two reads, as shown in figure 11.3.

A special case of an unrepeatable read is the *last commit wins* problem. Imagine that two concurrent transactions both read a data

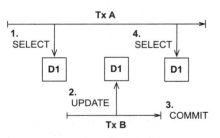

Figure 11.3 Unrepeatable read: transaction A executes two non-repeatable reads.

item, as shown in figure 11.4. One writes to it and commits, and then the second writes to it and commits. The changes made by the first writer are lost. This issue is especially frustrating for users: user A's changes are overwritten without warning, and B has potentially made a decision based on outdated information.

A *phantom read* is said to occur when a transaction executes a query twice, and the second result includes data that wasn't visible in the first result or less data because something was deleted. It need not necessarily be exactly the same query. Another transaction inserting or deleting data between the executions of the two queries causes this situation, as shown in figure 11.5.

Now that you understand all the bad things that can occur, we can define the transaction isolation levels and see what problems they prevent.

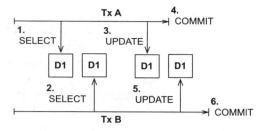

Figure 11.4 Last commit wins: transaction B overwrites changes made by A.

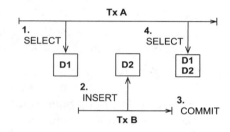

Figure 11.5 Phantom read: transaction A reads new data in the second SELECT.

ANSI ISOLATION LEVELS

The standard isolation levels are defined by the ANSI SQL standard, but they aren't specific to SQL databases. JTA defines exactly the same isolation levels, and you'll use these levels to declare your desired transaction isolation. With increased levels of isolation come higher cost and serious degradation of performance and scalability:

- *Read uncommitted isolation*—A system that permits dirty reads but not lost updates operates in read uncommitted isolation. One transaction may not write to a row if another uncommitted transaction has already written to it. Any transaction may read any row, however. A DBMS may implement this isolation level with exclusive write locks.
- *Read committed isolation*—A system that permits unrepeatable reads but not dirty reads implements read committed isolation. A DBMS may achieve this by using shared read locks and exclusive write locks. Reading transactions don't block other transactions from accessing a row, but an uncommitted writing transaction blocks all other transactions from accessing the row.
- *Repeatable read isolation*—A system operating in repeatable read isolation mode permits neither unrepeatable reads nor dirty reads. Phantom reads may occur. Reading transactions block writing transactions but not other reading transactions, and writing transactions block all other transactions.

- *Serializable isolation*—The strictest isolation, serializable, emulates serial execution, as if transactions were executed one after another, rather than concurrently. A DBMS may not implement serializable using only row-level locks. A DBMS must instead provide some other mechanism that prevents a newly inserted row from becoming visible to a transaction that has already executed a query that would return the row. A crude mechanism is exclusively locking the entire database table after a write, so no phantom reads can occur.

How exactly a DBMS implements its locking system varies significantly; each vendor has a different strategy. You should study the documentation of your DBMS to find out more about its locking system, how locks are escalated (from row-level, to pages, to entire tables, for example), and what impact each isolation level has on the performance and scalability of your system.

It's nice to know how all these technical terms are defined, but how does that help you choose an isolation level for your application?

CHOOSING AN ISOLATION LEVEL

Developers (ourselves included) are often unsure what transaction isolation level to use in a production application. Too high an isolation level harms the scalability of a highly concurrent application. Insufficient isolation may cause subtle, difficult-to-reproduce bugs in an application that you won't discover until the system is working under heavy load.

Note that we refer to *optimistic locking* (with versioning) in the following explanation, a concept explained later in this chapter. You may want to skip this section for now and come back to it later when it's time to pick an isolation level for your application. Choosing the correct isolation level is, after all, highly dependent on your particular scenario. Read the following discussion as recommendations, not dictums carved in stone.

Hibernate tries hard to be as transparent as possible regarding transactional semantics of the database. Nevertheless, persistence context caching and versioning affect these semantics. What is a sensible database isolation level to choose in a JPA application?

First, for almost all scenarios, eliminate the *read uncommitted* isolation level. It's extremely dangerous to use one transaction's uncommitted changes in a different transaction. The rollback or failure of one transaction will affect other concurrent transactions. Rollback of the first transaction could bring other transactions down with it, or perhaps even cause them to leave the database in an incorrect state (the seller of an auction item might be charged twice—consistent with database integrity rules but incorrect). It's possible that changes made by a transaction that ends up being rolled back could be committed anyway, because they could be read and then propagated by another transaction that is successful!

Second, most applications don't need *serializable* isolation. Phantom reads aren't usually problematic, and this isolation level tends to scale poorly. Few existing applications use serializable isolation in production, but rather rely on selectively applied pessimistic locks that effectively force a serialized execution of operations in certain situations.

Next, let's consider *repeatable read*. This level provides reproducibility for query result sets for the duration of a database transaction. This means you won't read committed updates from the database if you query it several times. But phantom reads are still possible: new rows might appear—rows you thought existed might disappear if another transaction committed such changes concurrently. Although you may sometimes want repeatable reads, you typically don't need them in every transaction.

The JPA specification assumes that *read committed* is the default isolation level. This means you have to deal with unrepeatable reads, phantom reads, and the last commit wins problem.

Let's assume you're enabling versioning of your domain model entities, something that Hibernate can do for you automatically. The combination of the (mandatory) persistence context cache and versioning already gives you most of the nice features of *repeatable read* isolation. The persistence context cache ensures that the state of the entity instances loaded by one transaction is isolated from changes made by other transactions. If you retrieve the same entity instance twice in a unit of work, the second lookup will be resolved within the persistence context cache and not hit the database. Hence, your read *is* repeatable, and you won't see conflicting committed data. (You still get phantom reads, though, which are typically much easier to deal with.) Additionally, versioning switches to *first commit wins*. Hence, for almost all multiuser JPA applications, *read committed* isolation for all database transactions is acceptable with enabled entity versioning.

Hibernate retains the isolation level of your database connection; it doesn't change the level. Most products default to *read committed* isolation. There are several ways you can change either the default transaction isolation level or the settings of the current transaction.

First, you can check whether your DBMS has a global transaction isolation level setting in its proprietary configuration. If your DBMS supports the standard SQL statement SET SESSION CHARACTERISTICS, you can execute it to set the transaction settings of all transactions started in this particular database *session* (which means a particular connection to the database, not a Hibernate Session). SQL also standardizes the SET TRANSACTION syntax, which sets the isolation level of the current transaction. Finally, the JDBC Connection API offers the setTransactionIsolation() method, which (according to its documentation) "attempts to change the transaction isolation level for this connection." In a Hibernate/JPA application, you can obtain a JDBC Connection from the native Session API; see section 17.1.

We recommend a different approach if you're using a JTA transaction manager or even a simple JDBC connection pool. JTA transaction management systems, such as Bitronix used for the examples of this book, allow you to set a default transaction isolation level for every connection obtained from the pool. In Bitronix, you can set the default isolation level on startup with `PoolingDataSource#setIsolationLevel()`. Check the documentation of your data source provider, application server, or JDBC connection pool for more information.

We assume from now on that your database connections are by default in *read committed* isolation level. From time to time, a particular unit of work in your application may require a different, usually stricter isolation level. Instead of changing the isolation level of the entire transaction, you should use the Java Persistence API to obtain additional locks on the relevant data. This fine-grained locking is more scalable in a highly concurrent application. JPA offers optimistic version checking and database-level pessimistic locking.

11.2.2 *Optimistic concurrency control*

Handling concurrency in an optimistic way is appropriate when concurrent modifications are rare and it's feasible to detect conflicts late in a unit of work. JPA offers automatic version checking as an optimistic conflict-detection procedure.

First you'll enable versioning, because it's turned off by default—that's why you get *last commit wins* if you don't do anything. Most multiuser applications, especially web applications, should rely on versioning for any concurrently modified `@Entity` instances, enabling the more user-friendly *first commit wins*.

The previous sections have been somewhat dry; it's time for code. After enabling automatic version checking, you'll see how manual version checking works and when you have to use it.

ENABLING VERSIONING

You enable versioning with an `@Version` annotation on a special additional property of your entity class, as shown next.

> **Listing 11.2   Enabling versioning on a mapped entity**
>
> PATH: /model/src/main/java/org/jpwh/model/concurrency/version/Item.java

```
@Entity
public class Item implements Serializable {

    @Version
    protected long version;

    // ...
}
```

In this example, each entity instance carries a numeric version. It's mapped to an additional column of the ITEM database table; as usual, the column name defaults to the property name, here VERSION. The actual name of the property and column doesn't matter—you could rename it if VERSION is a reserved keyword in your DBMS.

You could add a `getVersion()` method to the class, but you shouldn't have a setter method and the application shouldn't modify the value. Hibernate automatically changes the version value: it increments the version number whenever an Item instance has been found dirty during flushing of the persistence context. The version is a simple counter without any useful semantic value beyond concurrency control. You can use an int, an Integer, a short, a Short, or a Long instead of a long; Hibernate wraps and starts from zero again if the version number reaches the limit of the data type.

After incrementing the version number of a detected dirty Item during flushing, Hibernate compares versions when executing the UPDATE and DELETE SQL statements. For example, assume that in a unit of work, you load an Item and change its name, as follows.

> **Listing 11.3   Hibernate incrementing and checking the version automatically**
>
> **PATH:** /examples/src/test/java/org\jpwh/test/concurrency/Versioning.java

```
tx.begin();
em = JPA.createEntityManager();

Item item = em.find(Item.class, ITEM_ID);          ◁────❶ Retrieves by identifier
// select * from ITEM where ID = ?

assertEquals(item.getVersion(), 0);                ◁────❷ Instance version: 0

item.setName("New Name");
                                                        ❸ Flushes persistence context
em.flush();                                        ◁────
// update ITEM set NAME = ?, VERSION = 1 where ID = ? and VERSION = 0
```

❶ Retrieving an entity instance by identifier loads the current version from the database with a SELECT.

❷ The current version of the Item instance is 0.

❸ When the persistence context is flushed, Hibernate detects the dirty Item instance and increments its version to 1. SQL UPDATE now performs the version check, storing the new version in the database, but only if the database version is still 0.

Pay attention to the SQL statements, in particular the UPDATE and its WHERE clause. This update will be successful only if there *is* a row with VERSION = 0 in the database. JDBC returns the number of updated rows to Hibernate; if that result is zero, it means the ITEM row is either gone or doesn't have the version 0 anymore. Hibernate detects this conflict during flushing, and a javax.persistence.OptimisticLockException is thrown.

Now imagine two users executing this unit of work at the same time, as shown previously in figure 11.4. The first user to commit updates the name of the Item and flushes the incremented version 1 to the database. The second user's flush (and commit) will fail, because their UPDATE statement can't find the row in the database with version 0. The database version is 1. Hence, the *first commit wins*, and you can catch the OptimisticLockException and handle it specifically. For example, you could show the following message to the second user: "The data you have been working with has been modified by someone else. Please start your unit of work again with fresh data. Click the Restart button to proceed."

What modifications trigger the increment of an entity's version? Hibernate increments the version whenever an entity instance is dirty. This includes all dirty value-typed properties of the entity, no matter if they're single-valued (like a `String` or `int` property), embedded (like an `Address`), or collections. The exceptions are `@OneTo-Many` and `@ManyToMany` association collections that have been made read-only with `mappedBy`. Adding or removing elements to these collections doesn't increment the version number of the owning entity instance. You should know that none of this is standardized in JPA—don't rely on two JPA providers implementing the same rules when accessing a shared database.

> **Versioning with a shared database**
>
> If several applications access your database, and they don't all use Hibernate's versioning algorithm, you'll have concurrency problems. An easy solution is to use database-level triggers and stored procedures: An `INSTEAD OF` trigger can execute a stored procedure when any `UPDATE` is made; it runs instead of the update. In the procedure, you can check whether the application incremented the version of the row; if the version isn't updated or the version column isn't included in the update, you know the statement wasn't sent by a Hibernate application. You can then increment the version in the procedure before applying the `UPDATE`.

If you don't want to increment the version of the entity instance when a particular property's value has changed, annotate the property with `@org.hibernate.annotations.OptimisticLock(excluded = true)`. You may not like the additional `VERSION` column in your database schema. Alternatively, you may already have a "last updated" timestamp property on your entity class and a matching database column. Hibernate can check versions with timestamps instead of the extra counter field.

VERSIONING WITH TIMESTAMPS

If your database schema already contains a timestamp column such as `LASTUPDATED` or `MODIFIED_ON`, you can map it for automatic version checking instead of using a numeric counter.

Listing 11.4   Enabling versioning with timestamps

PATH: /model/src/main/java/org/jpwh/model/concurrency/versiontimestamp/
      Item.java

```
@Entity
public class Item {

    @Version
    // Optional: @org.hibernate.annotations.Type(type = "dbtimestamp")
    protected Date lastUpdated;

    // ...
}
```

This example maps the column LASTUPDATED to a java.util.Date property; a Calendar type would also work with Hibernate. The JPA standard doesn't define these types for version properties; JPA only considers java.sql.Timestamp portable. This is less attractive, because you'd have to import that JDBC class in your domain model. You should try to keep implementation details such as JDBC out of the domain model classes so they can be tested, instantiated, cross-compiled (to JavaScript with GWT, for example), serialized, and deserialized in as many environments as possible.

In theory, versioning with a timestamp is slightly less safe, because two concurrent transactions may both load and update the same Item in the same millisecond; this is exacerbated by the fact that a JVM usually doesn't have millisecond accuracy (you should check your JVM and operating system documentation for the guaranteed precision). Furthermore, retrieving the current time from the JVM isn' t necessarily safe in a clustered environment, where the system time of nodes may not be synchronized, or time synchronization isn't as accurate as you'd need for your transactional load.

Hibernate Feature

You can switch to retrieval of the current time from the database machine by placing an @org.hibernate.annotations.Type(type="dbtimestamp") annotation on the version property. Hibernate now asks the database, with for example call current _timestamp() on H2, for the current time before updating. This gives you a single source of time for synchronization. Not all Hibernate SQL dialects support this, so check the source of your configured dialect and whether it overrides the get-CurrentTimestampSelectString() method. In addition, there is always the overhead of hitting the database for every increment.

We recommend that new projects rely on versioning with a numeric counter, not timestamps. If you're working with a legacy database schema or existing Java classes, it may be impossible to introduce a version or timestamp property and column. If that's the case, Hibernate has an alternative strategy for you.

Hibernate Feature

VERSIONING WITHOUT VERSION NUMBERS OR TIMESTAMPS

If you don't have version or timestamp columns, Hibernate can still perform automatic versioning. This alternative implementation of versioning checks the current database state against the unmodified values of persistent properties at the time Hibernate retrieved the entity instance (or the last time the persistence context was flushed).

You enable this functionality with the proprietary Hibernate annotation @org.hibernate.annotations.OptimisticLocking:

PATH: \model\src\main\java\org\jpwh\model\concurrency\versionall\Item.java

```
@Entity
@org.hibernate.annotations.OptimisticLocking(
    type = org.hibernate.annotations.OptimisticLockType.ALL)
```

```
@org.hibernate.annotations.DynamicUpdate
public class Item {

    // ...
}
```

For this strategy, you also have to enable dynamic SQL generation of UPDATE statements, using `@org.hibernate.annotations.DynamicUpdate` as explained in section 4.3.2.

Hibernate now executes the following SQL to flush a modification of an Item instance:

```
update ITEM set NAME = 'New Name'
    where ID = 123
        and NAME = 'Old Name'
        and PRICE = '9.99'
        and DESCRIPTION = 'Some item for auction'
        and ...
        and SELLER_ID = 45
```

Hibernate lists all columns and their last known values in the WHERE clause. If any concurrent transaction has modified any of these values or even deleted the row, this statement returns with zero updated rows. Hibernate then throws an exception at flush time.

Alternatively, Hibernate includes only the modified properties in the restriction (only NAME, in this example) if you switch to OptimisticLockType.DIRTY. This means two units of work may modify the same Item concurrently, and Hibernate detects a conflict only if they both modify the same value-typed property (or a foreign key value). The WHERE clause of the last SQL excerpt would be reduced to where ID = 123 and NAME = 'Old Name'. Someone else could concurrently modify the price, and Hibernate wouldn't detect any conflict. Only if the application modified the name concurrently would you get a javax.persistence.OptimisticLockException.

In most cases, checking only dirty properties isn't a good strategy for business entities. It's probably not OK to change the price of an item if the description changes!

This strategy also doesn't work with detached entities and merging: if you merge a detached entity into a new persistence context, the "old" values aren't known. The detached entity instance will have to carry a version number or timestamp for optimistic concurrency control.

Automatic versioning in Java Persistence prevents lost updates when two concurrent transactions try to commit modifications on the same piece of data. Versioning can also help you to obtain additional isolation guarantees manually when you need them.

MANUAL VERSION CHECKING

Here's a scenario that requires repeatable database reads: imagine you have some categories in your auction system and that each Item is in a Category. This is a regular @ManyToOne mapping of an Item#category entity association.

Let's say you want to sum up all item prices in several categories. This requires a query for all items in each category, to add up the prices. The problem is, what happens if someone moves an `Item` from one `Category` to another `Category` while you're still querying and iterating through all the categories and items? With read-committed isolation, the same `Item` might show up twice while your procedure runs!

To make the "get items in each category" reads repeatable, JPA's `Query` interface has a `setLockMode()` method. Look at the procedure in the following listing.

Listing 11.5   Requesting a version check at flush time to ensure repeatable reads

PATH: /examples/src/test/java/org/jpwh/test/concurrency/Versioning.java

```
tx.begin();
EntityManager em = JPA.createEntityManager();

BigDecimal totalPrice = new BigDecimal(0);
for (Long categoryId : CATEGORIES) {                    ❶ Queries with
                                                          OPTIMISTIC lock mode
    List<Item> items =                            ◄─┘
        em.createQuery("select i from Item i where i.category.id = :catId")
            .setLockMode(LockModeType.OPTIMISTIC)
            .setParameter("catId", categoryId)
            .getResultList();

    for (Item item : items)
        totalPrice = totalPrice.add(item.getBuyNowPrice());
}

tx.commit();                    ◄────── ❷ Executes SELECT during flushing
em.close();

assertEquals(totalPrice.toString(), "108.00");
```

❶ For each `Category`, query all `Item` instances with an `OPTIMISTIC` lock mode. Hibernate now knows it has to check each `Item` at flush time.

❷ For each `Item` loaded earlier with the locking query, Hibernate executes a `SELECT` during flushing. It checks whether the database version of each `ITEM` row is still the same as when it was loaded. If any `ITEM` row has a different version or the row no longer exists, an `OptimisticLockException` is thrown.

Don't be confused by the *locking* terminology: The JPA specification leaves open how exactly each `LockModeType` is implemented; for `OPTIMISTIC`, Hibernate performs version checking. There are no actual locks involved. You'll have to enable versioning on the `Item` entity class as explained earlier; otherwise, you can't use the optimistic `LockModeTypes` with Hibernate.

Hibernate doesn't batch or otherwise optimize the `SELECT` statements for manual version checking: If you sum up 100 items, you get 100 additional queries at flush time. A pessimistic approach, as we show later in this chapter, may be a better solution for this particular case.

FAQ: Why can't the persistence context cache prevent this problem?

The "get all items in a particular category" query returns item data in a `ResultSet`. Hibernate then looks at the primary key values in this data and first tries to resolve the rest of the details of each `Item` in the persistence context cache—it checks whether an `Item` instance has already been loaded with that identifier. This cache, however, doesn't help in the example procedure: if a concurrent transaction moved an item to another category, that item might be returned several times in different `ResultSets`. Hibernate will perform its persistence context lookup and say, "Oh, I've already loaded that `Item` instance; let's use what we already have in memory." Hibernate isn't even aware that the category assigned to the item changed or that the item appeared again in a different result. Hence this is a case where the repeatable-read feature of the persistence context hides concurrently committed data. You need to manually check the versions to find out if the data changed while you were expecting it not to change.

As shown in the previous example, the `Query` interface accepts a `LockModeType`. Explicit lock modes are also supported by the `TypedQuery` and the `NamedQuery` interfaces, with the same `setLockMode()` method.

An additional optimistic lock mode is available in JPA, forcing an increment of an entity's version.

FORCING A VERSION INCREMENT

What happens if two users place a bid for the same auction item at the same time? When a user makes a new bid, the application must do several things:

1 Retrieve the currently highest `Bid` for the `Item` from the database.
2 Compare the new Bid with the highest `Bid`; if the new `Bid` is higher, it must be stored in the database.

There is the potential for a race condition in between these two steps. If, in between reading the highest `Bid` and placing the new `Bid`, another `Bid` is made, you won't see it. This conflict isn't visible; even enabling versioning of the `Item` doesn't help. The `Item` is never modified during the procedure. Forcing a version increment of the `Item` makes the conflict detectable.

Listing 11.6 Forcing a version increment of an entity instance

PATH: /examples/src/test/java/org/jpwh/test/concurrency/Versioning.java

```
tx.begin();
EntityManager em = JPA.createEntityManager();

Item item = em.find(                                    ❶ Tells Hibernate to
    Item.class,                                              increment Item version
    ITEM_ID,
    LockModeType.OPTIMISTIC_FORCE_INCREMENT
);

Bid highestBid = queryHighestBid(em, item);
```

```
try {
    Bid newBid = new Bid(                              ◁──────────❷ Persists Bid instance
        new BigDecimal("44.44"),
        item,
        highestBid
    );
    em.persist(newBid);
} catch (InvalidBidException ex) {                     ◁──────────❸ Checks bid
}

tx.commit();                          ◁──────────❹ INSERTs Bid
em.close();
```

❶ `find()` accepts a `LockModeType`. The `OPTIMISTIC_FORCE_INCREMENT` mode tells Hibernate that the version of the retrieved `Item` should be incremented after loading, even if it's never modified in the unit of work.

❷ The code persists a new `Bid` instance; this doesn't affect any values of the `Item` instance. A new row is inserted into the `BID` table. Hibernate wouldn't detect concurrently made bids without a forced version increment of the `Item`.

❸ You use a checked exception to validate the new bid amount. It must be greater than the currently highest bid.

❹ When flushing the persistence context, Hibernate executes an `INSERT` for the new `Bid` and forces an `UPDATE` of the `Item` with a version check. If someone modified the `Item` concurrently or placed a `Bid` concurrently with this procedure, Hibernate throws an exception.

For the auction system, placing bids concurrently is certainly a frequent operation. Incrementing a version manually is useful in many situations where you insert or modify data and want the version of some root instance of an aggregate to be incremented.

Note that if instead of a `Bid#item` entity association with `@ManyToOne`, you have an `@ElementCollection` of `Item#bids`, adding a `Bid` to the collection *will* increment the `Item` version. The forced increment then isn't necessary. You may want to review the discussion of parent/child ambiguity and how aggregates and composition work with ORM in section 7.3.

So far, we've focused on optimistic concurrency control: we expect that concurrent modifications are rare, so we don't prevent concurrent access and detect conflicts late. Sometimes you know that conflicts will happen frequently, and you want to place an exclusive lock on some data. This calls for a pessimistic approach.

11.2.3 *Explicit pessimistic locking*

Let's repeat the procedure shown in the section "Manual version checking" with a pessimistic lock instead of optimistic version checking. You again summarize the total price of all items in several categories. This is the same code as shown earlier in listing 11.5, with a different `LockModeType`.

Listing 11.7 Locking data pessimistically

PATH: /examples/src/test/java/org/jpwh/test/concurrency/Locking.java

```
tx.begin();
EntityManager em = JPA.createEntityManager();

BigDecimal totalPrice = new BigDecimal(0);
for (Long categoryId : CATEGORIES) {                    ❶ Queries all Item instances

    List<Item> items =
        em.createQuery("select i from Item i where i.category.id = :catId")
            .setLockMode(LockModeType.PESSIMISTIC_READ)
            .setHint("javax.persistence.lock.timeout", 5000)
            .setParameter("catId", categoryId)
            .getResultList();                           ❷ Query success means
                                                          exclusive lock
    for (Item item : items)
        totalPrice = totalPrice.add(item.getBuyNowPrice());
}

tx.commit();              ❸ Releases lock
em.close();

assertEquals(totalPrice.compareTo(new BigDecimal("108")), 0);
```

❶ For each `Category`, query all `Item` instances in `PESSIMISTIC_READ` lock mode. Hibernate locks the rows in the database with the SQL query. If possible, wait 5 seconds if another transaction holds a conflicting lock. If the lock can't be obtained, the query throws an exception.

❶ If the query returns successfully, you know that you hold an exclusive lock on the data and no other transaction can access it with an exclusive lock or modify it until this transaction commits.

❶ Your locks are released after commit, when the transaction completes.

The JPA specification defines that the lock mode `PESSIMISTIC_READ` guarantees repeatable reads. JPA also standardizes the `PESSIMISTIC_WRITE` mode, with additional guarantees: in addition to repeatable reads, the JPA provider must serialize data access, and no phantom reads can occur.

It's up to the JPA provider to implement these requirements. For both modes, Hibernate appends a "for update" clause to the SQL query when loading data. This places a lock on the rows at the database level. What kind of lock Hibernate uses depends on the `LockModeType` and your Hibernate database dialect.

On H2, for example, the query is `SELECT * FROM ITEM ... FOR UPDATE`. Because H2 supports only one type of exclusive lock, Hibernate generates the same SQL for all pessimistic modes.

PostgreSQL, on the other hand, supports shared read locks: the `PESSIMISTIC_READ` mode appends `FOR SHARE` to the SQL query. `PESSIMISTIC_WRITE` uses an exclusive write lock with `FOR UPDATE`.

On MySQL, PESSIMISTIC_READ translates to LOCK IN SHARE MODE, and PESSIMISTIC_ WRITE to FOR UPDATE. Check your database dialect. This is configured with the getReadLockString() and getWriteLockString() methods.

The duration of a pessimistic lock in JPA is a single database transaction. This means you can't use an exclusive lock to block concurrent access for longer than a single database transaction. When the database lock can't be obtained, an exception is thrown. Compare this with an optimistic approach, where Hibernate throws an exception at commit time, not when you query. With a pessimistic strategy, you know that you can read and write the data safely as soon as your locking query succeeds. With an optimistic approach, you hope for the best and may be surprised later, when you commit.

Offline locks

Pessimistic database locks are held only for a single transaction. Other lock implementations are possible: for example, a lock held in memory, or a so-called *lock table* in the database. A common name for these kinds of locks is offline locks.

Locking pessimistically for longer than a single database transaction is usually a performance bottleneck; every data access involves additional lock checks to a globally synchronized lock manager. Optimistic locking, however, is the perfect concurrency control strategy for long-running conversations (as you'll see in the next chapter) and performs well. Depending on your conflict-resolution strategy—what happens after a conflict is detected—your application users may be just as happy as with blocked concurrent access. They may also appreciate the application not locking them out of particular screens while others look at the same data.

You can configure how long the database will wait to obtain the lock and block the query in milliseconds with the javax.persistence.lock.timeout hint. As usual with hints, Hibernate might ignore it, depending on your database product. H2, for example, doesn't support lock timeouts per query, only a global lock timeout per connection (defaulting to 1 second). With some dialects, such as PostgreSQL and Oracle, a lock timeout of 0 appends the NOWAIT clause to the SQL string.

We've shown the lock timeout hint applied to a Query. You can also set the timeout hint for find() operations:

Path: /examples/src/test/java/org/jpwh/test/concurrency/Locking.java

```
tx.begin();
EntityManager em = JPA.createEntityManager();

Map<String, Object> hints = new HashMap<String, Object>();
hints.put("javax.persistence.lock.timeout", 5000);

Category category =
    em.find(
        Category.class,
        CATEGORY_ID,
        LockModeType.PESSIMISTIC_WRITE,
```

⊲— **Executes SELECT .. FOR UPDATE WAIT 5000 if supported by dialect**

```
        hints
    );

category.setName("New Name");

tx.commit();
em.close();
```

When a lock can't be obtained, Hibernate throws either a `javax.persistence.Lock-TimeoutException` or a `javax.persistence.PessimisticLockException`. If Hibernate throws a `PessimisticLockException`, the transaction must be rolled back, and the unit of work ends. A timeout exception, on the other hand, isn't fatal for the transaction, as explained in section 11.1.4. Which exception Hibernate throws again depends on the SQL dialect. For example, because H2 doesn't support per-statement lock timeouts, you always get a `PessimisticLockException`.

You can use both the `PESSIMISTIC_READ` and `PESSIMISTIC_WRITE` lock modes even if you haven't enabled entity versioning. They translate to SQL statements with database-level locks.

The special mode `PESSIMISTIC_FORCE_INCREMENT` requires versioned entities, however. In Hibernate, this mode executes a `FOR UPDATE NOWAIT` lock (or whatever your dialect supports; check its `getForUpdateNowaitString()` implementation). Then, immediately after the query returns, Hibernate increments the version and `UPDATE` (!) each returned entity instance. This indicates to any concurrent transaction that you have updated these rows, even if you haven't so far modified any data. This mode is rarely useful, mostly for aggregate locking as explained in the section "Forcing a version increment."

What about lock modes READ and WRITE?

These are older lock modes from Java Persistence 1.0, and you should no longer use them. `LockModeType.READ` is equivalent to `OPTIMISTIC`, and `LockModeType.WRITE` is equivalent to `OPTIMISTIC_FORCE_INCREMENT`.

If you enable pessimistic locking, Hibernate locks only rows that correspond to entity instance state. In other words, if you lock an `Item` instance, Hibernate will lock its row in the `ITEM` table. If you have a joined inheritance mapping strategy, Hibernate will recognize this and lock the appropriate rows in super- and sub-tables. This also applies to any secondary table mappings of an entity. Because Hibernate locks entire rows, any relationship where the foreign key is in that row will also effectively be locked: The `Item#seller` association is locked if the `SELLER_ID` foreign key column is in the `ITEM` table. The actual `Seller` instance isn't locked! Neither are collections or other associations of the `Item` where the foreign key(s) are in other tables.

With exclusive locking in the DBMS, you may experience transaction failures because you run into deadlock situations.

> ### Extending lock scope
>
> JPA 2.0 defines the `PessimisticLockScope.EXTENDED` option. It can be set as a query hint with `javax.persistence.lock.scope`. If enabled, the persistence engine expands the scope of locked data to include any data in collection and association join tables of locked entities. At the time of writing, Hibernate doesn't implement this feature.

11.2.4 Avoiding deadlocks

Deadlocks can occur if your DBMS relies on exclusive locks to implement transaction isolation. Consider the following unit of work, updating two `Item` entity instances in a particular order:

```
tx.begin();
EntityManager em = JPA.createEntityManager();

Item itemOne = em.find(Item.class, ITEM_ONE_ID);
itemOne.setName("First new name");

Item itemTwo = em.find(Item.class, ITEM_TWO_ID);
itemTwo.setName("Second new name");

tx.commit();
em.close();
```

Hibernate executes two SQL `UPDATE` statements when the persistence context is flushed. The first `UPDATE` locks the row representing `Item` one, and the second `UPDATE` locks `Item` two:

```
update ITEM set ... where ID = 1;      ⊲—— Locks row 1
update ITEM set ... where ID = 2;      ⊲—— Attempts to lock row 2
```

A deadlock may (or it may not!) occur if a similar procedure, with the opposite order of `Item` updates, executes in a concurrent transaction:

```
update ITEM set ... where ID = 2;      ⊲—— Locks row 2
update ITEM set ... where ID = 1;      ⊲—— Attempts to lock row 1
```

With a deadlock, both transactions are blocked and can't move forward, each waiting for a lock to be released. The chance of a deadlock is usually small, but in highly concurrent applications, two Hibernate applications may execute this kind of interleaved update. Note that you may not see deadlocks during testing (unless you write the right kinds of tests). Deadlocks can suddenly appear when the application has to handle a high transaction load in production. Usually the DBMS terminates one of the deadlocked transactions after a timeout period and fails; the other transaction can then proceed. Alternatively, depending on the DBMS, the DBMS may detect a deadlock situation automatically and immediately abort one of the transactions.

You should try to avoid transaction failures, because they're difficult to recover from in application code. One solution is to run the database connection in *serializable* mode when updating a single row locks the entire table. The concurrent transaction has to wait until the first transaction completes its work. Alternatively, the first transaction can obtain an exclusive lock on all data when you SELECT the data, as shown in the previous section. Then any concurrent transaction also has to wait until these locks are released.

An alternative pragmatic optimization that significantly reduces the probability of deadlocks is to order the UPDATE statements by primary key value: Hibernate should always update the row with primary key 1 before updating row 2, no matter in what order the data was loaded and modified by the application. You can enable this optimization for the entire persistence unit with the configuration property hibernate.order_updates. Hibernate then orders all UPDATE statements it executes in ascending order by primary key value of the modified entity instances and collection elements detected during flushing. (As mentioned earlier, make sure you fully understand the transactional and locking behavior of your DBMS product. Hibernate inherits most of its transaction guarantees from the DBMS; for example, your MVCC database product may avoid read locks but probably depends on exclusive locks for writer isolation, and you may see deadlocks.)

We didn't have an opportunity to mention the EntityManager#lock() method. It accepts an already-loaded persistent entity instance and a lock mode. It performs the same locking you've seen with find() and a Query, except that it doesn't load the instance. Additionally, if a versioned entity is being locked pessimistically, the lock() method performs an immediate version check on the database and potentially throws an OptimisticLockException. If the database representation is no longer present, Hibernate throws an EntityNotFoundException. Finally, the EntityManager#refresh() method also accepts a lock mode, with the same semantics.

We've now covered concurrency control at the lowest level—the database—and the optimistic and pessimistic locking features of JPA. We still have one more aspect of concurrency to discuss: accessing data outside of a transaction.

11.3   *Nontransactional data access*

A JDBC Connection is by default in *auto-commit* mode. This mode is useful for executing ad hoc SQL.

Imagine that you connect to your database with an SQL console and that you run a few queries, and maybe even update and delete rows. This interactive data access is ad hoc; most of the time you don't have a plan or a sequence of statements that you consider a unit of work. The default auto-commit mode on the database connection is perfect for this kind of data access—after all, you don't want to type begin transaction and end transaction for every SQL statement you write and execute. In auto-commit mode, a (short) database transaction begins and ends for each SQL statement you send to the database. You're working effectively in nontransactional mode, because there are no atomicity or isolation guarantees for your session with the SQL console. (The only guarantee is that a single SQL statement is atomic.)

An application, by definition, always executes a planned sequence of statements. It seems reasonable that you therefore always create transaction boundaries to group your statements into units that are atomic and isolated from each other. In JPA, however, special behavior is associated with auto-commit mode, and you may need it to implement long-running conversations. You can access the database in auto-commit mode and read data.

11.3.1 *Reading data in auto-commit mode*

Consider the following example, which loads an `Item` instance, changes its `name`, and then rolls back that change by refreshing.

Listing 11.8   Reading data in auto-commit mode

PATH: /examples/src/test/java/org/jpwh/test/concurrency/NonTransactional.java

```
EntityManager em = JPA.createEntityManager();          ①  Unsynchronized mode

Item item = em.find(Item.class, ITEM_ID);             ②  Accesses database
item.setName("New Name");
                                                       ③  Returns original value
assertEquals(
    em.createQuery("select i.name from Item i where i.id = :id)")
        .setParameter("id", ITEM_ID).getSingleResult(),
    "Original Name"
);                                                     ④  Returns already-
                                                          loaded instance
assertEquals(
    ((Item) em.createQuery("select i from Item i where i.id = :id)")
        .setParameter("id", ITEM_ID).getSingleResult()).getName(),
    "New Name"
);

// em.flush();                                         ⑤  Throws exception

em.refresh(item);                                      ⑥  Rolls back change
assertEquals(item.getName(), "Original Name");

em.close();
```

① No transaction is active when you create the EntityManager. The persistence context is now in a special *unsynchronized* mode; Hibernate won't flush automatically.

② You can access the database to read data; this operation executes a SELECT, sent to the database in auto-commit mode.

③ Usually Hibernate flushes the persistence context when you execute a Query. But because the context is unsynchronized, flushing doesn't occur, and the query returns the old, original database value. Queries with scalar results aren't repeatable: you see whatever values are in the database and given to Hibernate in the ResultSet. This also isn't a repeatable read if you're in synchronized mode.

❹ Retrieving a managed entity instance involves a lookup during JDBC result-set marshaling, in the current persistence context. The already-loaded `Item` instance with the changed name is returned from the persistence context; values from the database are ignored. This is a repeatable read of an entity instance, even without a system transaction.

❺ If you try to flush the persistence context manually, to store the new `Item#name`, Hibernate throws a `javax.persistence.TransactionRequiredException`. You can't execute an `UPDATE` in unsynchronized mode, because you wouldn't be able to roll back the change.

❻ You can roll back the change you made with the `refresh()` method. It loads the current `Item` state from the database and overwrites the change you made in memory.

With an unsynchronized persistence context, you read data in auto-commit mode with `find()`, `getReference()`, `refresh()`, or queries. You can load data on demand as well: proxies are initialized if you access them, and collections are loaded if you start iterating through their elements. But if you try to flush the persistence context or lock data with anything but `LockModeType.NONE`, a `TransactionRequiredException` will occur.

So far, auto-commit mode doesn't seem very useful. Indeed, many developers often rely on auto-commit for the wrong reasons:

- Many small per-statement database transactions (that's what auto-commit means) won't improve the performance of your application.
- You won't improve the scalability of your application: a longer-running database transaction, instead of many small transactions for every SQL statement, may hold database locks for a longer time. This is a minor issue, because Hibernate writes to the database as late as possible within a transaction (flush at commit), so the database already holds write locks for a short time.
- You also have weaker isolation guarantees if the application modifies data concurrently. Repeatable reads based on read locks are impossible with auto-commit mode. (The persistence context cache helps here, naturally.)
- If your DBMS has MVCC (for example, Oracle, PostreSQL, Informix, and Firebird), you likely want to use its capability for *snapshot isolation* to avoid unrepeatable and phantom reads. Each transaction gets its own personal snapshot of the data; you only see a (database-internal) version of the data as it was before your transaction started. With auto-commit mode, snapshot isolation makes no sense, because there is no transaction scope.
- Your code will be more difficult to understand. Any reader of your code now has to pay special attention to whether a persistence context is joined with a transaction, or if it's in unsynchronized mode. If you always group operations within a system transaction, even if you only read data, everyone can follow this simple rule, and the likelihood of difficult-to-find concurrency issues is reduced.

So, what are the benefits of an unsynchronized persistence context? If flushing doesn't happen automatically, you can prepare and *queue* modifications outside of a transaction.

11.3.2 *Queueing modifications*

The following example stores a new `Item` instance with an unsynchronized `Entity-Manager`:

> **PATH: /examples/src/test/java/org/jpwh/test/concurrency/NonTransactional.java**

```
EntityManager em = JPA.createEntityManager();

Item newItem = new Item("New Item");
em.persist(newItem)                             ◄────────── ❶ Saves transient instance
assertNotNull(newItem.getId());

tx.begin();                                     ◄────────── ❷ Stores changes
if (!em.isJoinedToTransaction())
    em.joinTransaction();
tx.commit();                                    ◄────────── Flush!
em.close();
```

❶ You can call `persist()` to save a transient entity instance with an unsynchronized persistence context. Hibernate only fetches a new identifier value, typically by calling a database sequence, and assigns it to the instance. The instance is now in persistent state in the context, but the SQL `INSERT` hasn't happened. Note that this is only possible with *pre-insert* identifier generators; see section 4.2.5.

❷ When you're ready to store the changes, join the persistence context with a transaction. Synchronization and flushing occur as usual, when the transaction commits. Hibernate writes all queued operations to the database.

Merged changes of a detached entity instance can also be queued:

> **PATH: /examples/src/test/java/org/jpwh/test/concurrency/NonTransactional.java**

```
detachedItem.setName("New Name");
EntityManager em = JPA.createEntityManager();

Item mergedItem = em.merge(detachedItem);

tx.begin();
em.joinTransaction();
tx.commit();                                    ◄────────── Flush!
em.close();
```

Hibernate executes a `SELECT` in auto-commit mode when you `merge()`. Hibernate defers the `UPDATE` until a joined transaction commits.

Queuing also works for removal of entity instances and `DELETE` operations:

PATH: /examples/src/test/java/org/jpwh/test/concurrency/NonTransactional.java

```
EntityManager em = JPA.createEntityManager();

Item item = em.find(Item.class, ITEM_ID);
em.remove(item);

tx.begin();
em.joinTransaction();
tx.commit();                                    <————— Flush!
em.close();
```

An unsynchronized persistence context therefore allows you to decouple persistence operations from transactions. This special behavior of the EntityManager will be essential later in the book, when we discuss application design. The ability to queue data modifications, independent from transactions (and client/server requests), is a major feature of the persistence context.

Hibernate's MANUAL flush mode

Hibernate offers a Session#setFlushMode() method, with the additional Flush-Mode.MANUAL. It's a much more convenient switch that disables any automatic flushing of the persistence context, even when a joined transaction commits. With this mode, you have to call flush() explicitly to synchronize with the database. In JPA, the idea was that a "transaction commit should always write any outstanding changes," so reading was separated from writing with the *unsynchronized* mode. If you don't agree with this and/or don't want auto-committed statements, enable manual flushing with the Session API. You can then have regular transaction boundaries for all units of work, with repeatable reads and even snapshot isolation from your MVCC database, but still queue changes in the persistence context for later execution and manual flush() before your transaction commits.

11.4   Summary

- You learned to use transactions, concurrency, isolation, and locking.
- Hibernate relies on a database's concurrency-control mechanism but provides better isolation guarantees in a transaction, thanks to automatic versioning and the persistence context cache.
- We discussed how to set transaction boundaries programmatically and handle exceptions.
- You explored optimistic concurrency control and explicit pessimistic locking.
- You saw how to work with auto-commit mode and an unsynchronized persistence context outside of a transaction, and how to queue modification.

Fetch plans, strategies, and profiles

In this chapter, we explore Hibernate's solution for the fundamental ORM problem of navigation, as mentioned in section 1.2.5. We show you how to retrieve data from the database and how you can optimize this loading.

Hibernate provides the following ways to get data out of the database and into memory:

- Retrieving an entity instance by identifier is the most convenient method when the unique identifier value of an entity instance is known: for example, `entityManager.find(Item.class, 123)`.
- You can navigate the entity graph, starting from an already-loaded entity instance, by accessing the associated instances through property accessor methods such as `someItem.getSeller().getAddress().getCity()`, and so on. Elements of mapped collections are also loaded on demand when you start iterating through a collection. Hibernate automatically loads nodes of

the graph if the persistence context is still open. What and how data is loaded when you call accessors and iterate through collections is the focus of this chapter.

- You can use the Java Persistence Query Language (JPQL), a full object-oriented query language based on strings such as `select i from Item i where i.id = ?`.
- The `CriteriaQuery` interface provides a type-safe and object-oriented way to perform queries without string manipulation.
- You can write native SQL queries, call stored procedures, and let Hibernate take care of mapping the JDBC result sets to instances of your domain model classes.

In your JPA applications, you'll use a combination of these techniques, but we won't discuss each retrieval method in much detail in this chapter. By now you should be familiar with the basic Java Persistence API for retrieval by identifier. We keep our JPQL and `CriteriaQuery` examples as simple as possible, and you won't need the SQL query-mapping features. Because these query options are sophisticated, we'll explore them further in chapters 15 and 17.

Major new features in JPA 2

- You can manually check the initialization state of an entity or an entity property with the new `PersistenceUtil` static helper class.
- You can create standardized declarative fetch plans with the new `Entity-Graph` API.

This chapter covers what happens behind the scenes when you navigate the graph of your domain model and Hibernate retrieves data on demand. In all the examples, we show you the SQL executed by Hibernate in a comment right immediately after the operation that triggered the SQL execution.

What Hibernate loads depends on the *fetch plan*: you define the (sub)graph of the network of objects that should be loaded. Then you pick the right *fetch strategy*, defining *how* the data should be loaded. You can store your selection of plan and strategy as a *fetch profile* and reuse it.

Defining fetch plans and *what* data should be loaded by Hibernate relies on two fundamental techniques: *lazy* and *eager* loading of nodes in the network of objects.

12.1 Lazy and eager loading

At some point, you must decide what data should be loaded into memory from the database. When you execute `entityManager.find(Item.class, 123)`, what is available in memory and loaded into the persistence context? What happens if you use `EntityManager#getReference()` instead?

In your domain-model mapping, you define the global *default fetch plan*, with the `FetchType.LAZY` and `FetchType.EAGER` options on associations and collections. This plan is the default setting for all operations involving your persistent domain model classes. It's always active when you load an entity instance by identifier and when you navigate the entity graph by following associations and iterating through persistent collections.

Our recommended strategy is a *lazy* default fetch plan for all entities and collections. If you map all of your associations and collections with `FetchType.LAZY`, Hibernate will only load the data you're accessing at this time. While you navigate the graph of your domain model instances, Hibernate will load data on demand, bit by bit. You then override this behavior on a per-case basis when necessary.

To implement lazy loading, Hibernate relies on runtime-generated entity place-holders called *proxies* and on *smart wrappers* for collections.

12.1.1 *Understanding entity proxies*

Consider the `getReference()` method of the `EntityManager` API. In section 10.2.3, you had a first look at this operation and how it may return a proxy. Let's further explore this important feature and find out how proxies work:

> PATH: /examples/src/test/java/org/jpwh/test/fetching/LazyProxyCollections.java

```
Item item = em.getReference(Item.class, ITEM_ID);        ⟵——— No SELECT

assertEquals(item.getId(), ITEM_ID);        ⟵—┐
                                              │ Calling the identifier getter (no field
                                              │ access!) doesn't trigger initialization.
```

This code doesn't execute any SQL against the database. All Hibernate does is create an `Item` proxy: it looks (and smells) like the real thing, but it's only a placeholder. In the persistence context, in memory, you now have this proxy available in persistent state, as shown in figure 12.1.

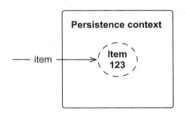

The proxy is an instance of a runtime-generated subclass of `Item`, carrying the identifier value of the entity instance it represents. This is why Hibernate (in line with JPA) requires that entity classes have at least a public or protected no-argument constructor (the class may have other constructors, too). The entity class and its methods must not be final; otherwise, Hibernate can't produce a proxy. Note that the JPA specification doesn't mention proxies; it's up to the JPA provider how lazy loading is implemented.

Figure 12.1 The persistence context contains an `Item` proxy.

If you call any method on the proxy that isn't the "identifier getter," you trigger initialization of the proxy and hit the database. If you call `item.getName()`, the SQL `SELECT` to load the `Item` will be executed. The previous example called `item.getId()` without triggering initialization because `getId()` *is* the identifier getter method in the given mapping; the `getId()` method was annotated with `@Id`. If `@Id` was on a field, then calling `getId()`, just like calling any other method, would initialize the proxy!

(Remember that we usually prefer mappings and access on fields, because this allows you more freedom when designing accessor methods; see section 3.2.3. It's up to you whether calling `getId()` without initializing a proxy is more important.)

With proxies, be careful how you compare classes. Because Hibernate generates the proxy class, it has a funny-looking name, and it is *not* equal to `Item.class`:

PATH: /examples/src/test/java/org/jpwh/test/fetching/LazyProxyCollections.java

```
assertNotEquals(item.getClass(), Item.class);        ⟵┤ Class is runtime generated,
                                                      │ named something like
assertEquals(                                         │ Item_$$_javassist_l
   HibernateProxyHelper.getClassWithoutInitializingProxy(item),
   Item.class
);
```

If you really must get the actual type represented by a proxy, use the `HibernateProxy-Helper`.

JPA provides `PersistenceUtil`, which you can use to check the initialization state of an entity or any of its attributes:

PATH: /examples/src/test/java/org/jpwh/test/fetching/LazyProxyCollections.java

```
PersistenceUtil persistenceUtil = Persistence.getPersistenceUtil();
assertFalse(persistenceUtil.isLoaded(item));
assertFalse(persistenceUtil.isLoaded(item, "seller"));

assertFalse(Hibernate.isInitialized(item));                        ┐ Would trigger
// assertFalse(Hibernate.isInitialized(item.getSeller()));  ⟵─────┘ initialization of
                                                                     item!
```

The static `isLoaded()` method also accepts the name of a property of the given entity (proxy) instance, checking its initialization state. Hibernate offers an alternative API with `Hibernate.isInitialized()`. If you call `item.getSeller()`, though, the item proxy is initialized first!

Hibernate Feature ──

Hibernate also offers a utility method for quick-and-dirty initialization of proxies:

PATH: /examples/src/test/java/org/jpwh/test/fetching/LazyProxyCollections.java

```
Hibernate.initialize(item);
// select * from ITEM where ID = ?
                                                             ┐ Make sure the
assertFalse(Hibernate.isInitialized(item.getSeller()));  ⟵──┤ default EAGER of
                                                             │ @ManyToOne has
Hibernate.initialize(item.getSeller());                      │ been overridden with
// select * from USERS where ID = ?                          │ LAZY.
```

The first call hits the database and loads the `Item` data, populating the proxy with the item's name, price, and so on.

The `seller` of the `Item` is an `@ManyToOne` association mapped with `FetchType.LAZY`, so Hibernate creates a `User` proxy when the `Item` is loaded. You can check the seller proxy state and load it manually, just like the `Item`. Remember that the JPA default for `@ManyToOne` is `FetchType.EAGER`! You usually want to override this to get a lazy default fetch plan, as first shown in section 7.3.1 and again here:

> PATH: /model/src/main/java/org/jpwh/model/fetching/proxy/Item.java

```java
@Entity
public class Item {

    @ManyToOne(fetch = FetchType.LAZY)
    public User getSeller() {
        return seller;
    }
    // ...
}
```

With such a lazy fetch plan, you might run into a `LazyInitializationException`. Consider the following code:

> PATH: /examples/src/test/java/org/jpwh/test/fetching/LazyProxyCollections.java

```java
Item item = em.find(Item.class, ITEM_ID);          // ❶ Loads Item instance
// select * from ITEM where ID = ?

em.detach(item);                                    // ❷ Detaches data
em.detach(item.getSeller());
// em.close();

PersistenceUtil persistenceUtil = Persistence.getPersistenceUtil();
assertTrue(persistenceUtil.isLoaded(item));
                                                    // PersistenceUtil
                                                    //   helper ❸
assertFalse(persistenceUtil.isLoaded(item, "seller"));

assertEquals(item.getSeller().getId(), USER_ID);    // ❹ Calls getter
//assertNotNull(item.getSeller().getUsername());    // Throws an exception!
```

❶ An `Item` entity instance is loaded in the persistence context. Its seller isn't initialized: it's a `User` proxy.

❷ You can manually detach the data from the persistence context or close the persistence context and detach everything.

❸ The static `PersistenceUtil` helper works without a persistence context. You can check at any time whether the data you want to access has been loaded.

❹ In detached state, you can call the identifier getter method of the `User` proxy. But calling any other method on the proxy, such as `getUsername()`, will throw a `LazyInitializationException`. Data can only be loaded on demand while the persistence context manages the proxy, not in detached state.

How does lazy loading of one-to-one associations work?

Lazy loading for *one-to-one* entity associations is sometimes confusing for new Hibernate users. If you consider *one-to-one* associations based on shared primary keys (see section 8.1.1), an association can be proxied only if it's `optional=false`. For example, an `Address` always has a reference to a `User`. If this association is nullable and optional, Hibernate must first hit the database to find out whether it should apply a proxy or a null—and the purpose of lazy loading is to not hit the database at all. You can enable lazy loading of optional one-to-one associations through bytecode instrumentation and interception, which we discuss later in this chapter.

Hibernate proxies are useful beyond simple lazy loading. For example, you can store a new `Bid` without loading any data into memory:

```
Item item = em.getReference(Item.class, ITEM_ID);
User user = em.getReference(User.class, USER_ID);

Bid newBid = new Bid(new BigDecimal("99.00"));
newBid.setItem(item);
newBid.setBidder(user);

em.persist(newBid);
// insert into BID values (?, ? ,? , ...)
```

There is no SQL SELECT in this procedure, only one INSERT.

The first two calls produce proxies of `Item` and `User`, respectively. Then the `item` and `bidder` association properties of the transient `Bid` are set with the proxies. The `persist()` call queues one SQL INSERT when the persistence context is flushed, and no SELECT is necessary to create the new row in the BID table. All (foreign) key values are available as identifier values of the `Item` and `User` proxy.

Runtime proxy generation as provided by Hibernate is an excellent choice for transparent lazy loading. Your domain model classes don't have to implement any special (super)type, as some older ORM solutions would require. No code generation or post-processing of bytecode is needed either, simplifying your build procedure. But you should be aware of some potentially negative aspects:

- Cases where runtime proxies aren't completely transparent are polymorphic associations that are tested with `instanceof`, a problem shown in section 6.8.1.
- With entity proxies, you have to be careful not to access fields directly when writing custom `equals()` and `hashCode()` methods, as discussed in section 10.3.2.
- Proxies can only be used to lazy-load entity associations. They can't be used to lazy load individual basic properties or embedded components, such as `Item#description` or `User#homeAddress`. If you set the `@Basic(fetch = FetchType.LAZY)` hint on such a property, Hibernate ignores it; the value is eagerly loaded when the owning entity instance is loaded. Although possible with bytecode instrumentation and interception, we consider this kind of optimization to be rarely useful. Optimizing at the level of individual columns selected in SQL is unnecessary if you aren't working with (a) a significant

number of optional/nullable columns or (b) columns containing large values that have to be retrieved on demand because of the physical limitations of your system. Large values are best represented with locator objects (LOBs) instead; they provide lazy loading by definition (see the section "Binary and large value types" in chapter 5).

Proxies enable lazy loading of entity instances. For persistent collections Hibernate has a slightly different approach.

12.1.2 *Lazy persistent collections*

You map persistent collections with either @ElementCollection for a collection of elements of basic or embeddable type or with @OneToMany and @ManyToMany for many-valued entity associations. These collections are, unlike @ManyToOne, lazy-loaded by default. You don't have to specify the FetchType.LAZY option on the mapping.

When you load an Item, Hibernate doesn't load its lazy collection of images right away. The lazy bids *one-to-many* collection is also only loaded on demand, when accessed and needed:

> **PATH: /examples/src/test/java/org/jpwh/test/fetching/LazyProxyCollections.java**

```
Item item = em.find(Item.class, ITEM_ID);
// select * from ITEM where ID = ?                          Collection isn't
                                                            initialized.
Set<Bid> bids = item.getBids();                     ◄──────
PersistenceUtil persistenceUtil = Persistence.getPersistenceUtil();
assertFalse(persistenceUtil.isLoaded(item, "bids"));

assertTrue(Set.class.isAssignableFrom(bids.getClass()));    ◄─────  It's a Set.

assertNotEquals(bids.getClass(), HashSet.class);     ◄─────  It's not a HashSet.
assertEquals(bids.getClass(),
    org.hibernate.collection.internal.PersistentSet.class);
```

The find() operation loads the Item entity instance into the persistence context, as you can see in figure 12.2. The Item instance has a reference to an uninitialized User proxy: the seller. It also has a reference to an uninitialized Set of bids and an uninitialized List of images.

Hibernate implements lazy loading (and dirty checking) of collections with its own special implementations called *collection wrappers*. Although the bids certainly look like a Set, Hibernate replaced the implementation with an org.hibernate.collection.internal .PersistentSet while you weren't looking.

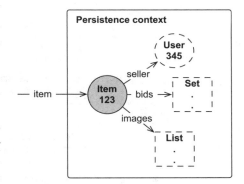

Figure 12.2 Proxies and collection wrappers represent the boundary of the loaded graph.

It's not a `HashSet`, but it has the same behavior. That's why it's so important to program with interfaces in your domain model and only rely on `Set` and not `HashSet`. Lists and maps work the same way.

These special collections can detect when you access them and load their data at that time. As soon as you start iterating through the `bids`, the collection and all bids made for the item are loaded:

PATH: /examples/src/test/java/org/jpwh/test/fetching/LazyProxyCollections.java
---

```
Bid firstBid = bids.iterator().next();
// select * from BID where ITEM_ID = ?

// Alternative: Hibernate.initialize(bids);
```

Alternatively, just as for entity proxies, you can call the static utility method `Hibernate.initialize()` to load a collection. It will be completely loaded; you can't say "only load the first two bids," for example. For this, you'd have to write a query.

Hibernate Feature

For convenience, so you don't have to write many trivial queries, Hibernate offers a proprietary setting on collection mappings:

PATH: /model/src/main/java/org/jpwh/model/fetching/proxy/Item.java
---

```
@Entity
public class Item {

    @OneToMany(mappedBy = "item")
    @org.hibernate.annotations.LazyCollection(
        org.hibernate.annotations.LazyCollectionOption.EXTRA
    )
    public Set<Bid> getBids() {
        return bids;
    }
    // ...
}
```

With `LazyCollectionOption.EXTRA`, the collection supports operations that don't trigger initialization. For example, you could ask for the collection's size:

```
Item item = em.find(Item.class, ITEM_ID);
// select * from ITEM where ID = ?

assertEquals(item.getBids().size(), 3);
// select count(b) from BID b where b.ITEM_ID = ?
```

The `size()` operation triggers a `SELECT COUNT()` SQL query but doesn't load the `bids` into memory. On all extra lazy collections, similar queries are executed for the `isEmpty()` and `contains()` operations. An extra lazy `Set` checks for duplicates with a simple query when you call `add()`. An extra lazy `List` only loads one element if you call `get(index)`. For `Map`, extra lazy operations are `containsKey()` and `containsValue()`.

Hibernate's proxies and smart collections are one possible implementation of lazy loading, with a good balance of features and cost. An alternative we've mentioned before is *interception*.

12.1.3 *Lazy loading with interception*

The fundamental problem with lazy loading is that the JPA provider must know when to load the `seller` of an `Item` or the collection of `bids`. Instead of runtime-generated proxies and smart collections, many other JPA providers rely exclusively on *interception* of method calls. For example, when you call `someItem.getSeller()`, the JPA provider would *intercept* this call and load the `User` instance representing the `seller`.

This approach requires special code in your `Item` class to implement the interception: the `getSeller()` method or the `seller` field must be wrapped. Because you don't want to write this code by hand, typically you run a *bytecode enhancer* (bundled with your JPA provider) after compiling your domain model classes. This enhancer injects the necessary interception code into your compiled classes, manipulating the fields and methods at the bytecode level.

Let's discuss lazy loading based on interception with a few examples. First, you probably want to disable Hibernate's proxy generation:

PATH: /model/src/main/java/org/jpwh/model/fetching/interception/User.java

```
@Entity
@org.hibernate.annotations.Proxy(lazy = false)
public class User {
    // ...
}
```

Hibernate will now no longer generate a proxy for the `User` entity. If you call `entityManager.getReference(User.class, USER_ID)`, a SELECT is executed, just as for `find()`:

PATH: /examples/src/test/java/org/jpwh/test/fetching/LazyInterception.java

```
User user = em.getReference(User.class, USER_ID);   ⟵   Proxies are disabled.
// select * from USERS where ID = ?                        getReference() will return
                                                           an initialized instance.
assertTrue(Hibernate.isInitialized(user));
```

For entity associations targeting `User`, such as the `seller` of an `Item`, the `FetchType.LAZY` hint has no effect:

PATH: /model/src/main/java/org/jpwh/model/fetching/interception/Item.java

```
@Entity
public class Item {                                    Has no effect—
                                                       no User proxy.
    @ManyToOne(fetch = FetchType.LAZY)          ⟵
```

```
@org.hibernate.annotations.LazyToOne(
    org.hibernate.annotations.LazyToOneOption.NO_PROXY
)
protected User seller;

// ...
}
```

⟵ **Requires bytecode enhancement!**

Instead, the proprietary `LazyToOneOption.NO_PROXY` setting tells Hibernate that the bytecode enhancer must add interception code for the `seller` property. Without this option, or if you don't run the bytecode enhancer, this association would be eagerly loaded and the field would be populated right away when the `Item` is loaded, because proxies for the `User` entity have been disabled.

If you run the bytecode enhancer, Hibernate intercepts access of the `seller` field and triggers loading when you touch the field:

PATH: /examples/src/test/java/org/jpwh/test/fetching/LazyInterception.java

```
Item item = em.find(Item.class, ITEM_ID);
// select * from ITEM where ID = ?
assertEquals(item.getSeller().getId(), USER_ID);
// select * from USERS where ID = ?
```

Even item.getSeller() would trigger the SELECT.

This is less lazy than proxies. Remember that you could call `User#getId()` on a proxy without initializing the instance, as explained in the previous sections. With interception, any access of the `seller` field, and calling `getSeller()`, will trigger initialization.

For lazy entity associations, proxies are usually a better choice than interception. A more common use case for interception is properties of basic type, such a `String` or `byte[]`, with potentially large values. We might argue that LOBs (see "Binary and large value types" in chapter 5) should be preferred for large strings or binary data, but you might not want to have the `java.sql.Blob` or `java.sql.Clob` type in your domain model. With interception and bytecode enhancement, you can load a simple `String` or `byte[]` field on demand:

PATH: /model/src/main/java/org/jpwh/model/fetching/interception/Item.java

```
@Entity
public class Item {

    @Basic(fetch = FetchType.LAZY)
    protected String description;

    // ...
}
```

The `Item#description` will be lazy loaded if you run the bytecode enhancer on the compiled class. If you don't run the bytecode enhancer—for example, during development—the `String` will be loaded together with the `Item` instance.

If you rely on interception, be aware that Hibernate will load *all* lazy fields of an entity or embeddable class, even if only one has to be loaded:

PATH: /examples/src/test/java/org/jpwh/test/fetching/LazyInterception.java

```
Item item = em.find(Item.class, ITEM_ID);
// select NAME, AUCTIONEND, ... from ITEM where ID = ?

assertTrue(item.getDescription().length() > 0);
// select DESCRIPTION from ITEM where ID = ?
// select * from USERS where ID = ?
```

Accessing one loads all lazy properties (description, seller, and so on).

When Hibernate loads the `description` of the `Item`, it loads the `seller` and any other intercepted field right away, too. There are no fetch groups in Hibernate at the time of writing: it's all or nothing.

The downside of interception is the cost of running a bytecode enhancer every time you build your domain model classes, and waiting for the instrumentation to complete. You may decide to skip the instrumentation during development, if the behavior of your application doesn't depend on an item's description load state. Then, when building the testing and production package, you can execute the enhancer.

The new Hibernate 5 bytecode enhancer

Unfortunately, we can't guarantee that the interception examples we show here will work with the latest Hibernate 5 version. The Hibernate 5 bytecode enhancer has been rewritten and now supports more than interception for lazy loading: the byte-code enhancer can inject code into your domain model classes to speed up dirty checking and automatically manage bidirectional entity associations. At the time of writing, however, we couldn't get this brand-new enhancer to work, and development was ongoing. We refer you to the current Hibernate documentation for more information about the enhancer feature and configuring it in your project using Maven or Gradle plug-ins.

We leave it to you to decide whether you want interception for lazy loading—in our experience, good use cases are rare. Note that we haven't talked about collection wrappers when discussing interception: although you could enable interception for collection fields, Hibernate would still use its smart collection wrappers. The reason is that these collection wrappers are, unlike entity proxies, needed for other purposes besides lazy loading. For example, Hibernate relies on them to track additions and removals of collection elements when dirty checking. You can't disable the collection wrappers in your mappings; they're always on. (Of course, you never *have* to map a persistent collection; they're a feature, not a requirement. See our earlier discussion in section 7.1.) Persistent arrays, on the other hand, can only be lazily loaded with field interception—they can't be wrapped like collections.

You've now seen all available options for lazy loading in Hibernate. Next, we look at the opposite of on-demand loading: the eager fetching of data.

12.1.4 *Eager loading of associations and collections*

We've recommended a lazy default fetch plan, with `FetchType.LAZY` on all your association and collection mappings. Sometimes, although not often, you want the opposite: to specify that a particular entity association or collection should always be loaded. You want the guarantee that this data is available in memory without an additional database hit.

More important, you want a guarantee that, for example, you can access the `seller` of an `Item` once the `Item` instance is in detached state. When the persistence context is closed, lazy loading is no longer available. If `seller` were an uninitialized proxy, you'd get a `LazyInitializationException` when you accessed it in detached state. For data to be available in detached state, you need to either load it manually while the persistence context is still open or, if you *always* want it loaded, change your fetch plan to be eager instead of lazy.

Let's assume that you always require loading of the `seller` and the `bids` of an `Item`:

PATH: /model/src/main/java/org/jpwh/model/fetching/eagerjoin/Item.java

```
@Entity
public class Item {

    @ManyToOne(fetch = FetchType.EAGER)              ◁——— The default
    protected User seller;

    @OneToMany(mappedBy = "item", fetch = FetchType.EAGER)  ◁— Not recommended
    protected Set<Bid> bids = new HashSet<>();

    // ...
}
```

Unlike `FetchType.LAZY`, which is a hint the JPA provider can ignore, a `FetchType.EAGER` is a hard requirement. The provider has to guarantee that the data is loaded and available in detached state; it can't ignore the setting.

Consider the collection mapping: is it really a good idea to say, "Whenever an item is loaded into memory, load the bids of the item right away, too"? Even if you only want to display the item's name or find out when the auction ends, all bids will be loaded into memory. Always eager-loading collections, with `FetchType.EAGER` as the default fetch plan in the mapping, usually isn't a great strategy. You'll also see the *Cartesian product problem* appear if you eagerly load several collections, which we discuss later in this chapter. It's best if you leave collections as the default `FetchType.LAZY`.

If you now `find()` an `Item` (or force the initialization of an `Item` proxy), both the `seller` and all the `bids` are loaded as persistent instances into your persistence context:

```
PATH: /examples/src/test/java/org/jpwh/test/fetching/EagerJoin.java
```

```java
Item item = em.find(Item.class, ITEM_ID);
// select i.*, u.*, b.*
//   from ITEM i
//     left outer join USERS u on u.ID = i.SELLER_ID
//     left outer join BID b on b.ITEM_ID = i.ID
//   where i.ID = ?

em.detach(item);
```
Done fetching: no more lazy loading

```java
assertEquals(item.getBids().size(), 3);
assertNotNull(item.getBids().iterator().next().getAmount());
```
In detached state, bids are available ...

```java
assertEquals(item.getSeller().getUsername(), "johndoe");
```
... and so is the seller

For the find(), Hibernate executes a single SQL SELECT and JOINs three tables to retrieve the data. You can see the contents of the persistence context in figure 12.3. Note how the boundaries of the loaded graph are represented: the collection of images hasn't been loaded, and each Bid has a reference to an uninitialized User proxy, the bidder. If you now detach the Item, you can access the loaded seller and bids without causing a LazyInitializationException. If you try to access the images or one of the bidder proxies, you'll get an exception!

In the following examples, we assume that your domain model has a lazy default fetch plan. Hibernate will only load the data you explicitly request and the associations and collections you access.

Next, we discuss *how* data should be loaded when you find an entity instance by identity and when you navigate the network, using the pointers of your mapped associations and collections. We're interested in what SQL is executed and finding the ideal *fetch strategy*.

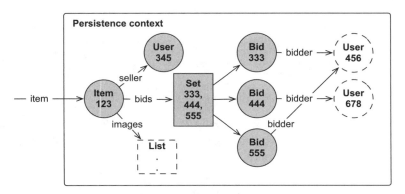

Figure 12.3   The seller and the bids of an Item are loaded.

12.2   *Selecting a fetch strategy*

Hibernate executes SQL SELECT statements to load data into memory. If you load an entity instance, one or more SELECT(s) are executed, depending on the number of tables involved and the *fetching strategy* you've applied. Your goal is to minimize the number of SQL statements and to simplify the SQL statements so that querying can be as efficient as possible.

Consider our recommended fetch plan from earlier in this chapter: every association and collection should be loaded on demand, lazily. This default fetch plan will most likely result in too many SQL statements, each loading only one small piece of data. This will lead to *n+1 selects problems*, and we discuss this issue first. The alternative fetch plan, using eager loading, will result in fewer SQL statements, because larger chunks of data are loaded into memory with each SQL query. You might then see the *Cartesian product problem*, as SQL result sets become too large.

You need to find the middle ground between these two extremes: the ideal fetching strategy for each procedure and use case in your application. Like fetch plans, you can set a global fetching strategy in your mappings: the default setting that is always active. Then, for a particular procedure, you might override the default fetching strategy with a custom JPQL, CriteriaQuery, or even SQL query.

First, let's discuss the fundamental problems you see, starting with the *n+1 selects* issue.

12.2.1   *The n+1 selects problem*

This problem is easy to understand with some example code. Let's assume that you mapped a lazy fetch plan, so everything is loaded on demand. The following example code checks whether the seller of each Item has a username:

> PATH: /examples/src/test/java/org/jpwh/test/fetching/NPlusOneSelects.java

```
List<Item> items = em.createQuery("select i from Item i").getResultList();
// select * from ITEM

for (Item item : items) {                                    Each seller must be loaded
    assertNotNull(item.getSeller().getUsername());  ◁──────  with an additional SELECT.
    // select * from USERS where ID = ?
}
```

You see one SQL SELECT to load the Item entity instances. Then, while you iterate through all the items, retrieving each User requires an additional SELECT. This amounts to one query for the Item plus *n* queries depending on how many items you have and whether a particular User is selling more than one Item. Obviously, this is a very inefficient strategy if you know you'll access the seller of each Item.

You can see the same issue with lazily loaded collections. The following example checks whether each Item has some bids:

```
PATH: /examples/src/test/java/org/jpwh/test/fetching/NPlusOneSelects.java
```

```
List<Item> items = em.createQuery("select i from Item i").getResultList();
// select * from ITEM

for (Item item : items) {                              Each bids collection has to be
    assertTrue(item.getBids().size() > 0);   ⟵┘      loaded with an additional SELECT.
    // select * from BID where ITEM_ID = ?
}
```

Again, if you know you'll access each `bids` collection, loading only one at a time is inefficient. If you have 100 items, you'll execute 101 SQL queries!

With what you know so far, you might be tempted to change the default fetch plan in your mappings and put a `FetchType.EAGER` on your `seller` or `bids` associations. But doing so can lead to our next topic: the *Cartesian product* problem.

12.2.2 The Cartesian product problem

If you look at your domain and data model and say, "Every time I need an `Item`, I also need the `seller` of that `Item`," you can map the association with `FetchType.EAGER` instead of a lazy fetch plan. You want a guarantee that whenever an `Item` is loaded, the `seller` will be loaded right away—you want that data to be available when the `Item` is detached and the persistence context is closed:

```
PATH: /model/src/main/java/org/jpwh/model/fetching/cartesianproduct/Item.java
```

```
@Entity
public class Item {

    @ManyToOne(fetch = FetchType.EAGER)
    protected User seller;

    // ...
}
```

To implement your eager fetch plan, Hibernate uses an SQL `JOIN` operation to load an `Item` and a `User` instance in one `SELECT`:

```
 item = em.find(Item.class, ITEM_ID);
// select i.*, u.*
//   from ITEM i
//   left outer join USERS u on u.ID = i.SELLER_ID
//   where i.ID = ?
```

The result set contains one row with data from the `ITEM` table combined with data from the `USERS` table, as shown in figure 12.4.

i.ID	i.NAME	i.SELLER_ID	...	u.ID	u.USERNAME	...
1	One	2	...	2	johndoe	...

Figure 12.4 Hibernate joins two tables to eagerly fetch associated rows.

Eager fetching with the default JOIN strategy isn't problematic for @ManyToOne and @OneToOne associations. You can eagerly load, with one SQL query and JOINs, an Item, its seller, the User's Address, the City they live in, and so on. Even if you map all these associations with FetchType.EAGER, the result set will have only one row. Now, Hibernate has to stop following your FetchType.EAGER plan at *some* point. The number of tables joined depends on the global hibernate.max_fetch_depth configuration property. By default, no limit is set. Reasonable values are small, usually between 1 and 5. You may even disable JOIN fetching of @ManyToOne and @OneToOne associations by setting the property to 0. If Hibernate reaches the limit, it will still eagerly load the data according to your fetch plan, but with additional SELECT statements. (Note that some database dialects may preset this property: for example, MySQL-Dialect sets it to 2.)

Eagerly loading collections with JOINs, on the other hand, can lead to serious performance issues. If you also switched to FetchType.EAGER for the bids and images collections, you'd run into the *Cartesian product problem*.

This issue appears when you eagerly load two collections with one SQL query and a JOIN operation. First, let's create such a fetch plan and then look at the SQL problem:

PATH: /model/src/main/java/org/jpwh/model/fetching/cartesianproduct/Item.java

```java
@Entity
public class Item {

    @OneToMany(mappedBy = "item", fetch = FetchType.EAGER)
    protected Set<Bid> bids = new HashSet<>();

    @ElementCollection(fetch = FetchType.EAGER)
    @CollectionTable(name = "IMAGE")
    @Column(name = "FILENAME")
    protected Set<String> images = new HashSet<String>();

    // ...
}
```

It doesn't matter whether both collections are @OneToMany, @ManyToMany, or @Element-Collection. Eager fetching more than one collection at once with the SQL JOIN operator is the fundamental issue, no matter what the collection content is. If you load an Item, Hibernate executes the problematic SQL statement:

PATH: /examples/src/test/java/org/jpwh/test/fetching/CartesianProduct.java

```java
Item item = em.find(Item.class, ITEM_ID);
// select i.*, b.*, img.*
//   from ITEM i
//     left outer join BID b on b.ITEM_ID = i.ID
//     left outer join IMAGE img on img.ITEM_ID = i.ID
//   where i.ID = ?

em.detach(item);

assertEquals(item.getImages().size(), 3);
assertEquals(item.getBids().size(), 3);
```

i.ID	i.NAME	...	b.ID	b.AMOUNT	img.FILENAME
1	One	...	1	99.00	foo.jpg
1	One	...	1	99.00	bar.jpg
1	One	...	1	99.00	baz.jpg
1	One	...	2	100.00	foo.jpg
1	One	...	2	100.00	bar.jpg
1	One	...	2	100.00	baz.jp
1	One	...	3	101.00	foo.jpg
1	One	...	3	101.00	bar.jpg
1	One	...	3	101.00	baz.jpg

Figure 12.5   A product is the result of two joins with many rows.

As you can see, Hibernate obeyed your eager fetch plan, and you can access the bids and images collections in detached state. The problem is *how* they were loaded, with an SQL JOIN that results in a product. Look at the result set in figure 12.5.

This result set contains many redundant data items, and only the shaded cells are relevant for Hibernate. The Item has three bids and three images. The size of the product depends on the size of the collections you're retrieving: three times three is nine rows total. Now imagine that you have an Item with 50 bids and 5 images—you'll see a result set with possibly 250 rows! You can create even larger SQL products when you write your own queries with JPQL or CriteriaQuery: imagine what happens if you load 500 items and eager-fetch dozens of bids and images with JOINs.

Considerable processing time and memory are required on the database server to create such results, which then must be transferred across the network. If you're hoping that the JDBC driver will compress the data on the wire somehow, you're probably expecting too much from database vendors. Hibernate immediately removes all duplicates when it marshals the result set into persistent instances and collections; information in cells that aren't shaded in figure 12.5 will be ignored. Obviously, you can't remove these duplicates at the SQL level; the SQL DISTINCT operator doesn't help here.

Instead of one SQL query with an extremely large result, three separate queries would be faster to retrieve an entity instance and two collections at the same time. Next, we focus on this kind of optimization and how you find and implement the best fetch strategy. We start again with a default lazy fetch plan and try to solve the *n+1 selects problem* first.

Hibernate Feature

12.2.3   *Prefetching data in batches*

If Hibernate fetches every entity association and collection only on demand, many additional SQL SELECT statements may be necessary to complete a particular procedure. As before, consider a routine that checks whether the seller of each Item has a username. With lazy loading, this would require one SELECT to get all Item instances and *n* more SELECTs to initialize the seller proxy of each Item.

Hibernate offers algorithms that can prefetch data. The first algorithm we discuss is *batch fetching*, and it works as follows: if Hibernate must initialize one User proxy, go ahead and initialize several with the same SELECT. In other words, if you already know that there are several Item instances in the persistence context and that they all have a proxy applied to their seller association, you may as well initialize several proxies instead of just one if you make the round trip to the database.

Let's see how this works. First, enable batch fetching of User instances with a proprietary Hibernate annotation:

PATH: /model/src/main/java/org/jpwh/model/fetching/batch/User.java

```
@Entity
@org.hibernate.annotations.BatchSize(size = 10)
@Table(name = "USERS")
public class User {
    // ...
}
```

This setting tells Hibernate that it may load up to 10 User proxies if one has to be loaded, all with the same SELECT. Batch fetching is often called a *blind-guess optimization*, because you don't know how many uninitialized User proxies may be in a particular persistence context. You can't say for sure that 10 is an ideal value—it's a guess. You know that instead of *n*+1 SQL queries, you'll now see *n*+1/10 queries, a significant reduction. Reasonable values are usually small, because you don't want to load too much data into memory either, especially if you aren't sure you'll need it.

This is the optimized procedure, which checks the username of each seller:

PATH: /examples/src/test/java/org/jpwh/test/fetching/Batch.java

```
List<Item> items = em.createQuery("select i from Item i").getResultList();
// select * from ITEM

for (Item item : items) {
    assertNotNull(item.getSeller().getUsername());
    // select * from USERS where ID in (?, ?, ?, ?, ?, ?, ?, ?, ?, ?)
}
```

Note the SQL query that Hibernate executes while you iterate through the items. When you call item.getSeller().getUserName() for the first time, Hibernate must initialize the first User proxy. Instead of only loading a single row from the USERS table, Hibernate retrieves several rows, and up to 10 User instances are loaded. Once you access the eleventh seller, another 10 are loaded in one batch, and so on, until the persistence context contains no uninitialized User proxies.

FAQ: What is the real batch-fetching algorithm?

Our explanation of batch loading was somewhat simplified, and you may see a slightly different algorithm in practice. As an example, imagine a batch size of 32. At startup time, Hibernate creates several batch loaders internally. Each loader knows how many proxies it can initialize: 32, 16, 10, 9, 8, 7, ..., 1. The goal is to minimize the memory consumption for loader creation and to create enough loaders that every possible batch fetch can be produced. Another goal is to minimize the number of SQL queries, obviously.

To initialize 31 proxies, Hibernate executes 3 batches (you probably expected 1, because 32 > 31). The batch loaders that are applied are 16, 10, and 5, as automatically selected by Hibernate. You can customize this batch-fetching algorithm with the property `hibernate.batch_fetch_style` in your persistence unit configuration. The default is `LEGACY`, which builds and selects several batch loaders on startup. Other options are `PADDED` and `DYNAMIC`. With `PADDED`, Hibernate builds only one batch loader SQL query on startup with placeholders for 32 arguments in the `IN` clause and then repeats bound identifiers if fewer than 32 proxies have to be loaded. With `DYNAMIC`, Hibernate dynamically builds the batch SQL statement at runtime, when it knows the number of proxies to initialize.

Batch fetching is also available for collections:

PATH: /model/src/main/java/org/jpwh/model/fetching/batch/Item.java

```java
@Entity
public class Item {

    @OneToMany(mappedBy = "item")
    @org.hibernate.annotations.BatchSize(size = 5)
    protected Set<Bid> bids = new HashSet<>();

    // ...
}
```

If you now force the initialization of one `bids` collection, up to five more `Item#bids` collections, if they're uninitialized in the current persistence context, are loaded right away:

PATH: /examples/src/test/java/org/jpwh/test/fetching/Batch.java

```java
List<Item> items = em.createQuery("select i from Item i").getResultList();
// select * from ITEM

for (Item item : items) {
    assertTrue(item.getBids().size() > 0);
    // select * from BID where ITEM_ID in (?, ?, ?, ?, ?)
}
```

When you call `item.getBids().size()` for the first time while iterating, a whole batch of `Bid` collections are preloaded for the other `Item` instances.

Batch fetching is a simple and often smart optimization that can significantly reduce the number of SQL statements that would otherwise be necessary to initialize all your proxies and collections. Although you may prefetch data you won't need in the end and consume more memory, the reduction in database round trips can make a huge difference. Memory is cheap, but scaling database servers isn't.

Another prefetching algorithm that isn't a blind guess uses subselects to initialize many collections with a single statement.

Hibernate Feature

12.2.4 *Prefetching collections with subselects*

A potentially better strategy for loading all `bids` of several `Item` instances is prefetching with a subselect. To enable this optimization, add a Hibernate annotation to your collection mapping:

PATH: /model/src/main/java/org/jpwh/model/fetching/subselect/Item.java

```java
@Entity
public class Item {

    @OneToMany(mappedBy = "item")
    @org.hibernate.annotations.Fetch(
        org.hibernate.annotations.FetchMode.SUBSELECT
    )
    protected Set<Bid> bids = new HashSet<>();

    // ...
}
```

Hibernate now initializes all `bids` collections for all loaded `Item` instances as soon as you force the initialization of one `bids` collection:

PATH: /examples/src/test/java/org/jpwh/test/fetching/Subselect.java

```java
List<Item> items = em.createQuery("select i from Item i").getResultList();
// select * from ITEM

for (Item item : items) {
    assertTrue(item.getBids().size() > 0);
    // select * from BID where ITEM_ID in (
    //   select ID from ITEM
    // )
}
```

Hibernate remembers the original query used to load the `items`. It then embeds this initial query (slightly modified) in a subselect, retrieving the collection of `bids` for each `Item`.

Prefetching using a subselect is a powerful optimization, but at the time of writing, it was only available for lazy collections, not for entity proxies. Also note that the original query that is rerun as a subselect is only remembered by Hibernate for a particular persistence context. If you detach an `Item` instance without initializing the collection of `bids`, and then merge it with a new persistence context and start iterating through the collection, no prefetching of other collections occurs.

Batch and subselect prefetching reduce the number of queries necessary for a particular procedure if you stick with a global lazy fetch plan in your mappings, helping mitigate the *n+1 selects problem*. If instead your global fetch plan has eager loaded associations and collections, you have to avoid the *Cartesian product problem*—for example, by breaking down a JOIN query into several SELECTs.

12.2.5 *Eager fetching with multiple SELECTs*

When you're trying to fetch several collections with one SQL query and JOINs, you run into the *Cartesian product problem*, as explained earlier. Instead of a JOIN operation, you can tell Hibernate to eagerly load data with additional SELECT queries and hence avoid large results and SQL products with duplicates:

> PATH: /model/src/main/java/org/jpwh/model/fetching/eagerselect/Item.java

```java
@Entity
public class Item {

    @ManyToOne(fetch = FetchType.EAGER)
    @org.hibernate.annotations.Fetch(
        org.hibernate.annotations.FetchMode.SELECT
    )
    protected User seller;

    @OneToMany(mappedBy = "item", fetch = FetchType.EAGER)
    @org.hibernate.annotations.Fetch(
        org.hibernate.annotations.FetchMode.SELECT
    )
    protected Set<Bid> bids = new HashSet<>();

    // ...
}
```

Defaults to JOIN

Now, when an `Item` is loaded, the `seller` and `bids` have to be loaded as well:

> PATH: /examples/src/test/java/org/jpwh/test/fetching/EagerSelect.java

```java
Item item = em.find(Item.class, ITEM_ID);
// select * from ITEM where ID = ?
// select * from USERS where ID = ?
// select * from BID where ITEM_ID = ?

em.detach(item);
```

```
assertEquals(item.getBids().size(), 3);
assertNotNull(item.getBids().iterator().next().getAmount());
assertEquals(item.getSeller().getUsername(), "johndoe");
```

Hibernate uses one SELECT to load a row from the ITEM table. It then immediately executes two more SELECTs: one loading a row from the USERS table (the seller) and the other loading several rows from the BID table (the bids).

The additional SELECT queries aren't executed lazily; the find() method produces several SQL queries. You can see how Hibernate followed the eager fetch plan: all data is available in detached state.

Still, all of these settings are global; they're always active. The danger is that adjusting one setting for one problematic case in your application might have negative side effects on some other procedure. Maintaining this balance can be difficult, so our recommendation is to map every entity association and collection as FetchType.LAZY, as mentioned before.

A better approach is to *dynamically* use eager fetching and JOIN operations only when needed, for a particular procedure.

12.2.6 Dynamic eager fetching

As in the previous sections, let's say you have to check the username of each Item#seller. With a lazy global fetch plan, load the data you need for this procedure and apply a *dynamic* eager fetch strategy in a query:

PATH: /examples/src/test/java/org/jpwh/test/fetching/EagerQuery.java

```
List<Item> items =
    em.createQuery("select i from Item i join fetch i.seller")
        .getResultList();
// select i.*, u.*
//  from ITEM i
//   inner join USERS u on u.ID = i.SELLER_ID
//  where i.ID = ?

em.close();                                        <— Detach all

for (Item item : items) {
    assertNotNull(item.getSeller().getUsername());
}
```

The important keywords in this JPQL query are join fetch, telling Hibernate to use a SQL JOIN (an INNER JOIN, actually) to retrieve the seller of each Item in the same query. The same query can be expressed with the CriteriaQuery API instead of a JPQL string:

PATH: /examples/src/test/java/org/jpwh/test/fetching/EagerQuery.java

```
CriteriaBuilder cb = em.getCriteriaBuilder();
CriteriaQuery criteria = cb.createQuery();
```

```
Root<Item> i = criteria.from(Item.class);
i.fetch("seller");
criteria.select(i);

List<Item> items = em.createQuery(criteria).getResultList();

em.close();                                        <— Detach all

for (Item item : items) {
    assertNotNull(item.getSeller().getUsername());
}
```

Dynamic eager join fetching also works for collections. Here you load all bids of each Item:

PATH: /examples/src/test/java/org/jpwh/test/fetching/EagerQuery.java

```
List<Item> items =
    em.createQuery("select i from Item i left join fetch i.bids")
        .getResultList();
// select i.*, b.*
//   from ITEM i
//     left outer join BID b on b.ITEM_ID = i.ID
//   where i.ID = ?

em.close();                                        <— Detach all

for (Item item : items) {
    assertTrue(item.getBids().size() > 0);
}
```

Now the same with the CriteriaQuery API:

PATH: /examples/src/test/java/org/jpwh/test/fetching/EagerQuery.java

```
CriteriaBuilder cb = em.getCriteriaBuilder();
CriteriaQuery criteria = cb.createQuery();

Root<Item> i = criteria.from(Item.class);
i.fetch("bids", JoinType.LEFT);
criteria.select(i);

List<Item> items = em.createQuery(criteria).getResultList();

em.close();                                        <— Detach all

for (Item item : items) {
    assertTrue(item.getBids().size() > 0);
}
```

Note that for collection fetching, a LEFT OUTER JOIN is necessary, because you also want rows from the ITEM table if there are no bids. We'll have much more to say about fetching with JPQL and CriteriaQuery later in this book, in chapter 15. You'll see many more examples then of inner, outer, left, and right joins, so don't worry too much about these details now.

Writing queries by hand isn't the only available option if you want to override the global fetch plan of your domain model dynamically. You can write *fetch profiles* declaratively.

12.3 Using fetch profiles

Fetch profiles complement the fetching options in the query languages and APIs. They allow you to maintain your profile definitions in either XML or annotation metadata. Early Hibernate versions didn't have support for special fetch profiles, but today Hibernate supports the following:

- *Fetch profiles*—A proprietary API based on declaration of the profile with `@org.hibernate.annotations.FetchProfile` and execution with `Session #enableFetchProfile()`. This simple mechanism currently supports overriding lazy-mapped entity associations and collections selectively, enabling a `JOIN` eager fetching strategy for a particular unit of work.
- *Entity graphs*—Specified in JPA 2.1, you can declare a graph of entity attributes and associations with the `@EntityGraph` annotation. This fetch plan, or a combination of plans, can be enabled as a hint when executing `EntityManager #find()` or queries (JPQL, criteria). The provided graph controls *what* should be loaded; unfortunately it doesn't control *how* it should be loaded.

It's fair to say that there is room for improvement here, and we expect future versions of Hibernate and JPA to offer a unified and more powerful API.

Don't forget that you can externalize JPQL and SQL statements and move them to metadata (see section 14.4). A JPQL query *is* a declarative (named) fetch profile; what you're missing is the ability to overlay different plans easily on the same base query. We've seen some creative solutions with string manipulation that are best avoided. With criteria queries, on the other hand, you already have the full power of Java available to organize your query-building code. Then the value of entity graphs is being able to reuse fetch plans across any kind of query.

Let's talk about Hibernate fetch profiles first and how you can override a global lazy fetch plan for a particular unit of work.

Hibernate Feature ───

12.3.1 Declaring Hibernate fetch profiles

Hibernate fetch profiles are global metadata: they're declared for the entire persistence unit. Although you could place the `@FetchProfile` annotation on a class, we prefer it as package-level metadata in a `package-info.java`:

> PATH: /model/src/main/java/org/jpwh/model/fetching/profile/package-info.java

```
@org.hibernate.annotations.FetchProfiles({
    @FetchProfile(name = Item.PROFILE_JOIN_SELLER,
        fetchOverrides = @FetchProfile.FetchOverride(
```

❶ Profile name

❷ Override

```
                    entity = Item.class,
                    association = "seller",
                    mode = FetchMode.JOIN        ◁————— ❸ JOIN mode
            )),
        @FetchProfile(name = Item.PROFILE_JOIN_BIDS,
            fetchOverrides = @FetchProfile.FetchOverride(
                entity = Item.class,
                association = "bids",
                mode = FetchMode.JOIN
            ))
    })
```

❶ Each profile has a name. This is a simple string isolated in a constant.

❷ Each override in a profile names one entity association or collection.

❸ The only supported mode at the time of writing is JOIN.

The profiles can now be enabled for a unit of work:

> PATH: /examples/src/test/java/org/jpwh/test/fetching/Profile.java

```
Item item = em.find(Item.class, ITEM_ID);          ◁————— ❶ Retrieves instance

em.clear();
em.unwrap(Session.class).enableFetchProfile(Item.PROFILE_JOIN_SELLER);  ◁┐
item = em.find(Item.class, ITEM_ID);                                     │
                                                        Enables profile ❷
em.clear();
em.unwrap(Session.class).enableFetchProfile(Item.PROFILE_JOIN_BIDS);  ◁┐
item = em.find(Item.class, ITEM_ID);                                   │
                                              Overlays second profile ❸
```

❶ The Item#seller is mapped lazy, so the default fetch plan only retrieves the Item instance.

❷ You need the Hibernate API to enable a profile. It's then active for any operation in that unit of work. The Item#seller is fetched with a join in the same SQL statement whenever an Item is loaded with this EntityManager.

❸ You can overlay another profile on the same unit of work. Now the Item#seller and the Item#bids collection are fetched with a join in the same SQL statement whenever an Item is loaded.

Although basic, Hibernate fetch profiles can be an easy solution for fetching optimization in smaller or simpler applications. With JPA 2.1, the introduction of *entity graphs* enables similar functionality in a standard fashion.

12.3.2 *Working with entity graphs*

An entity graph is a declaration of entity nodes and attributes, overriding or augmenting the default fetch plan when you execute an EntityManager#find() or with a hint on query operations. This is an example of a retrieval operation using an entity graph:

PATH: /examples/src/test/java/org/jpwh/test/fetching/FetchLoadGraph.java

```
Map<String, Object> properties = new HashMap<>();
properties.put(
    "javax.persistence.loadgraph",
    em.getEntityGraph(Item.class.getSimpleName())              ⟵ "Item"
);

Item item = em.find(Item.class, ITEM_ID, properties);
// select * from ITEM where ID = ?
```

The name of the entity graph you're using is Item, and the hint for the find() operation indicates it should be the *load graph*. This means attributes that are specified by attribute nodes of the entity graph are treated as FetchType.EAGER, and attributes that aren't specified are treated according to their specified or default FetchType in the mapping.

This is the declaration of this graph and the default fetch plan of the entity class:

PATH: /model/src/main/java/org/jpwh/model/fetching/fetchloadgraph/Item.java

```
@NamedEntityGraphs({
    @NamedEntityGraph                    ⟵ Default "Item" entity graph
})
@Entity
public class Item {

    @NotNull
    @ManyToOne(fetch = FetchType.LAZY)
    protected User seller;

    @OneToMany(mappedBy = "item")
    protected Set<Bid> bids = new HashSet<>();

    @ElementCollection
    protected Set<String> images = new HashSet<>();

    // ...
}
```

Entity graphs in metadata have names and are associated with an entity class; they're usually declared in annotations on top of an entity class. You can put them in XML if you like. If you don't give an entity graph a name, it gets the simple name of its owning entity class, which here is Item. If you don't specify any attribute nodes in the graph, like the empty entity graph in the last example, the defaults of the entity class are used. In Item, all associations and collections are mapped lazy; this is the default fetch plan. Hence, what you've done so far makes little difference, and the find() operation without any hints will produce the same result: the Item instance is loaded, and the seller, bids, and images aren't.

Alternatively, you can build an entity graph with an API:

> **PATH:** **/examples/src/test/java/org/jpwh/test/fetching/FetchLoadGraph.java**

```
EntityGraph<Item> itemGraph = em.createEntityGraph(Item.class);

Map<String, Object> properties = new HashMap<>();
properties.put("javax.persistence.loadgraph", itemGraph);

Item item = em.find(Item.class, ITEM_ID, properties);
```

This is again an empty entity graph with no attribute nodes, given directly to a retrieval operation.

Let's say you want to write an entity graph that changes the lazy default of Item#seller to eager fetching, when enabled:

> **PATH:** **/model/src/main/java/org\jpwh/model/fetching/fetchloadgraph/Item.java**

```
@NamedEntityGraphs({
    @NamedEntityGraph(
        name = "ItemSeller",
        attributeNodes = {
            @NamedAttributeNode("seller")
        }
    )
})
@Entity
public class Item {

    // ...
}
```

Now enable this graph by name when you want the Item and the seller eagerly loaded:

> **PATH:** **/examples/src/test/java/org/jpwh/test/fetching/FetchLoadGraph.java**

```
Map<String, Object> properties = new HashMap<>();
properties.put(
    "javax.persistence.loadgraph",
    em.getEntityGraph("ItemSeller")
);

Item item = em.find(Item.class, ITEM_ID, properties);
// select i.*, u.*
//   from ITEM i
//     inner join USERS u on u.ID = i.SELLER_ID
// where i.ID = ?
```

If you don't want to hardcode the graph in annotations, build it with the API instead:

```
PATH: /examples/src/test/java/org/jpwh/test/fetching/FetchLoadGraph.java
```

```
EntityGraph<Item> itemGraph = em.createEntityGraph(Item.class);
itemGraph.addAttributeNodes(Item_.seller);                          ⟵── Static
                                                                        metamodel
Map<String, Object> properties = new HashMap<>();
properties.put("javax.persistence.loadgraph", itemGraph);

Item item = em.find(Item.class, ITEM_ID, properties);
// select i.*, u.*
//   from ITEM i
//     inner join USERS u on u.ID = i.SELLER_ID
// where i.ID = ?
```

So far you've seen only properties for the find() operation. Entity graphs can also be enabled for queries, as hints:

```
PATH: /examples/src/test/java/org/jpwh/test/fetching/FetchLoadGraph.java
```

```
List<Item> items =
    em.createQuery("select i from Item i")
        .setHint("javax.persistence.loadgraph", itemGraph)
        .getResultList();
// select i.*, u.*
//   from ITEM i
//     left outer join USERS u on u.ID = i.SELLER_ID
```

Entity graphs can be complex. The following declaration shows how to work with reusable subgraph declarations:

```
PATH: /model/src/main/java/org/jpwh/model/fetching/fetchloadgraph/Bid.java
```

```java
@NamedEntityGraphs({
    @NamedEntityGraph(
        name = "BidBidderItemSellerBids",
        attributeNodes = {
            @NamedAttributeNode(value = "bidder"),
            @NamedAttributeNode(
                value = "item",
                subgraph = "ItemSellerBids"
            )
        },
        subgraphs = {
            @NamedSubgraph(
                name = "ItemSellerBids",
                attributeNodes = {
                    @NamedAttributeNode("seller"),
                    @NamedAttributeNode("bids")
                })
        }
    )
})
@Entity
public class Bid {
    // ...
}
```

This entity graph, when enabled as a load graph when retrieving `Bid` instances, also triggers eager fetching of `Bid#bidder`, the `Bid#item`, and furthermore the `Item#seller` and all `Item#bids`. Although you're free to name your entity graphs any way you like, we recommend that you develop a convention that everyone in your team can follow, and move the strings to shared constants.

With the entity graph API, the previous plan looks as follows:

> PATH: /examples/src/test/java/org/jpwh/test/fetching/FetchLoadGraph.java

```
EntityGraph<Bid> bidGraph = em.createEntityGraph(Bid.class);
bidGraph.addAttributeNodes(Bid_.bidder, Bid_.item);
Subgraph<Item> itemGraph = bidGraph.addSubgraph(Bid_.item);
itemGraph.addAttributeNodes(Item_.seller, Item_.bids);

Map<String, Object> properties = new HashMap<>();
properties.put("javax.persistence.loadgraph", bidGraph);

Bid bid = em.find(Bid.class, BID_ID, properties);
```

You've only seen entity graphs as *load* graphs so far. There is another option: you can enable an entity graph as a *fetch graph* with the `javax.persistence.fetchgraph` hint. If you execute a `find()` or query operation with a fetch graph, any attributes and collections not in your plan will be made `FetchType.LAZY`, and any nodes in your plan will be `FetchType.EAGER`. This effectively ignores all `FetchType` settings in your entity attribute and collection mappings, whereas the load graph feature was only augmenting.

Two weak points of the JPA entity graph operations are worth mentioning, because you'll run into them quickly. First, you can only modify fetch plans, not the Hibernate fetch strategy (batch/subselect/join/select). Second, declaring an entity graph in annotations or XML isn't fully type-safe: the attribute names are strings. The `Entity-Graph` API at least is type-safe.

12.4 Summary

- A fetch profile combines a fetch plan (what data should be loaded) with a fetch strategy (how the data should be loaded), encapsulated in reusable metadata or code.
- You created a global fetch plan and defined which associations and collections should be loaded into memory at all times. You defined the fetch plan based on use cases, how to access associated entities and iterate through collections in your application, and which data should be available in detached state.
- You learned to select the right fetching strategy for your fetch plan. Your goal is to minimize the number of SQL statements and the complexity of each SQL statement that must be executed. You especially want to avoid the *n+1 selects* and Cartesian product issues we examined in detail, using various optimization strategies.
- You explored Hibernate fetch profiles and entity graphs, the fetch profiles in JPA.

13
Filtering data

In this chapter, you see many different strategies for *filtering* data as it passes through the Hibernate engine. When Hibernate loads data from the database, you can transparently restrict the data seen by the application with a filter. When Hibernate stores data in the database, you can listen to such an event and execute some secondary routines: for example, write an audit log or assign a tenant identifier to the record.

We explore the following data-filtering features and APIs:

- In section 13.1, you learn to react to state changes of an entity instance and *cascade the state change* to associated entities. For example, when a User is saved, Hibernate can transitively and automatically save all related Billing-Details. When an Item is deleted, Hibernate can delete all Bid instances associated with that Item. You can enable this standard JPA feature with special attributes in your entity association and collection mappings.

312

- The Java Persistence standard includes life cycle *callbacks* and *event listeners*. An event listener is a class you write with special methods, called by Hibernate when an entity instance changes state: for example, after Hibernates loads it or is about to delete it from the database. These callback methods can also be on your entity classes and marked with special annotations. This gives you an opportunity to execute custom side effects when a transition occurs. Hibernate also has several proprietary extension points that allow interception of life cycle events at a lower level within its engine, which we discuss in section 13.2.

- A common side effect is writing an *audit log*; such a log typically contains information about the data that was changed, when the change was made, and who made the modification. A more sophisticated auditing system might require storing several versions of data and *temporal views*; you might want to ask Hibernate to load data "as it was last week." This being a complex problem, we introduce *Hibernate Envers* in section 13.3, a subproject dedicated to versioning and auditing in JPA applications.

- In section 13.4, you see that *data filters* are also available as a proprietary Hibernate API. These filters add custom restrictions to SQL SELECT statements executed by Hibernate. Hence, you can effectively define a custom limited view of the data in the application tier. For example, you could apply a filter that restricts loaded data by sales region, or any other authorization criteria.

We start with cascading options for transitive state changes.

Major new feature in JPA 2
- Injection of dependencies through CDI is now supported in JPA entity event listener classes.

13.1 Cascading state transitions

When an entity instance changes state—for example, when it was *transient* and becomes *persistent*—associated entity instances may also be included in this state transition. This *cascading* of state transitions isn't enabled by default; each entity instance has an independent life cycle. But for some associations between entities, you may want to implement fine-grained life cycle dependencies.

For example, in section 7.3, you created an association between the Item and Bid entity classes. In this case, not only did you make the bids of an Item automatically persistent when they were added to an Item, but they were also automatically deleted when the owning Item was deleted. You effectively made Bid an entity class that was dependent on another entity, Item.

The cascading settings you enabled in this association mapping were Cascade-Type.PERSIST and CascadeType.REMOVE. We also talked about the special switch orphanRemoval and how cascading deletion at the database level (with the foreign key ON DELETE option) affects your application.

You should review this association mapping and its cascading settings; we won't repeat it here. In this section, we look at some other, rarely used cascading options.

13.1.1 Available cascading options

Table 13.1 summarizes all available cascading options in Hibernate. Note how each is linked with an EntityManager or Session operation.

Table 13.1 Cascading options for entity association mappings

Option	Description
CascadeType.PERSIST	When an entity instance is stored with EntityManager #persist(), at flush time any associated entity instance(s) are also made persistent.
CascadeType.REMOVE	When an entity instance is deleted with EntityManager #remove(), at flush time any associated entity instance(s) are also removed.
CascadeType.DETACH	When an entity instance is evicted from the persistence context with EntityManager#detach(), any associated entity instance(s) are also detached.
CascadeType.MERGE	When a transient or detached entity instance is merged into a persistence context with EntityManager#merge(), any associated transient or detached entity instance(s) are also merged.
CascadeType.REFRESH	When a persistent entity instance is refreshed with EntityManager#refresh(), any associated persistent entity instance(s) are also refreshed.
org.hibernate.annotations .CascadeType.REPLICATE	When a detached entity instance is copied into a database with Session#replicate(), any associated detached entity instance(s) are also copied.
CascadeType.ALL	Shorthand to enable all cascading options for the mapped association.

If you're curious, you'll find more cascading options defined in the org.hibernate .annotations.CascadeType enumeration. Today, though, the only interesting option is REPLICATE and the Session#replicate() operation. All other Session operations have a standardized equivalent or alternative on the EntityManager API, so you can ignore these settings.

We've already covered the PERSIST and REMOVE options. Let's look at transitive detachment, merging, refreshing, and replication.

13.1.2 *Transitive detachment and merging*

Let's say you want to retrieve an `Item` and its `bids` from the database and work with this data in detached state. The `Bid` class maps this association with an `@ManyToOne`. It's bidirectional with this `@OneToMany` collection mapping in `Item`:

PATH: /model/src/main/java/org/jpwh/model/filtering/cascade/Item.java

```java
@Entity
public class Item {

    @OneToMany(
        mappedBy = "item",
        cascade = {CascadeType.DETACH, CascadeType.MERGE}
    )
    protected Set<Bid> bids = new HashSet<Bid>();

    // ...
}
```

Transitive detachment and merging is enabled with the DETACH and MERGE cascade types. Now you load the `Item` and initialize its `bids` collection:

PATH: /examples/src/test/java/org/jpwh/test/filtering/Cascade.java

```java
Item item = em.find(Item.class, ITEM_ID);
assertEquals(item.getBids().size(), 2);        ⟵── Initializes bids
em.detach(item);
```

The `EntityManager#detach()` operation is cascaded: it evicts the `Item` instance from the persistence context as well as all `bids` in the collection. If the `bids` aren't loaded, they aren't detached. (Of course, you could have closed the persistence context, effectively detaching *all* loaded entity instances.)

In detached state, you change the `Item#name`, create a new `Bid`, and link it with the `Item`:

PATH: /examples/src/test/java/org/jpwh/test/filtering/Cascade.java

```java
item.setName("New Name");

Bid bid = new Bid(new BigDecimal("101.00"), item);
item.getBids().add(bid);
```

Because you're working with detached entity state and collections, you have to pay extra attention to identity and equality. As explained in section 10.3, you should override the `equals()` and `hashCode()` methods on the `Bid` entity class:

PATH: **/model/src/main/java/org/jpwh/model/filtering/cascade/Bid.java**

```
@Entity
public class Bid {

    @Override
    public boolean equals(Object other) {
        if (this == other) return true;
        if (other == null) return false;
        if (!(other instanceof Bid)) return false;
        Bid that = (Bid) other;

        if (!this.getAmount().equals(that.getAmount()))
            return false;
        if (!this.getItem().getId().equals(that.getItem().getId()))
            return false;
        return true;
    }

    @Override
    public int hashCode() {
        int result = getAmount().hashCode();
        result = 31 * result + getItem().getId().hashCode();
        return result;
    }

    // ...
}
```

Two Bid instances are *equal* when they have the same amount and are linked with the same Item.

After you're done with your modifications in detached state, the next step is to store the changes. Using a new persistence context, merge the detached Item and let Hibernate detect the changes:

PATH: **/examples/src/test/java/org/jpwh/test/filtering/Cascade.java**

```
Item mergedItem = em.merge(item);            ◁——————— ❶ Merges item
// select i.*, b.*
//   from ITEM i
//     left outer join BID b on i.ID = b.ITEM_ID
//   where i.ID = ?

for (Bid b : mergedItem.getBids()) {         ◁——————— ❷ Bid has identifier value
    assertNotNull(b.getId());
}

em.flush();                                  ◁——————— ❸ Detects name change
// update ITEM set NAME = ? where ID = ?
// insert into BID values (?, ?, ?, ...)
```

❶ Hibernate merges the detached item. First it checks whether the persistence context already contains an Item with the given identifier value. In this case, there isn't any, so the Item is loaded from the database. Hibernate is smart enough to know that it will also need the bids during merging, so it fetches them right away in the same SQL query. Hibernate then copies the detached item values onto the loaded instance, which it returns to you in persistent state. The same procedure is applied to every Bid, and Hibernate will detect that one of the bids is new.

❷ Hibernate made the new Bid persistent during merging. It now has an identifier value assigned.

❸ When you flush the persistence context, Hibernate detects that the name of the Item changed during merging. The new Bid will also be stored.

Cascaded merging with collections is a powerful feature; consider how much code you would have to write without Hibernate to implement this functionality.

> ### Eagerly fetching associations when merging
>
> In the previous example, we said that Hibernate is smart enough to load the Item#bids collection when you merge a detached Item. Hibernate always loads entity associations eagerly with a JOIN when merging, if CascadeType.MERGE is enabled for the association. This is smart in the previous case, where the Item#bids were initialized, detached, and modified. Hibernate loading the collection when merging with a JOIN is therefore necessary and optimal. But if you merge an Item instance with an uninitialized bids collection or an uninitialized seller proxy, Hibernate will fetch the collection and proxy with a JOIN when merging. The merge initializes these associations on the managed Item it returns. CascadeType.MERGE causes Hibernate to ignore and effectively override any FetchType.LAZY mapping (as allowed by the JPA specification). This behavior may not be ideal in some cases, and at the time of writing, it isn't configurable.

Our next example is less sophisticated, enabling cascaded refreshing of related entities.

13.1.3 Cascading refresh

The User entity class has a *one-to-many* relationship with BillingDetails: each user of the application may have several credit cards, bank accounts, and so on. If you aren't familiar with the BillingDetails class, review the mappings in chapter 6.

You can map the relationship between User and BillingDetails as a unidirectional *one-to-many* entity association (there is no @ManyToOne):

PATH: /model/src/main/java/org/jpwh/model/filtering/cascade/User.java

```
@Entity
@Table(name = "USERS")
public class User {

    @OneToMany(cascade = {CascadeType.PERSIST, CascadeType.REFRESH})
    @JoinColumn(name = "USER_ID", nullable = false)
    protected Set<BillingDetails> billingDetails = new HashSet<>();

    // ...
}
```

The cascading options enabled for this association are PERSIST and REFRESH. The PERSIST option simplifies storing billing details; they become persistent when you add an instance of BillingDetails to the collection of an already persistent User.

In section 18.3, we'll discuss an architecture where the persistence context may be open for a long time, leading to managed entity instances in the context becoming stale. Therefore, in some long-running conversations, you'll want to reload them from the database. The REFRESH cascading option ensures that when you reload the state of a User instance, Hibernate will also refresh the state of each BillingDetails instance linked to the User:

PATH: /examples/src/test/java/org/jpwh/test/filtering/Cascade.java

```
User user = em.find(User.class, USER_ID);                    ◄──────── ❶ Loads User

assertEquals(user.getBillingDetails().size(), 2);            ◄──────    Initializes
for (BillingDetails bd : user.getBillingDetails()) {                ❷ collection
    assertEquals(bd.getOwner(), "John Doe");
}

// Someone modifies the billing information in the database!

em.refresh(user);                                            ◄──
// select * from CREDITCARD join BILLINGDETAILS where ID = ?
// select * from BANKACCOUNT join BILLINGDETAILS where ID = ?
// select * from USERS
//   left outer join BILLINGDETAILS                                Refreshes
//   left outer join CREDITCARD                                  ❸ BillingDetails
//   left outer JOIN BANKACCOUNT
// where ID = ?

for (BillingDetails bd : user.getBillingDetails()) {
    assertEquals(bd.getOwner(), "Doe John");
}
```

❶ An instance of User is loaded from the database.

❷ Its lazy billingDetails collection is initialized when you iterate through the elements or when you call size().

❸ When you refresh() the managed User instance, Hibernate cascades the operation to the managed BillingDetails and refreshes each with an SQL SELECT. If none of these instances remain in the database, Hibernate throws an EntityNotFoundException. Then, Hibernate refreshes the User instance and eagerly loads the entire billing-Details collection to discover any new BillingDetails.

This is a case where Hibernate isn't as smart as it could be. First it executes an SQL SELECT for each BillingDetails instance in the persistence context and referenced by the collection. Then it loads the entire collection again to find any added Billing-Details. Hibernate could obviously do this with one SELECT.

The last cascading option is for the Hibernate-only replicate() operation.

13.1.4 Cascading replication

You first saw replication in section 10.2.7. This nonstandard operation is available on the Hibernate `Session` API. The main use case is copying data from one database into another.

Consider this *many-to-one* entity association mapping between `Item` and `User`:

> **PATH: /model/src/main/java/org/jpwh/model/filtering/cascade/Item.java**

```
@Entity
public class Item {

    @ManyToOne(fetch = FetchType.LAZY)
    @JoinColumn(name = "SELLER_ID", nullable = false)
    @org.hibernate.annotations.Cascade(
        org.hibernate.annotations.CascadeType.REPLICATE
    )
    protected User seller;

    // ...
}
```

Here, you enable the `REPLICATE` cascading option with a Hibernate annotation. Next, you load an `Item` and its `seller` from the source database:

> **PATH: /examples/src/test/java/org/jpwh/test/filtering/Cascade.java**

```
tx.begin();
EntityManager em = JPA.createEntityManager();

Item item = em.find(Item.class, ITEM_ID);

assertNotNull(item.getSeller().getUsername());      <──── Initializes lazy Item#seller

tx.commit();
em.close();
```

After you close the persistence context, the `Item` and the `User` entity instances are in detached state. Next, you connect to the database and write the detached data:

> **PATH: /examples/src/test/java/org/jpwh/test/filtering/Cascade.java**

```
tx.begin();
EntityManager otherDatabase = // ... get EntityManager

otherDatabase.unwrap(Session.class)
    .replicate(item, ReplicationMode.OVERWRITE);
// select ID from ITEM where ID = ?
// select ID from USERS where ID = ?

tx.commit();
// update ITEM set NAME = ?, SELLER_ID = ?, ... where ID = ?
// update USERS set USERNAME = ?, ... where ID = ?
otherDatabase.close();
```

When you call `replicate()` on the detached `Item`, Hibernate executes SQL `SELECT` statements to find out whether the `Item` and its `seller` are already present in the database. Then, on commit, when the persistence context is flushed, Hibernate writes the values of the `Item` and the `seller` into the target database. In the previous example, these rows were already present, so you see an `UPDATE` of each, overwriting the values in the database. If the target database doesn't contain the `Item` or `User`, two `INSERT`s are made.

The last cascading option we're going to discuss is a global setting, enabling transitive persistence for all entity associations.

13.1.5 *Enabling global transitive persistence*

An object persistence layer is said to implement *persistence by reachability* if any instance becomes persistent whenever the application creates a reference to the instance from another instance that is already persistent. In the purest form of persistence by reachability, the database has some top-level or root object from which all persistent objects are reachable. Ideally, an instance should become transient and be deleted from the database if it isn't reachable via references from the root persistent object.

Neither Hibernate nor any other ORM solutions implement this. In fact, there is no analogue of the root persistent object in any SQL database, and no persistent garbage collector can detect unreferenced instances. Object-oriented (network) data stores may implement a garbage-collection algorithm, similar to the one implemented for in-memory objects by the JVM; but this option isn't available in the ORM world, and scanning all tables for unreferenced rows won't perform acceptably.

Still, there is some value in the concept of persistence by reachability. It helps you make transient instances persistent and propagate their state to the database without many calls to the persistence manager.

You can enable cascaded persistence for all entity associations in your orm.xml mapping metadata, as a default setting of the persistence unit:

PATH: /model/src/main/resources/filtering/DefaultCascadePersist.xml

```
<persistence-unit-metadata>
    <persistence-unit-defaults>
        <cascade-persist/>
    </persistence-unit-defaults>
</persistence-unit-metadata>
```

Hibernate now considers all entity associations in the domain model mapped by this persistence unit as `CascadeType.PERSIST`. Whenever you create a reference from an already persistent entity instance to a transient entity instance, Hibernate automatically makes that transient instance persistent.

Cascading options are effectively predefined reactions to life cycle events in the persistence engine. If you need to implement a custom procedure when data is stored or loaded, you can implement your own event listeners and interceptors.

13.2 Listening to and intercepting events

In this section, we discuss three different APIs for custom event listeners and persistence life cycle interceptors available in JPA and Hibernate. You can

- Use the standard JPA life cycle callback methods and event listeners.
- Write a proprietary `org.hibernate.Interceptor` and activate it on a `Session`.
- Use extension points of the Hibernate core engine with the `org.hibernate.event` SPI.

Let's start with the standard JPA callbacks. They offer easy access to persist, load, and remove life cycle events.

13.2.1 JPA event listeners and callbacks

Let's say you want to send a notification email to a system administrator whenever a new entity instance is stored. First, write a life cycle event listener with a callback method, annotated with `@PostPersist`, as shown in the following listing.

Listing 13.1 Notifying an admin when an entity instance was stored

PATH: /model/src/main/java/org/jpwh/model/filtering/callback/
       PersistEntityListener.java

```
public class PersistEntityListener {                    ◁——————— ❶ Entity listener constructor

    @PostPersist                                        ◁———┐
    public void notifyAdmin(Object entityInstance) {        │  Makes
                                                            │  notifyAdmin()
        User currentUser = CurrentUser.INSTANCE.get();      │  a callback
        Mail mail = Mail.INSTANCE;                        ❷ │  method

        mail.send(
            "Entity instance persisted by "
                + currentUser.getUsername()
                + ": "
                + entityInstance
        );
    }

}
```

Gets user info and email access ❸

❶ An entity listener class must have either no constructor or a public no-argument constructor. It doesn't have to implement any special interfaces. An entity listener is stateless; the JPA engine automatically creates and destroys it.

❷ You may annotate any method of an entity listener class as a callback method for persistence life cycle events. The `notifyAdmin()` method is invoked after a new entity instance is stored in the database.

❸ Because event listener classes are stateless, it can be difficult to get more contextual information when you need it. Here, you want the currently logged-in user and access to the email system to send a notification. A primitive solution is to use thread-local variables and singletons; you can find the source for `CurrentUser` and `Mail` in the example code.

A callback method of an entity listener class has a single `Object` parameter: the entity instance involved in the state change. If you only enable the callback for a particular entity type, you may declare the argument as that specific type. The callback method may have any kind of access; it doesn't have to be public. It must not be static or final and return nothing. If a callback method throws an unchecked `RuntimeException`, Hibernate will abort the operation and mark the current transaction for rollback. If a callback method declares and throws a checked `Exception`, Hibernate will wrap and treat it as a `RuntimeException`.

Injection in event listener classes

You often need access to contextual information and APIs when implementing an event listener. The previous example needs the currently logged-in user and an email API. A simple solution based on thread-locals and singletons might not be sufficient in larger and more complex applications. JPA also standardizes integration with CDI, so an entity listener class may rely on injection and the `@Inject` annotation to access dependencies. The CDI container provides the contextual information when the listener class is called. Note that even with CDI, you can't inject the current `Entity-Manager` to access the database in an event listener. We discuss a different solution for accessing the database in a (Hibernate) event listener later in this chapter.

You may only use each callback annotation once in an entity listener class; that is, only one method may be annotated `@PostPersist`. See table 13.2 for a summary of all available callback annotations.

Table 13.2   Life cycle callback annotations

Annotation	Description
`@PostLoad`	Triggered after an entity instance is loaded into the persistence context, either by identifier lookup, through navigation and proxy/collection initialization, or with a query. Also called after refreshing an already-persistent instance.
`@PrePersist`	Called immediately when `persist()` is called on an entity instance. Also called for `merge()` when an entity is discovered as transient, after the transient state is copied onto a persistent instance. Also called for associated entities if you enable `CascadeType.PERSIST`.
`@PostPersist`	Called after the database operation for making an entity instance persistent is executed and an identifier value is assigned. This may be at the time when `persist()` or `merge()` is invoked, or later when the persistence context is flushed if your identifier generator is *pre-insert* (see section 4.2.5). Also called for associated entities if you enable `CascadeType.PERSIST`.
`@PreUpdate, @PostUpdate`	Executed before and after the persistence context is synchronized with the database: that is, before and after flushing. Triggered only when the state of the entity requires synchronization (for example, because it's considered dirty).

Table 13.2 Life cycle callback annotations *(continued)*

Annotation	Description
`@PreRemove, @PostRemove`	Triggered when `remove()` is called or the entity instance is removed by cascading, and after deletion of the record in the database when the persistence context is flushed.

An entity listener class must be enabled for any entity you'd like to intercept, such as this `Item`:

PATH: /model/src/main/java/org/jpwh/model/filtering/callback/Item.java

```
@Entity
@EntityListeners(
    PersistEntityListener.class
)
public class Item {

    // ...

}
```

The `@EntityListeners` annotation accepts an array of listener classes, if you have several interceptors. If several listeners define callback methods for the same event, Hibernate invokes the listeners in the declared order. Alternatively, you can bind listener classes to an entity in XML metadata with the `<entity-listener>` sub-element of `<entity>`.

You don't have to write a separate entity listener class to intercept life cycle events. You can, for example, implement the `notifyAdmin()` method on the `User` entity class:

PATH: /model/src/main/java/org/jpwh/model/filtering/callback/User.java

```
@Entity
@Table(name = "USERS")
public class User {

    @PostPersist
    public void notifyAdmin(){
        User currentUser = CurrentUser.INSTANCE.get();
        Mail mail = Mail.INSTANCE;
        mail.send(
        "Entity instance persisted by "
                + currentUser.getUsername()
                + ": "
                + this
        );
    }

    // ...

}
```

Note that callback methods on an entity class don't have any arguments: the "current" entity involved in the state changes is this. Duplicate callbacks for the same event aren't allowed in a single class. But you can intercept the same event with callback methods in several listener classes or in a listener and an entity class.

You can also add callback methods on an entity superclass for the entire hierarchy. If, for a particular entity subclass, you want to disable the superclass's callbacks, annotate the subclass with @ExcludeSuperclassListeners or map it in XML metadata with <exclude-superclass-listeners>.

You can declare default entity listener classes, enabled for all entities in your persistence unit, in XML metadata:

PATH: /model/src/main/resources/filtering/EventListeners.xml

```
<persistence-unit-metadata>
  <persistence-unit-defaults>
    <entity-listeners>
      <entity-listener
        class="org.jpwh.model.filtering.callback.PersistEntityListener"/>
    </entity-listeners>
  </persistence-unit-defaults>
</persistence-unit-metadata>
```

If you want to disable a default entity listener for a particular entity, either map it with <exclude-default-listeners> in XML metadata or mark it with the @Exclude-DefaultListeners annotation:

PATH: /model/src/main/java/org/jpwh/model/filtering/callback/User.java

```
@Entity
@Table(name = "USERS")
@ExcludeDefaultListeners
public class User {

    // ...
}
```

Be aware that enabling entity listeners is additive. If you enable and/or bind entity listeners in XML metadata *and* annotations, Hibernate will call them all in the following order:

1 Default listeners for the persistence unit, in the order as declared in XML metadata.
2 Listeners declared on an entity with @EntityListeners, in the given order.
3 Callback methods declared in entity superclasses are first, starting with the most generic superclass. Callback methods on the entity class are last.

JPA event listeners and callbacks provide a rudimentary framework for reacting to life cycle events with your own procedures. Hibernate also has a more fine-grained and powerful alternative API: org.hibernate.Interceptor.

13.2.2 *Implementing Hibernate interceptors*

Let's assume that you want to write an audit log of data modifications in a separate database table. For example, you may record information about creation and update events for each Item. The audit log includes the user, the date and time of the event, what type of event occurred, and the identifier of the Item that was changed.

Audit logs are often handled using database triggers. On the other hand, it's sometimes better for the application to take responsibility, especially if portability between different databases is required.

You need several elements to implement audit logging. First, you have to mark the entity classes for which you want to enable audit logging. Next, you define what information to log, such as the user, date, time, and type of modification. Finally, you tie it all together with an org.hibernate.Interceptor that automatically creates the audit trail.

First, create a marker interface, Auditable:

PATH: /model/src/main/java/org/jpwh/model/filtering/interceptor/Auditable.java

```
public interface Auditable {
    public Long getId();
}
```

This interface requires that a persistent entity class expose its identifier with a getter method; you need this property to log the audit trail. Enabling audit logging for a particular persistent class is then trivial. You add it to the class declaration, such as for Item:

PATH: /model/src/main/java/org/jpwh/model/filtering/interceptor/Item.java

```
@Entity
public class Item implements Auditable {

    // ...
}
```

Now, create a new persistent entity class, AuditLogRecord, with the information you want to log in your audit database table:

PATH: /model/src/main/java/org/jpwh/model/filtering/interceptor/
      AuditLogRecord.java

```
@Entity
public class AuditLogRecord {

    @Id
    @GeneratedValue(generator = "ID_GENERATOR")
    protected Long id;

    @NotNull
    protected String message;
```

```
@NotNull
protected Long entityId;

@NotNull
protected Class entityClass;

@NotNull
protected Long userId;

@NotNull
@Temporal(TemporalType.TIMESTAMP)
protected Date createdOn = new Date();

// ...
}
```

You want to store an instance of `AuditLogRecord` whenever Hibernate inserts or updates an `Item` in the database. A Hibernate interceptor can handle this automatically. Instead of implementing all methods in `org.hibernate.Interceptor`, extend the `EmptyInterceptor` and override only the methods you need, as shown next.

> **Listing 13.2 Hibernate interceptor logging modification events**
>
> PATH: /examples/src/test/java/org/jpwh/test/filtering/AuditLogInterceptor.java

```
public class AuditLogInterceptor extends EmptyInterceptor {

    protected Session currentSession;                    ◀────── ❶ Accesses database
    protected Long currentUserId;
    protected Set<Auditable> inserts = new HashSet<Auditable>();
    protected Set<Auditable> updates = new HashSet<Auditable>();

    public void setCurrentSession(Session session) {
        this.currentSession = session;
    }                                                         ❷ Called
                                                                when
    public void setCurrentUserId(Long currentUserId) {          instance is
        this.currentUserId = currentUserId;                     made
    }                                                            persistent

    public boolean onSave(Object entity, Serializable id,   ◀──┐
                          Object[] state, String[] propertyNames,
                          Type[] types)
        throws CallbackException {

        if (entity instanceof Auditable)
            inserts.add((Auditable)entity);

        return false;                       Called if instance is dirty ❸
    }

    public boolean onFlushDirty(Object entity, Serializable id,   ◀──┐
                                Object[] currentState,
                                Object[] previousState,
                                String[] propertyNames, Type[] types)
        throws CallbackException {

        if (entity instanceof Auditable)
            updates.add((Auditable)entity);
```

You didn't modify the state. (annotation pointing to `return false;`)

```
        return false;                    ⟵── You didn't modify the currentState.
    }

    // ...
}
```

❶ You need to access the database to write the audit log, so this interceptor needs a Hibernate `Session`. You also want to store the identifier of the currently logged-in user in each audit log record. The `inserts` and `updates` instance variables are collections where this interceptor will hold its internal state.

❷ This method is called when an entity instance is made persistent.

❸ This method is called when an entity instance is detected as dirty during flushing of the persistence context.

The interceptor collects the modified `Auditable` instances in `inserts` and `updates`. Note that in `onSave()`, there may not be an identifier value assigned to the given entity instance. Hibernate guarantees to set entity identifiers during flushing, so the actual audit log trail is written in the `postFlush()` callback, which isn't shown in listing 13.2:

> PATH: /examples/src/test/java/org/jpwh/test/filtering/AuditLogInterceptor.java

```
public class AuditLogInterceptor extends EmptyInterceptor {

    // ...

    public void postFlush(Iterator iterator) throws CallbackException {

        Session tempSession =                              ⟵──  Creates
            currentSession.sessionWithOptions()                 temporary
                .transactionContext()                        ❷ Session
                .connection()
                .openSession();
                                                             ❸ Stores
        try {                                                   AuditLogRecords
            for (Auditable entity : inserts) {         ⟵──
                tempSession.persist(
                    new AuditLogRecord("insert", entity, currentUserId)
                );
            }
            for (Auditable entity : updates) {
                tempSession.persist(
                    new AuditLogRecord("update", entity, currentUserId)
                );
            }

            tempSession.flush();                       ⟵── ❹ Closes temporary Session
        } finally {
            tempSession.close();
            inserts.clear();
            updates.clear();
        }
    }
}
```

Writes audit log records ❶

❶ This method is called after flushing of the persistence context is complete. Here, you write the audit log records for all insertions and updates you collected earlier.

❷ You can't access the original persistence context: the Session that is currently executing this interceptor. The Session is in a fragile state during interceptor calls. Hibernate lets you create a new Session that inherits some information from the original Session with the sessionWithOptions() method. The new temporary Session works with the same transaction and database connection as the original Session.

❸ You store a new AuditLogRecord for each insertion and update using the temporary Session.

❹ You flush and close the temporary Session independently from the original Session.

You're now ready to enable this interceptor with a Hibernate property when creating an EntityManager:

PATH: /examples/src/test/java/org/jpwh/test/filtering/AuditLogging.java

```
EntityManagerFactory emf = JPA.getEntityManagerFactory();

Map<String, String> properties = new HashMap<String, String>();
properties.put(
    org.hibernate.jpa.AvailableSettings.SESSION_INTERCEPTOR,
    AuditLogInterceptor.class.getName()
);

EntityManager em = emf.createEntityManager(properties);
```

Enabling default interceptors
If you want to enable an interceptor by default for any EntityManager, you can set the property hibernate.ejb.interceptor in your persistence.xml to a class that implements org.hibernate.Interceptor. Note that unlike a session-scoped interceptor, Hibernate shares this default interceptor, so it must be thread-safe! The example AuditLogInterceptor is *not* thread-safe.

This EntityManager now has an enabled AuditLogInterceptor, but the interceptor must also be configured with the current Session and logged-in user identifier. This involves some typecasts to access the Hibernate API:

PATH: /examples/src/test/java/org/jpwh/test/filtering/AuditLogging.java

```
Session session = em.unwrap(Session.class);
AuditLogInterceptor interceptor =
    (AuditLogInterceptor) ((SessionImplementor) session).getInterceptor();
interceptor.setCurrentSession(session);
interceptor.setCurrentUserId(CURRENT_USER_ID);
```

The `EntityManager` is now ready for use, and an audit trail will be written whenever you store or modify an `Item` instance with it.

Hibernate interceptors are flexible, and, unlike JPA event listeners and callback methods, you have access to much more contextual information when an event occurs. Having said that, Hibernate allows you to hook even deeper into its core with the extensible event system it's based on.

13.2.3 *The core event system*

The Hibernate core engine is based on a model of events and listeners. For example, if Hibernate needs to save an entity instance, it triggers an event. Whoever listens to this kind of event can catch it and handle saving the data. Hibernate therefore implements all of its core functionality as a set of default listeners, which can handle all Hibernate events.

Hibernate is open by design: you can write and enable your own listeners for Hibernate events. You can either replace the existing default listeners or extend them and execute a side effect or additional procedure. Replacing the event listeners is rare; doing so implies that your own listener implementation can take care of a piece of Hibernate core functionality.

Essentially, all the methods of the `Session` interface (and its narrower cousin, the `EntityManager`) correlate to an event. The `find()` and `load()` methods trigger a `LoadEvent`, and by default this event is processed with the `DefaultLoadEvent-Listener`.

A custom listener should implement the appropriate interface for the event it wants to process and/or extend one of the convenience base classes provided by Hibernate, or any of the default event listeners. Here's an example of a custom load event listener.

Listing 13.3   Custom load event listener

PATH: /examples/src/test/java/org/jpwh/test/filtering/SecurityLoadListener.java

---

```java
public class SecurityLoadListener extends DefaultLoadEventListener {

    public void onLoad(LoadEvent event, LoadEventListener.LoadType loadType)
        throws HibernateException {

        boolean authorized =
            MySecurity.isAuthorized(
                event.getEntityClassName(), event.getEntityId()
            );

        if (!authorized)
            throw new MySecurityException("Unauthorized access");

        super.onLoad(event, loadType);
    }

}
```

This listener performs custom authorization code. A listener should be considered effectively a singleton, meaning it's shared between persistence contexts and thus shouldn't save any transaction-related state as instance variables. For a list of all events and listener interfaces in native Hibernate, see the API Javadoc of the `org.hibernate.event` package.

You enable listeners for each core event in your persistence.xml, in a `<persistence-unit>`:

PATH: /model/src/main/resources/META-INF/persistence.xml

```
<properties>
    <property name="hibernate.ejb.event.load"
              value="org.jpwh.test.filtering.SecurityLoadListener"/>
</properties>
```

The property name of the configuration setting always starts with `hibernate.ejb.event`, followed by the type of event you want to listen to. You can find a list of all event types in `org.hibernate.event.spi.EventType`. The value of the property can be a comma-separated list of listener class names; Hibernate will call each listener in the specified order.

You rarely have to extend the Hibernate core event system with your own functionality. Most of the time, an `org.hibernate.Interceptor` is flexible enough. It helps to have more options and to be able to replace any piece of the Hibernate core engine in a modular fashion.

The audit-logging implementation you saw in the previous section was very simple. If you need to log more information for auditing, such as the actual changed property values of an entity, consider *Hibernate Envers*.

13.3   *Auditing and versioning with Hibernate Envers*

Envers is a project of the Hibernate suite dedicated to audit logging and keeping multiple versions of data in the database. This is similar to version control systems you may already be familiar with, such as Subversion and Git.

With Envers enabled, a copy of your data is automatically stored in separate database tables when you add, modify, or delete data in the main tables of the application. Envers internally uses the Hibernate event SPI you saw in the previous section. Envers listens to Hibernate events, and when Hibernate stores changes in the database, Envers creates a copy of the data and logs a revision in its own tables.

Envers groups all data modifications in a unit of work—that is, in a transaction—as a change set with a revision number. You can write queries with the Envers API to retrieve historical data given a revision number or timestamp: for example, "find all `Item` instances as they were last Friday." First you have to enable Envers in your application.

13.3.1 Enabling audit logging

Envers is available without further configuration as soon as you put its JAR file on your classpath (or, as shown in the example code of this book, include it as a Maven dependency). You enable audit logging selectively for an entity class with the `@org.hibernate` `.envers.Audited` annotation.

Listing 13.4 Enabling audit logging for the `Item` entity

PATH: /model/src/main/java/org/jpwh/model/filtering/envers/Item.java

```
@Entity
@org.hibernate.envers.Audited
public class Item {

    @NotNull
    protected String name;

    @OneToMany(mappedBy = "item")
    @org.hibernate.envers.NotAudited
    protected Set<Bid> bids = new HashSet<Bid>();

    @ManyToOne(fetch = FetchType.LAZY)
    @JoinColumn(name = "SELLER_ID", nullable = false)
    protected User seller;

    // ...
}
```

You've now enabled audit logging for `Item` instances and all properties of the entity. To disable audit logging for a particular property, annotate it with `@NotAudited`. In this case, Envers ignores the `bids` but audits the `seller`. You also have to enable auditing with `@Audited` on the `User` class.

Hibernate will now generate (or expect) additional database tables to hold historical data for each `Item` and `User`. Figure 13.1 shows the schema for these tables.

The `ITEM_AUD` and `USERS_AUD` tables are where the modification history of `Item` and `User` instances is stored. When you modify data and commit a transaction, Hibernate inserts a new revision number with a timestamp into the `REVINFO` table. Then, for

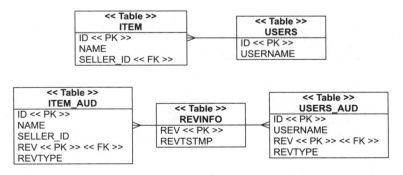

Figure 13.1 Audit logging tables for the `Item` and `User` entities

each modified and audited entity instance involved in the change set, a copy of its data is stored in the audit tables. Foreign keys on revision number columns link the change set together. The REVTYPE column holds the type of change: whether the entity instance was inserted, updated, or deleted in the transaction. Envers never automatically removes any revision information or historical data; even after you remove() an Item instance, you still have its previous versions stored in ITEM_AUD.

Let's run through some transactions to see how this works.

13.3.2 *Creating an audit trail*

In the following code examples, you see several transactions involving an Item and its seller, a User. You create and store an Item and User, then modify both, and then finally delete the Item.

You should already be familiar with this code. Envers automatically creates an audit trail when you work with the EntityManager:

PATH: /examples/src/test/java/org/jpwh/test/filtering/Envers.java

```
tx.begin();
EntityManager em = JPA.createEntityManager();

User user = new User("johndoe");
em.persist(user);

Item item = new Item("Foo", user);
em.persist(item);

tx.commit();
em.close();
```

PATH: /examples/src/test/java/org/jpwh/test/filtering/Envers.java

```
tx.begin();
EntityManager em = JPA.createEntityManager();

Item item = em.find(Item.class, ITEM_ID);
item.setName("Bar");
item.getSeller().setUsername("doejohn");

tx.commit();
em.close();
```

PATH: /examples/src/test/java/org/jpwh/test/filtering/Envers.java

```
tx.begin();
EntityManager em = JPA.createEntityManager();

Item item = em.find(Item.class, ITEM_ID);
em.remove(item);

tx.commit();
em.close();
```

Envers transparently writes the audit trail for this sequence of transactions by logging three change sets. To access this historical data, you first have to obtain the number of the revision, representing the change set you'd like to access.

13.3.3 *Finding revisions*

With the Envers `AuditReader` API, you can find the revision number of each change set:

> **Listing 13.5 Obtaining the revision numbers of change sets**
> PATH: /examples/src/test/java/org/jpwh/test/filtering/Envers.java

```
AuditReader auditReader = AuditReaderFactory.get(em);          ①  AuditReader API
Number revisionCreate =
        auditReader.getRevisionNumberForDate(TIMESTAMP_CREATE);        Gets
Number revisionUpdate =                                                revision
        auditReader.getRevisionNumberForDate(TIMESTAMP_UPDATE);   ②  number
Number revisionDelete  =
        auditReader.getRevisionNumberForDate(TIMESTAMP_DELETE);
List<Number> itemRevisions = auditReader.getRevisions(Item.class, ITEM_ID);
assertEquals(itemRevisions.size(), 3);
for (Number itemRevision : itemRevisions) {
    Date itemRevisionTimestamp = auditReader.getRevisionDate(itemRevision);
    // ...
}

List<Number> userRevisions = auditReader.getRevisions(User.class, USER_ID);
assertEquals(userRevisions.size(), 2);
```

Finds change sets ③

Gets timestamp ④

Counts revisions ⑤

❶ The main Envers API is `AuditReader`. It can be accessed with an `EntityManager`.

❷ Given a timestamp, you can find the revision number of a change set made before or on that timestamp.

❸ If you don't have a timestamp, you can get all revision numbers in which a particular audited entity instance was involved. This operation finds all change sets where the given `Item` was created, modified, or deleted. In our example, we created, modified, and then deleted the `Item`. Hence, we have three revisions.

❹ If you have a revision number, you can get the timestamp when Envers logged the change set.

❺ We created and modified the `User`, so there are two revisions.

In listing 13.5, we assumed that either you know the (approximate) timestamp for a transaction or you have the identifier value of an entity so you can obtain its revisions. If you have neither, you may want to explore the audit log with queries. This is also useful if you have to show a list of all change sets in the user interface of your application.

The following code discovers all revisions of the `Item` entity class and loads each `Item` version and the audit log information for that change set:

PATH: /examples/src/test/java/org/jpwh/test/filtering/Envers.java

```
AuditQuery query = auditReader.createQuery()                          ◄─┐  Query to get audit
    .forRevisionsOfEntity(Item.class, false, false);                   ❶  trail details

List<Object[]> result = query.getResultList();                       ◄─   Gets audit
for (Object[] tuple : result) {                                        ❷  trail details

    Item item = (Item) tuple[0];
    DefaultRevisionEntity revision = (DefaultRevisionEntity)tuple[1];
    RevisionType revisionType = (RevisionType)tuple[2];

    if (revision.getId() == 1) {                              ◄──── ❹ Gets revision type
        assertEquals(revisionType, RevisionType.ADD);
        assertEquals(item.getName(), "Foo");
    } else if (revision.getId() == 2) {
        assertEquals(revisionType, RevisionType.MOD);
        assertEquals(item.getName(), "Bar");
    } else if (revision.getId() == 3) {
        assertEquals(revisionType, RevisionType.DEL);
        assertNull(item);
    }
}
```

Gets revision details ❸ (pointing to the `Item item = (Item) tuple[0];` block)

❶ If you don't know modification timestamps or revision numbers, you can write a query with `forRevisionsOfEntity()` to obtain all audit trail details of a particular entity.

❷ This query returns the audit trail details as a `List` of `Object[]`.

❸ Each result tuple contains the entity instance for a particular revision, the revision details (including revision number and timestamp), as well as the revision type.

❹ The revision type indicates why Envers created the revision, because the entity instance was inserted, modified, or deleted in the database.

Revision numbers are sequentially incremented; a higher revision number is always a more recent version of an entity instance. You now have revision numbers for the three change sets in the audit trail, giving you access to historical data.

13.3.4 Accessing historical data

With a revision number, you can access different versions of the `Item` and its `seller`.

Listing 13.6   Loading historical versions of entity instances

PATH: /examples/src/test/java/org/jpwh/test/filtering/Envers.java

Returns audited instance ❶

```
Item item = auditReader.find(Item.class, ITEM_ID, revisionCreate);
assertEquals(item.getName(), "Foo");
assertEquals(item.getSeller().getUsername(), "johndoe");
```

```
Item modifiedItem = auditReader.find(Item.class,          ◀────②  Loads updated Item
     ITEM_ID, revisionUpdate);
assertEquals(modifiedItem.getName(), "Bar");
assertEquals(modifiedItem.getSeller().getUsername(), "doejohn");

Item deletedItem = auditReader.find(Item.class,           ◀────③  Handles deleted  Item
     ITEM_ID, revisionDelete);
assertNull(deletedItem);

User user = auditReader.find(User.class,                  ◀────④  Returns closest revision
     USER_ID, revisionDelete);
assertEquals(user.getUsername(), "doejohn");
```

❶ The `find()` method returns an audited entity instance version, given a revision. This operation loads the `Item` as it was after creation.

❷ This operation loads the `Item` after it was updated. Note how the modified `seller` of this change set is also retrieved automatically.

❸ In this revision, the `Item` was deleted, so `find()` returns `null`.

❹ The example didn't modify the `User` in this revision, so Envers returns its closest historical revision.

The `AuditReader#find()` operation retrieves only a single entity instance, like `EntityManager#find()`. But the returned entity instances are *not* in persistent state: the persistence context doesn't manage them. If you modify an older version of `Item`, Hibernate won't update the database. Consider the entity instances returned by the `AuditReader` API to be detached, or read-only.

    `AuditReader` also has an API for execution of arbitrary queries, similar to the native Hibernate `Criteria` API (see section 16.3).

Listing 13.7   Querying historical entity instances

PATH: /examples/src/test/java/org/jpwh/test/filtering/Envers.java

```
AuditQuery query = auditReader.createQuery()             ◀──┐   Return Items from
     .forEntitiesAtRevision(Item.class, revisionUpdate);    └─❶  particular revision

query.add(                                              ◀──┐   Adds
     AuditEntity.property("name").like("Ba", MatchMode.START)  └─❷  restriction
);

query.add(                                              ◀────❸  Adds restriction
     AuditEntity.relatedId("seller").eq(USER_ID)
);

query.addOrder(                                         ◀────❹  Orders results
     AuditEntity.property("name").desc()
);

query.setFirstResult(0);                               ◀────❺  Paginates
query.setMaxResults(10);

assertEquals(query.getResultList().size(), 1);
Item result = (Item)query.getResultList().get(0);
assertEquals(result.getSeller().getUsername(), "doejohn");
```

❶ This query returns Item instances restricted to a particular revision and change set.

❷ You can add further restrictions to the query; here the Item#name must start with "Ba".

❸ Restrictions can include entity associations: for example, you're looking for the revision of an Item sold by a particular User.

❹ You can order query results.

❺ You can paginate through large results.

Envers supports projection. The following query retrieves only the Item#name of a particular version:

PATH: /examples/src/test/java/org/jpwh/test/filtering/Envers.java

```
AuditQuery query = auditReader.createQuery()
    .forEntitiesAtRevision(Item.class, revisionUpdate);

query.addProjection(
    AuditEntity.property("name")
);

assertEquals(query.getResultList().size(), 1);
String result = (String)query.getSingleResult();
assertEquals(result, "Bar");
```

Finally, you may want to roll back an entity instance to an older version. This can be accomplished with the Session#replicate() operation and overwriting an existing row. The following example loads the User instance from the first change set and then overwrites the current User in the database with the older version:

PATH: /examples/src/test/java/org/jpwh/test/filtering/Envers.java

```
User user = auditReader.find(User.class, USER_ID, revisionCreate);

em.unwrap(Session.class)
    .replicate(user, ReplicationMode.OVERWRITE);
em.flush();
em.clear();

user = em.find(User.class, USER_ID);
assertEquals(user.getUsername(), "johndoe");
```

Envers will also track this change as an update in the audit log; it's just another new revision of the User instance.

Temporal data is a complex subject, and we encourage you to read the Envers reference documentation for more information. Adding details to the audit log, such as the user who made a change, isn't difficult. The documentation also shows how you can configure different tracking strategies and customize the database schema used by Envers.

Next, imagine that you don't want to see all the data in your database. For example, the currently logged-in application user may not have the rights to see everything.

Usually, you add a condition to your queries and restrict the result dynamically. This becomes difficult if you have to handle a concern such as security, because you'd have to customize most of the queries in your application. You can centralize and isolate these restrictions with Hibernate's dynamic data filters.

13.4 Dynamic data filters

The first use case for dynamic data filtering relates to data security. A User in Caveat-Emptor may have a ranking property, which is a simple integer:

> PATH: /model/src/main/java/org/jpwh/model/filtering/dynamic/User.java

```java
@Entity
@Table(name = "USERS")
public class User {

    @NotNull
    protected int rank = 0;

    // ...
}
```

Now assume that users can only bid on items that other users offer with an equal or lower rank. In business terms, you have several groups of users that are defined by an arbitrary rank (a number), and users can trade only with people who have the same or lower rank.

To implement this requirement, you'd have to customize all queries that load Item instances from the database. You'd check whether the Item#seller you want to load has an equal or lower rank than the currently logged-in user. Hibernate can do this work for you with a dynamic filter.

13.4.1 Defining dynamic filters

First, you define your filter with a name and the dynamic runtime parameters it accepts. You can place the Hibernate annotation for this definition on any entity class of your domain model or in a package-info.java metadata file:

> PATH: /model/src/main/java/org/jpwh/model/filtering/dynamic/package-info.java

```java
@org.hibernate.annotations.FilterDef(
    name = "limitByUserRank",
    parameters = {
        @org.hibernate.annotations.ParamDef(
            name = "currentUserRank", type = "int"
        )
    }
)
```

This example names this filter limitByUserRank; note that filter names must be unique in a persistence unit. It accepts one runtime argument of type int. If you have several filter definitions, declare them within @org.hibernate.annotations.FilterDefs.

The filter is inactive now; nothing indicates that it's supposed to apply to Item instances. You must apply and implement the filter on the classes or collections you want to filter.

13.4.2 Applying the filter

You want to apply the defined filter on the Item class so that no items are visible if the logged-in user doesn't have the necessary rank:

> PATH: /model/src/main/java/org/jpwh/model/filtering/dynamic/Item.java

```
@Entity
@org.hibernate.annotations.Filter(
    name = "limitByUserRank",
    condition =
        ":currentUserRank >= (" +
                "select u.RANK from USERS u " +
                "where u.ID = SELLER_ID" +
            ")"
)
public class Item {

    // ...
}
```

The condition is an SQL expression that's passed through directly to the database system, so you can use any SQL operator or function. It must evaluate to true if a record should pass the filter. In this example, you use a subquery to obtain the rank of the seller of the item. Unqualified columns, such as SELLER_ID, refer to the table mapped to the entity class. If the currently logged-in user's rank isn't greater than or equal to the rank returned by the subquery, the Item instance is filtered out. You can apply several filters by grouping them in an @org.hibernate.annotations.Filters.

A defined and applied filter, if enabled for a particular unit of work, filters out any Item instance that doesn't pass the condition. Let's enable it.

13.4.3 Enabling the filter

You've defined a data filter and applied it to a persistent entity class. It's still not filtering anything—it must be enabled and parameterized in the application for a particular unit of work, with the Session API:

> PATH: /examples/src/test/java/org/jpwh/test/filtering/DynamicFilter.java

```
org.hibernate.Filter filter = em.unwrap(Session.class)
    .enableFilter("limitByUserRank");

filter.setParameter("currentUserRank", 0);
```

You enable the filter by name; the method returns a Filter on which you set the runtime arguments dynamically. You must set the parameters you've defined; here it's set to rank 0. This example then filters out Items sold by a User with a higher rank in this Session.

Other useful methods of the `Filter` are `getFilterDefinition()` (which allows you to iterate through the parameter names and types) and `validate()` (which throws a `HibernateException` if you forget to set a parameter). You can also set a list of arguments with `setParameterList()`; this is mostly useful if your SQL restriction contains an expression with a quantifier operator (the `IN` operator, for example).

Now, every JPQL or criteria query that you execute on the filtered persistence context restricts the returned `Item` instances:

PATH: /examples/src/test/java/org/jpwh/test/filtering/DynamicFilter.java

```
List<Item> items = em.createQuery("select i from Item i").getResultList();
// select * from ITEM where 0 >=
//  (select u.RANK from USERS u  where u.ID = SELLER_ID)
```

PATH: /examples/src/test/java/org/jpwh/test/filtering/DynamicFilter.java

```
CriteriaBuilder cb = em.getCriteriaBuilder();
CriteriaQuery criteria = cb.createQuery();
criteria.select(criteria.from(Item.class));
List<Item> items = em.createQuery(criteria).getResultList();
// select * from ITEM where 0 >=
//  (select u.RANK from USERS u  where u.ID = SELLER_ID)
```

Note how Hibernate dynamically appends the SQL restriction conditions to the statement generated.

When you first experiment with dynamic filters, you'll most likely run into an issue with retrieval by identifier. You might expect that `em.find(Item.class, ITEM_ID)` will be filtered as well. This is not the case, though: Hibernate doesn't apply filters to retrieval by identifier operations. One of the reasons is that data-filter conditions are SQL fragments, and lookup by identifier may be resolved completely in memory, in the first-level persistence context cache. Similar reasoning applies to filtering of *many-to-one* or *one-to-one* associations. If a *many-to-one* association was filtered (for example, by returning `null` if you called `anItem.getSeller()`), the multiplicity of the association would change! You won't know if the item has a seller or if you aren't allowed to see it.

But you can dynamically filter collection access. Remember that persistent collections are shorthand for a query.

13.4.4 *Filtering collection access*

Until now, calling `someCategory.getItems()` has returned all `Item` instances that are referenced by that `Category`. This can be restricted with a filter applied to a collection:

PATH: /model/src/main/java/org/jpwh/model/filtering/dynamic/Category.java

```
@Entity
public class Category {

    @OneToMany(mappedBy = "category")
```

```
@org.hibernate.annotations.Filter(
    name = "limitByUserRank",
    condition =
        ":currentUserRank >= (" +
            "select u.RANK from USERS u " +
            "where u.ID = SELLER_ID" +
        ")"
)
protected Set<Item> items = new HashSet<Item>();

// ...
}
```

If you now enable the filter in a Session, all iteration through a collection of Category#items is filtered:

PATH: /examples/src/test/java/org/jpwh/test/filtering/DynamicFilter.java

```
filter.setParameter("currentUserRank", 0);
Category category = em.find(Category.class, CATEGORY_ID);
assertEquals(category.getItems().size(), 1);
```

If the current user's rank is 0, only one Item is loaded when you access the collection. Now, with a rank of 100, you see more data:

PATH: /examples/src/test/java/org/jpwh/test/filtering/DynamicFilter.java

```
filter.setParameter("currentUserRank", 100);
category = em.find(Category.class, CATEGORY_ID);
assertEquals(category.getItems().size(), 2);
```

You probably noticed that the SQL condition for both filter applications is the same. If the SQL restriction is the same for all filter applications, you can set it as the default condition when you define the filter, so you don't have to repeat it:

PATH: /model/src/main/java/org/jpwh/model/filtering/dynamic/package-info.java

```
@org.hibernate.annotations.FilterDef(
    name = "limitByUserRankDefault",
    defaultCondition=
        ":currentUserRank >= (" +
            "select u.RANK from USERS u " +
            "where u.ID = SELLER_ID" +
        ")",
    parameters = {
        @org.hibernate.annotations.ParamDef(
            name = "currentUserRank", type = "int"
        )
    }
)
```

There are many other excellent use cases for dynamic data filters. You've seen a restriction of data access given an arbitrary security-related condition. This can be the user rank, a particular group the user must belong to, or a role the user has been assigned. Data might be stored with a regional code (for example, all business contacts of a sales team). Or perhaps each salesperson works only on data that covers their region.

13.5 Summary

- Cascading state transitions are predefined reactions to life cycle events in the persistence engine.
- You learned about listening to and intercepting events. You implement event listeners and interceptors to add custom logic when Hibernate loads and stores data. We introduced JPA's event listener callbacks and Hibernate's `Interceptor` extension point, as well as the Hibernate core event system.
- You can use Hibernate Envers for audit logging and keeping multiple versions of data in the database (like the version control systems). Using Envers, a copy of your data is automatically stored in separate database tables when you add, modify, or delete data in application tables. Envers groups all data modifications as a change set, in a transaction, with a revision number. You can then query Envers to retrieve historical data.
- Using dynamic data filters, Hibernate can automatically append arbitrary SQL restrictions to queries it generates.

Part 4

Writing queries

In part 4, we introduce data-query features and cover query languages and APIs in detail. Not all chapters in this part are written in a tutorial style; we expect you'll browse this part of the book frequently when building an application and looking up a solution for a particular query problem.

Starting in chapter 14, we'll talk about creating and executing queries using the basic query APIs, preparing and executing queries, and optimizing query execution. Continuing in chapter 15, we'll cover the query languages, writing JPQL and criteria queries, retrieving data efficiently with joins, and reporting queries and subselects. Chapter 16 dives deeper into advanced query options: transforming query results, filtering collections, and query-by-criteria with the Hibernate API. Finally, chapter 17 describes customization techniques like falling back to JDBC, mapping SQL query results, customizing CRUD operations, and calling stored procedures.

After reading this part, you'll be able to get any data you want out of your database using various querying techniques, customizing access as needed.

14

Creating and executing queries

If you've been using handwritten SQL for a number of years, you may be concerned that ORM will take away some of the expressiveness and flexibility you're used to. This isn't the case with Hibernate and Java Persistence.

With Hibernate's and Java Persistence's powerful query facilities, you can express almost everything you commonly (or even uncommonly) need to express in SQL, but in object-oriented terms—using classes and properties of classes. Moreover, you can always fall back to SQL strings and let Hibernate do the heavy lifting of handling the query result. For additional SQL resources, consult our reference section.

Major new features in JPA 2
- A type-safe criteria API for the programmatic creation of queries is now available.
- You can now declare up front the type of a query result with the new `Typed-Query` interface.
- You can programmatically save a `Query` (JPQL, criteria, or native SQL) for later use as a named query.
- In addition to being able to set query parameters, hints, maximum results, and flush and lock modes, JPA 2 extends the `Query` API with various getter methods for obtaining the current settings.
- JPA now standardizes several query hints (timeout, cache usage).

In this chapter, we show you how to create and execute queries with JPA and the Hibernate API. The queries are as simple as possible so you can focus on the creation and execution API without unfamiliar languages possibly distracting. The next chapter will cover query languages.

Common to all APIs, a query must be prepared in application code before execution. There are three distinct steps:

1   Create the query, with any arbitrary selection, restriction, and projection of data that you want to retrieve.
2   Prepare the query: bind runtime arguments to query parameters, set hints, and set paging options. You can reuse the query with changing settings.
3   Execute the prepared query against the database and retrieve the data. You can control how the query is executed and how data should be retrieved into memory (all at once or piecemeal, for example).

Depending on the query options you use, your starting point for query creation is either the `EntityManager` or the native `Session` API. First up is creating the query.

14.1   Creating queries

JPA represents a query with a `javax.persistence.Query` or `javax.persistence.TypedQuery` instance. You create queries with the `EntityManager#createQuery()` method and its variants. You can write the query in the Java Persistence Query Language (JPQL), construct it with the `CriteriaBuilder` and `CriteriaQuery` APIs, or use plain SQL. (There is also `javax.persistence.StoredProcedureQuery`, covered in section 17.4.)

Hibernate has its own, older API to represent queries: `org.hibernate.Query` and `org.hibernate.SQLQuery`. We talk more about these in a moment. Let's start with the JPA standard interfaces and query languages.

14.1.1 *The JPA query interfaces*

Say you want to retrieve all `Item` entity instances from the database. With JPQL, this simple query string looks quite a bit like the SQL you know:

```
Query query = em.createQuery("select i from Item i");
```

The JPA provider returns a fresh `Query`; so far, Hibernate hasn't sent any SQL to the database. Remember that further preparation and execution of the query are separate steps.

JPQL is compact and will be familiar to anyone with SQL experience. Instead of table and column names, JPQL relies on entity class and property names. Except for these class and property names, JPQL is case-insensitive, so it doesn't matter whether you write `SeLEct` or `select`.

JPQL (and SQL) query strings can be simple Java literals in your code, as you saw in the previous example. Alternatively, especially in larger applications, you can move the query strings out of your data-access code and into annotations or XML. A query is then accessed by name with `EntityManager#createNamedQuery()`. We discuss externalized queries separately later in this chapter; there are many options to consider.

A significant disadvantage of JPQL surfaces as problems during refactoring of the domain model: if you rename the `Item` class, your JPQL query will break. (Some IDEs can detect and refactor JPQL strings, though.)

> ### JPA and query languages: HQL vs. JPQL
> Before JPA existed (and even today, in some documentation), the query language in Hibernate was called HQL. The differences between JPQL and HQL are insignificant now. Whenever you provide a query string to any query interface in Hibernate, either with the `EntityManager` or `Session`, it's a JPQL/HQL string. The same engine parses the query internally. The fundamental syntax and semantics are the same, although Hibernate, as always, supports some special constructs that aren't standardized in JPA. We'll tell you when a particular keyword or clause in an example only works in Hibernate. To simplify your life, think *JPQL* whenever you see *HQL*.

You can make query construction with `CriteriaBuilder` and `CriteriaQuery` APIs completely type-safe. JPA also calls this *query by criteria*:

```
CriteriaBuilder cb = em.getCriteriaBuilder();
// Also available on EntityManagerFactory:
// CriteriaBuilder cb = entityManagerFactory.getCriteriaBuilder();

CriteriaQuery criteria = cb.createQuery();
criteria.select(criteria.from(Item.class));

Query query = em.createQuery(criteria);
```

First you get a `CriteriaBuilder` from your `EntityManager` by calling `getCriteria-Builder()`. If you don't have an `EntityManager` ready, perhaps because you want to create the query independently from a particular persistence context, you may obtain the CriteriaBuilder from the usually globally shared EntityManagerFactory.

You then use the builder to create any number of CriteriaQuery instances. Each CriteriaQuery has at least one root class specified with from(); in the last example, that's Item.class. This is called *selection*; we'll talk more about it in the next chapter. The shown query returns all Item instances from the database.

The CriteriaQuery API will appear seamless in your application, without string manipulation. It's the best choice when you can't fully specify the query at development time and the application must create it dynamically at runtime. Imagine that you have to implement a search mask in your application, with many check boxes, input fields, and switches the user can enable. You must dynamically create a database query from the user's chosen search options. With JPQL and string concatenation, such code would be difficult to write and maintain.

You can write strongly typed CriteriaQuery calls, without strings, using the static JPA metamodel. This means your queries will be safe and included in refactoring operations, as already shown in the section "Using a static metamodel" in chapter 3.

> **Creating a detached criteria query**
>
> You always need an EntityManager or EntityManagerFactory to get the JPA CriteriaBuilder. With the older native org.hibernate.Criteria API, you only need access to the root entity class to create a detached query, as shown in section 16.3.

If you need to use features specific to your database product, your only choice is native SQL. You can directly execute SQL in JPA and let Hibernate handle the result for you, with the EntityManager#createNativeQuery() method:

```
Query query = em.createNativeQuery(
    "select * from ITEM", Item.class
);
```

After execution of this SQL query, Hibernate reads the java.sql.ResultSet and creates a List of managed Item entity instances. Of course, all columns necessary to construct an Item must be available in the result, and an error is thrown if your SQL query doesn't return them properly.

In practice, the majority of the queries in your application will be trivial—easily expressed in JPQL or with a CriteriaQuery. Then, possibly during optimization, you'll find a handful of complex and performance-critical queries. You may have to use special and proprietary SQL keywords to control the optimizer of your DBMS product. Most developers then write SQL instead of JPQL and move such complex queries into an XML file, where, with the help of a DBA, you change them independently from Java code. Hibernate can still handle the query result for you; hence you integrate SQL into your JPA application. There is nothing wrong with using SQL in Hibernate; don't let some kind of ORM "purity" get in your way. When you have a special case, don't try to hide it, but rather expose and document it properly so the next engineer will understand what's going on.

In certain cases, it's useful to specify the type of data returned from a query.

14.1.2 Typed query results

Let's say you want to retrieve only a single Item with a query, given its identifier value:

```
Query query = em.createQuery(
    "select i from Item i where i.id = :id"
).setParameter("id", ITEM_ID);

Item result = (Item) query.getSingleResult();
```

In this example, you see a preview of parameter binding and query execution. The important bit is the return value of the getSingleResult() method. It's java.lang.Object, and you have to cast it to an Item.

If you provide the class of your return value when creating the query, you can skip the cast. This is the job of the javax.persistence.TypedQuery interface:

```
TypedQuery<Item> query = em.createQuery(
    "select i from Item i where i.id = :id", Item.class
).setParameter("id", ITEM_ID);

Item result = query.getSingleResult();     ◁─── No cast needed
```

Query by criteria also supports the TypedQuery interface:

```
CriteriaBuilder cb = em.getCriteriaBuilder();

CriteriaQuery<Item> criteria = cb.createQuery(Item.class);
Root<Item> i = criteria.from(Item.class);
criteria.select(i).where(cb.equal(i.get("id"), ITEM_ID));

TypedQuery<Item> query = em.createQuery(criteria);

Item result = query.getSingleResult();     ◁─── No cast needed
```

Note that this CriteriaQuery isn't completely type-safe: the Item#id property is addressed with a string in get("id"). In chapter 3's "Using a static metamodel," you saw how you can make such queries completely type-safe with static metamodel classes.

Hibernate is older than even the first version of JPA, so it also has its own query APIs.

Hibernate Feature ┃───

14.1.3 Hibernate's query interfaces

Hibernate's own query representations are org.hibernate.Query and org.hibernate.SQLQuery. As usual, they offer more than is standardized in JPA, at the cost of portability. They're also much older than JPA, so there is some feature duplication.

Your starting point for Hibernate's query API is the `Session`:

```
Session session = em.unwrap(Session.class);
org.hibernate.Query query = session.createQuery("select i from Item i");
// Proprietary API: query.setResultTransformer(...);
```

You write the query string in standard JPQL. Compared with `javax.persistence.Query`, the `org.hibernate.Query` API has some additional proprietary methods that are only available in Hibernate. You see more of the API later in this and the following chapters.

Hibernate also has its own SQL result-mapping facility, with `org.hibernate.SQLQuery`:

```
Session session = em.unwrap(Session.class);

org.hibernate.SQLQuery query = session.createSQLQuery(
    "select {i.*} from ITEM {i}"
).addEntity("i", Item.class);
```

This example relies on placeholders in the SQL string to map columns of the `java.sql.ResultSet` to entity properties. We'll talk more about integration of SQL queries with this proprietary and the standard JPA result mapping in section 17.2.

Hibernate also has an older, proprietary `org.hibernate.Criteria` query API:

```
Session session = em.unwrap(Session.class);

org.hibernate.Criteria query = session.createCriteria(Item.class);
query.add(org.hibernate.criterion.Restrictions.eq("id", ITEM_ID));

Item result = (Item) query.uniqueResult();
```

You can also access the proprietary Hibernate query API given a `javax.persistence.Query`, by unwrapping an `org.hibernate.jpa.HibernateQuery` first:

```
javax.persistence.Query query = em.createQuery(
    // ...
);

org.hibernate.Query hibernateQuery =
    query.unwrap(org.hibernate.jpa.HibernateQuery.class)
        .getHibernateQuery();

hibernateQuery.getQueryString();
hibernateQuery.getReturnAliases();
// ... other proprietary API calls
```

We focus on the standard API and later show you some rarely needed advanced options only available with Hibernate's API, such as *scrolling with cursors* and *query by example*.

After writing your query, and before executing it, you typically want to further prepare the query by setting parameters applicable to a particular execution.

14.2 *Preparing queries*

A query has several aspects: it defines what data should be loaded from the database and the restrictions that apply, such as the identifier of an Item or the name of a User. When you write a query, you shouldn't code these arguments into the query string using string concatenation. You should use parameter placeholders instead and then bind the argument values before execution. This allows you to reuse the query with different argument values while keeping you're safe from SQL injection attacks.

Depending on your user interface, you frequently also need *paging*. You limit the number of rows returned from the database by your query. For example, you may want to return only result rows 1 to 20 because you can only show so much data on each screen, then a bit later you want rows 21 to 40, and so on.

Let's start with parameter binding.

14.2.1 *Protecting against SQL injection attacks*

Without runtime parameter binding, you're forced to write bad code:

```
String searchString = getValueEnteredByUser();    ◁——— Never do this!

Query query = em.createQuery(
    "select i from Item i where i.name = '" + searchString + "'"
);
```

You should never write code like this, because a malicious user could craft a search string to execute code on the database you didn't expect or want—that is, by entering the value of searchString in a search dialog box as foo' and callSomeStoredProcedure() and 'bar' = 'bar.

As you can see, the original searchString is no longer a simple search for a string but also executes a stored procedure in the database! The quote characters aren't escaped; hence the call to the stored procedure is another valid expression in the query. If you write a query like this, you open a major security hole in your application by allowing the execution of arbitrary code on your database. This is an *SQL injection* attack. Never pass unchecked values from user input to the database! Fortunately, a simple mechanism prevents this mistake.

The JDBC API includes functionality for safely binding values to SQL parameters. It knows exactly what characters in the parameter value to escape so the previous vulnerability doesn't exist. For example, the database driver escapes the single-quote characters in the given searchString and no longer treats them as control characters but as a part of the search string value. Furthermore, when you use parameters, the database can efficiently cache precompiled prepared statements, improving performance significantly.

There are two approaches to parameter binding: *named* and *positional* parameters. JPA support both options, but you can't use both at the same time for a particular query.

14.2.2 *Binding named parameters*

With named parameters, you can rewrite the query in the previous section as follows:

```
String searchString = // ...

Query query = em.createQuery(
    "select i from Item i where i.name = :itemName"
).setParameter("itemName", searchString);
```

The colon followed by a parameter name indicates a named parameter, here item-Name. In a second step, you bind a value to the itemName parameter. This code is cleaner, much safer, and performs better, because you can reuse a single compiled SQL statement if only parameter values change.

You can get a Set of Parameters from a Query, either to obtain more information about each parameter (such as name or required Java type) or to verify that you've bound all parameters properly before execution:

```
for (Parameter<?> parameter : query.getParameters()) {
    assertTrue(query.isBound(parameter));
}
```

The setParameter() method is a generic operation that can bind all types of arguments. It only needs a little help for temporal types:

```
Date tomorrowDate = // ...

Query query = em.createQuery(
    "select i from Item i where i.auctionEnd > :endDate"
).setParameter("endDate", tomorrowDate, TemporalType.TIMESTAMP);
```

Hibernate needs to know whether you want only the date or time or the full time-stamp bound.

For convenience, an entity instance can also be passed to the setParameter() method:

```
Item someItem = // ...

Query query = em.createQuery(
    "select b from Bid b where b.item = :item"
).setParameter("item", someItem);
```

Hibernate binds the identifier value of the given Item. You later see that b.item is a shortcut for b.item.id.

For criteria queries, there is a long way and a short way to bind parameters:

```
String searchString = // ...

CriteriaBuilder cb = em.getCriteriaBuilder();

CriteriaQuery criteria = cb.createQuery();
Root<Item> i = criteria.from(Item.class);

Query query = em.createQuery(
```

```
    criteria.select(i).where(
        cb.equal(
            i.get("name"),
            cb.parameter(String.class, "itemName")
        )
    )
).setParameter("itemName", searchString);
```

Here you put the `itemName` parameter placeholder of type `String` into the `Criteria-Query` and then bind a value to it as usual with the `Query#setParameter()` method.

Alternatively, with a `ParameterExpression`, you don't have to name the placeholder, and the binding of the argument is type-safe (you can't bind an `Integer` to a `ParameterExpression<String>`):

```
String searchString = // ...

CriteriaBuilder cb = em.getCriteriaBuilder();

CriteriaQuery criteria = cb.createQuery(Item.class);
Root<Item> i = criteria.from(Item.class);

ParameterExpression<String> itemNameParameter =
    cb.parameter(String.class);

Query query = em.createQuery(
    criteria.select(i).where(
        cb.equal(
            i.get("name"),
            itemNameParameter
        )
    )
).setParameter(itemNameParameter, searchString);
```

A rarely used and less safe option for value binding is positional query parameters.

14.2.3 *Using positional parameters*

If you prefer, you can use positional parameters instead of named parameters:

```
Query query = em.createQuery(
    "select i from Item i where i.name like ?1 and i.auctionEnd > ?2"
);
query.setParameter(1, searchString);
query.setParameter(2, tomorrowDate, TemporalType.TIMESTAMP);
```

In this example, the positional parameter markers are indexed ?1 and ?2. You may know this type of parameter placeholder from JDBC, but without the numbers and only the question marks. JPA requires that you enumerate the placeholders, starting with 1.

> **NOTE** In Hibernate both styles work, so be careful! Hibernate will warn you about a brittle query if you use JDBC-style positional parameters with only question marks.

Our recommendation is to avoid positional parameters. They may be more convenient if you build complex queries programmatically, but the `CriteriaQuery` API is a much better alternative for that purpose.

After binding parameters to your query, you may want to enable *pagination* if you can't display all results at once.

14.2.4 *Paging through large result sets*

A commonly used technique to process large result sets is *paging*. Users may see the result of their search request (for example, for specific items) as a page. This page shows a limited subset (say, 10 items) at a time, and users can navigate to the next and previous pages manually to view the rest of the result.

The `Query` interface supports paging of the query result. In this query, the requested page starts in the middle of the result set:

```
Query query = em.createQuery("select i from Item i");
query.setFirstResult(40).setMaxResults(10);
```

Starting from the fortieth row, you retrieve the next 10 rows. The call to `setFirstResults(40)` starts the result set at row 40. The call to `setMaxResults(10)` limits the query result set to 10 rows returned by the database. Because there is no standard way to express paging in SQL, Hibernate knows the tricks to make this work efficiently on your particular DBMS.

It's crucially important to remember that paging operates at the SQL level, on result rows. Limiting a result to 10 rows isn't necessarily the same as limiting the result to 10 instances of `Item`! In section 15.4.5, you'll see some queries with *dynamic fetching* that can't be combined with row-based paging at the SQL level, and we'll discuss this issue again.

You can even *add* this flexible paging option to an SQL query:

```
Query query = em.createNativeQuery("select * from ITEM");
query.setFirstResult(40).setMaxResults(10);
```

Hibernate will rewrite your SQL query to include the necessary keywords and clauses for limiting the number of returned rows to the page you specified.

In practice, you frequently combine paging with a special count-query. If you show a page of items, you also let the user know the total count of items. In addition, you need this information to decide whether there are more pages to show and whether the user can click to the next page. This usually requires two slightly different queries: for example, `select i from Item i` combined with `setMaxResults()` and `setFirstResult()` would retrieve a page of items, and `select count(i) from Item i` would retrieve the total number of items available.

Maintaining two almost identical queries is overhead you should avoid. A popular trick is to write only one query but execute it with a database cursor first to get the total result count:

```
Query query = em.createQuery("select i from Item i");

org.hibernate.Query hibernateQuery =
    query.unwrap(org.hibernate.jpa.HibernateQuery.class).getHibernateQuery();

org.hibernate.ScrollableResults cursor =
        hibernateQuery.scroll(org.hibernate.ScrollMode.SCROLL_INSENSITIVE);

cursor.last();
int count = cursor.getRowNumber()+1;

cursor.close();

query.setFirstResult(40).setMaxResults(10);
```

❶ Unwraps API
❷ Executes query with cursor
❸ Counts rows
❹ Closes cursor
❺ Gets arbitrary data

❶ Unwrap the Hibernate API to use scrollable cursors.

❷ Execute the query with a database cursor; this doesn't retrieve the result set into memory.

❸ Jump to the last row of the result in the database, and then get the row number. Because row numbers are zero-based, add 1 to get the total count of rows.

❹ You must close the database cursor.

❺ Execute the query again, and retrieve an arbitrary page of data.

There is one significant problem with this convenient strategy: your JDBC driver and/or DBMS may not support database cursors. Even worse, cursors seem to work, but the data is silently retrieved into application memory; the cursor isn't operating directly on the database. Oracle and MySQL drivers are known to be problematic, and we have more to say about scrolling and cursors in the next section. Later in this book, in section 19.2, we'll further discuss paging strategies in an application environment.

Your query is now ready for execution.

14.3 Executing queries

Once you've created and prepared a Query, you're ready to execute it and retrieve the result into memory. Retrieving the entire result set into memory in one go is the most common way to execute a query; we call this *listing*. Some other options are available that we also discuss next, such as *scrolling* and *iterating*.

14.3.1 Listing all results

The getResultList() method executes the Query and returns the results as a java.util.List:

```
Query query = em.createQuery("select i from Item i");
List<Item> items = query.getResultList();
```

Hibernate executes one or several SQL SELECT statements immediately, depending on your fetch plan. If you map any associations or collections with FetchType.EAGER, Hibernate must fetch them in addition to the data you want retrieved with your query. All data is loaded into memory, and any entity instances that Hibernate retrieves are in persistent state and managed by the persistence context.

Of course, the persistence context doesn't manage scalar projection results. The following query returns a List of Strings:

```
Query query = em.createQuery("select i.name from Item i");
List<String> itemNames = query.getResultList();
```

With some queries, you know the result is only a single result—for example, if you want only the highest Bid or only one Item.

14.3.2 *Getting a single result*

You may execute a query that returns a single result with the getSingleResult() method:

```
TypedQuery<Item> query = em.createQuery(
    "select i from Item i where i.id = :id", Item.class
).setParameter("id", ITEM_ID);

Item item = query.getSingleResult();
```

The call to getSingleResult() returns an Item instance. This also works for scalar results:

```
TypedQuery<String> query = em.createQuery(
    "select i.name from Item i where i.id = :id", String.class
).setParameter("id", ITEM_ID);

String itemName = query.getSingleResult();
```

Now, the ugly bits: if there are no results, getSingleResult() throws a NoResult-Exception. This query tries to find an item with a nonexistent identifier:

```
try {
    TypedQuery<Item> query = em.createQuery(
        "select i from Item i where i.id = :id", Item.class
    ).setParameter("id", 12341);

    Item item = query.getSingleResult();
    // ...

} catch (NoResultException ex) {
    // ...
}
```

You'd expect a `null` for this type of perfectly benign query. This is rather tragic, because it forces you to guard this code with a `try`/`catch` block. In fact, it forces you to *always* wrap a call of `getSingleResult()`, because you can't know whether the row(s) will be present.

If there's more than one result, `getSingleResult()` throws a `NonUniqueResultException`. This usually happens with this kind of query:

```
try {
    Query query = em.createQuery(
        "select i from Item i where name like '%a%'"
    );

    Item item = (Item) query.getSingleResult();
    // ...
} catch (NonUniqueResultException ex) {
    // ...
}
```

Retrieving all results into memory is the most common way to execute a query. Hibernate supports some other methods that you may find interesting if you want to optimize a query's memory consumption and execution behavior.

Hibernate Feature
───

14.3.3 *Scrolling with database cursors*

Plain JDBC provides a feature called *scrollable result sets*. This technique uses a cursor that the database management system holds. The cursor points to a particular row in the result of a query, and the application can move the cursor forward and backward. You can even directly jump to a row with the cursor.

One of the situations where you should scroll through the results of a query instead of loading them all into memory involves result sets that are too large to fit into memory. Usually you try to restrict the result further by tightening the conditions in the query. Sometimes this isn't possible, maybe because you need all the data but want to retrieve it in several steps. We'll show such a batch-processing routine in section 20.1.

JPA doesn't standardize scrolling through results with database cursors, so you need the `org.hibernate.ScrollableResults` interface available on the proprietary `org.hibernate.Query`:

```
Session session = em.unwrap(Session.class);

org.hibernate.Query query = session.createQuery(          ①  Creates query
    "select i from Item i order by i.id asc"
);
                                                          ②  Opens cursor
org.hibernate.ScrollableResults cursor =
        query.scroll(org.hibernate.ScrollMode.SCROLL_INSENSITIVE);

cursor.setRowNumber(2);                                   ③  Jumps to third row
```

```
Item item = (Item) cursor.get(0);          ◁————❹ Gets column value

cursor.close();                            ◁————❺ Closes cursor
```

Start by creating an `org.hibernate.Query` ❶ and opening a cursor ❷. You then ignore the first two result rows, jump to the third row ❸, and get that row's first "column" value ❹. There are no columns in JPQL, so this is the first projection element: here, i in the `select` clause. More examples of projection are available in the next chapter. *Always* close the cursor ❺ before you end the database transaction!

As mentioned earlier in this chapter, you can also `unwrap()` the Hibernate query API from a regular `javax.persistence.Query` you've constructed with `Criteria-Builder`. A proprietary `org.hibernate.Criteria` query can also be executed with scrolling instead of `list()`; the returned `ScrollableResults` cursor works the same.

The `ScrollMode` constants of the Hibernate API are equivalent to the constants in plain JDBC. In the previous example, `ScrollMode.SCROLL_INSENSITIVE` means the cursor isn't sensitive to changes made in the database, effectively guaranteeing that no dirty reads, unrepeatable reads, or phantom reads can slip into your result set while you scroll. Other available modes are `SCROLL_SENSITIVE` and `FORWARD_ONLY`. A sensitive cursor exposes you to committed modified data while the cursor is open; and with a forward-only cursor, you can't jump to an absolute position in the result. Note that the Hibernate persistence context cache still provides repeatable read for entity instances even with a sensitive cursor, so this setting can only affect modified scalar values you project in the result set.

Be aware that some JDBC drivers don't support scrolling with database cursors properly, although it might seem to work. With MySQL drivers, for example, the drivers always retrieve the entire result set of a query into memory immediately; hence you only scroll through the result set in application memory. To get real row-by-row streaming of the result, you have to set the JDBC fetch size of the query to `Integer.MIN_VALUE` (as explained in section 14.5.4) and only use `ScrollMode.FORWARD_ONLY`. Check the behavior and documentation of your DBMS and JDBC driver before using cursors.

An important limitation of scrolling with a database cursor is that it can't be combined with dynamic fetching with the `join fetch` clause in JPQL. Join fetching works with potentially several rows at a time, so you can't retrieve data row by row. Hibernate will throw an exception if you try to `scroll()` a query with dynamic fetch clauses.

Another alternative to retrieving all data at once is *iteration*.

Hibernate Feature ——

14.3.4 *Iterating through a result*

Let's say you know that most of the entity instances your query will retrieve are already present in memory. They may be in the persistence context or in the second-level shared cache (see section 20.2). In such a case, it might make sense to *iterate* the query result with the proprietary `org.hibernate.Query` API:

```
Session session = em.unwrap(Session.class);

org.hibernate.Query query = session.createQuery(
    "select i from Item i"
);

Iterator<Item> it = query.iterate(); // select ID from ITEM
while (it.hasNext()) {
    Item next = it.next(); // select * from ITEM where ID = ?
    // ...
}
Hibernate.close(it);
```

Iterator must be closed, either when the Session is closed or manually

When you call `query.iterate()`, Hibernate executes your query and sends an SQL SELECT to the database. But Hibernate slightly modifies the query and, instead of retrieving all columns from the ITEM table, only retrieves the identifier/primary key values.

Then, every time you call `next()` on the Iterator, an additional SQL query is triggered and the rest of the ITEM row is loaded. Obviously, this will cause an *n+1 selects problem* unless Hibernate can avoid the additional queries on `next()`. This will be the case if Hibernate can find the item's data in either the persistence context cache or the second-level cache.

The Iterator returned by `iterate()` must be closed. Hibernate closes it automatically when the EntityManager or Session is closed. If your iteration procedure exceeds the maximum number of open cursors in your database, you can close the Iterator manually with `Hibernate.close(iterator)`.

Iteration is rarely useful, considering that in the example all auction items would have to be in the caches to make this routine perform well. Like scrolling with a cursor, you can't combine it with dynamic fetching and `join fetch` clauses; Hibernate will throw an exception if you try.

So far, the code examples have all embedded query string literals in Java code. This isn't unreasonable for simple queries, but when you begin considering complex queries that must be split over multiple lines, it gets a bit unwieldy. Instead, you can give each query a name and move it into annotations or XML files.

14.4 *Naming and externalizing queries*

Externalizing query strings lets you store all queries related to a particular persistent class (or a set of classes) with the other metadata for that class. Alternatively, you can bundle your queries into an XML file, independent of any Java class. This technique is often preferred in larger applications; hundreds of queries are easier to maintain in a few well-known places rather than scattered throughout the code base in various classes accessing the database. You reference and access an externalized query by its name.

14.4.1 Calling a named query

The `EntityManager#getNamedQuery()` method obtains a `Query` instance for a named query:

```
Query query = em.createNamedQuery("findItems");
```

You can also obtain a `TypedQuery` instance for a named query:

```
TypedQuery<Item> query = em.createNamedQuery("findItemById", Item.class);
```

Hibernate's query API also supports accessing named queries:

```
org.hibernate.Query query = session.getNamedQuery("findItems");
```

Named queries are global—that is, the name of a query is a unique identifier for a particular persistence unit or `org.hibernate.SessionFactory`. How and where they're defined, in XML files or annotations, is no concern of your application code. On startup, Hibernate loads named JPQL queries from XML files and/or annotations and parses them to validate their syntax. (This is useful during development, but you may want to disable this validation in production, for a faster bootstrap, with the persistence unit configuration property `hibernate.query.startup_check`.)

Even the query language you use to write a named query doesn't matter. It can be JPQL or SQL.

14.4.2 Defining queries in XML metadata

You can place a named query in any JPA <entity-mappings> element in your orm.xml metadata. In larger applications, we recommend isolating and separating all named queries into their own file. Alternatively, you may want the same XML mapping file to define the queries and a particular class.

The <named-query> element defines a named JPQL query:

PATH: **/model/src/main/resources/querying/ExternalizedQueries.xml**

```xml
<entity-mappings
    version="2.1"
    xmlns="http://xmlns.jcp.org/xml/ns/persistence/orm"
    xmlns:xsi="http://www.w3.org/2001/XMLSchema-instance"
    xsi:schemaLocation="http://xmlns.jcp.org/xml/ns/persistence/orm
            http://xmlns.jcp.org/xml/ns/persistence/orm_2_1.xsd">

    <named-query name="findItems">
        <query><![CDATA[
            select i from Item i
        ]]></query>
    </named-query>

</entity-mappings>
```

You should wrap the query text into a `CDATA` instruction so any characters in your query string that may accidentally be considered XML (such as the *less than* operator) don't confuse the XML parser. We omit `CDATA` from most other examples for clarity.

Named queries don't have to be written in JPQL. They may even be native SQL queries—and your Java code doesn't need to know the difference:

> **PATH: /model/src/main/resources/querying/ExternalizedQueries.xml**

```
<named-native-query name="findItemsSQL"
                    result-class="org.jpwh.model.querying.Item">
    <query>select * from ITEM</query>
</named-native-query>
```

This is useful if you think you may want to optimize your queries later by fine-tuning the SQL. It's also a good solution if you have to port a legacy application to JPA/Hibernate, where SQL code can be isolated from the hand-coded JDBC routines. With named queries, you can easily port the queries one by one to mapping files.

Hibernate Feature

Hibernate also has its own, nonstandard facility for externalized queries in Hibernate XML metadata files:

> **PATH: /model/src/main/resources/querying/ExternalizedQueries.hbm.xml**

```
<?xml version="1.0"?>
<hibernate-mapping xmlns="http://www.hibernate.org/xsd/orm/hbm">

    <query name="findItemsOrderByAuctionEndHibernate">
        select i from Item i order by i.auctionEnd asc
    </query>

    <sql-query name="findItemsSQLHibernate">
        <return class="org.jpwh.model.querying.Item"/>
        select * from ITEM order by NAME asc
    </sql-query>

</hibernate-mapping>
```

You'll see more examples of externalized and especially custom SQL queries later in chapter 17.

If you don't like XML files, you can bundle and name your queries in Java annotation metadata.

14.4.3 *Defining queries with annotations*

JPA supports named queries with the `@NamedQuery` and `@NamedNativeQuery` annotations. You can only place these annotations on a mapped class. Note that the query name must again be globally unique in all cases; no class or package name is automatically prefixed to the query name:

```
@NamedQueries({
    @NamedQuery(
        name = "findItemById",
        query = "select i from Item i where i.id = :id"
    )
})
@Entity
public class Item {
    // ...
}
```

The class is annotated with an @NamedQueries containing an array of @NamedQuery. A single query can be declared directly; you don't need to wrap it in @NamedQueries. If you have an SQL instead of a JPQL query, use the @NamedNativeQuery annotation. There are many options to consider for mapping SQL result sets, so we'll show you how this works later, in a dedicated section in chapter 17.

Hibernate Feature

Unfortunately, JPA's named query annotations only work when they're on a mapped class. You can't put them into a package-info.java metadata file. Hibernate has some proprietary annotations for that purpose:

> PATH: /model/src/main/java/org/jpwh/model/querying/package-info.java

```
@org.hibernate.annotations.NamedQueries({
    @org.hibernate.annotations.NamedQuery(
        name = "findItemsOrderByName",
        query = "select i from Item i order by i.name asc"
    )
})

package org.jpwh.model.querying;
```

If neither XML files nor annotations seem to be the right place for defining your named queries, you might want to construct them programmatically.

14.4.4 *Defining named queries programmatically*

You can "save" a Query as a named query with the EntityManagerFactory#addNamedQuery() method:

```
Query findItemsQuery = em.createQuery("select i from Item i");
em.getEntityManagerFactory().addNamedQuery(
    "savedFindItemsQuery", findItemsQuery
);

Query query =

em.createNamedQuery("savedFindItemsQuery");     <-- Later, with the same
                                                    EntityManagerFactory
```

This registers your query with the persistence unit, the `EntityManagerFactory`, and make it reusable as a named query. The saved `Query` doesn't have to be a JPQL statement; you can also save a criteria or native SQL query. Typically, you register your queries once, on startup of your application.

We leave it to you to decide whether you want to use the named query feature. But we consider query strings in the application code (unless they're in annotations) to be the second choice; you should always externalize query strings if possible. In practice, XML files are probably the most versatile option.

Finally, for some queries, you may need extra settings and hints.

14.5 Query hints

In this section, we introduce some additional query options from the JPA standard and some proprietary Hibernate settings. As the name implies, you probably won't need them right away, so you can skip this section if you like and read it later as a reference.

All the examples use the same query, shown here:

```
String queryString = "select i from Item i";
```

In general, you can set a hint on a `Query` with the `setHint()` method. All the other query APIs, such as `TypedQuery` and `StoredProcedureQuery`, also have this method. If the persistence provider doesn't support a hint, the provider will ignore it silently.

JPA standardizes the hints shown in table 14.1.

Table 14.1 Standardized JPA query hints

Name	Value	Description
`javax.persistence.query.timeout`	(Milliseconds)	Sets the timeout for query execution. This hint is also available as a constant on `org.hibernate.annotations.Query-Hints.TIMEOUT_JPA`.
`javax.persistence.cache.retrieveMode`	`USE` | `BYPASS`	Controls whether Hibernate tries to read data from the second-level shared cache when marshaling a query result, or bypasses the cache and only reads data from the query result.
`javax.persistence.cache.storeMode`	`USE` | `BYPASS` |`REFRESH`	Controls whether Hibernate stores data in the second-level shared cache when marshaling a query result.

Hibernate Feature

Hibernate has its own vendor-specific hints for queries, also available as constants on `org.hibernate.annotations.QueryHints`; see table 14.2.

Table 14.2   Hibernate query hints

Name	Value	Description
`org.hibernate.flushMode`	`org.hibernate.FlushMode` (Enum)	Controls whether and when the persistence context should be flushed before execution of the query
`org.hibernate.readOnly`	`true` | `false`	Enables or disables dirty checking for the managed entity instances returned by the query
`org.hibernate.fetchSize`	(JDBC fetch size)	Calls the JDBC `PreparedStatement#setFetchSize()` method before executing the query, an optimization hint for the database driver
`org.hibernate.comment`	(SQL comment string)	A comment to prepend to the SQL, useful for (database) logging

Second-level shared caching (especially query caching) is a complex issue, so we'll dedicate section 20.2 to it. You should read that section before enabling the shared cache: setting caching to "enabled" for a query will have no effect.

Some of the other hints also deserve a longer explanation.

14.5.1   Setting a timeout

You can control how long to let a query run by setting a *timeout*:

```
Query query = em.createQuery(queryString)
    .setHint("javax.persistence.query.timeout", 60000);    ◁——— 1 minute
```

With Hibernate, this method has the same semantics and consequences as the `setQueryTimeout()` method on the JDBC `Statement` API.

Note that a JDBC driver doesn't necessarily cancel the query precisely when the timeout occurs. The JDBC specification says, "Once the data source has had an opportunity to process the request to terminate the running command, a `SQLException` will be thrown to the client …." Hence, there is room for interpretation as to when exactly the data source has an opportunity to terminate the command. It might only be after the execution completes. You may want to test this with your DBMS product and driver.

You can also specify this timeout hint as a global default property in persistence.xml as a property when creating the `EntityManagerFactory` or as a named query option. The `Query#setHint()` method then overrides this global default for a particular query.

14.5.2 *Setting the flush mode*

Let's assume that you make modifications to persistent entity instances before executing a query. For example, you modify the `name` of managed `Item` instances. These modifications are only present in memory, so Hibernate by default *flushes* the persistence context and all changes to the database before executing your query. This guarantees that the query runs on current data and that no conflict between the query result and the in-memory instances can occur.

This may be impractical at times, if you execute a sequence that consists of many query-modify-query-modify operations, and each query is retrieving a different data set than the one before. In other words, you sometimes know you don't need to flush your modifications to the database before executing a query, because conflicting results aren't a problem. Note that the persistence context provides repeatable read for entity instances, so only scalar results of a query are a problem anyway.

You can disable flushing of the persistence context before a query with the `org.hibernate.flushMode` hint on a `Query` and the value `org.hibernate.Flush-Mode.COMMIT`. Fortunately, JPA has a standard `setFlushMode()` method on the `Entity-Manager` and `Query` API, and `FlushModeType.COMMIT` is also standardized. So, if you want to disable flushing only before a particular query, use the standard API:

```
Query query = em.createQuery(queryString)
    .setFlushMode(FlushModeType.COMMIT);
```

With the flush mode set to `COMMIT`, Hibernate won't flush the persistence context before executing the query. The default is `AUTO`.

14.5.3 *Setting read-only mode*

In section 10.2.8, we talked about how you can reduce memory consumption and prevent long dirty-checking cycles. You can tell Hibernate that it should consider all entity instances returned by a query as read-only (although not detached) with a hint:

```
Query query = em.createQuery(queryString)
    .setHint(
        org.hibernate.annotations.QueryHints.READ_ONLY,
        true
    );
```

All `Item` instances returned by this query are in persistent state, but Hibernate doesn't enable snapshot for automatic dirty checking in the persistence context. Hibernate doesn't persist any modifications automatically unless you disable read-only mode with `session.setReadOnly(item, false)`.

14.5.4 Setting a fetch size

The *fetch size* is an optimization hint for the database driver:

```
Query query = em.createQuery(queryString)
    .setHint(
        org.hibernate.annotations.QueryHints.FETCH_SIZE,
        50
    );
```

This hint may not result in any performance improvement if the driver doesn't implement this functionality. If it does, it can improve the communication between the JDBC client and the database by retrieving many rows in one batch when the client (Hibernate) operates on a query result (that is, on a ResultSet).

14.5.5 Setting an SQL comment

When you optimize an application, you often have to read complex SQL logs. We highly recommend that you enable the property hibernate.use_sql_comments in your persistence.xml configuration. Hibernate will then add an auto-generated comment to each SQL statement it writes to the logs.

You can set a custom comment for a particular Query with a hint:

```
Query query = em.createQuery(queryString)
    .setHint(
        org.hibernate.annotations.QueryHints.COMMENT,
        "Custom SQL comment"
    );
```

The hints you've been setting so far are all related to Hibernate or JDBC handling. Many developers (and DBAs) consider a query hint to be something completely different. In SQL, a query hint is an instruction in the SQL statement for the optimizer of the DBMS. For example, if the developer or DBA thinks the execution plan selected by the database optimizer for a particular SQL statement isn't the fastest, they use a hint to force a different execution plan. Hibernate and Java Persistence don't support arbitrary SQL hints with an API; you'll have to fall back to native SQL and write your own SQL statement—you can of course execute that statement with the provided APIs.

On the other hand, with some DBMS products, you can control the optimizer with an SQL comment at the beginning of an SQL statement. In that case, use the comment hint as shown in the last example.

In all previous examples, you've set the query hint directly on the Query instance. If you have externalized and named queries, you must set hints in annotations or XML.

14.5.6 Named query hints

All the query hints set earlier with setHint() can also be set in XML metadata in a <named-query> or <named-native-query> element:

```xml
<entity-mappings
    version="2.1"
    xmlns="http://xmlns.jcp.org/xml/ns/persistence/orm"
    xmlns:xsi="http://www.w3.org/2001/XMLSchema-instance"
    xsi:schemaLocation="http://xmlns.jcp.org/xml/ns/persistence/orm
              http://xmlns.jcp.org/xml/ns/persistence/orm_2_1.xsd">

    <named-query name="findItems">
        <query><![CDATA[
            select i from Item i
        ]]></query>
        <hint name="javax.persistence.query.timeout" value="60000"/>
        <hint name="org.hibernate.comment" value="Custom SQL comment"/>
    </named-query>

</entity-mappings>
```

You can set hints on named queries defined in annotations:

```java
@NamedQueries({
    @NamedQuery(
        name = "findItemByName",
        query = "select i from Item i where i.name like :name",
        hints = {
            @QueryHint(
                name = org.hibernate.annotations.QueryHints.TIMEOUT_JPA,
                value = "60000"),
            @QueryHint(
                name = org.hibernate.annotations.QueryHints.COMMENT,
                value = "Custom SQL comment")
        }
    )
})
```

Hibernate Feature

Hints can be set on named queries in Hibernate annotations in a package-info.java file:

```java
@org.hibernate.annotations.NamedQueries({
    @org.hibernate.annotations.NamedQuery(
        name = "findItemBuyNowPriceGreaterThan",
        query = "select i from Item i where i.buyNowPrice > :price",
        timeout = 60,                                              // ⟵ Seconds!
        comment = "Custom SQL comment"
    )
})

package org.jpwh.model.querying;
```

In addition, of course, hints can be set on named queries externalized into a Hibernate XML metadata file:

```xml
<?xml version="1.0"?>
<hibernate-mapping xmlns="http://www.hibernate.org/xsd/orm/hbm">

    <query name="findItemsOrderByAuctionEndHibernateWithHints"
           cache-mode="ignore"
           comment="Custom SQL comment"
           fetch-size="50"
           read-only="true"
           timeout="60">
        select i from Item i order by i.auctionEnd asc
    </query>

</hibernate-mapping>
```

14.6   *Summary*

- You learned how to create and execute queries. To create queries, you use the JPA query interfaces and process typed query results. You also saw Hibernate's own query interfaces.

- You then looked at how to prepare queries, taking care to protect against SQL injection attacks. You learned how to use bound and positional parameters, and you paged through large result sets.

- Instead of embedding JPQL in Java sources, you can name and externalize queries. You saw how to call a named query and different ways to define queries: in XML metadata, with annotations, and programmatically.

- We discussed the query hints you can give Hibernate: setting a timeout, flush mode, read-only mode, fetch size, and SQL comment. As with JPQL, you saw how to name and externalize query hints.

The query languages

Queries are the most interesting part of writing good data access code. A complex query may require a long time to get right, and its impact on the performance of the application can be tremendous. On the other hand, writing queries becomes much easier with more experience, and what seemed difficult at first is only a matter of knowing the available *query languages*.

This chapter covers the query languages available in JPA: JPQL and the criteria query API. We always show the same query example with both languages/API, where the result of the queries is equivalent.

Major new features in JPA 2

- There is now support for CASE, NULLIF, and COALESCE operators, with the same semantics as their SQL counterparts.
- You can downcast with the TREAT operator in restrictions and selections.
- You can call arbitrary SQL database functions in restrictions and projections.
- You can append additional join conditions for outer joins with the new ON keyword.
- You can use joins in subselect FROM clauses.

We expect that you won't read this chapter just once but will rely on it as a reference to look up the correct syntax for a particular query when coding your application. Hence, our writing style is less verbose, with many small code examples for different use cases. We also sometimes simplify parts of the CaveatEmptor application for better readability. For example, instead of referring to MonetaryAmount, we use a simple BigDecimal amount in comparisons.

Let's start with some query terminology. You apply *selection* to define where the data should be retrieved from, *restriction* to match records to a given criteria, and *projection* to select the data you want returned from a query. You'll find this chapter organized in this manner.

When we talk about queries in this chapter, we usually mean SELECT statements: operations that retrieve data from the database. JPA also supports UPDATE, DELETE, and even INSERT ... SELECT statements in JPQL, criteria, and SQL flavors, which we'll discuss in section 20.1. We won't repeat those bulk operations here and will focus on SELECT statements. We start with some basic selection examples.

15.1 Selection

First, when we say *selection*, we don't mean the SELECT clause of a query. We aren't talking about the SELECT statement as such, either. We are referring to *selecting a relation variable*—or, in SQL terms, the FROM clause. It declares where data for your query should come from: simplifying, which tables you "select" for a query. Alternatively, with classes instead of table names in JPQL:

```
from Item
```

The following query (just a FROM clause) retrieves all Item entity instances. Hibernate generates the following SQL:

```
select i.ID, i.NAME, ... from ITEM i
```

The equivalent criteria query can be built with the from() method, passing in the entity name:

```
CriteriaQuery criteria = cb.createQuery(Item.class);
criteria.from(Item.class);
```

Hibernate understands queries with only a FROM clause or criterion. Unfortunately, the JPQL and criteria queries we've just shown aren't portable; they aren't JPA-compliant. The JPA specification requires that a JPQL query have a SELECT clause and that portable criteria queries call the select() method.

This requires assignment of aliases and query roots, our next topic.

15.1.1 *Assigning aliases and query roots*

Adding a SELECT clause to a JPQL query requires assignment of an *alias* to the queried class in the FROM clause, such that you can reference it in other parts of the query:

```
select i from Item as i
```

The following query is now JPA-compliant. The as keyword is always optional. The following is equivalent:

```
select i from Item i
```

You assign the alias i to queried instances of the Item class. Think of this as being a bit like the temporary variable declaration in the following Java code:

```
for(Iterator i = result.iterator(); i.hasNext();) {
    Item item = (Item) i.next();
    // ...
}
```

Aliases in queries aren't case-sensitive, so select iTm from Item itm works. We prefer to keep aliases short and simple, though; they only need to be unique within a query (or subquery).

Portable criteria queries must call the select() method:

```
CriteriaQuery criteria = cb.createQuery();
Root<Item> i = criteria.from(Item.class);
criteria.select(i);
```

We'll skip the cb.createQuery() line in most other criteria examples; it's always the same. Whenever you see a criteria variable, it was produced with Criteria-Builder#createQuery(). The previous chapter explains how to obtain a Criteria-Builder.

The Root of a criteria query always references an entity. Later we show you queries with several roots. You can abbreviate this query by inlining the Root:

```
criteria.select(criteria.from(Item.class));
```

Alternatively, you may look up the entity type dynamically with the Metamodel API:

```
EntityType entityType = getEntityType(
    em.getMetamodel(), "Item"
);

criteria.select(criteria.from(entityType));
```

The `getEntityType()` method is our own trivial addition: It iterates through `Metamodel#getEntities()`, looking for a match with the given entity name.

The `Item` entity doesn't have subclasses, so let's look at polymorphic selection next.

15.1.2 *Polymorphic queries*

JPQL, as an object-oriented query language, supports *polymorphic queries*—queries for instances of a class and all instances of its subclasses, respectively. Consider the following queries:

```
select bd from BillingDetails bd
```

```
criteria.select(criteria.from(BillingDetails.class));
```

These queries return all instances of the type `BillingDetails`, which is an abstract class. In this case, each instance is of a subtype of `BillingDetails`: `CreditCard` or `BankAccount`. If you want only instances of a particular subclass, you may use this:

```
select cc from CreditCard cc
```

```
criteria.select(criteria.from(CreditCard.class));
```

The class named in the `FROM` clause doesn't even need to be a mapped persistent class; any class will do. The following query returns all persistent objects:

```
select o from java.lang.Object o
```

Hibernate Feature

Yes, you can select all the tables of your database with such a query and retrieve all data into memory! This also works for arbitrary interfaces—for example, selecting all serializable types:

```
select s from java.io.Serializable s
```

The bad news is that JPA doesn't standardize polymorphic JPQL queries with arbitrary interfaces. They work in Hibernate, but portable applications should only reference mapped entity classes in the `FROM` clause (such as `BillingDetails` or `CreditCard`). The `from()` method in the criteria query API only accepts mapped entity types.

You can perform *non-polymorphic* queries by restricting the scope of selected types with the `TYPE` function. If you only want instances of a particular subclass, you may use

```
select bd from BillingDetails bd where type(bd) = CreditCard
```

```
Root<BillingDetails> bd = criteria.from(BillingDetails.class);
criteria.select(bd).where(
```

```
        cb.equal(bd.type(), CreditCard.class)
);
```

If you need to parameterize such a query, add an `IN` clause and a named parameter:

```
select bd from BillingDetails bd where type(bd) in :types
```

```
Root<BillingDetails> bd = criteria.from(BillingDetails.class);
criteria.select(bd).where(
    bd.type().in(cb.parameter(List.class, "types"))
);
```

You bind the argument to the parameter by providing a `List` of types you'd like to match:

```
Query query = // ...
query.setParameter("types", Arrays.asList(CreditCard.class,
    BankAccount.class));
```

If you want all instances of a particular subclass *except* a given class, use the following:

```
select bd from BillingDetails bd where not type(bd) = BankAccount
```

```
Root<BillingDetails> bd = criteria.from(BillingDetails.class);
criteria.select(bd).where(
    cb.not(cb.equal(bd.type(), BankAccount.class))
);
```

Polymorphism applies not only to explicitly named classes but also to polymorphic associations, as you'll see later in this chapter.

You're now done with the first step of writing a query, the *selection*. You picked the tables from which to query data. Next, you'd probably like to limit the rows you want to retrieve with a *restriction*.

15.2 Restriction

Usually, you don't want to retrieve all instances of a class from the database. You must be able to express constraints on the data returned by the query. We call this *restriction*. The `WHERE` clause declares restriction conditions in SQL and JPQL, and the `where()` method is the equivalent in the criteria query API.

This is a typical `WHERE` clause that restricts the results to all `Item` instances with a given name:

```
select i from Item i where i.name = 'Foo'
```

```
Root<Item> i = criteria.from(Item.class);
criteria.select(i).where(
    cb.equal(i.get("name"), "Foo")
);
```

The query expresses the constraint in terms of a property, `name`, of the `Item` class.

The SQL generated by these queries is

```
select i.ID, i.NAME, ... from ITEM i where i.NAME = 'Foo'
```

You can include string literals in your statements and conditions, with single quotes. For date, time, and timestamp literals, use the JDBC escape syntax: `...  where i.auctionEnd = {d '2013-26-06'}`. Note that your JDBC driver and DBMS define how to parse this literal and what other variations they support. Remember our advice from the previous chapter: don't concatenate unfiltered user input into your query string—use parameter binding. Other common literals in JPQL are `true` and `false`:

```
select u from User u where u.activated = true
```

```
Root<User> u = criteria.from(User.class);
criteria.select(u).where(
    cb.equal(u.get("activated"), true)
);
```

SQL (JPQL and criteria queries) expresses restrictions with ternary logic. The `WHERE` clause is a logical expression that evaluates to `true`, `false`, or `null`.

> ## What is ternary logic?
>
> A row is included in an SQL query result if and only if the `WHERE` clause evaluates to `true`. In Java, `nonNullObject == null` evaluates to `false`, and `null == null` evaluates to `true`. In SQL, `NOT_NULL_COLUMN = null` and `null = null` both evaluate to `null`, not `true`. Thus, SQL needs special operators, `IS NULL` and `IS NOT NULL`, to test whether a value is `null`. *Ternary logic* is a way of handling expressions you may apply to nullable column values. Treating `null` not as a special marker but as a regular value is an SQL extension of the familiar binary logic of the relational model. Hibernate has to support this ternary logic with ternary operators in JPQL and criteria queries.

Let's walk through the most common comparison operators in logical expressions, including ternary operators.

15.2.1 *Comparison expressions*

JPQL and the criteria API support the same basic comparison operators as SQL. Here are a few examples that should look familiar if you know SQL.

The following query returns all bids with amounts in a given range:

```
select b from Bid b where b.amount between 99 and 110
```

```
Root<Bid> b = criteria.from(Bid.class);
criteria.select(b).where(
    cb.between(
        b.<BigDecimal>get("amount"),                            ⟵── Type of path required
        new BigDecimal("99"), new BigDecimal("110")             ⟵── Must be the same type
    )
);
```

The criteria query may look a bit strange; you probably haven't seen generics in the middle of expressions often in Java. The `Root#get()` method produces a `Path<X>` of an entity attribute. To preserve type safety, you must specify the attribute type of that `Path`, as in `<BigDecimal>get("amount")`. The other two arguments of the `between()` method then must be of the same type, or the comparison wouldn't make sense or compile.

The following query returns all bids with amounts greater than the given value:

```
select b from Bid b where b.amount > 100
```

```
Root<Bid> b = criteria.from(Bid.class);
criteria.select(b).where(
    cb.gt(                                          ⟵——— gt() only works with Number;
        b.<BigDecimal>get("amount"),                       use greaterThan() otherwise.
        new BigDecimal("100")
    )
);
```

The `gt()` method only accepts arguments of `Number` type, such as `BigDecimal` or `Integer`. If you need to compare values of other types, for example a `Date`, use `greaterThan()` instead:

```
Root<Item> i = criteria.from(Item.class);
criteria.select(i).where(
    cb.greaterThan(
        i.<Date>get("auctionEnd"),
        tomorrowDate
    )
);
```

The following query returns all users with the user names "johndoe" and "janeroe":

```
select u from User u where u.username in ('johndoe', 'janeroe')
```

```
Root<User> u = criteria.from(User.class);
criteria.select(u).where(
    cb.<String>in(u.<String>get("username"))
        .value("johndoe")
        .value("janeroe")
);
```

For restrictions with enums, use the fully qualified literal:

```
select i from Item i
    where i.auctionType = org.jpwh.model.querying.AuctionType.HIGHEST_BID
```

```
Root<Item> i = criteria.from(Item.class);
criteria.select(i).where(
    cb.equal(
        i.<AuctionType>get("auctionType"),
        AuctionType.HIGHEST_BID
    )
);
```

Because SQL relies on ternary logic, testing for `null` values requires special care. You use the `IS [NOT] NULL` operators in JPQL and `isNull()` and `isNotNull()` in the criteria query API.

Here are IS NULL and isNull() in action, getting items without a buy-now price:

```
select i from Item i where i.buyNowPrice is null
```

```
Root<Item> i = criteria.from(Item.class);
criteria.select(i).where(
    cb.isNull(i.get("buyNowPrice"))
);
```

Using IS NOT NULL and isNotNull(), you return items with a buy-now price:

```
select i from Item i where i.buyNowPrice is not null
```

```
Root<Item> i = criteria.from(Item.class);
criteria.select(i).where(
    cb.isNotNull(i.get("buyNowPrice"))
);
```

The LIKE operator allows wildcard searches, where the wildcard symbols are % and _, as in SQL:

```
select u from User u where u.username like 'john%'
```

```
Root<User> u = criteria.from(User.class);
criteria.select(u).where(
    cb.like(u.<String>get("username"), "john%")
);
```

The expression john% restricts the result to users with a username starting with "john". You may also negate the LIKE operator, for example, in a substring match expression:

```
select u from User u where u.username not like 'john%'
```

```
Root<User> u = criteria.from(User.class);
criteria.select(u).where(
    cb.like(u.<String>get("username"), "john%").not()
);
```

You can match any substring by surrounding the search string with percentage characters:

```
select u from User u where u.username like '%oe%'
```

```
Root<User> u = criteria.from(User.class);
criteria.select(u).where(
    cb.like(u.<String>get("username"), "%oe%")
);
```

The percentage symbol stands for any sequence of characters; the underscore can be used to wildcard a single character. You can escape with a character of your choice if you want a literal percentage or underscore:

```
select i from Item i
    where i.name like 'Name\_with\_underscores' escape :escapeChar
query.setParameter("escapeChar", "\\");
```

```
Root<Item> i = criteria.from(Item.class);
criteria.select(i).where(
    cb.like(i.<String>get("name"), "Name\\_with\\_underscores", '\\')
);
```

These queries return all items with Name_with_underscores. In Java strings, the character \ is the escape character, so you must escape it, which explains the double-back-slash in the example.

JPA also supports arithmetic expressions:

```
select b from Bid b where (b.amount / 2) - 0.5 > 49
```

```
Root<Bid> b = criteria.from(Bid.class);
criteria.select(b).where(
    cb.gt(
        cb.diff(
            cb.quot(b.<BigDecimal>get("amount"), 2),
            0.5
        ),
        49
    )
);
```

Logical operators (and parentheses for grouping) combine expressions:

```
select i from Item i
    where (i.name like 'Fo%' and i.buyNowPrice is not null)
        or i.name = 'Bar'/
```

```
Root<Item> i = criteria.from(Item.class);

Predicate predicate = cb.and(
    cb.like(i.<String>get("name"), "Fo%"),
    cb.isNotNull(i.get("buyNowPrice"))
);

predicate = cb.or(
    predicate,
    cb.equal(i.<String>get("name"), "Bar")
);

criteria.select(i).where(predicate);
```

Hibernate Feature

If instead you combine all predicates with the logical AND, we prefer this fluent criteria query API style:

```
Root<Item> i = criteria.from(Item.class);

criteria.select(i).where(
```

```
        cb.like(i.<String>get("name"), "Fo%"),
        // AND
        cb.isNotNull(i.get("buyNowPrice"))
        // AND ...
);
```

We summarize all operators, including some we haven't shown so far, and their precedence from top to bottom, in table 15.1.

Table 15.1 JPQL operator precedence

JPQL operator	Criteria query API	Description
.	N/A	Navigation path expression operator
+, -	neg()	Unary positive or negative signing (all unsigned numeric values are considered positive)
*, /	prod(), quot()	Multiplication and division of numeric values
+, -	sum(), diff()	Addition and subtraction of numeric values
=, <>, <, >, >=, <	equal(), notEqual(), lessThan(), lt(), greaterThan(), gt(), greaterThanEqual(), ge(), lessThan(), lt()	Binary comparison operators with SQL semantics
[NOT] BETWEEN, [NOT] LIKE, [NOT] IN, IS [NOT] NULL	between(), like(), in(), isNull(), isNotNull()	Binary comparison operators with SQL semantics
IS [NOT] EMPTY, [NOT] MEMBER [OF]	isEmpty(), isNotEmpty(), isMember(), isNotMember()	Binary operators for persistent collections
NOT, AND, OR	not(), and(), or()	Logical operators for ordering of expression evaluation

You've already seen how binary comparison expressions have the same semantics as their SQL counterparts and how to group and combine them with logical operators. Let's discuss collection handling.

15.2.2 Expressions with collections

All expressions in the previous sections had only single-valued path expressions: `user.username`, `item.buyNowPrice`, and so on. You can also write path expressions that end in collections, and apply some operators and functions.

For example, let's assume you want to restrict your query result to `Category` instances that have an element in their `items` collection:

```
select c from Category c
    where c.items is not empty
```

```
Root<Category> c = criteria.from(Category.class);
criteria.select(c).where(
    cb.isNotEmpty(c.<Collection>get("items"))
);
```

The c.items path expression in the JPQL query terminates in a collection property: the items of a Category. Note that it's always illegal to continue a path expression after a collection-valued property: you can't write c.items.buyNowPrice.

You can restrict the result depending on the size of the collection, with the size() function:

```
select c from Category c
    where size(c.items) > 1
```

```
Root<Category> c = criteria.from(Category.class);
criteria.select(c).where(
    cb.gt(
        cb.size(c.<Collection>get("items")),
        1
    )
);
```

You can also express that you require a particular element to be present in a collection:

```
select c from Category c
    where :item member of c.items
```

```
Root<Category> c = criteria.from(Category.class);
criteria.select(c).where(
    cb.isMember(
        cb.parameter(Item.class, "item"),
        c.<Collection<Item>>get("items")
    )
);
```

For persistent maps, the special operators key(), value(), and entry() are available. Let's say you have a persistent map of Image embeddables for each Item, as shown in section 7.2.4. The filename of each Image is the map key. The following query retrieves all Image instances with a .jpg suffix in the filename:

```
select value(img)
    from Item i join i.images img
    where key(img) like '%.jpg'
```

The value() operator returns the values of the Map, and the key() operator returns the key set of the Map. If you want to return Map.Entry instances, use the entry() operator.

Let's look at other available functions next, not limited to collections.

15.2.3 *Calling functions*

An extremely powerful feature of the query languages is the ability to call functions in the WHERE clause. The following queries call the lower() function for case-insensitive searching:

```
select i from Item i where lower(i.name) like 'ba%'
```

```
Root<Item> i = criteria.from(Item.class);
criteria.select(i).where(
    cb.like(cb.lower(i.<String>get("name")), "ba%")
);
```

Look at the summary of all available functions in table 15.2. For criteria queries, the equivalent methods are in CriteriaBuilder, with slightly different name formatting (using camelCase and no underscores).

Table 15.2 JPA query functions (overloaded methods not listed)

Function	Applicability
upper(s), lower(s)	String values; returns a string value.
concat(s, s)	String values; returns a string value.
current_date, current_time, current_timestamp	Returns the date and/or time of the database management system machine.
substring(s, offset, length)	String values (offset starts at 1); returns a string value.
trim([[both|leading|trailing] char [from]] s)	Trims spaces on both sides of s if no char or other specification is given; returns a string value.
length(s)	String value; returns a numeric value.
locate(search, s, offset)	Returns the position of search in s starting to search at offset; returns a numeric value.
abs(n), sqrt(n), mod(dividend, divisor)	Numeric values; returns an absolute of same type as input, square root as Double, and the remainder of a division as an Integer.
treat(x as Type)	Downcast in restrictions; for example, retrieve all users with credit cards expiring in 2013: select u from User u where treat(u.billingDetails as CreditCard).expYear = '2013'. (Note that this isn't necessary in Hibernate. It automatically downcasts if a subclass property path is used.)
size(c)	Collection expressions; returns an Integer, or 0 if empty.
index(orderedCollection)	Expression for collections mapped with @OrderColumn; returns an Integer value corresponding to the position of its argument in the list. For example, select i.name from Category c join c.items i where index(i) = 0 returns the name of the first item in each category.

Hibernate Feature

Hibernate offers additional functions for JPQL, as shown in table 15.3. There is no equivalent for these functions in the standard JPA criteria API.

Table 15.3   Hibernate query functions

Function	Description
`bit_length(s)`	Returns the number of bits in `s`
`second(d)`, `minute(d)`, `hour(d)`, `day(d)`, `month(d)`, `year(d)`	Extracts the time and date from a temporal argument
`minelement(c)`, `maxelement(c)`, `minindex(c)`, `maxindex(c)`, `elements(c)`, `indices(c)`	Returns an element or index of an indexed collections (maps, lists, arrays)
`str(x)`	Casts the argument to a character string

Most of these Hibernate-only functions translate into SQL counterparts you've probably seen before. You can also call SQL functions supported by your DBMS that aren't listed here.

Hibernate Feature

With Hibernate, any function call in the WHERE clause of a JPQL statement that isn't known to Hibernate is passed directly to the database as an SQL function call. For example, the following query returns all items with an auction period longer than one day:

```
select i from Item i
    where
        datediff('DAY', i.createdOn, i.auctionEnd)
    > 1
```

Here you call the proprietary `datediff()` function of the H2 database system, it returns the difference in days between the creation date and the auction end date of an `Item`. This syntax only works in Hibernate though; in JPA, the standardized invocation syntax for calling arbitrary SQL functions is

```
select i from Item i
    where
        function('DATEDIFF', 'DAY', i.createdOn, i.auctionEnd)
    > 1
```

The first argument of `function()` is the name of the SQL function you want to call in single quotes. Then, you append any additional operands for the actual function; you may have none or many. This is the same criteria query:

```
Root<Item> i = criteria.from(Item.class);
criteria.select(i).where(
```

```
        cb.gt(
            cb.function(
                "DATEDIFF",
                Integer.class,
                cb.literal("DAY"),
                i.get("createdOn"),
                i.get("auctionEnd")
            ),
            1
        )
);
```

The `Integer.class` argument is the return type of the `datediff()` function and is irrelevant here because you aren't returning the result of the function call in a restriction.

A function call in the `SELECT` clause would return the value to the Java layer; you can also invoke arbitrary SQL database functions in the `SELECT` clause. Before we talk about this clause and *projection*, let's see how results can be ordered.

15.2.4 *Ordering query results*

All query languages provide some mechanism for ordering query results. JPQL provides an `ORDER BY` clause, similar to SQL.

The following query returns all users, ordered by username, ascending by default:

```
select u from User u order by u.username
```

You specify ascending or descending order with the `asc` and `desc` keywords:

```
select u from User u order by u.username desc
```

With the criteria query API, you *must* specify ascending and descending order with `asc()` or `desc()`:

```
Root<User> u = criteria.from(User.class);
criteria.select(u).orderBy(
    cb.desc(u.get("username"))
);
```

You may order by multiple properties:

```
select u from User u order by u.activated desc, u.username asc
```

```
Root<User> u = criteria.from(User.class);
criteria.select(u).orderBy(
    cb.desc(u.get("activated")),
    cb.asc(u.get("username"))
);
```

> **Order of nulls**
>
> If the column you're ordering by can be NULL, rows with NULL may be first or last in the query result. This behavior depends on your DBMS, so for portable applications you should specify whether NULL should be first or last with the clause ORDER BY ... NULLS FIRST|LAST. Hibernate supports this clause in JPQL, however, this isn't standardized in JPA. Alternatively, you can set a default order with the persistence unit configuration property hibernate.order_by.default_null_ordering set to none (the default), first, or last.

Hibernate Feature

The JPA specification only allows properties/paths in the ORDER BY clause if the SELECT clause projects the same properties/paths. The following queries may be non-portable but work in Hibernate:

```
select i.name from Item i order by i.buyNowPrice asc
```

```
select i from Item i order by i.seller.username desc
```

Be careful with implicit inner joins in path expressions and ORDER BY: The last query returns only Item instances that have a seller. This may be unexpected, as the same query without the ORDER BY clause would retrieve all Item instances. (Ignoring for a moment that in our model the Item always has a seller, this issue is visible with optional references.) You'll find a more detailed discussion of inner joins and path expressions later in this chapter.

You now know how to write the FROM, WHERE, and ORDER BY clauses. You know how to select the entities you want to retrieve instances of and the necessary expressions and operations to restrict and order the result. All you need now is the ability to project the data of this result to what you need in your application.

15.3 Projection

In simple terms, selection and restriction in a query is the process of declaring which tables and rows you want to query. *Projection* is defining the "columns" you want returned to the application: the data you need. The SELECT clause in JPQL performs projections.

15.3.1 Projection of entities and scalar values

For example, consider the following queries:

```
select i, b from Item i, Bid b
```

```
Root<Item> i = criteria.from(Item.class);
Root<Bid> b = criteria.from(Bid.class);
criteria.select(cb.tuple(i, b));
```

```
/* Convenient alternative:
criteria.multiselect(
    criteria.from(Item.class),
    criteria.from(Bid.class)
);
*/
```

As promised earlier, this criteria query shows how you can add several Roots by calling the from() method several times. To add several elements to your projection, either call the tuple() method of CriteriaBuilder, or the shortcut multiselect().

You're creating a Cartesian product of all Item and Bid instances. The queries return ordered pairs of Item and Bid entity instances:

```
List<Object[]> result = query.getResultList();          ◄———❶ Returns List of Object[]

Set<Item> items = new HashSet();
Set<Bid> bids = new HashSet();

for (Object[] row : result) {
    assertTrue(row[0] instanceof Item);          ◄———❷ Index 0
    items.add((Item) row[0]);

    assertTrue(row[1] instanceof Bid);          ◄———❸ Index 1
    bids.add((Bid)row[1]);
}
assertEquals(items.size(), 3);
assertEquals(bids.size(), 4);
assertEquals(result.size(), 12);          ◄——— Cartesian product
```

The query returns a List of Object[] ❶. At index 0 is the Item ❷, and at index 1 is the Bid ❸.

Because this is a product, the result contains every possible combination of Item and Bid rows found in the two underlying tables. Obviously, this query isn't useful, but you shouldn't be surprised to receive a collection of Object[] as a query result. Hibernate manages all Item and Bid entity instances in persistent state, in the persistence context. Note how the HashSets filter out duplicate Item and Bid instances.

Alternatively, with the Tuple API, in criteria queries you get typed access to the result list. Start by calling createTupleQuery() to create a CriteriaQuery<Tuple>. Then, refine the query definition by adding aliases for the entity classes:

```
CriteriaQuery<Tuple> criteria = cb.createTupleQuery();

// Or: CriteriaQuery<Tuple> criteria = cb.createQuery(Tuple.class);

criteria.multiselect(
    criteria.from(Item.class).alias("i"),          ◄——— Aliases optional
    criteria.from(Bid.class).alias("b")
);

TypedQuery<Tuple> query = em.createQuery(criteria);
List<Tuple> result = query.getResultList();
```

The `Tuple` API offers several ways to access the result, by index, by alias, or untyped meta access:

```
for (Tuple tuple : result) {
    Item item = tuple.get(0, Item.class);          <--- Indexed
    Bid bid = tuple.get(1, Bid.class);

    item = tuple.get("i", Item.class);             <--- Alias
    bid = tuple.get("b", Bid.class);

    for (TupleElement<?> element : tuple.getElements()) {   <--- Meta
        Class clazz = element.getJavaType();
        String alias = element.getAlias();
        Object value = tuple.get(element);
    }
}
```

The following projection also returns a collection of `Object[]`s:

```
select u.id, u.username, u.homeAddress from User u
```

```
Root<User> u = criteria.from(User.class);          | Returns a List
criteria.multiselect(                          <--- | of Object[]
    u.get("id"), u.get("username"), u.get("homeAddress")
);
```

The `Object[]`s returned by this query contain a `Long` at index 0, a `String` at index 1, and an `Address` at index 2. The first two are scalar values; the third is an embedded class instance. None are managed entity instances! Therefore, these values aren't in any persistent state, like an entity instance would be. They aren't transactional and obviously aren't checked automatically for dirty state. We say that all of these values are *transient*. This is the kind of query you need to write for a simple reporting screen, showing all user names and their home addresses.

You have now seen *path expressions* several times: using dot-notation, you can reference properties of an entity, such as `User#username` with `u.username`. For a nested embedded property, for example, you can write the path `u.homeAddress.city.zip-code`. These are single-valued path expressions, because they don't terminate in a mapped collection property.

A more convenient alternative than `Object[]` or `Tuple`, especially for report queries, is dynamic instantiation in projections, which is next.

15.3.2 Using dynamic instantiation

Let's say you have a reporting screen in your application where you need to show some data in a list. You want to show all auction items and when each auction ends. You don't want to load managed `Item` entity instances, because no data will be modified: you only read data.

First, write a class called `ItemSummary` with a constructor that takes a `Long` for the item's identifier, a `String` for the item's name, and a `Date` for the item's auction end timestamp:

```
public class ItemSummary {

    public ItemSummary(Long itemId, String name, Date auctionEnd) {
        // ...
    }

    // ...
}
```

We sometimes call these kinds of classes *data transfer objects* (DTOs), because their main purpose is to shuttle data around in the application. The ItemSummary class isn't mapped to the database, and you can add arbitrary methods (getter, setter, printing of values) as needed by your reporting user interface.

Hibernate can directly return instances of ItemSummary from a query with the new keyword in JPQL and the construct() method in criteria:

```
select new org.jpwh.model.querying.ItemSummary(
    i.id, i.name, i.auctionEnd
) from Item i
```

```
Root<Item> i = criteria.from(Item.class);
criteria.select(
    cb.construct(                                  Must have the
        ItemSummary.class,          ◄─────────    right constructor
        i.get("id"), i.get("name"), i.get("auctionEnd")
    )
);
```

In the result list of this query, each element is an instance of ItemSummary. Note that in JPQL, you must use a fully qualified class name, which means including the package name. Also note that nesting constructor calls isn't supported: you can't write new ItemSummary(..., new UserSummary(...)).

Dynamic instantiation isn't limited to non-persistent data transfer classes like ItemSummary. You can construct a new Item or a User in a query, which is a mapped entity class. The only important rule is that the class must have a matching constructor for your projection. But if you construct entity instances dynamically, they won't be in persistent state when returned from the query! They will be in *transient* or *detached* state, depending on whether you set the identifier value. One use case for this feature is simple data duplication: Retrieve a "new" transient Item with some values copied into the constructor from the database, set some other values in the application, and then store it in the database with persist().

If your DTO class doesn't have the right constructor, and you want to populate it from a query result through setter methods or fields, apply a ResultTransformer, as shown in in section 16.1.3. Later, we have more examples of aggregation and grouping.

Next, we're going to look at an issue with projection that is frequently confusing for many engineers: handling duplicates.

15.3.3 Getting distinct results

When you create a projection in a query, the elements of the result aren't guaranteed to be unique. For example, item names aren't unique, so the following query may return the same name more than once:

```
select i.name from Item i
```

```
CriteriaQuery<String> criteria = cb.createQuery(String.class);

criteria.select(
    criteria.from(Item.class).<String>get("name")
);
```

It's difficult to see how it could be meaningful to have two identical rows in a query result, so if you think duplicates are likely, you normally apply the DISTINCT keyword or distinct() method:

```
select distinct i.name from Item i
```

```
CriteriaQuery<String> criteria = cb.createQuery(String.class);

criteria.select(
    criteria.from(Item.class).<String>get("name")
);
criteria.distinct(true);
```

This eliminates duplicates from the returned list of Item descriptions and translates directly into the SQL DISTINCT operator. The filtering occurs at the database level. Later in this chapter, we show you that this isn't always the case.

Earlier, you saw function calls in restrictions, in the WHERE clause. You can also call functions in projections, to modify the returned data within the query.

15.3.4 Calling functions in projections

The following queries return a custom String with the concat() function in the projection:

```
select concat(concat(i.name, ': '), i.auctionEnd) from Item i
```

```
Root<Item> i = criteria.from(Item.class);
criteria.select(
    cb.concat(
        cb.concat(i.<String>get("name"), ":"),
        i.<String>get("auctionEnd")          <───── Note the cast of Date.
    )
);
```

This query returns a List of Strings, each with the form "[Item name]:[Auction end date]". This example also shows that you can write nested function calls.

Next, the coalesce() function returns null if all its arguments evaluate to null; otherwise it returns the value of the first non-null argument:

```
select i.name, coalesce(i.buyNowPrice, 0) from Item i
```

```
Root<Item> i = criteria.from(Item.class);
criteria.multiselect(
    i.get("name"),
    cb.coalesce(i.<BigDecimal>get("buyNowPrice"), 0)
);
```

If an `Item` doesn't have a `buyNowPrice`, a `BigDecimal` for the value zero is returned instead of `null`.

Similar to `coalesce()` but more powerful are `case/when` expressions. The following query returns the `username` of each `User` and an additional `String` with either "Germany", "Switzerland", or "Other", depending on the length of the user's address `zipcode`:

```
select
    u.username,
    case when length(u.homeAddress.zipcode) = 5 then 'Germany'
         when length(u.homeAddress.zipcode) = 4 then 'Switzerland'
         else 'Other'
    end
from User u
```

```
// Check String literal support; see Hibernate bug HHH-8124
Root<User> u = criteria.from(User.class);
criteria.multiselect(
    u.get("username"),
    cb.selectCase()
        .when(
            cb.equal(
                cb.length(u.get("homeAddress").<String>get("zipcode")), 5
            ), "Germany"
        )
        .when(
            cb.equal(
                cb.length(u.get("homeAddress").<String>get("zipcode")), 4
            ), "Switzerland"
        )
        .otherwise("Other")
);
```

For the built-in standard functions, refer to the tables in the previous section. Unlike function calls in restrictions, Hibernate won't pass on an unknown function call in a projection to the database as a plain direct SQL function call. Any function you'd like to call in a projection *must* be known to Hibernate and/or invoked with the special `function()` operation of JPQL.

This projection returns the name of each auction `Item` and the number of days between item creation and auction end, calling the SQL `datediff()` function of the H2 database:

```
select
    i.name,
    function('DATEDIFF', 'DAY', i.createdOn, i.auctionEnd)
from Item i
```

```
Root<Item> i = criteria.from(Item.class);
criteria.multiselect(
    i.get("name"),
    cb.function(
        "DATEDIFF",
        Integer.class,
        cb.literal("DAY"),
        i.get("createdOn"),
        i.get("auctionEnd")
    )
);
```

If instead you want to call a function directly, you give Hibernate the function's return type, so it can parse the query. You add functions for invocation in projections by extending your configured `org.hibernate.Dialect`. The `datediff()` function is already registered for you in the H2 dialect. Then, you can either call it as shown with `function()`, which works in other JPA providers when accessing H2, or directly as `datediff()`, which most likely only works in Hibernate. Check the source code of the dialect for your database; you'll probably find many other proprietary SQL functions already registered there.

Furthermore, you can add SQL functions programmatically on boot to Hibernate by calling the method `applySqlFunction()` on a Hibernate `MetadataBuilder`. The following example adds the SQL function `lpad()` to Hibernate before it's started:

```
...
MetadataBuilder metadataBuilder = metadataSources.getMetadataBuilder();
metadataBuilder.applySqlFunction(
    "lpad",
    new org.hibernate.dialect.function.StandardSQLFunction(
        "lpad", org.hibernate.type.StringType.INSTANCE
    )
);
```

See the Javadoc of `SQLFunction` and its subclasses for more information.

Next, we look at aggregation functions, which are the most useful functions in reporting queries.

15.3.5 Aggregation functions

Reporting queries take advantage of the database's ability to perform efficient grouping and aggregation of data. For example, a typical report query would retrieve the highest initial item price in a given category. This calculation can occur in the database, and you don't have to load many `Item` entity instances into memory.

The aggregation functions standardized in JPA are `count()`, `min()`, `max()`, `sum()`, and `avg()`.

The following query counts all `Items`:

```
select count(i) from Item i
```

```
criteria.select(
    cb.count(criteria.from(Item.class))
);
```

The query returns the result as a `Long`:

```
Long count = (Long)query.getSingleResult();
```

The special `count(distinct)` JPQL function and `countDistinct()` method ignore duplicates:

```
select count(distinct i.name) from Item i
```

```
criteria.select(
    cb.countDistinct(
        criteria.from(Item.class).get("name")
    )
);
```

The following query calculates the total value of all `Bids`:

```
select sum(b.amount) from Bid b
```

```
CriteriaQuery<Number> criteria = cb.createQuery(Number.class);
criteria.select(
    cb.sum(
        criteria.from(Bid.class).<BigDecimal>get("amount")
    )
);
```

This query returns a `BigDecimal`, because the `amount` property is of type `BigDecimal`. The `sum()` function also recognizes the `BigInteger` property type and returns `Long` for all other numeric property types.

The next query returns the minimum and maximum bid amounts for a particular `Item`:

```
select min(b.amount), max(b.amount) from Bid b
    where b.item.id = :itemId
```

```
Root<Bid> b = criteria.from(Bid.class);
criteria.multiselect(
    cb.min(b.<BigDecimal>get("amount")),
    cb.max(b.<BigDecimal>get("amount"))
);
criteria.where(
    cb.equal(
        b.get("item").<Long>get("id"),
        cb.parameter(Long.class, "itemId")
    )
);
```

The result is an ordered pair of `BigDecimals` (two instances of `BigDecimals`, in an `Object[]` array).

When you call an aggregation function in the SELECT clause, without specifying any grouping in a GROUP BY clause, you collapse the results down to a single row, containing the aggregated value(s). This means (in the absence of a GROUP BY clause) any SELECT clause that contains an aggregation function must contain *only* aggregation functions.

For more advanced statistics and for reporting, you need to be able to perform *grouping*, which is up next.

15.3.6 *Grouping*

JPA standardizes several features of SQL that are most commonly used for reporting—although they're also used for other things. In reporting queries, you write the SELECT clause for projection and the GROUP BY and HAVING clauses for aggregation.

Just like in SQL, any property or alias that appears outside of an aggregate function in the SELECT clause must also appear in the GROUP BY clause. Consider the next query, which counts the number of users with each last name:

```
select u.lastname, count(u) from User u
    group by u.lastname
```

```
Root<User> u = criteria.from(User.class);
criteria.multiselect(
    u.get("lastname"),
    cb.count(u)
);
criteria.groupBy(u.get("lastname"));
```

In this example, the u.lastname property isn't inside an aggregation function, so projected data has to be "grouped by" u.lastname. You also don't need to specify the property you want to count; the count(u) expression is automatically translated into count(u.id).

The next query finds the average Bid#amount for each Item:

```
select i.name, avg(b.amount)
    from Bid b join b.item i
    group by i.name
```

```
Root<Bid> b = criteria.from(Bid.class);
criteria.multiselect(
    b.get("item").get("name"),
    cb.avg(b.<BigDecimal>get("amount"))
);
criteria.groupBy(b.get("item").get("name"));
```

Hibernate Feature

When grouping, you may run into a Hibernate limitation. The following query is specification compliant but not properly handled in Hibernate:

```
select i, avg(b.amount)
    from Bid b join b.item i
    group by i
```

The JPA specification allows grouping by an entity path expression, group by i. But Hibernate doesn't automatically expand the properties of Item in the generated SQL GROUP BY clause, which then doesn't match the SELECT clause. You have to expand the grouped/projected properties manually in your query, until this Hibernate issue is fixed (this is one of the oldest and most "persistent" Hibernate issues, HHH-1615):

```
select i, avg(b.amount)
    from Bid b join b.item i
    group by i.id, i.name, i.createdOn, i.auctionEnd,
             i.auctionType, i.approved, i.buyNowPrice,
             i.seller
```

```
Root<Bid> b = criteria.from(Bid.class);
Join<Bid, Item> i = b.join("item");
criteria.multiselect(
    i,
    cb.avg(b.<BigDecimal>get("amount"))
);
criteria.groupBy(
    i.get("id"), i.get("name"), i.get("createdOn"), i.get("auctionEnd"),
    i.get("auctionType"), i.get("approved"), i.get("buyNowPrice"),
    i.get("seller")
);
```

Sometimes you want to restrict the result further by selecting only particular values of a group. Use the WHERE clause to perform the relational operation of restriction on rows. The HAVING clause performs restriction upon groups.

For example, the next query counts users with each last name that begins with "D":

```
select u.lastname, count(u) from User u
    group by u.lastname
    having u.lastname like 'D%'
```

```
Root<User> u = criteria.from(User.class);
criteria.multiselect(
    u.get("lastname"),
    cb.count(u)
);
criteria.groupBy(u.get("lastname"));
criteria.having(cb.like(u.<String>get("lastname"), "D%"));
```

The same rules govern the SELECT and HAVING clauses: only grouped properties may appear outside of an aggregate function.

The previous sections should get you started with basic queries. It's time to look at some more complex options. For many engineers, the most difficult to understand but also one of most powerful benefits of the relational model is the ability to *join* arbitrary data.

15.4 *Joins*

Join operations combine data in two (or more) relations. Joining data in a query also enables you to fetch several associated instances and collections in a single query: for example, to load an Item and all its bids in one round trip to the database. We now show you how basic join operations work and how to use them to write such *dynamic fetching* strategies. Let's first look at how joins work in SQL queries, without JPA.

15.4.1 *Joins with SQL*

Let's start with the example we already mentioned: joining the data in the ITEM and BID tables, as shown in figure 15.1. The database contains three items: the first has three bids, the second has one bid, and the third has no bids. Note that we don't show all columns; hence the dotted lines.

ITEM

ID	NAME	...
1	Foo	...
2	Bar	...
3	Baz	...

BID

ID	ITEM_ID	AMOUNT	...
1	1	99.00	...
2	1	100.00	...
3	1	101.00	...
4	2	4.99	...

Figure 15.1 The ITEM and BID tables are obvious candidates for a join operation.

What most people think of when they hear the word *join* in the context of SQL databases is an *inner join*. An inner join is the most important of several types of joins and the easiest to understand. Consider the SQL statement and result in figure 15.2. This SQL statement contains an *ANSI-style inner join* in the FROM clause.

If you join the ITEM and BID tables with an inner join, with the condition that the ID of an ITEM row must match the ITEM_ID value of a BID row, you get items combined with their bids in the result. Note that the result of this operation contains only items that *have* bids.

You can think of a join as working as follows: first you take a product of the two tables, by taking all possible combinations of ITEM rows with BID rows. Second, you filter these combined rows with a *join condition*: the expression in the ON clause. (Any good database engine has much more sophisticated algorithms to evaluate a join; it usually doesn't build a memory-consuming product and then filter out rows.) The join condition is a Boolean expression that evaluates to true if the combined row is to be included in the result.

It's crucial to understand that the join condition can be any expression that evaluates to true. You can join data in arbitrary ways; you aren't limited to comparisons of identifier values. For example, the join condition on i.ID = b.ITEM_ID and b.AMOUNT > 100 would only include rows from the BID table that also have an AMOUNT greater than 100. The ITEM_ID column in the BID table has a foreign key constraint, ensuring

```
select i.*, b.*
  from ITEM i
    inner join BID b on i.ID = b.ITEM_ID
```

i.ID	i.NAME	...	b.ID	b.ITEM_ID	b.AMOUNT
1	Foo	...	1	1	99.00
1	Foo	...	2	1	100.00
1	Foo	...	3	1	101.00
2	Bar	...	4	2	4.99

Figure 15.2 The result of an ANSI-style inner join of two tables

```
select i.*, b.*
   from ITEM i
      left outer join BID b on i.ID = b.ITEM_ID
```

i.ID	i.NAME	...	b.ID	b.ITEM_ID	b.AMOUNT
1	Foo	...	1	1	99.00
1	Foo	...	2	1	100.00
1	Foo	...	3	1	101.00
2	Bar	...	4	2	4.99
3	Baz	...			

Figure 15.3   The result of an ANSI-style left outer join of two tables

that a BID has a reference to an ITEM row. This doesn't mean you can only join by comparing primary and foreign key columns. Key columns are of course the most common operands in a join condition, because you often want to retrieve related information together.

If you want *all* items, not just the ones which have related bids, and NULL instead of bid data when there is no corresponding bid, then you write a *(left) outer join*, as shown in figure 15.3.

In case of the left outer join, each row in the (left) ITEM table that *never* satisfies the join condition is also included in the result, with NULL returned for all columns of BID. Right outer joins are rarely used; developers always think from left to right and put the "driving" table of a join operation first. In figure 15.4, you can see the same result with BID instead of ITEM as the driving table, and a right outer join.

In SQL, you usually specify the join condition explicitly. Unfortunately, it isn't possible to use the name of a foreign key constraint to specify how two tables are to be joined: select * from ITEM join BID on FK_BID_ITEM_ID doesn't work.

You specify the join condition in the ON clause for an ANSI-style join or in the WHERE clause for a so-called *theta-style join*: select * from ITEM i, BID b where i.ID = b.ITEM_ID. This is an inner join; here you see that a product is created first in the FROM clause.

We now discuss JPA join options. Remember that Hibernate eventually translates all queries into SQL, so even if the syntax is slightly different, you should always refer to the illustrations shown in this section and verify that you understand what the resulting SQL and result set looks like.

```
select b.*, i.*
   from BID b
      right outer join ITEM i on b.ITEM_ID = i.ID
```

b.ID	b.ITEM_ID	b.AMOUNT	i.ID	i.NAME	...
1	1	99.00	1	Foo	...
2	1	100.00	1	Foo	...
3	1	101.00	1	Foo	...
4	2	4.99	2	Bar	...
			3	Baz	...

Figure 15.4   The result of an ANSI-style right outer join of two tables

15.4.2 *Join options in JPA*

JPA provides four ways of expressing (inner and outer) joins in queries:

- An *implicit* association join with path expressions
- An *ordinary* join in the FROM clause with the join operator
- A *fetch* join in the FROM clause with the join operator and the fetch keyword for eager fetching
- A *theta-style* join in the WHERE clause

Let's start with implicit association joins.

15.4.3 *Implicit association joins*

In JPA queries, you don't have to specify a join condition explicitly. Rather, you specify the name of a mapped Java class association. This is the same feature we'd prefer to have in SQL: a join condition expressed with a foreign key constraint name. Because you've mapped most, if not all, foreign key relationships of your database schema, you can use the names of these mapped associations in the query language. This is syntactical sugar, but it's convenient.

For example, the Bid entity class has a mapped *many-to-one* association named item, with the Item entity class. If you refer to this association in a query, Hibernate has enough information to deduce the join expression with a key column comparison. This helps make queries less verbose and more readable.

Earlier in this chapter, we showed you property path expressions, using dot-notation: single-valued path expressions such as user.homeAddress.zipcode and collection-valued path expressions such as item.bids. You can create a path expression in an implicit inner join query:

```
select b from Bid b where b.item.name like 'Fo%'
```

```
Root<Bid> b = criteria.from(Bid.class);
criteria.select(b).where(
    cb.like(
        b.get("item").<String>get("name"),
        "Fo%"
    )
);
```

The path b.item.name creates an implicit join on the *many-to-one* associations from Bid to Item—the name of this association is item. Hibernate knows that you mapped this association with the ITEM_ID foreign key in the BID table and generates the SQL join condition accordingly. Implicit joins are always directed along *many-to-one* or *one-to-one* associations, never through a collection-valued association (you can't write item.bids.amount).

Multiple joins are possible in a single path expression:

```
select b from Bid b where b.item.seller.username = 'johndoe'
```

```
Root<Bid> b = criteria.from(Bid.class);
criteria.select(b).where(
    cb.equal(
        b.get("item").get("seller").get("username"),
        "johndoe"
    )
);
```

This query joins rows from the BID, the ITEM, and the USER tables.

We frown on the use of this syntactic sugar for more complex queries. SQL joins are important, and especially when optimizing queries, you need to be able to see at a glance exactly how many of them there are. Consider the following query:

```
select b from Bid b where b.item.seller.username = 'johndoe'
    and b.item.buyNowPrice is not null
```

```
Root<Bid> b = criteria.from(Bid.class);
criteria.select(b).where(
    cb.and(
        cb.equal(
            b.get("item").get("seller").get("username"),
            "johndoe"
        ),
        cb.isNotNull(b.get("item").get("buyNowPrice"))
    )
);
```

How many joins are required to express such a query in SQL? Even if you get the answer right, it takes more than a few seconds to figure out. The answer is two. The generated SQL looks something like this:

```
select b.*
    from BID b
        inner join ITEM i on b.ITEM_ID = i.ID
        inner join USER u on i.SELLER_ID = u.ID
        where u.USERNAME = 'johndoe'
            and i.BUYNOWPRICE is not null;
```

Alternatively, instead of joins with such complex path expressions, you can write ordinary joins explicitly in the FROM clause.

15.4.4 Explicit joins

JPA differentiates between purposes you may have for joining. Suppose you're querying items; there are two possible reasons you may be interested in joining them with bids.

You may want to limit the items returned by the query based on some criterion to apply to their bids. For example, you may want all items that have a bid of more than 100, which requires an *inner join*. Here, you aren't interested in items that have no bids.

On the other hand, you may be primarily interested in the items but may want to execute an outer join just because you want to retrieve all bids for the queried items in a single SQL statement, something we called *eager join fetching* earlier. Remember that you prefer to map all associations *lazily* by default, so an eager fetch query will override the default fetching strategy at runtime for a particular use case.

Let's first write some queries that use joins for the purpose of restriction. If you want to retrieve Item instances and restrict the result to items that have bids with a certain amount, you have to assign an alias to a joined association. Then you refer to the alias in a WHERE clause to restrict the data you want:

```
select i from Item i
    join i.bids b
    where b.amount > 100
```

```
Root<Item> i = criteria.from(Item.class);
Join<Item, Bid> b = i.join("bids");
criteria.select(i).where(
    cb.gt(b.<BigDecimal>get("amount"), new BigDecimal(100))
);
```

This query assigns the alias b to the collection bids and limits the returned Item instances to those with Bid#amount greater than 100.

So far, you've only written inner joins. Outer joins are mostly used for dynamic fetching, which we discuss soon. Sometimes, you want to write a simple query with an outer join without applying a dynamic fetching strategy. For example, the following query and retrieves items that have no bids, and items with bids of a minimum bid amount:

```
select i, b from Item i
    left join i.bids b on b.amount > 100
```

```
Root<Item> i = criteria.from(Item.class);
Join<Item, Bid> b = i.join("bids", JoinType.LEFT);
b.on(
    cb.gt(b.<BigDecimal>get("amount"), new BigDecimal(100))
);
criteria.multiselect(i, b);
```

This query returns ordered pairs of Item and Bid, in a List<Object[]>.

The first thing that is new in this query is the LEFT keyword and JoinType.LEFT in the criteria query. Optionally you can write LEFT OUTER JOIN and RIGHT OUTER JOIN in JPQL, but we usually prefer the short form.

The second change is the additional join condition following the ON keyword. If instead you place the b.amount > 100 expression into the WHERE clause, you restrict the result to Item instances that have bids. This isn't what you want here: you want to retrieve items and bids, and even items that don't have bids. If an item *has* bids, the bid amount must be greater than 100. By adding an additional join condition in the FROM clause, you can restrict the Bid instances and still retrieve all Item instances, whether they have bids or not.

This is how the additional join condition translates into SQL:

```
... from ITEM i
    left outer join BID b
        on i.ID = b.ITEM_ID and (b.AMOUNT > 100)
```

The SQL query will always contain the implied join condition of the mapped association, i.ID = b.ITEM_ID. You can only append additional expressions to the join condition. JPA and Hibernate don't support arbitrary outer joins without a mapped entity association or collection.

Hibernate has a proprietary WITH keyword, it's the same as the ON keyword in JPQL. You may see it in older code examples, because JPA only recently standardized ON.

You can write a query returning the same data with a right outer join, switching the driving table:

```
select b, i from Bid b
    right outer join b.item i
    where b is null or b.amount > 100
```

```
Root<Bid> b = criteria.from(Bid.class);
Join<Bid, Item> i = b.join("item", JoinType.RIGHT);
criteria.multiselect(b, i).where(
    cb.or(
        cb.isNull(b),
        cb.gt(b.<BigDecimal>get("amount"), new BigDecimal(100)))
);
```

This right outer join query is more important than you may think. Earlier in this book, we told you to avoid mapping a persistent collection whenever possible. If you don't have a *one-to-many* Item#bids collection, you need a right outer join to retrieve all Items and their Bid instances. You drive the query from the "other" side: the *many-to-one* Bid#item.

Left outer joins also play an important role with eager dynamic fetching.

15.4.5 *Dynamic fetching with joins*

All the queries you saw in the previous sections have one thing in common: the returned Item instances have a collection named bids. This @OneToMany collection, if mapped as FetchType.LAZY (the default for collections), isn't initialized, and an additional SQL statement is triggered as soon as you access it. The same is true for all single-valued associations, like the @ManyToOne association seller of each Item. By default, Hibernate generates a proxy and loads the associated User instance lazily and only on demand.

What options do you have to change this behavior? First, you can change the fetch plan in your mapping metadata and declare a collection or single-valued association as FetchType.EAGER. Hibernate then executes the necessary SQL to guarantee that the desired network of instances is loaded at all times. This also means a single JPA query may result in several SQL operations! As an example, the simple query select i from Item i may trigger additional SQL statements to load the bids of each Item, the seller of each Item, and so on.

In chapter 12, we made the case for a lazy global fetch plan in mapping metadata, where you shouldn't have FetchType.EAGER on association and collection mappings. Then, for a particular use case in your application, you *dynamically* override the lazy fetch plan and write a query that fetches the data you need as efficiently as possible. For example, there is no reason you need several SQL statements to fetch all Item instances and to initialize their bids collections, or to retrieve the seller for each Item. You can do this at the same time, in a single SQL statement, with a join operation.

Eager fetching of associated data is possible with the FETCH keyword in JPQL and the fetch() method in the criteria query API:

```
select i from Item i
    left join fetch i.bids
```

```
Root<Item> i = criteria.from(Item.class);
i.fetch("bids", JoinType.LEFT);
criteria.select(i);
```

You've already seen the SQL query this produces and the result set in figure 15.3.

This query returns a List<Item>; each Item instance has its bids collection fully initialized. This is different than the ordered pairs returned by the queries in the previous section!

Be careful—you may not expect the duplicate results from the previous query:

```
List<Item> result = query.getResultList();          3 items, 4 bids, 5 "rows"
assertEquals(result.size(), 5);                      in the result

Set<Item> distinctResult = new LinkedHashSet<Item>(result);      In-memory
assertEquals(distinctResult.size(), 3);                          "distinct"

              Only three items all along
```

Make sure you understand why these duplicates appear in the result List. Verify the number of Item "rows" in the result set, as shown in figure 15.3. Hibernate preserves the rows as list elements; you may need the correct row count to make rendering a report table in the user interface easier.

You can filter out duplicate Item instances by passing the result List through a LinkedHashSet, which doesn't allow duplicate elements but preserves the order of elements. Alternatively, Hibernate can remove the duplicate elements with the DISTINCT operation and distinct() criteria method:

```
select distinct i from Item i
    left join fetch i.bids
```

```
Root<Item> i = criteria.from(Item.class);
i.fetch("bids", JoinType.LEFT);
criteria.select(i).distinct(true);
```

Understand that in this case the DISTINCT operation does *not* execute in the database. There will be no DISTINCT keyword in the SQL statement. Conceptually, you *can't* remove the duplicate rows at the SQL ResultSet level. Hibernate performs deduplication in memory, just as you would manually with a LinkedHashSet.

You can also prefetch *many-to-one* or *one-to-one* associations with the same syntax:

```
select distinct i from Item i
    left join fetch i.bids b
        join fetch b.bidder
        left join fetch i.seller
```

```
Root<Item> i = criteria.from(Item.class);
Fetch<Item, Bid> b = i.fetch("bids", JoinType.LEFT);
b.fetch("bidder");
i.fetch("seller", JoinType.LEFT);
criteria.select(i).distinct(true);
```

Non-nullable foreign key columns. Inner join or outer doesn't make a difference.

This query returns a List<Item>, and each Item has its bids collection initialized. The seller of each Item is loaded as well. Finally, the bidder of each Bid instance is loaded. You can do this in one SQL query by joining rows of the ITEM, BID, and USERS tables.

If you write JOIN FETCH without LEFT, you get eager loading with an inner join (also if you use INNER JOIN FETCH). An eager inner join fetch makes sense if there must be a fetched value: an Item must have a seller, and a Bid must have a bidder.

There are limits to how many associations you should eagerly load in one query and how much data you should fetch in one round trip. Consider the following query, which initializes the Item#bids and Item#images collections:

```
select distinct i from Item i
    left join fetch i.bids
    left join fetch i.images
```

```
Root<Item> i = criteria.from(Item.class);
i.fetch("bids", JoinType.LEFT);
i.fetch("images", JoinType.LEFT);          ◁——— Cartesian product: bad
criteria.select(i).distinct(true);
```

This is a bad query, because it creates a Cartesian product of bids and images, with a potentially extremely large result set. We covered this issue in section 12.2.2.

To summarize, eager dynamic fetching in queries has the following caveats:

- Never assign an alias to any fetch-joined association or collection for further restriction or projection. The query left join fetch i.bids b where b.amount . . . is invalid. You can't say, "Load the Item instances and initialize their bids collections, but only with Bid instances that have a certain amount." You *can* assign an alias to a fetch-joined association for further fetching: for example, retrieving the bidder of each Bid: left join fetch i.bids b join fetch b.bidder.
- You shouldn't fetch more than one collection; otherwise, you create a Cartesian product. You can fetch as many single-valued associations as you like without creating a product.

- Queries ignore any fetching strategy you've defined in mapping metadata with `@org.hibernate.annotations.Fetch`. For example, mapping the `bids` collection with `org.hibernate.annotations.FetchMode.JOIN` has no effect on the queries you write. The dynamic fetching strategy of your query ignores the global fetching strategy. On the other hand, Hibernate doesn't ignore the mapped *fetch plan*: Hibernate always considers a `FetchType.EAGER`, and you may see several additional SQL statements when you execute your query.

- If you eager-fetch a collection, the `List` returned by Hibernate preserves the number of rows in the SQL result as duplicate references. You can filter out the duplicates in-memory either manually with a `LinkedHashSet` or with the special `DISTINCT` operation in the query.

There is one more issue to be aware of, and it deserves some special attention. You can't paginate a result set at the database level if you eagerly fetch a collection. For example, for the query `select i from Item i fetch i.bids`, how should `Query#setFirstResult(21)` and `Query#setMaxResults(10)` be handled?

Clearly, you expect to get only 10 items, starting with item 21. But you also want to load all `bids` of each `Item` eagerly. Therefore, the database can't do the paging operation; you can't limit the SQL result to 10 arbitrary rows. Hibernate will execute paging in-memory if a collection is eagerly fetched in a query. This means *all* `Item` instances will be loaded into memory, each with the `bids` collection fully initialized. Hibernate then gives you the requested page of items: for example, only items 21 to 30.

Not all items might fit into memory, and you probably expected the paging to occur in the database before it transmitted the result to the application! Therefore, Hibernate will log a warning message if your query contains `fetch [collectionPath]` and you call `setFirstResult()` or `setMaxResults()`.

We don't recommend the use of `fetch [collectionPath]` with `setMaxResults()` or `setFirstResult()` options. Usually there is an easier query you can write to get the data you want to render—and we don't expect that you load data page by page to modify it. For example, if you want to show several pages of items and for each item the number of bids, write a report query:

```
select i.id, i.name, count(b)
    from Item i left join i.bids b
        group by i.id, i.name
```

The result of this query can be paged by the database with `setFirstResult()` and `setMaxResults()`. It's much more efficient than retrieving *any* `Item` or `Bid` instances into memory, so let the database create the report for you.

The last JPA join option on the list is the *theta-style join*.

15.4.6 *Theta-style joins*

In traditional SQL, a theta-style join is a Cartesian product together with a join condition in the `WHERE` clause, which is applied on the product to restrict the result. In JPA queries, the theta-style syntax is useful when your join condition isn't a foreign key relationship mapped to a class association.

For example, suppose you store the User's name in log records instead of mapping an association from LogRecord to User. The classes don't know anything about each other, because they aren't associated. You can then find all the Users and their Log-Records with the following theta-style join:

```
select u, log from User u, LogRecord log
    where u.username = log.username
```

```
Root<User> u = criteria.from(User.class);
Root<LogRecord> log = criteria.from(LogRecord.class);
criteria.where(
    cb.equal(u.get("username"), log.get("username")));
criteria.multiselect(u, log);
```

The join condition here is a comparison of username, present as an attribute in both classes. If both rows have the same username, they're joined (with an inner join) in the result. The query result consists of ordered pairs:

```
List<Object[]> result = query.getResultList();
for (Object[] row : result) {
    assertTrue(row[0] instanceof User);
    assertTrue(row[1] instanceof LogRecord);
}
```

You probably won't need to use the theta-style joins often. Note that it's currently not possible in JPA to outer join two tables that don't have a mapped association—theta-style joins are inner joins.

Another more common case for theta-style joins is comparisons of primary key or foreign key values to either query parameters or other primary or foreign key values in the WHERE clause:

```
select i, b from Item i, Bid b
    where b.item = i and i.seller = b.bidder
```

```
Root<Item> i = criteria.from(Item.class);
Root<Bid> b = criteria.from(Bid.class);
criteria.where(
    cb.equal(b.get("item"), i),
    cb.equal(i.get("seller"), b.get("bidder"))
);
criteria.multiselect(i, b);
```

This query returns pairs of Item and Bid instances, where the bidder is also the seller. This is an important query in CaveatEmptor because it lets you detect people who bid on their own items. You probably should translate this query into a database constraint and not allow such a Bid instance to be stored.

The previous query also has an interesting comparison expression: i.seller = b.bidder. This is an identifier comparison, our next topic.

15.4.7 *Comparing identifiers*

JPA supports the following implicit identifier comparison syntax in queries:

```
select i, u from Item i, User u
    where i.seller = u and u.username like 'j%'
```

```
Root<Item> i = criteria.from(Item.class);
Root<User> u = criteria.from(User.class);
criteria.where(
    cb.equal(i.get("seller"), u),
    cb.like(u.<String>get("username"), "j%")
);
criteria.multiselect(i, u);
```

In this query, i.seller refers to the SELLER_ID foreign key column of the ITEM table, referencing the USERS table. The alias u refers to the primary key of the USERS table (on the ID column). Hence, this query has a theta-style join and is equivalent to the easier, readable alternative:

```
select i, u from Item i, User u
    where i.seller.id = u.id and u.username like 'j%'
```

```
Root<Item> i = criteria.from(Item.class);
Root<User> u = criteria.from(User.class);
criteria.where(
    cb.equal(i.get("seller").get("id"), u.get("id")),
    cb.like(u.<String>get("username"), "j%")
);
criteria.multiselect(i, u);
```

Hibernate Feature

A path expression ending with id is special in Hibernate: the id name always refers to the identifier property of an entity. It doesn't matter what the actual name of the property annotated with @Id is; you can always reach it with entityAlias.id. That's why we recommend you always name the identifier property of your entity classes id, to avoid confusion in queries. Note that this isn't a requirement or standardized in JPA; only Hibernate treats an id path element specially.

You may also want to compare a key value to a query parameter, perhaps to find all Items for a given seller (a User):

```
select i from Item i where i.seller = :seller
```

```
Root<Item> i = criteria.from(Item.class);
criteria.where(
    cb.equal(
        i.get("seller"),
        cb.parameter(User.class, "seller")
    )
);
criteria.select(i);
query.setParameter("seller", someUser);
List<Item> result = query.getResultList();
```

Alternatively, you may prefer to express these kinds of queries in terms of identifier values rather than object references. These queries are equivalent to the earlier queries:

```
select i from Item i where i.seller.id = :sellerId
```

```
Root<Item> i = criteria.from(Item.class);
criteria.where(
    cb.equal(
        i.get("seller").get("id"),
        cb.parameter(Long.class, "sellerId")
    )
);
criteria.select(i);
query.setParameter("sellerId", USER_ID);
List<Item> result = query.getResultList();
```

Considering identifier attributes, there is a world of difference between this query pair

```
select b from Bid b where b.item.name like 'Fo%'
```

```
Root<Bid> b = criteria.from(Bid.class);
criteria.select(b).where(
    cb.like(
        b.get("item").<String>get("name"),
        "Fo%"
    )
);
```

and this similar-looking query pair:

```
select b from Bid b where b.item.id = :itemId
```

```
CriteriaQuery<Bid> criteria = cb.createQuery(Bid.class);
Root<Bid> b = criteria.from(Bid.class);
criteria.where(
    cb.equal(
        b.get("item").get("id"),
        cb.parameter(Long.class, "itemId")
    )
);
criteria.select(b);
```

The first query pair uses an implicit table join; the second has no joins at all!

This completes our discussion of queries that involve joins. Our final topic is nesting selects within selects: *subselects.*

15.5   Subselects

Subselects are an important and powerful feature of SQL. A subselect is a select query embedded in another query, usually in the SELECT, FROM, or WHERE clause.

JPA supports subqueries in the WHERE clause. Subselects in the FROM clause aren't supported because the query languages doesn't have *transitive closure.* The result of a query may not be usable for further selection in a FROM clause. The query language also doesn't support subselects in the SELECT clause, but you map can subselects to derived properties with @org.hibernate.annotations.Formula, as shown in section 5.1.3.

Subselects can be either correlated with the rest of the query or uncorrelated.

15.5.1 *Correlated and uncorrelated nesting*

The result of a subquery may contain either a single row or multiple rows. Typically, subqueries that return single rows perform aggregation. The following subquery returns the total number of items sold by a user; the outer query returns all users who have sold more than one item:

```
select u from User u
    where (
        select count(i) from Item i where i.seller = u
    ) > 1
```

```
Root<User> u = criteria.from(User.class);

Subquery<Long> sq = criteria.subquery(Long.class);
Root<Item> i = sq.from(Item.class);
sq.select(cb.count(i))
    .where(cb.equal(i.get("seller"), u)
    );

criteria.select(u);
criteria.where(cb.greaterThan(sq, 1L));
```

The inner query is a *correlated subquery*—it refers to an alias (u) from the outer query.

The next query contains an *uncorrelated subquery*:

```
select b from Bid b
    where b.amount + 1 >= (
        select max(b2.amount) from Bid b2
    )
```

```
Root<Bid> b = criteria.from(Bid.class);

Subquery<BigDecimal> sq = criteria.subquery(BigDecimal.class);
Root<Bid> b2 = sq.from(Bid.class);
sq.select(cb.max(b2.<BigDecimal>get("amount")));

criteria.select(b);
criteria.where(
    cb.greaterThanOrEqualTo(
        cb.sum(b.<BigDecimal>get("amount"), new BigDecimal(1)),
        sq
    )
);
```

The subquery in this example returns the maximum bid amount in the entire system; the outer query returns all bids whose amount is within one (U.S. dollar, Euro, and so on) of that amount. Note that in both cases, parentheses enclose the subquery in JPQL. This is always required.

Uncorrelated subqueries are harmless, and there is no reason not to use them when convenient. You can always rewrite them as two queries, because they don't reference each other. You should think more carefully about the performance impact of correlated subqueries. On a mature database, the performance cost of a simple correlated subquery is similar to the cost of a join. But it isn't necessarily possible to rewrite a correlated subquery using several separate queries.

If a subquery returns multiple rows, you combine it with *quantification.*

15.5.2 *Quantification*

The following quantifiers are standardized:

- ALL—The expression evaluates to true if the comparison is true for all values in the result of the subquery. It evaluates to false if a single value of the subquery result fails the comparison test.
- ANY—The expression evaluates to true if the comparison is true for some (any) value in the result of the subquery. If the subquery result is empty or no value satisfies the comparison, it evaluates to false. The keyword SOME is a synonym for ANY.
- EXISTS—Evaluates to true if the result of the subquery consists of one or more values.

For example, the following query returns items where all bids are less or equal than 10:

```
select i from Item i
    where 10 >= all (
        select b.amount from i.bids b
    )
```

```
Root<Item> i = criteria.from(Item.class);

Subquery<BigDecimal> sq = criteria.subquery(BigDecimal.class);
Root<Bid> b = sq.from(Bid.class);
sq.select(b.<BigDecimal>get("amount"));
sq.where(cb.equal(b.get("item"), i));

criteria.select(i);
criteria.where(
    cb.greaterThanOrEqualTo(
        cb.literal(new BigDecimal(10)),
        cb.all(sq)
    )
);
```

The following query returns items with a bid of exactly 101:

```
select i from Item i
    where 101.00 = any (
        select b.amount from i.bids b
    )
```

```
Root<Item> i = criteria.from(Item.class);

Subquery<BigDecimal> sq = criteria.subquery(BigDecimal.class);
Root<Bid> b = sq.from(Bid.class);
```

```
sq.select(b.<BigDecimal>get("amount"));
sq.where(cb.equal(b.get("item"), i));

criteria.select(i);
criteria.where(
    cb.equal(
        cb.literal(new BigDecimal("101.00")),
        cb.any(sq)
    )
);
```

To retrieve all items that have bids, check the result of the subquery with `EXISTS`:

```
select i from Item i
    where exists (
        select b from Bid b where b.item = i
    )
```

```
Root<Item> i = criteria.from(Item.class);

Subquery<Bid> sq = criteria.subquery(Bid.class);
Root<Bid> b = sq.from(Bid.class);
sq.select(b).where(cb.equal(b.get("item"), i));

criteria.select(i);
criteria.where(cb.exists(sq));
```

This query is more important than it looks. You can find all items that have bids with the following query: `select i from Item i where i.bids is not empty`. This, however, requires a mapped *one-to-many* collection `Item#bids`. If you follow our recommendations, you probably only have the "other" side mapped: the *many-to-one* `Bid#item`. With an `exists()` and a subquery, you can get the same result.

Subqueries are an advanced technique; you should question frequent use of subqueries, because queries with subqueries can often be rewritten using only joins and aggregation. But they're powerful and useful from time to time.

15.6　*Summary*

- If you knew SQL coming into this chapter, you're now able to write a wide variety of queries in JPQL and with the criteria query API. If you aren't comfortable with SQL, consult our reference section.
- With selection, you pick the source(s) of your query: the "tables" you want to query. Then you apply restriction expressions to limit the queried "rows" to the relevant subset. The projection of your query defines the returned "columns": the data retrieved by your query. You can also direct the database to aggregate and group data efficiently, before returning it.
- We discussed joins: how you select, restrict, and combine data from several tables. A JPA application relies on joins to fetch associated entity instances and collections in a single database round-trip. This is a critical feature when you're trying to reduce database load, and we recommend you repeat these examples to get a firm grasp of joining data and eager fetching.
- You can nest queries inside each other as subselects.

Advanced query options *16*

This chapter explains query options that you may consider optional or advanced: transforming query results, filtering collections, and the Hibernate criteria query API. First, we discuss Hibernate's ResultTransformer API, with which you can apply a result transformer to a query result to filter or marshal the result with your own code instead of Hibernate's default behavior.

In previous chapters, we always advised you to be careful when mapping collections, because it's rarely worth the effort. In this chapter, we introduce *collection filters*, a native Hibernate feature that makes persistent collections more valuable. Finally, we look at another proprietary Hibernate feature, the org.hibernate.Criteria query API, and some situations when you might prefer it to the standard JPA query-by-criteria.

Let's start with the transformation of query results.

16.1 *Transforming query results*

You can apply a result transformer to a query result so that you can filter or marshal the result with your own procedure instead of the Hibernate default behavior. Hibernate's default behavior provides a set of default transformers that you can replace and/or customize.

The result you're going to transform is that of a simple query, but you need to access the native Hibernate API `org.hibernate.Query` through the `Session`, as shown in the following listing.

> **Listing 16.1 Simple query with several projected elements**
>
> PATH: /examples/src/test/java/org/jpwh/test/querying/advanced/
>   TransformResults.java

```
Session session = em.unwrap(Session.class);
org.hibernate.Query query = session.createQuery(
    "select i.id as itemId, i.name as name, i.auctionEnd as auctionEnd from
        Item i"
);
```

Without any custom result transformation, this query returns a `List` of `Object[]`:

> PATH: /examples/src/test/java/org/jpwh/test/querying/advanced/
>   TransformResults.java

```
List<Object[]> result = query.list();

for (Object[] tuple : result) {
    Long itemId = (Long) tuple[0];
    String name = (String) tuple[1];
    Date auctionEnd = (Date) tuple[2];
    // ...
}
```

Each object array is a "row" of the query result. Each element of that tuple can be accessed by index: here index 0 is a `Long`, index 1 a `String`, and index 2 a `Date`. The first result transformer we introduce instead returns a `List` of `Lists`.

Transforming criteria query results

All the mples in this section are for queries written in JPQL created with the `org.hibernate.Query` API. If you write a JPA `CriteriaQuery` using a `Criteria-Builder`, you can't apply a Hibernate `org.hibernate.transform.Result-Transformer`: this is a Hibernate-only interface. Even if you obtain the native API for your criteria query (through `HibernateQuery` casting, as shown in section 14.1.3), you can't set a custom transformer. For JPA `CriteriaQuery`, Hibernate applies a built-in transformer to implement the JPA contracts; using a custom transformer

(Continued)

would override this and cause problems. You can set a custom transformer for JPQL queries created with `javax.persistence.Query`, though, after obtaining the native API with `HibernateQuery`. In addition, later in this chapter, you see the native `org.hibernate.Criteria` API, an alternative query-by-criteria facility that supports overriding the `org.hibernate.transform.ResultTransformer`.

16.1.1 Returning a list of lists

Let's say you want to use indexed access but are unhappy with the `Object[]` result. Instead of a list of `Object[]`s, each tuple can also be represented as a `List`, using the `ToListResultTransformer`:

> PATH: /examples/src/test/java/org/jpwh/test/querying/advanced/
> TransformResults.java

```
query.setResultTransformer(
    ToListResultTransformer.INSTANCE
);

List<List> result = query.list();

for (List list : result) {
    Long itemId = (Long) list.get(0);
    String name = (String) list.get(1);
    Date auctionEnd = (Date) list.get(2);
    // ...
}
```

This is a minor difference but a convenient alternative if code in other layers of your application already works with lists of lists.

The next transformer converts the query result to a `Map` for each tuple, where the query projection assigns aliases mapped to the projection elements.

16.1.2 Returning a list of maps

The `AliasToEntityMapResultTransformer` returns a `List` of `java.util.Map`, one map per "row." The aliases in the query are `itemId`, `name`, and `auctionEnd`:

> PATH: /examples/src/test/java/org/jpwh/test/querying/advanced/
> TransformResults.java

```
query.setResultTransformer(
    AliasToEntityMapResultTransformer.INSTANCE
);

List<Map> result = query.list();

assertEquals(                          ⟵── Accesses query aliases
    query.getReturnAliases(),
```

```
        new String[]{"itemId", "name", "auctionEnd"}
);

for (Map map : result) {
    Long itemId = (Long) map.get("itemId");
    String name = (String) map.get("name");
    Date auctionEnd = (Date) map.get("auctionEnd");
    // ...
}
```

If you don't know the aliases used in the query and need to obtain them dynamically, call org.hibernate.Query#getReturnAliases().

The example query returns scalar values; you may also want to transform results that contain persistent entity instances. This example uses aliases for projected entities and a List of Maps:

> **PATH:** **/examples/src/test/java/org/jpwh/test/querying/advanced/**
>   **TransformResults.java**

```
org.hibernate.Query entityQuery = session.createQuery(
    "select i as item, u as seller from Item i join i.seller u"
);

entityQuery.setResultTransformer(
    AliasToEntityMapResultTransformer.INSTANCE
);

List<Map> result = entityQuery.list();

for (Map map : result) {
    Item item = (Item) map.get("item");
    User seller = (User) map.get("seller");

    assertEquals(item.getSeller(), seller);
    // ...
}
```

More useful is the next transformer, mapping the query result to JavaBean properties by alias.

16.1.3 *Mapping aliases to bean properties*

In section 15.3.2, we showed how a query can return instances of a JavaBean dynamically by calling the ItemSummary constructor. In JPQL, you achieve this with the new operator. For criteria queries, you use the construct() method. The ItemSummary class must have a constructor that matches the projected query result.

Alternatively, if your JavaBean doesn't have the right constructor, you can still instantiate and populate its values through setters and/or fields with the AliasTo-BeanResultTransformer. The following example transforms the query result shown in listing 16.1:

```
PATH: /examples/src/test/java/org/jpwh/test/querying/advanced/
      TransformResults.java
```

```java
query.setResultTransformer(
    new AliasToBeanResultTransformer(ItemSummary.class)
);

List<ItemSummary> result = query.list();

for (ItemSummary itemSummary : result) {
    Long itemId = itemSummary.getItemId();
    String name = itemSummary.getName();
    Date auctionEnd = itemSummary.getAuctionEnd();
    // ...
}
```

You create the transformer with the JavaBean class you want to instantiate, here Item-
Summary. Hibernate requires that this class either has no constructor or a public no-
argument constructor.

When transforming the query result, Hibernate looks for setter methods and fields
with the same names as the aliases in the query. The ItemSummary class must either
have the fields itemId, name, andauctionEnd, or the setter methods setItemId(),
setName(), and setAuctionEnd(). The fields or setter method parameters must be of
the right type. If you have fields that map to some query aliases and setter methods for
the rest, that's fine too.

You should also know how to write your own ResultTransformer when none of
the built-in ones suits you.

16.1.4 *Writing a ResultTransformer*

The built-in transformers in Hibernate aren't sophisticated; there isn't much difference between result tuples represented as lists, maps, or object arrays. Implementing
the ResultTransformer interface is trivial, though, and custom conversion of query
results can tighten the integration between the layers of code in your application. If
your user interface code already knows how to render a table of List<ItemSummary>,
let Hibernate return it directly from a query.

Next, we show you how to implement a ResultTransformer. Let's assume that you
want a List<ItemSummary> returned from the query shown in listing 16.1, but you
can't let Hibernate create an instance of ItemSummary through reflection on a constructor. Maybe your ItemSummary class is predefined and doesn't have the right constructor, fields, and setter methods. Instead, you have an ItemSummaryFactory to
produce instances of ItemSummary.

The ResultTransformer interface requires that you implement the methods
transformTuple() and transformList():

```
PATH:  /examples/src/test/java/org/jpwh/test/querying/advanced/
       TransformResults.java
```

```
query.setResultTransformer(
    new ResultTransformer() {                    ❶ Transforms
                                                    result rows
        @Override
        public Object transformTuple(Object[] tuple, String[] aliases) {

            Long itemId = (Long) tuple[0];
            String name = (String) tuple[1];
            Date auctionEnd = (Date) tuple[2];

            assertEquals(aliases[0], "itemId");        ⟵    Access query
            assertEquals(aliases[1], "name");                aliases if needed
            assertEquals(aliases[2], "auctionEnd");

            return ItemSummaryFactory.newItemSummary(
                itemId, name, auctionEnd
            );
        }                                            ❷ Modifies result list

        @Override
        public List transformList(List collection) {
            return Collections.unmodifiableList(collection);   ⟵
        }
    }                                                    Collection is a
);                                                       List<ItemSummary>
```

❶ For each result "row," an `Object[]` tuple must be transformed into the desired result value for that row. Here you access each projection element by index in the tuple array and then call the `ItemSummaryFactory` to produce the query result value. Hibernate passes the method the aliases found in the query, for each tuple element. You don't need the aliases in this transformer, though.

❷ You can wrap or modify the result list after transforming the tuples. Here you make the returned `List` unmodifiable: ideal for a reporting screen where nothing should change the data.

As you can see in the example, you transform query results in two steps: first you customize how to convert each "row" or tuple of the query result to whatever value you desire. Then you work on the entire `List` of these values, wrapping or converting again.

Next, we discuss another convenient Hibernate feature (where JPA doesn't have an equivalent): collection filters.

Hibernate Feature

16.2 *Filtering collections*

In chapter 7, you saw reasons you should (or rather, shouldn't) map a collection in your Java domain model. The main benefit of a collection mapping is easier access to data: you can call item.getImages() or item.getBids() to access all images and bids associated with an Item. You don't have to write a JPQL or criteria query; Hibernate will execute the query for you when you start iterating through the collection elements.

The most obvious problem with this automatic data access is that Hibernate will always write the same query, retrieving *all* images or bids for an Item. You can customize the order of collection elements, but even that is a static mapping. What would you do to render two lists of bids for an Item, in ascending *and* descending order by creation date? You could go back to writing and executing custom queries and not call item.getBids(); the collection mapping might not even be necessary.

Instead, you can use a Hibernate proprietary feature, *collection filters*, that makes writing these queries easier, using the mapped collection. Let's say you have a persistent Item instance in memory, probably loaded with the EntityManager API. You want to list all bids made for this Item but further restrict the result to bids made by a particular User. You also want the list sorted in descending order by Bid#amount.

Listing 16.2   Filtering and ordering a collection

Path: /examples/src/test/java/org/jpwh/test/querying/advanced/
       FilterCollections.java

```
Item item = em.find(Item.class, ITEM_ID);
User user = em.find(User.class, USER_ID);

org.hibernate.Query query = session.createFilter(
    item.getBids(),
    "where this.bidder = :bidder order by this.amount desc"
);

query.setParameter("bidder", user);
List<Bid> bids = query.list();
```

The session.createFilter() method accepts a persistent collection and a JPQL query fragment. This query fragment doesn't require a select or from clause; here it only has a restriction with the where clause and an order by clause. The alias this always refers to elements of the collection, here Bid instances. The filter created is an ordinary org.hibernate.Query, prepared with a bound parameter and executed with list(), as usual.

Hibernate doesn't execute collection filters in memory. The Item#bids collection may be uninitialized when you call the filter and, and if so, remains uninitialized. Furthermore, filters don't apply to transient collections or query results. You may only apply them to a mapped persistent collection currently referenced by an entity instance managed by the persistence context. The term *filter* is somewhat misleading, because the result of filtering is a completely new and different collection; the original collection isn't touched.

To the great surprise of everyone, including the designer of this feature, even trivial filters turn out to be useful. For example, you can use an empty query to paginate collection elements:

> **PATH: /examples/src/test/java/org/jpwh/test/querying/advanced/**
> **FilterCollections.java**

```
Item item = em.find(Item.class, ITEM_ID);

org.hibernate.Query query = session.createFilter(
    item.getBids(),
    ""
);

query.setFirstResult(0);              ⟵── Retrieves only two bids
query.setMaxResults(2);
List<Bid> bids = query.list();
```

Here, Hibernate executes the query, loading the collection elements and limiting the returned rows to two, starting with row zero of the result. Usually, you'd use an `order by` with paginated queries.

You don't need a `from` clause in a collection filter, but you can have one if that's your style. A collection filter doesn't even need to return elements of the collection being filtered.

This next filter returns any `Item` sold by any of the bidders:

> **PATH: /examples/src/test/java/org/jpwh/test/querying/advanced/**
> **FilterCollections.java**

```
Item item = em.find(Item.class, ITEM_ID);

org.hibernate.Query query = session.createFilter(
    item.getBids(),
    "from Item i where i.seller = this.bidder"
);

List<Item> items = query.list();
```

With a `select` clause, you can declare a projection. The following filter retrieves the names of users who made the bids:

> **PATH: /examples/src/test/java/org/jpwh/test/querying/advanced/**
> **FilterCollections.java**

```
Item item = em.find(Item.class, ITEM_ID);

org.hibernate.Query query = session.createFilter(
    item.getBids(),
    "select distinct this.bidder.username order by this.bidder.username asc"
);

List<String> bidders = query.list();
```

All this is a lot of fun, but the most important reason for the existence of collection filters is to allow your application to retrieve collection elements without initializing the entire collection. For large collections, this is important to achieve acceptable performance. The following query retrieves all `bids` made for the `Item` with an amount greater or equal to 100:

> PATH: /examples/src/test/java/org/jpwh/test/querying/advanced/
> FilterCollections.java

```
Item item = em.find(Item.class, ITEM_ID);

org.hibernate.Query query = session.createFilter(
    item.getBids(),
    "where this.amount >= :param"
);

query.setParameter("param", new BigDecimal(100));
List<Bid> bids = query.list();
```

Again, this doesn't initialize the `Item#bids` collection but returns a new collection.

Before JPA 2, query-by-criteria was only available as a proprietary Hibernate API. Today, the standardized JPA interfaces are equally as powerful as the old `org.hibernate.Criteria` API, so you'll rarely need it. But several features are still only available in the Hibernate API, such as *query-by-example* and embedding of arbitrary SQL fragments. In the following section, you find a short overview of the `org.hibernate.Criteria` API and some of its unique options.

Hibernate Feature

16.3   *The Hibernate criteria query API*

Using the `org.hibernate.Criteria` and `org.hibernate.Example` interfaces, you can build queries programmatically by creating and combining `org.hibernate.criterion.*` instances. You see how to use these APIs and how to express selection, restriction, joins, and projection. We assume that you've read the previous chapter and that you know how these operations are translated into SQL. All query examples shown here have an equivalent JPQL or JPA criteria example in the previous chapter, so you can easily flip back and forth if you need to compare all three APIs.

Let's start with some basic selection examples.

16.3.1 *Selection and ordering*

The following query loads all `Item` instances:

> PATH: /examples/src/test/java/org/jpwh/test/querying/advanced/
> HibernateCriteria.java

```
org.hibernate.Criteria criteria = session.createCriteria(Item.class);
List<Item> items = criteria.list();
```

You create an `org.hibernate.Criteria` using the `Session`. Alternatively, you can create a `DetachedCriteria` without an open persistence context:

> **PATH: /examples/src/test/java/org/jpwh/test/querying/advanced/**
> **HibernateCriteria.java**

```
DetachedCriteria criteria = DetachedCriteria.forClass(Item.class);

List<Item> items = criteria.getExecutableCriteria(session).list();
```

When you're ready to execute the query, "attach" it to a `Session` with `getExecutableCriteria()`.

Note that this is a unique feature of the Hibernate criteria API. With JPA, you always need at least an `EntityManagerFactory` to get a `CriteriaBuilder`.

You can declare the order of the results, equivalent to an `order` by clause in JPQL. The following query loads all `User` instances sorted in ascending order by first and last name:

> **PATH: /examples/src/test/java/org/jpwh/test/querying/advanced/**
> **HibernateCriteria.java**

```
List<User> users =
    session.createCriteria(User.class)
        .addOrder(Order.asc("firstname"))
        .addOrder(Order.asc("lastname"))
        .list();
```

In this example, the code is written in the fluent style (using method chaining); methods such as `addOrder()` return the original `org.hibernate.Criteria`.

Next, we look at restricting the selected records.

16.3.2 *Restriction*

The following query returns all `Item` instances with name "Foo":

> **PATH: /examples/src/test/java/org/jpwh/test/querying/advanced/**
> **HibernateCriteria.java**

```
List<Item> items =
    session.createCriteria(Item.class)
        .add(Restrictions.eq("name", "Foo"))
        .list();
```

The `Restrictions` interface is the factory for individual `Criterion` you can add to the `Criteria`. Attributes are addressed with simple strings, here `Item#name` with `"name"`.

You can also match substrings, similar to the `like` operator in JPQL. The following query loads all `User` instances with username starting with "j" or "J":

> PATH: /examples/src/test/java/org/jpwh/test/querying/advanced/
>   HibernateCriteria.java

```
List<User> users =
    session.createCriteria(User.class)
        .add(Restrictions.like("username", "j",
    MatchMode.START).ignoreCase())
        .list();
```

MatchMode.START is equivalent to the wildcard j% in JPQL. The other modes are
EXACT, END, and ANYWHERE.

You can name nested attributes of embeddable types, such as the Address of a
User, using dot-notation

> PATH: /examples/src/test/java/org/jpwh/test/querying/advanced/
>   HibernateCriteria.java

```
List<User> users =
    session.createCriteria(User.class)
        .add(Restrictions.eq("homeAddress.city", "Some City"))
        .list();
```

A unique feature of the Hibernate Criteria API is the ability to write plain SQL fragments in restrictions. This query loads all User instances with a username shorter than
eight characters:

> PATH: /examples/src/test/java/org/jpwh/test/querying/advanced/
>   HibernateCriteria.java

```
List<User> users =
    session.createCriteria(User.class)
        .add(Restrictions.sqlRestriction(
            "length({alias}.USERNAME) < ?",
            8,
            StandardBasicTypes.INTEGER
        )).list();
```

Hibernate sends the SQL fragment to the database as is. You need the {alias} placeholder to prefix any table alias in the final SQL; it always refers to the table the root
entity is mapped to (USERS, in this case). You also apply a position parameter (named
parameters aren't supported by this API) and specify its type as StandardBasic-
Types.INTEGER.

Extending the Hibernate criteria system

The Hibernate criteria query system is extensible: you could wrap the LENGTH() SQL
function in your own implementation of the org.hibernate.criterion.Criterion
interface.

After you perform selection and restriction, you want to add projection to your query to declare the data you want to retrieve.

16.3.3 *Projection and aggregation*

The following query returns the identifier value, the `username`, and the `homeAddress` of all `User` entities:

> PATH: /examples/src/test/java/org/jpwh/test/querying/advanced/
> HibernateCriteria.java

```
List<Object[]> result =
    session.createCriteria(User.class)
        .setProjection(Projections.projectionList()
            .add(Projections.property("id"))
            .add(Projections.property("username"))
            .add(Projections.property("homeAddress"))
        ).list();
```

The result of this query is a `List` of `Object[]`, one array for each tuple. Each array contains a `Long` (or whatever the type of the user's identifier is), a `String`, and an `Address`.

Just as with restrictions, you can add arbitrary SQL expressions and function calls to projections:

> PATH: /examples/src/test/java/org/jpwh/test/querying/advanced/
> HibernateCriteria.java

```
List<String> result =
    session.createCriteria(Item.class)
        .setProjection(Projections.projectionList()
            .add(Projections.sqlProjection(
                "NAME || ':' || AUCTIONEND as RESULT",
                new String[]{"RESULT"},
                new Type[]{StandardBasicTypes.STRING}
            ))
        ).list();
```

This query returns a `List` of `Strings`, where strings have the form "[Item name]:[Auction end date]". The second parameter for the projection is the name of the alias(es) you used in the query: Hibernate needs this to read the value of the `ResultSet`. The type of each projected element/alias is also needed: here, `StandardBasic-Types.STRING`.

Hibernate supports grouping and aggregation. This query counts users' last names:

> **PATH:** /examples/src/test/java/org/jpwh/test/querying/advanced/
> HibernateCriteria.java

```
List<Object[]> result =
    session.createCriteria(User.class)
        .setProjection(Projections.projectionList()
            .add(Projections.groupProperty("lastname"))
            .add(Projections.rowCount())
        ).list();
```

The rowCount() method is equivalent to a count() function call in JPQL. The follow-ing aggregation query returns average Bid amounts grouped by Item:

> **PATH:** /examples/src/test/java/org/jpwh/test/querying/advanced/
> HibernateCriteria.java

```
List<Object[]> result =
    session.createCriteria(Bid.class)
        .setProjection(Projections.projectionList()
            .add(Projections.groupProperty("item"))
            .add(Projections.avg("amount"))
        ).list();
```

Next, you see that joins are also available with the Criteria API.

16.3.4 *Joins*

You express *inner joins* of an associated entity with nested Criterias:

> **PATH:** /examples/src/test/java/org/jpwh/test/querying/advanced/
> HibernateCriteria.java

```
List<Bid> result =
    session.createCriteria(Bid.class)
        .createCriteria("item")
        .add(Restrictions.isNotNull("buyNowPrice"))          Inner join
        .createCriteria("seller")
        .add(Restrictions.eq("username", "johndoe"))
        .list();
```

This query returns all Bid instances of any Item sold by User "johndoe" that doesn't have a buyNowPrice. The first inner join of the Bid#item association is made with createCriteria("item") on the root Criteria of the Bid. This nested Criteria now represents the association path, on which another inner join is made with createCri-teria("seller"). Further restrictions are placed on each join Criteria; they will be combined with logical and in the where clause of the final SQL query.

Alternatively, inner joins can be expressed with createAlias() on a Criteria. This is the same query:

```
PATH:  /examples/src/test/java/org/jpwh/test/querying/advanced/
       HibernateCriteria.java
```

```
List<Bid> result =
    session.createCriteria(Bid.class)
        .createCriteria("item")
        .createAlias("seller", "s")            Inner join
        .add(Restrictions.and(
            Restrictions.eq("s.username", "johndoe"),
            Restrictions.isNotNull("buyNowPrice")
        ))
        .list();
```

Dynamic eager fetching with *outer joins* are declared with `setFetchMode()`:

```
PATH:  /examples/src/test/java/org/jpwh/test/querying/advanced/
       HibernateCriteria.java
```

```
List<Item> result =
    session.createCriteria(Item.class)
        .setFetchMode("bids", FetchMode.JOIN)
        .list();
```

This query returns all `Item` instances with their `bids` collection initialized in the same SQL query.

Look out for duplicates

As with JPQL and JPA criteria queries, Hibernate may return duplicate `Item` references! See our previous discussion in section 15.4.5.

Similar to JPQL and JPA criteria, Hibernate can filter out duplicate references in-memory with a "distinct" operation:

```
PATH:  /examples/src/test/java/org/jpwh/test/querying/advanced/
       HibernateCriteria.java
```

```
List<Item> result =
    session.createCriteria(Item.class)
        .setFetchMode("bids", FetchMode.JOIN)
        .setResultTransformer(Criteria.DISTINCT_ROOT_ENTITY)
        .list();
```

Here, you can also see that a `ResultTransformer`, as discussed earlier in this chapter, can be applied to a `Criteria`.

You can fetch multiple associations/collections in one query:

> PATH: /examples/src/test/java/org/jpwh/test/querying/advanced/
> HibernateCriteria.java

```
List<Item> result =
    session.createCriteria(Item.class)
        .createAlias("bids", "b", JoinType.LEFT_OUTER_JOIN)
        .setFetchMode("b", FetchMode.JOIN)
        .createAlias("b.bidder", "bdr", JoinType.INNER_JOIN)
        .setFetchMode("bdr", FetchMode.JOIN)
        .createAlias("seller", "s", JoinType.LEFT_OUTER_JOIN)
        .setFetchMode("s", FetchMode.JOIN)
        .list();
```

This query returns all `Item` instances, loads the `Item#bids` collection with an outer join, and loads `Bid#bidder` with an inner join. The `Item#seller` is also loaded: because it can't be `null`, it doesn't matter whether an inner or outer join is used. As always, don't fetch several collections in one query, or you'll create a Cartesian product (see section 15.4.5).

Next, you see that subqueries with criteria also work with nested `Criteria` instances.

16.3.5 Subselects

The following subquery returns all `User` instances who are selling more than one item:

> PATH: /examples/src/test/java/org/jpwh/test/querying/advanced/
> HibernateCriteria.java

```
DetachedCriteria sq = DetachedCriteria.forClass(Item.class, "i");
sq.add(Restrictions.eqProperty("i.seller.id", "u.id"));
sq.setProjection(Projections.rowCount());

List<User> result =
    session.createCriteria(User.class, "u")
        .add(Subqueries.lt(11, sq))
        .list();
```

The `DetachedCriteria` is a query that returns the number of items sold restricted by a given `User`. The restriction relies on the alias u, so this is a correlated subquery. The "outer" query then embeds the `DetachedCriteria` and provides the alias u. Note that the subquery is the right operand of the `lt()` (less than) operation, which translates into `1 < ([Result of count query])` in SQL.

Hibernate also supports quantification. This query returns items where all bids are less or equal than 10:

PATH: /examples/src/test/java/org/jpwh/test/querying/advanced/
HibernateCriteria.java

```
DetachedCriteria sq = DetachedCriteria.forClass(Bid.class, "b");
sq.add(Restrictions.eqProperty("b.item.id", "i.id"));
sq.setProjection(Projections.property("amount"));

List<Item> result =
    session.createCriteria(Item.class, "i")
        .add(Subqueries.geAll(new BigDecimal(10), sq))
        .list();
```

Again, the position of the operands dictates that the comparison is based on `geAll()` (greater or equal than all) to find the bids with "less or equal than 10" amount.

So far, there are a few good reasons to use the old `org.hibernate.Criteria` API. You really should use the standardized JPA query languages in new applications, though. The most interesting features of the old proprietary API we've shown are embedded SQL expressions in restrictions and projections. Another Hibernate-only feature you may find interesting is *query-by-example*.

16.3.6 *Example queries*

The idea behind example queries is that you provide an example entity instance, and Hibernate loads all entity instances that "look like the example." This can be convenient if you have a complex search screen in your user interface, because you don't have to write extra classes to hold the entered search terms.

Let's say you have a search form in your application where you can search for `User` instances by last name. You can bind the form field for "last name" directly to the `User#lastname` property and then tell Hibernate to load "similar" `User` instances:

PATH: /examples/src/test/java/org/jpwh/test/querying/advanced/
HibernateCriteria.java

```
User template = new User();                                          ①  Creates empty User instance
template.setLastname("Doe");

org.hibernate.criterion.Example example = Example.create(template);
example.ignoreCase();                                                    Creates
example.enableLike(MatchMode.START);                                     Example
example.excludeProperty("activated");           Ignores              ②  instance
                                                activate
List<User> users =                              ③  property
    session.createCriteria(User.class)
        .add(example)                           Adds Example
        .list();                            ④  as a restriction
```

① Create an "empty" instance of `User` as a template for your search, and set the property values you're looking for: people with the last name "Doe".

❷ Create an instance of `Example` with the template. This API allows you to fine-tune the search. You want the case of the last name to be ignored, and a substring search, so "Doe", "DoeX", or "Doe Y" will match.

❸ The `User` class has a `boolean` property called `activated`. As a primitive, it can't be `null`, and its default value is `false`, so Hibernate would include it in the search and only return users that aren't activated. You want all users, so tell Hibernate to ignore that property.

❹ The `Example` is added to a `Criteria` as a restriction.

Because you've written the `User` entity class following JavaBean rules, binding it to a UI form should be trivial. It has regular getter and setter methods, and you can create an "empty" instance with the public no-argument constructor (remember our discussion of constructor design in section 3.2.3.)

One obvious disadvantage of the `Example` API is that any string-matching options, such as `ignoreCase()` and `enableLike()`, apply to *all* string-valued properties of the template. If you searched for both `lastname` and `firstname`, both would be case-insensitive substring matches.

By default, all non-null valued properties of the given entity template are added to the restriction of the example query. As shown in the last code snippet, you can manually exclude properties of the entity template by name with `excludeProperty()`. Other exclusion options are exclusion of zero-valued properties (such as `int` or `long`) with `excludeZeroes()` and disabling exclusion altogether with `excludeNone()`. If no properties are excluded, any `null` property of the template is added to the restriction in the SQL query with an `is null` check.

If you need more control over exclusion and inclusion of properties, you can extend `Example` and write your own `PropertySelector`:

> **PATH:** /examples/src/test/java/org/jpwh/test/querying/advanced/
> HibernateCriteria.java

```
class ExcludeBooleanExample extends Example {
    ExcludeBooleanExample(Object template) {
        super(template, new PropertySelector() {
            @Override
            public boolean include(Object propertyValue,
                                   String propertyName,
                                   Type type) {
                return propertyValue != null
                    && !type.equals(StandardBasicTypes.BOOLEAN);
            }
        });
    }
}
```

This selector excludes any `null` properties (like the default selector) and additional excludes any Boolean properties (such as `User#activated`).

After adding an `Example` restriction to a `Criteria`, you can add further restrictions to the query. Alternatively, you can add multiple example restrictions to a single query. The following query returns all `Item` instances with `names` starting with "B" or "b" and a `seller` matching a `User` example:

> **PATH:** /examples/src/test/java/org/jpwh/test/querying/advanced/
>   HibernateCriteria.java

```
Item itemTemplate = new Item();
itemTemplate.setName("B");

Example exampleItem = Example.create(itemTemplate);
exampleItem.ignoreCase();
exampleItem.enableLike(MatchMode.START);
exampleItem.excludeProperty("auctionType");
exampleItem.excludeProperty("createdOn");

User userTemplate = new User();
userTemplate.setLastname("Doe");

Example exampleUser = Example.create(userTemplate);
exampleUser.excludeProperty("activated");

List<Item> items =
    session
        .createCriteria(Item.class)
        .add(exampleItem)
        .createCriteria("seller").add(exampleUser)
        .list();
```

At this point, we invite you to take a step back and consider how much code would be required to implement such a search using hand-coded SQL/JDBC.

16.4 Summary

- You used the `ResultTransformer` API to write custom code to process a query result, returning a list of lists and a list of maps, and mapping aliases to bean properties.
- We covered Hibernate's collection-filtering interfaces as well as making better use of mapped persistent collections.
- You explored the older Hibernate `Criteria` query facility and when you might use it instead of the standardized criteria queries in JPA. We covered all the relational and Hibernate goodies using this API: selection and ordering, restriction, projection and aggregation, joins, subselects, and example queries.

Customizing SQL

In this chapter, we cover customizing and embedding SQL in a Hibernate application. SQL was created in the 1970s, but ANSI didn't standardized it until 1986. Although each update of the SQL standard has seen new (and many controversial) features, every DBMS product that supports SQL does so in its own unique way. The burden of portability is again on the database application developers. This is where Hibernate helps: its built-in query languages produce SQL that depends on the configured database dialect. Dialects also help produce all other automatically generated SQL (for example, when Hibernate has to retrieve a collection on demand). With a simple dialect switch, you can run your application on a different DBMS. Hibernate generates all SQL statements for you, for all create, read, update, and delete (CRUD) operations.

Sometimes, though, you need more control than Hibernate and the Java Persistence API provide: you need to work at a lower level of abstraction. With Hibernate, you can write your own SQL statements:

426

- Fall back to the JDBC API, and work directly with the `Connection`, `Prepared-Statement`, and `ResultSet` interfaces. Hibernate provides the `Connection`, so you don't have to maintain a separate connection pool, and your SQL statements execute within the same (current) transaction.

- Write plain SQL `SELECT` statements, and either embed them within your Java code or externalize them (in XML files or annotations) as named queries. You execute these SQL queries with the Java Persistence API, just like a regular JPQL query. Hibernate can then transform the query result according to your mapping. This also works with stored procedure calls.

- Replace SQL statements generated by Hibernate with your own hand-written SQL. For example, when Hibernate loads an entity instance with `em.find()` or loads a collection on-demand, your own SQL query can perform the load. You can also write your own Data Manipulation Language (DML) statements, such as `UPDATE`, `INSERT`, and `DELETE`. You might even call a stored procedure to perform a CRUD operation. You can replace all SQL statements automatically generated by Hibernate with custom statements.

We start with JDBC fallback usage and then discuss Hibernate's automatic result-mapping capabilities. Then, we show you how to override queries and DML statements in Hibernate. Last, we discuss integration with stored database procedures.

Major new features in JPA 2

- You can map a SQL query result to a constructor.
- You can call stored procedures and functions directly with the new `Stored-ProcedureQuery` API.

Hibernate Feature

17.1 *Falling back to JDBC*

Sometimes you want Hibernate to get out of the way and directly access the database through the JDBC API. To do so, you need a `java.sql.Connection` interface to write and execute your own `PreparedStatement` and direct access to your statement `ResultSet`. Because Hibernate already knows how to obtain and close database connections, it can provide your application with a `Connection` and release it when you're done.

This functionality is available with the `org.hibernate.jdbc.Work` API, a callback-style interface. You encapsulate your JDBC "work" by implementing this interface; Hibernate calls your implementation providing a `Connection`. The following example executes an SQL `SELECT` and iterates through the `ResultSet`.

Listing 17.1   Encapsulating "work" with the JDBC interfaces

PATH: /examples/src/test/java/org/jpwh/test/querying/sql/JDBCFallback.java

```java
public class QueryItemWork implements org.hibernate.jdbc.Work {

    final protected Long itemId;                          ①  Item identifier

    public QueryItemWork(Long itemId) {
        this.itemId = itemId;
    }
                                                          ②  Calls execute()
    @Override
    public void execute(Connection connection) throws SQLException {
        PreparedStatement statement = null;
        ResultSet result = null;
        try {
            statement = connection.prepareStatement(
                "select * from ITEM where ID = ?"
            );
            statement.setLong(1, itemId);

            result = statement.executeQuery();

            while (result.next()) {
                String itemName = result.getString("NAME");
                BigDecimal itemPrice = result.getBigDecimal("BUYNOWPRICE");
                // ...
            }
        } finally {
            if (result != null)                           ③  Closes resources
                result.close();
            if (statement != null)
                statement.close();
        }
    }
}
```

① For this "work," an item identifier is needed, enforced with the final field and the constructor parameter.

② The execute() method is called by Hibernate with a JDBC Connection. You don't have to close the connection when you're done.

③ You have to close and release other resources you've obtained, though, such as the PreparedStatement and ResultSet.

You execute the Work with the Hibernate Session API:

PATH: /examples/src/test/java/org/jpwh/test/querying/sql/JDBCFallback.java

```java
UserTransaction tx = TM.getUserTransaction();
tx.begin();
EntityManager em = JPA.createEntityManager();

Session session = em.unwrap(Session.class);
session.doWork(new QueryItemWork(ITEM_ID));
```

```
tx.commit();
em.close();
```

In this case, Hibernate has already enlisted the JDBC `Connection` it provides with the current system transaction. Your statements are committed when the system transaction is committed, and all operations, whether executed with the `EntityManager` or `Session` API, are part of the same unit of work. Alternatively, if you want to return a value from your JDBC "work" to the application, implement the interface `org.hibernate.jdbc.ReturningWork`.

There are no limits on the JDBC operations you can perform in a `Work` implementation. Instead of a `PreparedStatement`, you may use a `CallableStatement` and execute a stored procedure in the database; you have full access to the JDBC API.

For simple queries and working with a `ResultSet`, such as the one in the previous example, a more convenient alternative is available.

17.2 Mapping SQL query results

When you execute an SQL `SELECT` query with the JDBC API or execute a stored procedure that returns a `ResultSet`, you iterate through each row of this result set and retrieve the data you need. This is a labor-intensive task, and you end up duplicating the same lines of code repeatedly.

> **Quickly testing SQL statements**
>
> For an easy way to test SQL scripts with several DBMSs, without starting a local server, check out the online service SQL Fiddle at http://sqlfiddle.com.

Hibernate offers an alternative: execute the native SQL query or stored procedure call with the Hibernate/Java Persistence API and, instead of a `ResultSet`, get a `List` of instances of your choice. You can map the `ResultSet` to any class you like, and Hibernate will perform the transformation for you.

NOTE In this section, we only talk about native `SELECT` SQL queries. You can also write `UPDATE` and `INSERT` statements with the same API, which we cover in section 20.1.

Hibernate Feature

Today, two APIs are available for executing native SQL queries and transforming their result:

- The standardized Java Persistence API with `EntityManager#createNativeQuery()` for embedded SQL statements, and `@NamedNativeQuery` for externalized queries. You can map result sets with the `@SqlResultSetMapping` annotation or in JPA orm.xml files. You may also externalize named SQL queries to JPA XML files.

- The proprietary and older Hibernate API, with `Session#createSQLQuery()` and `org.hibernate.SQLQuery` for result-set mapping. You can also define externalized named SQL queries and result mappings in Hibernate XML metadata files.

The Hibernate API has more features. For example, it also supports eager loading of collections and entity associations in an SQL result mapping. In the following sections, you see both APIs side by side for each query. Let's start with a simple embedded SQL query and mapping of scalar projection results.

17.2.1 *Projection with SQL queries*

The following query returns a `List` of `Object[]`, each array representing a tuple (row) of the SQL projection:

> PATH: /examples/src/test/java/org/jpwh/test/querying/sql/NativeQueries.java

```
Query query = em.createNativeQuery(
    "select NAME, AUCTIONEND from {h-schema}ITEM"
);
List<Object[]> result = query.getResultList();

for (Object[] tuple : result) {
    assertTrue(tuple[0] instanceof String);
    assertTrue(tuple[1] instanceof Date);}
```

> PATH: /examples/src/test/java/org/jpwh/test/querying/sql/
>   HibernateSQLQueries.java

```
org.hibernate.SQLQuery query = session.createSQLQuery(
    "select NAME, AUCTIONEND from {h-schema}ITEM"
);
List<Object[]> result = query.list();

for (Object[] tuple : result) {
    assertTrue(tuple[0] instanceof String);
    assertTrue(tuple[1] instanceof Date);
}
```

The `em.createNativeQuery()` and `session.createSQLQuery()` methods accept a plain SQL query string.

The query retrieves the `NAME` and `AUCTIONEND` column values of the `ITEM` table, and Hibernate automatically maps them to `String` and `java.util.Date` values. Hibernate reads the `java.sql.ResultSetMetaData` to determine the type of each projection element, and it knows that a `VARCHAR` column type maps to a `String` and a `TIMESTAMP` to a `java.util.Date` (as explained in section 5.3).

Hibernate's SQL query engine supports several handy placeholders, like `{h-schema}` in the previous examples. Hibernate replaces this placeholder with the default schema of your persistence unit (the `hibernate.default_schema` configuration property). The other supported placeholders are `{h-catalog}` for the default SQL catalog and `{h-domain}`, which combines the catalog and schema values.

The biggest advantage of executing an SQL statement within Hibernate is automatic marshaling of the result set into instances of your domain model (entity) classes.

17.2.2 Mapping to an entity class

This SQL query returns a `List` of `Item` entity instances:

> **PATH:** /examples/src/test/java/org/jpwh/test/querying/sql/NativeQueries.java

```
Query query = em.createNativeQuery(
    "select * from ITEM",
    Item.class
);

List<Item> result = query.getResultList();
```

> **PATH:** /examples/src/test/java/org/jpwh/test/querying/sql/
> HibernateSQLQueries.java

```
org.hibernate.SQLQuery query = session.createSQLQuery(
    "select * from ITEM"
);
query.addEntity(Item.class);

List<Item> result = query.list();
```

The returned `Item` instances are in persistent state, managed by the current persistence context. The result is therefore the same as with the JPQL query `select i from Item i`.

For this transformation, Hibernate reads the result set of the SQL query and tries to discover the column names and types as defined in your entity mapping metadata. If the column AUCTIONEND is returned, and it's mapped to the `Item#auctionEnd` property, Hibernate knows how to populate that property and returns fully loaded entity instances.

Note that Hibernate expects the query to return all columns required to create an instance of `Item`, including all properties, embedded components, and foreign key columns. If Hibernate can't find a mapped column (by name) in the result set, an exception is thrown. You may have to use aliases in SQL to return the same column names as defined in your entity mapping metadata.

The interfaces `javax.persistence.Query` and `org.hibernate.SQLQuery` both support parameter binding. The following query returns only a single `Item` entity instance:

> **PATH:** /examples/src/test/java/org/jpwh/test/querying/sql/NativeQueries.java

```
Query query = em.createNativeQuery(
    "select * from ITEM where ID = ?",
    Item.class
);
```

```
query.setParameter(1, ITEM_ID);                    ◁—— Starts at one

List<Item> result = query.getResultList();
```

> **PATH:** /examples/src/test/java/org/jpwh/test/querying/sql/
>   HibernateSQLQueries.java

```
org.hibernate.SQLQuery query = session.createSQLQuery(
    "select * from ITEM where ID = ?"
);
query.addEntity(Item.class);
query.setParameter(0, ITEM_ID);                    ◁—— Starts at zero

List<Item> result = query.list();
```

For historical reasons, Hibernate counts positional parameters starting at zero, whereas JPA starts at one. Named parameter binding is usually more robust:

> **PATH:** /examples/src/test/java/org/jpwh/test/querying/sql/NativeQueries.java

```
Query query = em.createNativeQuery(
    "select * from ITEM where ID = :id",
    Item.class
);
query.setParameter("id", ITEM_ID);

List<Item> result = query.getResultList();
```

> **PATH:** /examples/src/test/java/org/jpwh/test/querying/sql/
>   HibernateSQLQueries.java

```
org.hibernate.SQLQuery query = session.createSQLQuery(
    "select * from ITEM where ID = :id"
);
query.addEntity(Item.class);
query.setParameter("id", ITEM_ID);

List<Item> result = query.list();
```

Although available in Hibernate for both APIs, the JPA specification doesn't consider named parameter binding for native queries portable. Therefore, some JPA providers may not support named parameters for native queries.

If your SQL query doesn't return the columns as mapped in your Java entity class, and you can't rewrite the query with aliases to rename columns in the result, you must create a result-set mapping.

17.2.3 *Customizing result mappings*

The following query returns a List of managed Item entity instances. All columns of the ITEM table are included in the SQL projection, as required for the construction of an Item instance. But the query renames the NAME column to EXTENDED_NAME with an alias in the projection:

> **PATH:** /examples/src/test/java/org/jpwh/test/querying/sql/NativeQueries.java

```
Query query = em.createNativeQuery(
    "select " +
        "i.ID, " +
        "'Auction: ' || i.NAME as EXTENDED_NAME, " +
        "i.CREATEDON, " +
        "i.AUCTIONEND, " +
        "i.AUCTIONTYPE, " +
        "i.APPROVED, " +
        "i.BUYNOWPRICE, " +
        "i.SELLER_ID " +
        "from ITEM i",
    "ItemResult"
);

List<Item> result = query.getResultList();
```

Hibernate can no longer automatically match the result set fields to Item properties: the NAME column is missing from the result set. You therefore specify a "result mapping" with the second parameter ofcreateNativeQuery(), here ItemResult.

MAPPING RESULT FIELDS TO ENTITY PROPERTIES
You can declare this mapping with annotations, for example, on the Item class:

> **PATH:** /model/src/main/java/org/jpwh/model/querying/Item.java

```
@SqlResultSetMappings({
    @SqlResultSetMapping(
        name = "ItemResult",
        entities =
        @EntityResult(
            entityClass = Item.class,
            fields = {
                @FieldResult(name = "id", column = "ID"),
                @FieldResult(name = "name", column = "EXTENDED_NAME"),
                @FieldResult(name = "createdOn", column = "CREATEDON"),
                @FieldResult(name = "auctionEnd", column = "AUCTIONEND"),
                @FieldResult(name = "auctionType", column = "AUCTIONTYPE"),
                @FieldResult(name = "approved", column = "APPROVED"),
                @FieldResult(name = "buyNowPrice", column = "BUYNOWPRICE"),
                @FieldResult(name = "seller", column = "SELLER_ID")
            }
        )
    )
})
@Entity
public class Item {
    // ...
}
```

You map all fields of the result set to properties of the entity class. Even if only one field/column doesn't match the already mapped column name (here EXTENDED_NAME), all other columns and properties have to be mapped as well.

SQL result mappings in annotations are difficult to read and as usual with JPA annotations, they only work when declared on a class, not in a package-info.java metadata file. We prefer externalizing such mappings into XML files. The following provides the same mapping:

PATH: /model/src/main/resources/querying/NativeQueries.xml

```xml
<sql-result-set-mapping name="ExternalizedItemResult">
    <entity-result entity-class="org.jpwh.model.querying.Item">
        <field-result name="id" column="ID"/>
        <field-result name="name" column="EXTENDED_NAME"/>
        <field-result name="createdOn" column="CREATEDON"/>
        <field-result name="auctionEnd" column="AUCTIONEND"/>
        <field-result name="auctionType" column="AUCTIONTYPE"/>
        <field-result name="approved" column="APPROVED"/>
        <field-result name="buyNowPrice" column="BUYNOWPRICE"/>
        <field-result name="seller" column="SELLER_ID"/>
    </entity-result>
</sql-result-set-mapping>
```

If both result-set mappings have the same name, the mapping declared in XML overrides the one defined with annotations.

You can also externalize the actual SQL query with @NamedNativeQuery or <named-native-query>, as shown in section 14.4. In all following examples, we keep the SQL statement embedded in the Java code, because this will make it easier for you to understand what the code does. But most of the time, you'll see result-set mappings in the more succinct XML syntax.

Let's first repeat the last query with the proprietary Hibernate API:

PATH: /examples/src/test/java/org/jpwh/test/querying/sql/
      HibernateSQLQueries.java

```java
org.hibernate.SQLQuery query = session.createSQLQuery(
    "select " +
        "i.ID as {i.id}, " +
        "'Auction: ' || i.NAME as {i.name}, " +
        "i.CREATEDON as {i.createdOn}, " +
        "i.AUCTIONEND as {i.auctionEnd}, " +
        "i.AUCTIONTYPE as {i.auctionType}, " +
        "i.APPROVED as {i.approved}, " +
        "i.BUYNOWPRICE as {i.buyNowPrice}, " +
        "i.SELLER_ID as {i.seller} " +
        "from ITEM i"
);
query.addEntity("i", Item.class);

List<Item> result = query.list();
```

With the Hibernate API, you can perform the result-set mapping directly within the query through alias placeholders. When calling addEntity(), you provide an alias, here i. In the SQL string, you then let Hibernate generate the actual aliases in the projection with placeholders such as {i.name} and {i.auctionEnd}, which refer to properties of the Item entity. No additional result-set mapping declaration is necessary; Hibernate generates the aliases in the SQL string and knows how to read the property values from the query ResultSet. This is much more convenient than the JPA result-set mapping option.

Or, if you can't or don't want to modify the SQL statement, use addRoot() and addProperty() on the org.hibernate.SQLQuery to perform the mapping:

PATH: /examples/src/test/java/org/jpwh/test/querying/sql/
        HibernateSQLQueries.java

```java
org.hibernate.SQLQuery query = session.createSQLQuery(
    "select " +
        "i.ID, " +
        "'Auction: ' || i.NAME as EXTENDED_NAME, " +
        "i.CREATEDON, " +
        "i.AUCTIONEND, " +
        "i.AUCTIONTYPE, " +
        "i.APPROVED, " +
        "i.BUYNOWPRICE, " +
        "i.SELLER_ID " +
        "from ITEM i"
);
query.addRoot("i", Item.class)
    .addProperty("id", "ID")
    .addProperty("name", "EXTENDED_NAME")
    .addProperty("createdOn", "CREATEDON")
    .addProperty("auctionEnd", "AUCTIONEND")
    .addProperty("auctionType", "AUCTIONTYPE")
    .addProperty("approved", "APPROVED")
    .addProperty("buyNowPrice", "BUYNOWPRICE")
    .addProperty("seller", "SELLER_ID");

List<Item> result = query.list();
```

As with the standard API, you can also rely on an existing result-set mapping by name with the Hibernate API:

PATH: /examples/src/test/java/org/jpwh/test/querying/sql/
        HibernateSQLQueries.java

```java
org.hibernate.SQLQuery query = session.createSQLQuery(
    "select " +
        "i.ID, " +
        "'Auction: ' || i.NAME as EXTENDED_NAME, " +
        "i.CREATEDON, " +
        "i.AUCTIONEND, " +
        "i.AUCTIONTYPE, " +
        "i.APPROVED, " +
        "i.BUYNOWPRICE, " +
        "i.SELLER_ID " +
        "from ITEM i"
```

```
);
query.setResultSetMapping("ItemResult");

List<Item> result = query.list();
```

Another case where you need custom result-set mapping are duplicate column names in the result set of your SQL query.

MAPPING DUPLICATE FIELDS

The following query loads the seller of each Item in a single statement, joining ITEM and USERS tables:

> **PATH:** /examples/src/test/java/org/jpwh/test/querying/sql/NativeQueries.java

```
Query query = em.createNativeQuery(
    "select " +
        "i.ID as ITEM_ID, " +
        "i.NAME, " +
        "i.CREATEDON, " +
        "i.AUCTIONEND, " +
        "i.AUCTIONTYPE, " +
        "i.APPROVED, " +
        "i.BUYNOWPRICE, " +
        "i.SELLER_ID, " +
        "u.ID as USER_ID, " +
        "u.USERNAME, " +
        "u.FIRSTNAME, " +
        "u.LASTNAME, " +
        "u.ACTIVATED, " +
        "u.STREET, " +
        "u.ZIPCODE, " +
        "u.CITY " +
        "from ITEM i join USERS u on u.ID = i.SELLER_ID",
    "ItemSellerResult"
);
List<Object[]> result = query.getResultList();

for (Object[] tuple : result) {
    assertTrue(tuple[0] instanceof Item);
    assertTrue(tuple[1] instanceof User);
    Item item = (Item) tuple[0];
    assertTrue(Persistence.getPersistenceUtil().isLoaded(item, "seller"));
    assertEquals(item.getSeller(), tuple[1]);
}
```

This is effectively an eager fetch of the association Item#seller. Hibernate knows that each row contains the fields for an Item and a User entity instance, linked by the SELLER_ID.

The duplicate columns in the result set would be i.ID and u.ID, which both have the same name. You've renamed them with an alias to ITEM_ID and USER_ID, so you have to map how the result set is to be transformed:

PATH: /model/src/main/resources/querying/NativeQueries.xml

```xml
<sql-result-set-mapping name="ItemSellerResult">
    <entity-result entity-class="org.jpwh.model.querying.Item">
        <field-result name="id" column="ITEM_ID"/>
        <field-result name="name" column="NAME"/>
        <field-result name="createdOn" column="CREATEDON"/>
        <field-result name="auctionEnd" column="AUCTIONEND"/>
        <field-result name="auctionType" column="AUCTIONTYPE"/>
        <field-result name="approved" column="APPROVED"/>
        <field-result name="buyNowPrice" column="BUYNOWPRICE"/>
        <field-result name="seller" column="SELLER_ID"/>
    </entity-result>
    <entity-result entity-class="org.jpwh.model.querying.User">
        <field-result name="id" column="USER_ID"/>
        <field-result name="name" column="NAME"/>
        <field-result name="username" column="USERNAME"/>
        <field-result name="firstname" column="FIRSTNAME"/>
        <field-result name="lastname" column="LASTNAME"/>
        <field-result name="activated" column="ACTIVATED"/>
        <field-result name="homeAddress.street" column="STREET"/>
        <field-result name="homeAddress.zipcode" column="ZIPCODE"/>
        <field-result name="homeAddress.city" column="CITY"/>
    </entity-result>
</sql-result-set-mapping>
```

As before, you have to map all fields of each entity result to column names, even if only two have different names as the original entity mapping.

This query is much easier to map with the Hibernate API:

PATH: /examples/src/test/java/org/jpwh/test/querying/sql/
      HibernateSQLQueries.java

```java
org.hibernate.SQLQuery query = session.createSQLQuery(
    "select " +
        "{i.*}, {u.*} " +
        "from ITEM i join USERS u on u.ID = i.SELLER_ID"
);
query.addEntity("i", Item.class);
query.addEntity("u", User.class);

List<Object[]> result = query.list();
```

Hibernate will add auto-generated unique aliases to the SQL statement for the {i.*} and {u.*} placeholders, so the query won't return duplicate column names.

You may have noticed the dot syntax in the previous JPA result mapping for the homeAddress embedded component in a User. Let's look at this special case again.

MAPPING FIELDS TO COMPONENT PROPERTIES

The User has a homeAddress, an embedded instance of the Address class. The following query loads all User instances:

PATH: **/examples/src/test/java/org/jpwh/test/querying/sql/NativeQueries.java**

```java
Query query = em.createNativeQuery(
    "select " +
        "u.ID, " +
        "u.USERNAME, " +
        "u.FIRSTNAME, " +
        "u.LASTNAME, " +
        "u.ACTIVATED, " +
        "u.STREET as USER_STREET, " +
        "u.ZIPCODE as USER_ZIPCODE, " +
        "u.CITY as USER_CITY " +
        "from USERS u",
    "UserResult"
);

List<User> result = query.getResultList();
```

In this query, you rename the STREET, ZIPCODE, and CITY columns, so you have to map them manually to the embedded component properties:

PATH: **/model/src/main/resources/querying/NativeQueries.xml**

```xml
<sql-result-set-mapping name="UserResult">
    <entity-result entity-class="org.jpwh.model.querying.User">
        <field-result name="id" column="ID"/>
        <field-result name="name" column="NAME"/>
        <field-result name="username" column="USERNAME"/>
        <field-result name="firstname" column="FIRSTNAME"/>
        <field-result name="lastname" column="LASTNAME"/>
        <field-result name="activated" column="ACTIVATED"/>
        <field-result name="homeAddress.street" column="USER_STREET"/>
        <field-result name="homeAddress.zipcode" column="USER_ZIPCODE"/>
        <field-result name="homeAddress.city" column="USER_CITY"/>
    </entity-result>
</sql-result-set-mapping>
```

We've shown this dot syntax several times before when discussing embedded components: you reference the street property of homeAddress with homeAddress.street. For nested embedded components, you can write homeAddress.city.name if City isn't just a string but another embeddable class.

Hibernate's SQL query API also supports the dot syntax in alias placeholders for component properties. Here are the same query and result-set mapping:

PATH: **/examples/src/test/java/org/jpwh/test/querying/sql/**
        HibernateSQLQueries.java

```java
org.hibernate.SQLQuery query = session.createSQLQuery(
    "select " +
        "u.ID as {u.id}, " +
        "u.USERNAME as {u.username}, " +
        "u.FIRSTNAME as {u.firstname}, " +
```

```
        "u.LASTNAME as {u.lastname}, " +
        "u.ACTIVATED as {u.activated}, " +
        "u.STREET as {u.homeAddress.street}, " +
        "u.ZIPCODE as {u.homeAddress.zipcode}, " +
        "u.CITY as {u.homeAddress.city} " +
        "from USERS u"
);
query.addEntity("u", User.class);

List<User> result = query.list();
```

Eager fetching of collections with an SQL query is only available with the Hibernate API.

Hibernate Feature

EAGER-FETCHING COLLECTIONS

Let's say you want to load all Item instances with an SQL query and have the bids collection of each Item initialized at the same time. This requires an outer join in the SQL query:

> PATH: /examples/src/test/java/org/jpwh/test/querying/sql/
>   HibernateSQLQueries.java

```
org.hibernate.SQLQuery query = session.createSQLQuery(   ◄─❶ Joins ITEM and BID
    "select " +
        "i.ID as ITEM_ID, " +
        "i.NAME, " +
        "i.CREATEDON, " +
        "i.AUCTIONEND, " +
        "i.AUCTIONTYPE, " +
        "i.APPROVED, " +
        "i.BUYNOWPRICE, " +
        "i.SELLER_ID, " +
        "b.ID as BID_ID," +
        "b.ITEM_ID as BID_ITEM_ID, " +
        "b.AMOUNT, " +
        "b.BIDDER_ID " +
        "from ITEM i left outer join BID b on i.ID = b.ITEM_ID"
);
query.addRoot("i", Item.class)              ◄─❷ Maps columns to entity properties
    .addProperty("id", "ITEM_ID")
    .addProperty("name", "NAME")
    .addProperty("createdOn", "CREATEDON")
    .addProperty("auctionEnd", "AUCTIONEND")
    .addProperty("auctionType", "AUCTIONTYPE")
    .addProperty("approved", "APPROVED")
    .addProperty("buyNowPrice", "BUYNOWPRICE")
    .addProperty("seller", "SELLER_ID");

query.addFetch("b", "i", "bids")            ◄─❸ Maps Bid properties to result set
    .addProperty("key", "BID_ITEM_ID")
    .addProperty("element", "BID_ID")
    .addProperty("element.id", "BID_ID")
    .addProperty("element.item", "BID_ITEM_ID")
```

```
        .addProperty("element.amount", "AMOUNT")
        .addProperty("element.bidder", "BIDDER_ID");
List<Object[]> result = query.list();
                                                          4  5 rows
                                                             in result
assertEquals(result.size(), 5);

for (Object[] tuple : result) {                           5  First result is
    Item item = (Item) tuple[0];                             Item instance
    assertTrue(Persistence.getPersistenceUtil().isLoaded(item, "bids"));

    Bid bid = (Bid) tuple[1];                           6  Second result is each Bid
    if (bid != null)
        assertTrue(item.getBids().contains(bid));
}
```

❶ The query (outer) joins the ITEM and BID tables. The projection returns all columns required to construct Item and Bid instances. The query renames duplicate columns such as ID with aliases, so field names are unique in the result.

❷ Because of the renamed fields, you have to map each column to its respective entity property.

❸ Add a FetchReturn for the bids collection with the alias of the owning entity i, and map the key and element special properties to the foreign key column BID_ITEM_ID and the identifier of the Bid. Then the code maps each property of Bid to a field of the result set. Some fields are mapped twice, as required by Hibernate for construction of the collection.

❹ The number of rows in the result set is a product: one item has three bids, one item has one bid, and the last item has no bids, for a total of five rows in the result.

❺ The first element of the result tuple is the Item instance; Hibernate initialized the bids collection.

❻ The second element of the result tuple is each Bid.

Alternatively, if you don't have to manually map the result because the field names returned by your SQL query match the already-mapped columns of the entities, you can let Hibernate insert aliases into your SQL statement with placeholders:

> **PATH:** /examples/src/test/java/org/jpwh/test/querying/sql/
>   HibernateSQLQueries.java

```
org.hibernate.SQLQuery query = session.createSQLQuery(
    "select " +
        "{i.*}, " +
        "{b.*} " +
        "from ITEM i left outer join BID b on i.ID = b.ITEM_ID"
);
query.addEntity("i", Item.class);
query.addFetch("b", "i", "bids");

List<Object[]> result = query.list();
```

Eager fetching of collections with dynamic SQL result mappings is only available with the Hibernate API; it's not standardized in JPA.

Limitations of collection fetching with SQL queries

With the org.hibernate.SQLQuery API, you can only fetch a collection of entity associations: that is, *one-to-many* or *many-to-many* collections. At the time of writing, Hibernate doesn't support ad hoc dynamic mapping of SQL result sets to collections of basic or embeddable type. This means you can't, for example, eagerly load the Item#images collection with a custom SQL query and the org .hibernate.SQLQuery API.

So far, you've seen SQL queries returning managed entity instances. You can also return transient instances of any class with the right constructor.

MAPPING THE RESULT TO A CONSTRUCTOR

We covered dynamic instantiation in a query with JPQL and criteria examples in section 15.3.2. JPA supports the same feature with native queries. The following query returns a List of ItemSummary instances:

PATH: /examples/src/test/java/org/jpwh/test/querying/sql/NativeQueries.java

```
Query query = em.createNativeQuery(
    "select ID, NAME, AUCTIONEND from ITEM",
    "ItemSummaryResult"
);
List<ItemSummary> result = query.getResultList();
```

The ItemSummaryResult mapping transforms each column of the query result into a parameter for the ItemSummary constructor:

PATH: /model/src/main/resources/querying/NativeQueries.xml

```
<sql-result-set-mapping name="ItemSummaryResult">
    <constructor-result target-class="org.jpwh.model.querying.ItemSummary">
        <column name="ID" class="java.lang.Long"/>
        <column name="NAME"/>
        <column name="AUCTIONEND"/>
    </constructor-result>
</sql-result-set-mapping>
```

The returned column types have to match the constructor parameter types; Hibernate would default to BigInteger for the ID column, so you map it to a Long with the class attribute.

The Hibernate API gives you a choice. You can either use an existing result mapping for the query by name, or apply a *result transformer*, as you saw for JPQL queries in section 16.1:

> PATH: /examples/src/test/java/org/jpwh/test/querying/sql/
>   HibernateSQLQueries.java

```
org.hibernate.SQLQuery query = session.createSQLQuery(
    "select ID, NAME, AUCTIONEND from ITEM"
);

// query.setResultSetMapping("ItemSummaryResult");

query.addScalar("ID", StandardBasicTypes.LONG);
query.addScalar("NAME");
query.addScalar("AUCTIONEND");

query.setResultTransformer(
    new AliasToBeanConstructorResultTransformer(
        ItemSummary.class.getConstructor(
            Long.class,
            String.class,
            Date.class
        )
    )
);

List<ItemSummary> result = query.list();
```

❶ Uses existing result mapping

❷ Maps fields as scalars

❸ Applies result transformer

❶ You can use an existing result mapping.

❷ Alternatively, you can map the fields returned by the query as scalar values. Without a result transformer, you'd get an Object[] for each result row.

❸ Apply a built-in result transformer to turn the Object[] into instances of ItemSummary.

As explained in section 15.3.2, Hibernate can use any class constructor with such a mapping. Instead of ItemSummary, you can construct Item instances. They will be in either transient or detached state, depending on whether you return and map an identifier value in your query.

You can also mix different kinds of result mappings or return scalar values directly.

SCALAR AND MIXED RESULT MAPPINGS
The next query returns a List of Object[], where the first element is an Item entity instance and the second element is a scalar reflecting the number of bids for that item:

> PATH: /examples/src/test/java/org/jpwh/test/querying/sql/NativeQueries.java

```
Query query = em.createNativeQuery(
    "select " +
        "i.*, " +
        "count(b.ID) as NUM_OF_BIDS " +
        "from ITEM i left join BID b on b.ITEM_ID = i.ID " +
        "group by i.ID, i.NAME, i.CREATEDON, i.AUCTIONEND, " +
        "i.AUCTIONTYPE, i.APPROVED, i.BUYNOWPRICE, i.SELLER_ID",
    "ItemBidResult"
);
```

```
List<Object[]> result = query.getResultList();

for (Object[] tuple : result) {
    assertTrue(tuple[0] instanceof Item);
    assertTrue(tuple[1] instanceof Number);
}
```

The result mapping is simple, because the projection contains no duplicate columns:

PATH: /model/src/main/resources/querying/NativeQueries.xml

```
<sql-result-set-mapping name="ItemBidResult">
    <entity-result entity-class="org.jpwh.model.querying.Item"/>
    <column-result name="NUM_OF_BIDS"/>
</sql-result-set-mapping>
```

With the Hibernate API, the additional scalar result is mapped with addScalar():

**PATH: /examples/src/test/java/org/jpwh/test/querying/sql/
HibernateSQLQueries.java**

```
org.hibernate.SQLQuery query = session.createSQLQuery(
    "select " +
        "i.*, " +
        "count(b.ID) as NUM_OF_BIDS " +
        "from ITEM i left join BID b on b.ITEM_ID = i.ID " +
        "group by i.ID, i.NAME, i.CREATEDON, i.AUCTIONEND, " +
        "i.AUCTIONTYPE, i.APPROVED, i.BUYNOWPRICE, i.SELLER_ID"
);
query.addEntity(Item.class);
query.addScalar("NUM_OF_BIDS");

List<Object[]> result = query.list();

for (Object[] tuple : result) {
    assertTrue(tuple[0] instanceof Item);
    assertTrue(tuple[1] instanceof Number);
}
```

Finally, in a single result mapping, you can combine entity, constructor, and scalar column results. The following query returns a persistent and managed User entity instance that is the seller of the also-returned ItemSummary. You also get the number of bids for each item:

PATH: /examples/src/test/java/org/jpwh/test/querying/sql/NativeQueries.java

```
Query query = em.createNativeQuery(
    "select " +
        "u.*, " +
        "i.ID as ITEM_ID, i.NAME as ITEM_NAME, i.AUCTIONEND as
    ITEM_AUCTIONEND, " +
        "count(b.ID) as NUM_OF_BIDS " +
        "from ITEM i " +
        "join USERS u on u.ID = i.SELLER_ID " +
```

```
        "left join BID b on b.ITEM_ID = i.ID " +
        "group by u.ID, u.USERNAME, u.FIRSTNAME, u.LASTNAME, " +
        "u.ACTIVATED, u.STREET, u.ZIPCODE, u.CITY, " +
        "ITEM_ID, ITEM_NAME, ITEM_AUCTIONEND",
    "SellerItemSummaryResult"
);

List<Object[]> result = query.getResultList();
for (Object[] tuple : result) {
    assertTrue(tuple[0] instanceof User);
    assertTrue(tuple[1] instanceof BigInteger);
    assertTrue(tuple[2] instanceof ItemSummary);
}
```

Wrong order of results: Hibernate issue HHH-8678

The result mapping of this query is as follows:

> **PATH: /model/src/main/resources/querying/NativeQueries.xml**

```xml
<sql-result-set-mapping name="SellerItemSummaryResult">

    <entity-result entity-class="org.jpwh.model.querying.User"/>

    <constructor-result target-class="org.jpwh.model.querying.ItemSummary">
        <column name="ID" class="java.lang.Long"/>
        <column name="ITEM_NAME"/>
        <column name="ITEM_AUCTIONEND"/>
    </constructor-result>

    <column-result name="NUM_OF_BIDS"/>
</sql-result-set-mapping>
```

The JPA specification guarantees that in mixed result mappings, the produced `Object[]` of each tuple will contain elements in the following order: first all `<entity-result>` data, then `<constructor-result>`data, and then `<column-result>` data. The JPA XML schema enforces this order in the result mapping declaration; but even if you map elements in a different order with annotations (which can't enforce the order in which you declare mappings), the query result will have the standard order. Be aware that, as shown in the code example, Hibernate at the time of writing didn't return the right order.

Note that with the Hibernate query API, you can use the same result mapping by name, as we've shown previously. If you need more programmatic control over the result marshalling, you must write your own result transformer, because there is no built-in transformer to map such a mixed query result automatically.

Last, you'll see a more complex example with an SQL query declared in an XML file.

17.2.4 *Externalizing native queries*

We now show you how to declare an SQL query in an XML file, instead of embedding the string in the code. In real applications with long SQL statements, reading concatenated strings in Java code is unpleasant, so you'll almost always prefer having SQL statements in an XML file. This also simplifies ad hoc testing, because you can copy and paste SQL statements between an XML file and your SQL database console.

You've probably noticed that all the SQL examples in the previous sections were trivial. In fact, none of the examples required a query written in SQL—we could have used JPQL in each case. To make the next example more interesting, we write a query that can't be expressed in JPQL, only in SQL.

THE TREE OF CATEGORIES

Consider the `Category` class and its self-referencing *many-to-one* association, as shown in figure 17.1.

This is the mapping of the association—a regular `@ManyToOne` of the `PARENT_ID` foreign key column:

Figure 17.1 The `Category` has a self-referencing *many-to-one* association.

PATH: /model/src/main/java/org/jpwh/model/querying/Category.java

```
@Entity
public class Category {

    @ManyToOne
    @JoinColumn(
        name = "PARENT_ID",
        foreignKey = @ForeignKey(name = "FK_CATEGORY_PARENT_ID")
    )
    protected Category parent;        ◁─┐ Tree root has no parent;
                                        │ column must be nullable
    // ...
}
```

Categories form a tree. The root of the tree is a `Category` node without a `parent`. The database data for the example tree is in figure 17.2.

You can also represent this data as a tree diagram, as shown in figure 17.3. Alternatively, you can use a sequence of paths and the level of each node:

```
/One, 0
/One/Two, 1
/One/Three, 1
/One/Two/Four, 2
```

CATEGORY

ID	NAME	PARENT_ID
1	One	
2	Two	1
3	Three	1
4	Four	2

Figure 17.2 Database table and sample data for a tree of categories

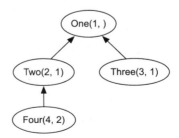

Figure 17.3 A tree of categories

Now, consider how your application loads `Category` instances. You may want to find the root `Category` of the tree. This is a trivial JPQL query:

```
select c from Category c where c.parent is null
```

You can easily query for the categories in a particular level of the tree, such as all children of the root:

```
select c from Category c, Category r where r.parent is null and c.parent = r
```

This query will only return direct children of the root: here, categories `Two` and `Three`.

How can you load the *entire* tree (or a subtree) in one query? This isn't possible with JPQL, because it would require recursion: "Load categories at this level, then all the children on the next level, then all the children of those, and so on." In SQL, you can write such a query, using a *common table expression* (CTE), a feature also known as *subquery factoring*.

LOADING THE TREE

The following SQL query loads the entire tree of `Category` instances, declared in a JPA XML file:

PATH: /model/src/main/resources/querying/NativeQueries.xml

```xml
<named-native-query name="findAllCategories"
                    result-set-mapping="CategoryResult">
    <query>
        with CATEGORY_LINK(ID, NAME, PARENT_ID, PATH, LEVEL) as (
            select
                ID,
                NAME,
                PARENT_ID,
                '/' || NAME,
                0
            from CATEGORY where PARENT_ID is null
            union all
            select
                c.ID,
                c.NAME,
                c.PARENT_ID,
                cl.PATH || '/' || c.NAME,
                cl.LEVEL + 1
            from CATEGORY_LINK cl
            join CATEGORY c on cl.ID = c.PARENT_ID
        )
        select
            ID,
            NAME as CAT_NAME,
            PARENT_ID,
            PATH,
            LEVEL
        from CATEGORY_LINK
        order by ID
    </query>
</named-native-query>
```

It's a complex query, and we won't spend too much time on it here. To understand it, read the last SELECT, querying the CATEGORY_LINK view. Each row in that view represents a node in the tree. The view is declared here in the WITH() AS operation. The CATEGORY_LINK view is a combined (union) result of two other SELECTs. You add additional information to the view during recursion, such as the PATH and the LEVEL of each node.

Let's map the result of this query:

PATH: /model/src/main/resources/querying/NativeQueries.xml

```xml
<sql-result-set-mapping name="CategoryResult">
    <entity-result entity-class="org.jpwh.model.querying.Category">
        <field-result name="id" column="ID"/>
        <field-result name="name" column="CAT_NAME"/>
        <field-result name="parent" column="PARENT_ID"/>
    </entity-result>
    <column-result name="PATH"/>
    <column-result name="LEVEL" class="java.lang.Integer"/>
</sql-result-set-mapping>
```

The XML maps the ID, CAT_NAME, and PARENT_ID fields to properties of the Category entity. The mapping returns the PATH and LEVEL as additional scalar values.

To execute the named SQL query and access the result, write the following:

PATH: /examples/src/test/java/org/jpwh/test/querying/sql/NativeQueries.java

```java
Query query = em.createNamedQuery("findAllCategories");
List<Object[]> result = query.getResultList();

for (Object[] tuple : result) {
    Category category = (Category) tuple[0];
    String path = (String) tuple[1];
    Integer level = (Integer) tuple[2];
    // ...
}
```

Each tuple contains a managed, persistent Category instance; its path in the tree as a string (such as /One, /One/Two, and so on); and the tree level of the node.

Alternatively, you can declare and map an SQL query in a Hibernate XML metadata file:

PATH: /model/src/main/resources/querying/SQLQueries.hbm.xml

```xml
<sql-query name="findAllCategoriesHibernate">
    <return class="org.jpwh.model.querying.Category">
        <return-property name="id" column="ID"/>
        <return-property name="name" column="CAT_NAME"/>
        <return-property name="parent" column="PARENT_ID"/>
    </return>
    <return-scalar column="PATH"/>
    <return-scalar column="LEVEL" type="integer"/>
    ...
</sql-query>
```

We left out the SQL query in this snippet; it's the same as the SQL statement shown earlier in the JPA example.

As mentioned in section 14.4, with regard to the execution in Java code, it doesn't matter which syntax you declare your named queries in: XML file or annotations. Even the language doesn't matter—it can be JPQL or SQL. Both Hibernate and JPA query interfaces have methods to "get a named query" and execute it independently from how you defined it.

This concludes our discussion of SQL result mapping for queries. The next subject is customization of SQL statements for CRUD operations, replacing the SQL automatically generated by Hibernate for creating, reading, updating, and deleting data in the database.

Hibernate Feature

17.3   *Customizing CRUD operations*

The first custom SQL you write loads an entity instance of the `User` class. All the following code examples show the same SQL that Hibernate executes automatically by default, without much customization—this helps you understand the mapping technique more quickly.

You can customize retrieval of an entity instance with a *loader*.

17.3.1   *Enabling custom loaders*

Hibernate has two requirements when you override an SQL query to load an entity instance:

- Write a named query that retrieves the entity instance. We show an example in SQL, but as always, you can also write named queries in JPQL. For an SQL query, you may need a custom result mapping, as shown earlier in this chapter.
- Activate the query on an entity class with `@org.hibernate.annotations` `.Loader`. This enables the query as the replacement for the Hibernate-generated query.

Let's override how Hibernate loads an instance of the `User` entity, as shown in the following listing.

> **Listing 17.2   Loading a `User` instance with a custom query**
>
> PATH: /model/src/main/java/org/jpwh/model/customsql/User.java

```
@NamedNativeQueries({                                    ◁──── ❶ Declares query to load User
    @NamedNativeQuery(
        name = "findUserById",                                      ❷ Parameter
        query = "select * from USERS where ID = ?",     ◁──┘          placeholder
        resultClass = User.class            ◁──┐
    )                                          ❸ No custom mapping needed
})
```

```
@org.hibernate.annotations.Loader(
    namedQuery = "findUserById"
)
@Entity
@Table(name = "USERS")
public class User {
    // ...
}
```

Sets loader to
❹ named query

❶ Annotations declare the query to load an instance of User; you can also declare it in an XML file (JPA or Hibernate metadata). You can call this named query directly in your data-access code when needed.

❷ The query must have exactly one parameter placeholder, which Hibernate sets as the identifier value of the instance to load. Here it's a positional parameter, but a named parameter would also work.

❸ For this trivial query, you don't need a custom result-set mapping. The User class maps all fields returned by the query. Hibernate can automatically transform the result.

❹ Setting the loader for an entity class to a named query enables the query for all operations that retrieve an instance of User from the database. There's no indication of the query language or where you declared it; this is independent of the loader declaration.

In a named loader query for an entity, you have to SELECT (that is, perform a projection for) the following properties of the entity class:

- The value of the identifier property or properties, if a composite primary key is used.
- All scalar properties of basic type.
- All properties of embedded components.
- An entity identifier value for each @JoinColumn of each mapped entity association such as @ManyToOne owned by the loaded entity class.
- All scalar properties, embedded component properties, and association join references that are inside a @SecondaryTable annotation.
- If you enable lazy loading for some properties, through interception and bytecode instrumentation, you don't need to load the lazy properties (see section 12.1.3).

Hibernate always calls the enabled loader query when a User has to be retrieved from the database by identifier. When you call em.find(User.class, USER_ID), your custom query will execute. When you call someItem.getSeller().getUsername(), and the Item#seller proxy has to be initialized, your custom query will load the data.

You may also want to customize how Hibernate creates, updates, and deletes an instance of User in the database.

17.3.2 *Customizing creation, updates, and deletion*

Hibernate usually generates CRUD SQL statements at startup. It caches the SQL statements internally for future use, thus avoiding any runtime costs of SQL generation for the most common operations. You've seen how you can override the R in CRUD, so now, let's do the same for CUD. For each entity, you can define custom CUD SQL statements with the Hibernate annotations `@SQLInsert`, `@SQLUpdate`, and `@SQLDelete`, respectively.

Listing 17.3   Custom DML for the `User` entity

PATH: /model/src/main/java/org/jpwh/model/customsql/User.java

```java
@org.hibernate.annotations.SQLInsert(
    sql = "insert into USERS " +
        "(ACTIVATED, USERNAME, ID) values (?, ?, ?)"
)
@org.hibernate.annotations.SQLUpdate(
    sql = "update USERS set " +
        "ACTIVATED = ?, " +
        "USERNAME = ? " +
        "where ID = ?"
)
@org.hibernate.annotations.SQLDelete(
    sql = "delete from USERS where ID = ?"
)
@Entity
@Table(name = "USERS")
public class User {
    // ...
}
```

You need to be careful with the binding of arguments for SQL statements and parameter placeholders (the ? in the statements). For CUD customization, Hibernate only supports positional parameters.

What is the right order for the parameters? There's an internal order to how Hibernate binds arguments to SQL parameters for CUD statements. The easiest way to figure out the right SQL statement and parameter order is to let Hibernate generate an example for you. Without any custom SQL statements, enable DEBUG logging for the `org.hibernate.persister.entity` category, and search the Hibernate startup output for lines like the following:

```
Static SQL for entity: org.jpwh.model.customsql.User
 Insert 0: insert into USERS (activated, username, id) values (?, ?, ?)
 Update 0: update USERS set activated=?, username=? where id=?
 Delete 0: delete from USERS where id=?
```

These automatically generated SQL statements show the right parameter order, and Hibernate always binds the values in that order. Copy the SQL statements you want to customize into annotations, and make the necessary changes.

A special case is properties of an entity class mapped to another table with `@SecondaryTable`. The CUD customization statements we've shown so far only refer to the columns of the main entity table. Hibernate still executes automatically generated SQL statements for insertion, updates, and deletion of rows in the secondary table(s).

You can customize this SQL by adding the @org.hibernate.annotations.Table annotation to your entity class and setting its sqlInsert, sqlUpdate, and sqlDelete attributes.

If you prefer to have your CUD SQL statements in XML, your only choice is to map the entire entity in a Hibernate XML metadata file. The elements in this proprietary mapping format for custom CUD statements are <sql-insert>, <sql-update>, and <sql-delete>. Fortunately, CUD statements are usually much more trivial than queries, so annotations are fine in most applications.

You've now added custom SQL statements for CRUD operations of an entity instance. Next, we show how to override SQL statements for loading and modifying a collection.

17.3.3 *Customizing collection operations*

Let's override the SQL statement Hibernate uses when loading the Item#images collection. This is a collection of embeddable components mapped with @Element-Collection; the procedure is the same for collections of basic types or many-valued entity associations (@OneToMany or @ManyToMany).

Listing 17.4 Loading a collection with a custom query

PATH: /model/src/main/java/org/jpwh/model/customsql/Item.java

```
@Entity
public class Item {

    @ElementCollection
    @org.hibernate.annotations.Loader(namedQuery = "loadImagesForItem")
    protected Set<Image> images = new HashSet<Image>();

    // ...
}
```

As before, you declare that a named query will load the collection. This time, however, you must declare and map the result of the query in a Hibernate XML metadata file, which is the only facility that supports mapping of query results to collection properties:

PATH: /model/src/main/resources/customsql/ItemQueries.hbm.xml

```
<sql-query name="loadImagesForItem">
    <load-collection alias="img" role="Item.images"/>
    select
        ITEM_ID, FILENAME, WIDTH, HEIGHT
    from
        ITEM_IMAGES
    where
        ITEM_ID = ?
</sql-query>
```

The query has to have one (positional or named) parameter. Hibernate sets its value to the entity identifier that owns the collection. Whenever Hibernate need to initialize the Item#images collection, Hibernate now executes your custom SQL query.

Sometimes you don't have to override the entire SQL statement for loading a collection: for example, if you only want to add a restriction to the generated SQL statement. Let's say the `Category` entity has a collection of `Item` references, and the `Item` has an activation flag. If the property `Item#active` is `false`, you don't want to load it when accessing the `Category#items` collection. You can append this restriction to the SQL statement with the Hibernate `@Where` annotation on the collection mapping, as a plain SQL fragment:

PATH: /model/src/main/java/org/jpwh/model/customsql/Category.java

```
@Entity
public class Category {

    @OneToMany(mappedBy = "category")
    @org.hibernate.annotations.Where(clause = "ACTIVE = 'true'")
    protected Set<Item> items = new HashSet<Item>();

    // ...
}
```

You can also write custom insertion and deletion SQL statements for collection elements, as shown next.

Listing 17.5   Custom CUD statements for collection modification

PATH: /model/src/main/java/org/jpwh/model/customsql/Item.java

```
@Entity
public class Item {

    @ElementCollection
    @org.hibernate.annotations.SQLInsert(
        sql = "insert into ITEM_IMAGES " +
              "(ITEM_ID, FILENAME, HEIGHT, WIDTH) " +
              "values (?, ?, ?, ?)"
    )
    @org.hibernate.annotations.SQLDelete(
        sql = "delete from ITEM_IMAGES " +
              "where ITEM_ID = ? and FILENAME = ? and HEIGHT = ? and WIDTH = ?"
    )
    @org.hibernate.annotations.SQLDeleteAll(
        sql = "delete from ITEM_IMAGES where ITEM_ID = ?"
    )
    protected Set<Image> images = new HashSet<Image>();

    // ...
}
```

To find the right parameter order, enable `DEBUG` logging for the `org.hibernate`
`.persister.collection` category and search the Hibernate startup output for the generated SQL statements for this collection, before you add your custom SQL annotations.

A new annotation here is `@SQLDeleteAll`, which only applies to collections of basic or embeddable types. Hibernate executes this SQL statement when the entire collection has to be removed from the database: for example, when you call `someItem` `.getImages().clear()` or `someItem.setImages(new HashSet())`.

No `@SQLUpdate` statement is necessary for this collection, because Hibernate doesn't update rows for this collection of embeddable type. When an `Image` property value changes, Hibernate detects this as a new `Image` in the collection (recall that images are compared "by value" of *all* their properties). Hibernate will `DELETE` the old row and `INSERT` a new row to persist this change.

Instead of lazily loading collection elements, you can eagerly fetch them when the owning entity is loaded. You can also override this query with a custom SQL statement.

17.3.4 *Eager fetching in custom loaders*

Let's consider the `Item#bids` collection and how it's loaded. Hibernate enables lazy loading by default because you mapped with `@OneToMany`, so it's only when you begin iterating through the collection's elements that Hibernate will execute a query and retrieve the data. Hence, when loading the `Item` entity, you don't have to load any collection data.

If instead you want to fetch the `Item#bids` collection eagerly when the `Item` is loaded, first enable a custom loader query on the `Item` class:

PATH: /model/src/main/java/org/jpwh/model/customsql/Item.java

```java
@org.hibernate.annotations.Loader(
    namedQuery = "findItemByIdFetchBids"
)
@Entity
public class Item {

    @OneToMany(mappedBy = "item")
    protected Set<Bid> bids = new HashSet<>();

    // ...
}
```

As in the previous section, you must declare this named query in a Hibernate XML metadata file; no annotations are available to fetch collections with named queries. Here is the SQL statement to load an `Item` and its `bids` collection in a single `OUTER JOIN`:

PATH: /model/src/main/resources/customsql/ItemQueries.hbm.xml

```xml
<sql-query name="findItemByIdFetchBids">
    <return alias="i" class="Item"/>
    <return-join alias="b" property="i.bids"/>
    select
        {i.*}, {b.*}
    from
        ITEM i
    left outer join BID b
        on i.ID = b.ITEM_ID
    where
        i.ID = ?
</sql-query>
```

You saw this query and result mapping in Java code earlier in this chapter in the section "Eager-fetching collections." Here, you apply an additional restriction to only one row of ITE, with the given primary key value.

You can also eagerly load single-valued entity associations such as a @ManyToOne with a custom SQL statement. Let's say you want to eagerly load the bidder when a Bid entity is retrieved from the database. First, enable a named query as the entity loader:

PATH: /model/src/main/java/org/jpwh/model/customsql/Bid.java

```
@org.hibernate.annotations.Loader(
    namedQuery = "findBidByIdFetchBidder"
)
@Entity
public class Bid {

    @ManyToOne(optional = false, fetch = FetchType.LAZY)
    protected User bidder;

    // ...
}
```

Unlike custom queries used to load collections, you can declare this named query with standard annotations (of course, you can also have it in an XML metadata file, in either the JPA or Hibernate syntax):

PATH: /model/src/main/java/org/jpwh/model/customsql/Bid.java

```
@NamedNativeQueries({
    @NamedNativeQuery(
        name = "findBidByIdFetchBidder",
        query =
            "select " +
                "b.ID as BID_ID, b.AMOUNT, b.ITEM_ID, b.BIDDER_ID, " +
                "u.ID as USER_ID, u.USERNAME, u.ACTIVATED " +
                "from BID b join USERS u on b.BIDDER_ID = u.ID " +
                "where b.ID = ?",
        resultSetMapping = "BidBidderResult"
    )
})
@Entity
public class Bid {
    // ...
}
```

An INNER JOIN is appropriate for this SQL query, because a Bid always has a bidder and the BIDDER_ID foreign key column is never NULL. You rename duplicate ID columns in the query, and because you rename them to BID_ID and USER_ID, a custom result mapping is necessary:

PATH: /model/src/main/java/org/jpwh/model/customsql/Bid.java

```
@SqlResultSetMappings({
    @SqlResultSetMapping(
        name = "BidBidderResult",
        entities = {
            @EntityResult(
                entityClass = Bid.class,
                fields = {
                    @FieldResult(name = "id", column = "BID_ID"),
                    @FieldResult(name = "amount", column = "AMOUNT"),
                    @FieldResult(name = "item", column = "ITEM_ID"),
                    @FieldResult(name = "bidder", column = "BIDDER_ID")
                }
            ),
            @EntityResult(
                entityClass = User.class,
                fields = {
                    @FieldResult(name = "id", column = "USER_ID"),
                    @FieldResult(name = "username", column = "USERNAME"),
                    @FieldResult(name = "activated", column = "ACTIVATED")
                }
            )
        }
    )
})
@Entity
public class Bid {
    // ...
}
```

Hibernate executes this custom SQL query and maps the result when loading an instance of the Bid class, either through em.find(Bid.class, BID_ID) or when it has to initialize a Bid proxy. Hibernate loads the Bid#bidder right away and overrides the FetchType.LAZY setting on the association.

You've now customized Hibernate operations with your own SQL statements. Let's continue with stored procedures and explore the options for integrating them into your Hibernate application.

17.4 Calling stored procedures

Stored procedures are common in database application development. Moving code closer to the data and executing it inside the database has distinct advantages. You end up not duplicating functionality and logic in each program that accesses the data. A different point of view is that a lot of business logic shouldn't be duplicated, so it can be applied all the time. This includes procedures that guarantee the integrity of the data: for example, constraints that are too complex to implement declaratively. You'll usually also find triggers in a database that contain procedural integrity rules.

Stored procedures have advantages for all processing on large amounts of data, such as reporting and statistical analysis. You should always try to avoid moving large data sets on your network and between your database and application servers, so a stored procedure is the natural choice for mass data operations.

There are of course (legacy) systems that implement even the most basic CRUD operations with stored procedures. In a variation on this theme, some systems don't allow any direct use of SQL INSERT, UPDATE, or DELETE, but only stored procedure calls; these systems also had (and sometimes still have) their place.

In some DBMSs, you can declare user-defined functions, in addition to, or instead of, stored procedures. The summary in table 17.1 shows some of the differences between procedures and functions.

Table 17.1 Comparing database procedures and functions

Stored procedure	Function
May have input and/or output parameters	May have input parameters
Returns zero, a single, or multiple values	Must return a value (although the value may not be scalar or even NULL)
Can only be called directly with JDBC CallableStatement	Can be called directly or inside a SELECT, WHERE, or other clauses of a CRUD statement

It's difficult to generalize and compare procedures and functions beyond these obvious differences. This is one area where DBMS support differs widely; some DBMSs don't support stored procedures or user-defined functions, whereas others roll both into one (for example, PostgreSQL has only user-defined functions). Programming languages for stored procedures are usually proprietary. Some databases even support stored procedures written in Java. Standardizing Java stored procedures was part of the SQLJ effort, which unfortunately hasn't been successful.

In this section, we show you how to integrate Hibernate with MySQL stored procedures and PostgreSQL user-defined functions. First, we look at defining and calling stored procedures with the standardized Java Persistence API and the native Hibernate API. Then, we customize and replace Hibernate CRUD operations with procedure calls. It's important that you read the previous sections before this one, because the integration of stored procedures relies on the same mapping options as other SQL customization in Hibernate.

As before in this chapter, the actual SQL stored procedures we cover in the examples are trivial so you can focus on the more important parts—how to call the procedures and use the API in your application.

When calling a stored procedure, you typically want to provide input and receive the output of the procedure. You can distinguish between procedures that

- Return a result set
- Return multiple result sets
- Update data and return the count of updated rows
- Accept input and/or output parameters
- Return a cursor, referencing a result in the database

Let's start with the simplest case: a stored procedure that doesn't have any parameters and only returns data in a result set.

17.4.1 *Returning a result set*

You can create the following procedure in MySQL. It returns a result set containing all rows of the ITEM table:

> **PATH:** **/model/src/main/resources/querying/StoredProcedures.hbm.xml**

```
create procedure FIND_ITEMS()
begin
    select * from ITEM;
end
```

Using an EntityManager, build a StoredProcedureQuery and execute it:

> **PATH:/examples/src/test/java/org/jpwh/test/querying/sql/**
> **CallStoredProcedures.java**

```
StoredProcedureQuery query = em.createStoredProcedureQuery(
    "FIND_ITEMS",
    Item.class                          ⟵── Or name of result-set mapping
);

List<Item> result = query.getResultList();
for (Item item : result) {
    // ...
}
```

As you've previously seen in this chapter, Hibernate automatically maps the columns returned in the result set to properties of the Item class. The Item instances returned by this query will be managed and in persistent state. To customize the mapping of returned columns, provide the name of a result-set mapping instead of the Item .class parameter.

Hibernate Feature

Using the Hibernate native API on a Session, you get the outputs of a Procedure-Call:

> **PATH:/examples/src/test/java/org/jpwh/test/querying/sql/**
> **CallStoredProcedures.java**

```
org.hibernate.procedure.ProcedureCall call =
    session.createStoredProcedureCall("FIND_ITEMS", Item.class);

org.hibernate.result.ResultSetOutput resultSetOutput =
    (org.hibernate.result.ResultSetOutput) call.getOutputs().getCurrent();

List<Item> result = resultSetOutput.getResultList();
```

The Hibernate `getCurrent()` method already indicates that a procedure may return more than a single `ResultSet`. A procedure may return multiple result sets and even return update counts if it modified data.

17.4.2 *Returning multiple results and update counts*

The following MySQL procedure returns all rows of the `ITEM` table that weren't approved and all rows that were already approved, and also sets the `APPROVED` flag for these rows:

> PATH: **/model/src/main/resources/querying/StoredProcedures.hbm.xml**

```
create procedure APPROVE_ITEMS()
begin
    select * from ITEM where APPROVED = 0;
    select * from ITEM where APPROVED = 1;
    update ITEM set APPROVED = 1 where APPROVED = 0;
end
```

In the application, you get two result sets and an update count. Accessing and processing the results of a procedure call is a bit more involved, but JPA is closely aligned to plain JDBC, so this kind of code should be familiar if you've worked with stored procedures:

> PATH: **/examples/src/test/java/org/jpwh/test/querying/sql/**
>   **CallStoredProcedures.java**

```
StoredProcedureQuery query = em.createStoredProcedureQuery(
    "APPROVE_ITEMS",
    Item.class                              ⟵——— Or name of result-set mapping
);

boolean isCurrentReturnResultSet = query.execute();   ⟵——❶ Calls execute()
while (true) {
    if (isCurrentReturnResultSet) {          ⟵——❸ Processes result sets
        List<Item> result = query.getResultList();
        // ...
    } else {                                          No more update
        int updateCount = query.getUpdateCount();  ⟵—┘ counts: exit the loop
        if (updateCount > -1) {
            // ...
        } else {
            break;                            ⟵——❹ Processes update counts
        }
    }
                                                     ❺ Advances to
    isCurrentReturnResultSet = query.hasMoreResults();  ⟵—┘ next result
}
```

Processes results ❷

❶ Execute the procedure call with `execute()`. This method returns `true` if the first result of the call is a result set and `false` if the first result is an update count.

❷ Process all results of the call in a loop. Stop looping when no more results are available, which is always indicated by hasMoreResults() returning false and getUpdate-Count() returning -1.

❸ If the current result is a result set, read and process it. Hibernate maps the columns in each result set to managed instances of the Item class. Alternatively, provide a result-set mapping name applicable to all result sets returned by the call.

❹ If the current result is an update count, getUpdateCount() returns a value greater than -1.

❺ hasMoreResults() advances to the next result and indicates the type of that result.

Hibernate Feature

The alternative—procedure execution with the Hibernate API—may seem more straightforward. It hides some of the complexity of testing the type of each result and whether there is more procedure output to process:

> **PATH:** **/examples/src/test/java/org/jpwh/test/querying/sql/**
> **CallStoredProcedures.java**

```
org.hibernate.procedure.ProcedureCall call =
    session.createStoredProcedureCall("APPROVE_ITEMS", Item.class);

org.hibernate.procedure.ProcedureOutputs callOutputs = call.getOutputs();

org.hibernate.result.Output output;
while ((output = callOutputs.getCurrent()) != null) {          ❶ Checks for
    if (output.isResultSet()) {                                    more outputs
        List<Item> result =
            ((org.hibernate.result.ResultSetOutput) output)     ❷ Is output a
                .getResultList();                                    result set?
        // ...
    } else {                                     ❸ Output is an update count.
        int updateCount =
            ((org.hibernate.result.UpdateCountOutput) output)
                .getUpdateCount();
        // ...
    }
    if (!callOutputs.goToNext())          ❹ Continues
        break;
}
```

❶ As long as getCurrent() doesn't return null, there are more outputs to process.

❷ An output may be a result set: test and cast it.

❸ If an output isn't a result set, it's an update count.

❹ Proceed with the next output, if any.

Next, we consider stored procedures with input and output parameters.

17.4.3   *Setting input and output parameters*

The following MySQL procedure returns a row for the given identifier from the ITEM table, as well as the total number of items:

> **PATH: /model/src/main/resources/querying/StoredProcedures.hbm.xml**

```
create procedure FIND_ITEM_TOTAL(in PARAM_ITEM_ID bigint,
                                 out PARAM_TOTAL bigint)
begin
    select count(*) into PARAM_TOTAL from ITEM;
    select * from ITEM where ID = PARAM_ITEM_ID;
end
```

This next procedure returns a result set with the data of the ITEM row. Additionally, the output parameter PARAM_TOTAL is set. To call this procedure in JPA, you must first register all parameters:

> **PATH: /examples/src/test/java/org/jpwh/test/querying/sql/
>   CallStoredProcedures.java**

```
StoredProcedureQuery query = em.createStoredProcedureQuery(
    "FIND_ITEM_TOTAL",
    Item.class                                            Registers      ❶
);                                                        parameters

query.registerStoredProcedureParameter(1, Long.class, ParameterMode.IN);
query.registerStoredProcedureParameter(2, Long.class, ParameterMode.OUT);

query.setParameter(1, ITEM_ID);              ◁——❷ Binds parameter values

List<Item> result = query.getResultList();   ◁——❸ Retrieves results
for (Item item : result) {
    // ...                                       Accesses parameter values  ❹
}

Long totalNumberOfItems = (Long) query.getOutputParameterValue(2);   ◁—┘
```

❶ Register all parameters by position (starting at 1) and their type.

❷ Bind values to the input parameters.

❸ Retrieve the result set returned by the procedure.

❹ After you've retrieved the result sets, you can access the output parameter values.

You can also register and use named parameters, but you can't mix named and positional parameters in a particular call. Also, note that any parameter names you choose in your Java code don't have to match the names of the parameters in your stored procedure declaration. Ultimately, you must register the parameters in the same order as declared in the signature of the procedure.

Hibernate Feature

The native Hibernate API simplifies parameter registration and usage:

```
PATH:  /examples/src/test/java/org/jpwh/test/querying/sql/
       CallStoredProcedures.java
```

Registers parameters ❶

```
org.hibernate.procedure.ProcedureCall call =
    session.createStoredProcedureCall("FIND_ITEM_TOTAL", Item.class);

call.registerParameter(1, Long.class, ParameterMode.IN)
    .bindValue(ITEM_ID);

ParameterRegistration<Long> totalParameter =
    call.registerParameter(2, Long.class, ParameterMode.OUT);

org.hibernate.procedure.ProcedureOutputs callOutputs = call.getOutputs();

org.hibernate.result.Output output;
while ((output = callOutputs.getCurrent()) != null) {
    if (output.isResultSet()) {
        org.hibernate.result.ResultSetOutput resultSetOutput =
            (org.hibernate.result.ResultSetOutput) output;
        List<Item> result = resultSetOutput.getResultList();
        for (Item item : result) {
            // ...
        }
    }
    if (!callOutputs.goToNext())
        break;
}
Long totalNumberOfItems =
    callOutputs.getOutputParameterValue(totalParameter);
```

❷ **Gets registrations**

❸ **Processes result sets**

❹ **Accesses parameter values**

❶ Register all parameters; you can bind input values directly.

❷ Output parameter registrations can be reused later to read the output value.

❸ Process all returned result sets before you access any output parameters.

❹ Access the output parameter value through the registration.

The following MySQL procedure uses input parameters to update a row in the ITEM table with a new item name:

```
PATH:  /model/src/main/resources/querying/StoredProcedures.hbm.xml
```

```
create procedure UPDATE_ITEM(in PARAM_ITEM_ID bigint,
                            in PARAM_NAME varchar(255))
begin
    update ITEM set NAME = PARAM_NAME where ID = PARAM_ITEM_ID;
end
```

No result sets are returned by this procedure, so execution is simple, and you only get an update count:

> PATH: /examples/src/test/java/org/jpwh/test/querying/sql/
>   CallStoredProcedures.java

```
StoredProcedureQuery query = em.createStoredProcedureQuery(
    "UPDATE_ITEM"
);

query.registerStoredProcedureParameter("itemId", Long.class,
    ParameterMode.IN);
query.registerStoredProcedureParameter("name", String.class,
    ParameterMode.IN);
query.setParameter("itemId", ITEM_ID);
query.setParameter("name", "New Item Name");

assertEquals(query.executeUpdate(), 1);              ◁—— Update count is 1

// Alternative:
// assertFalse(query.execute());                     ◁—— First result is NOT a result set
// assertEquals(query.getUpdateCount(), 1);
```

In this example, you can also see how named parameters work and that names in the Java code don't have to match names in the stored procedure declaration. The order of parameter registrations is still important, though; PARAM_ITEM_ID must be first, and PARAM_ITEM_NAME must be second.

Hibernate Feature

A shortcut for calling procedures that don't return a result set but modify data is executeUpdate(): its return value is your update count. Alternatively, you can execute() the procedure and call getUpdateCount().

This is the same procedure execution using the Hibernate API:

> PATH: /examples/src/test/java/org/jpwh/test/querying/sql/
>   CallStoredProcedures.java

```
org.hibernate.procedure.ProcedureCall call =
    session.createStoredProcedureCall("UPDATE_ITEM");

call.registerParameter(1, Long.class, ParameterMode.IN)
    .bindValue(ITEM_ID);

call.registerParameter(2, String.class, ParameterMode.IN)
    .bindValue("New Item Name");

org.hibernate.result.UpdateCountOutput updateCountOutput =
    (org.hibernate.result.UpdateCountOutput) call.getOutputs().getCurrent();

assertEquals(updateCountOutput.getUpdateCount(), 1);
```

Because you know there is no result set returned by this procedure, you can directly cast the first (current) output to UpdateCountOutput.

Next, instead of returning a result set, we see procedures that return a cursor reference.

17.4.4 *Returning a cursor*

MySQL doesn't support returning cursors from stored procedures. The following example only works on PostgreSQL. This stored procedure (or, because this is the same in PostgreSQL, this user-defined function) returns a cursor to all rows of the ITEM table:

PATH: /model/src/main/resources/querying/StoredProcedures.hbm.xml

```
create function FIND_ITEMS() returns refcursor as $$
    declare someCursor refcursor;
    begin
        open someCursor for select * from ITEM;
        return someCursor;
    end;
$$ language plpgsql;
```

JPA always registers cursor results as parameters, using the special ParameterMode .REF_CURSOR:

**PATH: /examples/src/test/java/org/jpwh/test/querying/sql/
        CallStoredProcedures.java**

```
StoredProcedureQuery query = em.createStoredProcedureQuery(
    "FIND_ITEMS",
    Item.class
);

query.registerStoredProcedureParameter(
    1,
    void.class,
    ParameterMode.REF_CURSOR
);
List<Item> result = query.getResultList();
for (Item item : result) {
    // ...
}
```

The type of the parameter is void, because its only purpose is to prepare the call internally for reading data with the cursor. When you call getResultList(), Hibernate knows how to get the desired output.

The Hibernate API also offers automatic handling of cursor output parameters:

> **PATH:** /examples/src/test/java/org/jpwh/test/querying/sql/
>   CallStoredProcedures.java

```
org.hibernate.procedure.ProcedureCall call =
    session.createStoredProcedureCall("FIND_ITEMS", Item.class);

call.registerParameter(1, void.class, ParameterMode.REF_CURSOR);

org.hibernate.result.ResultSetOutput resultSetOutput =
    (org.hibernate.result.ResultSetOutput) call.getOutputs().getCurrent();

List<Item> result = resultSetOutput.getResultList();
for (Item item : result) {
    // ...
}
```

Scrolling stored procedure cursors

In section 14.3.3, we discussed how to use a database cursor to *scroll* through a potentially large result set. Unfortunately, at the time of writing, this feature isn't available for stored procedure calls in JPA or in the Hibernate API. Hibernate will always retrieve in memory the result set represented by the stored procedure cursor reference.

Supporting database cursors across DBMS dialects is difficult, and Hibernate has some limitations. For example, with PostgreSQL, a cursor parameter must always be the first registered parameter, and (because it's a function) only one cursor should be returned by the database. With the PostgreSQL dialect, Hibernate doesn't support named parameter binding if a cursor return is involved: you must use positional parameter binding. Consult your Hibernate SQL dialect for more information; the relevant methods are `Dialect#getResultSet(CallableStatement)` and so on.

This completes our discussion of APIs for direct stored procedure calls. Next, you can also use stored procedures to override the statements generated by Hibernate when it loads or stores data.

17.5   *Using stored procedures for CRUD*

The first customized CRUD operation you write loads an entity instance of the User class. Previously in this chapter, you used a native SQL query with a loader to implement this requirement. If you have to call a stored procedure to load an instance of User, the process is equally straightforward.

17.5.1 *Custom loader with a procedure*

First, write a named query that calls a stored procedure—for example, in annotations on the User class:

> **PATH:** /model/src/main/java/org/jpwh/model/customsql/procedures/User.java

```
@NamedNativeQueries({
    @NamedNativeQuery(
        name = "findUserById",
        query = "{call FIND_USER_BY_ID(?)}",
        resultClass = User.class
    )
})
@org.hibernate.annotations.Loader(
    namedQuery = "findUserById"
)
@Entity
@Table(name = "USERS")
public class User {
    // ...
}
```

Compare this with the previous customization in section 17.3.1: the declaration of the loader is still the same, and it relies on a defined named query in any supported language. You've only changed the named query, which you can also move into an XML metadata file to further isolate and separate this concern.

JPA doesn't standardize what goes into a @NamedNativeQuery, you're free to write any SQL statement. With the JDBC escape syntax in curly braces, you're saying, "Let the JDBC driver figure out what to do here." If your JDBC driver and DBMS understand stored procedures, you can invoke a procedure with {call PROCEDURE}. Hibernate expects that the procedure will return a result set, and the first row in the result set is expected to have the columns necessary to construct a User instance. We listed the required columns and properties earlier, in section 17.3.1. Also remember that you can always apply a result-set mapping if the column (names) returned by your procedure aren't quite right or you can't change the procedure code.

The stored procedure must have a signature matching the call with a single argument. Hibernate sets this identifier argument when loading an instance of User. Here's an example of a stored procedure on MySQL with such a signature:

> **PATH:** /model/src/main/resources/customsql/CRUDProcedures.hbm.xml

```
create procedure FIND_USER_BY_ID(in PARAM_USER_ID bigint)
begin
    select * from USERS where ID = PARAM_USER_ID;
end
```

Next, we map creating, updating, and deleting a User to a stored procedure.

17.5.2 *Procedures for CUD*

You use the Hibernate annotations @SQLInsert, @SQLUpdate, and @SQLDelete to customize how Hibernate creates, updates, and deletes an entity instance in the database. Instead of a custom SQL statement, you can call a stored procedure to perform the operation:

PATH: /model/src/main/java/org/jpwh/model/customsql/procedures/User.java

```java
@org.hibernate.annotations.SQLInsert(
    sql = "{call INSERT_USER(?, ?, ?)}",
    callable = true
)
@org.hibernate.annotations.SQLUpdate(
    sql = "{call UPDATE_USER(?, ?, ?)}",
    callable = true,
    check = ResultCheckStyle.NONE
)
@org.hibernate.annotations.SQLDelete(
    sql = "{call DELETE_USER(?)}",
    callable = true
)
@Entity
@Table(name = "USERS")
public class User {
    // ...
}
```

You have to indicate that Hibernate must execute an operation with a JDBC Callable-Statement instead of a PreparedStatement; hence set the callable=true option.

As explained in section 17.3.2, argument binding for procedure calls is only possible with positional parameters, and you must declare them in the order Hibernate expects. Your stored procedures must have a matching signature. Here are some procedure examples for MySQL that insert, update, and delete a row in the USERS table:

PATH: /model/src/main/resources/customsql/CRUDProcedures.hbm.xml

```sql
create procedure INSERT_USER(in PARAM_ACTIVATED bit,
                            in PARAM_USERNAME varchar(255),
                            in PARAM_ID bigint)
begin
    insert into USERS (ACTIVATED, USERNAME, ID)
        values (PARAM_ACTIVATED, PARAM_USERNAME, PARAM_ID);
end
```

PATH: /model/src/main/resources/customsql/CRUDProcedures.hbm.xml

```sql
create procedure UPDATE_USER(in PARAM_ACTIVATED bit,
                            in PARAM_USERNAME varchar(255),
                            in PARAM_ID bigint)
begin
    update USERS set
```

```
        ACTIVATED = PARAM_ACTIVATED,
        USERNAME = PARAM_USERNAME
    where ID = PARAM_ID;
end
```

PATH: /model/src/main/resources/customsql/CRUDProcedures.hbm.xml

```
create procedure DELETE_USER(in PARAM_ID bigint)
begin
    delete from USERS where ID = PARAM_ID;
end
```

When a stored procedure inserts, updates, or deletes an instance of `User`, Hibernate has to know whether the call was successful. Usually, for dynamically generated SQL, Hibernate looks at the number of updated rows returned from an operation. If you enabled versioning (see section 11.2.2), and the operation didn't or couldn't update any rows, an optimistic locking failure occurs. If you write your own SQL, you can customize this behavior as well. It's up to the stored procedure to perform the version check against the database state when updating or deleting rows. With the `check` option in your annotations, you can let Hibernate know how the procedure will implement this requirement.

The default is `ResultCheckStyle.NONE`, and the following settings are available:

- `NONE`—The procedure will throw an exception if the operation fails. Hibernate doesn't perform any explicit checks but instead relies on the procedure code to do the right thing. If you enable versioning, your procedure must compare/increment versions and throw an exception if it detects a version mismatch.
- `COUNT`—The procedure will perform any required version increments and checks and return the number of updated rows to Hibernate as an update count. Hibernate uses `CallableStatement#getUpdateCount()` to access the result.
- `PARAM`—The procedure will perform any required version increments and checks and return the number of updated rows to Hibernate in its first output parameter. For this check style, you need to add an additional question mark to your call and, in your stored procedure, return the row count of your DML operation in this (first) output parameter. Hibernate automatically registers the parameter and reads its value when the call completes.

Availability of ResultCheckStyle options
At the time of writing, Hibernate only implements `ResultCheckStyle.NONE`.

Finally, remember that stored procedures and functions sometimes can't be mapped in Hibernate. In such cases, you have to fall back to plain JDBC. Sometimes you can wrap a legacy stored procedure with another stored procedure that has the parameter interface Hibernate expects.

17.6   *Summary*

- You saw how to fall back to the JDBC API when necessary. Even for custom SQL queries, Hibernate can do the heavy lifting and transform the ResultSet into instances of your domain model classes, with flexible mapping options, including customizing result mapping. You can also externalize native queries for a cleaner setup.

- We discussed how to override and provide your own SQL statements for regular create, read, update, and delete (CRUD) operations, as well as for collection operations.

- You can enable custom loaders and use eager fetching in such loaders.

- You learned how to call database stored procedures directly and integrate them into Hibernate. You explored processing a single result set as well as multiple result sets and update counts. You set stored procedure (input and output) parameters and learned how to return a database cursor. You also saw how to use stored procedures for CRUD.

Part 5

Building applications

In part 5, the last part of this book, we'll discuss the design and implementation of layered and conversation-aware Java database applications. We'll discuss the most common design patterns used with Hibernate, such as the Data Access Object (DAO). You'll see how you can test your Hibernate application easily and what other best practices are relevant if you work with ORM software in web and client/server applications in general.

Chapter 18 is all about designing client/server applications. You'll learn patterns for client/server architecture, write and test a persistence layer, and integrate EJBs with JPA. In chapter 19, we'll look at building web applications and integrating JPA with CDI and JSF. We'll cover browsing data in tables, implementing long-running conversations, and customizing entity serialization. Finally, in chapter 20, we'll look at scaling Hibernate by performing bulk and batch data operations, and improving scalability with the shared cache.

After reading this part, you'll have gathered the architectural-level knowledge to put together an application and let it scale as it succeeds.

18

Designing client/server applications

Most JPA developers build client/server applications with a Java-based server accessing the database tier through Hibernate. Knowing how the EntityManager and system transactions work, you could probably come up with your own server architecture. You'd have to figure out where to create the EntityManager, when and how to close it, and how to set transaction boundaries.

You may be wondering what the relationship is between requests and responses from and to your client, and the persistence context and transactions on the server. Should a single system transaction handle each client request? Can several consecutive requests hold a persistence context open? How does detached entity state fit into this picture? Can you and should you serialize entity data between client and server? How will these decisions affect your client design?

Before we start answering these questions, we have to mention that we won't talk about any specific frameworks besides JPA and EJB in this chapter. There are several reasons the code examples use EJBs in addition to JPA:

- Our goal is to focus on client/server design patterns with JPA. Many cross-cutting concerns, such as data serialization between client and server, are standardized in EJB, so we don't have to solve every problem immediately. We know you probably won't write an EJB client application. With the example EJB client code in this chapter, though, you'll have the foundation to make informed decisions when choosing and working with a different framework. We'll discuss custom serialization procedures in the next chapter and explain how to exchange your JPA-managed data with any client.
- We can't possibly cover every combination of client/server frameworks in the Java space. Note that we haven't even narrowed our scope to web server applications. Of course, web applications are important, so we'll dedicate the next chapter to JPA with JSF and JAX-RS. In this chapter, we're concerned with any client/server system relying on JPA for persistence, and abstractions like the *DAO pattern*, which are useful no matter what frameworks you use.
- EJBs are effective even if you only use them on the server side. They offer transaction management, and you can bind the persistence context to stateful session beans. We'll discuss these details as well, so if your application architecture calls for EJBs on the server side, you'll know how to build them.

Throughout this chapter, you implement two simple use cases with straightforward workflows as an actual working application: editing an auction item, and placing bids for an item. First we look at the persistence layer and how you can encapsulate JPA operations into reusable components: in particular, using the *DAO pattern*. This will give you a solid foundation to build more application functionality.

Then you implement the use cases as *conversations*: units of work from the perspective of your application users. You see the code for *stateless* and *stateful* server-side components and the impact this has on client design and overall application architecture. This affects not only the behavior of your application but also its scalability and robustness. We repeat all the examples with both strategies and highlight the differences.

Let's start with fleshing out a persistence layer and the DAO pattern.

18.1   *Creating a persistence layer*

In section 3.1.1, we introduced the encapsulation of persistence code in a separate layer. Although JPA already provides a certain level of abstraction, there are several reasons you should consider hiding JPA calls behind a facade:

- A custom persistence layer can provide a higher level of abstraction for data-access operations. Instead of basic CRUD and query operations as exposed by the `EntityManager`, you can expose higher-level operations, such as `get-MaximumBid(Item i)` and `findItems(User soldBy)` methods. This abstraction is the primary reason to create a persistence layer in larger applications: to support reuse of the same data-access operations.

- The persistence layer can have a generic interface without exposing implementation details. In other words, you can hide the fact that you're using Hibernate (or Java Persistence) to implement the data-access operations from any client of the persistence layer. We consider persistence-layer portability an unimportant concern because full object/relational mapping solutions like Hibernate already provide database portability. It's highly unlikely that you'll rewrite your persistence layer with different software in the future and still not want to change any client code. Furthermore, Java Persistence is a standardized and fully portable API; there is little harm in occasionally exposing it to clients of the persistence layer.

The persistence layer can unify data-access operations. This concern relates to portability, but from a slightly different angle. Imagine that you have to deal with mixed data-access code, such as JPA and JDBC operations. By unifying the facade that clients see and use, you can hide this implementation detail from the client. If you have to deal with different types of data stores, this is a valid reason to write a persistence layer.

If you consider portability and unification to be side effects of creating a persistence layer, your primary motivation is achieving a higher level of abstraction and improve the maintainability and reuse of data-access code. These are good reasons, and we encourage you to create a persistence layer with a generic facade in all but the simplest applications. But always first consider using JPA directly without any additional layering. Keep it as simple as possible, and create a lean persistence layer on top of JPA when you realize you're duplicating the same query and persistence operations.

Many tools available claim to simplify creating a persistence layer for JPA or Hibernate. We recommend that you try to work without such tools first, and only buy into a product when you need a particular feature. Be especially wary of code and query generators: the frequently heard claims of a holistic solution to every problem, in the long term, can become a significant restriction and maintenance burden. There can also be a huge impact on productivity if the development process depends on running a code-generation tool. This is of course also true for Hibernate's own tools: for example, if you have to generate the entity class source from an SQL schema every time you make a change. The persistence layer is an important part of your application, and you must be aware of the commitment you're making by introducing additional dependencies. You see in this chapter and the next how to avoid the repetitive code often associated with persistence-layer components without using any additional tools.

There is more than one way to design a persistence layer facade—some small applications have a single `DataAccess` class; others mix data-access operations into domain classes (the Active Record pattern, not discussed in this book)—but we prefer the DAO pattern.

18.1.1 A generic data access object pattern

The DAO design pattern originated in Sun's Java Blueprints more than 15 years ago; it's had a long history. A DAO class defines an interface to persistence operations relating to a particular entity; it advises you to group together code that relates to the persistence of that entity. Given its age, there are many variations of the DAO pattern. The basic structure of our recommended design is shown in figure 18.1.

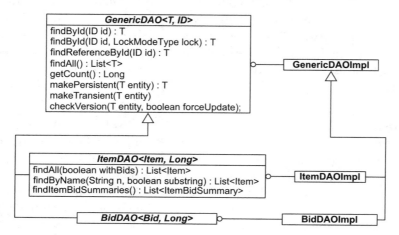

Figure 18.1   Generic DAO interfaces support arbitrary implementations.

We designed the persistence layer with two parallel hierarchies: interfaces on one side, implementations on the other. The basic instance-storage and -retrieval operations are grouped in a generic super-interface and a superclass that implements these operations with a particular persistence solution (using Hibernate, of course). The generic interface is extended by interfaces for particular entities that require additional business-related data-access operations. Again, you may have one or several implementations of an entity DAO interface.

Let's quickly look at some of the interfaces and methods shown in this illustration. There are a bunch of *finder* methods. These typically return managed (in persistent state) entity instances, but they may also return arbitrary data-transfer objects such as ItemBidSummary. Finder methods are your biggest code duplication issue; you may end up with dozens if you don't plan carefully. The first step is to try to make them as generic as possible and move them up in the hierarchy, ideally into the top-level interface. Consider the findByName() method in the ItemDAO: you'll probably have to add more options for item searches soon, or you may want the result presorted by the database, or you may implement some kind of paging feature. We'll elaborate on this again later and show you a generic solution for sorting and paging in section 19.2.

The methods offered by the DAO API indicate clearly that this is a *state-managing* persistence layer. Methods such as makePersistent() and makeTransient() change an entity instance's state (or the state of many instances at once, with cascading enabled). A client can expect that updates are executed automatically (flushed) by the persistence engine when an entity instance is modified (there is no `perform-Update()` method). You'd write a completely different DAO interface if your persistence layer were statement-oriented: for example, if you weren't using Hibernate to implement it, but rather only plain JDBC.

The persistence layer facade we introduce here doesn't expose any Hibernate or Java Persistence interface to the client, so theoretically you can implement it with any software without making changes to the client code. You may not want or need persistence-layer portability, as explained earlier. In that case, you should consider exposing Hibernate or Java Persistence interfaces—for example, you could allow clients to access the JPA `CriteriaBuilder` and then have a generic `findBy(CriteriaQuery)` method. This decision is up to you; you may decide that exposing Java Persistence interfaces is a safer choice than exposing Hibernate interfaces. You should know, however, that although it's possible to change the implementation of the persistence layer from one JPA provider to another, it's almost impossible to rewrite a persistence layer that is state-oriented with plain JDBC statements.

Next, you implement the DAO interfaces.

18.1.2 *Implementing the generic interface*

Let's continue with a possible implementation of the `GenericDAO` interface:

> **PATH: /apps/app-model/src/main/java/org/jpwh/dao/GenericDAOImpl.java**

```
public abstract class GenericDAOImpl<T, ID extends Serializable>
    implements GenericDAO<T, ID> {

  @PersistenceContext
  protected EntityManager em;

  protected final Class<T> entityClass;

  protected GenericDAOImpl(Class<T> entityClass) {
    this.entityClass = entityClass;
  }
  public void setEntityManager(EntityManager em) {
    this.em = em;
  }

    // ...

}
```

This generic implementation needs two things to work: an `EntityManager` and an entity class. A subclass must provide the entity class as a constructor argument. The `EntityManager`, however, can be provided either by a runtime container that understands the `@PersistenceContext` injection annotation (for example, any standard Java EE container) or through `setEntityManager()`.

Next, let's look at the finder methods:

```
PATH:  /apps/app-model/src/main/java/org/jpwh/dao/GenericDAOImpl.java
```

```java
public abstract class GenericDAOImpl<T, ID extends Serializable>
    implements GenericDAO<T, ID> {

    // ...

    public T findById(ID id) {
        return findById(id, LockModeType.NONE);
    }

    public T findById(ID id, LockModeType lockModeType) {
        return em.find(entityClass, id, lockModeType);
    }

    public T findReferenceById(ID id) {
        return em.getReference(entityClass, id);
    }

    public List<T> findAll() {
        CriteriaQuery<T> c =
            em.getCriteriaBuilder().createQuery(entityClass);
        c.select(c.from(entityClass));
        return em.createQuery(c).getResultList();
    }

    public Long getCount() {
        CriteriaQuery<Long> c =
            em.getCriteriaBuilder().createQuery(Long.class);
        c.select(em.getCriteriaBuilder().count(c.from(entityClass)));
        return em.createQuery(c).getSingleResult();
    }

    // ...
}
```

You can see how the code uses the entity class to perform the query operations. We've written some simple criteria queries, but you could use JPQL or SQL.

Finally, here are the state-management operations:

```
PATH:  /apps/app-model/src/main/java/org/jpwh/dao/GenericDAOImpl.java
```

```java
public abstract class GenericDAOImpl<T, ID extends Serializable>
    implements GenericDAO<T, ID> {

    // ...

    public T makePersistent(T instance) {
        // merge() handles transient AND detached instances
        return em.merge(instance);
    }

    public void makeTransient(T instance) {
        em.remove(instance);
    }
```

```
    public void checkVersion(T entity, boolean forceUpdate) {
        em.lock(
            entity,
            forceUpdate
                ? LockModeType.OPTIMISTIC_FORCE_INCREMENT
                : LockModeType.OPTIMISTIC
        );
    }
}
```

An important decision is how you implement the makePersistent() method. Here we've chosen EntityManager#merge() because it's the most versatile. If the given argument is a transient entity instance, merging will return a persistent instance. If the argument is a detached entity instance, merging will also return a persistent instance. This provides clients with a consistent API without worrying about the state of an entity instance before calling makePersistent(). But the client needs to be aware that the returned value of makePersistent() is *always* the current instance and that the argument it has given must now be thrown away (see section 10.3.4).

You've now completed building the basic machinery of the persistence layer and the generic interface it exposes to the upper layer of the system. In the next step, you create entity-related DAO interfaces and implementations by extending the generic interface and implementation.

18.1.3 *Implementing entity DAOs*

Everything you've created so far is abstract and generic—you can't even instantiate GenericDAOImpl. You now implement the ItemDAO interface by extending GenericDAOImpl with a concrete class.

First you must make choices about how callers will access the DAOs. You also need to think about the life cycle of a DAO instance. With the current design, the DAO classes are stateless except for the EntityManager member.

Caller threads can share a DAO instance. In a multithreaded Java EE environment, for example, the automatically injected EntityManager is effectively thread-safe, because internally it's often implemented as a proxy that delegates to some thread- or transaction-bound persistence context. Of course, if you call setEntityManager() on a DAO, that instance can't be shared and should only be used by one (for example, integration/unit test) thread.

An EJB stateless session bean pool would be a good choice, and thread-safe persistence context injection is available if you annotate the concrete ItemDAOImpl as a stateless EJB component:

PATH: /apps/app-model/src/main/java/org/jpwh/dao/ItemDAOImpl.java

```
@Stateless
public class ItemDAOImpl extends GenericDAOImpl<Item, Long>
    implements ItemDAO {
```

```
    public ItemDAOImpl() {
        super(Item.class);
    }

    // ...
}
```

You see in a minute how the EJB container selects the "right" persistence context for injection.

> **Thread-safety of an injected EntityManager**
>
> The Java EE specifications don't document clearly the thread-safety of injected `EntityManager`s with `@PersistenceContext`. The JPA specification states that an `EntityManager` may "only be accessed in a single-threaded manner." This would imply that it can't be injected into inherently multithreaded components such as EJBs, singleton beans, and servlets that, because it's the default, don't run with `Single-ThreadModel`. But the EJB specification requires that the EJB container serializes calls to each stateful and stateless session bean instance. The injected `Entity-Manager` in stateless or stateful EJBs is therefore thread-safe; containers implement this by injecting an `EntityManager` placeholder. Additionally, your application server *might* (it doesn't have to) support thread-safe access to injected `EntityManager`s in a singleton bean or multithreaded servlet. If in doubt, inject the thread-safe `Entity-ManagerFactory`, and then create and close your own application-managed `Entity-Manager` in your component's service methods.

Next are the finder methods defined in `ItemDAO`:

> **PATH:** /apps/app-model/src/main/java/org/jpwh/dao/ItemDAOImpl.java

```
@Stateless
public class ItemDAOImpl extends GenericDAOImpl<Item, Long>
    implements ItemDAO {

    // ...

    @Override
    public List<Item> findAll(boolean withBids) {
        CriteriaBuilder cb = em.getCriteriaBuilder();
        CriteriaQuery<Item> criteria = cb.createQuery(Item.class);
        // ...
        return em.createQuery(criteria).getResultList();
    }

    @Override
    public List<Item> findByName(String name, boolean substring) {
        // ...
    }

    @Override
    public List<ItemBidSummary> findItemBidSummaries() {
        CriteriaBuilder cb = em.getCriteriaBuilder();
```

```
        CriteriaQuery<ItemBidSummary> criteria =
            cb.createQuery(ItemBidSummary.class);
        // ...
        return em.createQuery(criteria).getResultList();
    }
}
```

You shouldn't have any problem writing these queries after reading the previous chapters; they're straightforward: Either use the criteria query APIs or call externalized JPQL queries by name. You should consider the static metamodel for criteria queries, as explained in the section "Using a static metamodel" in chapter 3.

With the `ItemDAO` finished, you can move on to `BidDAO`:

> **PATH:** /apps/app-model/src/main/java/org/jpwh/dao/BidDAOImpl.java

```
@Stateless
public class BidDAOImpl extends GenericDAOImpl<Bid, Long>
    implements BidDAO {

    public BidDAOImpl() {
        super(Bid.class);
    }
}
```

As you can see, this is an empty DAO implementation that only inherits generic methods. In the next section, we discuss some operations you could potentially move into this DAO class. We also haven't shown any `UserDAO` or `CategoryDAO` code and assume that you'll write these DAO interfaces and implementations as needed.

Our next topic is testing this persistence layer: Should you, and if so, how?

18.1.4 *Testing the persistence layer*

We've pulled almost all the examples in this book so far directly from actual test code. We continue to do so in all future examples, but we have to ask: should you write tests for the persistence layer to validate its functionality?

In our experience, it doesn't usually make sense to test the persistence layer separately. You could instantiate your domain DAO classes and provide a mock `EntityManager`. Such a unit test would be of limited value and quite a lot of work to write. Instead, we recommend that you create *integration* tests, which test a larger part of the application stack and involve the database system. All the rest of the examples in this chapter are from such integration tests; they simulate a client calling the server application, with an actual database back end. Hence, you're testing what's important: the correct behavior of your services, the business logic of the domain model they rely on, and database access through your DAOs, all together.

The problem then is preparing such integration tests. You want to test in a real Java EE environment, in the actual runtime container. For this, we use *Arquillian* (http://arquillian.org), a tool that integrates with TestNG. With Arquillian, you prepare a virtual archive in your test code and then execute it on a real application server. Look at the examples to see how this works.

A more interesting problem is preparing test data for integration tests. Most meaningful tests require that *some* data exists in the database. You want to load that test data into the database before your test runs, and each test should work with a clean and well-defined data set so you can write reliable assertions.

Based on our experience, here are three common techniques to import test data:

- Your test fixture executes a method before every test to obtain an Entity-Manager. You manually instantiate your test data entities and persist them with the EntityManager API. The major advantage of this strategy is that you test quite a few of your mappings as a side effect. Another advantage is easy programmatic access to test data. For example, if you need the identifier value of a particular test Item in your test code, it's already there in Java because you can pass it back from your data-import method. The disadvantage is that test data can be hard to maintain, because Java code isn't a great data format. You can clear test data from the database by dropping and re-creating the schema after every test using Hibernate's schema-export feature. All integration tests in this book so far have used this approach; you can find the test data-import procedure next to each test in the example code.

- Arquillian can execute a DbUnit (http://dbunit.sourceforge.net) data-set import before every test run. DbUnit offers several formats for writing data sets, including the commonly used flat XML syntax. This isn't the most compact format but is easy to read and maintain. The examples in this chapter use this approach. You can find Arquillian's @UsingDataSet on the test classes with a path to the XML file to import. Hibernate generates and drops the SQL schema, and Arquillian, with the help of DbUnit, loads the test data into the database. If you like to keep your test data independent of tests, this may be the right approach for you. If you don't use Arquillian, manually importing a data set is pretty easy with DbUnit—see the SampleDataImporter in this chapter's examples. We deploy this importer when running the example applications during development, to have the same data available for interactive use as in automated tests.

- In section 9.1.1, you saw how to execute custom SQL scripts when Hibernate starts. The *load script* executes after Hibernate generates the schema; this is a great utility for importing test data with plain INSERT SQL statements. The examples in the next chapter use this approach. The major advantage is that you can copy/paste the INSERT statements from an SQL console into your test fixture and vice versa. Furthermore, if your database supports the SQL row value constructor syntax, you can write compact multirow insertion statements like insert into MY_TABLE (MY_COLUMN) values (1), (2), (3), ...

We leave it up to you to pick a strategy. This is frequently a matter of taste and how much test data you have to maintain. Note that we're talking about test data for integration tests, not performance or scalability tests. If you need large amounts of (mostly random) test data for load testing, consider data-generation tools such as *Benerator* (http://databene.org/databene-benerator.html).

This completes the first iteration of the persistence layer. You can now obtain `ItemDAO` instances and work with a higher level of abstraction when accessing the database. Let's write a client that calls this persistence layer and implement the rest of the application.

18.2 Building a stateless server

The application will be a stateless server application, which means no application state will be managed on the server between client requests. The application will be simple, in that it supports only two use cases: editing an auction item and placing a bid for an item.

Consider these workflows to be *conversations*: units of work from the perspective of the application user. The point of view of application users isn't necessarily the same that we as developers have on the system; developers usually consider one system transaction to be a unit of work. We now focus on this mismatch and how a user's perspective influences the design of server and client code. We start with the first conversation: editing an item.

18.2.1 Editing an auction item

The client is a trivial text-based EJB console application. Look at the "edit an auction item" user conversation with this client in figure 18.2.

The client presents the user with a list of auction items; the user picks one. Then the client asks which operation the user would like to perform. Finally, after entering a new name, the client shows a success confirmation message. The system is now ready for the next conversation. The example client starts again and presents a list of auction items.

```
>>> Starting dialog, connecting to server (press CTRL+C to exit)...
--------------------------------------------------------------------
ID  | Name                 | Auction End          |   Highest Bid
--------------------------------------------------------------------
1   | Baseball Glove       | 06. Mar 2015 15:00   |          13.00
2   | Aquarium             | 07. Mar 2015 16:00   |              -
3   | Golf GTI             | 08. Mar 2015 09:30   |       30000.00
4   | Blade Runner Bluray  | 09. Mar 2015 10:20   |              -
5   | Coffee Machine       | 10. Mar 2015 14:55   |           6.00
--------------------------------------------------------------------
Please enter an item ID:
1
Would you like to rename (n) the item or place a bid (b):
n
New name for item 'Baseball Glove':
Pretty Baseball Glove
=> Item name changed successfully!
```

Figure 18.2 This conversation is a unit of work from a user's perspective.

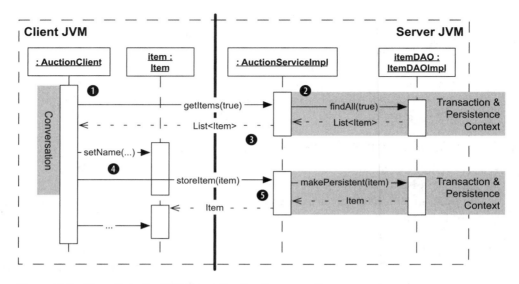

Figure 18.3   The calls in the "Edit an auction item" conversation

The sequence of calls for this conversation is shown in figure 18.3. This is your road map for the rest of the section.

Let's have a closer look at this in code; you can refer to the bullet items in the illustration to keep track of where we are. The code you see next is from a test case simulating the client, followed by code from the server-side components handling these client calls.

The client retrieves a list of Item instances from the server to start the conversation ❶ and also requests with true that the Item#bids collection be eagerly fetched. Because the server doesn't hold the conversation state, the client must do this job:

```
PATH: /apps/app-stateless-server/src/test/java/org/jpwh/test/stateless/
      AuctionServiceTest.java
```

```
List<Item> items;                          ⟵── Client must manage application state: a list of items.

items = service.getItems(true);            ⟵── Get all items in detached state, and load bids.
```

The server-side code handles the call with the help of DAOs:

```
PATH: /apps/app-stateless-server/src/main/java/org/jpwh/stateless/
      AuctionServiceImpl.java
```

```
@javax.ejb.Stateless
@javax.ejb.Local(AuctionService.class)
@javax.ejb.Remote(RemoteAuctionService.class)
public class AuctionServiceImpl implements AuctionService {
```

```
@Inject
protected ItemDAO itemDAO;

@Inject
protected BidDAO bidDAO;

@Override
@TransactionAttribute(TransactionAttributeType.REQUIRED)          <──── Default
public List<Item> getItems(boolean withBids) {
    return itemDAO.findAll(withBids);
}

// ...

}
```

(You can ignore the interfaces declared here; they're trivial but necessary for remote calls and local testing of an EJB.) Because no transaction is active when the client calls getItems(), a new transaction is started. The transaction is committed automatically when the method returns. The @TransactionAttribute annotation is optional in this case; the default behavior requires a transaction on EJB method calls.

The getItems() EJB method calls the ItemDAO to retrieve a List of Item instances ❷. The Java EE container automatically looks up and injects the ItemDAO, and the EntityManager is set on the DAO. Because no EntityManager or persistence context is associated with the current transaction, a new persistence context is started and joined with the transaction. The persistence context is flushed and closed when the transaction commits. This is a convenient feature of stateless EJBs; you don't have to do much to use JPA in a transaction.

A List of Item instances in detached state (after the persistence context is closed) is returned to the client ❸. You don't have to worry about serialization right now; as long as List and Item and all other reachable types are Serializable, the EJB framework takes care of it.

Next, the client sets the new name of a selected Item and asks the server to store that change by sending the detached and modified Item ❹:

> PATH: /apps/app-stateless-server/src/test/java/org/jpwh/test/stateless/
> AuctionServiceTest.java

```
detachedItem.setName("Pretty Baseball Glove");        Call service and make
                                                      change permanent. Current
detachedItem = service.storeItem(detachedItem);  <──┘ Item instance is returned.
```

The server takes the detached Item instance and asks the ItemDAO to make the changes persistent ❺, internally merging modifications:

PATH: /apps/app-stateless-server/src/main/java/org/jpwh/stateless/
      AuctionServiceImpl.java

```java
public class AuctionServiceImpl implements AuctionService {

    // ...

    @Override
    public Item storeItem(Item item) {
        return itemDAO.makePersistent(item);
    }

    // ...
}
```

The updated state—the result of the merge—is returned to the client.

The conversation is complete, and the client may ignore the returned updated Item. But the client knows that this return value is the latest state and that any previous state it was holding during the conversation, such as the List of Item instances, is outdated and should probably be discarded. A subsequent conversation should begin with fresh state: using the latest returned Item, or by obtaining a fresh list.

You've now seen how to implement a single conversation—the entire unit of work, from the user's perspective—with two system transactions on the server. Because you only loaded data in the first system transaction and deferred writing changes to the last transaction, the conversation was atomic: changes aren't permanent until the last step completes successfully. Let's expand on this with the second use case: placing a bid for an item.

18.2.2 Placing a bid

In the console client, a user's "placing a bid" conversation looks like figure 18.4. The client presents the user with a list of auction items again and asks the user to pick one. The user can place a bid and receives a success-confirmation message if the bid was stored successfully. The sequence of calls and the code road map are shown in figure 18.5.

```
>>> Starting dialog, connecting to server (press CTRL+C to exit)...
------------------------------------------------------------------------
ID  | Name                | Auction End         |     Highest Bid
------------------------------------------------------------------------
1   | Baseball Glove      | 06. Mar 2015 15:00  |           13.00
2   | Aquarium            | 07. Mar 2015 16:00  |               -
3   | Golf GTI            | 08. Mar 2015 09:30  |        30000.00
4   | Blade Runner Bluray | 09. Mar 2015 10:20  |               -
5   | Coffee Machine      | 10. Mar 2015 14:55  |            6.00
------------------------------------------------------------------------
Please enter an item ID:
1
Would you like to rename (n) the item or place a bid (b):
b
Your bid for item 'Baseball Glove':
15
=> Bid placed successfully!
```

Figure 18.4   A user placing a bid: a unit of work from the user's perspective

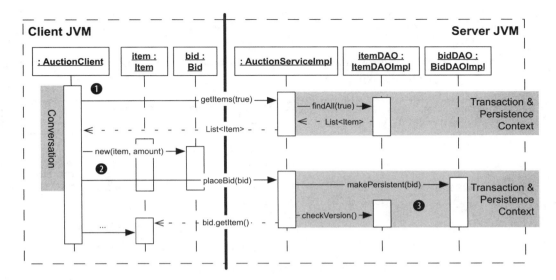

Figure 18.5   The calls in the "Placing a bid" conversation

We again step through the test client and server-side code. First ❶, the client gets a list of `Item` instances and eagerly fetches the `Item#bids` collection. You saw the code for this in the previous section.

Then, the client creates a new `Bid` instance after receiving user input for the amount ❷, linking the new transient `Bid` with the detached selected `Item`. The client has to store the new `Bid` and send it to the server. If you don't document your service API properly, a client may attempt to send the detached `Item`:

> PATH: /apps/app-stateless-server/src/test/java/org/jpwh/test/stateless/
> AuctionServiceTest.java

```
item.getBids().add(newBid);

item = service.storeItem(item);
```
"Maybe this service has cascading persistence on the Item#bids @OneToMany?" Afterward, nothing happens—bid isn't stored.

Here, the client assumes that the server knows it added the new `Bid` to the `Item#bids` collection and that it must be stored. Your server could implement this functionality, maybe with merge cascading enabled on the `@OneToMany` mapping of that collection. Then, the `storeItem()` method of the service would work as in the previous section, taking the `Item` and calling the `ItemDAO` to make it (and its transitive dependencies) persistent.

This isn't the case in this application: the service offers a separate `placeBid()` method. You have to perform additional validation before a bid is stored in the database, such as checking whether it was higher than the last bid. You also want to force an increment of the `Item` version, to prevent concurrent bids. Hence, you document the cascading behavior of your domain model entity associations: Item#bids isn't transitive, and new Bid instances must be stored through the service's placeBid() method exclusively.

The implementation of the placeBid() method on the server takes care of validation and version checking:

> PATH: /apps/app-stateless-server/src/main/java/org/jpwh/stateless/
> AuctionServiceImpl.java

```
public class AuctionServiceImpl implements AuctionService {

    // ...

    @Override
    public Item placeBid(Bid bid) throws InvalidBidException {
        bid = bidDAO.makePersistent(bid);

        if (!bid.getItem().isValidBid(bid))
            throw new InvalidBidException("Bid amount too low!");

        itemDAO.checkVersion(bid.getItem(), true);

        return bid.getItem();
    }
}
```

Checks that business rules are met.

Two interesting things are happening here. First, a transaction is started and spans the placeBid() method call. The nested EJB method calls to ItemDAO and BidDAO are in that same transaction context and inherit the transaction. The same is true for the persistence context: it has the same scope as the transaction ❸. Both DAO classes declare that they need the current @PersistenceContext injected; the runtime container provides the persistence context bound to the current transaction. Transaction and persistence-context creation and propagation with stateless EJBs is straightforward, always "along with the call."

Second, the validation of the new Bid is business logic encapsulated in the domain model classes. The service calls Item#isValid(Bid) and delegates the responsibility for validation to the Item domain model class. Here's how you implement this in the Item class:

> PATH: /apps/app-model/src/main/java/org/jpwh/model/Item.java

```
@Entity
public class Item implements Serializable {
    // ...
    public boolean isValidBid(Bid newBid) {
        Bid highestBid = getHighestBid();
        if (newBid == null)
            return false;
        if (newBid.getAmount().compareTo(new BigDecimal("0")) != 1)
            return false;
        if (highestBid == null)
```

```
            return true;
        if (newBid.getAmount().compareTo(highestBid.getAmount()) == 1)
            return true;
        return false;
    }

    public Bid getHighestBid() {
        return getBids().size() > 0
            ? getBidsHighestFirst().get(0) : null;
    }

    public List<Bid> getBidsHighestFirst() {
        List<Bid> list = new ArrayList<>(getBids());
        Collections.sort(list);
        return list;
    }

    // ...
}
```

The isValid() method performs several checks to find out whether the Bid is higher than the last bid. If your auction system has to support a "lowest bid wins" strategy at some point, all you have to do is change the Item domain-model implementation; the services and DAOs using that class won't know the difference. (Obviously, you'd need a different message for the InvalidBidException.)

What is debatable is the efficiency of the getHighestBid() method. It loads the entire bids collection into memory, sorts it there, and then takes just one Bid. An optimized variation could look like this:

> **PATH:** **/apps/app-model/src/main/java/org/jpwh/model/Item.java**

```
@Entity
public class Item implements Serializable {

    // ...

    public boolean isValidBid(Bid newBid,
                              Bid currentHighestBid,
                              Bid currentLowestBid) {

        // ...
    }

}
```

The service (or controller, if you like) is still completely unaware of any business logic—it doesn't need to know whether a new bid must be higher or lower than the last one. The service implementation must provide the currentHighestBid and currentLowestBid when calling the Item#isValid() method. This is what we hinted at earlier: that you may want to add operations to the BidDAO. You could write database queries to find those bids in the most efficient way possible without loading all the item bids into memory and sorting them there.

The application is now complete. It supports the two use cases you set out to implement. Let's take a step back and analyze the result.

18.2.3 *Analyzing the stateless application*

You've implemented code to support conversations: units of work from the perspective of the users. The users expect to perform a series of steps in a workflow and that each step will be only temporary until they finalize the conversation with the last step. That last step is usually a final request from the client to the server, ending the conversation. This sounds a lot like transactions, but you may have to perform several system transactions on the server to complete a particular conversation. The question is how to provide atomicity across several requests and system transactions.

Conversations by users can be of arbitrary complexity and duration. More than one client request in a conversation's flow may load detached data. Because you're in control of the detached instances on the client, you can easily make a conversation atomic if you don't merge, persist, or remove any entity instances on the server until the final request in your conversation workflow. It's up to you to somehow queue modifications and manage detached data where the list of items is held during user think-time. Just don't call any service operation from the client that makes permanent changes on the server until you're sure you want to "commit" the conversation.

One issue you have to keep an eye on is equality of detached references: for example, if you load several `Item` instances and put them in a `Set` or use them as keys in a `Map`. Because you're then comparing instances outside the guaranteed scope of object identity—the persistence context—you must override the `equals()` and `hashCode()` methods on the `Item` entity class as explained in section 10.3.1. In the trivial conversations with only one detached list of `Item` instances, this wasn't necessary. You never compared them in a `Set`, used them as keys in a `HashMap`, or tested them explicitly for equality.

You should enable versioning of the `Item` entity for multiuser applications, as explained in the section "Enabling versioning" in chapter 11. When entity modifications are merged in `AuctionService#storeItem()`, Hibernate increments the `Item`'s version (it doesn't if the `Item` wasn't modified, though). Hence, if another user has changed the name of an `Item` concurrently, Hibernate will throw an exception when the system transaction is committed and the persistence context is flushed. The first user to commit their conversation always wins with this optimistic strategy. The second user should be shown the usual error message: "Sorry, someone else modified the same data; please restart your conversation."

What you've created is a system with a *rich client* or *thick client*; the client isn't a dumb input/output terminal but an application with an internal state independent of the server (recall that the server doesn't hold any application state). One of the advantages of such a stateless server is that any server can handle any client request. If a server fails, you can route the next request to a different server, and the conversation process continues. The servers in a cluster *share nothing*; you can easily scale up your system horizontally by adding more servers. Obviously, all application servers still share the database system, but at least you only have to worry about scaling up one tier of servers.

Keeping changes after race conditions

In acceptance testing, you'll probably discover that users don't like to restart conversations when a race condition is detected. They may demand pessimistic locking: while user A edits an item, user B shouldn't even be allowed to load it into an editor dialog. The fundamental problem isn't the optimistic version checks at the end of a conversation; it's that you lose all your work when you start a conversation from scratch.

Instead of rendering a simple concurrency error message, you could offer a dialog that allows the user to keep their now invalid changes, merge them manually with the modifications made by the other user, and then save the combined result. Be warned, though: implementing this feature can be time-consuming, and Hibernate doesn't help much.

The downside is that you need to write rich-client applications, and you have to deal with network communication and data-serialization issues. Complexity shifts from the server side to the client side, *and* you have to optimize communication between the client and server.

If, instead of on an EJB client, your (JavaScript) client has to work on several web browsers or even as a native application on different (mobile) operating systems, this can certainly be a challenge. We recommend this architecture if your rich client runs in popular web browsers, where users download the latest version of the client application every time they visit your website. Rolling out native clients on several platforms, and maintaining and upgrading the installations, can be a significant burden even in medium-sized intranets where you control the user's environment.

Without an EJB environment, you have to customize serialization and transmission of detached entity state between the client and the server. Can you serialize and deserialize an Item instance? What happens if you didn't write your client in Java? We'll look at this issue in section 19.4.

Next, you implement the same use cases again, but with a very different strategy. The server will now hold the conversational state of the application, and the client will only be a dumb input/output device. This is an architecture with a *thin client* and a stateful server.

18.3   *Building a stateful server*

The application you'll write is still simple. It supports the same two uses cases as before: editing an auction item and placing a bid for an item. No difference is visible to the users of the application; the EJB console client still looks like figures 18.2 and 18.4.

With a thin client, it's the server's job to transform data for output into a display format understood by the thin client—for example, into HTML pages rendered by a web browser. The client transmits user input operations directly to the server—for example, as simple HTML form submissions. The server is responsible for decoding and transforming the input into higher-level domain model operations. We keep this part simple for now, though, and use only remote method invocation with an EJB client.

The server must then also hold conversational data, usually stored in some kind of server-side session associated with a particular client. Note that a client's session has a larger scope than a single conversation; a user may perform several conversations during a session. If the user walks away from the client and doesn't complete a conversation, temporary conversation data must be removed on the server at some point. The server typically handles this situation with timeouts; for example, the server may discard a client's session and all the data it contains after a certain period of inactivity. This sounds like a job for EJB stateful session beans, and, indeed, they're ideal for this kind of architecture if you're in need of a standardized solution.

Keeping those fundamental issues in mind, let's implement the first use case: editing an auction item.

18.3.1 Editing an auction item

The client presents the user again with a list of auction items, and the user picks one. This part of the application is trivial, and you don't have to hold any conversational state on the server. Have a look at the sequence of calls and contexts in figure 18.6.

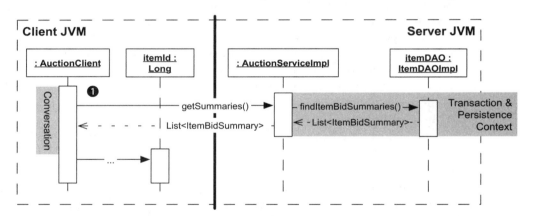

Figure 18.6   The client retrieves data already transformed for immediate display.

Because the client isn't very smart, it doesn't and shouldn't understand what an `Item` entity class is. It loads ❶ a `List` of `ItemBidSummary` data-transfer objects:

> PATH: /apps/app-stateful-server/src/test/java/org/jpwh/test/stateful/
> AuctionServiceTest.java

```
List<ItemBidSummary> itemBidSummaries = auctionService.getSummaries();
```

The server implements this with a stateless component because there is no need for it to hold any conversational state at this time:

```
PATH:  /apps/app-stateful-server/src/main/java/org/jpwh/stateful/
       AuctionServiceImpl.java
```

```java
@javax.ejb.Stateless
@javax.ejb.Local(AuctionService.class)
@javax.ejb.Remote(RemoteAuctionService.class)
public class AuctionServiceImpl implements AuctionService {

    @Inject
    protected ItemDAO itemDAO;

    @Override
    public List<ItemBidSummary> getSummaries() {
        return itemDAO.findItemBidSummaries();
    }
}
```

Even if you have a stateful server architecture, there will be many short conversations in your application that don't require any state to be held on the server. This is both normal and important: holding state on the server consumes resources. If you implemented the getSummaries() operation with a stateful session bean, you'd waste resources. You'd only use the stateful bean for a single operation, and then it would consume memory until the container expired it. Stateful server architecture doesn't mean you can only use stateful server-side components.

Next, the client renders the ItemBidSummary list, which only contains the identifier of each auction item, its description, and the current highest bid. This is exactly what the user sees on the screen, as shown in figure 18.2. The user then enters an item identifier and starts a conversation that works with this item. You can see the road map for this conversation in figure 18.7.

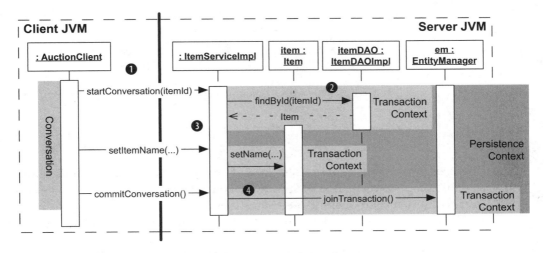

Figure 18.7 The client controls the conversation boundaries on the server.

The client notifies the server that it should now start a conversation, passing an item identifier value **❶**:

> PATH: /apps/app-stateful-server/src/test/java/org/jpwh/test/stateful/
>   **AuctionServiceTest.java**

```
itemService.startConversation(itemId);
```

The service called here isn't the pooled stateless `AuctionService` from the last section. This new `ItemService` is a stateful component; the server will create an instance and assign it to this client exclusively. You implement this service with a stateful session bean:

> PATH: /apps/app-stateful-server/src/main/java/org/jpwh/stateful/
>   **ItemServiceImpl.java**

```
@javax.ejb.Stateful(passivationCapable = false)
@javax.ejb.StatefulTimeout(10)                          <──── Minutes
@javax.ejb.Local(ItemService.class)
@javax.ejb.Remote(RemoteItemService.class)
public class ItemServiceImpl implements ItemService {

    @PersistenceContext(type = EXTENDED, synchronization = UNSYNCHRONIZED)
    protected EntityManager em;

    @Inject
    protected ItemDAO itemDAO;

    @Inject
    protected BidDAO bidDAO;

    // Server-side conversational state
    protected Item item;
    // ...

    @Override
    public void startConversation(Long itemId) {
        item = itemDAO.findById(itemId);
        if (item == null)
            throw new EntityNotFoundException(
                "No Item found with identifier: " + itemId
            );
    }

    // ...

}
```

There are many annotations on this class, defining how the container will handle this stateful component. With a 10-minute timeout, the server removes and destroys an instance of this component if the client hasn't called it in the last 10 minutes. This handles dangling conversations: for example, when a user walks away from the client.

You also disable passivation for this EJB: an EJB container may serialize and store the stateful component to disk, to preserve memory or to transmit it to another node in a cluster when session-failover is needed. This passivation won't work because of one member field: the `EntityManager`. You're attaching a persistence context to this stateful component with the `EXTENDED` switch, and the `EntityManager` isn't `java.io.Serializable`.

FAQ: Why can't you serialize an EntityManager?

There is no technical reason why a persistence context and an `EntityManager` can't be serialized. Of course, the `EntityManager` would have to reattach itself upon deserialization to the right `EntityManagerFactory` on the target machine, but that's an implementation detail. Passivation of persistence contexts has so far been out of scope of the JPA and Java EE specifications.

Most vendors, however, have an implementation that is serializable and knows how to deserialize itself correctly. Hibernate's `EntityManager` can be serialized and deserialized and tries to be smart when it has to find the right persistence unit upon deserialization.

With Hibernate and a Wildfly server, you *could* enable passivation in the previous example, and you'd get session failover and high availability with a stateful server and extended persistence contexts. This isn't standardized, though; and as we discuss later, this strategy is difficult to scale.

There was also a time when not even Hibernate's `EntityManager` was serializable. You may encounter legacy framework code that tries to work around this entire issue, such as the Seam framework's `ManagedEntityInterceptor`. You should avoid this and look for a simpler solution, which usually means sticky sessions in a cluster, stateless server design, or the CDI server-side conversation-management solution we'll discuss in the next chapter with a request-scoped persistence context.

You use `@PersistenceContext` to declare that this stateful bean needs an `Entity-Manager` and that the container should *extend* the persistence context to span the same duration as the life cycle of the stateful session bean. This extended mode is an option exclusively for stateful EJBs. Without it, the container will create and close a persistence context whenever a transaction commits. Here, you want the persistence context to stay open beyond any transaction boundaries and remain attached to the stateful session bean instance.

Furthermore, you don't want the persistence context to be flushed automatically when a transaction commits, so you configure it to be `UNSYNCHRONIZED`. Hibernate will only flush the persistence context after you manually join it with a transaction. Now Hibernate won't automatically write to the database changes you make to loaded persistent entity instances; instead, you queue them until you're ready to write everything.

At the start of the conversation, the server loads an `Item` instance and holds it as conversational state in a member field ❷ (figure 18.7). The `ItemDAO` also needs an `EntityManager`; remember that it has a `@PersistenceContext` annotation without any options. The rules for persistence context propagation in EJB calls you've seen before still apply: Hibernate propagates the persistence context along with the transaction context. The persistence context rides along into the `ItemDAO` with the transaction that was started for the `startConversation()` method call. When `startConversation()` returns, the transaction is committed, but the persistence context is neither flushed nor closed. The `ItemServiceImpl` instance waits on the server for the next call from the client.

The next call from the client instructs the server to change the item's name ❸:

> PATH: /apps/app-stateful-server/src/test/java/org/jpwh/test/stateful/
>   AuctionServiceTest.java

```
itemService.setItemName("Pretty Baseball Glove");
```

On the server, a transaction is started for the `setItemName()` method. But because no transactional resources are involved (no DAO calls, no `EntityManager` calls), nothing happens but a change to the `Item` you hold in conversational state:

> PATH: /apps/app-stateful-server/src/main/java/org/jpwh/stateful/
>   ItemServiceImpl.java

```
public class ItemServiceImpl implements ItemService {

    // ...
    @Override
    public void setItemName(String newName) {          Persistence context isn't
        item.setName(newName);                         flushed when transaction of
    }                                                  this method commits; it's
                                            <────────  unsynchronized.
    // ...
}
```

Note that the `Item` is still be in persistent state—the persistence context is still open! But because it isn't synchronized, it won't detect the change you made to the `Item`, because it won't be flushed when the transaction commits.

Finally, the client ends the conversation, giving the OK to store all changes on the server ❹ (figure 18.7):

> PATH: /apps/app-stateful-server/src/test/java/org/jpwh/test/stateful/
>   AuctionServiceTest.java

```
itemService.commitConversation();
```

On the server, you can flush changes to the database and discard the conversational state:

> **PATH:** /apps/app-stateful-server/src/main/java/org/jpwh/stateful/
> ItemServiceImpl.java

```
public class ItemServiceImpl implements ItemService {          Bean is removed
                                                               after method
    @Override                                                  completes.
    @javax.ejb.Remove
    public void commitConversation() {          ◄────┘
        em.joinTransaction();                              Persistence context is joined with
    }                                     ◄────────────────current transaction and flushed when
}                                                          this method returns, saving changes.
```

You've now completed the implementation of the first use case. We'll skip the implementation of the second use case (placing a bid) and refer you to the example code for details. The code for the second case is almost the same as the first, and you shouldn't have any problems understanding it. The important aspect you must understand is how persistence context and transaction handling work in EJBs.

NOTE There are additional rules for EJBs about persistence-context propagation between different types of components. They're extremely complex, and we've never seen any good use cases for them in practice. For example, you probably wouldn't call a stateful EJB from a stateless EJB. Another complication is disabled or optional EJB method transactions, which also influence how the persistence context is propagated along with component calls. We explained these propagation rules in the previous edition of this book. We recommend that you try to work only with the strategies shown in this chapter, and keep things simple.

Let's discuss some of the differences between a stateful and a stateless server architecture.

18.3.2 *Analyzing the stateful application*

As in our analysis of the stateless application, the first question is how the unit of work is implemented from the perspective of the user. In particular, you need to ask how atomicity of the conversation works and how you can make all steps in the workflow appear as a single unit.

At some point, usually when the last request in a conversation occurs, you commit the conversation and write the changes to the database. The conversation is atomic if you don't join the extended `EntityManager` with a transaction until the last event in the conversation. No dirty checking and flushing will occur if you only read data in unsynchronized mode.

While you keep the persistence context open, you can keep loading data lazily by accessing proxies and unloaded collections; this is obviously convenient. The loaded `Item` and other data become stale, however, if the user needs a long time to trigger the next request. You may want to `refresh()` some managed entity instances during the conversation if you need updates from the database, as explained in section 10.2.6. Alternatively, you can refresh to undo an operation during a conversation. For example, if the user changes the `Item#name` in a dialog but then decides to undo this, you can `refresh()` the persistent `Item` instance to retrieve the "old" name from the database. This is a nice feature of an extended persistence context and allows the `Item` to be always available in managed persistent state.

> ### Savepoints in conversations
>
> You may be familiar with savepoints in JDBC transactions: after changing some data in a transaction, you set a savepoint; later you roll back the transaction to the savepoint, undoing some work but keeping changes made before the savepoint was set. Unfortunately, Hibernate doesn't offer a concept similar to savepoints for the persistence context. You can only roll back an entity instance to its database state with the `refresh()` operation. Regular JDBC savepoints in a transaction can be used with Hibernate (you need a `Connection`; see section 17.1), but they won't help you implement undo in a conversation.

The stateful server architecture may be more difficult to scale horizontally. If a server fails, the state of the current conversation and indeed the entire session is lost. Replicating sessions on several servers is a costly operation, because any modification of session data on one server involves network communication to (potentially all) other servers.

With stateful EJBs and a member-extended `EntityManager`, serialization of this extended persistence context isn't possible. If you use stateful EJBs and an extended persistence context in a cluster, consider enabling *sticky sessions*, causing a particular client's requests to always route to the same server. This allows you to handle more load with additional servers easily, but your users must accept losing session state when a server fails.

On the other hand, stateful servers can act as a first line of caches with their extended persistence contexts in user sessions. Once an `Item` has been loaded for a particular user conversation, that `Item` won't be loaded again from the database in the same conversation. This can be a great tool to reduce the load on your database servers (the most expensive tier to scale).

An extended persistence-context strategy requires more memory on the server than holding only detached instances: the persistence context in Hibernate contains a snapshot copy of all managed instances. You may want to manually `detach()` managed instances to control what is held in the persistence context, or disable dirty checking and snapshots (while still being able to lazy load) as explained in section 10.2.8.

There are alternative implementations of thin clients and stateful servers, of course. You can use regular request-scoped persistence contexts and manage detached (not persistent) entity instances on the server manually. This is certainly possible with detaching and merging but can be much more work. One of the main advantages of the extended persistence context, transparent lazy loading even across requests, would no longer be available either. In the next chapter, we'll show you such a stateful service implementation with request-scoped persistence contexts in CDI and JSF, and you can compare it with the extended persistence context feature of EJBs you've seen in this chapter.

Thin client systems typically produce more load on servers than rich clients do. Every time the user interacts with the application, a client event results in a network request. This can even happen for every mouse click in a web application. Only the server knows the state of the current conversation and has to prepare and render all information the user is viewing. A rich client, on the other hand, can load raw data needed for a conversation in one request, transform it, and bind it locally to the user interface as needed. A dialog in a rich client can queue modifications on the client side and fire a network request only when it has to make changes persistent at the end of a conversation.

An additional challenge with thin clients is parallel conversations by one user: what happens if a user is editing two items at the same time—for example, in two web browser tabs? This means the user has two parallel conversations with the server. The server must separate data in the user session by conversation. Client requests during a conversation must therefore contain some sort of conversation identifier so you can select the correct conversation state from the user's session for each request. This happens automatically with EJB clients and servers but probably isn't built into your favorite web application framework (unless it's JSF and CDI, as you'll see in the next chapter).

One significant benefit of a stateful server is less reliance on the client platform; if the client is a simple input/output terminal with few moving parts, there is less chance for things to go wrong. The only place you have to implement data validation and security checks is the server. There are no deployment issues to deal with; you can roll out application upgrades on servers without touching clients.

Today, there are few advantages to thin client systems, and stateful server installations are declining. This is especially true in the web application sector, where easy scalability is frequently a major concern.

18.4 Summary

- You implemented simple conversations—units of work, from the perspective of your application user.
- You saw two server and client designs, with stateless and stateful servers, and learned how Hibernate fits into both these architectures.
- You can work with either detached entity state or an extended conversation-scoped persistence context.

Building web applications 19

In this chapter, you see how Hibernate works in a typical web application environment. There are dozens of web application frameworks for Java, so we apologize if we don't cover your favorite combination here. We discuss JPA in the standard Java Enterprise Edition environment, in particular combined with standards Contexts and Dependency Injection (CDI), JavaServer Faces (JSF), and Java API for RESTful web services (JAX-RS). As always, we show patterns you can apply in other proprietary environments.

First we revisit the persistence layer and introduce CDI management for the DAO classes. Then we extend these classes with a generic solution for sorting and paging data. This solution is useful whenever you have to display data in tables, no matter what framework you choose.

Next, you write a fully functional JSF application on top of the persistence layer and look at the Java EE *conversation* scope, where CDI and JSF work together to provide a simple stateful model for server-side components. If you didn't like the stateful EJBs with the extended persistence context in the last chapter, maybe these conversation examples with detached entity state on the server are what you're looking for.

Finally, if you prefer writing web applications with rich clients, a stateless server, and frameworks such as JAX-RS, GWT, or AngularJS, we show you how to customize serialization of JPA entity instances into XML and JSON formats. We start with migrating the persistence layer from EJB components to CDI.

19.1 Integrating JPA with CDI

The CDI standard offers a type-safe dependency injection and component life-cycle management system in a Java EE runtime environment. You saw the `@Inject` annotation in the previous chapter and used it to wire the `ItemDAO` and `BidDAO` components together with the service EJB classes.

The JPA `@PersistenceContext` annotation you used *inside* the DAO classes is just another special injection case: you tell the runtime container to provide and automatically handle an `EntityManager` instance. This is a *container-managed* `EntityManager`. There are some strings attached, though, such as the persistence-context propagation and transaction rules we discussed in the previous chapter. Such rules are convenient when all of your service and DAO classes are EJBs, but if you don't employ EJBs, you may not want to follow these rules. With an *application-managed* `EntityManager`, you can create your own persistence context management, propagation, and injection rules.

You now rewrite the DAO classes as simple CDI managed beans, which are just like EJBs: plain Java classes with extra annotations. You want to `@Inject` an `EntityManager` and drop the `@PersistenceContext` annotation, and thus have full control over the persistence context. Before you can inject your own `EntityManager`, you must *produce* it.

19.1.1 Producing an EntityManager

A *producer* in CDI parlance is a factory used to customize creation of an instance and tell the runtime container to call a custom routine whenever the application needs an instance based on the declared scope. For example, the container will create an application-scoped instance only once during the life cycle of the application. The container creates a request-scoped instance once for every request handled by a server and a session-scoped instance once for every session a user has with a server.

The CDI specification maps the abstract notions of *request* and *session* to servlet requests and sessions. Remember that both JSF and JAX-RS build on top of servlets, so CDI works well with those frameworks. In other words, don't worry much about this: in a Java EE environment, all the integration work has already been done for you.

Let's create a producer of request-scoped `EntityManager` instances:

```
PATH:  /apps/app-web/src/main/java/org/jpwh/web/dao/
       EntityManagerProducer.java
```

```
@javax.enterprise.context.ApplicationScoped        ⊲──❶ Only 1 producer needed
public class EntityManagerProducer {

    @PersistenceUnit                                ⊲──❷ Gets persistence unit
    private EntityManagerFactory entityManagerFactory;

    @javax.enterprise.inject.Produces              ⊲──❸ Gets EntityManager
    @javax.enterprise.context.RequestScoped
    public EntityManager create() {
        return entityManagerFactory.createEntityManager();
    }

    public void dispose(
        @javax.enterprise.inject.Disposes          ⊲──┐  Closes
        EntityManager entityManager) {                │  persistence
        if (entityManager.isOpen())                 ❹  context
            entityManager.close();
    }
}
```

❶ This CDI annotation declares that only one producer is needed in the entire application: there will only ever be one instance of EntityManagerProducer.

❷ The Java EE runtime gives you the persistence unit configured in persistence.xml, which is also an application-scoped component. (If you use CDI standalone and outside a Java EE environment, you can instead use the static Persistence.createEntity-ManagerFactory() bootstrap.)

❸ Whenever an EntityManager is needed, create() is called. The container reuses the same EntityManager during a request handled by your server. (If you forget @RequestScoped on the method, the EntityManager will be application-scoped like the producer class!)

❹ When a request is over and the request context is being destroyed, the CDI container calls this method to get rid of an EntityManager instance. You created this application-managed persistence context (see section 10.1.2), so it's your job to close it.

A common issue with CDI-annotated classes is mistaken imports of annotations. In Java EE 7, there are two annotations called @Produces; the other one is in javax.ws .rs (JAX-RS). This isn't the same as the CDI producer annotation and you can spend hours looking for this error in your code if you pick the wrong one. Another duplicate is @RequestScoped, also in javax.faces.bean (JSF). Like all other outdated JSF bean management annotations in the javax.faces.bean package, don't use them when you have the more modern CDI available. We hope that future Java EE specification versions will resolve these ambiguities.

You now have a producer of application-managed EntityManagers and request-scoped persistence contexts. Next, you must find a way to let the EntityManager know about your system transactions.

19.1.2 *Joining the EntityManager with transactions*

When your server must handle a servlet request, the container creates the Entity-Manager automatically when it first needs it for injection. Remember that an Entity-Manager you manually create will only join a system transaction automatically if the transaction is already in progress. Otherwise, it will be *unsynchronized*: you'll read data in auto-commit mode, and Hibernate won't flush the persistence context.

It's not always obvious when the container will call the EntityManager producer or exactly when during a request the first EntityManager injection takes place. Of course, if you process a request without a system transaction, the EntityManager you get is always unsynchronized. Hence, you must ensure that the EntityManager knows you have a system transaction.

You add a method for this purpose to the persistence layer, in the super-interface:

PATH: /apps/app-web/src/main/java/org/jpwh/web/dao/GenericDAO.java

```
public interface GenericDAO<T, ID extends Serializable>
    extends Serializable {

    void joinTransaction();

    // ...
}
```

You should call this method on any DAO before storing data, when you're sure you're in a transaction. If you forget, Hibernate will throw a TransactionRequiredException when you try to write data, indicating that the EntityManager has been created before a transaction was started and that nobody told it about the transaction. If you want to exercise your CDI skills, you could try to implement this aspect with a CDI *decorator* or *interceptor*.

Let's implement this GenericDAO interface method and wire the new Entity-Manager to the DAO classes.

19.1.3 *Injecting an EntityManager*

The old GenericDAOImpl relies on the @PersistenceContext annotation for injection of an EntityManager in a field, or someone calling setEntityManager() before the DAO is used. With CDI, you can use the safer constructor-injection technique:

PATH: /apps/app-web/src/main/java/org/jpwh/web/dao/GenericDAOImpl.java

```
public abstract class GenericDAOImpl<T, ID extends Serializable>
        implements GenericDAO<T, ID> {

    protected final EntityManager em;
    protected final Class<T> entityClass;

    protected GenericDAOImpl(EntityManager em, Class<T> entityClass) {
        this.em = em;
        this.entityClass = entityClass;
    }
```

```
    public EntityManager getEntityManager() {
        return em;
    }

    @Override
    public void joinTransaction() {
        if (!em.isJoinedToTransaction())
            em.joinTransaction();
    }
    // ...
}
```

Anyone who wants to instantiate a DAO must provide an EntityManager. This declaration of an invariant of the class is a much stronger guarantee; hence, although we frequently use field injection in our examples, you should always first think about constructor injection. (We don't do it in some examples because they would be even longer, and this book is already quite big.)

In the concrete (entity DAO) subclasses, declare the necessary injection on the constructor:

PATH: /apps/app-web/src/main/java/org/jpwh/web/dao/ItemDAOImpl.java

```
public class ItemDAOImpl
    extends GenericDAOImpl<Item, Long>
    implements ItemDAO {

    @Inject
    public ItemDAOImpl(EntityManager em) {
        super(em, Item.class);
    }

    // ...

}
```

When your application needs an ItemDAO, the CDI runtime will call your Entity-ManagerProducer and then call the ItemDAOImpl constructor. The container will reuse the same EntityManager for any injection in any DAO during a particular request.

What scope then is ItemDAO? Because you don't declare a scope for the implementation class, it's *dependent*. An ItemDAO is created whenever someone needs it, and the ItemDAO instance is then in the same context and scope as its caller and belongs to that

---

FAQ: How can I handle multiple persistence units with CDI?

If you have more than one database—more than one persistence unit—you can use CDI *qualifiers* to differentiate them. A qualifier is a custom annotation. You write that annotation, such as @BillingDatabase, and mark it as a qualifier. Then you place it next to @Produces on the method that creates an EntityManager from that particular persistence unit. Anyone who wants this EntityManager now also adds @BillingDatabase right next to @Inject.

calling object. This is a good choice for the persistence layer API, because you delegate scoping decisions to the upper layer with the services calling the persistence layer.

You're now ready to `@Inject` an `ItemDAO` field in a service class. Before you use your CDI-enabled persistence layer, let's add some functionality for paging and sorting data.

19.2 Paging and sorting data

A very common task is loading data from the database with a query and then displaying that data on a web page in a table. Frequently you must also implement dynamic *paging* and *sorting* of the data:

- Because the query returns much more information than can be displayed on a single page, you only show a subset of the data. You only render a certain number of rows in a data table and give users the options to go to the next, previous, first, or last page of rows. Users also expect the application to preserve sorting when they switch pages.
- Users want to be able to click a column header in the table and sort the rows of the table by the values of this column. Typically, you can sort in either *ascending* or *descending* order; this can be switched by subsequent clicks the column header.

You now implement a generic solution for browsing through pages of data, based on the metamodel of persistent classes provided by JPA.

Page browsing can be implemented in two variations: using the *offset* or the *seek* technique. Let's look first at the differences and what you want to implement.

19.2.1 Offset paging vs. seeking

Figure 19.1 shows an example of a browsing UI with an offset-based paging mechanism. You see that there's a handful of auction items and that a small page size of three records is used. Here, you're on the first page; the application renders links to the other pages dynamically. The current sort order is by ascending item name. You can click the column header and change the sorting to descending (or ascending) by name, auction end date, or highest bid amount. Clicking the item name in each table row opens the item detail view, where you can make bids for an item. We take on this use case later in this chapter.

Catalog

|<	<	Items 1 to 3 of 7	>	>|

Item ↑	Auction End	Highest Bid
Aquarium	07. Mar 2018 15:00	-
Baseball Glove	06. Mar 2018 14:00	13.00
Coffee Machine	10. Mar 2018 10:11	6.00

Figure 19.1 Browsing the catalog pages by offset

Behind this page are database queries with an offset and a limit condition, based on row numbers. The Java Persistence API for this are `Query#setFirstResult()` and `Query#setMaxResults()`, which we discussed in section 14.2.4. You write a query and then let Hibernate wrap the offset and limit clauses around it, depending on your database SQL dialect.

Now consider the alternative: paging with a seek method, as shown in figure 19.2. Here you don't offer users the option to jump to any page by offset; you only allow them to seek forward, to the next page. This may seem restrictive, but you've probably seen or even implemented such a paging routine when you needed *infinite scrolling*. You can, for example, automatically load and display the next page of data when the user reaches the bottom of the table/screen.

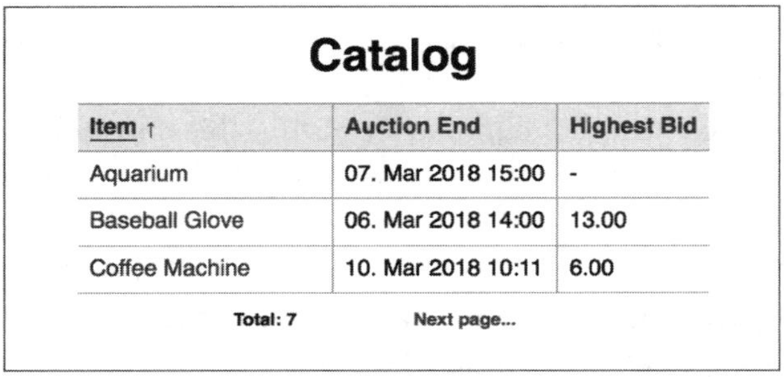

Catalog

Item ↑	Auction End	Highest Bid
Aquarium	07. Mar 2018 15:00	-
Baseball Glove	06. Mar 2018 14:00	13.00
Coffee Machine	10. Mar 2018 10:11	6.00

Total: 7   Next page...

Figure 19.2   Browsing the catalog by seeking the next page

The seek method relies on a special additional restriction in the query retrieving the data. When the next page has to be loaded, you query for all items with a name "greater than [Coffee Machine]". You seek forward not by offset of result rows with `setFirstResult()`, but by restricting the result based on the ordered values of some key. If you're unfamiliar with seek paging (sometimes called *keyset* paging), we're sure you won't find this difficult once you see the queries later in this section.

Let's compare the advantages and disadvantages of both techniques. You can of course implement an endless-scrolling feature with offset paging or direct-page navigation with the seek technique; but they each have their strength and weaknesses:

- The offset method is great when users want to jump to pages directly. For example, many search engines offer the option to jump directly to page 42 of a query result or directly to the last page. Because you can easily calculate the offset and limit of a range of rows based on the desired page number, you can implement this with little effort. With the seek method, providing such a page-jumping UI is more difficult; you must know the value to seek. You don't know what item name the client displayed just before page 42, so you can't seek forward to items with names "greater than X." Seeking is best suited for a UI where users only move forward or backward page by page through a data list or table, and if you can easily remember the last value shown to the user.
- A great use case for seeking is paging based on anchor values that you don't have to remember. For example, all customers whose names start with *C* could

be on one page and those starting with *D* on the next page. Alternatively, each page shows auction items that have reached a certain threshold value for their highest bid amount.

- The offset method performs much worse if you fetch higher page numbers. If you jump to page 5,000, the database must count all the rows and prepare 5,000 pages of data before it can skip 4,999 of them to give you the result. A common workaround is to restrict how far a user can jump: for example, only allowing direct jumps to the first 100 pages and forcing the user to refine the query restrictions to get a smaller result. The seek method is usually faster than the off-set method, even on low page numbers. The database query optimizer can skip directly to the start of the desired page and efficiently limit the index range to scan. Records shown on previous pages don't have to be considered or counted.

- The offset method may sometimes show incorrect results. Although the result may be consistent with what's in the database, your users may consider it incorrect. When applications insert new records or delete existing records while the user is browsing, anomalies may occur. Imagine the user looking at page 1 and someone adding a new record that would appear on page 1. If the user now retrieves page 2, some record they may have seen on page 1 is pushed forward onto page 2. If a record on page 1 was deleted, the user may miss data on page 2 because a record was pulled back to page 1. The seek method avoids these anomalies; records don't mysteriously reappear or vanish.

We now show you how to implement both paging techniques by extending the persistence layer. You start with a simple model that holds the current paging and sorting settings of a data table view.

19.2.2 *Paging in the persistence layer*

When you want to coordinate querying and rendering data pages, you need to keep some details about the size of the pages and what page you're currently viewing. Following is a simple model class encapsulating this information; it's an abstract super-class that will work for both the offset and seek techniques:

> PATH: /apps/app-web/src/main/java/org/jpwh/web/dao/Page.java

```
public abstract class Page {

    public static enum SortDirection {
        ASC,
        DESC
    }

    protected int size = -1;                                    ❶ Shows all records

    protected long totalRecords;                                ❷ Keeps record count

    protected SingularAttribute sortAttribute;                  ❸ Sorts records
    protected SortDirection sortDirection;

    protected SingularAttribute[] allowedAttributes;            ❹ Restricts sortable
                                                                    attributes
```

```
    // ...

    abstract public <T> TypedQuery<T> createQuery(
        EntityManager em,
        CriteriaQuery<T> criteriaQuery,
        Path attributePath
    );
}
```

❶ The model holds the size of each page and the number of records shown per page. The value -1 is special, meaning "no limit; show all records."

❷ Keeping the number of total records is necessary for some calculations: for example, to determine whether there is a "next" page.

❸ Paging always requires a deterministic record order. Typically, you sort by a particular attribute of your entity classes in ascending or descending order. javax.persistence .metamodel.SingularAttribute is an attribute of either an entity or an embeddable class in JPA; it's not a collection (you can't "order by collection" in a query).

❹ The allowedAttributes list is set when creating the page model. It restricts the possible sortable attributes to the ones you can handle in your queries.

Some methods of the Page class that we haven't shown are trivial—mostly getters and setters. The abstract createQuery() method, however, is what subclasses must implement: it's how paging settings are applied to a CriteriaQuery before the query is executed.

First you introduce the Page interface in the persistence layer. In a DAO interface, an API accepts a Page instance where you want to support retrieving data page by page:

PATH: /apps/app-web/src/main/java/org/jpwh/web/dao/ItemDAO.java

```
public interface ItemDAO extends GenericDAO<Item, Long> {

    List<ItemBidSummary> getItemBidSummaries(Page page);

    // ...

}
```

The data table you want to render shows a List of ItemBidSummary data-transfer objects. The result of the query is not important in this example; you could just as easily retrieve a list of Item instances. This is a brief excerpt of the DAO implementation:

PATH: /apps/app-web/src/main/java/org/jpwh/web/dao/ItemDAOImpl.java

```
public class ItemDAOImpl
    extends GenericDAOImpl<Item, Long>
    implements ItemDAO {

    // ...

    @Override
    public List<ItemBidSummary> getItemBidSummaries(Page page) {
```

```
CriteriaBuilder cb =                              ◄──────────❶ Criteria query
    getEntityManager().getCriteriaBuilder();

CriteriaQuery<ItemBidSummary> criteria =
    cb.createQuery(ItemBidSummary.class);

Root<Item> i = criteria.from(Item.class);

// Some query details...
// ...

TypedQuery<ItemBidSummary> query =               ◄──────────❷ Finishes query
    page.createQuery(em, criteria, i);

    return query.getResultList();
    }

    // ...
}
```

❶ This is a regular criteria query you've seen many times before.

❷ Delegate finishing the query to the given Page.

The concrete Page implementation prepares the query, setting the necessary offset, limit, and seek parameters.

IMPLEMENTING OFFSET PAGING
For example, here is the implementation of the offset paging strategy:

PATH: /apps/app-web/src/main/java/org/jpwh/web/dao/OffsetPage.java

```
public class OffsetPage extends Page {

    protected int current = 1;             ◄──────────❶ Current page

    // ...

    @Override
    public <T> TypedQuery<T> createQuery(EntityManager em,
                                          CriteriaQuery<T> criteriaQuery,
                                          Path attributePath) {

        throwIfNotApplicableFor(attributePath);

        CriteriaBuilder cb = em.getCriteriaBuilder();
                                                                    ❸ Adds
        Path sortPath = attributePath.get(getSortAttribute());  ◄──┘  ORDER BY
        criteriaQuery.orderBy(
            isSortedAscending() ? cb.asc(sortPath) : cb.desc(sortPath)
        );

        TypedQuery<T> query = em.createQuery(criteriaQuery);

        query.setFirstResult(getRangeStartInteger());  ◄──────────❹ Sets offset

        if (getSize() != -1)                           ◄──┐
            query.setMaxResults(getSize());               ❺ Sets result size

        return query;
    }
}
```

Tries to resolve sorting attribute ❷

❶ For offset-based paging, you need to know which page you're on. By default, you start with page 1.

❷ Test whether the sorting attribute of this page can be resolved against the attribute path and therefore the model used by the query. The method throws an exception if the sorting attribute of the page wasn't available on the model class referenced in the query. This is a safety mechanism that produces a meaningful error message if you pair the wrong paging settings with the wrong query.

❸ Add an ORDER BY clause to the query.

❹ Set the offset of the query: the starting result row.

❺ Cut the result off with the desired page size.

We haven't shown all the methods involved here, such as getRangeStartInteger(), which calculates the number of the first row that must be retrieved for the current page based on page size. You can find other simple convenience methods in the source code.

Note that the result order may not be deterministic: if you sort by ascending item name, and several items have the same name, the database will return them in whatever order the DBMS creators deemed appropriate. You should either sort by a unique key attribute or add an additional order criterion with a key attribute. Although many developers get away with ignoring deterministic sorting problems with the offset method, a predictable record order is mandatory for the seek strategy.

IMPLEMENTING SEEK PAGING

For seek paging, you need to add restrictions to a query. Let's assume that the previous page showed all items sorted by ascending name up to Coffee Machine, as shown in figure 19.2, and that you want to retrieve the next page with an SQL query. You remembered the last value of the previous page, the Coffee Machine record and its identifier value (let's say 5), so you can write in SQL:

```
select i.* from ITEM i
where
    i.NAME >= 'Coffee Machine'
    and (
        i.NAME <> 'Coffee Machine'
        or i.ID > 5
    )
order by
    i.NAME asc, i.ID asc
```

The first restriction of the query says, "Give me all items with a name greater than or equal to [Coffee Machine]," which seeks forward to the end of the previous page. The database may perform this efficient restriction with an index scan. Then you further restrict the result by saying you want no records named Coffee Machine, thus skipping the last record you've already shown on the previous page.

But there may be two items named Coffee Machine in the database. A unique key is necessary to prevent items from falling through the cracks between pages. You must order by and restrict the result with that unique key. Here you use the primary key, thus guaranteeing that the database includes only items *not* named Coffee Machine *or* (even if named Coffee Machine) with a greater identifier value than the one you showed on the previous page.

Of course, if the item name (or any other column you sort by) is unique, you won't need an additional unique key. The generic example code assumes that you always provide an explicit unique key attribute. Also note that the fact that item identifiers are incremented numerical values isn't important; the important aspect is that this key allows deterministic sorting.

You can write this same query in a more compact form in SQL with the row-value constructor syntax:

```
select i.* from ITEM i
where
    (i.NAME, i.ID) > ('Coffee Machine', 5)
order by
    i.NAME asc, i.ID asc
```

This kind of restriction expression works even in JPQL in Hibernate. JPA doesn't standardized this, though; it's unavailable with the criteria API and not supported by all database products. We prefer the slightly more verbose variation, which works everywhere. If you sort in descending order, you invert the comparisons from *greater than* to *less than*.

The following code in the SeekPage implementation adds such a restriction to a criteria query:

PATH: /apps/app-web/src/main/java/org/jpwh/web/dao/SeekPage.java

```
public class SeekPage extends Page {

    protected SingularAttribute uniqueAttribute;         ◁─❶ Adds paging attribute

    protected Comparable lastValue;                       ◁─┐
    protected Comparable lastUniqueValue;                    ├ Remembers
                                                           ❷ values from
    // ...                                                     last page

    @Override
    public <T> TypedQuery<T> createQuery(EntityManager em,
                                         CriteriaQuery<T> criteriaQuery,
                                         Path attributePath) {

        throwIfNotApplicableFor(attributePath);

        CriteriaBuilder cb = em.getCriteriaBuilder();       ❸ Sorts
                                                               result
        Path sortPath = attributePath.get(getSortAttribute());  ◁─┐
        Path uniqueSortPath = attributePath.get(getUniqueAttribute());
        if (isSortedAscending()) {
            criteriaQuery.orderBy(cb.asc(sortPath), cb.asc(uniqueSortPath));
```

```
        } else {
            criteriaQuery.orderBy(cb.desc(sortPath),
                cb.desc(uniqueSortPath));
        }
```

**Adds
restrictions** ❹

```
    applySeekRestriction(em, criteriaQuery, attributePath);

    TypedQuery<T> query = em.createQuery(criteriaQuery);

    if (getSize() != -1)                          ⟵ ❺ Sets result size
        query.setMaxResults(getSize());

    return query;
}

// ...
}
```

❶ In addition to the regular sorting attribute, the seek technique requires a paging attribute that's a guaranteed unique key. This can be any unique attribute of your entity model, but it's usually the primary key attribute.

❷ For both the sorting attribute and the unique key attribute, you must remember their values from the "last page." You can then retrieve the next page by seeking those values. Any Comparable value is fine, as required by the restriction API in criteria queries.

❸ You must always sort the result by both the sorting attribute and the unique key attribute.

❹ Add any necessary additional restrictions (not shown) to the where clause of the query, seeking beyond the last known values to the target page.

❺ Cut off the result with the desired page size.

The full applySeekRestriction() method can be found in the example code; this is criteria query code we don't have enough space for here. The final query is equivalent to the SQL example you saw earlier.

Let's test the new paging feature of the persistence layer.

Finding page boundaries for the seek method

We said earlier that jumping directly to a page with the seek technique isn't easy because you don't know what the last values to seek for are, given a particular page number. You can find out what those values are with an SQL statement like this:

```
select i.NAME, i.ID
from ITEM i
where
    (select count(i2.*)
      from ITEM i2
      where (i2.NAME, i2.ID) <= (i.NAME, i.ID)
    ) % :pageSizeParameter = 0
order by i.NAME asc, i.ID asc
```

This query with a modulo (%) operation returns all (NAME, ID) pairs that are page-boundary values: they're the last values on each page. We've included a criteria version of this query in the example code.

19.2.3 *Querying page-by-page*

When you call the ItemDAO#getItemBidSummaries() method now, you must provide a Page instance. A service or UI layer client on top of the persistence layer executes the following code:

> PATH: /apps/app-web/src/test/java/org/jpwh/test/service/PagingTest.java

```
OffsetPage page = new OffsetPage(              Total records
    3,                                         available
    itemDAO.getCount(),
    Item_.name, ASC,
    Item_.name, Item_.auctionEnd, Item_.maxBidAmount
);

List<ItemBidSummary> result = itemDAO.getItemBidSummaries(page);
```

Page size ⟶ (label pointing to `3,`)

Total records available ⟵ (label pointing to `itemDAO.getCount(),`)

Default sort attribute and sort direction ⟵ (label pointing to `Item_.name, ASC,`)

All attributes allowed as sort attributes for this page ⟵ (label pointing to `Item_.name, Item_.auctionEnd, Item_.maxBidAmount`)

Advancing to the next page is easy, and you can jump directly to any page number:

```
page.setCurrent(2);
result = itemDAO.getItemBidSummaries(page);
```

The seek technique needs a bit more information. First you instantiate a SeekPage with the additional required unique key attribute:

> PATH: /apps/app-web/src/test/java/org/jpwh/test/service/PagingTest.java

```
SeekPage page = new SeekPage(
    3,
    itemDAO.getCount(),          Additional unique key
    Item_.name, ASC,             attribute for ordering
    Item_.id,                    and seeking
    Item_.name, Item_.auctionEnd, Item_.maxBidAmount
);

List<ItemBidSummary> result = itemDAO.getItemBidSummaries(page);
```

Additional unique key attribute for ordering and seeking ⟵ (label pointing to `Item_.id,`)

With the offset strategy, all you had to know to jump to a page was the page number. With the seek strategy, you must remember the last values shown on the previous page:

```
ItemBidSummary lastShownOnPreviousPage = // ...

page.setLastValue(lastShownOnPreviousPage.getName());
page.setLastUniqueValue(lastShownOnPreviousPage.getItemId());

result = itemDAO.getItemBidSummaries(page);
```

This is clearly more work for a client of the persistence layer. Instead of a simple number, it must be able to remember the last values dynamically, depending on the sort and the unique attribute.

We implemented the UIs for earlier screenshots with JSF and CDI, including the necessary glue code for our paging API. Look at the source code for inspiration on how to integrate this technique with your own service and UI layer.

Even if you don't use JSF, it should be straightforward to adapt our paging and sorting solutions to other web frameworks. If you plan to use JSF, the next section is for you: we dive into complex use cases such as placing a bid and editing an auction item with a JSF web interface and a stateful service layer.

19.3 Building JSF applications

In the previous example, you can click an auction item name in the catalog. This brings you to the auction page for that item, with more detailed information, as shown in figure 19.3.

The item auction page has one form, allowing you to place a bid on the item. This is the first use case to implement: placing a bid. You can handle this with a simple request-scoped service.

Figure 19.3   Viewing item details and placing a bid

19.3.1 *Request-scoped services*

Let's start with some important excerpts from the XHTML template for the page:

> **PATH:** **/apps/app-web/src/main/webapp/auction.xhtml**

```
<f:metadata>
    <f:viewParam name="id" value="#{auctionService.id}"/>
</f:metadata>
```

The page is bookmarkable—that is, it can and will be called with a query parameter, the identifier value of an `Item`. The view metadata tells JSF it should bind this parameter value to the back-end property `id` of the `AuctionService`. You implement this new service in a minute.

You render some item details on the page, asking the `AuctionService` for the data:

> **PATH:** **/apps/app-web/src/main/webapp/auction.xhtml**

```
<h:outputText value="Auction End:"/>
<h:outputText value="#{auctionService.item.auctionEnd}">
    <f:convertDateTime pattern="dd. MMM yyyy HH:mm"/>
</h:outputText>

<h:outputText value="Starting Price:"/>
<h:outputText value="#{auctionService.item.initialPrice}"/>
```

Rendering this information repeatedly calls the `AuctionService#getItem()` method, something you have to keep in mind when you work on the service implementation. Finally, here's the form for placing a bid:

> **PATH:** **/apps/app-web/src/main/webapp/auction.xhtml**

```
<h:form>
    <h:inputHidden value="#{auctionService.id}"/>                    ◄──❶ Sends identifier

    <h:inputText value="#{auctionService.newBidAmount}"
                 size="6"/>                                          ◄──❷ Sets bid amount

    <h:commandButton value="Place Bid"
      action="#{auctionService.placeBid}"/>                          ◄──❸ Places bid
</h:form>
```

❶ You need to transmit the identifier value of the item when the form is submitted. The back-end service is request-scoped, so it needs to be initialized for every request: this calls the `AuctionService#setId()` method.

❷ The entered bid amount is set by JSF with the `AuctionService#setNewBidAmount()` method when the POSTback of this form is processed.

❸ After all values have been bound, the action method `AuctionService#placeBid()` is called.

Let's now move on to the back-end service class, which is a simple CDI managed bean:

PATH: /apps/app-web/src/main/java/org/jpwh/web/jsf/AuctionService.java

```
@Named
@RequestScoped                              ◁────── 1  No need to hold state
public class AuctionService {

    @Inject
    ItemDAO itemDAO;

    @Inject
    BidDAO bidDAO;
    long id;                                ◁────── 2  Defines state
    Item item;
    BigDecimal highestBidAmount;
    BigDecimal newBidAmount;

    // ...

}
```

1 You don't need to hold state across requests for this use case. A service instance is created when the auction page view is rendered with a GET request, and JSF binds the request parameter by calling setId(). The service instance is destroyed after rendering is complete. Your server doesn't hold any state between requests. When the auction form is submitted and processing of that POST request starts, JSF calls setId() to bind the hidden form field, and you can again initialize the state of the service.

2 The state you hold for each request is the identifier value of the Item the user is working on, the Item after it was loaded, the currently highest bid amount for that item, and the new bid amount entered by the user.

Remember that in JSF, any property accessor methods bound in an XHTML template may be called multiple times. In the AuctionService, data will be loaded when accessor methods are called, and you have to make sure you don't load from the database multiple times by accident:

PATH: /apps/app-web/src/main/java/org/jpwh/web/jsf/AuctionService.java

```
public class AuctionService {

    public void setId(long id) {
        this.id = id;
        if (item == null) {
            item = itemDAO.findById(id);
            if (item == null)
                throw new EntityNotFoundException();
            highestBidAmount = itemDAO.getMaxBidAmount(item);
        }
    }

    // Other plain getters and setters...

}
```

When JSF calls `setId()` for the first time in a request, you load the `Item` with that identifier value once. Fail immediately if the entity instance can't be found. You also load the currently highest bid amount to initialize the state of this service fully, before the view can be rendered or the action method called.

Note that this is a nontransactional method! Unlike EJBs, methods in a simple CDI bean don't require a transaction to be active by default. The produced `EntityManager` and the persistence context used by the DAOs are unsynchronized, and you read data from the database in auto-commit mode. Even if later, while still processing the same request, a transactional method is called, the same unsynchronized, already-produced, request-scoped `EntityManager` is reused.

The `placeBid()` method is such a transactional method:

PATH: /apps/app-web/src/main/java/org/jpwh/web/jsf/AuctionService.java

```
public class AuctionService {

    // ...
                                                    ❶ Interceptor wraps
                                                      method call in
    @Transactional                                    transaction context
    public String placeBid() {
        itemDAO.joinTransaction();                  ❷ Stores bid

        if (!getItem().isValidBidAmount(            ❸ Checks for higher bid
                getHighestBidAmount(),
                getNewBidAmount()
            )) {
            ValidationMessages.addFacesMessage("Auction.bid.TooLow");
            return null;
        }                                           ❹ Forces version
                                                       increment
        itemDAO.checkVersion(getItem(), true);

        bidDAO.makePersistent(new Bid(getNewBidAmount(), getItem()));

        return "auction?id=" + getId() + "&faces-redirect=true";

    }                                               Redirects ❺
}
```

❶ The `@Transactional` annotation is new in Java EE 7 (from JTA 1.2) and similar to `@TransactionAttribute` on EJB components. Internally, an interceptor wraps the method call in a system transaction context, just like an EJB method.

❷ Perform transactional work and store a new bid in the database, and prevent concurrent bids. You must join the persistence context with the transaction. It doesn't matter which DAO you call: all of them share the same request-scoped `EntityManager`.

❸ If another transaction is committed for a higher bid in the time the user was thinking and looking at the rendered auction page, fail and re-render the auction page with a message.

❹ You must force a version increment of the `Item` at flush time to prevent concurrent bids. If another transaction runs at the same time as this and loads the same `Item` version and current highest bid from the database in setId(), one of the transactions must fail in placeBid().

❺ This is a simple redirect-after-POST in JSF, so users can safely reload the page after submitting a bid.

When the placeBid() method returns, the transaction is committed, and the joined persistence context flushes changes to the database automatically. In Java EE 7, you can finally have the most convenient feature of EJBs: the declarative transaction demarcation, independent from EJBs.

Another new feature in Java EE is the CDI conversation scope and its integration in JSF.

19.3.2 *Conversation-scoped services*

You can declare beans and produced instances in Java EE as @ConversationScoped. This special scope is manually controllable with the standard javax.enterprise .context.Conversation API. To understand conversation scope, think about the examples in the previous chapter.

The shortest possible conversation, a unit of work from the perspective of the application user, is a single request/response cycle. A user sends a request, and the server starts a conversation context to hold the data for that request. When the response is returned, this short-running transient conversation context ends and is closed. Transient conversation scope is therefore the same as the request scope; both contexts have the same life cycle. This is how the CDI specification maps the conversation scope to servlet requests and therefore also JSF and JAX-RS requests.

With the Conversation API, you can promote a conversation on the server and make it long-running and no longer transient. If you promote the conversation during a request, the same conversation context is then available to the next request. You can use the context to transport data from one request to the next. Usually you'd need the session context for this, but the data from several parallel conversations (a user opens two browser tabs) would have to be manually isolated in the session. This is what the conversation context provides: automatic data isolation in a controllable context, which is more convenient than the regular session context.

You implement the conversation context with server-side sessions, of course, and store the data in the user's session. To isolate and identify conversations within a session, each conversation has an identifier value; you must transmit that value with every request. The parameter name cid has even been standardized for this purpose. Each conversation also has an individual timeout setting so the server can free resources if a user stops sending requests. This allows the server to clean up expired conversation state automatically without waiting until the entire user session expires.

Another nice feature of the long-running (not transient) conversation context is that the server protects concurrent access to conversation-scoped data automatically: if a user quickly clicks an action button several times, and each request transmits the

FAQ: What about the JSF flow scope?

The flow scope added in recent JSF versions is similar to the CDI conversation scope. It's focused on how the view templates of a workflow are grouped and discovered, and how navigation rules in a workflow can be automated. You can also use it to hold state across requests. Unfortunately, flow-context timeouts within a session aren't specified, and neither is there a control API for manually ending or promoting workflow contexts. We think flow scope isn't usable in its current incarnation beyond the most trivial cases—only where excessive resource consumption on the server doesn't matter. We hope that future versions of Java EE will align CDI conversation and JSF flow-scope features and combine the strengths of both.

identifier value of a particular conversation, the server will terminate all except one of the requests with `BusyConversationExceptions`.

We now walk through an example of conversation scope usage in JSF. You implement a use case with a workflow that takes the user several requests to complete: putting an item up for auction.

THE "EDIT ITEM" CONVERSATION WORKFLOW

If you think about it for a minute, creating and editing an auction item are very similar tasks. These workflows are conversations: units of work from the perspective of the application user, and your users will expect them to look similar. Your goal is therefore to avoid code duplication; you should implement both cases with a single UI and backend service. Your application guides the user through the workflow; figure 19.4 shows a graphical representation as a state chart.

Here's how to read this diagram. The user may start the conversation without any data, if no item exists. Alternatively, the user may have the identifier value of an existing item, which is probably a simple numeric value. How the user obtained this identifier isn't important; maybe they executed some kind of search in a previous conversation. This is a common scenario, and many conversation workflows have several entry points (the solid filled circles in the state chart).

From the perspective of the user, editing an item is a multistep process: each box with rounded corners represents a state of the application. In the Edit Item state, the

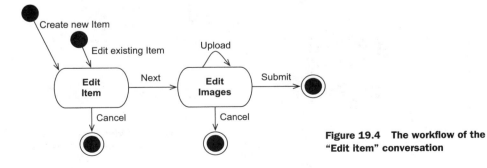

Figure 19.4 The workflow of the "Edit item" conversation

application presents the user with a dialog or form where they can change the item's description or the starting price for the auction. Meanwhile, the application waits for the user to trigger an event; we call this *user think-time*.

When the user triggers the Next event, the application processes it, and the user proceeds to the next (wait) state, Edit Images. When the user finishes working on the item images, they end the conversation by submitting the item and images (the solid circles with an outer circle). Clicking Cancel on any page aborts everything. From the application user's perspective, the entire conversation is an atomic unit: all changes are committed and final when the user clicks Submit. No other transition or outcome should result in any permanent changes to the database.

You'll implement this with a wizard-style user interface with two web pages. On the first page, the user enters the details of the item to sell or edit, as shown in figure 19.5.

Sell Item

Name:
Description:
Auction End:
Cancel   Next

Figure 19.5   The first page in the item auction wizard

Note that rendering this page won't start a long-running conversation context on the server. This would waste resources, because you don't know yet whether the user wants to follow through and work on the item details. You begin the long-running conversation context and hold state across requests on the server when the user clicks the Next button for the first time. If form validation passes, the server stores the conversational data in the user's session and advances the user to the Edit Images page (see figure 19.6).

The unit of work is complete when the user submits the item after uploading images for the item. The user may at any time click Cancel to end the conversation or walk away from the terminal and let the conversation expire. The user may work in two browser tabs and run several conversations in parallel, so they must be isolated from each other on the server within the same user session. All conversation data for a

Figure 19.6   Editing images on the second page of the wizard

user is removed if the user session expires (or if, in a cluster of servers with sticky sessions, a server fails).

The XHTML templates for this wizard have no markup relevant for the conversation; JSF with CDI automates this. Conversation identifiers are transmitted automatically with regular JSF form submissions in a generated hidden field, if a long-running conversation context was discovered when the form was rendered. This works even across JSF redirects: the cid parameter is appended automatically to the redirect destination URL.

The conversation-scoped back-end service bound to those pages—the EditItem-Service—is where everything happens and where you control the contexts.

THE PERSISTENCE CONTEXT IN A CONVERSATION

The EditItemService is the back end for the entire wizard and workflow:

```
PATH: /apps/app-web/src/main/java/org/jpwh/web/jsf/EditItemService.java
```

```
@Named                                                    ➊ Behaves as
@ConversationScoped                                          request-scoped
public class EditItemService implements Serializable {
    @Inject                                                       Must be
    ItemDAO itemDAO;                                          ➋ serializable

                                          ➌ Serializable
    @Inject
    ImageDAO imageDAO;

    // ...

    @Inject                                              ➍ Calls Conversation API
    Conversation conversation;

    Long itemId;                                         ➎ Service state
    Item item = new Item();

    transient Part imageUploadPart;                      ➏ Service transient state

    public void setItemId(Long itemId) {                 ➐ Loads item
        this.itemId = itemId;
        if (item.getId() == null && itemId != null) {
            item = itemDAO.findById(itemId);                    Gets item
            if (item == null)                                   from
                throw new EntityNotFoundException();      ➑ database
        }
    }

    // ...

}
```

➊ The service instance is conversation-scoped. By default, the conversation context is transient and therefore behaves as a request-scoped service.

➋ The class must be Serializable, unlike a request-scope implementation. An instance of EditItemService may be stored in the HTTP session, and that session data may be serialized to disk or sent across the network in a cluster. We took the easy way out in chapter 18 by using a stateful EJB, saying, "It's not passivation capable." Anything in the CDI conversation scope must be passivation-capable and therefore serializable.

❸ The injected DAO instances have dependent scope and are serializable. You may think they aren't, because they have an EntityManager field, which isn't serializable. We talk about this mismatch in a second.

❹ The Conversation API is provided by the container. Call it to control the conversation context. You need it when the user clicks the Next button for the first time, promoting the transient conversation to long-running.

❺ This is the state of the service: the item the user is editing on the pages of the wizard. You start with a fresh Item entity instance in transient state. If this service is initialized with an item identifier value, load the Item in setItemId().

❻ This is a transient state of the service. You only need it temporarily when the user clicks Upload on the Edit Images page. The Part class of the Servlet API isn't serializable. It's not uncommon to have some transient state in a conversational service, but you must initialize it for every request when it's needed.

❼ setItemId() is called only if the request contains an item identifier value. You therefore have two entry points into this conversation: with or without an existing item's identifier value.

❽ If the user is editing an item, you must load it from the database. You're still relying on a request-scoped persistence context, so as soon as the request is complete, this Item instance is in detached state. You can hold detached entity instances in a conversational service's state and merge it when needed to persist changes (see section 10.3.4).

Unlike stateful EJBs, you can't disable passivation of the conversation context. The CDI specification requires that the class and all non-transient dependencies of a conversation-scoped component be serializable. In fact, you'll get a deployment error if you make a mistake and include state that can't be serialized in a conversation-scoped bean or any of its dependencies.

To pass this test, we lied earlier by saying that GenericDAO is java.io.Serializable. The EntityManager field in GenericDAOImpl is *not* serializable! This works because CDI uses *contextual references*—smart placeholders.

The EntityManager field of the DAOs isn't an actual instance of a persistence context at runtime. The field holds a reference to some EntityManager: some current persistence context. Remember that CDI produces and injects the dependency through the constructor. Because you declared it request-scoped, at runtime a special proxy is injected that only looks like a real EntityManager. This proxy delegates all calls to an actual EntityManager it finds in the current request context. The proxy *is* serializable and doesn't hold a reference to an EntityManager after a request is complete. It can then be easily serialized; and when it's deserialized, maybe even on a different JVM, it will continue to do its work and obtain a request-scoped EntityManager whenever called. Therefore, you're not serializing the entire persistence context— only a proxy that can look up the current request-scoped persistence context.

This may sound strange at first, but it's how CDI works: if a request-scoped bean is injected into a conversation-, session-, or application-scoped bean, an indirect reference is required. If you try to call the `EntityManager` proxy through a DAO when no request context is active (say, in a servlet's `init()` method), you'll get a `ContextNotActiveException` because the proxy can't obtain a current `EntityManager`. The CDI specification also defines that such proxies may be passivated (serialized), even when the component they represent may not be.

Assume now that the user has filled out the form on the first page of the wizard with the item details and clicks Next. You have to promote the transient conversation context.

BEGINNING LONG-RUNNING CONVERSATIONS

Clicking Next in the wizard submits the form with the `Item` details and takes the user to the Edit Images page. Because the `EditItemService` is bound to a transient conversation context, processing this request happens in a new, transient conversation context. Remember that the transient conversation scope is the same as the request scope.

When you process the request with an action method, you call the `Conversation` API to control the current transient conversation context:

PATH: **/apps/app-web/src/main/java/org/jpwh/web/jsf/EditItemService.java**

```
public class EditItemService implements Serializable {

    // ...

    public String editImages() {
        if (conversation.isTransient()) {
            conversation.setTimeout(10 * 60 * 1000);      ⟵—— 10 minutes
            conversation.begin();
        }
        return "editItemImages";
    }

    // ...

}
```

The action method is called after all the `Item` details have been set on the `EditItemService#item` property by the JSF engine. You make the transient conversation long-running with an individual timeout setting. This timeout is obviously shorter than or equal to the timeout of the user's session; larger values don't make sense. The server preserves the state of the service in the user's session and renders an automatically generated conversation identifier as a hidden field on any action form on the Edit Images page. If you need it, you can also obtain the identifier value of the conversation with `Conversation#getId()`. You can even set your own identifier value in the `Conversation#begin()` method call.

The server now waits for the next request with the identifier of the conversation, most likely originating from the Edit Images page. If this takes too long, because either the long-running conversation or the entire session expired, a `NonexistentConversationException` is thrown on request.

If the user wants to attach an image to the auction item, the next request may be an Upload action bound to this service method:

PATH: /apps/app-web/src/main/java/org/jpwh/web/jsf/EditItemService.java

```
public class EditItemService implements Serializable {

    // ...

    public void uploadImage() throws Exception {
        if (imageUploadPart == null)
            return;

        Image image =                                          ❶ Creates instance
            imageDAO.hydrateImage(imageUploadPart.getInputStream());
        image.setName(imageUploadPart.getSubmittedFileName());
        image.setContentType(imageUploadPart.getContentType());

        image.setItem(item);                          ❷ Adds transient Image
        item.getImages().add(image);
    }

    // ...

}
```

❶ Create the Image entity instance from the submitted multipart form.

❷ You must add the transient Image to the transient or detached Item. This conversation will consume more and more memory on the server as uploaded image data is added to conversational state and therefore the user's session.

One of the most important issues when building a stateful server system is memory consumption and how many concurrent user sessions the system can handle. You must be careful with conversational data. Always question whether you must hold data you get from the user or data you load from the database for the entire conversation.

When the user clicks Submit Item, the conversation ends, and all transient and detached entity instances must be stored.

ENDING LONG-RUNNING CONVERSATIONS

The conversation workflow ends when the transient or detached Item and its images are stored:

PATH: /apps/app-web/src/main/java/org/jpwh/web/jsf/EditItemService.java

```
public class EditItemService implements Serializable {

    // ...

    @Transactional                                    ❶ Wraps method call
    public String submitItem() {
        itemDAO.joinTransaction();                    ❷ Joins persistence
                                                        context with transaction
        // ...

        item = itemDAO.makePersistent(item);          ❸ Makes Item persistent
```

```
    if (!conversation.isTransient())          ◄————————④ Ends conversation
        conversation.end();

    return "auction?id=" + item.getId() + "&faces-redirect=true"; ◄┐
}                                                                   │
// ...                                                       Redirects ⑤

}
```

① The system transaction interceptor wraps the method call.

② You must join the unsynchronized request-scoped persistence context with the system transaction if you want to store data.

③ This DAO call makes the transient or detached `Item` persistent. Because you enabled it with a cascading rule on the `@OneToMany`, it also stores any new transient or old detached `Item#images` collection elements. According to the DAO contract, you must take the returned instance as the current state.

④ Manually end the long-running conversation. This is effectively a demotion: the long-running conversation becomes transient. You destroy the conversation context and this service instance when the request is complete. All conversational state is removed from the user's session.

⑤ This is a redirect-after-`POST` in JSF to the auction item details page, with the new identifier value of the now-persistent `Item`.

Alternatively, the user may click Cancel at any time to exit the wizard:

> PATH: /apps/app-web/src/main/java/org/jpwh/web/jsf/EditItemService.java

```
public class EditItemService implements Serializable {

    // ...

    public String cancel() {
        if (!conversation.isTransient())
            conversation.end();
        return "catalog?faces-redirect=true";
    }

    // ...
}
```

This completes our example of stateful services with JSF, CDI, and a JPA persistence layer. We think JSF and CDI are great in combination with JPA; you get a well-tested and standardized programming model with little overhead, both in terms of resource consumption and lines of code.

We now continue with CDI but, instead of JSF, introduce JAX-RS combined with JPA in a stateless server design for any rich clients. One of the challenges you face in this architecture is serializing data.

19.4   *Serializing domain model data*

When we first talked about writing persistence-capable classes in section 3.2.3, we briefly mentioned that the classes don't have to implement `java.io.Serializable`. You can apply this marker interface when needed.

One of the cases when this was necessary so far was in chapter 18. Domain model instances were transmitted between EJB client and server systems, and they were automatically serialized on one end into some wire format and deserialized on the other end. This worked flawlessly and without customization because both client and server are Java virtual machines, and the Hibernate libraries were available on both systems. The client used Remote Method Invocation (RMI) and the standardized Java serialization format (a stream of bytes representing Java objects).

If your client isn't running in a Java virtual machine, you probably don't want to receive a stream of bytes representing Java objects from the server. A common scenario is a stateless server system that handles a rich client, such as a JavaScript application running in a web browser or a mobile device application. To implement this, you typically create a *Web API* on the server that speaks HTTP and transmit either XML or JSON payloads, which clients must then parse. The clients also send XML or JSON data when changes must be stored on the server, so your server must be able to produce and consume the desired media types.

Designing RESTful hypermedia-driven applications

Many people call a system with HTTP remote communication and JSON or XML media types *RESTful*. But one of the most important aspects of an architecture with representational state transfer is that client and server exchange hypermedia documents. These hypermedia documents contain the data and the affordances (actions) available on that data: Thus, the name Hypermedia As The Engine Of Application State (HATEOAS). Because this is a book about Hibernate and not Web API design, we can only show you how to build a simple HTTP API that exchanges basic XML documents, which isn't RESTful and doesn't use hypermedia.

When you design your own API, consider the *H Factor* of your chosen media type (see http://amundsen.com/hypermedia/hfactor/) and study the excellent book *RESTful Web APIs* by Leonard Richardson, Mike Amundsen, and Sam Ruby (Richardson, 2013). We recommend that you avoid using JSON, because it requires proprietary extensions to improve its H-Factor.

Designing your own XML-based hypermedia format, perhaps by extending the example shown in this chapter, isn't much better. Our favorite media type is plain XHTML: it has a great H-Factor, and it's easy to write and read with APIs available everywhere. Compressed, it can be more efficient than JSON, and it's a joy to work with interactively when building and testing your API. Jon Moore presents a great example of such a design in "Building Hypermedia APIs with HTML" (www.infoq.com /presentations/web-api-html).

You now write an HTTP server with the JAX-RS framework, producing and consuming XML documents. Although the examples are in XML, they're equally applicable to JSON, and the fundamental problems we discuss are the same in both.

19.4.1 *Writing a JAX-RS service*

Let's start with the JAX-RS service. One service method delivers an XML document representing an `Item` entity instance when a client sends a GET HTTP request. Another service method accepts an XML document for updating an Item in a PUT request:

PATH: **/apps/app-web/src/main/java/org/jpwh/web/jaxrs/ItemService.java**

```
@Path("/item")                                    ◄─────── ❶ Request path
public class ItemService {

    @Inject
    ItemDAO itemDAO;
GET ❷
request
    @GET
    @Path("{id}")                                 ◄─────── ❸ Argument for call
    @Produces(APPLICATION_XML)                    ◄─────── ❹ Serializes value into XML
    public Item get(@PathParam("id") Long id) {
        Item item = itemDAO.findById(id);
        if (item == null)
            throw new WebApplicationException(NOT_FOUND);
        return item;
    }

    @PUT                                          ❺ Deserializes XML
    @Path("{id}")
    @Consumes(APPLICATION_XML)                     ◄─────── ❻ Starts transaction
    @Transactional                                 ◄───────
    public void put(@PathParam("id") Long id, Item item) {
        itemDAO.joinTransaction();
        itemDAO.makePersistent(item);
    }

    // ...
}
```

❶ When the server receives a request with the request path `/item`, the method on this service handles it. By default, the service instance is request-scoped, but you can apply CDI scoping annotations to change that.

❷ An HTTP GET request maps to this method.

❸ The container uses the path segment after `/item` as an argument value for the call, such as `/item/123`. You map it to a method parameter with `@PathParam`.

❹ This method produces XML media; therefore, someone has to serialize the method's returned value into XML. Be careful: this annotation isn't the same producer annotation as in CDI. It's in a different package!

❺ This method consumes XML media; therefore, someone has to deserialize the XML document and transform it into a detached `Item` instance.

6 You want to store data in this method, so you must start a system transaction and join the persistence context with it.

The JAX-RS standard covers automatic marshalling for the most important media types and a whole range of Java types. A JAX-RS implementation, for example, must be able to produce and consume XML media for an application-supplied Java Architecture for XML Binding (JAXB) class. The domain model entity class Item must therefore become a JAXB class.

19.4.2 Applying JAXB mappings

JAXB, much like JPA, works with annotations to declare a class's capabilities. These annotations map the properties of a class to elements and attributes in an XML document. The JAXB runtime automatically reads and writes instances from and to XML documents. This should sound familiar to you by now; JAXB is a great companion for JPA-enabled domain models.

Here's an XML document for a sample Item:

```
<item id="1" auctionEnd="2018-03-06T15:00:00+01:00">
    <name>Baseball Glove</name>
    <description>It is brown.</description>
    <initialPrice>5.00</initialPrice>
    <bids>
        <bid id="1" createdOn="2018-03-06T15:01:00+01:00">
            <amount>11.00</amount>
        </bid>
        <bid id="2" createdOn="2018-03-06T15:02:00+01:00">
            <amount>12.00</amount>
        </bid>
        <bid id="3" createdOn="2018-03-06T15:03:00+01:00">
            <amount>13.00</amount>
        </bid>
    </bids>
</item>
```

Where is the seller? We talk about it in a minute.

Several design decisions were made to come up with this XML schema. Let's look at the JAXB annotations in the Item class to explore the available options:

PATH: /apps/app-web/src/main/java/org/jpwh/web/model/Item.java

```
@Entity
@XmlRootElement                                          ❶ Maps to XML
@XmlAccessorType(XmlAccessType.FIELD)
public class Item implements Serializable {              ❷ Calls fields

    @Id
    @GeneratedValue(generator = Constants.ID_GENERATOR)
    @XmlAttribute
    protected Long id;

    @NotNull
    @Future(message = "{Item.auctionEnd.Future}")
```

```
@XmlAttribute
protected Date auctionEnd;

    // ...
}
```

❶ An `Item` instance maps to an `<item>` XML element. This annotation effectively enables JAXB on the class.

❷ When serializing or deserializing an instance, JAXB should call the fields directly and not the getter or setter methods. The reasoning behind this is the same as for JPA: freedom in method design.

The identifier and auction end date of the item become XML attributes, and all other properties are nested XML elements. You don't have to put any JAXB annotations on `description` and `initialPrice`; they map to elements by default. Singular attributes of the domain model class are easy: they're either XML attributes or nested XML elements with some text. What about entity associations and collections?

You can embed a collection directly in the XML document and thus eagerly include it, as you did with the `Item#bids`:

> **PATH:** **/apps/app-web/src/main/java/org/jpwh/web/model/Item.java**

```
public class Item implements Serializable {

    @OneToMany(mappedBy = "item")
    @XmlElementWrapper(name = "bids")
    @XmlElement(name = "bid")
    protected Set<Bid> bids = new HashSet<>();

    // ...
}
```

There is some optimization potential here: if you say, "Always eagerly include bids" when your service returns an `Item`, then you should load them eagerly. Right now, several queries are necessary in JPA to load the `Item` and the default lazy-mapped `Item#bids`. The JAXB serializer automatically iterates through the collection elements when the response is prepared.

Hibernate initializes the collection data either lazily or eagerly, and JAXB (or any other serializer you have) serializes each element in turn. The fact that Hibernate uses special collections internally, as discussed in section 12.1.2, makes no difference when you serialize. It will later be important when you deserialize an XML document, but let's ignore this issue for now.

When you don't want to include a collection or a property in the XML document, use the `@XmlTransient` annotation:

PATH: **/apps/app-web/src/main/java/org/jpwh/web/model/Item.java**

```
public class Item implements Serializable {

    @OneToMany(mappedBy = "item", cascade = MERGE)
    @XmlTransient
    protected Set<Image> images = new HashSet<>();

    // ...
}
```

Collections are easy to handle, regardless of whether they're collections of primitives, embeddables, or many-valued entity associations. Of course, you must be careful with circular references, such as each `Bid` having a (back) reference to an `Item`. At some point, you must make a break and declare a reference transient.

The most difficult issue you face when serializing an entity instance loaded by Hibernate is internal proxies: the placeholders used for lazy loading of entity associations. In the `Item` class, this is the `seller` property, referencing a `User` entity.

19.4.3 *Serializing Hibernate proxies*

`Item#seller` is mapped with `@ManyToOne(fetch = LAZY)`, a lazy entity association. When you load an `Item` entity instance, its `seller` property isn't a real `User`: it's a `User` proxy, a runtime-generated class from Hibernate.

If you don't declare anything else, this is how JAXB will render the property:

```
<item id="1" auctionEnd="2018-03-06T15:00:00+01:00">
    <!-- ... -->
    <seller/>
    <!-- ... -->
</item>
```

Such a document would indicate to a client that the item has no seller. This is of course wrong; an uninitialized proxy is *not* the same as `null`! You could assign special meaning to an empty XML element and say, on the client, "An empty element means a proxy" and "A missing element means `null`." Unfortunately, we've seen serialization solutions, even designed for Hibernate, that don't make this distinction. Some serialization solutions, not designed for Hibernate, may even stumble and fail as soon as they discover a Hibernate proxy.

Usually, you must customize your serialization tool to deal with Hibernate proxies in some meaningful way. In this application, you want the following XML data for an uninitialized entity proxy:

```
<item id="1" auctionEnd="2018-03-06T15:00:00+01:00">
    <!-- ... -->
    <seller type="org.jpwh.web.model.User" id="123"/>
    <!-- ... -->
</item>
```

This is the same data as the proxy: the entity class and the identifier value represented by the proxy. A client now knows that there is indeed a seller for this item and the identifier of that user; it can request this data if needed. If you receive this XML document on the server when a user updates an item, you can reconstruct a proxy from the entity class name and identifier value.

You should write a model class that represents such an entity reference and map it to XML elements and attributes:

PATH: **/apps/app-web/src/main/java/org/jpwh/web/model/EntityReference.java**

```java
@XmlRootElement
@XmlAccessorType(XmlAccessType.FIELD)
public class EntityReference {

    @XmlAttribute
    public Class type;

    @XmlAttribute
    public Long id;

    public EntityReference() {
    }

    public EntityReference(Class type, Long id) {
        this.type = type;
        this.id = id;
    }
}
```

Next, you must customize marshalling and unmarshalling the `Item`, so instead of a real `User`, an `EntityReference` handles the `Item#seller` property. In JAXB, you apply a custom type adapter on the property:

PATH: **/apps/app-web/src/main/java/org/jpwh/web/model/Item.java**

```java
public class Item implements Serializable {

    @NotNull
    @ManyToOne(fetch = LAZY)
    @XmlJavaTypeAdapter(EntityReferenceAdapter.class)
    protected User seller;

    // ...
}
```

You can use the `EntityReferenceAdapter` for any entity association property. It knows how to read and write an `EntityReference` from and to XML:

PATH: **/apps/app-web/src/main/java/org/jpwh/web/jaxrs/**
EntityReferenceAdapter.java

```java
public class EntityReferenceAdapter
    extends XmlAdapter<EntityReference, Object> {
```

```
EntityManager em;

public EntityReferenceAdapter() {                    ◁———————● Writes EntityReference
}

public EntityReferenceAdapter(EntityManager em) {  ◁
    this.em = em;                                              ● Reads
}                                                             ❷ EntityReference

@Override
public EntityReference marshal(Object entityInstance)
    throws Exception {

    Class type = getType(entityInstance);        ◁———        Creates
    Long id = getId(type, entityInstance);              ┐    serialization
    return new EntityReference(type, id);              ❸    representation
}

@Override
public Object unmarshal(EntityReference entityReference)
    throws Exception {
    if (em == null)
        throw new IllegalStateException(
            "Call Unmarshaller#setAdapter() and " +
                "provide an EntityManager"
        );

    return em.getReference(              ◁————— ❹ Creates proxy
        entityReference.type,
        entityReference.id
    );
}

}
```

❶ JAXB calls this constructor when it generates an XML document. In that case, you don't need an EntityManager: the proxy contains all the information you need to write an EntityReference.

❷ JAXB must call this constructor when it reads an XML document. You need an Entity-Manager to get a Hibernate proxy from an EntityReference.

❸ When writing an XML document, take the Hibernate proxy and create a serializable representation. This calls internal Hibernate methods that we haven't shown here.

❹ When reading an XML document, take the serialized representation and create a Hibernate proxy attached to the current persistence context.

Finally, you need an extension for JAX-RS that will automatically initialize this adapter with the current request-scoped EntityManager when an XML document has to be unmarshalled on the server. You can find this EntityReferenceXMLReader extension in the example code for this book.

There are a few remaining points we need to discuss. First, we haven't talked about unmarshalling collections. Any <bids> element in the XML document will be deserialized when the service is called, and detached instances of Bid will be created from that data. You can access them on the detached `Item#bids` when your service runs. Nothing else will happen or can happen, though: the collection created during unmarshalling by JAXB isn't one of the special Hibernate collections. Even if you had enabled cascaded merging of the `Item#bids` collection in your mapping, it would be ignored by `EntityManager#merge()`.

This is similar to the proxy problem you solved in the previous section. You would have to detect that you must create a special Hibernate collection when a particular property is unmarshalled in an XML document. You'd have to call some Hibernate internal APIs to create that magic collection. We recommend that you consider collections to be read-only; collection mappings in general are a shortcut for embedding data in query results when you send data to the client. When the client sends an XML document to the server, it shouldn't include any `<bids>` element. On the server, you only access the collection on the persistent `Item` after it's merged (ignoring the collection during merge).

Second, you're probably wondering where our JSON examples are. We know you're most likely relying on JSON right now in your applications and not on a custom XML media type. JSON is a convenient format to parse in a JavaScript client. The bad news is that we couldn't figure out a way to customize JSON marshalling and unmarshalling in JAX-RS without relying on a proprietary framework. Although JAX-RS may be standardized, how it generates and reads JSON isn't standardized; some JAX-RS implementations use Jackson, whereas others use Jettison. There is also the new standard Java API for JSON Processing (JSONP), which some JAX-RS implementations may rely on in the future.

If you want to use JSON with Hibernate, you must write the same extension code we wrote for JAXB, but for your favorite JSON marshalling tool. You'll have to customize proxy handling, how proxy data is sent to the client, and how proxy data is turned back into entity references with `em.getReference()`. You'll certainly have to rely on some extension API of your framework, just as we did with JAXB, but the same pattern applies.

19.5 *Summary*

- You've seen many ways to integrate Hibernate and JPA in a web application environment. You enabled the EntityManager for CDI injection and improved the persistence layer with CDI and a generic sorting and paging solution for finder queries.
- You looked at JPA in a JSF web application: how to write request- and conversation-scoped services with a JPA persistence context.
- We discussed problems and solutions associated with entity data serialization, and how to resolve those in an environment with stateless clients and a JAX-RS server.

Scaling Hibernate

You use object/relational mapping to move data into the application tier in order to use an object-oriented programming language to process that data. This is a good strategy when implementing a multiuser online transaction-processing application with small to medium size data sets involved in each unit of work.

On the other hand, operations that require massive amounts of data aren't best-suited for the application tier. You should move the operation closer to where the data lives, rather than the other way around. In an SQL system, the DML statements UPDATE and DELETE execute directly in the database and are often sufficient if you have to implement an operation that involves thousands of rows. Operations that are more complex may require additional procedures to run inside the database; therefore, you should consider stored procedures as one possible strategy. You can fall back to JDBC and SQL at any time in Hibernate applications. We discussed some these options earlier, in chapter 17. In this chapter, we show you how to avoid falling back to JDBC and how to execute bulk and batch operations with Hibernate and JPA.

A major justification for our claim that applications using an object/relational persistence layer outperform applications built using direct JDBC is caching. Although we argue passionately that most applications should be designed so that it's possible to achieve acceptable performance without the use of a cache, there's no doubt that for some kinds of applications, especially read-mostly applications or applications that keep significant metadata in the database, caching can have an enormous impact on performance. Furthermore, scaling a highly concurrent application to thousands of online transactions per second usually requires some caching to reduce the load on the database server(s). After discussing bulk and batch operations, we explore Hibernate's caching system.

Major new features in JPA 2
- Bulk update and delete operations, which translate directly into SQL UPDATE and DELETE statements, are now standardized and available in the JPQL, criteria, and SQL execution interfaces.
- The configuration settings and annotations to enable a shared entity data cache are now standardized.

20.1 Bulk and batch processing

First we look at standardized bulk statements in JPQL, such as UPDATE and DELETE, and their equivalent criteria versions. After that, we repeat some of these operations with SQL native statements. Then, you learn how to insert and update a large number of entity instances in batches. Finally, we introduce the special org.hibernate.State-lessSession API.

20.1.1 Bulk statements in JPQL and criteria

The Java Persistence Query Language is similar to SQL. The main difference between the two is that JPQL uses class names instead of table names and property names instead of column names. JPQL also understands inheritance—that is, whether you're querying with a superclass or an interface. The JPA criteria query facility supports the same query constructs as JPQL but in addition offers type-safe and easy programmatic statement creation.

The next statements we show you support updating and deleting data directly in the database without the need to retrieve them into memory. We also provide a statement that can select data and insert it as new entity instances, directly in the database.

UPDATING AND DELETING ENTITY INSTANCES

JPA offers DML operations that are a little more powerful than plain SQL. Let's look at the first operation in JPQL: an UPDATE.

Listing 20.1   Executing a JPQL UPDATE statement

```
Query query = em.createQuery(
    "update Item i set i.active = true where i.seller = :s"
).setParameter("s", johndoe);

int updatedEntities = query.executeUpdate();

assertEquals(updatedEntities, 2);            ⟵——   Entity instances, not "rows"
```

This JPQL statement looks like an SQL statement, but it uses an entity name (class name) and property names. The aliases are optional, so you can also write `update Item set active = true`. You use the standard query API to bind named and positional parameters. The `executeUpdate` call returns the number of updated entity instances, which may be different from the number of updated database rows, depending on the mapping strategy.

This `UPDATE` statement only affects the database; Hibernate doesn't update any `Item` instance you've already retrieved into the (current) persistence context. In the previous chapters, we've repeated that you should think about state management of entity instances, not how SQL statements are managed. This strategy assumes that the entity instances you're referring to are available in memory. If you update or delete data directly in the database, what you've already loaded into application memory, into the persistence context, isn't updated or deleted.

A pragmatic solution that avoids this issue is a simple convention: execute any direct DML operations first in a fresh persistence context. Then, use the `Entity-Manager` to load and store entity instances. This convention guarantees that the persistence context is unaffected by any statements executed earlier. Alternatively, you can selectively use the `refresh()` operation to reload the state of an entity instance in the persistence context from the database, if you know it's been modified outside of the persistence context.

Bulk JPQL/criteria statements and the second-level cache

Executing a DML operation directly on the database automatically clears the optional Hibernate second-level cache. Hibernate parses your JPQL and criteria bulk operations and detects which cache regions are affected. Hibernate then clears the regions in the second-level cache. Note that this is a coarse-grained invalidation: although you may only update or delete a few rows in the `ITEM` table, Hibernate clears and invalidates *all* cache regions where it holds `Item` data.

This is the same operation with the criteria API:

```
CriteriaUpdate<Item> update =
    criteriaBuilder.createCriteriaUpdate(Item.class);
Root<Item> i = update.from(Item.class);
update.set(i.get(Item_.active), true);
```

```
update.where(
    criteriaBuilder.equal(i.get(Item_.seller), johndoe)
);

int updatedEntities = em.createQuery(update).executeUpdate();
```

Another benefit is that the JPQL UPDATE statement and a `CriteriaUpdate` work with inheritance hierarchies. The following statement marks all credit cards as stolen if the owner's name starts with "J" :

Hibernate even creates a temporary table for this update.

```
Query query = em.createQuery(  ⟵┘
    "update CreditCard c set c.stolenOn = :now where c.owner like 'J%'"
).setParameter("now", new Date());
```

Hibernate knows how to execute this update, even if several SQL statements have to be generated or some data needs to be copied into a temporary table; it updates rows in several base tables (because `CreditCard` is mapped to several superclass and subclass tables).

JPQL UPDATE statements can reference only a single entity class, and criteria bulk operations may have only one root entity; you can't write a single statement to update `Item` and `CreditCard` data simultaneously, for example. Subqueries are allowed in the WHERE clause, and any joins are allowed only in these subqueries.

You can update values of an embedded type: for example, `update User u set u.homeAddress.street = ....` You *can't* update values of an embeddable type in a collection. This isn't allowed: `update Item i set i.images.title = ....`

<hr/>

Hibernate Feature

Direct DML operations, by default, don't affect any version or timestamp values in the affected entities (as standardized by JPA). But a Hibernate extension lets you increment the version number of directly modified entity instances:

```
int updatedEntities =
    em.createQuery("update versioned Item i set i.active = true")
        .executeUpdate();
```

The version of each updated `Item` entity instance will now be directly incremented in the database, indicating to any other transaction relying on optimistic concurrency control that you modified the data. (Hibernate doesn't allow use of the versioned keyword if your version or timestamp property relies on a custom `org.hibernate.usertype.UserVersionType`.)

With the JPA criteria API, you have to increment the version yourself:

```
CriteriaUpdate<Item> update =
    criteriaBuilder.createCriteriaUpdate(Item.class);

Root<Item> i = update.from(Item.class);

update.set(i.get(Item_.active), true);
```

```
update.set(
    i.get(Item_.version),
    criteriaBuilder.sum(i.get(Item_.version), 1)
);

int updatedEntities = em.createQuery(update).executeUpdate();
```

The second bulk operation we introduce is DELETE:

```
em.createQuery("delete CreditCard c where c.owner like 'J%'")
    .executeUpdate();
CriteriaDelete<CreditCard> delete =
    criteriaBuilder.createCriteriaDelete(CreditCard.class);

Root<CreditCard> c = delete.from(CreditCard.class);

delete.where(
    criteriaBuilder.like(
        c.get(CreditCard_.owner),
        "J%"
    )
);

em.createQuery(delete).executeUpdate();
```

The same rules for UPDATE statements and CriteriaUpdate apply to DELETE and CriteriaDelete: no joins, single entity class only, optional aliases, or subqueries allowed in the WHERE clause.

Another special JPQL bulk operation lets you create entity instances directly in the database.

Hibernate Feature

CREATING NEW ENTITY INSTANCES

Let's assume that some of your customers' credit cards have been stolen. You write two bulk operations to mark the day they were stolen (well, the day you discovered the theft) and to remove the compromised credit-card data from your records. Because you work for a responsible company, you have to report the stolen credit cards to the authorities and affected customers. Therefore, before you delete the records, you extract everything stolen and create a few hundred (or thousand) StolenCreditCard records. You write a new mapped entity class just for this purpose:

```
@Entity
public class StolenCreditCard {

    @Id                              <──── Application-assigned
    public Long id;
    public String owner;
    public String cardNumber;
    public String expMonth;
    public String expYear;
    public Long userId;
    public String username;
```

```
    public StolenCreditCard() {
    }

    public StolenCreditCard(Long id,
                            String owner, String cardNumber,
                            String expMonth, String expYear,
                            Long userId, String username) {

    }
}
```

Hibernate maps this class to the STOLENCREDITCARD table. Next, you need a statement that executes directly in the database, retrieves all compromised credit cards, and creates new StolenCreditCard records. This is possible with the Hibernate-only INSERT ... SELECT statement:

```
int createdRecords =
    em.createQuery(
        "insert into" +
            " StolenCreditCard(id, owner, cardNumber, expMonth, expYear,
    ➥userId, username)" +
            " select c.id, c.owner, c.cardNumber, c.expMonth, c.expYear, u.id,
    ➥u.username" +
            " from CreditCard c join c.user u where c.owner like 'J%'"
    ).executeUpdate();
```

This operation does two things. First, it selects the details of CreditCard records and the respective owner (a User). Second, it inserts the result directly into the table mapped by the StolenCreditCard class.

Note the following:

- The properties that are the target of an INSERT ... SELECT (in this case, the StolenCreditCard properties you list) have to be for a particular subclass, not an (abstract) superclass. Because StolenCreditCard isn't part of an inheritance hierarchy, this isn't an issue.
- The types returned by the projection in the SELECT must match the types required for the arguments of the INSERT.
- In the example, the identifier property of StolenCreditCard is in the list of inserted properties and supplied through selection; it's the same as the original CreditCard identifier value. Alternatively, you can map an identifier generator for StolenCreditCard; but this works only for identifier generators that operate directly inside the database, such as sequences or identity fields.
- If the generated records are of a versioned class (with a version or timestamp property), a fresh version (zero, or the current timestamp) is also generated. Alternatively, you can select a version (or timestamp) value and add the version (or timestamp) property to the list of inserted properties.

The INSERT ... SELECT statement was, at the time of writing, not supported by the JPA or Hibernate criteria APIs.

JPQL and criteria bulk operations cover many situations in which you'd usually resort to plain SQL. In some cases, you may want to execute SQL bulk operations without falling back to JDBC.

20.1.2   *Bulk statements in SQL*

In the previous section, you saw JPQL UPDATE and DELETE statements. The primary advantage of these statements is that they work with class and property names and that Hibernate knows how to handle inheritance hierarchies and versioning when generating SQL. Because Hibernate parses JPQL, it also knows how to efficiently dirty-check and flush the persistence context before the query and how to invalidate second-level cache regions.

If JPQL doesn't have the features you need, you can execute native SQL bulk statements:

```
Query query = em.createNativeQuery(
    "update ITEM set ACTIVE = true where SELLER_ID = :sellerId"
).setParameter("sellerId", johndoe.getId());        All second-level cache
                                                     regions are cleared.
int updatedEntities = query.executeUpdate();

assertEquals(updatedEntities, 2);                    Updated rows, not
                                                     entity instances
```

With JPA native bulk statements, you must be aware of one important issue: Hibernate will *not* parse your SQL statement to detect the affected tables. This means Hibernate doesn't know whether a flush of the persistence context is required before the query executes. In the previous example, Hibernate doesn't know you're updating rows in the ITEM table. Hibernate has to dirty-check and flush *any* entity instances in the persistence context when you execute the query; it can't only dirty-check and flush Item instances in the persistence context.

You must consider another issue if you enable the second-level cache (if you don't, don't worry): Hibernate has to keep your second-level cache synchronized to avoid returning stale data, so it will invalidate and clear *all* second-level cache regions when you execute a native SQL UPDATE or DELETE statement. This means your second-level cache will be empty after this query!

Hibernate Feature

You can get more fine-grained control over dirty checking, flushing, and second-level cache invalidation with the Hibernate API for SQL queries:

```
org.hibernate.SQLQuery query =
    em.unwrap(org.hibernate.Session.class).createSQLQuery(
        "update ITEM set ACTIVE = true where SELLER_ID = :sellerId"
    );
query.setParameter("sellerId", johndoe.getId());     Only second-level cache regions
                                                     with Item data are cleared.
query.addSynchronizedEntityClass(Item.class);
```

```
int updatedEntities = query.executeUpdate();
assertEquals(updatedEntities, 2);
```

Updated rows, not entity instances

With the addSynchronizedEntityClass() method, you can let Hibernate know which tables are affected by your SQL statement and Hibernate will clear only the relevant cache regions. Hibernate now also knows that it has to flush only modified Item entity instance in the persistence context, before the query.

Sometimes you can't exclude the application tier in a mass data operation. You have to load data into application memory and work with the EntityManager to perform your updates and deletions, which brings us to batch processing.

20.1.3 *Processing in batches*

If you have to create or update a few hundred or thousand entity instances in one transaction and unit of work, you may run out of memory. Furthermore, you have to consider the time it takes for the transaction to complete. Most transaction managers have a low transaction timeout, in the range of seconds or minutes. The Bitronix transaction manager used for the examples in this book has a default transaction timeout of 60 seconds. If your unit of work takes longer to complete, you should first override this timeout for a particular transaction:

```
tx.setTransactionTimeout(300);
```
5 minutes

This is the UserTransaction API. Only future transactions started on this thread will have the new timeout. You must set the timeout before you begin() the transaction.

Next, let's insert a few thousand Item instances into the database in a batch.

INSERTING ENTITY INSTANCES IN BATCHES
Every transient entity instance you pass to EntityManager#persist() is added to the persistence context cache, as explained in section 10.2.8. To prevent memory exhaustion, you flush() and clear() the persistence context after a certain number of insertions, effectively batching the inserts.

Listing 20.2 Inserting a large number of entity instances

```
tx.begin();
EntityManager em = JPA.createEntityManager();

for (int i = 0; i < ONE_HUNDRED_THOUSAND; i++) {          ❶ Creates instances
    Item item = new Item(
        // ...
    );
    em.persist(item);

    if (i % 100 == 0) {                                   ❷ Executes INSERTs
        em.flush();
        em.clear();
    }
}
```

```
tx.commit();
em.close();
```

❶ Create and persist 100,000 `Item` instances.

❷ After 100 operations, flush and clear the persistence context. This executes the SQL `INSERT` statements for 100 `Item` instances, and because they're now in detached state and no longer referenced, the JVM garbage collection can reclaim that memory.

You should set the `hibernate.jdbc.batch_size` property in the persistence unit to the same size as your batch, here 100. With this setting, Hibernate will batch the `INSERT` statements at the JDBC level, with `PreparedStatement#addBatch()`.

> **Batching interleaved SQL statements**
>
> A batch procedure persisting several different entity instances in an interleaved fashion, let's say an `Item`, then a `User`, then another `Item`, another `User`, and so on, isn't efficiently batched at the JDBC level. When flushing, Hibernate generates an `insert into ITEM` SQL statement, then an `insert into USERS` statement, then another `insert into ITEM` statement, and so on. Hibernate can't execute a larger batch at once, given that each statement is different from the last. If you enable the property `hibernate.order_inserts` in the persistence unit configuration, Hibernate sorts the operations before trying to build a batch of statements. Hibernate then executes all `INSERT` statements for the `ITEM` table and all `INSERT` statements for the `USERS` table. Then, Hibernate can batch the statements at the JDBC level.

If you enable the shared second-level cache for the `Item` entity, you should then bypass the cache for your batch (insertion) procedure; see section 20.2.5.

A serious problem with mass insertions is contention on the identifier generator: every call of `EntityManager#persist()` must obtain a new identifier value. Typically, the generator is a database sequence, called once for every persisted entity instance. You have to reduce the number of database round trips for an efficient batch procedure.

Hibernate Feature

In section 4.2.5, we recommended the Hibernate-specific `enhanced-sequence` generator, not least because it supports certain optimizations ideal for batch operations. First, define the generator in the package-info.java metadata:

```
@org.hibernate.annotations.GenericGenerator(
  name = "ID_GENERATOR_POOLED",
  strategy = "enhanced-sequence",
  parameters = {
    @org.hibernate.annotations.Parameter(
      name = "sequence_name",
      value = "JPWH_SEQUENCE"
    ),
```

```
    @org.hibernate.annotations.Parameter(
        name = "increment_size",
        value = "100"
    ),
    @org.hibernate.annotations.Parameter(
        name = "optimizer",
        value = "pooled-lo"
    )
})
```

Now use the generator with `@GeneratedValue` in your mapped entity classes.

With `increment_size` set to 100, the sequence produces the "next" values 100, 200, 300, 400, and so on. The `pooled-lo` optimizer in Hibernate generates intermediate values each time you call `persist()`, without another round trip to the database. Therefore, if the next value obtained from the sequence is 100, Hibernate will generate the identifier values 101, 102, 103, and so on in the application tier. Once the optimizer's pool of 100 identifier values is exhausted, the database obtains the next sequence value, and the procedure repeats. This means you only make one round trip to get an identifier value from the database per batch of 100 insertions. Other identifier generator optimizers are available, but the `pooled-lo` optimizer covers virtually all use cases and is the easiest to understand and configure.

Be aware that an increment size of 100 will leave large gaps in between numeric identifiers if an application uses the same sequence but doesn't apply the same algorithm as Hibernate's optimizer. This shouldn't be too much of a concern; instead of being able to generate a new identifier value each millisecond for 300 million years, you might exhaust the number space in 3 million years.

You can use the same batching technique to update large number of entity instances.

UPDATING ENTITY INSTANCES IN BATCHES

Imagine that you have to manipulate many `Item` entity instances and that the changes you need to make aren't as trivial as setting a flag (which you've done with a single `UPDATE` JPQL statement previously). Let's also assume that you can't create a database stored procedure, for whatever reason (maybe because your application has to work on database-management systems that don't support stored procedures). Your only choice is to write the procedure in Java and to retrieve a massive amount of data into memory to run it through the procedure.

This requires working in batches and scrolling through a query result with a database cursor, which is a Hibernate-only query feature. Please review our explanation of scrolling with cursors in section 14.3.3 and make sure database cursors are properly supported by your DBMS and JDBC driver. The following code loads 100 `Item` entity instances at a time for processing.

Listing 20.3   Updating a large number of entity instances

```
tx.begin();
EntityManager em = JPA.createEntityManager();

org.hibernate.ScrollableResults itemCursor =        ◁——————❶ Opens cursor
    em.unwrap(org.hibernate.Session.class)
        .createQuery("select i from Item i")
        .scroll(org.hibernate.ScrollMode.SCROLL_INSENSITIVE);

int count = 0;                                          ❷ Moves cursor
while (itemCursor.next()) {                          ◁——┘
    Item item = (Item) itemCursor.get(0);           ◁——
                                                       ❸ Retrieves instance
    modifyItem(item);

    if (++count % 100 == 0) {          ◁——
        em.flush();                       ❹ Flushes persistence context
        em.clear();
    }
}

itemCursor.close();
tx.commit();
em.close();
```

❶ You use a JPQL query to load all Item instances from the database. Instead of retrieving the result of the query completely into application memory, you open an online database cursor.

❷ You control the cursor with the ScrollableResults API and move it along the result. Each call to next() forwards the cursor to the next record.

❸ The get(int i) call retrieves a single entity instance into memory: the record the cursor is currently pointing to.

❹ To avoid memory exhaustion, you flush and clear the persistence context before loading the next 100 records into it.

For the best performance, you should set the size of the property hibernate.jdbc.batch_size in the persistence unit configuration to the same value as your procedure batch: 100. Hibernate batches at the JDBC level all UPDATE statements executed while flushing. By default, Hibernate won't batch at the JDBC level if you've enabled versioning for an entity class—some JDBC drivers have trouble returning the correct updated row count for batch UPDATE statements (Oracle is known to have this issue). If you're sure your JDBC driver supports this properly, and your Item entity class has an @Version annotation, enable JDBC batching by setting the property hibernate.jdbc.batch_versioned_data to true. If you enable the shared second-level cache for the Item entity, you should then bypass the cache for your batch (update) procedure; see section 20.2.5.

Another option that avoids memory consumption in the persistence context (by effectively disabling it) is the org.hibernate.StatelessSession interface.

20.1.4 *The Hibernate StatelessSession interface*

The persistence context is an essential feature of the Hibernate engine. Without a persistence context, you can't manipulate entity state and have Hibernate detect your changes automatically. Many other things wouldn't also be possible.

Hibernate offers an alternative interface, however, if you prefer to work with your database by executing statements. The statement-oriented interface `org.hibernate.StatelessSession`, feels and works like plain JDBC, except that you get the benefit of mapped persistent classes and Hibernate's database portability. The most interesting methods in this interface are `insert()`, `update()`, and `delete()`, which all map to the equivalent immediately executed JDBC/SQL operation.

Let's write the same "update all item entity data" procedure from the earlier example with this interface.

Listing 20.4 Updating data with a `StatelessSession`

```
tx.begin();                                          ❶ Opens StatelessSession

org.hibernate.SessionFactory sf =
    JPA.getEntityManagerFactory().unwrap(org.hibernate.SessionFactory.class);
org.hibernate.StatelessSession statelessSession = sf .openStatelessSession();

org.hibernate.ScrollableResults itemCursor =
    statelessSession                                 ❷ Loads Item instances
        .createQuery("select i from Item i")
        .scroll(org.hibernate.ScrollMode.SCROLL_INSENSITIVE);

while (itemCursor.next()) {                           ❸ Retrieves instance
    Item item = (Item) itemCursor.get(0);

    modifyItem(item);

    statelessSession.update(item);                    ❹ Executes UPDATE
}

itemCursor.close();
tx.commit();
statelessSession.close();
```

❶ Open a `StatelessSession` on the Hibernate `SessionFactory`, which you can unwrap from an `EntityManagerFactory`.

❷ Use a JPQL query to load all `Item` instances from the database. Instead of retrieving the result of the query completely into application memory, open an online database cursor.

❸ Scroll through the result with the cursor, and retrieve an `Item` entity instance. This instance is in detached state; there is no persistence context!

❹ Because Hibernate doesn't detect changes automatically without a persistence context, you have to execute SQL UPDATE statements manually.

Disabling the persistence context and working with the `StatelessSession` interface has some other serious consequences and conceptual limitations (at least, if you compare it to a regular `EntityManager` and `org.hibernate.Session`):

- The `StatelessSession` doesn't have a persistence context cache and doesn't interact with any other second-level or query cache. There is no automatic dirty checking or SQL execution when a transaction commits. Everything you do results in immediate SQL operations.

- No modification of an entity instance and no operation you call are cascaded to any associated instance. Hibernate ignores any cascading rules in your mappings. You're working with instances of a single entity class.

- You have no guaranteed scope of object identity. The same query executed twice in the same `StatelessSession` produces two different in-memory detached instances. This can lead to data-aliasing effects if you don't carefully implement the `equals()` and `hashCode()` methods in your persistent classes.

- Hibernate ignores any modifications to a collection that you mapped as an entity association (*one-to-many, many-to-many*). Only collections of basic or embeddable types are considered. Therefore, you shouldn't map entity associations with collections—but only *many-to-one* or *one-to-one*—and handle the relationship through that side only. Write a query to obtain data you'd otherwise retrieve by iterating through a mapped collection.

- Hibernate doesn't invoke JPA event listeners and event callback methods for operations executed with `StatelessSession`. `StatelessSession` bypasses any enabled `org.hibernate.Interceptor`, and you can't intercept it through the Hibernate core event system.

Good use cases for a `StatelessSession` are rare; you may prefer it if manual batching with a regular `EntityManager` becomes cumbersome.

In the next section, we introduce the Hibernate shared caching system. Caching data on the application tier is a complementary optimization that you can utilize in any sophisticated multiuser application.

20.2   *Caching data*

In this section, we show you how to enable, tune, and manage the shared data caches in Hibernate. The shared data cache is *not* the persistence context cache, which Hibernate never shares between application threads. For reasons explained in section 10.1.2, this isn't optional. We call the persistence context a *first-level cache*. The shared data cache—the *second-level cache*—*is* optional, and although JPA standardizes some configuration settings and mapping metadata for shared caching, every vendor has different solutions for optimization. Let's start with some background information and explore the architecture of Hibernate's shared cache.

20.2.1 *The Hibernate shared cache architecture*

A cache keeps a representation of current database state close to the application, either in memory or on disk of the application server machine. A *cache* is a local copy of the data and sits between your application and the database. Simplified, to Hibernate a cache looks like a map of key/value pairs. Hibernate can store data in the cache by providing a key and a value, and it can look up a value in the cache with a key.

Hibernate has several types of shared caches available. You may use a cache to avoid a database hit whenever the following take place:

- The application performs an entity instance lookup by identifier (primary key); this may get a hit in the *entity data cache*. Initializing an entity proxy on demand is the same operation and, internally, may hit the entity data cache instead of the database. The cache key is the identifier value of the entity instance, and the cache value is the data of the entity instance (its property values). The actual data is stored in a special disassembled format, and Hibernate assembles an entity instance again when it reads from the entity data cache.
- The persistence engine initializes a collection lazily; a *collection cache* may hold the elements of the collection. The cache key is the collection role: for example, "Item[1234]#bids" would be the `bids` collection of an `Item` instance with identifier `1234`. The cache value in this case would be a set of `Bid` identifier values, the elements of the collection. (Note that this collection cache does *not* hold the `Bid` entity data, only the data's identifier values!)
- The application performs an entity instance lookup by a unique key attribute. This is a special *natural identifier cache* for entity classes with unique properties: for example, `User#username`. The cache key is the unique property, such as the `username`, and the cached value is the `User`'s entity instance identifier.
- You execute a JPQL, criteria, or SQL query, and the result of the actual SQL query is already stored in the *query result cache*. The cache key is the rendered SQL statement including all its parameter values, and the cache value is some representation of the SQL result set, which may include entity identifier values.

It's critically important to understand that the entity data cache is the only type of cache that holds actual entity data values. The other three cache types only hold entity identifier information. Therefore, it doesn't make sense to enable the natural identifier cache, for example, without also enabling the entity data cache. A lookup in the natural identifier cache will, when a match is found, always involve a lookup in the entity data cache. We'll further analyze this behavior below with some code examples.

As we hinted earlier, Hibernate has a two-level cache architecture.

Enabling reference storage for immutable data

Hibernate holds data in the second-level entity cache as a copy in a disassembled format and reassembles it when read from the cache. Copying data is an expensive operation; so, as an optimization, Hibernate allows you to specify that immutable data may be stored as is rather than copied into the second-level cache. This is useful for reference data. Let's say you have a `City` entity class with the properties `zipcode` and `name`, annotated `@Immutable`. If you enable the configuration property `hibernate.cache.use_reference_entries` in your persistence unit, Hibernate will try to (and can't in some special cases) to store a reference of `City` directly in the second-level data cache. One caveat is that if you accidentally modify an instance of `City` in your application, the change will effectively write-through to all concurrent users of the (local) cache region, because they all get the same reference.

THE SECOND-LEVEL CACHE

You can see the various elements of Hibernate's caching system in figure 20.1. The first-level cache is the persistence context cache, which we discussed in section 10.1.2. Hibernate does *not* share this cache between threads; each application thread has its own copy of the data in this cache. Hence, there are *no* issues with transaction isolation and concurrency when accessing this cache.

The second-level cache system in Hibernate may be process-scoped in the JVM or may be a cache system that can work in a cluster of JVMs. Multiple application threads may access the shared second-level caches concurrently. The *cache concurrency strategy* defines the transaction isolation details for entity data, collection elements, and

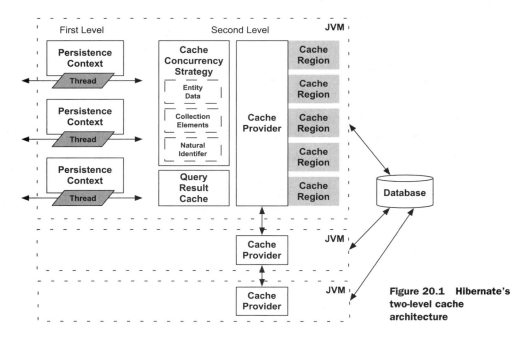

Figure 20.1 Hibernate's two-level cache architecture

natural identifier caches. Whenever an entry is stored or loaded in these caches, Hibernate will coordinate access with the configured strategy. Picking the right cache concurrency strategy for entity classes and their collections can be challenging, and we'll guide you through the process with several examples later on.

The query result cache also has its own, internal strategy for handling concurrent access and keeping the cached results fresh and coordinated with the database. We show you how the query cache works and for which queries it makes sense to enable result caching.

The *cache provider* implements the physical caches as a pluggable system. For now, Hibernate forces you to choose a single cache provider for the entire persistence unit. The cache provider is responsible for handling physical cache regions—the buckets where the data is held on the application tier (in memory, in indexed files, or even replicated in a cluster). The cache provider controls expiration policies, such as when to remove data from a region by timeout, or keeping only the most-recently used data when the cache is full. The cache provider implementation may be able to communicate with other instances in a cluster of JVMs, to synchronize data in each instance's buckets. Hibernate itself doesn't handle any clustering of caches; this is fully delegated to the cache provider engine.

In this section, you set up caching on a single JVM with the *Ehcache* provider, a simple but very powerful caching engine (originally developed for Hibernate specifically as the *easy Hibernate cache*). We only cover some of Ehcache's basic settings; consult its manual for more information.

Frequently, the first question many developers have about the Hibernate caching system is, "Will the cache know when data is modified in the database?" Let's try to answer this question before you get hands-on with cache configuration and usage.

CACHING AND CONCURRENCY

If an application does *not* have exclusive access to the database, shared caching should only be used for data that changes rarely and for which a small window of inconsistency is acceptable after an update. When another application updates the database, your cache may contain stale data until it expires. The other application may be a database-triggered stored procedure or even an ON DELETE or ON UPDATE foreign key option. There is no way for Hibernate's cache system to know when another application or trigger updates the data in the database; the database can't send your application a message. (You could implement such a messaging system with database triggers and JMS, but doing so isn't exactly trivial.) Therefore, using caching depends on the type of data and the freshness of the data required by your business case.

Let's assume for a moment that your application has exclusive access to the database. Even then, you must ask the same questions as a shared cache makes data retrieved from the database in one transaction visible to another transaction. What transaction isolation guarantees should the shared cache provide? The shared cache will affect the isolation level of your transactions, whether you read only committed data or if reads are repeatable. For some data, it may be acceptable that updates by one application thread aren't immediately visible by other application threads, providing an acceptable window of inconsistency. This would allow a much more efficient and aggressive caching strategy.

Start this design process with a diagram of your domain model, and look at the entity classes. Good candidates for caching are classes that represent

- Data that changes rarely
- Noncritical data (for example, content-management data)
- Data that's local to the application and not modified by other applications

Bad candidates include

- Data that is updated often
- Financial data, where decisions must be based on the latest update
- Data that is shared with and/or written by other applications

These aren't the only rules we usually apply. Many applications have a number of classes with the following properties:

- A small number of instances (thousands, not millions) that all fit into memory
- Each instance referenced by many instances of another class or classes
- Instances that are rarely (or never) updated

We sometimes call this kind of data *reference data*. Examples of reference data are Zip codes, locations, static text messages, and so on. Reference data is an excellent candidate for shared caching, and any application that uses reference data heavily will benefit greatly from caching that data. You allow the data to be refreshed when the cache timeout period expires, and some small window of inconsistency is acceptable after an update. In fact, some reference data (such as country codes) may have an extremely large window of inconsistency or may be cached eternally if the data is read-only.

You must exercise careful judgment for each class and collection for which you want to enable caching. You have to decide which concurrency strategy to use.

SELECTING A CACHE CONCURRENCY STRATEGY

A cache concurrency strategy is a mediator: it's responsible for storing items of data in the cache and retrieving them from the cache. This important role defines the transaction isolation semantics for that particular item. You'll have to decide, for each persistent class and collection, which cache concurrency strategy to use if you want to enable the shared cache.

The four built-in Hibernate concurrency strategies represent decreasing levels of strictness in terms of transaction isolation:

- TRANSACTIONAL—Available only in environments with a system transaction manager, this strategy guarantees full transactional isolation up to *repeatable read*, if supported by the cache provider. With this strategy, Hibernate assumes that the cache provider is aware of and participating in system transactions. Hibernate doesn't perform any kind of locking or version checking; it relies solely on the cache provider's ability to isolate data in concurrent transactions. Use this strategy for read-mostly data where it's critical to prevent stale data in concurrent transactions, in the rare case of an update. This strategy also works in a cluster if the cache provider engine supports synchronous distributed caching.

- READ_WRITE—Maintains *read committed* isolation where Hibernate can use a time-stamping mechanism; hence, this strategy only works in a non-clustered environment. Hibernate may also use a proprietary locking API offered by the cache provider. Enable this strategy for read-mostly data where it's critical to prevent stale data in concurrent transactions, in the rare case of an update. You shouldn't enable this strategy if data is concurrently modified (by other applications) in the database.

- NONSTRICT_READ_WRITE—Makes no guarantee of consistency between the cache and the database. A transaction may read stale data from the cache. Use this strategy if data hardly ever changes (say, not every 10 seconds) and a window of inconsistency isn't of critical concern. You configure the duration of the inconsistency window with the expiration policies of your cache provider. This strategy is usable in a cluster, even with asynchronous distributed caching. It may be appropriate if other applications change data in the same database.

- READ_ONLY—Suitable for data that never changes. You get an exception if you trigger an update. Use it for reference data only.

With decreasing strictness come increasing performance and scalability. A clustered asynchronous cache with NONSTRICT_READ_WRITE can handle many more transactions than a synchronous cluster with TRANSACTIONAL. You have to evaluate carefully the performance of a clustered cache with full transaction isolation before using it in production. In many cases, you may be better off not enabling the shared cache for a particular class, if stale data isn't an option!

You should benchmark your application with the shared cache disabled. Enable it for good candidate classes, one at a time, while continuously testing the scalability of your system and evaluating concurrency strategies. You must have automated tests available to judge the impact of changes to your cache setup. We recommend that you write these tests first, for the performance and scalability hotspots of your application, before you enable the shared cache.

With all this theory under your belt, it's time to see how caching works in practice. First, you configure the shared cache.

20.2.2 Configuring the shared cache

You configure the shared cache in your persistence.xml configuration file.

Listing 20.5 Shared cache configuration in persistence.xml

PATH: /model/src/main/resources/META-INF/persistence.xml

```
<persistence-unit name="CachePU">
    ...
    <shared-cache-mode>ENABLE_SELECTIVE</shared-cache-mode>   <—  ❶ Shared
    <properties>                                                     cache mode
        <property name="hibernate.cache.use_second_level_cache"
```

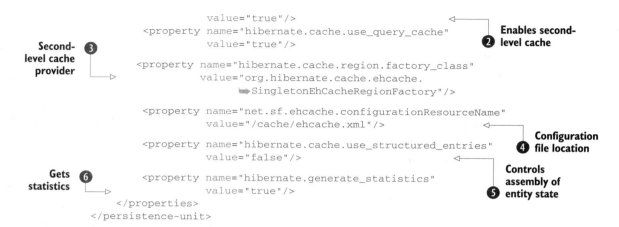

❶ The shared cache mode controls how entity classes of this persistence unit become cacheable. Usually you prefer to enable caching selectively for only some entity classes. Options: DISABLE_SELECTIVE, ALL, and NONE.

❷ Hibernate's second-level cache system has to be enabled explicitly; it isn't enabled by default. You can separately enable the query result cache; it's disabled by default as well.

❸ Pick a provider for the second-level cache system. For Ehcache, add the org.hibernate :hibernate-ehcache Maven artifact dependency to your classpath. Then, choose how Hibernate uses Ehcache with this region factory setting; here you tell Hibernate to manage a single Ehcache instance internally as the second-level cache provider.

❹ Hibernate passes this property to Ehcache when the provider is started, setting the location of the Ehcache configuration file. All physical cache settings for cache regions are in this file.

❺ This controls how Hibernate disassembles and assembles entity state when data is stored and loaded from the second-level cache. The structured cache entry format is less efficient but necessary in a clustered environment. For a nonclustered second-level cache like the singleton Ehcache on this JVM, you can disable this setting and use a more efficient format.

❻ When you experiment with the second-level cache, you usually want to see what's happening behind the scenes. Hibernate has a statistics collector and an API to access these statistics. For performance reasons, it's disabled by default (and should be disabled in production).

The second-level cache system is now ready, and Hibernate will start Ehcache when you build an EntityManagerFactory for this persistence unit. Hibernate won't cache anything by default, though; you have to enable caching selectively for entity classes and their collections.

20.2.3 *Enabling entity and collection caching*

We now look at entity classes and collections of the CaveatEmptor domain model and enable caching with the right concurrency strategy. In parallel, you'll configure the necessary physical cache regions in the Ehcache configuration file.

First the `User` entity: this data rarely changes, but, of course, a user may change their user name or address from time to time. This isn't critical data in a financial sense; few people make buying decisions based on a user's name or address. A small window of inconsistency is acceptable when a user changes name or address information. Let's say there is no problem if, for a maximum of one minute, the old information is still visible in some transactions. This means you can enable caching with the `NONSTRICT_READ_WRITE` strategy:

PATH: /model/src/main/java/org/jpwh/model/cache/User.java

```
@Entity
@Table(name = "USERS")
@Cacheable
@org.hibernate.annotations.Cache(
    usage = org.hibernate.annotations
                .CacheConcurrencyStrategy.NONSTRICT_READ_WRITE,
    region = "org.jpwh.model.cache.User"          <--- Default name
)
@org.hibernate.annotations.NaturalIdCache
public class User {                                    Ignored for schema generation
                                                       because of @NaturalId
    @NotNull
    @org.hibernate.annotations.NaturalId(mutable = true)  <--
    @Column(nullable = false)               <--         Makes it UNIQUE
    protected String username;
                                            For schema
    // ...                                  generation
}
```

Hibernate Feature

The `@Cacheable` annotation enables the shared cache for this entity class, but a Hibernate annotation is necessary to pick the concurrency strategy. Hibernate stores and loads `User` entity data in the second-level cache, in a cache region named `your.package.name.User`. You can override the name with the `region` attribute of the `@Cache` annotation. (Alternatively, you can set a global region name prefix with the `hibernate.cache.region_prefix` property in the persistence unit.)

You also enable the natural identifier cache for the `User` entity with `@org.hibernate.annotations.NaturalIdCache`. The natural identifier properties are marked with `@org.hibernate.annotations.NaturalId`, and you have to tell Hibernate whether the property is mutable. This enables you to look up `User` instances by `username` without hitting the database.

Next, configure the cache regions for both the entity data and the natural identifier caches in Ehcache:

PATH: **/model/src/main/resources/cache/ehcache.xml**

```
<ehcache xmlns:xsi="http://www.w3.org/2001/XMLSchema-instance"
         xsi:noNamespaceSchemaLocation="http://ehcache.org/ehcache.xsd">

    <cache name="org.jpwh.model.cache.User"
           maxElementsInMemory="500"
           eternal="false"
           timeToIdleSeconds="30"
           timeToLiveSeconds="60"/>

    <cache name="org.jpwh.model.cache.User##NaturalId"
           maxElementsInMemory="500"
           eternal="false"
           timeToIdleSeconds="30"
           timeToLiveSeconds="60"/>

</ehcache>
```

You can store a maximum 500 entries in both caches, and Ehcache won't keep them eternally. Ehcache will remove an element if it hasn't been accessed for 30 seconds and will remove even actively accessed entries after 1 minute. This guarantees that your window of inconsistency from cache reads is never more than 1 minute. In other words, the cache region(s) will hold up to the 500 most-recently used user accounts, none older than 1 minute, and shrink automatically.

Let's move on to the Item entity class. This data changes frequently, although you still have many more reads than writes. If the name or description of an item is changed, concurrent transactions should see this update immediately. Users make financial decisions, whether to buy an item, based on the description of an item. Therefore, READ_WRITE is an appropriate strategy:

PATH: **/model/src/main/java/org/jpwh/model/cache/Item.java**

```
@Entity
@Cacheable
@org.hibernate.annotations.Cache(
    usage = org.hibernate.annotations.CacheConcurrencyStrategy.READ_WRITE
)
public class Item {

    // ...
}
```

Hibernate will coordinate reads and writes when Item changes are made, ensuring that you can always read committed data from the shared cache. If another application is modifying Item data directly in the database, all bets are off! You configure the cache region in Ehcache to expire the most-recently used Item data after one hour, to avoid filling up the cache bucket with stale data:

```
PATH:  /model/src/main/resources/cache/ehcache.xml
```

```xml
<cache name="org.jpwh.model.cache.Item"
       maxElementsInMemory="5000"
       eternal="false"
       timeToIdleSeconds="600"
       timeToLiveSeconds="3600"/>
```

Consider the `bids` collection of the `Item` entity class: A particular `Bid` in the `Item#bids` collection is immutable, but the collection itself is mutable, and concurrent units of work need to see any addition or removal of a collection element immediately:

```
PATH:  /model/src/main/java/org/jpwh/model/cache/Item.java
```

```java
public class Item {

    @OneToMany(mappedBy = "item")
    @org.hibernate.annotations.Cache(
        usage = org.hibernate.annotations.CacheConcurrencyStrategy.READ_WRITE
    )
    protected Set<Bid> bids = new HashSet<>();

    // ...
}
```

You configure the cache region with the same settings as for the entity class owning the collection, because each `Item` has one `bids` collection:

```
PATH:  /model/src/main/resources/cache/ehcache.xml
```

```xml
<cache name="org.jpwh.model.cache.Item.bids"
       maxElementsInMemory="5000"
       eternal="false"
       timeToIdleSeconds="600"
       timeToLiveSeconds="3600"/>
```

It's critical to remember that the collection cache will *not* contain the actual `Bid` data. The collection cache only holds a set of `Bid` identifier values. Therefore, you must enable caching for the `Bid` entity as well. Otherwise, Hibernate may hit the cache when you start iterating through `Item#bids`, but then, due to cache misses, load each `Bid` separately from the database. This is a case where enabling the cache will result in *more* load on your database server!

We've said that `Bids` are immutable, so you can cache this entity data as READ_ONLY:

```
PATH:  /model/src/main/java/org/jpwh/model/cache/Bid.java
```

```java
@Entity
@org.hibernate.annotations.Immutable
@Cacheable
@org.hibernate.annotations.Cache(
    usage = CacheConcurrencyStrategy.READ_ONLY
```

```
)
public class Bid {

    // ...
}
```

Even though `Bids` are immutable, you should configure an expiration policy for the cache region, to prevent old bid data from clogging up the cache eternally:

PATH: /model/src/main/resources/cache/ehcache.xml

```
<cache name="org.jpwh.model.cache.Bid"
       maxElementsInMemory="100000"
       eternal="false"
       timeToIdleSeconds="600"
       timeToLiveSeconds="3600"/>
```

You're now ready to test the cache and explore Hibernate's caching behavior.

20.2.4 *Testing the shared cache*

Hibernate's transparent caching behavior can be difficult to analyze. The API for loading and storing data is still the `EntityManager`, with Hibernate automatically writing and reading data in the cache. Of course, you can see actual database access by logging Hibernate's SQL statements, but you should familiarize yourself with the `org.hibernate.stat.Statistics` API to obtain more information about a unit of work and see what's going on behind the scenes. Let's run through some examples to see how this works.

You enabled the statistics collector earlier in the persistence unit configuration, in section 20.2.2. You access the statistics of the persistence unit on the `org.hibernate.SessionFactory`:

PATH: /examples/src/test/java/org/jpwh/test/cache/SecondLevel.java

```
Statistics stats =
    JPA.getEntityManagerFactory()
        .unwrap(SessionFactory.class)
        .getStatistics();

SecondLevelCacheStatistics itemCacheStats =
    stats.getSecondLevelCacheStatistics(Item.class.getName());
assertEquals(itemCacheStats.getElementCountInMemory(), 3);
assertEquals(itemCacheStats.getHitCount(), 0);
```

Here, you also get statistics for the data cache region for `Item` entities, and you can see that there are several entries already in the cache. This is a *warm* cache; Hibernate stored data in the cache when the application saved `Item` entity instances. However, the entities haven't been read from the cache, and the hit count is zero.

When you now look up an `Item` instance by identifier, Hibernate attempts to read the data from the cache and avoids executing an SQL SELECT statement:

> **PATH: /examples/src/test/java/org/jpwh/test/cache/SecondLevel.java**

```
Item item = em.find(Item.class, ITEM_ID);
assertEquals(itemCacheStats.getHitCount(), 1);
```

You also have some `User` entity data in the cache, so initializing the `Item#seller` proxy hits the cache, too:

> **PATH: /examples/src/test/java/org/jpwh/test/cache/SecondLevel.java**

```
SecondLevelCacheStatistics userCacheStats =
    stats.getSecondLevelCacheStatistics(User.class.getName());
assertEquals(userCacheStats.getElementCountInMemory(), 3);
assertEquals(userCacheStats.getHitCount(), 0);

User seller = item.getSeller();
assertEquals(seller.getUsername(), "johndoe");            ◁—— Initializes proxy

assertEquals(userCacheStats.getHitCount(), 1);
```

When you iterate through the `Item#bids` collection, Hibernate uses the cache:

> **PATH: /examples/src/test/java/org/jpwh/test/cache/SecondLevel.java**

```
SecondLevelCacheStatistics bidsCacheStats =                        ◁—
    stats.getSecondLevelCacheStatistics(Item.class.getName() + ".bids");
assertEquals(bidsCacheStats.getElementCountInMemory(), 3);
assertEquals(bidsCacheStats.getHitCount(), 0);            Counts
                                                          Item#bids
SecondLevelCacheStatistics bidCacheStats =                collections ❶
    stats.getSecondLevelCacheStatistics(Bid.class.getName());
assertEquals(bidCacheStats.getElementCountInMemory(), 5);
assertEquals(bidCacheStats.getHitCount(), 0);

Set<Bid> bids = item.getBids();                      ◁——— ❸ Reads caches
assertEquals(bids.size(), 3);

assertEquals(bidsCacheStats.getHitCount(), 1);       ◁——— ❹ Cache results
assertEquals(bidCacheStats.getHitCount(), 3);
```

Counts Bids ❷ (label for `bidCacheStats` block)

❶ The statistics tell you that there are three `Item#bids` collections in the cache (one for each `Item`). No successful cache lookups have occurred so far.

❷ The entity cache of `Bid` has five records, and you haven't accessed it either.

❸ Initializing the collection reads the data from both caches.

❹ The cache found one collection as well as the data for its three `Bid` elements.

The special natural identifier cache for Users is *not* completely transparent. You need to call a method on the org.hibernate.Session to perform a lookup by natural identifier:

PATH: /examples/src/test/java/org/jpwh/test/cache/SecondLevel.java

```
                                                        ❶ Counts Users
NaturalIdCacheStatistics userIdStats =          ⟵
    stats.getNaturalIdCacheStatistics(User.class.getName() + "##NaturalId");
assertEquals(userIdStats.getElementCountInMemory(), 1);

User user = (User) session.byNaturalId(User.class)          ⟵         Natural
    .using("username", "johndoe")                                     identifier
    .load();                                                    ❷    lookup

assertNotNull(user);                                        ❸ Natural
                                                              identifier hit
assertEquals(userIdStats.getHitCount(), 1);          ⟵

SecondLevelCacheStatistics userStats =               ⟵    ❹ Entity hit
    stats.getSecondLevelCacheStatistics(User.class.getName());
assertEquals(userStats.getHitCount(), 1);
```

❶ The natural identifier cache region for Users has one element.

❷ The org.hibernate.Session API performs natural identifier lookup; this is the only API for accessing the natural identifier cache.

❸ You had a cache hit for the natural identifier lookup. The cache returned the identifier value "johndoe".

❹ You also had a cache hit for the entity data of that User.

The statistics API offers much more information than we've shown in these simple examples; we encourage you to explore this API further. Hibernate collects information about all its operations, and these statistics are useful for finding hotspots such as the queries taking the longest time and the entities and collections most accessed.

Accessing statistics with JMX
You can analyze Hibernate statistics at runtime through the standard Java Management Extension (JMX) system. Bind the Hibernate Statistics object as an MBean; this is only a few lines of code with a dynamic proxy. We've included an example in org.jpwh.test.cache.SecondLevel.

As mentioned at the beginning of this section, Hibernate transparently writes and reads the cached data. For some procedures, you need more control over cache usage, and you may want to bypass the caches explicitly. This is where cache modes come into play.

20.2.5 Setting cache modes

JPA standardizes control of the shared cache with several *cache modes*. The following `EntityManager#find()` operation, for example, doesn't attempt a cache lookup and hits the database directly:

PATH: /examples/src/test/java/org/jpwh/test/cache/SecondLevel.java

```
Map<String, Object> properties = new HashMap<String, Object>();
properties.put("javax.persistence.cache.retrieveMode",
    CacheRetrieveMode.BYPASS);
Item item = em.find(Item.class, ITEM_ID, properties);    <--- Hits database
```

The default `CacheRetrieveMode` is `USE`; here, you override it for one operation with `BYPASS`.

A more common usage of cache modes is the `CacheStoreMode`. By default, Hibernate puts entity data in the cache when you call `EntityManager#persist()`. It also puts data in the cache when you load an entity instance from the database. But if you store or load a large number of entity instances, you may not want to fill up the available cache. This is especially important for batch procedures, as we showed earlier in this chapter.

You can disable storage of data in the shared entity cache for the entire unit of work by setting a `CacheStoreMode` on the `EntityManager`:

PATH: /examples/src/test/java/org/jpwh/test/cache/SecondLevel.java

```
em.setProperty("javax.persistence.cache.storeMode", CacheStoreMode.BYPASS);

Item item = new Item(
    // ...
);

em.persist(item);                        <--- Not stored in cache
```

Let's look at the special cache mode `CacheStoreMode.REFRESH`. When you load an entity instance from the database with the default `CacheStoreMode.USE`, Hibernate first asks the cache whether it already has the data of the loaded entity instance. Then, if the cache already contains the data, Hibernate doesn't put the loaded data into the cache. This avoids a cache write, assuming that cache reads are cheaper. With the `REFRESH` mode, Hibernate always puts loaded data into the cache without first querying the cache

In a cluster with synchronous distributed caching, writing to all cache nodes is usually a very expensive operation. In fact, with a distributed cache, you should set the configuration property `hibernate.cache.use_minimal_puts` to `true`. This optimizes second-level cache operation to minimize writes, at the cost of more frequent reads. If, however, there is no difference for your cache provider and architecture between reads and writes, you may want to disable the additional read with `CacheStore-Mode.REFRESH`. (Note that some cache providers in Hibernate may set `use_minimal_puts`: for example, with Ehcache this setting is enabled by default.)

Cache modes, as you've seen, can be set on the `find()` operation and for the entire `EntityManager`. You can also set cache modes on the `refresh()` operation and on individual `Query`s as hints, as discussed in section 14.5. The per-operation and per-query settings override the cache mode of the `EntityManager`.

The cache mode only influences how Hibernate works with the caches internally. Sometimes you want to control the cache system programmatically: for example, to remove data from the cache.

20.2.6 *Controlling the shared cache*

The standard JPA interface for controlling the caches is the `Cache` API:

> **PATH: /examples/src/test/java/org/jpwh/test/cache/SecondLevel.java**

```
EntityManagerFactory emf = JPA.getEntityManagerFactory();
Cache cache = emf.getCache();

assertTrue(cache.contains(Item.class, ITEM_ID));
cache.evict(Item.class, ITEM_ID);
cache.evict(Item.class);
cache.evictAll();
```

This is a simple API, and it only allows you to access cache regions of entity data. You need the `org.hibernate.Cache` API to access the other cache regions, such as the collection and natural identifier cache regions:

> **PATH: /examples/src/test/java/org/jpwh/test/cache/SecondLevel.java**

```
org.hibernate.Cache hibernateCache =
    cache.unwrap(org.hibernate.Cache.class);

assertFalse(hibernateCache.containsEntity(Item.class, ITEM_ID));
hibernateCache.evictEntityRegions();
hibernateCache.evictCollectionRegions();
hibernateCache.evictNaturalIdRegions();
hibernateCache.evictQueryRegions();
```

You'll rarely need these control mechanisms. Also, note that eviction of the second-level cache is nontransactional: that is, Hibernate doesn't lock the cache regions during eviction.

Let's move on to the last part of the Hibernate caching system: the query result cache.

20.2.7 *The query result cache*

The query result cache is by default disabled, and every JPA, criteria, or native SQL query you write always hits the database first. In this section, we show you why Hibernate disables the query cache by default and then how to enable it for particular queries when needed.

The following procedure executes a JPQL query and stores the result in a special cache region for query results:

> **PATH:** /examples/src/test/java/org/jpwh/test/cache/SecondLevel.java

```
String queryString = "select i from Item i where i.name like :n";

Query query = em.createQuery(queryString)                    ◄────❶ Enables caching
    .setParameter("n", "I%")
    .setHint("org.hibernate.cacheable", true);

List<Item> items = query.getResultList();                    ◄────❷ Executes query
assertEquals(items.size(), 3);

QueryStatistics queryStats = stats.getQueryStatistics(queryString); ◄─┐ Gets
assertEquals(queryStats.getCacheHitCount(), 0);                       │ ❸ details
assertEquals(queryStats.getCacheMissCount(), 1);
assertEquals(queryStats.getCachePutCount(), 1);

SecondLevelCacheStatistics itemCacheStats =                  ◄────────┐ Stores data in
    stats.getSecondLevelCacheStatistics(Item.class.getName()); │ ❹ entity cache
assertEquals(itemCacheStats.getElementCountInMemory(), 3);
```

❶ You have to enable caching for a particular query. Without the org.hibernate .cachable hint, the result won't be stored in the query result cache.

❷ Hibernate executes the SQL query and retrieves the result set into memory.

❸ Using the statistics API, you can find out more details. This is the first time you execute this query, so you get a cache miss, not a hit. Hibernate puts the query and its result into the cache. If you run the same query again, the result will be from the cache.

❹ The entity instance data retrieved in the result set is stored in the entity cache region, not in the query result cache.

The org.hibernate.cachable hint is set on the Query API, so it also works for criteria and native SQL queries. Internally, the cache key is the SQL Hibernate uses to access the database, with arguments rendered into the string where you had parameter markers.

The query result cache doesn't contain the entire result set of the SQL query. In the last example, the SQL result set contained rows from the ITEM table. Hibernate ignores most of the information in this result set; only the ID value of each ITEM record is stored in the query result cache. The property values of each Item are stored in the entity cache region.

Now, when you execute the same query again, with the same argument values for its parameters, Hibernate first accesses the query result cache. It retrieves the identifier values of the ITEM records from the cache region for query results. Then, Hibernate looks up and assembles each Item entity instance by identifier from the entity cache region. If you query for entities and decide to enable caching, make sure you also enable regular data caching for these entities. If you don't, you may end up with *more* database hits after enabling the query result cache!

If you cache the result of a query that doesn't return entity instances but returns only scalar or embeddable values (for example, select i.name from Item i or select u.homeAddress from User), the values are held in the query result cache region directly.

The query result cache uses two physical cache regions:

PATH: /model/src/main/resources/cache/ehcache.xml

```
<cache name="org.hibernate.cache.internal.StandardQueryCache"
       maxElementsInMemory="500"
       eternal="false"
       timeToIdleSeconds="600"
       timeToLiveSeconds="3600"/>

<cache name="org.hibernate.cache.spi.UpdateTimestampsCache"
       maxElementsInMemory="50"
       eternal="true"/>
```

The first cache region is where the query results are stored. You should let the cache provider expire the most-recently used result sets over time, such that the cache uses the available space for recently executed queries.

The second region, org.hibernate.cache.spi.UpdateTimestampsCache, is special: Hibernate uses this region to decide whether a cached query result set is stale. When you re-execute a query with caching enabled, Hibernate looks in the timestamp cache region for the timestamp of the most recent insert, update, or delete made to the queried table(s). If the timestamp found is later than the timestamp of the cached query results, Hibernate discards the cached results and issues a new database query. This effectively guarantees that Hibernate won't use the cached query result if any table that may be involved in the query contains updated data; hence, the cached result may be stale. You should disable expiration of the update timestamp cache so that the cache provider never removes an element from this cache. The maximum number of elements in this cache region depends on the number of tables in your mapped model.

The majority of queries don't benefit from result caching. This may come as a surprise. After all, it sounds like avoiding a database hit is always a good thing. There are two good reasons this doesn't always work for arbitrary queries, compared to entity retrieval by identifier or collection initialization.

First, you must ask how often you're going to execute the same query repeatedly, with the same arguments. Granted, your application may execute a few queries repeatedly with exactly the same arguments bound to parameters and the same automatically generated SQL statement. We consider this a rare case, but when you're certain you're executing a query repeatedly, it becomes a good candidate for result set caching.

Second, for applications that perform many queries and few inserts, deletes, or updates, caching query results can improve performance and scalability. On the other hand, if the application performs many writes, Hibernate won't use the query result cache efficiently. Hibernate expires a cached query result set when there is any insert, update, or delete of any row of a table that appears in the cached query result. This means cached results may have a short lifetime, and even if you execute a query repeatedly, Hibernate won't use cached results due to concurrent modifications of rows in the tables referenced by the query.

For many queries, the benefit of the query result cache is nonexistent or, at least, doesn't have the impact you'd expect. But if your query restriction is on a unique natural identifier, such as `select u from User u where u.username = ?`, you should consider natural identifier caching and lookup as shown earlier in this chapter.

20.3 *Summary*

- You saw options you need to scale up your application and handle many concurrent users and larger data sets.
- With bulk `UPDATE` and `DELETE` operations, you can modify data directly in the database and still benefit from JPQL and criteria APIs without falling back to SQL.
- You learned about batch operations that let you work with large numbers of records in the application tier.
- We discussed the Hibernate caching system in detail: how you can selectively enable and optimize shared caching of entity, collection, and query result data.
- You configured Ehcache as a cache provider and learned how to peek under the hood with the Hibernate statistics API.

references

Ambler, Scott W. 2002. "Data Modeling 101." *Agile Data.* www.agiledata.org/essays/dataModeling101.html.

Bernard, Emmanuel. 2008. *Hibernate Search in Action.* Manning Publications.

Bloch, Joshua. 2008. *Effective Java,* 2nd ed. Prentice Hall.

Booch, Grady, James Rumbaugh, and Ivar Jacobson. 2005. *The Unified Modeling Language User Guide,* 2nd ed. Addison-Wesley Professional.

Codd, E.F. 1970. "A Relational Model of Data for Large Shared Data Banks." *Communications of the ACM* 13 (6): 377-87. www.acm.org/classics/nov95/toc.html.

Date, C.J. 2003. *An Introduction to Database Systems,* 8th ed. Addison-Wesley.

———. 2009. *SQL and Relational Theory.* O'Reilly Media.

Fowler, Martin. 1999. *Refactoring: Improving the Design of Existing Code.* Addison-Wesley Professional.

———. 2003. *Patterns of Enterprise Application Architecture.* Addison-Wesley Professional.

Gamma, E., R. Helm, R. Johnson, and J. Vlissides. 1995. *Design Patterns: Elements of Reusable Object-Oriented Software.* Addison-Wesley Professional.

Karwin, Bill. 2010. *SQL Antipatterns: Avoiding the Pitfalls of Database Programming.* The Pragmatic Bookshelf.

Morgan, Timothy D. 2010. *Weaning the Web off of Session Cookies: Making Digest Authentication Viable.* Virtual Security Research. www.vsecurity.com/download/papers/WeaningTheWebOffOfSessionCookies.pdf.

Pascal, Fabian. 2000. *Practical Issues in Database Management: A Reference for the Thinking Practitioner.* Addison-Wesley Professional.

Richardson, Leonard, Mike Amundsen, and Sam Ruby. 2013. *RESTful Web APIs.* O'Reilly Media.

Shute, Jeff, et al. 2012. "F1 - The Fault-Tolerant Distributed RDBMS Supporting Google's Ad Business." *Research at Google.* http://research.google.com/pubs/pub38125.html.

Tow, Dan. 2003. *SQL Tuning.* O'Reilly Media.

Walls, Craig, and Norman Richards. 2004. *XDoclet in Action.* Manning Publications.

Watterson, Bill. 1992. *The Indispensable Calvin and Hobbes: A Calvin and Hobbes Treasury.* Andrews McMeel Publishing.

index